EARLY MUSIC DISCOGRAPHY

From Plainsong to the Sons of Bach

Volume 2: Composer, Plainsong, Anonymous Work and Performer Indexes

W9-AED-699

1981 Edition

**Compiled by
Trevor Croucher**

ORYX PRES

The rare Arabian Oryx is believed to have inspired the myth of the unicorn. This desert antelope became virtually extinct in the early 1960s. At that time several groups of international conservationists arranged to have 9 animals sent to the Phoenix Zoo to be the nucleus of a captive breeding herd. Today the Oryx population is nearing 300 and herds have been returned to reserves in Israel, Jordan, and Oman.

Copyright © 1981 by Trevor Croucher

Published by The Oryx Press
2214 North Central at Encanto
Phoenix, AZ 85004

Published simultaneously in Canada

Printed and Bound in the United States of America

Library of Congress Cataloging in Publication Data

Croucher, Trevor.
    Early music discography from plainsong to the sons of Bach.

    Contents: v. 1. Record index—v. 2. Composer, plainsong, anonymous, and performer indexes.
    1. Music—Discography.   I. Title.
ML156.2.C76   016.789'12   81-16794
ISBN 0-89774-018-1   AACR2

Contents

Introduction

The Composer Index consists of a straight alphabetical listing of composers (with their dates), along with the major source collections (Codices, Cancioneros, Liederbücher, and the like). The works of any composer have been grouped – as far as this is possible – into the major headings of orchestral, chamber and instrumental, keyboard, secular vocal, and sacred vocal works. Cross references are made to the Record Index by way of the location number. The first two letters (AA, ER, LB, etc) refer to the period division, and the following letter and number refer to the section within the period division and the record's exact location within that section.

The Plainsong Index lists all individual chants separately and in alphabetical order. Each chant is classified (Antiphon, Responsory, Hymn, etc), and separate references are given for Mass Ordinaries, Propers and Offices. Unless they occur in isolation, individual items from Propers and Offices are not given separate entries but will be found under the general headings, eg. FUNERAL SERVICE, MASS FOR THE FEAST OF... etc.

The Anonymous Work Index lists all anonymous works alphabetically and identifies them according to date of composition, country of origin, and, whenever possible, source. In most cases capitalized sources may be cross-checked for further entries within the Composer Index.

The final index is devoted to Performers and includes references to all individuals, ensembles, orchestras, choirs, etc, that occur in the Record Index. A considerable problem here is the complete identification of all personnel in an ensemble. This is particularly difficult – but ultimately highly desirable – for important ensembles such as the Academy of Ancient Music, the Consort of Musicke, Hesperion XX, and La Petite Bande, to name but a few, since the individual members are seemingly ubiquitous, being interchangeable between ensembles and often soloists in their own right. For the present edition the names of soloists only have been given entries.

The Composer, Plainsong, Anonymous Work and Performer Indexes

Composer Index

AGRELL, Johan (1701–1765)
  a. Orchestral
  Concerto in A maj for flute, harpsichord and strings, Op.
    4, No. 1.
  LB:A1.
  Concerto in B min for flute, harpsichord and strings, Op.
    4, No. 2.
  LB:A1.

AGRICOLA, Alexander. (1446–1506)
  b. Instrumental
  Comme femme.
  ER:A2.
  De tous bien plaine.
  ER:A1.
  Fortuna desperata.
  ER:A1.
  Oublier veul.
  LR:Ga11.

AGRICOLA, Martin (1486–1556)
  e. Sacred Vocal.
  Gelobet seist du, Jesu Christ.
  LR:F103.
  Weihnachtsgesang.
  LR:F104.

AHLE, Johann Rudolf. (1625–1673)
  e. Sacred Vocal.
  Merk auf, mein Herz.
  EB:G131.

AICHINGER, Gregor. (1546–1628)
  e. Sacred Vocal.
  Regina caeli.
  LR:F77.

A KEMPIS, Nicolaus (17th. cent.)
  b. Chamber and Instrumental
  Sinfonia IV for violin, viola da gamba and continuo.
  EB:B35.
  Sinfonia V for violin, viola da gamba and continuo.
  EB:B35.

ALA DA MONZA (17th./18th. cent.)
  b. Chamber and Instrumental.
  Concerto Ecclesiastico for sackbutt and organ.
  LB:B202.

ALANUS (14th. cent.)
  e. Sacred Vocal.
  Sub Arcturo plebs.
  LR:A4.

ALBERCH I VILA, Pere (1517–1582)
  c. Keyboard.
  Fantasia.
  AN:B15.
  Tiento.
  EB:D28.
  5 Versos de 1o tono.
  LR:D13.

ALBERT, Heinrich (1604–1651)
  d. Secular Vocal.
  Musikalische Kurbishütte.
  LB:G318.
  e. Sacred Vocal.
  Der Tag beginnet zu vergehen.
  EB:G132.
  Du mein einzig Licht.
  LR:E22.
  Gott des Himmels und der Erden.
  EB:G132.

ALBERTI, Domenico (1710–1740)
  c. Keyboard

Sonata in A maj.
EB:D29.
LB:D213.

ALBERTIN, Alfons (18th. cent.)
  b. Instrumental
  Sonata in D maj per la festa di Pasqua for 4 organs, 4
    trumpets, 4 horns and tympani.
  LB:B203.

ALBERTO, Luys (17th. cent.)
  c. Keyboard
  3 Glosadas.
  LR:D13.
  EB:D28.

ALBERTUS PARISIENSIS (13th. cent.)
  e. Sacred Vocal.
  Con gaudent catholici.
  AA:E6.

ALBINONI, Tommaso (1671–1750)
  a. Orchestral.
  Adagio in G min for organ and strings (Spurious).
  LB:A9, A10, A15, A229, A442, A476, A580, A581,
    A582, A583, A585, A589, A590, A591, A619, A620,
    A623, A625, A671, B206.
  Concertos and Sonatas (Sinfonias) for strings. Op. 2.
    Nos. 1–12.
    Concertos 1 in F maj; 2 in E min; 3 in B flat maj; 4 in G
      maj; 5 in C maj; 6 in D maj.
    Sonatas 1 in G maj; 2 in C maj; 3 in A maj; 4 in G min; 5
      in B flat maj; 6 in G min.
  LB:A2.
  Sonata in A maj for strings and continuo, Op. 2, No. 3.
  LB:A3, A584.
  Concerto in F maj for trumpet and organ, Arr. Op. 2, No.
    4.
  LB:B204.
  Sonata in G min for strings and continuo, Op. 2, No. 6.
  LB:A3, A20.
  Concertos for strings and continuo, Op. 5, Nos. 1–12.
    1 in B flat maj; 2 in F maj; 3 in D maj; 4 in G maj; 5 in A
      min; 6 in C maj; 7 in D min; 8 in F maj; 9 in E min; 10 in A
      maj; 11 in G min; 12 in C maj.
  LB:A4.
  Concerto in B flat maj for strings and continuo, Op. 5, No.
    1.
  LB:A5.
  Concerto in A min for strings and continuo, Op. 5, No. 5.
  LB:A3, A4, A588.
  Concerto in A min for cello and strings, Arr. Op. 5, No. 5.
  LB:A17.
  Concerto in D min for strings and continuo, Op. 5, No. 7.
  LB:A3.
  Concertos for strings or oboe and strings, Op. 7, Nos.
    1–12.
    1 in D maj for strings; 2 in C maj for 2 oboes; 3 in B flat
      maj for oboe; 4 in G maj for strings; 5 in C maj for 2
      oboes; 6 in D maj for oboe; 7 in G maj for strings; 8 in D
      maj for 2 oboes; 9 in F maj for oboe; 10 in B flat maj for
      strings; 11 in C maj for 2 oboes; 12 in C maj for oboe.
  LB:A6, A7.
  Concerto in D maj for strings and continuo, Op. 7, No. 1.
  LB:A9, A11.
  Concerto in C maj for 2 oboes and strings, Op. 7, No. 2.
  LB:A8, A11.
  Concerto in B flat maj for oboe and strings, Op. 7, No. 3.
  LB:A5, A8, A19, A21, A592, A621, A624.
  Concerto in B flat maj for trumpet and strings, Arr. Op. 7,
    No. 3.
  LB:A650, A655.
  Concerto in G maj for strings and continuo, Op. 7, No. 4.
  LB:A9, A11.
  Concerto in C maj for 2 oboes and strings, Op. 7, No. 5.
  LB:A8, A622.

Concerto in C maj for trumpet and strings, Arr. Op. 7, No. 5.
LB:A651, A654.
Concerto in D maj for oboe and strings, Op. 7, No. 6.
LB:A5, A8, A21, A621.
Concerto in D maj for trumpet and strings, Arr. Op. 7, No. 6.
LB:A10, A650.
Concerto in G maj for strings and continuo, Op. 7, No. 7.
LB:A9.
Concerto in D maj for 2 oboes and strings, Op. 7, No. 8.
LB:A8.
Concerto in F maj for oboe and strings, Op. 7, No. 9.
LB:A5, A8.
Concerto in B flat maj for strings and continuo, Op. 7, No. 10.
LB:A9.
Concerto in C maj for 2 oboes and strings, Op. 7, No. 11.
LB:A8.
Concerto in C maj for oboe and strings, Op. 7, No. 12.
LB:A5, A8.
Concertos for oboe or violin and strings, Op. 9, Nos. 1-12.
1 in B flat maj for violin; 2 in D min for oboe; 3 in F maj for 2 oboes; 4 in A maj for violin; 5 in C maj for oboe; 6 in G maj for violin; 7 in D maj for violin; 8 in G min for oboe; 9 in C maj for 2 oboes; 10 in F maj for violin; 11 in B flat maj for oboe; 12 in D maj for 2 oboes.
LB:A12, A13.
Concerto in B flat maj for violin and strings, Op. 9, No. 1.
LB:A15.
Concerto in D min for oboe and strings, Op. 9, No. 2.
LB:A10, A618, A619, A626.
Concerto in D min for trumpet and organ, Arr. Op. 9, No. 2.
LB:B205, B208.
Concerto in F maj for 2 oboes and strings, Op. 9, No. 3.
LB:A11, A15.
Concerto in F maj for trumpet and strings, Arr. Op. 9, No. 3.
LB:A14.
Concerto in C maj for trumpet and organ, Arr. Op. 9, No. 5.
LB:B209.
Concerto in G maj for trumpet and strings, Arr. Op. 9, No. 6.
LB:A14.
Concerto in G min for violin and strings, Op. 9, No. 8.
LB:A15, F71.
Concerto in C maj for trumpet and strings, Arr. Op. 9, No. 9.
LB:A14.
Concerto in D maj for trumpet and strings, Arr. Op. 9, No. 12.
LB:A14.
Concertos for violin and strings, Op. 10, Nos. 1-12.
1 in B flat maj; 2 in G min; 3 in C maj; 4 in G maj; 5 in A maj; 6 in D maj; 7 in F maj; 8 in G min; 9 in C maj; 10 in F maj; 11 in C min; 12 in B flat maj.
LB:A16.
Concerto in B flat maj for strings and continuo, Op. 10, No. 1.
LB:A11.
Concerto in G min for violin and strings, Op. 10, No. 9.
LB:A15.
Concerto in A maj for trumpet and 6 clarinets.
LB:A649.
Concerto in B flat maj for trumpet and strings.
LB:A648, A652.
Concerto in C maj for trumpet, 3 oboes, bassoon and continuo.
LB:A647.
Concerto in C maj for violin and strings.
LB:A3, A18.

Sinfonia in B flat maj for strings and continuo.
LB:A10.
Sinfonia a 4 No. 2 in G maj for strings and continuo.
LB:A587.
Sinfonia a 4 No. 3 in G min for strings and continuo.
LB:A586.
Sonata a 5 in D maj for 2 oboes, bassoon and 2 horns.
LB:A627.
Sonata a 5 in G min for strings and continuo.
LB:A10.
b. Chamber and Instrumental
Sonata in D min for organ, Arr. Op. 1, No. 1.
LB:E1.
Sonata in F maj for organ, Arr. Op. 1, No. 2.
LB:E1.
Sonata in C maj for organ, Arr. Op. 1, No. 5.
LB:E1.
Sonata in E min for organ, Arr. Op. 1, No. 11.
LB:E1.
Sonata in A min for violin and continuo, Op. 6, No. 4.
LB:B3.
Concerto in D min for trumpet and strings, Arr. Op. 6, No. 4.
LB:A653.
Sonata in F maj for violin and strings, Op. 6, No. 5.
LB:B3.
Sonata in F maj for trumpet and organ, Arr. Op. 6, No. 5.
LB:B207.
Sonata in D min for violin and continuo, Op. 6, No. 6.
LB:B3.
Sonata in A min for 2 flutes and continuo, Op. 6, No. 6.
LB:B226.
Sonata in D maj for trumpet and organ, Arr. Op. 6, No. 7.
LB:B207.
Sonata in A maj for violin and continuo, Op. 6, No. 11.
LB:B3.
Concerto in B flat maj for trumpet and strings, Arr. Op. 6, No. 11
LB:A655.

ALBRICI, Vincenzo (1631-1696)
b. Chamber and Instrumental
Sinfonia in D min.
LB:B1.

ALDER, Cosmas (1497-1550)
e. Sacred Vocal
Da Jacob nu das Klein ansach.
LR:A2, F78.

ALDOMAR, Juan (16th. cent.)
d. Secular Vocal
Ah, Pelayo, que desmayo! (Cancionero de Upsala)
LR:E23.

ALDROVANDINI, Giuseppe (1673-1707)
e. Sacred Vocal
O bambino mio divino.
LB:E182.

ALISON, Richard (d.1609)
b. Instrumental
The Batchelar's Delight.
LR:Ga12, Ga13, Gd21.
De la tromba pavan.
LR:Ga12, Gd21.
Dolorosa pavan.
LR:A1, E24.
Goe from my window.
LR:Ga12, Ga13, Gd19.
Lady Frances Sidney's Almain.
LR:Gd19.
d. Secular Vocal
Shall I abide this jesting.
LR:Gd19.

ALLEGRI, Gregorio (1582-1652)
　a. Orchestral
　Sinfonia in G maj for strings and continuo.
　EB:G11.
　e. Sacred Vocal
　Miserere (Psalm 50)
　LR:Ge30, Ge31.
　EB:G133.
　LB:G319, G320.

ALMOROX, (15th. cent.)
　d. Secular Vocal
　O dichoso!
　LR:E25.

ALONSO (16th. cent.)
　d. Secular Vocal
　Gritos davan en aquella sierra.
　LR:E27.
　La Tricotea Samartin.
　LR:A3, A8, E26, E28.

ALTENBURG, Johann Ernst (1734-1801)
　b. Instrumental
　Concerto in D maj for 7 trumpets and tympani.
　LB:A656.

ALTNIKOL, Johann Christoph (1720-1759)
　e. Sacred Vocal
　Befiehl du deine Wege.
　LR:E29.
　LB:G321.
　Nun danket alle Gott.
　LB:G318.

ALVARADO, Diego de (16th. cent.)
　c. Keyboard – Organ
　Tiento por de la sol re sobre el pange lingua Espagnol.
　LR:D13.

AMIENS – *see* GUILLAUME D'AMIENS

AMMERBACH, Elias Nicolaus (1530-1597)
　c. Keyboard
　Ich sage ade.
　LR:D14.
　Passamezzo.
　LR:B11, B13.
　Wer das Töchterlein haben will.
　EB:E56.

AMNER, John (d.1641)
　c. Keyboard – Organ
　3 Verses on 'O Lord, in thee is all my trust.'
　LB:D214.

ANCHIETA, Juan de (1462-1523)
　d. Secular Vocal
　Con amores la mi madre.
　LR:E31.
　Dos anades, Madre.
　LR:E30.
　En memoria d'Alixandre.
　LR:E26.
　e. Sacred Vocal
　Kyrie.
　LR:E27.

ANDREA DE FLORENTIA (14th. cent.)
　d. Secular Vocal
　Presunzion da ignoranca.
　AN:B3.
　Sotto candido vel.
　AN:B3.

ANDREU, Francisco (17th. cent.)
　c. Keyboard – Organ
　Tiento llano a 3.

LR:D13.
Tiento partido de mane derecha a 3.
LR:D13.
Versos de 4o tono para despues de la Epistola.
LR:D13.

ANDRIEU, Francescus (15th. cent.)
　d. Secular Vocal
　Armes amours – O flour des flours.
　AN:A1.
　ER:A11.
　Phiton, Phiton.
　AN:A2.

ANERIO, Giovanni Francesco (1567-1630)
　e. Sacred Vocal
　Christus factus est.
　LR:F79, F80.

ANGLEBERT – *see* D'ANGLEBERT, Jean-Henri.

ANTEGNATI, Costanzo (1549-1624)
　c. Keyboard – Organ
　Ricercar III del decimo tono.
　LR:D15.

ANTHONELLO DA CASERTA (14th./15th. cent.)
　d. Secular Vocal
　Amour m'a le cuer mis.
　AN:A2.
　Beaute parfaite.
　AN:B4.

ANTONI, Giovanni Battista degli (1660-1700)
　b. Chamber and Instrumental
　Ricercata VIII for solo cello.
　LB:B309.
　Ricercata XI for solo cello.
　LB:B308.

APPENZELLER, Benedictus (c.1550)
　d. Secular Vocal
　Plangite Pierides.
　LR:A2, E32.

APT MS (c.1380-1420)
　e. Sacred Vocal
　Agnus Dei.
　AN:B5.
　Benedictus.
　AN:B5.
　Jesu nostra redemptio.
　ER:B6.

ARANIES, Juan (c.1600)
　b. Instrumental
　A la vida bona – Chaconne.
　LR:E30.

ARAUJO, Pedro de (d.1684)
　c. Keyboard – Organ
　Battallia de 6o tono.
　EB:E57, E58.
　Obra de 1o tono.
　EB:E57, E58.
　Tiento de 2o tono.
　EB:E58.
　LB:D215.

ARAUXO – *see* CORREA DE ARAUXO, Francisco.

ARBEAU, Thoinot (1519-1595)
　b. Instrumental (Orchesographie)
　Allemande.
　LR:B1.
　LB:A593.
　Antoinette – Galliard.
　LR:B1.

Sonata in D min for viola d'amore and continuo.
LB:B310.

ARNAUD, Pascal (18th. cent.)
  b. Instrumental
  Tambourin.
  LR:B12.

ARNAUT DE MARVELH (c.1195)
  d. Secular Vocal
  Na carenza al bel cors avinen.
  AA:D1.

ARNE, Thomas Augustine (1710–1778)
  a. Orchestral
  Concerto No. 1 for organ and orchestra: Allegro.
  LB:E184.
  Concerto No. 4 in B flat maj for organ and strings.
  LB:A23.
  Concerto No. 5 in G min for organ and strings.
  LB:A23, A24, A594, A595.
  Concerto No. 6 in B flat maj for organ and strings.
  LB:A23.
  Con spirito (from unspec. Organ Concerto.)
  LB:E183.
  Overtures, Nos. 1–8.
    1 in E min; 2 in A maj; 3 in G maj; 4 in F maj; 5 in D maj; 6
    in B flat maj; 7 in D maj; 8 in G min.
  LB:A22.
  Overture No. 1 in E min.
  LB:A24.
  Symphony No. 1 in C maj.
  LB:A25.
  Symphony No. 2 in F maj.
  LB:A25.
  Symphony No. 3 in E flat maj.
  LB:A25.
  Symphony No. 4 in C min.
  LB:A25.
  b. Chamber and Instrumental
  Trio Sonata in A maj for violin(s) and continuo, Op. 3, No.
    1.
  LB:B4.
  Trio Sonata in E flat maj for violin(s) and continuo, Op. 3,
    No. 3.
  LB:B4.
  c. Keyboard – Harpsichord
  Sonatas for harpsichord, Nos. 1–8.
    1 in F maj; 2 in E min; 3 in G maj; 4 in D min; 5 in B flat
    maj; 6 in G min; 7 in A maj; 8 in G maj.
  LB:D1.
  Sonata No. 1 in F maj.
  LR:Gc7.
  LB:A24.
  Sonata No. 2 in E min.
  LR:Gc7.
  Sonata No. 3 in G maj.
  LB:D216, D217.
  Sonata No. 5 in B flat maj.
  LB:B4.
  Sonata No. 6 in G maj.
  EB:D30.
  Allegro in F maj (Sonata No. 1).
  LR:Gc6.
  d. Secular Vocal
  Blow, blow, thou winter wind.
  LB:B319.
  SI:B2.
  Come away death.
  LR:Gd23.
  SI:B2.
  Come unto these yellow sands.
  LB:B4.
  Fair Celia love pretended (Bacchus and Ariadne).
  LB:F78.

The Miller on the Dee (Love in a Village)
EB:B37.
The Morning – Cantata.
LB:B4.
Under the Greenwood tree.
LB:B227.
When daisies pied.
LB:B319.
Where the bee sucks.
LR:Gd22, Gd23.
LB:B4, B319.
  e. Sacred Vocal
  Libera me.
  LR:Ge32.

ARNT VON AICH LIEDERBUCH
  d. Secular Vocal
  Ein meidlein tet mir klagen.
  ER:A22, A25.
  Ein pauer gab seim son ein weib.
  ER:A22.
  Vil hinderlist.
  ER:A22.

ARRAS – *see* MONIOT D'ARRAS.

ASCANIO, Jusquin d' (c.1445–1521)
  e. Sacred Vocal
  In te Domine speravi.
  LR:E26:

ASTON, Hugh (1485–1522)
  b. Instrumental
  Hornepype.
  LR:B10, B11, Ga14.

ATTIAGNANT, Pierre (1480–1552)
  b. Instrumental
  Au joly bois – Basse danse.
  LR:E42.
  SI:C6.
  Basse danse (Unsp.)
  ER:A8, A22.
  LR:B19, D16, D17, E25, E37.
  EB:C5.
  Belfiore – Pavan.
  EB:D29.
  LB:D213.
  Branle.
  LR:D16.
  Branle de Champagne.
  LR:B19, E45.
  Branle de Poictou.
  LR:C15, E45.
  Branle des Lavandieres.
  LR:B19.
  Branle Double.
  EB:D29.
  LB:D213.
  Branle gai.
  LR:B14, C14, C15.
  Branle gai de Poictou.
  LR:D17.
  EB:D29.
  LB:D213.
  Branles I and II.
  LR:F103.
  Branles I–V.
  ER:A22.
  LR:E36.
  La Brosse – Basse danse.
  ER:A8.
  LR:B16, C9.
  C'est boucaner.
  ER:A8.
  LR:C15.

C'est mon amy.
LR:C15.
Content desir – Basse danse.
LR:A1, E42.
Cortesana padoana.
LR:B10.
Destre amoureux.
LR:C9, C14.
L'Espoir que j'ay.
LR:D12, D16.
SI:C6.
Galliards I and II.
LR:D16, F103.
Galliard (Unsp.)
LR:B10, B14, B17, B18, C9, D14, D17, E25, E43, E45.
EB:C5, D29.
LB:D213.
La Gatta – Basse danse.
LR:B16.
La Guerre.
LR:C11.
Haulberroys.
LR:C14.
Il est jour dit l'Alouette.
SI:C6.
Kyrie (Keyboard Tablature)
LR:Gf1.
Kyrie cunctipotens (Keyboard Tablature)
LR:D16.
La Madelena – Basse danse.
LR:B14, B16, C11, C14, C15, E44.
Magnificat in 1re ton.
ER:A7.
Magnificat in 4me ton.
LR:D16.
Pavan.
EB:C5.
O vos omnes (after Compere)
LR:Gf1.
Pavan.
ER:A22.
LR:B10, B17, B18, B19, D17, E25, E37, E45, Gf1.
2 Pavanes, 2 Galliards.
ER:A8.
Prelude.
LR:C15, D16.
Puis qu'en deux cueurs – Basse danse.
LR:C15.
Recoup et Tourdion.
LR:C9, C15.
La Roque – Basse danse.
LR:C9.
La Rote de ronde – Pavane.
LR:C9.
Sans roche – Basse danse.
LR:C9.
EB:D29.
LB:D213.
Sanssere – Basse danse.
LR:C14, C15, E43.
Suite of Dances (Unsp.)
LR:D12.
Tablature – Excpts.
ER:A7.
Tant que vivray.
LR:C9, C14, D16.
EB:C5.
Te Deum (Keyboard Tablature)
ER:A7.
LR:D16.
Tourdion.
ER:A8, A22.
LR:B10, B12, B14, B16.
EB:C5.

Tourdions I–III.
LR:E43.
Tous mes amys – Basse danse.
LR:C9.
Tripla.
LR:B16.

ATTEY, John (d.c.1640)
d. Secular Vocal
My days, my months, my years.
LR:Gd24.

AUVERGNE – *see* D'AUVERGNE, Antoine.

AVISON, Charles (1709–1770)
a. Orchestral
12 Concerti Grossi after Domenico Scarlatti.
1 in A maj; 2 in G maj; 3 in D min; 4 in A min; 5 in D min; 6 in D maj; 7 in G min; 8 in E min; 9 in C maj; 10 in D maj; 11 in G maj; 12 in D maj.
LB:A27.
Concerto in G min for strings and continuo, Op. 2, No. 1.
LB:A26.
Concerto in E min for strings and continuo, Op. 2, No. 3.
LB:A26.
Concerto No. 8 in E min for strings and continuo (1758)
LB:A26.
Concerto No. 9 in D maj for strings and continuo (1758)
LB:A26.
Concerto No. 10 in E maj for strings and continuo (1758)
LB:A26.
Concerto No. 12 in A maj for strings and continuo (1758)
LB:A26.

AZALAIS DE PORCAIRAGUES (12th. cent.)
d. Secular Vocal
Ar em al freg temps vengut.
AA:D2.
Vida.
AA:D2.

AZZAIOLA, Filippo (1535–1569)
b. Instrumental
Girometta.
LR:A1.
d. Secular Vocal
Al di dolce.
LR:E42.
Chi passa per sta strada.
LR:E20, E42.
Gentil Madonna.
LR:E20.
Quanda la sera.
LR:A1.
Sentomi la formicula.
LR:A1, E24.
Ti partit cor mio caro.
LR:E20.

BABELL, William (1690–1723)
b. Instrumental and Chamber
Concerto a 7 in D maj for recorder, strings and continuo.
LB:B229, B230.
Sonata No. 1 in B flat maj for oboe and continuo.
LB:B228.
Sonata in F min for oboe and organ.
LB:B210.
c. Keyboard
Grand Lesson for the forte-piano on an air from Handel's 'Rinaldo'.
LR:Gc7.

BABOU, 'Monsieur' Rene (c.1710)
c. Keyboard – Organ
Fantasia des trompettes basse et haute.
PS:A47.

BACH, Carl Philip Emmanuel (1714–1788)
a. Orchestral
Concerto in E maj for harpsichord and orchestra, Wq. 14.
LB:A38.
Concerto in D min for flute and strings, Wq. 22.
LB:A32, A33, A45, A47.
Concerto in D min for harpsichord, 2 violins, viola and continuo, Wq. 23.
LB:A30, A628.
Concerto in D maj for harpsichord and orchestra, Wq. 27.
LB:A29.
Concerto in A maj for harpsichord and orchestra, Wq. 29.
LB:A29.
Concerto in G maj for organ and strings, Wq. 34.
LB:A31.
Concerto in E flat maj for organ and strings, Wq. 35.
LB:A31.
Concerto in C min for harpsichord and orchestra, Wq. 43/4.
LB:A24.
Concerto in G maj for harpsichord and orchestra, Wq. 43/5.
LB:A38.
Concerto in F maj for harpsichord, forte-piano and orchestra, Wq. 46.
LB:A28, A42.
Concerto in E flat maj for harpsichord, forte-piano, 2 flutes, 2 horns and strings, Wq. 47.
LB:A40, A44.
Sonatina in D min for 2 harpsichords and orchestra, Wq. 107.
LB:A28.
Sonatina in D maj for 2 harpsichords and orchestra, Wq. 109.
LB:A28.
Concerto in E flat maj for oboe and strings, Wq. 165.
LB:A30, A43.
Concerto in A min for flute and strings, Wq. 166.
LB:A34.
Concerto in G maj for flute and strings, Wq. 169.
LB:A32, A34.
Concerto in A maj for cello and strings, Wq. 172.
LB:A33.
Concerto in A min for flute and strings.
LB:A46.
Concerto in B flat maj for oboe and strings.
LB:A43.
Sinfonia in C maj, Wq. 174.
LB:A35.
Sinfonia in D maj, Wq. 176.
LB:A35.
Sinfonias for strings, Wq. 182, 'Hamburg'. Nos. 1–6.
    1 in C maj; 2 in B flat maj; 3 in C maj; 4 in A maj; 5 in B min; 6 in E maj.
LB:A35.
Sinfonia in B flat maj, Wq. 182/2.
LB:A36.
Sinfonia in C maj, Wq. 182/3.
LB:A36.
Sinfonia in A maj, Wq. 182/4.
LB:A36.
Sinfonia in B min, Wq. 182/5.
LB:A36.
Orchestral Trios, Wq. 183, Nos. 1–4.
    1 in D maj; 2 in E flat maj; 3 in F maj; 4 in G maj.
LB:A37.
Orchestral Trio in G maj, Wq. 183/4.
LB:A41.
Sinfonia in B flat maj.
LB:A39.
b. Chamber and Instrumental Music

Sonata in D maj for flute and harpsichord, Wq. 83.
LB:B5, B239.
Sonata in C maj for flute and harpsichord, Wq. 87.
LB:B5.
Quartet in A min for flute, violin, cello and keyboard, Wq. 93.
LB:B7.
Quartet in D maj for flute, violin, cello and keyboard, Wq. 94.
LB:B7.
Quartet in G maj for flute, violin, cello and keyboard, Wq. 95.
LB:B7.
Sonata in E min for flute and continuo, Wq. 124.
LB:B5.
Sonata in A min for flute and continuo, Wq. 128.
LB:B5.
Sonata in A min for solo flute, Wq. 132.
LB:B234, B236, B238, B240.
Sonata in G maj for flute and continuo, Wq. 133.
LB:B5, B235.
Sonata in G min for oboe and continuo, Wq. 135.
LB:A618, B211, B228, B241.
Solo in C maj for harp, Wq. 139.
LB:B320.
Trio Sonata in B min for flute, violin and continuo, Wq. 143.
LB:B6.
Trio Sonata in A min for flute, violin and continuo, Wq. 145.
LB:B6.
Trio Sonata in D min for flute, violin and continuo, Wq. 145.
LB:A629.
Trio Sonata in D min for flute, violin and continuo, Wq. 147.
LB:B6.
Trio Sonata in C maj for flute, violin and continuo, Wq. 148.
LB:B6.
Trio Sonata in E maj for 2 flutes and continuo, Wq. 162.
LB:B233.
March in D maj, Wq. 185/1.
EB:B38.
LB:A657.
Minuet and Trio.
LB:B48.
5 Polonaises, Wq. 190.
LB:A48.
Duo in G maj for flute and violin.
LB:B240.
6 Little Sonatas for harpsichord, clarinet and bassoon.
LB:B232.
Sonata in D maj for flute and continuo.
LB:B237.
Trio Sonata in E flat maj for flute, violin, and continuo.
LB:B231.
Trio Sonata in F maj for bass flute, viola and continuo.
LB:B240.
c. Keyboard – Harpsichord and Organ
Sonata in A min, Wq. 33.
LB:B305.
Sonatas, Wq. 48, Nos. 1–6, 'Prussian'.
LB:D3.
Sonata in C maj, Wq. 48/5.
SI:A1.
Sonatas, Wq. 49, Nos. 1–6, 'Württemburg'.
    1 in A min; 2 in A flat maj; 3 in E min; 4 in B flat maj; 5 in E flat maj; 6 in B min.
LB:D2.
Sonata in A min, Wq. 49/1.
EB:D31.
Sonata in C maj, Wq. 55/1.
LB:D4.

Sonata in B min, Wq. 55/3.
LB:D7.
Sonata in F maj, Wq. 55/5.
LB:D7.
Rondo in C maj, Wq. 56/1.
LB:D4, D5.
Sonata in G maj, Wq. 56/2.
LB:D5.
Rondo, Wq. 56/5.
LB:D8.
Sonata, Wq. 56/6.
LB:D8.
Rondo in E maj, Wq. 57/1.
LB:D4.
Sonata in D min, Wq. 57/4.
LB:D4.
Fantasia in E flat maj, Wq. 58/6.
LB:D4.
Fantasia in F maj, Wq. 59/5.
LB:D4.
Fantasia in C maj, Wq. 59/6.
LB:D5, D9.
Rondo in D min, Wq. 61/4.
LB:D4.
Fantasia in C maj, Wq. 61/6.
LB:D9.
Adagio in D min, Wq. 66.
LB:E2.
Sonatas for organ, Wq. 70, Nos. 1-6.
LB:E2.
Sonata in B flat maj, Wq. 70/2.
LB:E186.
Sonata in G min, Wq. 70/4.
LB:E187.
Sonata in G min, Wq. 70/4: 1st. Movement.
LB:A186.
Sonata in D maj, Wq. 70/5.
LB:E188.
Praeludium in D maj, Wq. 70/7.
LB:E2.
4 Small Duets for 2 keyboards, Wq. 115.
LB:D6.
Variations on 'Les Folies d'Espagne', Wq. 118.
LB:A24, D8, D220.
Fugue in E flat maj, Wq. 119/6.
LB:E2.
Fantasia and fugue in C min, Wq. 119/7.
LB:A31, E2, E186.
Sonata in G maj, Wq. 139.
LB:D218.
Fantasia in C min, Wq. 254.
LB:D9.
Fantasia in C maj.
LB:B7.
Fantasia in F sharp min.
LB:D219.
Fugue in D min.
LB:E2, E185.
e. Sacred Vocal
Magnificat in D maj, Wq. 215.
LB:G1, G2.

BACH, Heinrich (1615-1692)
e. Sacred Vocal
Nun ist alles über wunden.
LB:G323.

BACH, Johann (1604-1673)
e. Sacred Vocal
Unser Leben ist ein Schatten.
LB:G323.

BACH, Johann Bernard (1676-1749)
c. Keyboard - Organ
Du Friedefürst, Herr Jesu Christ.

LB:E185, E190.
Passacaglia.
LB:E190.

BACH, Johann Christian (1735-1782)
a. Orchestral
Concertos for keyboard and orchestra, Op. 1, Nos. 1-6.
    1 in B flat maj; 2 in A maj; 3 in F maj; 4 in G maj; 5 in C
    maj; 6 in D maj.
LB:A49.
Concertos for keyboard and orchestra, Op. 7, Nos. 1-6.
    1 in C maj; 2 in F maj; 3 in D maj; 4 in B flat maj; 5 in E
    flat maj; 6 in G maj.
LB:A49.
Concerto in E flat maj for harpsichord and orchestra, Op.
    7, No. 5.
LB:A57.
Concertos for keyboard and orchestra, Op. 13, Nos. 1-6.
    1 in C maj; 2 in D maj; 3 in F maj; 4 in B flat maj; 5 in G
    maj; 6 in E flat maj.
LB:A49.
Concerto in D maj for harpsichord and orchestra, Op. 13,
    No. 2.
LB:A50.
Concerto in B flat maj for harpsichord and orchestra, Op.
    13, No. 4.
LB:A50.
Concerto in B flat maj for harpsichord and orchestra, Op.
    13, No. 4: Andante con moto.
LB:D221.
Concerto in A maj for harpsichord and strings.
LB:A66.
Concerto in C min for cello and strings.
LB:A17.
Concerto in C min for harpsichord and strings.
LB:A51.
Concerto in C min for viola and orchestra (Cassadesus).
LB:A64.
Concerto in D maj for flute and orchestra.
LB:A51.
Concerto in D maj for harpsichord and orchestra.
LB:A38.
Concerto in E flat maj for bassoon and strings.
LB:A63.
Concerto in F maj for oboe and strings.
LB:A51.
Overtures, Nos. 1-6.
    1 in D maj; 2 in D maj; 3 in D maj; 4 in C maj; 5 in G maj;
    6 in G maj.
LB:A54.
Overture in D maj, 'La Calamita de cuori.'
LB:A55, A596.
Sinfonia Concertante in A maj for violin, cello and
    orchestra.
LB:A53.
Sinfonia Concertante in C maj for flute, oboe, violin, cello
    and orchestra.
LB:A52, A67.
Sinfonia Concertante in E flat maj for 2 violins and
    orchestra.
LB:A52.
Sinfonia Concertante in F maj for oboe, cello and
    orchestra.
LB:A52.
Sinfonia Concertante in F maj for oboe, cello, 2 oboes, 2
    horns and strings.
LB:A40.
Sinfonias, Op. 6, Nos. 1-6.
    1 in G maj; 2 in D maj; 3 in E flat maj; 4 in B flat maj; 5 in
    E flat maj; 6 in G min.
LB:A55.
Sinfonia in G maj, Op. 6, No. 1.
LB:A65.
Sinfonia in E flat maj, Op. 6, No. 3.

LB:A56.
Sinfonia in G min, Op. 6, No. 6.
LB:A39, A57, A58.
Sinfonias, Op. 8, Nos. 2-4.
  2 in G maj; 3 in D maj; 4 in F maj.
LB:A55.
Sinfonias, Op. 9, Nos. 1-3.
  1 in B flat maj; 2 in E flat maj; 3 in B flat maj.
LB:A55.
Sinfonia in B flat maj, Op. 9, No. 1.
LB:A65.
Sinfonia in E flat maj, Op. 9, No. 2.
LB:A56, A60, A67.
Sinfonia in B flat maj, Op. 9, No. 3.
LB:A59.
Sinfonias, Op. 18, Nos. 1-6.
  1 in E flat maj for double orchestra; 2 in B flat maj; 3 in
  D maj for double orchestra; 4 in D maj; 5 in E flat maj
  for double orchestra; 6 in D maj.
LB:A60.
Sinfonia in E flat maj for double orchestra, Op. 18, No. 1.
LB:A53, A59, A61, A68.
Sinfonia in B flat maj, Op. 18, No. 2.
LB:A56.
Sinfonia in D maj for double orchestra, Op. 18, No. 3.
LB:A59, A61.
Sinfonia in D maj, Op. 18, No. 4.
LB:A56, A58, A59.
Sinfonia in E flat maj for double orchestra, Op. 18, No. 5.
LB:A61, A62.
Sinfonia in D maj, Op. 18, No. 6.
LB:A58.
b. Chamber and Instrumental
Concerto in E flat maj for trumpet and organ (Arr. Sonata
  in F maj for flute and harpsichord).
LB:B204.
Quartet in C maj for 2 flutes, violin and cello.
LB:B243.
Quartet in D maj for 2 flutes, viola and cello.
LB:B243.
Quartet in C maj for oboe and string trio, Op. 8, No. 1.
LB:B2.
Quartet in E flat maj for oboe and string trio, Op. 8, No. 3.
LB:B2.
Quartet in G maj for oboe and string trio, Op. 8, No. 6.
LB:B2.
Quintet in E flat maj for flute, oboe, violin, viola and
  harpsichord, Op. 11, No. 4.
LB:B242.
Quintet in D maj for flute, oboe, violin, viola and harpsi-
  chord, Op. 11, No. 6.
LB:B231, B232.
Quintet in D maj for flute, oboe, violin, cello and harpsi-
  chord, Op. 22.
LB:B244.
Quintet in F maj for flute, oboe; violin and continuo, Op.
  22, No. 2.
LB:B242.
Sonatas for flute and keyboard, Op. 16, Nos. 1-6.
  1 in D maj; 2 in G maj; 3 in C maj; 4 in A maj; 5 in D maj;
  6 in F maj.
LB:B8.
Sonatas for flute and keyboard, Op. 18, Nos. 1-4.
  1 in C maj; 2 in D maj; 3 in E flat maj; 4 in G maj.
LB:B9.
Sonatas for flute and keyboard, Op. 19, Nos. 1-6.
  1 in C maj; 2 in G maj; 3 in D maj; 4 in A maj; 5 in E flat
  maj; 6 in B flat maj.
LB:B10.
c. Keyboard – Harpsichord
Aria and 15 Variations.
LB:D222.
Sonata in D maj, Op. 5, No. 5.
LB:D223.

Sonata in C min, Op. 5, No. 6.
LB:D216.
Sonata in A maj for 2 keyboards, Op. 15.
LB:D10.
Sonata in C maj for 2 keyboards, Op. 15.
LB:D10.
Sonata in F maj for 2 keyboards, Op. 15.
LB:D10.
Sonata in G maj for 2 keyboards, Op. 15.
LB:D6.
Sonata in G maj, Op. 17, No. 4: Presto.
LB:D221.
Duet in A maj, Op. 18, No. 5.
LB:B9.
Duet in F maj, Op. 18, No. 6.
LB:B9.

BACH, Johann Christoph (1642-1703)
c. Keyboard – Organ
Aria in A min.
EB:D32.
Praeludium and fugue in E flat maj.
LB:E190.
Aus meines Herzuns Grunde.
LB:E190.
Wachet auf mein Herz.
LB:E190.
Warum betrübst du dich.
LB:E185, E190.
e. Sacred Vocal
Ach, dass ich Wassers g'nug hätte.
EB:G134, G324.
Der Mensch vom Weibe geboren.
LR:F27.
Ich lasse dich nicht.
LB:G323.

BACH, Johann Christoph Friedrich (1732-1795)
b. Chamber and Instrumental
Sextet in C maj for harpsichord, oboe, 2 horns, violin and
  cello.
LB:B242.
Sonata in D maj for forte-piano concertante, flute and
  cello.
LB:B245.
c. Keyboard – Harpsichord and Organ
Allegretto con variazione.
LB:E191.
Prelude in E min.
LB:E185.
Sonata in A maj for 2 keyboards.
LB:D10.
Sonatine in A min.
LB:D7.
Variations on 'Ah vous dirai-je Maman.'
LB:D8.

BACH, Johann Ernst (1722-1777)
c. Keyboard – Organ
Fantasia and fugue in D min.
LB:E185.
Fantasia and fugue in F maj.
LB:E190.

BACH, Johann Lorenz (1695-1773)
c. Keyboard – Organ
Praeludium and fugue in D maj.
LB:E190.

BACH, Johann Ludwig (1677-1731)
a. Orchestral
Orchestral Suite in G maj.
LB:A41.
e. Sacred Vocal
Das ist meine Freude.
LB:G323.

Es danken dir Gott.
LB:G323.

BACH, Johann Michael (1648–1694)
  c. Keyboard – Organ
  Allein Gott in der Höh' sei Ehr'.
  LB:E190.
  Chorale Variations (Unsp.)
  LB:E186.
  Wenn wir in höchsten Nöten sein.
  LB:E185, E190.
  e. Sacred Vocal
  Ich weiss das mein Erlöser lebt.
  LB:G323.

BACH, Johann Nikolaus (1669–1753)
  e. Sacred Vocal
  Auf meinen lieben Gott.
  LB:G323.

BACH, Johann Sebastian (1685–1750)
  a. Orchestral, BWV 1041–1070
  Concerto in A min for violin and strings, BWV 1041.
  LB:A69, A70, A71, A72, A73, A74, A75, A76, A77, A78,
    A79, A80, A81, A82, A83, A84, A86, A174, A175,
    A213, A214.
  Concerto in A min for flute and strings, BWV 1041.
  LB:A176.
  Concerto in E maj for violin and strings, BWV 1042.
  LB:A69, A70, A71, A72, A73, A74, A75, A76, A77, A78,
    A79, A80, A81, A82, A83, A84, A85, A86, A174,
    A177, A178, A213, A214, A597.
  Concerto in D min for 2 violins and strings, BWV 1043.
  LB:A69, A71, A72, A73, A74, A75, A76, A77, A78, A79,
    A81, A82, A83, A84, A173, A177, A179, A213, A214.
  Concerto in A min for flute, violin, harpsichord and
    strings, BWV 1044.
  LB:A69, A163, A180, A181, A182, A183, A184, A185,
    A186, A213, A214.
  Concerto in D maj for violin and strings, BWV 1045:
    Sinfonia.
  LB:A187.
  Brandenburg Concertos, Nos. 1–6, BWV 1046–1051.
    1 in F maj; 2 in F maj; 3 in G maj; 4 in G maj; 5 in D maj; 6
      in B flat maj.
  LB:A87, A88, A89, A90, A91, A92, A93, A94, A95, A96,
    A97, A98, A99, A100, A101, A102, A103, A104,
    A105, A106, A107, A108, A109, A110, A111, A112,
    A113, A114, A115, A116, A117, A213, A214.
  Brandenburg Concerto No. 3 in G maj, BWV 1048.
  LB:A188, A582.
  Brandenburg Concerto No. 5 in D maj, BWV 1050.
  LB:A180, A181, A189, A600.
  Concertos for harpsichord and strings, BWV
    1052–1058.
    1 in D min; 2 in E maj; 3 in D maj; 4 in A maj; 5 in F min;
      6 in F maj; 7 in G min.
  LB:A118, A119, A120, A121, A122, A213.
  Concerto in D min for harpsichord and strings, BWV
    1052.
  LB:A42, A117, A123, A124, A125, A126, A127, A128,
    A129, A130, A131, A132, A187, A193, A214.
  Concerto in D min for violin and strings, BWV 1052.
  LB:A80, A175, A190, A191.
  Concerto in E maj for harpsichord and strings, BWV
    1053.
  LB:A117, A123, A124, A125, A126, A127, A133.
  Concerto in F maj for oboe and strings, BWV 1053.
  LB:A191, A192, A194.
  Concerto in D maj for harpsichord and strings, BWV
    1054.
  LB:A123, A135, A136, A137, A138, A195.
  Concerto in A maj for harpsichord and strings, BWV
    1055.
  LB:A123, A127, A128, A129, A130, A131, A133,

A134, A135, A136, A137, A196, A214.
  Concerto in A maj for viola d'amore and strings, BWV
    1055.
  LB:A190, A191, A197, A213.
  Concerto in A maj for oboe d'amore and strings, BWV
    1055.
  LB:A192, A195.
  Concerto in F min for harpsichord and strings, BWV
    1056.
  LB:A123, A128, A129, A130, A131, A133, A134,
    A136, A139, A140, A178, A214.
  Concerto in F min for harpsichord and strings, BWV
    1056: Largo.
  LB:A580, D65.
  Concerto in A min for flute and strings, BWV 1056.
  LB:A198.
  Concerto in G min for flute and strings, BWV 1056.
  LB:A176, A191, A199, A594.
  Concerto in G min for oboe d'amore and strings, BWV
    1056.
  LB:A190.
  Concerto in G min for violin and strings, BWV 1056.
  LB:A177, A195, A196.
  Concerto in F maj for harpsichord and strings, BWV
    1057.
  LB:A137, A138, A139, A141, A214.
  Concerto in G min for harpsichord and strings, BWV
    1058.
  LB:A123, A136, A138, A139, A140, A194.
  Concerto in D min for harpsichord and strings, BWV
    1059.
  LB:A118, A122, A142.
  Concerto in E min for flute and strings, BWV 1059.
  LB:A198, A200.
  Concertos for 2 harpsichords and strings, BWV
    1060–1062.
    1 in C min; 2 in C maj; 3 in C min.
  LB:A118, A143, A213.
  Concerto in C min for 2 harpsichords and strings, BWV
    1060.
  LB:A134, A140, A144, A174.
  Concerto in C min for 2 harpsichords and strings, BWV
    1060: Adagio.
  LB:A580.
  Concerto in C min for violin, oboe and strings, BWV
    1060.
  LB:A174, A175, A199.
  Concerto in C min for violin, trumpet and strings, BWV
    1060.
  LB:A206.
  Concerto in D min for violin, oboe and strings, BWV
    1060.
  LB:A69, A179, A182, A183, A187, A191, A202, A203,
    A204, A205, A213, A214, A594, A630.
  Concerto in C maj for 2 harpsichords and strings, BWV
    1061.
  LB:A119, A134, A140, A145, A184.
  Concerto in C min for 2 harpsichords and strings, BWV
    1062.
  LB:A119.
  Concertos for 3 harpsichords and strings, BWV
    1063–1064.
    1 in D min; 2 in C maj.
  LB:A118, A119, A134, A146, A147, A148, A213.
  Concerto in D min for 3 harpsichords and strings, BWV
    1063.
  LB:A142.
  Concerto in D min for violin, oboe, flute and strings, BWV
    1063.
  LB:A192.
  Concerto in C maj for 3 harpsichords and strings, BWV
    1064.
  LB:A132, A141, A142.
  Concerto in D maj for 3 violins and strings, BWV 1064.

LB:A191, A199, A602.
Concerto in D maj for flute, oboe, violin and strings, BWV 1064.
LB:A205.
Concerto in A min for 4 harpsichords and strings, BWV 1065.
LB:A118, A119, A132, A134, A141, A144, A146, A147, A148, A149, A213.
Orchestral Suites, BWV 1066-1069.
  1 in C maj; 2 in B min; 3 in D maj; 4 in D maj.
LB:A117, A150, A151, A152, A153, A154, A155, A156, A157, A158, A159, A160, A161, A162, A213.
Orchestral Suite in C maj, BWV 1066.
LB:A163, A164.
Orchestral Suite in B min, BWV 1067.
LB:A163, A165, A166, A167, A171, A172, A173, A185, A188, A193, A198, A200, A206, A214.
Orchestral Suite in B min, BWV 1067: Badinerie.
LB:A658.
Orchestral Suite in D maj, BWV 1068.
LB:A163, A165, A166, A167, A168, A169, A170, A178, A214.
Orchestral Suite in D maj, BWV 1068: Air.
LB:A83, A211, A580, A601, A658, B206, B226.
Orchestral Suite in D maj, BWV 1069.
LB:A164, A168, A189.
Orchestral Suite in G min, BWV 1070 (See also W.F.BACH).
LB:A162.

b. Chamber and Instrumental – Lute Works, BWV 995–1000 and arrangements
Suite for lute in G min, BWV 995.
LR:C10.
LB:B111, C2, C3, C5, C6, C7, C11, C12, C13, C21.
Allemande in G min, BWV 995.
LB:C8.
Bourree in G min, BWV 995.
LB:C8, C10.
Sarabande in G min, BWV 995.
LB:B253, C10.
Gavotte I in G min, BWV 995.
LB:B253.
Gavottes I and II in G min, BWV 995.
LB:B322.
Suite for lute in E min, BWV 996.
LB:B111, C1, C4, C6, C7, C9, C11.
Suite for lute in C min, BWV 997.
LB:B111, C4, C6, C7, C9, C22, C23, D92.
Sarabande in C min, BWV 997.
LB:B58.
Suite in C min for flute and continuo, Arr. BWV 997.
LB:B258.
Prelude, fugue and allegro in E flat maj, BWV 998.
LR:C10.
EB:D31.
LB:B111, C1, C4, C6, C7, C11, C21, D88.
Prelude in C min, BWV 999.
LB:B111, B249, C1, C4, C5, C6, C7, C8, C11, C24, D64, D78, D106.
Fugue in G min, BWV 1000 (after BWV 1001).
LR:C10.
LB:B111, B249, C5, C6, C7, C8, C14, C25.
Fugue in A min, BWV 1001.
LB:C1, C3, C9, C11, C24.
Adagio in G min, BWV 1001.
LB:C14.
Bourree in G min, BWV 1001.
LB:C25.
Sarabande in B min, BWV 1002.
LB:C1.
Chaconne in D min, BWV 1004.
LB:C10, D105.
Suite for lute in E maj, BWV 1006a.
LB:B111, C2, C3, C5, C6, C7, C8.

Gavotte in E maj, BWV 1006.
LB:C10.
Suite for lute in A maj, BWV 1007a.
LB:C8.
Prelude and Courante in C maj, BWV 1009.
LB:C10.
Prelude and Presto in C min, BWV 1011.
LB:C11.
Gavotte in D maj, BWV 1012.
LB:C10.

b. Chamber and Instrumental – Works for solo violin, solo cello, BWV 1001–1012 and arrangements
Sonatas and Partitas for solo violin, BWV 1001-1006.
  Sonata 1 in G min; Partita 1 in B min; Sonata 2 in A min; Partita 2 in D min; Sonata 3 in C maj; Partita 3 in E maj.
LB:B11, B12, B13, B14, B15, B16, B17, B18, B19, B20, B21, B22, B23, B111.
Sonata in G min for solo violin, BWV 1001.
LB:B24, B25.
Partita in B min for solo violin, BWV 1002.
LB:B25.
Sonata in A min for solo violin, BWV 1003.
LB:B26, B28.
Partita in D min for solo violin, BWV 1004.
LB:B26, B28, B29, B30.
Chaconne in D min, BWV 1004.
LB:A211, D76.
Sonata in C maj for solo violin, BWV 1005.
LB:B27, B30.
Adagio in C maj, BWV 1005.
LB:A209.
Partita in E maj for solo violin, BWV 1006.
LB:B24, B27, B29.
Prelude in E maj, BWV 1006.
LB:A209, A211.
Gavotte in E maj, BWV 1006.
LB:A209.
Gavotte and Rondeau in E maj, BWV 1006.
LB:B206.
Sonata in D min for solo flute, Arr. BWV 1001/2/3.
LB:B91.
Sonata in G min for solo flute, Arr. BWV 1004/5.
LB:B91.
Sonata in G maj for solo flute, Arr. BWV 1005/6.
LB:B91.

b. Chamber and Instrumental – Works for solo cello, BWV 1007–1012
Suites for solo cello, BWV 1007-1012.
  1 in G maj; 2 in D min; 3 in C maj; 4 in E flat maj; 5 in C min; 6 in D maj.
LB:B31, B32, B33, B34, B35, B36, B37, B38, B39, B40, B112.
Suite in G maj for solo cello, BWV 1007.
LB:B41.
Menuetto and Courante in G maj, BWV 1007, Arr. for brass.
EB:B38.
Suite in D min for solo cello, BWV 1008.
LB:B41, B42, B43.
Suite in C maj for solo cello, BWV 1009.
LB:B41, B44.
Bourree in C maj, BWV 1009.
LB:B322.
Bourree in E flat maj, BWV 1010.
LB:B206.
Suite in C min for solo cello, BWV 1011.
LB:B43, B45.
Suite in D maj for viola pomposa, BWV 1012.
LB:C12.

b. Chamber and Instrumental – Partita for solo flute, BWV 1013
Partita (sonata) in A min for solo flute, BWV 1013.
LB:A173, B66, B67, B70, B71, B73, B74, B86, B91,

B112.
Partita (sonata) in G min for solo oboe, BWV 1013.
LB:B72, B234, B236.
b.Chamber and Instrumental – Works for solo instrument and continuo, BWV 1014–1035
Sonatas for violin and harpsichord, BWV 1014–1019.
  1 in B min; 2 in A maj; 3 in E maj; 4 in C min; 5 in F min; 6 in G maj.
LB:B46, B47, B48, B49, B50, B51, B52, B53, B54, B55, B111.
Sonata in B min for violin and harpsichord, BWV 1014.
LB:B56, B57.
Sonata in B min for recorder and harpsichord, BWV 1014.
LB:B58.
Sonata in A maj for violin and harpsichord, BWV 1015.
LB:B57.
Andante in F sharp min, BWV 1015.
LB:E138..
Sonata in E maj for violin and harpsichord, BWV 1016.
LB:B56, B57.
Sonata in C min for violin and harpsichord, BWV 1017.
LB:B250.
Sonata in F min for violin and harpsichord, BWV 1018.
LB:B56.
Sonata in G min for flute and harpsichord, BWV 1020.
LB:B66, B68, B69, B70, B71, B75, B76, B77, B86, B112.
Sonata in G min for oboe and harpsichord, BWV 1020.
LB:B72, B250, B252, B254, B255, B256.
Sonata in C min for flute and continuo, BWV 1024.
LB:B246.
Sonatas for viola da gamba and harpsichord, BWV 1027–1029.
  1 in G maj; 2 in D maj; 3 in G min.
LB:B59, B60, B61, B62, B63, B64, B65, B112.
Sonata in G maj for viola da gamba and harpsichord, BWV 1027.
SI:C4.
Sonata in B min for flute and harpsichord, BWV 1030.
LB:B66, B67, B68, B69, B70, B71, B73, B74, B75, B76, B78, B79, B80, B81, B82, B85, B86, B112, B235, B246.
SI:C7.
Sonata in G min for oboe and harpsichord, BWV 1030.
LB:A72, B89, B248.
Sonata in E flat maj for flute and harpsichord, BWV 1031.
LB:B58, B66, B67, B68, B69, B70, B71, B73, B74, B75, B76, B78, B79, B86, B112.
SI:C18.
Sonata in E flat maj for flute and harpsichord, BWV 1031: Siciliano.
LB:D65, D67, D76.
Sonata in A maj for flute and harpsichord, BWV 1032.
LB:B66, B67, B69, B70, B71, B73, B74, B78, B79, B80, B81, B82, B85, B86, B112.
Sonata in C maj for flute and harpsichord, BWV 1033.
LB:B66, B67, B69, B70, B71, B73, B74, B75, B77, B83, B84, B86, B112.
Sonata in E min for flute and harpsichord, BWV 1034.
LB:B66, B67, B69, B70, B71, B73, B74, B75, B77, B80, B81, B82, B83, B84, B86, B112.
Sonata in E maj for flute and harpsichord, BWV 1035.
LB:B66, B67, B69, B70, B71, B73, B74, B75, B77, B80, B81, B82, B83, B84, B85, B86, B87, B112, B247.
b.Chamber and Instrumental – Trio Sonatas, BWV 1036–1039 and miscellaneous arrangements
Trio Sonata in D min for 2 violins and harpsichord, BWV 1036.
LB:B88, B251.
Trio Sonata in C maj for 2 violins and continuo, BWV 1037.
LB:B65, B88.

Trio Sonata in D maj for flute, violin and continuo, BWV 1038.
LB:B85, B86, B88, B246.
Trio Sonata in G maj for 2 flutes and continuo, BWV 1039.
LB:A631, B64, B85, B86, B88, B112, B231, B233, B257.
Instrumental Movement in F maj for violin, oboe and continuo, BWV 1040.
LB:A62, B88.
Trio Sonata in E flat maj for lute and continuo, Arr. BWV 525.
LB:C9.
Trio Sonata in G maj for flute and harpsichord, Arr. BWV 525.
LB:B90.
Trio Sonata in E flat maj for oboe, clarinet and bassoon, Arr. BWV 525.
LB:B92.
Trio Sonata in E min for flute and continuo, Arr. BWV 526.
LB:B90.
Trio Sonata in C min for recorder and harpsichord, Arr. BWV 527.
LB:B58.
Trio Sonata in D min for flute and harpsichord, Arr. BWV 527.
LB:B90.
Trio Sonata in D min for oboe, clarinet and bassoon, Arr. BWV 527.
LB:B92.
Trio Sonata in A min for flute and harpsichord, Arr. BWV 528.
LB:B90.
Trio Sonata in C maj for lute and continuo, Arr. BWV 529.
LB:C9.
Trio Sonata in F maj for flute and harpsichord, Arr. BWV 529.
LB:B90.
Trio Sonata in C maj for flute and harpsichord, Arr. BWV 530.
LB:B90.
Concerto in G maj for harp and orchestra, Arr. BWV 973.
LB:A201.
Concerto in C maj for harp and orchestra, Arr. BWV 976.
LB:A201.
Concerto in F maj for harp and orchestra, Arr. BWV 978.
LB:A201.
b.Chamber and Instrumental – Musical Offering, Art of Fugue, etc.
Canon in C maj a 8, BWV 1072.
LB:E138.
Canon in A min a 4, BWV 1073.
LB:E138, G175.
Canon in C maj a 4, BWV 1074.
LB:E138.
Canon in C maj a 2, BWV 1075.
LB:E138, G175.
Canon in G maj a 6, BWV 1076.
LB:A148.
Canon in G maj a 3, BWV 1077.
LB:G175.
Canon in F maj a 7, BWV 1078.
LB:E138, G175.
The Musical Offering, BWV 1079.
LB:B65, B93, B94, B95, B96, B97, B98, B99, B100, B101, B102, B103, B112.
The Musical Offering, BWV 1079: 10 Canons.
LB:E138.
  : Canon perpetuo.
LB:B88.
SI:A1.
  : Ricercar a 3.
SI:A1.

Toccata, adagio and fugue in C maj, BWV 564.
LB:E12, E17, E21, E25, E26, E30, E39, E41, E51, E59,
  E61, E66, E67, E73, E94, E116, E145, E146, E198.
Toccata and fugue in D min, BWV 565.
LB:A84, A209, A210, D76, E11, E17, E21, E23, E25,
  E26, E27, E30, E33, E36, E40, E41, E42, E44, E45,
  E46, E47, E51, E55, E56, E60, E61, E65, E66, E67,
  E70, E71, E72, E74, E75, E122, E145, E146, E190,
  E194, E197.
Toccata and fugue in E maj (C maj), BWV 566.
LB:E14, E21, E50, E127, E141, E144, E146.
Prelude in C maj, BWV 567.
LB:E143, E146.
Prelude in G maj, BWV 568.
LB:E9, E50, E144, E146.
Prelude in A min, BWV 569.
LB:E9, E50, E143, E144, E146.
Fantasia in C maj, BWV 570.
LB:E9, E53, E146, E215.
Fantasia in G maj, BWV 571.
LB:E143, E146.
Fantasia in G maj, BWV 572.
EB:E64.
LB:A248, E12, E15, E21, E33, E40, E46, E53, E60, E64,
  E68, E70, E73, E111, E127, E140, E145, E146,
  E197, E207.
Fantasia in C maj, BWV 573.
LB:E80, E188.
Fantasia in C min, Ohne BWV.
LB:E80, E146.
Fugue in C min on a theme of Legrenzi, BWV 574.
LB:E21, E53, E143, E145, E146.
Fugue in C min, BWV 575.
LB:E9, E53, E57, E146.
Fugue in G maj, BWV 576.
LB:E143, E146.
Fugue in G maj, BWV 577.
LB:A209, E35, E54, E57, E80, E146, E196, E210.
Fugue in G min, BWV 578.
LB:A209, A211, C10, E9, E11, E18, E37, E39, E53, E57,
  E69, E143, E145, E146.
Fugue in B min on a theme of Corelli, BWV 579.
LB:E21, E53, E57, E142, E145, E147.
Fugue in D maj, BWV 580.
LB:E146.
Fugue in G maj, BWV 581.
LB:E146.
Passacaglia (and fugue) in C min, BWV 582.
EB:E63.
LB:A84, A210, E3, E13, E21, E22, E24, E25, E26, E34,
  E40, E43, E46, E47, E55, E56, E68, E71, E73, E74,
  E94, E95, E143, E144, E145, E146, E185, E206,
  E228.
Trio in D min, BWV 583.
LB:E21, E26, E31, E54, E127, E142, E146.
Trio in G min, BWV 584.
LB:E9, E146.
Trio in C min, BWV 585.
LB:E146, E205.
Trio in G maj after Telemann, BWV 586.
LB:E54, E80, E146.
Aria in F maj after Couperin, BWV 587.
LB:E54, E143, E146.
Canzona in D min, BWV 588.
LB:E4, E21, E54, E57, E143, E145, E146.
Allabreve in D maj, BWV 589.
LB:E4, E21, E54, E57, E118, E142, E145, E146, E197.
Pastorale in F maj, BWV 590.
LR:F107, F108.
EB:E70.
LB:D95, E21, E24, E34, E36, E54, E57, E64, E65, E69,
  E72, E99, E115, E117, E120, E143, E145, E146,
  E182, E207.
Kleines Harmonisches Labyrinth, BWV 591.

LB:E54, E76, E146.
Concerto in G maj after Ernst, BWV 592.
LB:E42, E77, E78, E79, E80, E116, E140, E146, E205.
Concerto in A min after Vivaldi, BWV 593.
LB:A671, E35, E77, E78, E79, E80, E140, E146.
Concerto in C maj after Vivaldi, BWV 594.
LB:E77, E78, E79, E80, E146.
Concerto in C maj after Ernst, BWV 595.
LB:E77, E78, E79, E80, E146.
Concerto in D min after Vivaldi, BWV 596.
LB:A671, E77, E78, E79, E80, E146.
Concerto in E flat maj, BWV 597.
LB:E79, E80, E142, E146.
Pedal Exercitium, BWV 598.
LB:E75, E143, E146.
Canon discordia discors, BWV Ohne.
LB:E138.
Das Orgelbüchlein, BWV 599-644.
LB:E81, E82, E83, E84, E85, E86, E87, E88, E89, E145,
  E146.
Nun komm' der Heiden Heiland, BWV 599.
LR:F105.
EB:E65.
LB:E27, E90, E91, E92, E115, E119, E125, E186, E196,
  E216, G176.
Gottes Sohn ist kommen, BWV 600.
LB:E90, E91, E92, E115, E119, E125.
Herr Christ, der ein'ge Gottes Sohn, BWV 601.
LB:E90, E91, E92, E115, E119, E125, E205.
Lob sei dem allmächtigen Gott, BWV 602.
LB:E90, E91, E115, E119, E125.
Puer natus in Bethlehem, BWV 603.
LB:E90, E92, E115, E119.
Gelobet seist du, Jesu Christ, BWV 604.
PS:B2.
LB:E90, E91, E92, E115, E119, E120, E205, E216.
Der Tag der ist so freudenreich, BWV 605.
LB:A84, E90, E115, E119, E205.
Vom Himmel hoch, da komm' ich her, BWV 606.
LB:A84, A212, E90, E91, E92, E111, E115, E119.
Vom Himmel kam der Engel Schar, BWV 607.
LB:E90, E91, E92, E115, E119, E120, E125, E216.
In dulci jubilo, BWV 608.
AA:B2.
LB:E72, E90, E91, E92, E111, E115, E119, E120.
Lobt Gott, ihr Christen, BWV 609.
PS:A71.
LB:A84, E91, E115, E119, E120, E125.
Jesu, meine Freude, BWV 610.
LR:F101.
LB:E66, E90, E119, E125.
Christum wir sollen loben schon, BWV 611.
PS:B2.
LB:E90, E91, E119, E120.
Wir Christenleut', BWV 612.
LB:E90, E119, E120.
Helft mir Gottes Güte preisen, BWV 613.
LB:E28, E90, E91, E119.
Das alte Jahr vergangen ist, BWV 614.
LB:E37, E91, E119, E121, E125, E225.
In dir ist Freude, BWV 615.
PS:A71, B2.
LB:E91, E204, E215.
Mit Fried' und Freud' ich fahr, dahin, BWV 616.
LB:A84.
Herr Gott, nun schleuss den Himmel auf, BWV 617.
PS:B2.
Christe, du Lamm Gottes, BWV 619.
LB:E28.
Christus, der uns selig macht, BWV 620.
LR:Ge30.
O Mensch, bewein' dein' Sünde gross, BWV 622.
LB:E27, E37, E98, E130, E199.
Jesus Christus unser Heiland, BWV 626.

LB:A84.
Erstanden ist der heil'ge Christ, BWV 628.
LB:A84, E209.
Komm, Gott Schöpfer, Heiliger Geist, BWV 631.
LB:G176.
Herr Jesu Christ, dich zu uns wend', BWV 632.
LR:F101.
LB:A84, E199, E205.
Liebster Jesu, wir sind hier, BWV 633.
LR:F101.
LB:A84.
Durch Adams Fall ist ganz verderbt, BWV 637.
LB:E90.
Es ist das Heil uns kommen her, BWV 638.
LB:A84, E205.
Ich ruf' zu dir, Herr Jesu Christ, BWV 639.
LR:Ge30.
LB:D62, D65, D67, E28, E66, E98, E130, E187, E197,
    E205, E225, G176.
In dich hab' ich gehoffet, Herr, BWV 640.
LB:E187.
Wenn wir in höchsten Nöten sein, BWV 641.
PS:B2.
EB:E65.
LB:E23, E130, E190, E205.
Wer nur den lieben Gott lässt walten, BWV 642.
LB:E205.
Ach wie nichtig, ach wie flüchtig, BWV 644.
LB:A212.
Schübler Chorales, BWV 645–650.
LB:E93, E94, E95, E96, E97, E98, E99, E142, E145,
    E146.
Wachet auf ruft uns die Stimme, BWV 645.
LB:D65, E27, E45, E66, E75, E114, E204, E205, E219,
    E220, G176.
Auf meinen lieben Gott – See: Wo soll ich fliehen hin,
    BWV 646.
LB:E33, E197.
Wer nur den lieben Gott lässt walten, BWV 647.
LB:E112.
Meine Seele erhabet den Herren, BWV 648.
LB:E112, E208.
Ach bleib' bei uns, Herr Jesu Christ, BWV 649.
LB:E112, E187, E213.
Kommst du nun, Jesu, vom Himmel herunter, BWV 650.
LB:E45, E112, E208.
Leipzig Chorales (The '18'), BWV 651–668.
LB:E100, E101, E102, E103, E104, E105, E145, E146.
Komm, heiliger Geist, herre Gott, BWV 651.
LB:E33.
An Wasserflüssen Babylon, BWV 653.
LB:E124, E128.
An Wasserflüssen Babylon, BWV 653b.
LB:E6, E80, E136, E145, E146.
Schmücke dich, O liebe Seele, BWV 654.
LB:E33, E197.
Herr Jesu Christ, dich zu uns wend', BWV 655.
LB:E125.
O Lamm Gottes unschuldig, BWV 656.
EB:E62.
LB:E38.
Nun danket alle Gott, BWV 657.
EB:B38, E68.
Von Gott will ich nicht lassen, BWV 658.
LB:E38.
Nun komm' der Heiden Heiland, BWV 659.
EB:E67.
LB:D62, D65, D76, D119, E125, E136, E200.
Nun komm', der Heiden Heiland, BWV 661.
LB:D67.
Allein Gott in der Höh' sei Ehr', BWV 662.
LB:E28, E213.
Vor deinen Thron tret' ich = Wenn wir in höchsten Nöten
    sein, BWV 668.

LB:E33, E38, E114.
Clavierübung, Part III, BWV 669–689 (See also Duets,
    BWV 802–805, and Prelude and fugue in E flat maj,
    BWV 552).
LB:D22, E106, E107, E108, E109, E110, E141, E145,
    E146.
Kyrie, Gott Vater in Ewigkeit, BWV 669.
LB:E224.
Christe, aller Welt Trost, BWV 670.
LB:E224.
Kyrie, Gott heiliger Geist, BWV 671.
LB:E186, E224.
Allein Gott in der Höh' sei Ehr', BWV 675.
LB:E213.
Allein Gott in der Höh' sei Ehr', BWV 677.
LB:E213.
Wir glauben all' an einen Gott, BWV 680.
LB:A210, E98, E214.
Wir glauben all' an einen Gott, BWV 681.
LB:E121.
Vater unser im Himmelreich, BWV 683.
EB:E65.
LB:E37, E121.
Aus tiefer Not schrei' ich zu dir, BWV 687.
LB:E192.
Jesus Christus, unser Heiland, BWV 688.
EB:E67.
Wer nur den lieben Gott lässt walten, BWV 690
    (Kirnberger).
LB:E113, E124, E140, E146, G175.
SI:C1.
Wer nur den lieben Gott lässt walten, BWV 691
    (Kirnberger).
LB:D104, E113, E124, E130, E140, E146, G175, G177,
    G178.
SI:C1.
Ach Gott und Herr, BWV 692. (Kirnberger).
LB:E140, E146.
Ach Gott und Herr, BWV 693 (Kirnberger).
LB:E140, E146.
Wo soll ich fliehen hin, BWV 694 (Kirnberger).
LB:E112, E124, E140, E146.
Christ lag in Todesbanden, BWV 695 (Kirnberger).
LB:E112, E124, E140, E146, E209.
Christum wir sollen loben schon, BWV 696 (Kirnberger).
LB:E112, E119, E124, E140, E146.
Gelobet seist du, Jesu Christ, BWV 697 (Kirnberger).
LB:E112, E119, E124, E140, E146.
Herr Christ, der ein'ge Gottes Sohn, BWV 698
    (Kirnberger).
LB:E112, E119, E124, E140, E146.
Nun komm' der Heiden Heiland, BWV 699 (Kirnberger).
LB:E112, E119, E124, E140, E146.
Vom Himmel hoch da komm' ich her, BWV 700
    (Kirnberger).
LB:E72, E112, E119, E124, E140, E145, E146.
Vom Himmel hoch da komm' ich her, BWV 701
    (Kirnberger).
LB:E112, E124, E125, E140, E146.
Das Jesulein soll doch mein Trost, BWV 702 (Kirn-
    berger).
LB:E96, E112, E140, E146.
Gottes Sohn ist kommen, BWV 703 (Kirnberger).
LB:E37, E112, E119, E124, E125, E140, E146.
Lob sei dem allmächtigen Gott, BWV 704 (Kirnberger).
LB:E112, E119, E124, E140, E146.
Durch Adams Fall ist ganz verderbt, BWV 705 (Kirn-
    berger).
LB:E140, E145, E146.
Liebster Jesu, wir sind hier, BWV 706 (Kirnberger).
LB:E96, E113, E140, E146.
Ich hab' mein' Sach' Gott heimgestellt, BWV 707 (Kirn-
    berger).
LB:E140, E146.

Ich hab' mein' Sach' Gott heimgestellt, BWV 708 (Kirnberger).
LB:E140, E146.
Herr Jesu Christ, dich zu uns wend', BWV 709 (Kirnberger).
LB:E82, E96, E113, E130, E140, E146.
Wir Christenleut, BWV 710 (Kirnberger).
LB:E112, E119, E124, E125, E140, E146.
Allein Gott in der Höh' sei Ehr', BWV 711 (Kirnberger).
LB:E96, E112, E140, E146.
In dich hab' ich gehoffet, Herr, BWV 712 (Kirnberger).
LB:E112, E124, E140, E146.
Jesu, meine Freude, BWV 713 (Kirnberger).
LB:E96, E112, E140, E146.
Ach, Gott und Herr, BWV 714.
LB:E96, E113, E141, E146.
Allein Gott in der Höh' sei Ehr', BWV 715.
LB:E96, E112, E146, G176.
Allein Gott in der Höh' sei Ehr', BWV 716.
LB:E141, E146.
Allein Gott in der Höh' sei Ehr', BWV 717.
LB:E112, E146.
Christ lag in Todesbanden, BWV 718.
LB:E6, E112, E124, E146.
Der Tag, der ist so freudenreich, BWV 719.
LB:E141, E146.
Ein' feste Burg ist unser Gott, BWV 720.
LB:A211, E96, E113, E128, E146.
Erbarm' dich mein, O Herr Gott, BWV 721.
LB:E61, E96, E113, E141, E146.
Gelobet seist du, Jesu Christ, BWV 722.
LB:E96, E112, E119, E146, E208.
Gelobet seist du, Jesu Christ, BWV 723.
LB:E119, E141, E146.
Gottes Sohn ist kommen, BWV 724.
LB:E112, E119, E141, E146.
Herr Gott, dich loben wir, BWV 725.
LB:E113, E146.
Herr Jesu Christ, dich zu uns wend, BWV 726.
LB:E96, E113, E142, E146.
Herzlich tut mich verlangen, BWV 727.
LB:A212, E6, E37, E61, E72, E82, E96, E113, E121, E128, E130, E140, E146, E203.
Jesus, meine Zuversicht, BWV 728.
LB:E96, E113, E130, E142, E146.
In dulci jubilo, BWV 729.
EB:E64.
LB:E96, E112, E120, E142, E146, E202, E203, E220.
Liebster Jesu, wir sind hier, BWV 730.
LB:E96, E113, E142, E146, E222.
Liebster Jesu wir sind hier, BWV 731.
LB:E96, E111, E113, E130, E142, E146, E183, E184, E195, E220, E222.
Lobt Gott, ihr Christen allzugleich, BWV 732.
LB:E96, E142, E146, E208, G176.
Fugue on the Magnificat, BWV 733.
LB:E38, E95, E96, E112, E115, E141, E145, E146, E208, E221.
Nun freut euch, lieben Christen g'mein, BWV 734.
LB:D76, E72, E96, E113, E128, E140, E145, E146, E208, E219.
Valet will ich dir geben, BWV 735.
LB:E96, E113, E142, E146.
Valet will ich dir geben, BWV 736.
LB:E6, E96, E113, E114, E128, E140, E145, E146, E183.
Vater unser im Himmelreich, BWV 737.
LB:E96, E113, E128, E142, E146.
Vom Himmel hoch, da komm' ich her, BWV 738.
LB:E96, E112, E119, E148, E208.
Wie schön leuchtet uns der morgenstern, BWV 739.
LB:E146.
Wir glauben all' an einen Gott, BWV 740.
LB:A212, E61, E76, E96, E114, E146.

Ach Gott, vom Himmel sich' darein, BWV 741.
LB:E80, E96, E146.
Ach Herr, mich armen Sünder, BWV 742.
LB:E146.
Ach, wast ist doch unser Leben, BWV 743.
LB:E146.
Auf meinen lieben Gott, BWV 744.
LB:E146.
Aus der Tiefe rufe ich, BWV 745.
EB:E66.
LB:E146.
Christ ist erstanden, BWV 746.
LB:E146.
Christus der uns selig macht, BWV 747.
LB:E146.
Gott der Vater wohn uns bei, BWV 748.
LB:E146, E187.
Herr Jesu Christ, dich zu uns wend', BWV 749.
LB:E146.
Herr Jesu Christ, mein's Lebens Licht, BWV 750.
LB:E146.
In dulci jubilo, BWV 751.
LB:D65, E115, E124, E146, E182, E208, G176.
Jesu, der du meine Seele, BWV 752.
LB:E146.
Liebster, Jesu, wir sind hier, BWV 754.
LB:E146.
Nun freut euch, lieben Christen, BWV 755.
LB:E146.
Nun ruhen alle Wälder, BWV 756.
LB:E146, G176.
O Herr Gott, dein göttlich's Wort, BWV 757.
LB:E146.
O Vater, allmächtiger Gott, BWV 758.
LB:E146.
Schmücke dich O liebe Seele, BWV 759.
LB:E146.
Vater unser im Himmelreich, BWV 760.
LB:E146.
Vater unser im Himmelreich, BWV 761.
LB:E146.
Vater unser im Himmelreich, BWV 762.
LB:E146.
Wie schön leuchtet der Morgenstern, BWV 763.
LB:E146.
Wir glauben all' an einem Gott, BWV 765.
LB:E146.
Christ der Du bist der helle Tag, BWV 766 (Partita).
LB:E113, E126, E129, E146.
O Gott, du frommer Gott, BWV 767 (Partita).
LB:E23, E41, E113, E114, E118, E126, E129, E146.
Sei gegrüsset Jesu gütig, BWV 768 (Partita).
LB:E93, E113, E117, E122, E123, E126, E129, E142, E145, E146.
Vom Himmel hoch da komm' ich her, BWV 769 (Canonic Variations).
LB:E38, E64, E93, E112, E116, E120, E122, E124, E125, E127, E142, E145, E146.
Ach was soll ich Sünder machen, BWV 770 (Partita).
LB:E143, E146.
Allein Gott in der Höh' sei Ehr', BWV 771.
LB:E143, E146.
O Lamm Gottes unschuldig, Ohne BWV.
EB:E63, E80, E96, E146, E225.
Duets, BWV 802-805.
  1 in E min; 2 in F maj; 3 in G maj; 4 in A min.
LB:D22, D73, D97, D102, E4, E106, E108, E145, E146.
c.Keyboard – Harpsichord: BWV 772-994.
Anna-Magdalena Bach Notebook, Clavierbüchlein
for W.F.Bach and miscellany
15 2-Part Inventions, BWV 772-786.
LB:D57, D58, D59, D78, D92, D103, D106.
2-Part Invention in C maj, BWV 772.
LB:B321, D90.

LB:D78, D104, D106.
SI:C4.
Prelude in F maj, BWV 927.
LB:D64, D78, D104, D106, G175.
Prelude in F maj, BWV 928.
LB:D64, D78, D104, D106.
Prelude in G min, BWV 929.
LB:D78, D104, D106, G175.
Prelude in G min, BWV 930.
LB:D78, D104, D106.
Prelude in C maj, BWV 931.
LB:D104.
Little Preludes, BWV 933-938.
    1 in C maj; 2 in C min; 3 in D min; 4 in D maj; 5 in E maj;
    6 in E min.
LB:D80, D99, D106.
Prelude in C maj, BWV 933.
LB:D64.
SI:C12.
Prelude in C min, BWV 934.
SI:C12.
Prelude in D min, BWV 935.
LB:D64.
SI:C12.
Prelude in D maj, BWV 936.
LB:D64.
SI:C12.
Prelude in E maj, BWV 937.
LB:D64, G175.
SI:C12.
Prelude in E min, BWV 938.
LB:D64.
Prelude in C maj, BWV 939.
LB:D78, D106, G175.
Prelude in D min, BWV 940.
LB:D78, D106, G175.
Prelude in E min, BWV 941.
LB:D78, D106.
Prelude in A min, BWV 942.
LB:D78, D106.
Prelude in C maj, BWV 943.
LB:E6, E50, E144.
Fugue in A min, BWV 944.
LB:D64.
Fugue in C maj, BWV 952.
LB:G175.
Fugue in C maj, BWV 953.
LB:D104.
Sonata in D min, BWV 964 (after BWV 1003).
LB:D87, D98.
Sonata in C maj, BWV 966 (after Reinken).
LB:D98.
Adagio in G maj, BWV 968.
EB:D31.
LB:D98.
Italian Concerto in F maj, BWV 971.
LB:D22, D41, D62, D63, D64, D71, D73, D74, D77,
    D79, D84, D85, D86, D88, D89, D90, D92, D93,
    D94, D95, D97, D99, D101, D102, D103, D107.
Concerto in D maj, BWV 972 (after Vivaldi).
LB:D82, D93, D96, D97.
Concerto in G maj, BWV 973 (after Vivaldi).
LB:D96.
Concerto in D min, BWV 974 (after Marcello).
LB:D82, D100.
Concerto in G min, BWV 975 (after Vivaldi).
LB:D82, D96.
Concerto in C maj, BWV 976 (after Vivaldi).
LB:D82, D96.
Concerto in F maj, BWV 978 (after Vivaldi).
LB:A149, D96.
Concerto in G maj, BWV 980 (after Vivaldi).
LB:D96.
Concerto in C maj, BWV 984 (after Ernst).

LB:D100.
Concerto in G min, BWV 985 (after Telemann).
LB:D100.
Concerto in G maj, BWV 986 (after Telemann).
LB:D100.
Concerto in D min, BWV 987 (after Ernst).
LB:D100.
Goldberg Variations, BWV 988.
LB:D22, D43, D44, D45, D46, D47, D48, D49, D50,
    D51, D52, D53, D54, D55, D56, D106.
Aria in G maj, BWV 988(i).
LB:D69, G177, G178.
Aria variata in the Italian Manner in A min, BWV 989.
LB:D55, D107.
Capriccio in B flat maj on the departure of a beloved
    brother, BWV 992.
LB:D17, D41, D64, D66, D77, D83, D107.
Capriccio in B flat maj on the departure of a beloved
    brother, BWV 922: Aria and fugue in imitation of the
    postillion's horn.
EB:B38.
LB:A659.
Capriccio in E maj in honour of Johann Christoph Bach,
    BWV 993.
LB:E190.
Applicatio in C maj, BWV 994 (Clavierbüchlein für WFB).
LB:D104, D106.
Allegro in E min, BWV 1019.
LB:D98.
(Clavierbüchlein für W.F.Bach: Minuets, BWV 841-843;
    Little Preludes, BWV 924-932; Applicatio, BWV 994.)
    (Notebook for Anna-Magdalena Bach: Chorale, BWV
    691; Arias and Chorales, BWV 82, 299, 508-518;
    Harpsichord pieces, BWV Anh 113-132, BWV Anh
    183, BWV 812, 827, 830, 846(P), 933; Aria, BWV
    988(i); Air, BWV 991; Prelude in C min, BWV 999.)
Minuet in F maj, BWV Anh 113.
LB:D69, G177.
Minuet in G maj, BWV Anh 114.
LB:D69, G177, G178, G182.
Minuet in G min, BWV Anh 115.
LB:D69, G177, G178, G182.
Minuet in G maj, BWV Anh 116.
LB:D69, G177, G178.
Polonaise in F maj, BWV Anh 117.
LB:D69, G177.
Minuet in B flat maj, BWV Anh 118.
LB:D69, G177.
Polonaise in G min, BWV Anh 119.
LB:D69, G177, G178.
Minuet in A min, BWV Anh 120.
LB:D69.
Minuet in C min, BWV Anh 121.
LB:D69, G177.
March in D maj, BWV Anh 122 (C.P.E.Bach).
LB:D69, G177, G178.
Polonaise in G min, BWV Anh 123 (C.P.E.Bach).
LB:D69.
March in G maj, BWV Anh 124 (C.P.E.Bach).
LB:D69, G177, G178.
Polonaise in G min, BWV Anh 125 (C.P.E.Bach).
LB:D69, G177.
Musette in D maj, BWV Anh 126.
LB:D69, G178.
March in E flat maj, BWV Anh 127.
LB:D69, G177, G178.
Polonaise in D min, BWV Anh 128.
LB:D69, G177.
Solo in E flat maj, BWV Anh 129.
LB:G177, G182.
Polonaise in G maj, BWV Anh 130.
LB:G177.
Minuet in D min, BWV Anh 132.
LB:D69, G177.

Rondeau in B maj. 'Les Bergeries'. BWV Anh 183 (after
    Couperin).
LB:G177, G178.
Aria in D min.
LB:D69.
Aria harmonise in G min.
LB:D69.
Chorale in C maj.
LB:D69.
Menuet by Böhm (Anna-Magdalena Bach Notebook).
LB:D69.

d.Secular Vocal – Cantatas 201–215, 249a
Cantata 201: Geschwinde, geschwinde, ihr wirbelhden
    Winde.
LB:F1, G93.
Cantata 202: Weichet nur, betrübte Schatten (Wedding,
    1720?).
LB:F2, F3, F4, G43, G44.
Cantata 203: Amore traditore (c.1735).
LB:F5.
Cantata 204: Ich bin in mir vergnügt (before 1728).
LB:F2, F6.
Cantata 205: Zerreisset, zersprenget, zertrümmert die
    Gruft.
LB:F7, G93.
Cantata 206: Schleicht, spielende Wellen (Birthday,
    1733).
LB:F8, F9, G93.
Cantata 207: Vereinigte zwietracht der wechseinden
    Saiten (In Honour of Dr. G. Kortte, 1726).
LB:F10.
Cantata 207a: Auf, schmetternde Töne der muntern
    Trompetten.
LB:F11.
Cantata 208: Was mir behagt, das ist die muntre Jagd
    (Hunt, 1716).
LB:F9, F12, F13.
Cantata 208: Excpt: Sinfonia.
LB:A62, A599.
Cantata 208: Excpt: Jagen ist die Lust der Götter.
LB:B227.
Cantata 208: Excpt: 'Sheep may safely graze.'
LB:A209, A590.
Cantata 209: Non sa che sia dolore (1729).
LB:F3, F6.
Cantata 209: Excpt: Sinfonia.
LB:A183, A200, B88.
Cantata 210: O holder Tag, erwünschte Zeit.
LB:F14.
Cantata 211: Schweigt still, plaudert nicht (Coffee,
    c.1723).
LB:F3, F5, F15, F16, F17, G93.
Cantata 212: Mer hahn en neue Oberkeet (Peasant,
    1742).
LB:F3, F4, F16, F17, G93.
Cantata 213: Lasst uns sorgen, lasst uns wachen.
LB:F18.
Cantata 214: Tönet, ihr Pauken! Erschallet, Trompeten!
    (Birthday of Maria Josepha, 1733).
LB:F10, F11.
Cantata 215: Preise dein Glücke, gesegnetes Sachsen
    (Music Drama).
LB:F19.
Cantata 249a: Entfliehet verschwindet, entweicht, ihr
    Sorgen (Shepherd Cantata).
LB:F20.

d.Secular Vocal – Arias, BWV 504–518, 524
Vergiss mein nicht, dass ich dein vergesse, BWV 505.
LB:G105, G175, G181.
Wo ist mein Schäflein, das ich liebe, BWV 507.
LB:G105, G181.
Bist du bei mir, BWV 508.
LB:A212, E201, G174, G177, G178, G182.
Gedenke doch, mein Geist zurücke, BWV 509.

LB:G177.
Gib dich zufrieden und sei stille, BWV 510.
LB:G177.
Gib dich zufrieden und sei stille, BWV 511.
LB:G175.
Gib dich zufrieden und sei stille, BWV 512.
LB:G105.
O Ewigkeit, du Donnerwort, BWV 513.
LB:G177.
Schaffs mit mir, Gott, nach deinem Willen, BWV 514.
LB:G177.
Sooft ich meine Tobackspfeife, BWV 515a.
LB:G175, G177, G178, G182.
Warum betrübst du dich, mein Herz, BWV 516.
LB:G177.
Wie wohl ist mir, O Freund der Seelen, BWV 517.
LB:G105, G177.
Willst du dein Herz mir schenken, BWV 518.
LB:G177, G178, G182.
Quodlibet, BWV 524.
LB:G175.

e.Sacred Vocal – Cantatas, BWV 1–200
Cantata 1: Wie schön leuchtet der Morgenstern
    (Annunciation, c.1740).
LB:G3, G87, G92.
Cantata 2: Ach Gott vom Himmel sieh darein (2nd.
    Sunday after Trinity, c.1740).
LB:G3.
Cantata 3: Ach Gott, wie manches Herzeleid (2nd.
    Sunday after Epiphany, c.1740).
LB:G3.
Cantata 4: Christ lag in Todesbanden (Easter, 1724).
LB:G3, G4, G87, G92.
Cantata 4: Excpt: Christ lag in Todesbanden.
LB:G183.
Cantata 4: Excpt: Wir essen und leben wohl.
LB:G176.
Cantata 4: Excpt: O'er death no man prevail.
EB:G135.
Cantata 5: Wo soll ich fliehen hin (19th. Sunday after
    Trinity, 1935).
LB:G5, G88.
Cantata 6: Bleib bei uns, denn es will Abend werden
    (Easter Monday, 1736).
LB:G5, G87, G92.
Cantata 6: Excpt: Hochgelobter Gottes Sohn.
LB:G174.
Cantata 7: Christ unser Herr zum Jordan kam (St. John
    the Baptist, c.1740).
LB:G5.
Cantata 8: Liebster Gott, wann werd ich sterben? (16th.
    Sunday after Trinity, c.1725).
LB:G5.
Cantata 9: Es ist das Heil uns kommen her (6th. Sunday
    after Trinity, 1731).
LB:G6.
Cantata 9: Excpt: Ob sichs anliess, als wollt er nicht.
LR:F101.
Cantata 10: Meine Seel erhebt den Herrn (Visitation,
    c.1740).
LB:G6, G7, G8, G90, G128.
Cantata 11: Lobet Gott in seinen Reichen (Ascension
    Oratorio, 1735/6).
LB:G6, G9, G10, G11, G90, G92.
Cantata 11: Excpt: Ach, bleibe doch.
LB:G174.
Cantata 12: Weinen, Klagen, Sorgen, Zagen (3rd.
    Sunday after Easter, c.1714).
LB:G12, G87, G92.
Cantata 12: Excpt: Sinfonia.
LB:A43, B88.
Cantata 13: Meine Seufzer, meine Tränen (2nd. Sunday
    after Epiphany, 1738).
LB:G12, G13, G91.

LB:G40, G46, G93.
Cantata 56: Ich will den Kreuzstab gerne tragen (19th.
Sunday after Trinity, c.1731).
LB:G40, G47, G48, G49, G50, G93.
Cantata 57: Selig ist der Mann (Day after Christmas,
c.1740).
LB:G26, G51.
Cantata 58: Ach Gott, wie manches Herzeleid (Sunday
after Circumcision, 1733).
LB:G10, G51, G91.
Cantata 59: Wer nich liebet der wird mein Wort halten
(Whitsun, 1716).
LB:G51.
Cantata 60: O Ewigkeit, du Donnerwort (24th. Sunday
after Trinity, 1732).
LB:G51.
Cantata 61: Nun komm, der Heiden Heiland (1st. Sunday
in Advent, 1714).
LB:G52, G53, G91.
Cantata 61: Excpt: Nun komm, der Heiden Heiland.
LB:G183.
Cantata 61: Excpt: Lob sei Gott.
LB:G176.
Cantata 62: Nun komm, der Heiden Heiland (1st. Sunday
in Advent, c.1740).
LB:G47, G52, G92.
Cantata 63: Christen ätzet diesen Tag (Christmas,
c.1733).
LB:G52, G91.
Cantata 64: Sehet, welche eine Liebe (3rd. Day of
Christmas, 1723).
LB:G31, G52, G91, G92.
Cantata 65: Sie werden aus Saba alle kommen
(Epiphany, c.1724).
LB:G36, G54, G91, G92.
Cantata 66: Erfreut euch, ihr Herzen (Anniversary, 1731).
LB:G54.
Cantata 67: Halt im Gedächtnis Jesum Christ (1st.
Sunday after Easter, 1723/7).
LB:G11, G54, G87, G92.
Cantata 67: Excpt: Opening Chorale.
LB:E209.
Cantata 68: Also hat Gott die Welt geliebt (Whit Monday,
1735).
LB:G28, G54, G55, G90, G93.
Cantata 68: Excpt: Mein glaubiges Herze.
LB:B206.
Cantata 69: Lobe den Herrn, meine Seele (Council,
1723).
LB:G66.
Cantata 70: Wachet! betet! seid bereit allezeit (26th.
Sunday after Trinity, 1716).
LB:G56, G88.
Cantata 71: Gott ist mein König (Council Election,
1708).
LB:G56.
Cantata 72: Alles nur nach Gottes willen (3rd. Sunday
after Epiphany, c.1726).
LB:G56.
Cantata 73: Herr, wie du willst, so schicks mit mir (3rd.
Sunday after Epiphany, c.1725).
LB:G57.
Cantata 74: Wer mich liebet, der wird mein Wort halten,
(Whitsun, 1735).
LB:G57.
Cantata 75: Die Elenden sollen essen (1st. Sunday after
Trinity, 1723).
LB:G57.
Cantata 75: Excpt: Sinfonia.
LB:A62.
Cantata 76: Die Himmel erzählen die Ehre Gottes (2nd.
Sunday after Trinity, 1723).
LB:G32, G58, G59, G90, G93.
Cantata 77: Du sollst Gott, deinen Herrn, lieben (13th.

Sunday after Trinity, 1723/7).
LB:G59.
Cantata 78: Jesu, der du meine Seele (15th. Sunday after
Trinity, 1735/44).
LB:G10, G59, G60, G121.
Cantata 78: Excpt: Duetto allegro.
LB:A599.
Cantata 79: Gott der Herr, ist Sonn' und Schild (Reforma-
tion, 1735).
LB:G59, G61.
Cantata 80: Ein feste Burg ist unser Gott (Reformation,
1715/30).
LB:G62, G63, G64, G88.
Cantata 81: Jesus schläft, was soll ich hoffen? (4th.
Sunday after Epiphany, 1724).
LB:G63, G91.
Cantata 82: Ich hab genug (Purification, c.1731).
LB:A204, G48, G49, G50, G63, G65, G66, G91.
Cantata 82: Excpt: Schlummert ein, ihr matten Augen.
LB:G178, G182.
Cantata 83: Erfreute Zeit im neuen Bunde (Purification,
1724?).
LB:G63.
Cantata 84: Ich bin vergnugt mit meinem Glücke
(Septuagesima, c.1732).
LB:G38, G67.
Cantata 85: Ich bin ein guter Hirt (2nd. Sunday after
Easter, 1735).
LB:G67.
Cantata 86: Wahrlich, wahrlich, ich sage euch.
LB:G67.
Cantata 87: Bisher habt ihr nichts gebeten in meinen
Namen (5th. Sunday after Easter, 1735).
LB:G19, G67, G87.
Cantata 88: Siehe, ich will viel Fischer aussenden (5th.
Sunday after Trinity, 1732).
LB:G67.
Cantata 89: Was soll ich aus dir machen, Ephraim?
(22nd. Sunday after Trinity, c.1732).
LB:G67.
Cantata 90: Es reifet euch ein schrecklich Ende (25th.
Sunday after Trinity, c.1740).
LB:G67.
Cantata 91: Gelobet seist du, Jesu Christ (Christmas,
c.1740).
LB:G68.
Cantata 92: Ich habe in Gottes Herz und Sinn (Septua-
gesima, c.1740).
LB:G68, G69, G92.
Cantata 93: Wer nur den lieben Gott lässt walten (5th.
Sunday after Trinity, 1728?).
LB:G68, G70, G71, G90, G93.
Cantata 93: Excpt: Wer nur den lieben Gott lässt walten.
LB:B207.
Cantata 93: Excpt: Sing, bet, und geh' auf Gottes Wegen.
LR:F101.
Cantata 94: Was frag ich nach der Welt (9th. Sunday
after Trinity, 1735?).
LB:G27, G68.
Cantata 95: Christus, der ist mein Leben (16th. Sunday
after Trinity, c.1732).
LB:G72.
Cantata 96: Herr Christ, der einge Gottes sohn (18th.
Sunday after Trinity, c.1740).
LB:G72, G88.
Cantata 97: In allen meinen Taten (1734).
LB:G72.
Cantata 98: Was Gott tut, das ist Wohlgetan.
LB:G72.
Cantata 100: Was Gott tut, das ist Wohlgetan (15th.
Sunday after Trinity, c.1732).
LB:G73, G89.
Cantata 102: Herr, deine Augen sehen nach dem
Glauben (10th. Sunday after Trinity, 1731?).

Cantata 13: Excpt: Der Gott, der mit hat versprochen.
LB:G183.

Cantata 14: Wär Gott nicht mit uns diese Zeit (4th. Sunday after Epiphany, 1735).
LB:G12.

Cantata 16: Herr Gott, dich loben wir (Circumcision, 1714).
LB:G12.

Cantata 17: Wer Dank opfert der prieiset mich (14th. Sunday after Trinity, 1732).
LB:G14, G15, G89.

Cantata 18: Gleich wie der Regen und Schnee vom Himmel fällt (Sexuagesima, 1714).
LB:G14.

Cantata 18: Excpt: Sinfonia.
LB:A207.

Cantata 19: Es erhub sich ein Streit (St. Michael, 1726).
LB:G14.

Cantata 20: O Ewigkeit, du Donnerwort (1st. Sunday after Trinity, c.1725).
LB:G14, G93.

Cantata 21: Ich hatte viel Bekümmernis (3rd. Sunday after Trinity, 1714.)
LB:G16, G17, G18, G93.

Cantata 21: Excpt: Sinfonia.
LB:A43, A62, A207.

Cantata 22: Jesus nahm zu sich die Zwölfe (Quinquagesima, 1723).
LB:G18.

Cantata 23: Du wahrer Gott und Davids Sohn (Quinquagesima, 1724).
LB:G18, G19, G20, G87.

Cantata 23: Excpt: Christe, du Lamm Gottes.
LB:G183.

Cantata 24: Ein ungefärbt Gemüte (4th. Sunday after Trinity, 1723).
LB:G21, G90.

Cantata 25: es ist nichts gesundes an meinen Leibe (14th. Sunday after Trinity, c.1731).
LB:G21.

Cantata 26: Ach wie flüchtig, ach wie nichtig (24th. Sunday after Trinity, c.1740).
LB:G21, G88.

Cantata 27: Wer weiss wie nahe mir mein Ende (16th. Sunday after Trinity, c.1731).
LB:G21, G89.

Cantata 28: Gottlob! nun geht das Jahr zu Ende (Sunday after Christmas, c.1736).
LB:G22, G91.

Cantata 28: Excpt: Nun lob, mein Seele, den Herren.
LB:G325.

Cantata 29: Wie danken dir, Gott (Council Election, 1731).
LB:G22, G23.

Cantata 29: Excpt: Sinfonia.
LB:A62, A207, A208, D65.

Cantata 30: Freue dich, erlöste Schar (St. John the Baptist, 1738).
LB:G22, G24, G90.

Cantata 31: Der Himmel lacht, die Erde jubiliert (Easter, 1715).
LB:G25.

Cantata 31: Excpt: Sinfonia.
LB:A207.

Cantata 32: Liebster Jesu, mein Verlangen (1st. Sunday after Epiphany, 1740).
LB:G25, G26.

Cantata 33: Allein zu dir, Herr Jesu Christ (13th. Sunday after Trinity, c.1740).
LB:G25, G27, G89.

Cantata 34: O ewiges Feuer, O ursprung der Liebe (Pentecost, c.1740).
LB:G25, G28, G93.

Cantata 34: Excpt. Wohl euch, ihr auswewahlten Seele.

LB:G174, G184

Cantata 35: Geist und Seele wird verwirret (12th. Sunday after Trinity, 1731).
LB:G29, G30.

Cantata 35: Excpt: Sinfonia.
LB:A207, A208.

Cantata 36: Schwingt freudig euch empor (1st. Sunday in Advent, c.1730).
LB:G29, G31.

Cantata 36: Excpt: Chorale.
LR:F105.

Cantata 37: Wer da glaubet und getauft wird (Ascension, 1731).
LB:G29, G32.

Cantata 38: Aus tiefer Not schrei ich zu dir (21st. Sunday after Trinity, c.1740).
LB:G29, G88.

Cantata 39: Brich dem Hungrigen dein Brot (1st. Sunday after Trinity, c.1725).
LB:G33, G90, G93.

Cantata 40: Dazu ist erscheinen der Sohn Gottes (Day after Christmas, 1723).
LB:G33.

Cantata 40: Excpt: Freut euch, ihr Christen alle.
LR:F109.

Cantata 41: Jesu, nun sei gepreiset (Circumcision, 1736).
LB:G33.

Cantata 42: Am Abend aber desselbigen Sabbats (1st. Sunday after Easter, 1731).
LB:G33.

Cantata 42: Excpt: Sinfonia.
LB:A39, A207.

Cantata 43: Gott fähret auf mit Jauchzen (Ascension, 1735).
LB:G34.

Cantata 44: Sie werden euch in den Bann tun (1st. Sunday after Ascension, c.1725).
LB:G9, G34, G90, G92.

Cantata 45: Es ist dir gesagt, Mensch, was gut ist (8th. Sunday after Trinity, c.1740).
LB:G34, G35.

Cantata 46: Schauet doch und sehet (10th. Sunday after Trinity, c.1725).
LB:G34, G36.

Cantata 47: Wer sich selbst erhöht (17th. Sunday after Trinity, 1720).
LB:G7, G37.

Cantata 48: Ich elender Mensch, were wird mich erlösen (19th. Sunday after Trinity, c.1740).
LB:G37.

Cantata 49: Ich geh und suche mit Verlangen (20th. Sunday after Trinity, c.1731).
LB:G37, G38.

Cantata 49: Excpt: Sinfonia.
LB:A207, A208.

Cantata 49: Excpt: Dich hab ich je und je geliebet.
LB:G183.

Cantata 50: Nun ist das Heil und die Kraft (St. Michael, 1735/44.)
LB:G37, G39.

Cantata 51: Jauchzet Gott in allen Landen (15th. Sunday after Trinity, c.1731).
LB:G40, G41, G42, G43, G44, G93.

Cantata 52: Falsche Welt, dir trau ich nicht (23rd. Sunday after Trinity, c.1730).
LB:G40.

Cantata 53: Schlage doch, gewünschte Stunde (c.1730).
LB:G45.

Cantata 54: Widerstehe doch der Sünde (1723/34?).
LB:G40, G45.

Cantata 55: Ich armer Mensche, ich Sünderknecht (22nd. Sunday after Trinity, c.1731).

LB:G40, G46, G93.
Cantata 56: Ich will den Kreuzstab gerne tragen (19th. Sunday after Trinity, c.1731).
LB:G40, G47, G48, G49, G50, G93.
Cantata 57: Selig ist der Mann (Day after Christmas, c.1740).
LB:G26, G51.
Cantata 58: Ach Gott, wie manches Herzeleid (Sunday after Circumcision, 1733).
LB:G10, G51, G91.
Cantata 59: Wer nich liebet der wird mein Wort halten (Whitsun, 1716).
LB:G51.
Cantata 60: O Ewigkeit, du Donnerwort (24th. Sunday after Trinity, 1732).
LB:G51.
Cantata 61: Nun komm, der Heiden Heiland (1st. Sunday in Advent, 1714).
LB:G52, G53, G91.
Cantata 61: Excpt: Nun komm, der Heiden Heiland.
LB:G183.
Cantata 61: Excpt: Lob sei Gott.
LB:G176.
Cantata 62: Nun komm, der Heiden Heiland (1st. Sunday in Advent, c.1740).
LB:G47, G52, G92.
Cantata 63: Christen ätzet diesen Tag (Christmas, c.1733).
LB:G52, G91.
Cantata 64: Sehet, welche eine Liebe (3rd. Day of Christmas, 1723).
LB:G31, G52, G91, G92.
Cantata 65: Sie werden aus Saba alle kommen (Epiphany, c.1724).
LB:G36, G54, G91, G92.
Cantata 66: Erfreut euch, ihr Herzen (Anniversary, 1731).
LB:G54.
Cantata 67: Halt im Gedächtnis Jesum Christ (1st. Sunday after Easter, 1723/7).
LB:G11, G54, G87, G92.
Cantata 67: Excpt: Opening Chorale.
LB:E209.
Cantata 68: Also hat Gott die Welt geliebt (Whit Monday, 1735).
LB:G28, G54, G55, G90, G93.
Cantata 68: Excpt: Mein glaubiges Herze.
LB:B206.
Cantata 69: Lobe den Herrn, meine Seele (Council, 1723).
LB:G66.
Cantata 70: Wachet! betet! seid bereit allezeit (26th. Sunday after Trinity, 1716).
LB:G56, G88.
Cantata 71: Gott ist mein König (Council Election, 1708).
LB:G56.
Cantata 72: Alles nur nach Gottes willen (3rd. Sunday after Epiphany, c.1726).
LB:G56.
Cantata 73: Herr, wie du willst, so schicks mit mir (3rd. Sunday after Epiphany, c.1725).
LB:G57.
Cantata 74: Wer mich liebet, der wird mein Wort halten, (Whitsun, 1735).
LB:G57.
Cantata 75: Die Elenden sollen essen (1st. Sunday after Trinity, 1723).
LB:G57.
Cantata 75: Excpt: Sinfonia.
LB:A62.
Cantata 76: Die Himmel erzählen die Ehre Gottes (2nd. Sunday after Trinity, 1723).
LB:G32, G58, G59, G90, G93.
Cantata 77: Du sollst Gott, deinen Herrn, lieben (13th.

Sunday after Trinity, 1723/7).
LB:G59.
Cantata 78: Jesu, der du meine Seele (15th. Sunday after Trinity, 1735/44).
LB:G10, G59, G60, G121.
Cantata 78: Excpt: Duetto allegro.
LB:A599.
Cantata 79: Gott der Herr, ist Sonn' und Schild (Reformation, 1735).
LB:G59, G61.
Cantata 80: Ein feste Burg ist unser Gott (Reformation, 1715/30).
LB:G62, G63, G64, G88.
Cantata 81: Jesus schläft, was soll ich hoffen? (4th. Sunday after Epiphany, 1724).
LB:G63, G91.
Cantata 82: Ich hab genug (Purification, c.1731).
LB:A204, G48, G49, G50, G63, G65, G66, G91.
Cantata 82: Excpt: Schlummert ein, ihr matten Augen.
LB:G178, G182.
Cantata 83: Erfreute Zeit im neuen Bunde (Purification, 1724?).
LB:G63.
Cantata 84: Ich bin vergnugt mit meinem Glücke (Septuagesima, c.1732).
LB:G38, G67.
Cantata 85: Ich bin ein guter Hirt (2nd. Sunday after Easter, 1735).
LB:G67.
Cantata 86: Wahrlich, wahrlich, ich sage euch.
LB:G67.
Cantata 87: Bisher habt ihr nichts gebeten in meinen Namen (5th. Sunday after Easter, 1735).
LB:G19, G67, G87.
Cantata 88: Siehe, ich will viel Fischer aussenden (5th. Sunday after Trinity, 1732).
LB:G67.
Cantata 89: Was soll ich aus dir machen, Ephraim? (22nd. Sunday after Trinity, c.1732).
LB:G67.
Cantata 90: Es reifet euch ein schrecklich Ende (25th. Sunday after Trinity, c.1740).
LB:G67.
Cantata 91: Gelobet seist du, Jesu Christ (Christmas, c.1740).
LB:G68.
Cantata 92: Ich habe in Gottes Herz und Sinn (Septuagesima, c.1740).
LB:G68, G69, G92.
Cantata 93: Wer nur den lieben Gott lässt walten (5th. Sunday after Trinity, 1728?).
LB:G68, G70, G71, G90, G93.
Cantata 93: Excpt: Wer nur den lieben Gott lässt walten.
LB:B207.
Cantata 93: Excpt: Sing, bet, und geh' auf Gottes Wegen.
LR:F101.
Cantata 94: Was frag ich nach der Welt (9th. Sunday after Trinity, 1735?).
LB:G27, G68.
Cantata 95: Christus, der ist mein Leben (16th. Sunday after Trinity, c.1732).
LB:G72.
Cantata 96: Herr Christ, der einge Gottes sohn (18th. Sunday after Trinity, c.1740).
LB:G72, G88.
Cantata 97: In allen meinen Taten (1734).
LB:G72.
Cantata 98: Was Gott tut, das ist Wohlgetan.
LB:G72.
Cantata 100: Was Gott tut, das ist Wohlgetan (15th. Sunday after Trinity, c.1732).
LB:G73, G89.
Cantata 102: Herr, deine Augen sehen nach dem Glauben (10th. Sunday after Trinity, 1731?).

LB:G89.
Cantata 104: Du Hirte Israel, Höre (2nd. Sunday after Easter, c.1725).
LB:G87, G92.
Cantata 104: Excpt: Der Herr ist mein getreuer Hirt.
LB:G176.
Cantata 105: Herr, gehe nicht ins Gericht (9th. Sunday after Trinity, 1723).
LB:G89.
Cantata 106: Gottes Zeit ist die allerbeste Zeit (Actus tragicus, 1707?).
LB:G60, G74, G75, G76, G93.
Cantata 106: Excpt: Sonata.
LB:B227.
Cantata 108: Es ist euch gut, dass ich hingehe (4th. Sunday after Easter, 1735?).
LB:G87.
Cantata 110: Unser Mund sei voll Lachens (Christmas, after 1734).
LB:G15, G125.
Cantata 110: Excpt: Ihr Gedanken und ihr Sinnen.
LB:G184.
Cantata 111: Was mein Gott will, das g'scheh allzeit (3rd. Sunday after Epiphany, c.1740).
LB:G91, G92.
Cantata 113: Herr Jesu Christ, du höchstes Gut (11th. Sunday after Trinity, c.1740): Excpt: Jesus nimmt die Sünder an.
LB:G184.
Cantata 114: Ach lieben Christen, sei getrost (17th. Sunday after Trinity, c.1740): Excpt: Wo wird in diesem Jammertale.
LB:G184.
Cantata 115: Mache dich, mein Geist, bereit (22nd. Sunday after Trinity, c.1740).
LB:G88.
Cantata 116: Du Friedefürst, Herr Jesu Christ (25th. Sunday after Trinity, 1744).
LB:G88.
Cantata 117: Sei Lob und Ehr dem höchsten Gut.
LB:G70, G183.
Cantata 118: O Jesu Christ, mein Lebens Licht (Funeral, 1740).
LB:G130.
Cantata 121: Christum wir sollen loben schon (Day after Christmas, c.1740).
LB:G91, G92.
Cantata 124: Meinem Jesus lass ich nicht (1st. Sunday after Epiphany, c.1740).
LB:G91, G92.
Cantata 125: Mit Fried und Freud fahr ich dahin (Purification, c.1740): Excpt: Ich will auch mit gebrochen Augen.
LB:G184.
Cantata 126: Erhalt uns, Herr, bei deinem Wort (Sexuagesima, c.1740).
LB:G69, G87.
Cantata 127: Herr Jesu Christ, wahr' Mensch und Gott.
LB:G77.
Cantata 129: Gelobet sei der Herr (Trinity, 1732).
LB:G90, G93.
Cantata 129: Excpt: Chorale.
LB:A212.
Cantata 130: Herr Gott, dich loben alle wir (St. Michael, c.1740).
LB:G88.
Cantata 131: Aus der Tiefe rufe ich, Herr (1707).
LB:G71, G78.
Cantata 131: Excpt: Fugue in G maj. (Arr.)
EB:E65.
Cantata 132: Bereitet die Wege (4th. Sunday in Advent, 1715).
LB:G53, G91.
Cantata 135: Ach Herr, mich armen Sünder (3rd. Sunday

after Trinity, c.1740).
LB:G8, G23, G90.
Cantata 135: Excpt: Ach Herr, mich armen Sünder.
LB:G183.
Cantata 137: Lobe den Herren, den mächtigen König der Ehren (12th. Sunday after Trinity, 1732).
LB:G61, G79, G80, G81, G89.
Cantata 139: Wohl dem, der sich auf seinen Gott (23rd. Sunday after Trinity, c.1740).
LB:G88.
Cantata 140: Wachet auf, ruft uns die Stimme (27th. Sunday after Trinity, c.1731).
LB:G64, G74, G79, G82, G88.
Cantata 140: Excpt: Chorale.
LB:A206, A211.
Cantata 140: Excpt: Gloria sei dir gesungen.
LB:G176.
Cantata 142: Uns ist ein Kind geboren (Christmas, c.1714).
LB:G123.
Cantata 146: Wir müssen durch viel Trübsal (3rd. Sunday after Easter, c.1740): Excpt: Sinfonia.
LB:A208.
Cantata 146: Excpt: Ich säe meine Zähren.
LB:G184.
Cantata 147: Herz und Mund und Tat und Leben (Visitation, 1716).
LB:G83, G129.
Cantata 147: Excpt: Jesu, bleibet meine Freude.
LB:A209, A583, A590, B205, B207, B212, B213, D65, D67, D76, E27, E227, G11, G176.
Cantata 147: Excpt: Chorale prelude.
EB:E67.
Cantata 148: Bringet dem Herr Ehre seines Namens (17th. Sunday after Trinity, 1723?).
LB:G82, G89.
Cantata 151: Süsser Trost, mein Jesus kommt (3rd. Day after Christmas): Excpt: Süsser Trost, mein Jesus kommt.
LB:G184.
Cantata 152: Tritt auf die Glaubensbahn (Sunday after Christmas, 1715): Excpt: Concerto.
LB:B88.
Cantata 154: Mein liebster Jesus ist verloren: Excpt: Jesu, mein Hort und Erretter.
LB:G176.
Cantata 156: Ich steh mit einem Fuss im Grabe (3rd. Sunday after Epiphany, 1730?): Excpt: Sinfonia.
LB:B88.
Cantata 157: Ich lasse dich nicht, du segnest mich denn.
LB:G84.
Cantata 158: Der Friede sei mit dir (Purification, 1714/5).
LB:G30, G87, G92.
Cantata 158: Excpt: Welt, ade, ich bin dein müde.
LB:G183.
Cantata 159: Sehet, wir gehen hinauf gegen Jerusalem (Quinquagesima, 1729?).
LB:G20, G85.
Cantata 159: Excpt: Ich folge nach.
LB:G183.
Cantata 161: Komm, du süsse Todesstunde (16th. Sunday after Trinity, 1715).
LB:G86.
Cantata 161: Excpt: Gelobet sei der Herr.
LB:G174.
Cantata 166: Wo gehest du hin.
LB:G13.
Cantata 169: Got soll allein mein Herze haben (18th. Sunday after Trinity, c.1731).
LB:G45, G65, G84, G86.
Cantata 169: Excpt: Sinfonia.
LB:A208.
Cantata 170: Vergnügte Ruh' (6th. Sunday after Trinity,

1732).
LB:G85.
Cantata 171: Gott wie dein Name, so ist auch dein Ruhm
(Circumcision, 1730).
LB:G77, G91, G92.
Cantata 172: Erschallet, ihr Lieder (Whitsun, 1714).
LB:G55.
Cantata 175: Er rufet seinem Schafen mit Namen (Whit
Tuesday, c.1735).
LB:G28, G73, G90.
Cantata 176: Es ist ein trotzig und verzagt Ding.
LB:G35.
Cantata 177: Ich ruf zu dir, Herr Jesu Christ (4th. Sunday
after Trinity, 1732): Excpt: Ich lieg im Streit.
LR:F101.
LB:G176.
Cantata 178: Wo Gott der Herr nicht bei uns hält (8th.
Sunday after Trinity, c.1740).
LB:G89.
Cantata 179: Siehe zu, dass deine Gottesfurcht nicht
Heuchelei sei (11th. Sunday after Trinity, 1724?).
LB:G89.
Cantata 180: Schmücke dich, O liebe Seele (20th.
Sunday after Trinity, c.1740).
LB:G88.
Cantata 182: Himmelskönig, sei willkommen (Palm
Sunday, 1714).
LB:G4, G75, G92.
Cantata 182: Excpt: Sinfonia.
LB:A62, B88.
Cantata 187: Es wartet alles auf dich (7th. Sunday after
Trinity, 1732).
LB:G89, G127.
Cantata 189: Meine Seele rühmt und preist (Visitation,
1707/10).
LB:G46, G93.
Cantata 190: Singet dem Herrn ein neues Lied (Circum-
cision, c.1725).
LB:G80, G81.
Cantata 190: Excpt: Bebe, Zion, deinen Gott.
LB:G174.
Cantata 190: Excpt: Komm, du süsses Todesstunde.
LB:G174.
Cantata 191: Gloria in excelsis Deo (Christmas, c.1740):
Excpt: Gloria Patri et Filio et Spiritu Sancto.
LB:G184.
Cantata 196: Der Herr denket an uns (1708): Excpt:
Sinfonia.
LB:A39.
Cantata 198: Lass Fürstin, lass noch einem Strahl
(Funeral Ode, 1727).
LB:G10.
Cantata 199: Mein Herze schwimmt im Blut (11th.
Sunday after Trinity, c.1714).
LB:G41, G42.
**e. Sacred Vocal – Motets, BWV 225-231, BWV Anh
159**
Singet dem Herrn ein neues Lied, BWV 225.
EB:G136.
LB:G58, G94, G95, G96, G97, G98, G99, G100, G102,
G104, G105.
Der Geist hilft unserer Schwachheit auf, BWV 226.
LR:F27.
LB:B88, G83, G95, G96, G97, G98, G99, G100, G104,
G105, G325.
Jesu, Meine Freude, BWV 227.
LB:G62, G94, G95, G96, G97, G98, G100, G101, G102,
G103, G105, G186, G319.
Jesu, Meine Freude, BWV 227: Excpt: Jesu, Meine
Freude.
LR:F101.
Fürchte dich nicht ich bin bei mir, BWV 228.
LB:G83, G94, G96, G97, G98, G100, G104, G105,
G325.

Komm, Jesu, komm, BWV 229.
LR:F83.
LB:G96, G97, G98, G99, G100, G101, G102, G104,
G105.
Lobet den Herrn, alle Heiden, BWV 230.
LB:G83, G96, G97, G98, G100, G101, G103, G105.
Sei Lob und Preis mit Ehren, BWV 231.
LB:G96, G103, G105.
Ich lasse dich nicht, BWV Anh 159.
LB:G96, G105.
**e. Sacred Vocal – Masses and Mass movements, BWV
232-242**
Mass in B min, BWV 232.
LB:G105, G106, G107, G108, G109, G110, G111,
G112, G113, G114, G115, G116, G117.
Mass in B min, BWV 232: Excpt: Qui sedes.
LB:G185.
Mass in B min, BWV 232: Excpt: Agnus Dei.
LB:G185.
Mass in F maj, BWV 233.
LB:G105, G118, G119.
Mass in A maj, BWV 234.
LB:G105, G118, G119.
Mass in G min, BWV 235.
LB:G105, G118, G120.
Mass in G maj, BWV 236.
LB:G105, G118, G120.
Sanctus in C maj, BWV 237.
LB:G118.
Sanctus in D maj, BWV 238.
LB:G118.
Sanctus in D min, BWV 239.
LB:G118.
Sanctus in G maj, BWV 240.
LB:G118.
Sanctus in D maj, BWV 241.
LB:G118.
Christe in G min, BWV 242.
LB:G118.
e. Sacred Vocal – Magnificat, BWV 243, 243a
Magnificat in D maj, BWV 243.
LB:G92, G121, G122, G123, G124, G125, G127, G128,
G129, G130, G131, G132, G133.
Magnificat in D maj, BWV 243, with Interpolations from
Magnificat in E flat maj, BWV 243a.
LB:G124, G126, G130, G133.
Magnificat in D maj, BWV 243: Excpt: Esurientes
implevit bonis
LB:B227.
Magnificat in D maj, BWV 243: Excpt: Et exultavit.
LB:G174.
Magnificat in E flat maj, BWV 243a.
LB:G126.
Magnificat in E flat maj, BWV 243a: Excpt: Virga Jesse
floruit.
LR:F105.
Magnificat in E flat maj, BWV 243a: Excpt: Vom Himmel
hoch.
LR:F108.
e. Sacred Vocal – Passions, BWV 244-247
St. Matthew Passion, BWV 244.
LB:G134, G135, G136, G137, G138, G139, G140,
G141, G142, G143, G144, G145, G146, G147, G148,
G149.
Excerpts:
1. Kommt, ihr Tochter.
LB:G150.
2. Da Jesus diese Rede vollen.
LB:G150.
3. Herzliebster Jesu.
LB:G150.
Da versammleten sich die Hohenpriester.
LB:G150.
5. Ja nicht auf das Fest.

LB:G150.
10. Buss' und Reu'.
LB:G185.
11. Da ging hin der Zwolfen einer.
LB:G150.
16. Ich bin's.
LB:G176.
24. Da kam Jesus mit ihnen.
LB:G150.
35. O Mensch bewein' dein' Sunde gross.
LB:G150.
47. Erbarme dich.
LB:G150.
54. Auf das Fest aber hatte der Land.
LB:G150.
62. Da nahmen die Kriegsknechte.
LB:G150.
63. Haupt voll Blut.
LB:G150.
66. Komm susses Kreuz.
SI:C8.
71. Und von der sechsten Stunde.
LB:G150.
72. Wenn ich einmal soll scheiden.
LB:G150.
78. Wir setzen uns.
LB:G150.
St. John Passion, BWV 245.
LB:G134, G151, G152, G153, G154, G155, G156, G157, G158, G159, G160, G161.
Excerpts:
58. Es ist vollbracht.
LB:G174, G185.
67. Ruht wehl.
LB:G319.
68. Ach Herr, lass dein lieb.
LB:G319.
St. Luke Passion, BWV 246.
LB:G162.
e. Sacred Vocal – Oratorios, BWV 248–249
Christmas Oratorio, BWV 248.
LB:G92, G163, G164, G165, G166, G167, G168, G169, G170, G171.
Excerpts:
Miscellaneous.
LB:G326.
4. Bereite dich, Zion.
LB:G174.
10. Sinfonia.
LB:A178, A208.
Easter Oratorio, BWV 249.
LB:G172, G173.
Excerpts:
Chorale.
LB:A210.
Sinfonia/Adagio in B min.
LB:A183, A188, A204, A209, A581.
e. Sacred Vocal – Sacred Songs and Arias, BWV 250–503
Befiehl du deine Wege, BWV 270.
LB:D65.
Dir, dir, Jehova, will ich singen, BWV 299.
LB:G175, G177, G178.
Es ist gewisslich an der Zeit, BWV 307.
LB:D65.
Gott lebet noch, BWV 320.
LB:E209.
Herr Jesu Christ, dich zu uns wend, BWV 322.
LR:F101.
In dulci jubilo, BWV 368.
LR:F109.
LB:G176.
Komm, Gott, Schöpfer, heiliger Geist, BWV 370.
LB:G176.

Liebster Jesu, wir sind hier, BWV 373.
LR:F101.
Lobt Gott, ihr Christen allegleich, BWV 375.
LB:G176.
Nicht so traurig, nicht so sehr, BWV 384.
LB:G175.
Nun ruhen alle Wälder, BWV 392.
EB:G132.
O Ewigkeit, du Donnerwort, BWV 397.
LB:G178.
O Herzensangst, O Bangigkeit und Zagen, BWV 400.
LB:G175.
Uns ist ein Kindlein heut geborn, BWV 414.
LR:F108, F109.
Vater unser im Himmelreich, BWV 416.
LR:F101.
Was betrübst du dich, mein Herz, BWV 423.
LB:G175.
Wenn wir in höchsten Nöten sein, BWV 431.
LR:F101.
Wer nur den lieben Gott lässt walten, BWV 434.
LB:G175, G321.
Ach, dass nicht die letze Stunde, BWV 439.
LB:G105, G181.
Brich entzwei mein armes Herze, BWV 444.
LB:G105, G181.
Brunnquell aller Güter, Herrscher der Gemüter, BWV 445.
LB:G186.
Der lieben Sonne Licht und Pracht, BWV 446.
LB:G105, G181.
Die bittre Leidenszeit beginnet abermal, BWV 450.
LB:G105, G181, G186.
Die Goldne Sonne, BWV 451.
LB:G105, G181.
Dir, dir, Jehova, BWV 452.
LB:G105, G181.
Eins ist Not, ach Herr, BWV 453.
LB:G105, G181.
Es ist vollbracht! Vergis ja nicht, BWV 458.
LB:G181, G186.
Es kostet viel, ein Christ zu sein, BWV 459.
LB:G105, G181.
Gott lebet noch, BWV 461.
LB:G105, G181, G186.
Gott, wie gross ist, BWV 462.
LB:G105, G181.
Herr, nicht schicke, BWV 463.
LB:G186.
Ich lass dich nicht, BWV 467.
LB:G105, G181.
Ich steh an deiner Krippen hier, BWV 469.
LR:F106, F109.
LB:G105, G181.
Jesus ist das schönste Licht, BWV 474.
LB:G186.
Ihr Gestirn', ihr hohen Lüfte, BWV 476.
LB:G105, G181.
Komm, Süsser Tod, BWV 478.
LB:A211, G105, G181.
Kommt, Seelen dieser Tag, BWV 479.
LB:G105, G181.
Kommt wieder aus der finstern Gruft, BWV 480.
LB:G105, G181.
Liebster Herr Jesu, BWV 484.
LB:G105, G181.
Mein Jesu, was für Seelenweh, BWV 487.
LB:A210, G105, G181.
O Jesulein suss, BWV 493.
LR:F77, F107, F108.
LB:G105, G181, G320.
So gehst du nun, BWV 500.
LB:G105, G181.
So gibst du nun, mein Jesu, BWV 501.

LB:G105, G181.
Steh' ich bei meinem Gott, BWV 503.
LB:G105, G181.
**e. Sacred Vocal – Miscellaneous arrangements of
Chorales, etc.**
Allein Gott in der Höh' sei Ehr'.
LB:G179.
Befiehl du deine Wege.
LB:G179.
Christ ist erstanden.
LB:G180.
Christ lag in Todesbanden.
LB:G179, G180.
Christum wir sollen loben schon.
LB:G180.
Christus der ist mein Leben.
LB:G179.
Christus, der uns selig macht.
LB:G180.
Der Tag der ist so freudenreich.
LB:G180.
Die Nacht ist kommen.
LB:G179.
Ein feste Burg ist unser Gott.
LB:G179.
Erscheinen ist der herrlich Tag.
LB:G180.
Es woll uns Gott genädig sein.
LB:G179.
Gelobet seist du, Jesu Christ.
LB:G179, G180.
Gottes Sohn ist kommen.
LB:G179, G180.
Herr Christ, der einig Gottes Sohn.
LB:G180.
Herr Gott, dich loben alle wir.
LB:G179.
Herzliebster Jesu.
LB:G179.
Heut triumphiert Gottes Sohn.
LB:G180.
In dulci jubilo.
LB:G180.
Jesus Christus unser Heiland.
LB:G180.
Lobe den Herren.
LB:G179.
Lobt Gott, ihr Christen allzugleich.
LB:G180.
Nun danket alle Gott.
LB:G179.
Nun komm, der Heiden Heiland.
LB:G180.
Nun lässt uns Gott dem Herren.
LB:G179.
Nun ruhen alle Wälder.
LB:G179.
O Haupt voll Blut und Wunden.
LB:G179.
O Lamm Gottes, unschuldig.
LB:G180.
O Mensch bewein dein Sünde gross.
LB:G180.
Puer natus in Bethlehem.
LB:G180.
Vom Himmel hoch, da komm ich her.
LB:G180.
Wachet auf, ruft uns die stimme.
LB:G179.
Wass Gott tut, das ist wohlgetan.
LB:G179.
Wer nur den lieben Gott lässt walten.
LB:G179.
Wie schön leuchtet der Morgenstern.

LB:G179.
Wir Christenleut.
LB:G180.
Wir danken dir, Herr Jesu Christ.
LB:G180.

BACH, Wilhelm Friedemann (1710–1784)
a. Orchestral
Concerto in D maj for harpsichord and strings, F41.
LB:A215.
Concerto in E min for harpsichord and strings, F43.
LB:A215.
Concerto in F maj for harpsichord and strings, F44.
LB:A216.
Concerto in F maj for harpsichord and strings, F44:
   Presto.
LB:D221.
Concerto in A min for harpsichord and strings, F45.
LB:A216.
Concerto in E flat maj for 2 harpsichords, 2 trumpets, 2
   horns and strings.
LB:A40.
Concerto in F min for harpsichord and strings.
LB:A584.
Orchestral Suite in G min (Attrib. J.S Bach, BWV 1070).
LB:A162.
Sinfonia in D min.
LB:A39.
Sinfonia in F maj, 'Dissonanzen', F67.
LB:A41.
b. Chamber and Instrumental
Duo in F maj for 2 flutes.
LB:B233, B243, B246.
Trio Sonata in D maj for flute and harpsichord, F48.
LB:B226.
c. Keyboard – Harpsichord
Capriccio and fugue in B min, F19.
LB:D108.
Concerto in F maj for 2 keyboards, F10.
LB:D6, D229.
Fantasia in A min, F23.
LB:D108.
Fantasia in D min, F19.
LB:D9.
Fantasia in E min, F20.
LB:D108.
Fugues, F31, Nos. 1–8.
   1 in C maj; 2 in C min; 3 in D maj; 4 in D min; 5 in E flat
   maj; 6 in E min; 7 in B flat maj; 8 in F min.
LB:D108.
Polonaise in C maj.
LB:B242.
Polonaise in D maj.
LB:B242.
Polonaise in D min.
LB:B242.
Polonaise in F min.
LB:B242.
Polonaise in G maj.
LB:B242.
Prelude in B flat maj.
LB:E186.
Prelude in C min, F29.
LB:D108.
Sonata in B flat maj.
LB:D7.
c. Keyboard – Organ
Chorale Prelude (Unsp.)
LB:E186.
Jesu meine Freude.
LB:E185.
Was mein Gott will.
LB:E185.

BACH, Wilhelm Friedrich Ernst (1759-1845)
  b. Chamber and Instrumental
  Trio in G maj for 2 flutes and viola.
  LB:B243.

BAKFARK, Balint (= Valentin GREFF) (1507-1576)
  b. Instrumental - Lute
  Aspice Domine (after Gombert).
  LR:C2.
  Aspice Domine (after Jachet de Mantua).
  LR:C3.
  Benedicta es - Per illud ave (after Pieton).
  LR:C2.
  Le Corps absent (after Crecquillon).
  LR:C1.
  Circumdederunt me (after Clemens non Papa).
  LR:C3.
  Czarna krowa.
  LR:C1.
  D'amours me plains (after Rogier).
  LR:C1, C17.
  Delicta juventis (after Clemens non Papa).
  LR:C3.
  Domine si tu es (after Gombert).
  LR:C19.
  Dormend' un giorno (after Verdelot).
  LR:C3.
  Erravi sicut ovis (after Clemens non Papa).
  LR:C3.
  Fantasia (Unsp.)
  LR:C16.
  Fantasia I.
  LR:C1, C18, C19.
  Fantasia II.
  LR:C18, C20.
  Fantasia III.
  LR:C2.
  Fantasia IV.
  LR:A5, C2, C19.
  Fantasia V.
  LR:C3.
  Fantasia VI.
  LR:C3.
  Fantasia VII.
  LR:C20.
  Fantasia VIII.
  LR:C1, C18, C20.
  Fantasia IX.
  LR:A6, C1, C19.
  Fantasia X.
  LR:C1, C18.
  Un Gay bergier (after Crecquillon).
  LR:C1.
  Hierusalem luge - Deduc quasi torrentem (after Richafort).
  LR:C2.
  Il ciel che rado (after Arcadelt).
  LR:C1.
  Martin menoit (after Jannequin).
  LR:C2.
  Non dit mai - Galliard.
  LR:C1.
  O combien (after Sandrin).
  LR:C1.
  Or vien ca vien (after Jannequin).
  LR:C1.
  Passamezzo I.
  LR:C3.
  Quand' io pens' al martire (after Arcadelt).
  LR:C3.
  Quoniam tribulatio.
  LR:C3.
  Schoner Deutscher Danz - Galliard.
  LR:C1.

  Si grand' e la pieta (after Arcadelt).
  LR:C1.
  Ultimi mei sospiri (after Jannequin).
  LR:C2.

BALASSI, Balint (1554-1594)
  d. Secular Vocal
  Who would not trust (after Regnart).
  LR:A5.

BALBASTRE, Claude (1729-1799)
  c. Keyboard - Harpsichord
  La Belland.
  LB:D110.
  La Boullonge.
  LB:D111.
  La Castelmore.
  LB:D110.
  La de Caze (Book 1).
  LB:D109, D111.
  La Courteille (Book 1).
  LB:D109.
  La Genty.
  LB:D110.
  La d'Hericourt (Book 1).
  LB:D109, D110.
  La Lamarke.
  LB:D111.
  La Laporte.
  LB:D110.
  La Lugeac (Book 1).
  LB:D109, D110.
  La Malesherbe.
  LB:D110.
  La Monmartel ou Le Brunoy.
  LB:D111.
  La Morisseau.
  LB:D111.
  Romance in C maj (?).
  LB:D224.
  La Segue.
  LB:D110.
  La Suzanne.
  LB:D111.
  c. Keyboard - Organ: Noëls
  A cei-ci le moitre de to l'univar.
  LB:E148.
  A la venue de Noël.
  LB:E147, E148, E193.
  Ah! ma voisin es-tu fachee.
  LB:E147, E148.
  Au jo deu de pubelle.
  LB:E147, E148, E232.
  Comment tu oze petite Rose.
  LB:E147.
  Fugue en duo.
  LB:E230.
  Grand dei, ribon, ribeine.
  LB:E147, E148, E232.
  Il est un petite l'ange.
  LB:E147, E148.
  Joseph est bien marie.
  LB:E147, E148, E194, E232.
  Joseph revenant un jour.
  LB:E147, E148.
  Ou s'en vont ces gais bergers.
  LB:E147, E148.
  Quand Jesus naquit a Noël.
  LB:E147, E148, E229, E231.
  Que tu gro Jan, quei folie.
  LB:E147, E148.
  Tous les bourgeois de Chatres.
  LB:E147, E148.
  Votre bonte grand Dieu.

LB:E147, E148, E232.

BALDASSARE, Pietro (c.1700)
  c. Keyboard – Organ
  Sonata No. 1 in F maj for organ.
  LB:B212.

BALES, Alfonso (d.c.1635)
  d. Secular Vocal
  Chloris sighed.
  EB:F92.

BALLARD, Robert (1575–1650)
  b. Instrumental – Lute
  Allemande.
  LB:B306, C22.
  Ballade.
  LB:C22.
  2 Ballets a 4 (Terpsichore).
  EB:B40.
  Ballet des insencez.
  LB:C22.
  Ballet de Monsieur le Dauphin.
  LR:C11.
  Branle de la Cornemuse.
  LB:C22.
  Branle de Village.
  LR:C11, C14, E43.
  LB:B259.
  Branles de Village, 1–4.
  LR:C21, E21.
  Courant.
  LR:C14, C21.
  EB:B40.
  LB:B306, C22.
  Entrees de Luth, 1–3.
  LR:C14, C21.
  EB:B1.
  Grand Ballet de St. Germain.
  EB:B1.
  Prelude.
  LB:B306.
  Rocantins.
  LB:B306.

BAMBURG CODEX (13th. cent. – Ars Antiqua Motets)
  b. Instrumental Motets, etc.
  Flos filius.
  AA:D16.
  2 Hoquets.
  AA:D19.
  Hoquets 1–8.
  AA:B1.
  In saeculum vielatoris.
  AA:A3, B8, D18.
  ER:A7.
  Sine nomine.
  AA:D16.
  d/e. Secular and Sacred Vocal Motets
  Amor potest – Ad amorem.
  AA:B1, D18.
  Ave gloriosa – Ave virgo regia – Domine.
  AA:B2.
  Belle Ysabellot.
  ER:A5.
  Depositum – Ad solitum – Regnat.
  AN:A12.
  Dominator Domine – Ecce ministerium.
  AA:B1.
  Endurez le maux.
  AA:D16.
  Johannes postquam senuit.
  AA:C3.
  Ne m'oublier mie.
  AA:D16.
  O mitissima virgo – Quant voi – Virgo virginum.

AA:A3, B1.
On parole de batre – A Paris – Frese nouvele.
AA:A3, B1, D18.

BANCHIERI, Adriano (1567–1634)
  b. Instrumental
  La Battaglia.
  LR:D18.
  Dialogo acuto et grave.
  LR:D18.
  Bizaria del 1o tono.
  EB:E59.
  Bizaria del 1o tono alla quarta.
  EB:E59.
  Canzona VIII, 'La Banchierina.'
  EB:E59.
  Canzona XI, 'L'Organistina bella in echo.'
  EB:E59.
  Christe (Messa della Domenica).
  EB:E59.
  Fantasia del 12o e 11o modo.
  EB:E59.
  Fantasia in echo.
  LR:Ga14.
  Kyrie (Messa della Domenica).
  EB:E59.
  Sonata VIII in aria francese.
  EB:E59.
  Sonata sopra l'aria musicale del Gran Duca.
  EB:B41.
  Toccata I del 3o tono.
  LR:D18.
  Toccata (Unsp.)
  EB:E59.
  d. Secular Vocal
  Il Barca di Venetia per Padova.
  LR:E1.
  Contrapunto bestiale alla mente.
  LR:E46, Gd25.
  Dolcissimo usignuolo.
  LR:E47.
  Festina nella sera del giovedi grasso avanti cena.
  LR:E2.
  Restiva i corni.
  LR:E42.
  e. Sacred Vocal
  Omnes gentes.
  LR:Ge33.

BAPTISTA, Gracia (17th. cent.)
  c. Keyboard – Harpsichord
  Conditor alme – Hymn.
  EB:D28.

BARAHONA – see ESQUIVEL DE BARAHONA.

BARBELLA, Francesco (1692–1732)
  b. Chamber and Instrumental
  Concerto (Sonata) in G maj for recorder and strings.
  LB:A632.

BARBERIIS, Melchior de (c.1500–1550)
  b. Instrumental – Lute
  Fantasia.
  LR:C22, E2.
  d. Secular Vocal
  Madonna, qual certezza.
  LR:A1.

BARBETTA, Giulio Cesare (1540–c.1603)
  b. Instrumental – Lute
  Moresca detta le Canarie.
  LR:C23.

BARBION, Eustachias (d.c1556)
  d. Secular Vocal

Gallis hostibus in fugam coactis.
LR:E32.

BARBIREAU, Jacobus (= BERBIGANT) (1508–1591)
  b. Instrumental
  Au travail suis.
  ER:A9.
  Esperant que mon bien vendra.
  ER:A9.
  Gracuuly et biaulx.
  ER:A9.
  L'Omni banni.
  ER:A9.
  Die Pfoben swancz.
  ER:A9.
  LR:A6.
  d. Secular Vocal
  Ein frohlich wesen.
  ER:A1, A9.
  LR:Gf2.
  LB:B227.

BARDI, Giovanni de (1534–1612)
  d. Secular Vocal
  Miseri habitator.
  LR:E41.

BARKOCZY MS (16th./17th. cent. Hungarian.)
  b. Instrumental
  Dances.
  LR:A7.

BARON, Ernst Gottlieb (1696–1760)
  b. Instrumental – Lute and Guitar
  Sonata in B flat maj.
  LB:C15.
  Suite No. 2.
  LB:C16.

BARRE – *see* DE LA BARRE, Joseph.

BARRETT, John (1674–1735)
  b. Instrumental
  Voluntary in C maj for 2 trumpets and organ.
  LB:B214.

BARRIERE, Jean (d.1757)
  b. Chamber and Instrumental
  Sonata in D maj for viol and harpsichord.
  SI:C2.
  Sonata No. 3 in D min for cello and harpsichord.
  LB:B308.

BARSANTI, Francesco (1690–1772)
  a. Orchestral
  Concerto Grosso in D maj for 2 horns, tympani and
    strings, Op. 3, No. 4.
  LB:A586.
  Concerto Grosso in D maj for 2 oboes, trumpet, tympani
    and strings, Op. 3, No. 10.
  LB:A587.
  Overture in D maj for strings, Op. 4, No. 2.
  LB:A585.
  b. Chamber and Instrumental
  Sonata in C maj for recorder and continuo.
  LB:B260, B261, B262, B264.
  Sonata in C min for recorder and continuo.
  EB:B42.
  Sonata in G min for recorder and continuo.
  LB:B263.

BARTFA, COLLECTION OF (16th. Cent. Hungarian.)
  Collection of dances, songs, etc.
  LR:E42.

BARTHALI, Antonio (= BERTALI) (1605–1669)
  b. Chamber and Instrumental

Sonata for 2 violins and continuo, 'A Thousand Florins.'
EB:B43.

BARTLETT, John (fl.c.1600)
  d. Secular Vocal
  Of all the birds.
  LR:Gd18, Gd26.
  What thing is love?
  LR:Gd28.
  Sweet birds deprive us never.
  LR:Gd27.

BARTOLINO DA PADUA (14th. cent.)
  d. Secular Vocal
  La doulse cere.
  AN:B3.
  Per un verde boschetto.
  AN:B3, B6.
  e. Sacred Vocal
  Patrem omnipotem.
  AN:B5.

BARTOLOMEO, Padre Francesco (17th. cent.)
  b. Instrumental
  Canzon a due (Quarto Libro di Canzoni...1638).
  EB:B44.

BASSA, Jose (17th. cent.)
  c. Keyboard – Harpsichord
  Minue.
  EB:D33.

BASSANI – *see* BASSANO, Giovanni.

BASSANO, Giovanni (1560–1617)
  b. Instrumental
  Galliard.
  LR:B10.
  Oyme dolente.
  LR:Ga9.
  Ricercata III (Ricercate, Passagi, Cadentie, 1598).
  LB:B265.
  Ricercata V (Ricercate, Passagi, Cadentie, 1598).
  EB:E45, G56.
  Tirsir morir volea (after Marenzio).
  LR:B20.
  e. Sacred Vocal
  Ave regina.
  LR:F85.
  Dic nobis Maria.
  LR:F84.
  Hodie Christus natus est.
  LR:F86.

BASTON, John (18th. cent.)
  a. Orchestral
  Concerto in D maj for recorder and strings.
  LB:B227.

BATAILLE, Gabriel (1574–1630)
  d. Secular Vocal
  Baisez-moi.
  LR:E44.
  Belle qui de peur.
  LR:E44.
  Je ne sais s'il vous souvient.
  LR:E44.
  Ma bergere non legere.
  LR:E47.
  Qui veut chasser une migraine.
  LR:E43, E44, E48.
  Un jour que ma rebelle.
  LR:E48.
  Un satire cornu.
  LR:E43.
  Voici la bande des cornets.
  LR:E44.

BATCHELAR, Daniel (16th. cent.)
  b. Instrumental
  Mounsieur's Alman.
  LR:C10, Gb4, Gb5, Gb6.
  Pavan and Galliard.
  LR:Gb7.
  The Widowe's Mite.
  LR:Gd19.
  d. Secular Vocal
  To plead my faith.
  LR:Gd29, Gd30, Gd31.

BATESON, Thomas (c.1570–1630)
  d. Secular Vocal
  Come follow me, fair Nymphs.
  LR:Gd33.
  The Nightingale.
  LR:Gd29.
  Sister, awake.
  LR:Gd20.
  Those sweet delightful lilies.
  LR:Gd32.

BATIZI, Andras (16th. cent.)
  d. Secular Vocal The Book of the Prophet Jonah. (Verse
  Chronicle).
  LR:E49.

BATTEN, Adrian (d.1637)
  e. Sacred Vocal
  O sing joyfully.
  LB:G322.

BATTISHILL, Jonathan (1738–1801)
  e. Sacred Vocal
  O Lord, look down from heaven.
  LB:G322.

BAXTER, John (16th. cent.)
  b. Instrumental
  The Sacred End Pavan and Galliard.
  LR:Ga12.

BEATRICE DE DIA (12th. cent.)
  d. Secular Vocal
  A chantar.
  AA:D1, D2, D3.
  Plang.
  LR:B14.
  LB:B259.
  Vida.
  AA:D2.

BELLE, Jan van (16th. cent.)
  d. Secular Vocal
  O amoureusich mondeken root.
  EB:B35.

BELLINZANI, Paolo Benedetto (1690–1757)
  b. Instrumental
  Sonata in G min for recorder and continuo, Op. 3, No. 4.
  LB:B226.

BENDUSI, Francesco (16th. cent.)
  b. Instrumental
  Basse imperiale.
  LR:B10.
  Cortesa padoana e fusta.
  LR:B20.

BENEDETTI (17th. cent.)
  d. Secular Vocal
  Ch'io non senta per voi tormente guai.
  EB:F93.
  Cor mio, deh, non piangete.
  EB:F93.

BENESOV HYMNBOOK (16th. cent. Bohemian)
  e. Sacred Vocal
  Various Hymns.
  LR:F99.

BENET, John (15th. cent.)
  e. Sacred Vocal
  Jacet granum.
  ER:B1.

BENEVOLI, Orazio (1605–1672)
  e. Sacred Vocal
  Missa 'Salisburgensis.'
  EB:G1.
  Plaudite tympana.
  EB:G1.

BENNETT, John (1570–1615)
  d. Secular Vocal
  All creatures now are merry-minded (Triumphs of
  Oriana).
  LR:Gd20, Gd34, Gd35.
  The Hunt is up.
  LR:Gd33.
  Weep, O mine eyes.
  LR:E50, Gd25, Gd32.
  e. Sacred Vocal
  God is a spirit.
  LR:F77.

BERCHEM, Jachet de (d.1580)
  d. Secular Vocal
  Jehan de Lagny.
  LR:E38.
  Que feu craintif.
  EB:B35.
  e. Sacred Vocal
  Noë, Noë.
  LR:F118.
  O vos omnes.
  LR:F80.

BERENGUER DE PALOU (1150–1185)
  d. Secular Vocal
  De la iensor.
  AA:D4.
  Dona, la iensor.
  AA:D4.

BERGER, Andreas (17th. cent.)
  b. Instrumental
  Canzon octavi modi a 8 (Threnodiae Amatoriae)
  EB:B46.

BERMUDO, Juan (b.1510)
  c. Keyboard – Organ
  Cantus del primero tono, pour mi becarre.
  LR:D13.
  Conditor alme siderum.
  LR:D13.
  Modo primero por Mi y modo octavo por Elami.
  LR:E51.
  Vexilla regis procedunt.
  LR:D13.

BERNABE (16th. cent.)
  c. Keyboard – Organ
  Tiento de falsas de 2o tono por g sol re.
  LR:D13.

BERNARD DE CLUNY (14th. cent.)
  d. Secular Vocal
  Pantheon abluitur – Apollinis – Zodiacum.
  AA:B1.

BERNARD DE VENTADORN (b.1125)
  d. Secular Vocal
  Ab joi mou lo vers el momens.

AA:D1, D7.
Be m'an perdut.
AA:A3, D5.
Can l'erba fresc.
AA:D2, D5, D8.
LR:B14.
Can vei la lauzeta mover.
AA:D3, D5, D6, D8, D9, D10, D20.
Eram cosselhatz, senhor.
AA:D15.
Pois preyatz me, senhor.
AA:D7.
Pour oublier mon malheur il faut que je chante.
SI:C2.
Vida.
AA:D2.

BERNARDI, Steffano (1580–1638)
   d. Secular Vocal
   Il bianco e dolce cigno.
   LR:E39.
   O quam tu pulchra es.
   EB:G137.

BERNEVILLE – *see* GILLEBERT DE BERNEVILLE.

BERNARD, Christoph (1627–1692)
   e. Sacred Vocal
   Was betrübst du dich, meine Seele.
   LB:G324.

BERTOLDO, Sperandio (c.1530–1570)
   b. Instrumental
   Canzon francese.
   LR:B20.
   Petit fleur.
   LR:B20.

BERTOUCHE, Georg (1668–1743)
   b. Chamber and Instrumental
   Sonata No. 6 in C maj for organ solo.
   LB:B311.
   Sonata No. 18 in A flat maj for 2 violins and continuo.
   LB:B311.
   Sonata No. 21 in B flat min for 2 violins and continuo.
   LB:B311.

BERTRAND, Anthoine de (1540–1581)
   d. Secular Vocal
   Qui voudra voir dedans une jeunesse.
   LR:E52.

BESARD, Jean Baptiste (1567–1625)
   b. Instrumental – Lute
   Air de cour.
   LR:C14, C16.
   Allemande.
   LR:C14.
   2 Ballets a 4 (Terpsichore).
   EB:B40.
   Ballet pass' e mezzo.
   LR:C14.
   Branles.
   LR:B21, C9, C14, C16, C22, C24.
   Branle gai.
   LR:B21, C9, C14.
   Chorea rustica.
   LR:C14.
   Courante.
   LR:C9.
   Courante de Perichou (Terpsichore).
   EB:B40.
   Galliard.
   LR:C9, C14.
   Galliarda vulgo dolorata.
   LR:C14.
   Guillemette.

LR:C14, C16.
Ma belle si ton ame.
LR:E43.
Prelude.
LR:C9.
Villanelle.
LR:C9.
Volte.
LR:C9, C14, C16.
Volte de Tambour (Terpsichore).
EB:B40.

BESOZZI, Alessandro (1702–1775)
   b. Instrumental
   Sonata in C maj for oboe and continuo.
   LB:B248.
   Sonata in B flat maj for trombone and organ (Arr. Sonata
      in C maj for oboe and continuo).
   LB:B215.

BEVIN, Elway (1570–1640)
   b. Instrumental
   Browning a 3.
   LR:Ga15, Ga16.

BIBER, Heinrich Ignaz Franz (1644–1704)
   b. Chamber and Instrumental
   Ballettae I–VII a 4 violettae.
   EB:B3.
   Battalia.
   EB:B3, B4.
   LB:A597.
   Concerto in C maj for trumpet and strings.
   LB:A660.
   Partita I in D min for 2 violins in scordatura and continuo
      (Harmonia artificiosa-ariosa, 1712).
   EB:B48.
   Passacaglia in G min for violin and continuo.
   EB:B2.
   Serenade for strings, bass voice and continuo, 'Night-
      watchman.'
   LB:A604.
   Sonatas for violin in scordatura and continuo, Nos.
      1–15, 'Rosenkranz Sonaten.'
   EB:B2.
   Sonata for violin solo, 'Representativa avium.'
   EB:B50.
   Sonata a 4 for 2 violins, trombone and bass.
   EB:B4.
   Sonata a 4 for 2 violins, trombone and bass: Adagio and
      Allegro.
   AA:A1.
   Sonata a 6, 'Peasant's Church Procession.'
   EB:B3, B4.
   Sonata a 7 for 6 trombones, tramburin con organo.
   EB:B3, B38.
   Sonata I a 8 for 2 clarini and 6 violae.
   EB:B3.
   Sonata II a 8 for 2 clarini and 6 violae.
   EB:B3.
   Sonata III a 5 violae.
   EB:B3.
   Sonata IV a 5 violae.
   EB:B3.
   Sonata I (Fidicinium sacro-profanum).
   EB:B5.
   Sonata IV for 2 violins, 2 violas and continuo (Fidicinium
      sacro-profanum).
   EB:B49.
   Sonata V for 2 violins, 2 violas and continuo (Fidicinium
      sacro-profanum).
   EB:B49.
   Sonata VII in C min for 2 violins in scordatura and
      continuo: Sarabande (Fidicinium sacro-profanum).
   LB:B321.
   Sonata VIII in B flat maj (Fidicinium sacro-profanum).

EB:B4, B5.
Sonata X (Fidicinium sacro-profanum).
EB:B5.
Sonata III a 4 for violin, viola, 2 viols and continuo (Mensa Sonora, 1680).
EB:B51.
Sonata in C maj for 8 trumpets and continuo, 'St. Polycarpi.'
LB:A656.
Sonata IV in C maj for trumpet and organ.
LB:B205.
Suite for 2 clarinos.
EB:B47.

BIGAGLIA, Diogenio (1666–1733)
    b. Chamber and Instrumental
    Sonata in A min for recorder and continuo.
    LB:B260, B261, B267.

BINCHOIS, Gilles (c.1400–c.1460)
    d. Secular Vocal
    Adieu, adieu mon joieulx souvenir.
    ER:A10.
    Adieu ma douce.
    ER:A10.
    Adieu mon amoureuse.
    ER:A10.
    Amoureux suy.
    ER:A10, A12.
    Ay douloureux.
    ER:A10.
    Bien puist.
    ER:A12.
    De plus en plus.
    ER:A4.
    Deuil angoisseux.
    ER:A10, A11.
    En regardant.
    ER:A10.
    Esclave puist.
    ER:A10.
    Filles a marier.
    ER:A4, A12.
    LR:E25.
    Je loe amours.
    ER:A10, A12.
    Je ne fait tourjours.
    ER:A12.
    Plain de plours.
    ER:A10.
    Qui veut mesdire.
    ER:A10.
    Rondeau (Instrumental).
    LR:B22.
    Triste plaisire et douloureuse joie.
    SI:C6.
    Vostre allee.
    ER:A10.
    Vostre tres doulz regart.
    ER:A12.
    e. Sacred Vocal
    A solis ortus cardine.
    LR:F110.
    Agnus Dei.
    ER:B5.
    Asperges me.
    ER:B5.
    Gloria, laus et honor.
    ER:A11, B5.
    Veni creator spiritus.
    ER:B5.

BIONI, Antonio (b.1698)
    d. Secular Vocal
    Issipile – Opera, 1732: So che riduce a piangere.
    LB:F79.

BITTI, Martino (c.1720)
    b. Chamber and Instrumental
    Sonata in A min for recorder and continuo.
    LB:B262.

BITTNER, Jacques (17th. cent.)
    b. Instrumental – Lute
    Suite in G min.
    LR:C9.
    ER:C5.

BLANCHE DE CASTILLE (1188–1252)
    d. Secular Vocal
    Amours ou trop tard me suis pris.
    AA:D16.

BLANCO, Pedro Jose (c.1750–1811)
    c. Keyboard
    Concerto for 2 keyboards.
    LB:D229, E233.

BLASON – *see* **THIBAUT DE BLASON.**

BLAVET, Michael (1700–1786)
    a. Orchestral
    Concerto in A min for flute and orchestra.
    LB:A633.
    b. Chamber and Instrumental
    Sonata in D min for flute and continuo, 'La Vibray', Op. 2, No. 2.
    LB:B268, B269.
    Sonata in B min for flute and continuo, Op. 3, No. 2.
    LB:B215.
    Sonata in B min for flute and continuo, Op. 3, No. 2: Allegro.
    LB:B259.
    Sonata in G min for flute and continuo, 'La Lumagne.'
    LB:B237.

BLAYE, (13th. cent.)
    d. Secular Vocal
    Can lo rossinhols.
    AA:D5.
    Lanquan li jorn.
    AA:D5.

BLITHEMAN, William (d.1591)
    c. Keyboard
    Eterne rerum conditor (Mulliner Book).
    LR:Gc6.
    EB:E56.

BLONDEL DE NESLE (12th. cent.)
    d. Secular Vocal
    Quant je plus.
    AA:D17.

BLOW, John (1649–1708)
    c. Keyboard – Harpsichord
    Chaconne in F maj.
    EB:D1.
    2 Corants.
    LR:Gc6.
    Fugue in F maj.
    EB:B47.
    Ground in G maj.
    EB:D1.
    Jigg.
    LR:B10.
    Lesson in A min.
    EB:D1.
    Lesson in D min.
    EB:D1.
    Lesson in G min.
    EB:D1.
    Mortlack's Ground.
    EB:D30.

Praeludium in G maj.
EB:D1.
Sarabande.
LR:B10.
Suite in D maj.
LR:Gc7.
Suite in D min.
LB:D217.
c. Keyboard – Organ
Echo Voluntary in G maj.
EB:G3.
Verse for single organ.
LB:E195.
Voluntary for single organ.
LB:E195.
Voluntary for double organ.
LB:E184.
Voluntary in A maj.
EB:G3.
d. Secular Vocal
Cloe found Amyntas lying.
EB:F1.
Couched by the pleasant Heliconian spring.
EB:F94.
The Fair lover.
LR:Gd26.
Flavia grown old.
EB:F2.
Kellsea Coom.
EB:F94.
It grieves me.
EB:F1.
Marriage Ode.
EB:F1.
Ode on the Death of Henry Purcell.
EB:F1.
Oh, Nigrocella.
EB:F2.
Philander.
EB:F94.
Sabina.
EB:F2.
The Self-banished.
LR:Gd26.
EB:F94.
Tell me no more.
EB:F2, F94.
Why does my Laura.
EB:F2.
e. Sacred Vocal
Blessed is the man.
EB:G2.
Cry aloud and spare not.
EB:G2.
God spake sometimes in visions.
EB:G2.
LB:G319.
I was glad.
EB:G2.
Let thy hand be strengthened.
EB:G3.
Magnificat and Nunc dimittis – Evening Service in G maj.
EB:G3.
O pray for the peace of Jerusalem.
EB:G3.
O sing unto the Lord, all ye saints.
EB:G2.
Salvator mundi.
LR:Ge32.
EB:G3.

BODEL D'ARRAS, Jehan (1165–1210)
d. Secular Vocal
Contre le doux temps nouvel.
AA:D16.

LR:B14.
Pres d'un pin verdoyant.
AA:D16.

BODENSCHATZ, Erhard (1576–1636)
e. Sacred Vocal
Josef, lieber, Josef mein.
LR:F104, F111, F112, F113.

BODINUS, Sebastian (18th. cent.)
b. Chamber and Instrumental
Sonata in E maj for 2 flutes.
LB:B226.

BOESSET, Anthoine (1586–1643)
d. Secular Vocal
Ennuits, desespoirs et douleurs.
LR:E48.
Ils s'en vont ses rois de ma vie.
LR:E43.
N'esperez plus, mes yeux.
LR:E48.
Plaignez la rigueur de mon sort.
LR:E48.
Un jour Amarille et Tircis.
LR:E43.

BOHM, Georg (1661–1733)
b. Chamber and Instrumental
Concert en trio in F maj for viola d'amore, oboe d'amore and continuo.
LB:D226.
Suite in D maj for trumpet and organ (Arr. of Suite for solo harpsichord).
LB:B211.
c. Keyboard – Harpsichord
Suite No. 1 in C min.
LB:D225.
Suite No. 6 in E flat maj.
LB:D230.
Suite No. 7 in F maj.
LB:D225.
Suite No. 8 in F min.
LR:D16.
Suite No. 9 in F min.
LB:D230.
Menuet (Anna-Magdalena Bach Notebook).
LB:D69.
c. Keyboard – Organ
Capriccio.
EB:E73.
Christ lag in Todesbanden.
EB:E73, E75.
Christum wir sollen loben schon.
EB:E60.
Gelobet seist du.
EB:E60.
Prelude in D min.
LB:E234.
Prelude in F maj.
EB:E60.
Prelude and fugue in A min.
EB:E61.
Prelude and fugue in C maj.
EB:E62, E65, E71, E72.
Prelude, fugue and postlude in G min.
EB:E74.
Wer nur den lieben Gott lässt walten.
EB:E61.

BOISMORTIER, Joseph Bodin de (1691–1755)
b. Chamber and Instrumental
Daphnis et Cloe – Ballet: Menuet. Musette. Tambourin.
LB:B322.
1re. Divertissement de Champagne.
LB:B273.

Concerto in D maj for bassoon, strings and continuo.
LB:A635.
Concerto in D min for 5 recorders without bass.
LB:B271.
Concerto No. 4 in D min for 5 recorders without bass.
LB:A636.
Concerto in E min for recorder, flute, oboe, cello and
continuo, Op. 37, No. 6.
LB:B275, B276.
Sonata in F min for 3 recorders.
LB:B274.
Sonata in G min for flute and continuo, Op. 91, No. 2.
LB:B268.
Sonata in C maj for trombone and organ (Arr. Sonata in G
maj for cello or bassoon and continuo).
LB:B217.
Sonata in G maj for trumpet and orchestra (Arr. Sonata in
G maj for flute and continuo, Op. 91).
LB:B218.
Sonata No. 1 for viol and continuo (6 Sonatas, 1736).
SI:C19.
Sonata No. 2 for viol and continuo (6 Sonatas, 1736).
SI:C12.
Sonata No. 4 for viol and continuo (6 Sonatas, 1736).
SI:C15.
Sonata No. 6 in D min for viol and continuo (6 Sonatas,
1736).
SI:C10, C11.
Suite in D maj for solo flute, Op. 35, No. 4.
LB:B234.
Suite de Pieces de Violes: Prelude. Rondeau. Rigaudon.
Rondeau.
SI:C19.
Trio in E min for flute, recorder and bassoon.
LB:B270.
c. Keyboard - Harpsichord
La Belliqueuse (Suite 3).
LB:D112.
La Brunette - Doubles de la Brunette (Suite 4).
LB:D112.
La Caverneuse (Suite 1).
L:D112, D231.
La Choquante (Suite 2).
LB:D112.
La Decharnee (Suite 2).
LB:D112.
La Flagorneuse (Suite 3).
LB:D112.
La Frenetique (Book 4).
LB:D112.
La Gauloise (Suite 2).
LB:D112.
L'Imperieuse (Suite 3).
LB:D112.
L'Indeterminee (Suite 4).
LB:D112, D231.
La Marguilliere (Suite 1).
LB:D112.
La Navette (Suite 3).
LB:D112.
La Puce (Suite 3).
LB:D112.
La Rustique (Suite 2).
LB:D112.
La Serrenissime (Suite 2).
LB:D112.
La Transalpine (Suite 1).
LB:D112.
La Valtudiniere (Suite 1).
LB:D112.
La Veloutee (Suite 4).
LB:D112.
d. Secular Vocal
L'Hyver - Cantata.
LB:A634.

BOLOGNA – see JACOPO DA BOLOGNA.

BOND, Capel (d.1790)
a. Orchestral
Concerto in D maj for trumpet and strings.
LB:A661.

BONO, Pietro (1417-1497)
b. Instrumental
Balle.
ER:A9.
La Brosse.
ER:A9.
Le corps s'en va.
ER:A9.
Galliards 1 and 2.
ER:A9.
La Magdalena.
ER:A9.
Pavanes 1 and 2.
ER:A9.
Sans Roche.
ER:A9.
La Scarpa.
ER:A9.

BONONCINI, Antonio Maria (1677-1726)
e. Sacred Vocal
Stabat Mater.
LB:G187.

BONONCINI, Giovanni Battista (1670-1747)
a. Orchestral
Sinfonia No. 10 a 7 in D maj for 2 trumpets, strings and
continuo, Op. 3.
LB:A662.
Sinfonia da chiesa a 4, Op. 5, No. 1.
LB:A619.
b. Chamber and Instrumental
Divertimenti da Camera, Nos. 1-8.
1 in A min; 2 in G min; 3 in E min; 4 in G maj; 5 in F maj;
6 in D min; 7 in C min; 8 in B flat maj.
LB:B113.
Divertimento da camera No. 7 in C min.
LB:B262.
Divertimento da camera No. 5 in F maj.
LB:B263.
Sonata in A min for cello and continuo, No. 1.
LB:B309, B312.
d. Secular Vocal
Deh piu a me non v'ascondete - Air.
EB:F95.
Era, nella stagione - Cantata.
LB:F21.

BONPORTI, Francesco Antonio (1672-1749)
a. Orchestral
Concerto in F maj for violin and strings, Op. 11, No. 5:
Recitativo.
LB:A620.
Concerto in D maj for violin and strings, Op. 11, No. 8.
LB:A605.

BORCHGREVINCK, Melchior (d.1632)
b. Instrumental
Galliard.
LR:B23.
Paduana.
LR:B23.
d. Secular Vocal
Amatemi, ben mio.
LR:E19.
Baci amorosi e cari.
LR:E19.

BOREK, Krzysztof (17th. cent.)
e. Sacred Vocal

Missa 'Te Deum laudamus.'
EB:G4.

BORLET (14th. cent.)
  d.Secular Vocal
  He tres doulz roussignol.
  AA:A2.
  AN:A2, B16.
  ER:A4.
  Ma tredol rosignol joly.
  AA:A2.
  AN:A2, B16.

BORNELH – *see* GUIRAUT DE BORNELH.

BORNEMISZA, Peter (16th. cent.)
  d.Secular Vocal
  I am grieved to be parting from you (Cantio Optima,
    1553–1566).
  LR:A5, E49.
  I feel so sad.
  LR:A7.

BORRONO, Pietro Paolo (16th. cent.)
  b.Instrumental – Lute
  Pavana Milanese.
  LR:C26.
  Pescatore que va cantando.
  LR:C11, C25. ·
  Saltarello.
  LR:C26.

BOSSINIENSIS, Franciscus (15th./16th. cent.)
  c.Keyboard – Harpsichord
  3 Ricercares.
  LR:E53.

BOTTEGARI, Cosimo (16th. cent.)
  b.Instrumental
  Mi stare pone Totesche.
  LR:A1.

BOUIN, Francois (18th. cent.)
  b.Instrumental
  La Montauban.
  LB:B323.

BOUGEOIS, Loys (16th. cent.)
  b.Instrumental
  Psalm C: Vous tous qui sur la terre habitez.
  LB:B272.

BOURGES, Clement de (16th. cent.)
  c.Keyboard
  Fantasia.
  EB:E76.

BOUSSET – *see* DE BOUSSET, Jean-Baptiste.

BOUTMY, Guillaume (1723–1791)
  c.Keyboard – Harpsichord
  Sonata No. 4 in A maj.
  LB:D113.
  Sonata No. 6 in B flat maj.
  LB:D114.

BOUTMY, Jean-Baptiste Joseph (1725–1794)
  c.Keyboard – Harpsichord
  Divertimento in C maj.
  LB:D114.
  Divertimento in D maj.
  LB:D113.

BOUTMY, Josse (1697–1779)
  c.Keyboard – Harpsichord
  Tambourin in A maj.
  LB:D113.
  Suite in C min.

LB:D114.
Suite in D maj.
LB:D115.
Suite in D min.
LB:D114.

BOUTMY, Laurent (1756–1838)
  b.Instrumental and Chamber
  Sonata in D min for violin and harpsichord.
  LB:D113.
  Sonata in F min for violin and harpsichord.
  LB:D113.
  Sonata in G min for violin and harpsichord.
  LB:D113.
  c.Keyboard – Harpsichord
  Partant pour la Syrie.
  LB:D113.

BOUZIGNAC, Guillaume (17th. cent.?
  e.Sacred Vocal
  Noe, Noel! Pastores, cantate Domino.
  LR:F114.

BOYCE, William (1710–1779)
  a.Orchestral
  Concerto Grosso No. 1 in B flat maj.
  LB:A217.
  Concerto Grosso No. 2 in B min.
  LB:A217, A222, A606.
  Concerto Grosso No. 3 in E min.
  LB:A217, A222.
  Overture No. 5 in F maj for the New Year's Ode, 1762.
  LB:A217.
  Symphonies, Nos. 1–8.
    1 in B flat maj; 2 in A maj; 3 in C maj; 4 in F maj; 5 in D
    maj; 6 in F maj; 7 in B flat maj; 8 in D min.
  LB:A218, A219, A220, A221.
  Symphony No. 1 in B flat maj.
  LB:A595.
  Symphony No. 5 in D maj.
  LB:A657.
  b.Chamber and Instrumental
  Trio Sonata in D maj for 2 violins and continuo.
  SI:B2.
  c.Keyboard – Organ
  Voluntary in A min.
  LB:E195, E235.
  Voluntary in D maj.
  LB:E196.
  Voluntary No. 1.
  LB:B212, B214, G191.
  Voluntary No. 2.
  LB:G191.
  Voluntary No. 4.
  LB:G191.
  Voluntary No. 10.
  LB:G191.
  d.Secular Vocal
  From the mountains.
  EB:F92.
  Song of Momus to Mars.
  LB:F78.
  Tell me lovely shepherd (Solomon – Serenata, 1741).
  LR:Gd22.
  EB:F92.
  e.Sacred Vocal
  By the waters of Babylon.
  LB:G191.
  I have surely built Thee an house.
  LB:G190, G191, G322.
  O be joyful.
  LB:G190.
  O give thanks.
  LB:G190.
  O where shall wisdom be found?
  LB:G191.

Save me, O God.
LB:G190.
Turn Thee unto me.
LB:G190, G191.

BOYCE/HANDEL/STANLEY/STUBLEY
  b. Instrumental
  Suite of Trumpet Voluntaries in C maj.
  LB:B214.

BOYVIN, Jacques (c.1653–c.1706)
  c. Keyboard – Organ
  Livre d'Orgue I.
  EB:E1.
  Suite du 1re ton (Livre I).
  EB:E2.
  Suite du 4me ton (Livre I).
  EB:E2.
  LB:E197.

BRACHROGGE, Hans (16th./17th. cent.)
  d. Secular Vocal
  Alma cara gradita.
  LR:E19.
  Da la candida mano.
  LR:E19.

BRADE, William (c.1560–1630)
  b. Instrumental
  Alman.
  LR:B10, Ga10.
  3 Almans.
  LR:B23.
  Canzon.
  LR:Ga9.
  Coranto.
  LR:B10, Ga10.
  3 Corantos.
  LR:B23.
  Galliard.
  LR:B10, B23, Ga10, Ga14.
  Paduana.
  LR:B23.
  Pavane and Galliard a 6.
  LR:Ga17.
  Suite of 3 Dances.
  LB:A606.

BRAMIERI, Claudio (d.1594)
  b. Instrumental
  La Foccara – Canzone.
  LR:F87.

BRANDT, Jobst von (1517–1570)
  d. Secular Vocal
  Mir ist feins brauns meidelein.
  LR:E35.

BRASSART, Johannes (15th. cent.)
  e. Sacred Vocal
  O flos flagrans.
  ER:A11, B6.

BREHY, Pierre Hercule (1673–1737)
  a. Orchestral
  Sinfonia in C maj.
  LB:G188.

BREMON RICAS NOVAS, Peire (fl.1229–1241)
  d. Secular Vocal
  Ab marrimen.
  AA:D11.

BRENNENBURG – see REINMAR VON BRENNENBURG.

BRETEUILL – see GOTTFRIED VON BRETEUILL.

BREVI, Giovanni Battista (17th. cent.)
  e. Sacred Vocal
  O spiritus angeli.
  EB:G137.

BRIEGEL, Wolfgang Carl (1626–1712)
  e. Sacred Vocal
  Petite Cantate pour le temps de l'Avent.
  LR:F115.

BRIHUEGA (15th. cent.)
  b. Instrumental
  Villancico.
  ER:A7.

BRIVIO, Giuseppe Ferdinando (mid. 18th. cent.)
  d. Secular Vocal
  Demofoonte – Opera, 1738: Marcia in D maj.
    Par maggiore ogni diletto.
  LB:F79.

BRIXI, Simon (1693–1735)
  e. Sacred Vocal
  Missa Pastoralis.
  LB:G189.
  Offertorium solenne de Epiphanie Domini.
  LR:F116.
  Pastores.
  LR:F115.

BROSCHI, Riccardo (c.1700–1756)
  a. Orchestral
  Merope – Opera, 1736: Ballet Music, Act III.
  LB:F79.

BROWNE, John (1426–1498)
  d. Secular Vocal
  Margaret meek.
  LR:Gf3.
  Woefully arrayed.
  LR:Gf4.
  e. Sacred Vocal
  O mater venerabilis.
  LR:Gd36.
  Stabat juxta Christi crucem.
  SI:D4.
  Stabat mater.
  ER:B2.

BRUBIER, Antoine (16th. cent.)
  d. Secular Vocal
  Vivite felices.
  LR:E32.

BRUCK, Arnold von (1480–1554)
  d. Secular Vocal
  So trinken wir alle.
  LR:E35, E54.
  e. Sacred Vocal
  Aus tiefer Not.
  LR:F78.
  O du armer Judas.
  EB:G138.

BRUDIEU, Joan (16th. cent.)
  d. Secular Vocal
  Llir entre cards.
  AN:B15.
  No hi ha bens, no hi ha fortuna.
  AN:B15.

BRUHNS, Nicolaus (1665–1697)
  c. Keyboard – Organ
  Nun komm der Heiden Heiland (4).
  EB:E3, E4.
  Prelude and fugue in E min (2).
  EB:E3, E4, E63, E72, E77.

LB:E91, E198, E199, E200.
Prelude and fugue in E min (3).
EB:E3, E4.
Prelude and fugue in G maj (1).
EB:E3, E4, E71.

BRULE, Gace (c.1160–c.1212)
  d. Secular Vocal
  Biaus m'est estez.
  AA:D21.
  Cil qui d'amer me conseille.
  AA:D6.
  Contre temps que voy frimer.
  LR:B14.
  De bone amor.
  AA:D18.

BRUMEL, Anton (c.1460–c.1520)
  b. Instrumental
  Bicinium.
  EB:E78.
  d. Secular Vocal
  Ach, ghedeloos.
  EB:B35.
  Du tout plongiet – Fors seulement l'attente.
  ER:A1.
  Tous les regretz.
  ER:A8.
  Vray dieu d'amors.
  ER:A2, A7.
  e. Sacred Vocal
  Ave virgo gloriosa.
  ER:B7.
  Missa 'Et ecce terrae motus': Gloria.
  ER:A2.
  Noë, Noë.
  ER:B7.
  O Domine Jesu Christe.
  ER:B7.

BRUNA, Pablo (1611–1669)
  c. Keyboard – Organ
  Pange lingua.
  LR:D13.
  Tiento de dos tiples de 6o tono.
  LR:D13.
  Tiento de falsas de 2o tono.
  LR:D13.
  EB:E79.
  Tiento sobre la Litania de la Virgen.
  LR:D13.
  EB:E79.

BUCHNER, Hans (1483–1538)
  b. Instrumental
  Ach hülf mich Lied.
  LR:B10, B11, B13.
  Tanzmass Benzenauer: Nachtanz.
  LR:D19.

BULL, John (c.1562–1628)
  b. Instrumental
  Dorick.
  LR:Ga18.
  Prelude and In Nomine.
  LR:Gd40.
  In Nomine.
  LR:Ga17, Gd37.
  c. Keyboard – Harpsichord, virginals, organ
  Bonny sweet Robin.
  LR:Gc6.
  Les Buffons.
  LR:Gd38.
  Bull's Goodnight.
  LR:Gc6.
  Captain Piper's Galliard.

LR:Gc7, Gc16.
Chromatic Galliard.
LR:Gc10.
Chromatic Pavan – See Queen Elizabeth's Pavan.
Coranto.
LR:Ga19.
Coranto 'Alarm.'
SI:A2.
Coranto 'Battle.'
SI:A2.
Coranto 'Kingston.'
LR:Gc6.
Coranto 'The Princes.'
LR:Gc6.
Dallying Alman.
LR:Gc6.
Den luselijken mey, Christus plaisant.
LR:F117.
The Duchess of Brunswick's Toy.
LR:Ga19, Gc6, Gc13.
The Duke of Brunswick's Almain.
LR:Gc6.
Dutch Dance.
LR:Gc6.
Een kindeken is uns geboren.
LR:Gc6.
English Toy.
LR:Gc6, Gc11.
Fantasia.
EB:D34, E64.
Fantasia in D min.
LR:Gc11, Gc15.
Fantasia in G maj.
LR:Gc6.
Fantasia on a theme of Sweelinck.
LR:Gc6.
Galliard.
LR:D20, Gc6, Gc12, Gc13.
Galliard in D min.
LR:Gc6.
Galliard to My Lord Lumsley's Pavane.
LR:D20, Gc12.
La Guamina – Fantasia.
LR:Gc6.
In Nomine.
LR:Gc8.
EB:D24.
The King's Hunt.
LR:Gc8, Gc9, Gc11, Gc14, Gd41.
Laet ons met Herten reyne – Prelude and fantasia.
LR:Gc6.
EB:B47.
Lord Lumsley's Pavan and Galliard.
LR:Gc15.
My choice I will not change.
SI:B1.
My Grief.
LR:Gc6.
My Jewel.
LR:Ga19, Gc6, Gc8.
My Self.
LR:Gc6, Gc9, Gd39.
Pavana.
LR:D20, Gc12.
EB:E73.
Pavane in the 2nd. tone.
LR:Gc6.
Pavane and Galliard.
LR:Gc6.
Pavane and Galliard 'Sinfonie.'
LR:Gc6.
Prelude.
LR:Gc10, Gc15.
Prelude and fantasia on sol ut.

LR:Gc6.
The Prince's Galliard.
LR:Gc15.
Queen Elizabeth's Pavane (the Chromatic Pavane).
LR:Gc6, Gc10.
Regina Galliard.
LR:Gc6, Gd39.
SI:A2.
Salve regina.
LR:Gc6.
The Spanish Pavane.
LB:D220.
SI:A2.
Vexilla regis.
LR:Gc6.
Walsingham.
LR:Gc8.
Welsh Dance.
LR:Gc6.
Why ask you?
LR:Gc6, Gc10.
e. Sacred Vocal
Almighty God.
LR:F117.

BULMAN, Baruch (16th. cent.)
   b. Instrumental – Lute
   Pavan.
   LR:E54, Gb4, Gb5, Gb6.

BUONAMENTE, Giovanni Battista (d.1643)
   b. Chamber and Instrumental
   Sonata a 3 violini and continuo (Sonate...libro sesto...
      1636)
   EB:B52.

BURGK, Joachim (1546–1610)
   e. Sacred Vocal
   Der Herr mit seinem Jüngern.
   EB:G138.

BUSATTI, Cherubino (16th./17th. cent.)
   d. Secular Vocal
   Morte son io.
   LR:Gd42.
   EB:F96.
   e. Sacred Vocal
   Surrexit pastor bonus.
   EB:G139.

BUSNOIS, Antoine (d.1492)
   d. Secular Vocal
   Fortuna desperata.
   ER:A1, A13, B35.
   Fortune esperee.
   LR:Gf2.
   Je ne fay plus.
   ER:A13.
   LR:A1, E24.
   e. Sacred Vocal
   Missa 'L'Homme arme.'
   ER:B5.

BUTERNE, Jean-Baptiste (1650–1727)
   b. Instrumental
   Suite Pastorale.
   LB:A593.

BUXTEHUDE, Dietrich (1637–1707)
   b. Chamber and Instrumental
   Sonata in C maj for 2 viols and continuo.
   EB:B48.
   Suite in G maj for lute.
   LB:C13.
   **c. Keyboard – Organ: Free Organ Works, BuxWV
   136–176, 225**

Prelude and fugue in C maj, BuxWV 136 (H2:2).
EB:E8, E15, E17, E24.
Prelude, fugue and chaconne in C maj, BuxWV 137
   (H2:1).
EB:E7, E13, E16, E24, E66, E72.
LB:E198, E206.
Prelude and fugue in C maj, BuxWV 138.
EB:E12, E24.
Prelude and fugue in D maj, BuxWV 139 (H2:11).
EB:E7, E14, E18, E24, E72.
LB:E199, E200.
Prelude and fugue in D min, BuxWV 140 (H2:19).
EB:E7, E15, E17, E24, E72.
Prelude and fugue in E maj, BuxWV 141 (H2:14).
EB:E6, E15, E17, E24, E72, G6.
Prelude and fugue in E min, BuxWV 142 (H2:9).
EB:E6, E13, E24, E72, G6.
Prelude and fugue in E min, BuxWV 143 (H2:10).
EB:E6, E12, E18, E24.
Prelude and fugue in F maj, BuxWV 144 (H2:16).
EB:E11, E14, E22, E24.
Prelude and fugue in F maj, BuxWV 145 (H2:15).
EB:E5, E14, E23, E24, E72.
LB:E207.
Prelude and fugue in F sharp min, BuxWV 146 (H2:13).
EB:E8, E14, E23, E24, E62, E67, E72, E80.
LB:E229.
Prelude and fugue in G maj, BuxWV 147 (H2:7).
EB:E9, E19, E24.
Prelude, fugue and chaconne in G min, BuxWV 148
   (H2:22).
EB:D32, E10, E15, E21, E24, G6.
LB:D222, E201.
Prelude and fugue in G min, BuxWV 149 (H2:24).
EB:E5, E13, E24, E72, E83.
Prelude and fugue in G min, BuxWV 150 (H2:23).
EB:E9, E14, E18, E24.
Prelude and fugue in A maj, BuxWV 151 (H2:12a).
EB:E9, E13, E23, E24.
Prelude and fugue in A min, BuxWV 152 (H2:6).
EB:E10, E15, E20, E24.
Prelude and fugue in A min, BuxWV 153 (H2:4).
EB:E8, E14, E18, E24.
Prelude and fugue in B flat maj, BuxWV 154 (H2:21).
EB:E14, E24, E25.
Toccata in D min, BuxWV 155 (H2:20).
EB:E10, E12, E24.
Toccata in F maj, BuxWV 156 (H2:17).
EB:E6, E15, E19, E24.
Toccata and fugue in F maj, BuxWV 157 (H2:18).
EB:E7, E13, E16, E24, E65.
Prelude and fugue in A min, BuxWV 158 (H2:5).
EB:E8, E13, E21, E24.
Chaconne in C min, BuxWV 159 (H1:3).
EB:E6, E14, E21, E24, E72, E81.
Chaconne in E min, BuxWV 160 (H1:2).
EB:E11, E13, E17, E24, E72.
Passacaglia in D min, BuxWV 161 (H1:1).
EB:E7, E13, E18, E24, E25, E69, E72, E80.
Prelude and fugue in G maj, BuxWV 162 (H2:8).
EB:E15, E19, E24.
Prelude and fugue in G min, BuxWV 163 (H2:25).
EB:E12, E17, E24.
Toccata in G maj, BuxWV 164 (H2:27).
EB:E15, E20, E24, E74.
Toccata in G maj, BuxWV 165 (H2:26).
EB:E12, E19, E24.
Canzona in C maj, BuxWV 166 (H1:4).
EB:E11, E14, E19, E24.
Canzonetta in C maj, BuxWV 167 (H1:5).
EB:E14, E22, E24, E61, E74.
Canzona in D min, BuxWV 168 (H1:10).
EB:E11, E14, E20, E24.
Canzonetta in E min, BuxWV 169 (H1:9).

EB:E14, E16, E24.
Canzona in G maj, BuxWV 170 (H1:6).
EB:E15, E23, E24.
Canzonetta in G maj, BuxWV 171 (H1:7).
EB:E13, E16, E24.
Canzonetta in G maj, BuxWV 172.
EB:E15, E20, E24.
Canzonetta in G min, BuxWV 173 (H1:12).
EB:E15, E24, E74.
Fugue in C maj, BuxWV 174 (H2:3).
EB:E15, E22, E24, E25, E61.
Canzona (Fugue) in G maj, BuxWV 175 (H1:8).
EB:E13, E18, E24.
Canzona (Fugue) in B flat maj, BuxWV 176 (H1:11).
EB:E11, E15, E22, E24.
Canzonetta in A min, BuxWV 225.
EB:E22, E24.
Prelude and fugue in D maj, (H2:28).
EB:B53.
LB:E202, E203, E205, E206.

c.Keyboard – Organ: Chorale-Based Works, BuxWV 177–224

Ach Gott und Herr, BuxWV 177 (H3,1:1).
EB:E14, E18, E24.
Ach Herr, mich armen Sünder, BuxWV 178 (H4:1).
EB:E9, E14, E17, E24.
Auf meinen lieben Gott, BuxWV 179 (H3,1:7).
EB:E14, E18, E20, E24, E61.
Christ unser Herr zum Jordan kam, BuxWV 180 (H4:2).
EB:E8, E14, E22, E24.
Danket dem Herrn, denn er ist sehr freundlich, BuxWV 181 (H3,1:2).
EB:E7, E13, E19, E24.
Der Tag, der ist so freudenreich, BuxWV 182 (H4:3).
EB:E7, E13, E20, E24.
Durch Adams fall ist ganz verderbt, BuxWV 183 (H4:4).
EB:E8, E14, E22, E24, E68.
Ein feste Burg ist unser Gott, BuxWV 184 (H4:5).
EB:E8, E14, E20, E24.
LB:E196.
Erhalt uns Herr bei deinem Wort, BuxWV 185 (H4:6).
EB:E8, E15, E21, E24, E60.
Es ist das Heil uns kommen her, BuxWV 186 (H4:7).
EB:E8, E14, E18, E26.
Es spricht der unweisen Mund wohl, BuxWV 187 (H4:8).
EB:E8, E15, E22, E24.
Gelobet seist du, Jesu Christ, BuxWV 188 (H3,2:1).
EB:E5, E12, E24.
Gelobet seist du, Jesu Christ, BuxWV 189 (H4:9).
EB:E8, E13, E16, E24.
Gott der Vater, wohn uns bei, BuxWV 190 (H4:10).
EB:E8, E15, E16, E24.
Herr Christ, der einig Gottes Sohn, BuxWV 191 (H4:11a).
EB:E5, E14, E24.
Herr Christ, der einig Gottes Sohn, BuxWV 192 (H4:11b).
EB:E9, E13, E21, E22, E24.
Herr Christ, ich weiss gar wohl, BuxWV 193 (H4:12).
EB:E7, E15, E23, E24.
Ich danke dir, lieber Herre, BuxWV 194 (H3,2:2).
EB:E11, E15, E20, E24.
Ich danke dir schon durch deinem Sohn, BuxWV 195 (H3,2:3).
EB:E11, E15, E22, E24.
Ich ruf zu dir, Herr Jesu Christ, BuxWV 196 (H3,2:4).
EB:E11, E12, E21, E24.
In dulci jubilo, BuxWV 197 (H4:14).
LR:F111.
EB:E5, E13, E20, E24, E64, E67.
LB:E208.
Jesus Christus, unser Heiland, BuxWV 198 (H4:13).
EB:E9, E14, E18, E24.
Komm, heiliger Geist, Herre Gott, BuxWV 199 (H4:15a).
EB:E6, E14, E16, E24.
Komm, heiliger Geist, Herre Gott, BuxWV 200 (H4:15b).

EB:E9, E14, E19, E24.
Kommt her zu mir, spricht Gottes Sohn, BuxWV 201 (H4:16).
EB:E7, E15, E20, E24.
Lobt Gott, ihr Christen allzugleich, BuxWV 202 (H4:17).
EB:E5, E13, E23, E24, E60, E65, G6.
Magnificat primi toni, BuxWV 203 (H3,2:5).
EB:E9, E13, E19, E24, E68.
Magnificat primi toni, BuxWV 204 (H3,1:3a).
EB:E15, E19, E24, E60.
Magnificat noni toni, BuxWV 205 (H3,1:3b).
EB:E13, E18, E24.
Mensch, willt du leben seliglich, BuxWV 206 (H4:18).
EB:E9, E14, E23, E24.
Nimm vons uns, Herr – See Vater unser im Himmelreich.
Vater unser im Himmelreich, BuxWV 207 (H4:22).
EB:E7, E14, E16, E24.
Nun bitten wir den Heiligen Geist, BuxWV 208 (H4:19a).
EB:E9, E15, E21, E24, E60, G6.
Nun bitten wir den Heiligen Geist, BuxWV 209 (H4:19b).
EB:E9, E15, E20, E24.
Nun freut euch lieben Christen g'mein, BuxWV 210 (H3,2:6).
EB:E10, E13, E17, E24.
Nun komm, der Heiden heiland, BuxWV 211 (H4:20).
EB:E9, E13, E20, E24, E25, E65, E83.
LB:E202.
Nun lob mein Seel den Herren, BuxWV 212 (H3,1:4a).
EB:E11, E15, E19, E20, E24.
Nun lob mein Seel den Herren, BuxWV 213 (H3,1:4b).
EB:E15, E19, E20, E24.
Nun lob mein Seel den Herren, BuxWV 214 (H3,1:5a).
EB:E10, E15, E23, E24.
Nun lob mein Seel den Herren, BuxWV 215 (H3,1:5b).
EB:E23, E24.
Puer natus in Bethlehem, BuxWV 217 (H4:21).
EB:E10, E13, E17, E24, E60.
LB:E202.
Te Deum laudamus, BuxWV 218 (H3,2:7).
EB:E15, E14, E21, E24.
Vater unser im Himmelreich, BuxWV 219 (H3,1:6).
EB:E6, E14, E16, E24.
Von Gott will ich nicht lassen, BuxWV 220 (H4:23a).
EB:E10, E12, E17, E24.
Von Gott will ich nicht lassen, BuxWV 221 (H4:32b).
EB:E10, E12, E17, E24.
Wär Gott nicht mit uns diese Zeit, BuxWV 222 (H4:24).
EB:E10, E12, E19, E24.
Wie schön leuchtet der Morgenstern, BuxWV 223 (H3,2:8).
EB:E11, E13, E22, E24, E82.
Wir danken dir, Herr Jesu Christ, BuxWV 224 (H4:25).
EB:E10, E13, E24.

e.Sacred Vocal – Cantatas

Alles, was ihr tut mir Worten, BuxWV 4.
EB:G9.
Also hat Gott die Welt geliebet,. BuxWV 5.
EB:G8.
Befiehl dem Engel, dass er komm, BuxWV 10.
EB:G9.
Cantate Domino, BuxWV 12.
EB:G9.
Das neugeborne Kindelein, BuxWV 13.
EB:G131.
Herr, auf dich traue ich, BuxWV 35.
EB:G8.
Herr, ich lasse dich nicht, BuxWV 36.
EB:G7.
Herr, nun lässest du deinen Deiner, BuxWV 37.
EB:G5.
Herr, wenn ich nur dich habe, BuxWV 39.
EB:G5.
Herzlich lieb hab ich dich, O Herr, BuxWV 41.
EB:G10.

Ich bin eine Blume zu Saron, BuxWV 45.
EB:G5.
Ich suchte des Nachts, BuxWV 50.
EB:G7.
In dulci jubilo, BuxWV 52.
EB:G6.
Jesu, meine Freude, BuxWV 59.
EB:G10.
Jubilate Domino, BuxWV 64.
EB:G6, G134.
LB:G324.
Lauda Sion, BuxWV 68.
LR:F105.
EB:G9.
Laudate Dominum, BuxWV 69.
EB:G8.
Magnificat.
EB:G132.
Mein Herz ist bereit, BuxWV 73.
EB:G7.
Mit Fried und Freud fahr' ich dahin, BuxWV 76.
EB:G5, G9, E12, E22.
Muss der Tod denn nun doch treunen, BuxWV 76.
EB:G134.
O Gottes Stadt, BuxWV 87.
EB:G7.
Pastores loquebantur.
LR:F104.
Singet dem Herrn, BuxWV 98.
EB:F92, G8.
Wachet auf, ruft, uns die Stimme, BuxWV 100.
EB:G10.
Wie schmeckt es so lieblich und wohl, BuxWV 108.
EB:G5.

BYRD, William (1543–1623)
b. Instrumental (*see also* Keyboard)
Christe redemptor a 4.
LR:Ga18.
Fantasia a 3.
LR:Gd19.
Fantasia a 4.
AA:A1.
LR:Gd19.
Fantasia a 4 (I).
LR:Gd1.
Fantasia a 4 'Browning' (II).
LR:Gd37.
EB:B54.
Fantasia a 4 (III).
EB:B54.
Fantasia a 4 (IV).
LR:Gd1.
Fantasia (Unsp.)
LB:A585.
In Nomine a 4 (I).
LR:Gd1.
SI:B1.
In Nomine a 4 (II).
LR:Gd1.
In Nomine a 5.
LR:Ga16, Gd40.
EB:B49.
The Leaves be green – Browning a 5.
LR:Ga13, Ga16.
LB:B227, B271.
Lullaby.
LR:Gb1, Gd46.
Pavane.
LR:Gb1, Gd1, Gd21.
EB:D24.
Pavana Bray.
LR:Gb1, Gd1, Gd21.
Pavane and Galliard a 6.
EB:B54.

c. Keyboard – Harpsichord, virginals, organ (including lute and consort arrangements)
All in a garden green (N32).
LR:Gc1.
Almand.
LR:D20, Gc12.
The Bells.
LR:Gc14.
LB:D216.
The Barley Breake (N6).
LR:Gc1.
The Battell (N4).
LR:Gc1, Gc2, Gc14.
EB:D35.
Calleno castura me.
LR:D20, Gc7, Gc12.
EB:B37.
SI:C19.
The Carman's Whistle (N34).
LR:Gc1, Gc2, Gc9, Gc14.
Clarifica me pater (for organ).
LR:Gd19.
Coranto.
LR:Gc3, Gd1.
EB:D24.
SI:C7.
The Earl of Oxford's March.
LR:Ga11.
A Fancy (N36).
LR:Gc1.
A Fancy (N41).
LR:Gc1.
Fantasia (FVB).
LR:Gc17.
Fantasia in A min.
EB:E84.
Fantasia in D min.
LR:Gc3.
Fantasia No. 4.
LR:D21.
Fantasia No. 8.
EB:E66.
Fantasia for organ.
LR:Ge11.
EB:E73.
The First French Coranto.
LR:Gc6.
Fortune my foe.
LR:Gd43.
Gagliarda.
LR:B10, Gb1, Gc13.
Galliard.
LR:Ga15, Gd1, Gd21.
EB:D24.
Galliard in D min.
LR:Gc3.
Galliard for the Victory (N5).
LR:Gc1.
Galliards Gygge (N7).
LR:Gc1, Gc2.
Galliardas Passamezzo.
LR:D20, Gc8, Gc12.
Hugh Ashton's Ground (N35).
LR:Gc1, Gc2, Gc3.
The Hunt's Up (N8).
LR:Gc1, Gc10.
Lachrymae Pavane.
LR:Gc3, Gc16.
A Lesson of Voluntaries (N29).
LR:Gc1.
The Maiden's Song (N28).
LR:Gc1.
March before the Battel (N3).
LR:Gc1.
Miserere.

LR:Gc12, Gc17, Ge11.
EB:B54.
Mistress Mary Brownlow's Galliard.
LR:Gc3.
The Morris.
SI:B1.
Mounsier's Almain (N38).
LR:Ga20, Gc1, Gc2, Gd1, Gd21.
My Lady Nevell's Book (Cpte) (N).
LR:Gc1.
My Lady Nevell's Ground (N1).
LR:Gc1.
My Lord of Oxenford's Maske.
LR:Ga13, Ga20, Gd1, Gd21.
My Lord Salisbury's Pavane.
LR:Ga18, Gc6, Gc13, Gd40.
My Lord Salisbury's Pavane and Galliard.
LR:Gd38.
SI:C3.
My Lord Salisbury's Pavane - 2 Galliards.
LR:Gc6.
My Lord Willoughby's Welcome Home (N33).
LR:Gb1, Gc1, Gc6, Gc9, Gd1.
Pavan and Galliard No. 1 (N10-11).
LR:Gc1, Gc6.
Pavan and Galliard No. 3 (N14-15).
LR:Gc1.
Pavan and Galliard No. 4 (N16-17).
LR:Gc1, Gc2.
Pavan and Galliard No. 5 (N18-19).
LR:Gc1, Gc2, Gc6.
Pavan and Galliard No. 5 'Kinbrugh Goodd' (N20-21).
LR:Gc1.
Pavan No. 7 (N22).
LR:Gc1.
Pavan No. 8 (N23).
LR:Gc1.
Pavan and Galliard No. 9 'Passymeasures' (N24-25).
LR:Gc1, Gc10.
Pavan and Galliard No. 10 'Mr. Peter' (N30-31).
LR:Gc1, Gc11.
Pavan and Galliard in C min.
LR:Gc3.
Pavan and Galliard in G maj.
LR:Gc3.
Prelude.
LR:Gc10, Gc17.
EB:D35.
Prelude in C maj.
LR:Gc3.
Quadran Pavan and Galliard.
LR:Gc3.
The Queen's Almain.
LR:Gc6.
LB:D216.
Qui passe (N2).
LR:Gc1, Gc2.
Rowland.
LR:Gc13.
The Second Ground (N30).
LR:Gc1, Gc2.
Sellinger's Round (N37).
LR:Gc1, Gc2.
Souldier's Dance.
SI:B1.
Ut re mi fa sol la (N9).
LR:Gc1.
Verse for organ.
LR:Ge11.
La Volta.
LR:D20, Gc12, Gc13, Gd1, Gd46.
LB:B277.
SI:A1.
A Voluntary (N42).
LR:Gc1, Gc2.

A Voluntary for My Lady Nevell (N26).
LR:Gc1.
Walsingham (N31).
LR:Gc1, Gc11.
Walt's Come Down.
LR:Gc7.
Watkin's Ale.
LR:Gc9.
The Woods so Wild.
LR:Gb1, Gb4, Gb8, Gd1.
SI:B1.
Wolsey's Wilde (N27).
LR:E35, Gb1, Gc1, Gc13, Gd47.
d. Secular Vocal
Ah, silly soul.
LR:Gd44.
All is as a sea.
LR:Gd44.
As Caesar wept.
LR:Gd1.
Blame, I confess.
LR:Gd1.
Come to me grief, for ever.
LR:Gd29.
Come woeful Orpheus.
LR:Gd19.
Content is rich.
LR:Gd19.
Farewell delight.
SI:B1.
Farewell false love.
LR:Gd29.
I joy not in no earthly bliss.
SI:A2.
John come kiss me now.
LR:D20, Gc12.
Lullaby, my sweet little baby.
LR:F117, F118, F120, Gd20, Gd32.
My mistress had a little dog.
LR:Gd1.
The Noble famous Queen.
LR:Gd42.
O dear life.
LR:Gd44.
This sweet and merry month of May.
LR:E46, Gd20.
Though Amaryllis dance in green.
LR:Gd20, Gd32.
SI:A2.
Wedded to will is witless.
LR:Gd19.
What pleasures have great Princes.
LR:Gd19.
When I was otherwise.
LR:Gd44.
Ye Sacred Muses - Elegy on the Death of Thomas Tallis.
LR:Gd1, Gd40.
e. Sacred Vocal – Works with English texts
Bow thine ear O Lord.
LR:Ge8.
Christ rising from the dead.
LR:Ge11.
From Virgin's womb this day did come.
LR:Ge11.
Have mercy upon us.
LR:Gd36.
Lesser Litany.
LR:Ge31.
Lord, hear my prayer.
LR:Ge30.
Magnificat (Great Service).
LR:Ge1, Ge8.
Make ye joy to God.
LR:Ge11.
Nunc dimittis (Great Service).

LR:Ge1, Ge8.
O God, whom our offences.
LR:Ge10.
O Lord make thy servant Elizabeth.
LR:Ge38.
O Lord, how vain.
LR:Gd1, Gd29, Gd40.
Praise our Lord, all ye Gentiles.
LR:Gd19, Ge8, Ge11.
Preces and Responses.
LR:Ge31.
Prevent us, O Lord.
LR:Ge8.
Psalm XLVII.
LR:Ge8.
Psalm LIV.
LR:Ge8.
Psalm LV.
LR:Ge8.
Psalm CXIV.
LR:Ge8.
Psalm CXIX.
LR:Ge8.
Sing joyfully unto God.
LR:Gd39, Ge8, Ge10, Ge11.
This day Christ was born.
LR:Ge11, Ge35.
Turn our captivity, O Lord.
LR:Ge11.
Versicles and Responses.
LR:Ge31.

e. Sacred Vocal – Works with Latin Texts
Ad Dominum cum tribulare – Motet.
LR:Ge38.
Alleluia ascendit Deus (Gradualia, 1605).
LR:Ge4.
Ave Maria (Gradualia, 1605).
LR:Ge7.
Ave regina caelorun (Gradualia, 1605).
LR:Ge2.
Ave verum corpus (Gradualia, 1605).
LR:F77, F83, Ge1, Ge4, Ge8, Ge9, Ge37.
LB:G320.
Benedictio et claritas (Cantiones Sacrae, 1589).
LR:Ge4.
Christe qui lux es et dies – Motet.
LR:F120, Gd1, Ge7.
Cibavit eos (Gradualia, 1605).
LR:Ge2.
Civitas sancti tui (Cantiones Sacrae, 1589).
LR:F79, Ge7.
Cognoverunt discipuli.
LR:Ge7.
Domine, salva nos – Motet.
LR:Ge9.
Ego sum panus vivus (Gradualia, 1607).
LR:Ge2.
Emendemus in melius (Cantiones Sacrae, 1575).
LR:Gd19.
Gaudeamus omnes – Motet.
LR:Ge9.
Haec dicit Dominus – Motet.
LR:Gd19.
Haec dies – Graduale.
LR:F88, Ge9, Ge32, Ge35.
EB:G136.
LB:E209.
Hodie beata virgo.
LR:F119.
Hunc arguta (Cantiones Sacrae, 1591).
LR:Ge4.
In resurrectione tua – Motet.
LR:Ge10.
Justorum animae (Gradualia, 1605).
LR:Ge4.

Laetentur caeli (Cantiones Sacrae, 1589).
LR:Ge7, Ge10.
Laudibus in sanctis (Cantiones Sacrae, 1591).
LR:Ge4, Ge10.
Libera me, Domine (Cantiones Sacrae, 1575).
LR:Gd19.
Magnificum Domini (Cantiones Sacrae, 1591).
LR:Ge4.
Mass for 3vv.
LR:Ge1, Ge2, Ge3.
Mass for 4vv.
LR:Ge1, Ge4, Ge5, Ge6.
LB:G319.
Mass for 4vv: Agnus Dei.
LR:Gd39.
Mass for 5vv.
LR:Gd18, Ge1, Ge5, Ge6, Ge7.
Miserere mei (Cantiones Sacrae, 1591).
LR:D20, Ge7, Ge30.
Ne irasceris Domine (Cantiones Sacrae, 1589).
LR:Ge7, Ge9.
Non nobis, Domine – Motet.
LR:Gd45.
Non vos reliquam orphanos (Gradualia, 1607).
LR:Ge4, Ge10.
O magnum mysterium (Cantiones Sacrae, 1575).
LR:F81, Ge2.
O quam gloriosum (Gradualia, 1605).
LR:Ge4.
O sacrum convivium (Gradualia, 1605).
LR:Ge2.
Orietur in diebus (Cantiones Sacrae, 1589).
LR:Ge7.
Sacerdotes Domini (Gradualia, 1605).
LR:Ge2.
Senex puerum portabat (Gradualia, 1605).
LR:F119, Ge2.
Siderum rector (Cantiones Sacrae, 1575).
LR:Ge4.
Victimae paschali.
LR:Ge34.
Vide, Domine – Motet.
LR:Ge9.

CABANILLES, Juan Battista (1644–1712
c. Keyboard – Organ
Batalia Imperial.
EB:D33, E26, E27.
Corrente Italiana.
LR:D13.
EB:E79.
Entrada de 4o tono.
LR:D13.
Gallardas I de 1o tono.
EB:E26, F97.
Interludi per la Messa degli Angeli.
LB:E210.
Passacalles in D maj.
EB:E27.
Passacalles in G maj.
EB:E27.
Passacalles I de 1o tono.
LR:D13.
EB:E26.
Passacalles II.
EB:E57.
Passacalles IV de 4o tono.
LR:D13.
EB:E26.
Paseos II.
EB:E26.
Tiento II de falsas de 1o tono.
EB:E26.
Tiento XII de falsas de 4o tono.
EB:E26.

Tiento XVI lleno de 5o tono.
EB:E26.
Tiento XVII de 5o tono sobre 'Pange lingua.'
EB:E26.
Tiento XXIII por Alamire.
LR:D13.
EB:E57.
Tiento de falsas.
LR:D13.
Tiento de Battalla de 5o tono.
LR:D21.
EB:E26.
Toccata.
EB:F97.
Toccata II de 5o tono sobre 'Ma esquerra.'
EB:E26, E27.
Toccata de mano izquierda.
LR:D13.
Toccata II de mano izquierda.
EB:E57.

CABESTANH – *see* GUILHEM DE CABESTANH.

CABEZON, Antonio de (1510–1566)
c. Keyboard – Harpsichord and organ
Ad Dominum cum tribulare.
LR:D2.
Anchor che col partire (after De Rore).
LR:D8.
Ardenti mei sospiri (after Verdelot).
LR:D6, E51.
Ave Maris stella – Diferencias.
LR:D13, D14.
EB:D28.
Ave maris stella (III/H).
LR:D5.
Ave maris stella (IX/Ve).
LR:D6.
Ave maris stella (X/H).
LR:D5.
Ave maris stella (XI/H).
LR:B24.
Ay joli bois (after Lupus).
LR:D9.
Ayme qui voldra (after Gombert).
LR:D1, D9.
Beata viscera Mariae.
LR:D6.
Benedicta est caelorum Regina. Duo (II/H) (after Josquin).
LR:D3.
Cancion francesca (after Clemens non Papa).
LR:D1.
Dic nobis Maris – Faebordon glosada.
LR:D1, D13, E27.
EB:D28, E70, E86.
Diferencias sobre el 'Canto del Cavallero.'
LR:B24.
EB:D28, D33, E27, E66.
Diferencias sobre 'La dama le demanda.'
LR:A3, B24, C22, D9.
EB:D36, E84.
SI:A2.
Diferencias sobre la Galliarda Milanesa.
LR:B24, D3, D9, E26.
EB:D33, E66.
Diferencias sobre 'Guardame las vacas.' (I/H, II/H).
LR:D5, D8.
SI:C6.
Discante sobre la Pavana Italiana (I/H).
LR:B24, D3, D9.
D'ou vient cela.
LR:B24.
Duo (I/H, II/H).

LR:D6, D7, E27.
Durmendo un giorno (after Verdelot).
LR:D4.
E qui la dira.
LR:A1.
Fabordon de 1o tono.
LR:D9.
EB:D28.
Fabordon I de 1o tono.
LR:D4.
Fabordon II de 1o tono.
LR:D3.
Fabordon III de 1o tono.
LR:D4.
Fabordon IV de 1o tono.
LR:D4.
Fabordon I de 2o tono.
LR:D1.
Fabordon II de 2o tono.
LR:D6.
Fabordon III de 2o tono.
LR:D3.
Fabordon IV de 2o tono.
LR:D6.
Fabordon II de 4o tono.
LR:D6.
Fabordon IV de 4o tono.
LR:D6.
Fabordon IV de 5o tono.
LR:D6.
Fabordon II de 6o tono.
LR:D4.
Fabordon IV de 6o tono.
LR:D2.
Fabordon I de 7o tono.
LR:D7.
Fabordon II de 7o tono.
LR:D1.
Fabordon I de 8o tono.
LR:D2.
Fabordon II de 8o tono.
LR:D5.
Fabordon III de 8o tono.
LR:D7.
Fabordon IV de 8o tono.
LR:D5.
La Gamba – Pavan.
LR:E42.
Glosado sobre el Benedictus.
EB:D28.
Final (I/Ve).
LR:D4.
EB:D28.
Himno a tres (MUC/106).
LR:D1.
EB:D28.
Hosanna de la Missa 'L'Homme arme' (after Josquin).
LR:D3.
In te Domine speravi (after Lupus).
LR:D1.
Inviolata (I/H) (after Josquin).
LR:D2, D8.
Je ville quant (after Willaert).
LR:D2.
Je pres en grey (after Crecquillon).
LR:D2.
Je suis ayme (after Crecquillon).
LR:D3.
Jerusalem luge (after Richafort).
LR:D6.
Kyrie – 4 Versos.
LR:D13.
Kyrie III de 1o tono.
LR:D6.
Kyrie I de 2o tono.

LR:D1.
Kyrie VII de 2o tono.
LR:D3.
Kyrie II de 3o tono.
LR:D1.
Kyrie IV de 3o tono.
LR:D1.
Kyries I–IV de 4o tono.
LR:D8.
Kyrie I de 5o tono.
LR:D4.
Kyrie III de 5o tono.
LR:D4.
Kyrie IV de 5o tono.
LR:D7.
Kyrie I de 7o tono.
LR:D2.
Kyrie II de 7o tono.
LR:D2.
Kyrie III de 7o tono.
LR:D4.
Kyrie IV de 7o tono.
LR:D5.
Kyrie V sobre 'Rex virginum.'
LR:D6.
Kyrie VI sobre 'Rex virginum.'
LR:D6.
Magnificat de 1o tono.
LR:D13.
O lux beata trinitas – Himno (XIII/Ve).
LR:D7, D13.
Obra a cuatro de 8o tono (MUC/110).
LR:D7.
Obra a cuatro sobre 'Cantus firmus.' (MUC/110).
LR:D4.
Obra a tres (MUC/107).
LR:D4.
Pange lingua (I/Ve).
LR:D6.
Pange lingua (II/Ve).
LR:D6.
Pange lingua – Himno (III/Ve).
LR:D2.
Pange lingua (V/Ve).
LR:D4.
Pange lingua – Himno (VI/H).
LR:D7.
Pange lingua – Himno (VII/H).
LR:D5.
Pange lingua – Himno (XVII/H).
LR:D7.
Pange lingua – Himno (XVIII/H) (after Urreda).
LR:D5.
Para quien crie yo cabellos – Romance (I/Ve).
LR:D4.
EB:D28.
Para quien crie yo cabellos – Romance (II/Ve).
LR:B24, D3.
Pavana con su glosa.
LR:D4, D20.
EB:D28, D33, E27, E87.
Pavana Italiana.
LR:C22, E2.
Pavaniglia – Fantasia a 4.
SI:C6, C13.
Pis ne me peult venir (after Crecquillon).
LR:D5.
Pour un plaisir (after Crecquillon).
LR:D8.
Pues no me quereis hablar – Romance.
LR:D4.
Quaeramus (I/H) (after Mouton).
LR:D5.
Quaeramus (II/H) (after Mouton).

LR:D6.
Quem terra pontus – Himno (XVI/Ve).
LR:D2.
Sacris solemnis (I/Ve).
LR:D4.
Sacris solemnis (XVII/Ve).
LR:D6.
Saecularum Amen – Versos.
LR:D13.
Saname Domine (after Clemens non Papa).
LR:D6.
Sancta Maria (after Medinaceli).
LR:D7.
Sancta Maria (after Verdelot).
LR:D2.
Stabat mater (after Josquin) (I/H).
LR:D4, D8.
Susana (after Lassus).
LR:D3, D9.
Tiento de 1o tono (III/H).
LR:D8, D13.
Tiento de 1o tono (V/Ve).
LR:D5.
Tiento de 1o tono (IX/Ve).
LR:D5.
Tiento de 1o tono (X/H).
LR:D2.
Tiento de 1o tono (X/Ve).
LR:D8.
Tiento de 1o tono (XI/Ve).
LR:D3.
Tiento de 1o tono (Unsp.)
LR:D9.
EB:D28, E86.
Tiento de 2o tono.
LR:D13.
Tiento de 3o tono (III/Ve).
LR:D4.
Tiento de 3o tono – 'Fugas al contrario' (VI/H).
LR:D1.
Tiento de 4o tono. (Unsp.)
LR:D9, E51.
EB:E86.
Tiento de 4o tono sobre 'Malheur me bat' (XII/Ve).
LR:D1, D13.
Tiento de 4o tono (XIII/Ve).
LR:D8.
Tiento de 5o tono.
LR:E51.
Tiento de 5o tono (III/Ve).
LR:D5.
Tiento de 5o tono (IX/H).
LR:D7.
Tiento de 6o tono (XI/H).
LR:D3.
Tiento de 7o tono 'Cum sancto spirito' (XII/H).
LR:D7.
Tiento de 8o tono (IV/Ve).
LR:D8.
Tres (I/Ve).
LR:D1.
Ultimi mei sospiri (after Verdelot).
LR:D5, D9.
Un gay berger (after Crecquillon).
LR:D2.
Un joli bois sur la verdure.
LR:D4.
Ut queant laxis – Himno (XIV/H).
LR:D6.
Veni redemptor (MUC/32).
LR:D7.
Versillos a cuatro (MUC/111).
LR:D7.
Verso a cuatro (MUC/160).

LR:D1.
Versos (Unsp.)
LR:E27.
Versos de 1o tono.
LR:D1, D2, D3.
Versos de 2o tono.
LR:D1, D5, D7, D8.
Versos de 3o tono.
LR:D1, D4, D7.
Versos de 4o tono.
LR:D1, D4, D5, D6, D7, D8, D28.
Versos de 5o tono.
LR:D1, D2, D3, D4, D7.
Versos de 6o tono.
LR:D7, D8, D1, D5.
Versos de 7o tono.
LR:D3, D5, D7, D8, D9.
Versos de 7o tono – Magnificat.
LR:D9.
Versos de 8o tono.
LR:D1, D2, D7, D8.

CABEZON, Hernandez de (1541–1602)
  c. Keyboard – Organ and Harpsichord
  Dulce memoria.
  LR:D13.
  Fantasia a 3 sobre 'Ave maris stella.'
  SI:C10, C13.

CACCINI, Francesca (b.1581)
  d. Secular Vocal
  O che nuovo stupor.
  LB:B227.

CACCINI, Giulio (1545–1618)
  d. Secular Vocal
  Amarilli mia bella (Dowland's Musical Banquet).
  LR:Gd30, Gd31.
  EB:F93, F95, F96, F98, F106.
  Amor, ch'attendi.
  EB:F99.
  Aura amorosa.
  EB:F99
  Belle rose porporine.
  LR:E55, Gd41.
  EB:F98.
  Dovro dunque morire? (Dowland's Musical Banquet).
  LR:Gd30, Gd31.
  Io che dal ciel cader.
  LR:E41.
  Nell amoroso ciel del vostro volto.
  EB:F100
  O che giorno.
  EB:F99.
  Perfidissime volte.
  EB:F98.
  Pien d'amoroso affetto.
  EB:F106.
  Queste lagrim' amare.
  LR:Gd41.
  Udite amanti.
  EB:F98.

CADEAC, Pierre (16th. cent.)
  d. Secular Vocal
  Je suis desheritee.
  LR:E38.

CADENAL, Piere (or CARDENAL) (fl. after 1204).
  d. Secular Vocal
  Ben volgra (See also NOVELLA).
  AA:D11.
  Razos es qui'ieu m'esbaude.
  AA:D11.
  Tartarassa ni voutor.
  AA:D11.

  Un sirventes.
  AA:D4.

CADENET (1200–1230)
  d. Secular Vocal
  S'au fui belha ni prezada.
  AA:D1.

CAIMO, Giuseppe (1540–1584
  d. Secular Vocal
  Mentre, il cuculo.
  LR:Gd25.

CAIX D'HERVELOIS, Louis de (1680–1760)
  b. Chamber and Instrumental
  Pieces de Violes, Book 1: Excpts.
  LB:B114.
  Pieces de Violes, Book 3: Suite No. 1.
  LB:B114.
  Suite in A maj for viol and continuo.
  LB:B306.
  Suite No. 2 in D maj for viol and continuo.
  SI:C5, C16.
  Suite No. 4 for viol and continuo.
  SI:C8.

CALABRIA, Duke of – See CANCIONERO DE UPSALA

CALDARA, Antonio (1671–1736)
  d. Secular Vocal
  Come raggio di sol.
  EB:F95, F101.
  Mirti, faggi, tronchi.
  EB:F102.
  Sebben crudele mi far languir.
  EB:F95.
  Selve amiche.
  EB:F95, F101.
  Atalo, ossia la verita nell'Inganno - Opera, 1717: Quando
    empieta.
  LB:F79.
  e. Sacred Vocal
  Crucifixus.
  LB:G187.

CALESTANI, Vincenzo (16th./17th. cent.)
  d. Secular Vocal
  Damigella tutta bella.
  EB:F98.

CALIXTINE CODEX (12th.–14th. cent. Spanish)
  e. Sacred Vocal
  Ad honorem regis.
  PS:B22.
  Benedicamus Domino.
  AA:B3, B4.
  Cunctipotens genitor.
  AA:B3, B4, B9.
  Dum pater familias.
  PS:B22.
  AA:E7.
  Rex immense.
  AA:B3, B4.
  (See also items in PLAINSONG INDEX.)

CALVI, Carlo (17th. cent.)
  b. Instrumental
  La Bertazzina.
  EB:B41.

CALVIERE, Guillaume Antoine (c.1695–1755)
  c. Keyboard – Organ
  Piece in D min.
  LB:E230

CALVISIUS, Sethus (1556–1615)
  e. Sacred Vocal
  Freut euch und Jubiliert.

LR:F115.
Unser Leben währet siebzig Jahr.
LB:G325.

CAMPIAN, Thomas (1567–1620)
b. Instrumental
Move now with measured step.
LR:Gd2.
What if a day.
LR:Gd2.
While dancing rests.
LR:Gd2.
d Secular Vocal
All looks be pale.
LR:Gd2.
Author of light.
LR:Gd3, Gd48.
Beauty is but a painted hell.
LR:Gd28.
Beauty since you so much desire.
LR:Gd24.
Come ashore, merry mates.
LR:Gd2.
Come let us sound.
LR:Gd27, Gd28.
The Cypress curtain of the night.
LR:Gd2, Gd18, Gd26, Gd28, Gd48.
Fain would I wed.
LR:Gd2, Gd22.
Fair if you expect admiring.
LR:Gd2, Gd48.
Fire, fire.
LR:Gd2.
Harden now thy tired heart.
LR:Gd2.
I care not for these ladies.
LR:Gd2, Gd18, Gd26, Gd46.
If any hath the heart to kill.
LR:Gd24.
If thou long'st so much to learn.
LR:Gd22.
It fell upon a summer's day.
LR:Gd2, Gd21, Gd48.
Jack and Joan they think no ill.
LR:Gd2, Gd33, Gd49.
Never love unless you can.
LR:Gd2, Gd22.
Never weather-beaten sail.
LR:Gd2, Gd3.
EB:B47.
Now hath Flora robed her bowers.
LR:Gd2.
Oft have I sighed.
LR:Gd22, Gd38.
Shall I come, sweet love?
EB:F103.
So sweet is thy discourse to me.
LR:Gd2.
Sweet, exclude me not.
LR:Gd2.
There is a garden in her face.
LR:Gd38, Gd48.
To music bent.
LR:Gd3.
Turn back, you wanton flyer.
LR:Gd37.
When to her lute.
LR:Gd27.
e Sacred Vocal
Most sweet and pleasing are thy ways, O God.
LR:Gd3.

CAMPION, Francois (1686–1748)
b. Instrumental – Guitar
Suite in D maj.

LB:C26.
Suite in D min.
LB:C27.

CAMPRA, Andre (1660–1744)
d. Secular Vocal – Stage Works
L'Europe Galante – Opera Ballet, 1697.
LB:F22.
L'Europe Galante – Orchestral Suite.
LB:A223.
Les Fetes Venitienes – Opera Ballet, 1710:
Excerpts:
Bourrees I and II.
SI:C19.
Contredanse.
SI:C19.
Entree.
SI:C17.
Pastre et Pastourelle.
SI:C17.
Tancrede: Orchestral Suite.
LB:A580, A634.
e. Sacred Vocal
De profundis – Psalm CXXIX.
LB:G192.
Ecce panis angelorum.
LB:G192.
Laudate Dominum.
LB:G192.

CANCIONERO DE LA COLOMBINA (late 15th. cent. Spanish)
d. Secular Vocal
Como no lo and are yo?
ER:A26.
Filles a marier.
ER:A4.
Nina y vina.
ER:A26.
Propinan de melyor.
ER:A26.

CANCIONERO HORTENSA (early 16th. cent. Spanish)
d. Secular Vocal
Venid a sospirar.
ER:A4.

CANCIONERO MEDINACELLI (16th. cent. Spanish)
d. Secular Vocal
A biente y siete de marco.
SI:A2.
Corten espadas afiladas.
SI:A2.
El fresco ayre.
ER:A4.

CANCIONERO DEL PALACIO (1490–1530, Spanish)
d. Secular Vocal
A los banos del amor.
ER:A26.
Al alva venid.
ER:A26.
LR:E25.
Dale si le das.
ER:A4.
LR:A2, E27, E28.
Dindirindin.
LR:E31, E62, E64, E65.
Fantasia.
ER:A26.
Pase el agoa.
LR:E64, A3, E31.
Perdi la mia rrueca.
ER:A26.
Rodrigo Martinez.
ER:A4.

LR:A3, E27.
Romanesca.
ER:A26.
Si aveis dicho, marido.
ER:A26.
Tres morillas m'enamoran.
LR:E30, E31.

CANCIONERO DE SABLONARA (16th./17th. cent. Spanish)
    d. Secular Vocal
Du visita celoso ~ Seguidillas en eco.
LR:E30.

CANCIONERO DE UPSALA (1500–1550, Spanish – Duke of Calabria.)
    d. Secular Vocal
Alca la nina los ojos.
LR:E23.
Alta estava la pena.
LR:E23.
Ay, luna que reluzes!
LR:E23.
Con que la lavare.
ER:A26.
LR:E23.
E la don don, verges Maria.
ER:A24.
LR:F120.
Dadme albricias.
LR:E23, E27, F120
Estas noches a tan largas.
LR:E23.
Llaman a Teresica.
LR:E23.
No la devomos dormir.
LR:E23.
Ojos garcos la la nina.
LR:E23.
Riu, riu, chiu.
LR:E27, F120, F127.
Serrana, donde dormistes?
LR:E23.
Si la noce haze escura.
ER:A26.
LR:E23.
Si no's huviera mirado.
LR:E23.
Si te vas a banar Juanilla.
LR:E23.
Soleta so jo aci.
AN:B15.
ER:A26.
Soy serranica.
ER:A26.
LR:E23.
Vi los barcos, madre.
LR:E23.
Y dezid serranicas, he.
LR:E23.
Yo me soy la morenica.
ER:A26.
LR:E23.

CANTIGAS DE AMIGO – See CODAX, Martim.

CANTIGAS DE SANTA MARIA (13th. cent. Spanish – Attr. to Alfonso el Sabio, 1230–1284)
    d/e. Secular Vocal/Sacred Vocal
Prologue. Porque trobar.
AA:A2, D9, E1, E4, E5.
1. Des oge.
AA:E4.
2. Muito devomos varoes.
AA:E1.
2. Pois que dos reys.
AA:E4.

5. Instrumental Version.
AA:E1.
7. Santa Maria amar.
AA:E3, E5.
11. Nembressete Madre de Deus.
AA:D9, E4.
LR:A8.
13. Assi como Jesu Christe.
AA:E2.
20. Virga da Jesse.
AA:E4.
25. Pagar ben.
AA:E2, E4.
26. Non egran causa.
AA:E6.
29. Mas mentes.
AA:E4.
30. Muito valuera mais.
AA:E1.
36. Muit' amar devemos.
AA:E3, E5.
37: Instrumental Version.
AA:E1.
40. Deus te salve.
AA:E4.
47. Virgen Santa Maria, guarda nos.
AA:E1.
49. Ben com.
AA:E7.
58. De muitas guisas.
AA:E4.
59. Instrumental Version.
AA:E1.
73. Instrumental Version.
AA:E2.
77. Instrumental Version.
LB:B273.
79. Ay, Santa Maria.
AA:E3, E4.
97. A virgen sempr' acorrer.
AA:E5.
100. Santa Maria, strela do dia.
AA:E2, E3, E4.
103. Quen a Virgen.
AA:E6.
111. En todo tempo faz ben.
AA:E5.
118. Fazer pode d'outri vivelos seus fillos.
AA:D9, E4, E5.
139. Maravillosos et piadosos.
AA:D9.
159. Non sofre Santa Maria.
AA:E3, E4.
160. Quen boa dona querra.
AA:E5.
166. Como poden per sas culpas.
AA:E2, E4.
176. Instrumental Version.
LB:B273.
179. Ben sab.
AA:E4.
184. A madre.
AA:E7.
190. Instrumental Version.
AA:E3.
205. Oracon com piadade.
AA:E5.
207: Se ome fezer.
AA:E3.
216. En Santa Maria.
AA:E4.
222. Quen ouver.
AA:E4.
226. Asi pod'a Virgen.
AA:A2, D9.

230. Instrumental Version.
AA:E3.
244. Grande reif'e que mal venna.
AA:D9.
253. De grad.
AA:E7.
261. Quen Jesu Christe.
AA:E5.
264. Pois aos seus que ama.
AA:E1.
279. Santa Maria, valed.
AA:E4.
290. Instrumental Version.
AA:E3.
302. A madre de Jhesucristo.
AA:E4.
303. Instrumental Version.
AA:E2.
320. Santa Maria leva.
AA:D9, E3, E4.
322. Instrumental Version.
AA:E1.
330. Qual e a santiuigada.
AA:E5.
340. Virgen, madre groriosa.
AA:E2, E5.
353. Quen a omagen.
AA:E3, E4.
LR:B19.
364. Quen por servico.
AA:E5.
370. Loemos mui' a Virgen.
AA:E2.
380. Sen Calar.
AA:E4.
383. Offondo do mar tan chao faz.
AA:D9.
384. Por muy gran fremosura.
AA:E4.
401. Peticon.
AA:E4.
A madre do qui liurou.
AA:A3.
Aque serven todo' los celestiaes.
AA:A3.
Aquel que de voontade.
AA:A1.
Mais nos faz Sancta Maria.
AA:A3.
Rosa das Rosas.
LR:BA19, E34, E62.
LB:B259.

CAPIROLA, Giovanni Paolo (1474–1547)
 b. Instrumental – Lute
 De tous bien plaine.
 LR:Gf5.
 Ricercar I.
 LR:C23.
 Ricercar II.
 LR:C23.
 Ricercar X.
 LR:C23.
 Ricercar XIII.
 LR:C23.
 La Spagna.
 ER:A13.

CAPRICORNUS, Samuel (17th. cent.)
 e. Sacred Vocal
 Dixit Dominus.
 LR:F116.
 Magnificat.
 LR:F116.
 Te Deum.

EB:G140.

CAPUA, Marcello di (= BERNARDINI) (18th. cent.)
 d. Secular Vocal
 Serenade for Chorus and orchestra.
 EB:G141.

CARA, Marchetto (1495–1530)
 b. Instrumental
 Per fuggir d'amor le punte.
 LB:B265.
 d. Secular Vocal
 Io non compro.
 LR:E56.
 Non e tempo.
 LR:A3, E55.
 O che aiuto, o che conforto.
 LR:E53.
 Quei che sempre han da pendare.
 LR:E53.

CARCASIO, Giuseppe (18th. cent.)
 b. Instrumental
 Sonata for organ with trumpet and oboe.
 LB:A662.

CARCERES (16th. cent.)
 d. Secular Vocal
 E la don don (Cancionero de Upsala)
 LR:E23.

CARISSIMI, Giacomo (1605–1674)
 d. Secular Vocal
 Amor mio, che cosa e questo?
 EB:F3, F4.
 Apritevi, Inferni.
 EB:F3.
 Beltempo per me se n'ando.
 EB:F3.
 Deh, memoria.
 EB:F3, F4.
 In un mar di pensieri.
 EB:F3, F4.
 Lamento della Maria Stuarda.
 EB:F4.
 No, no, mio core.
 EB:F3, F101.
 No, non si speri.
 EB:F102.
 Suonera l'ultima tromba.
 EB:F3, F4.
 V'intendo, v'intendo, occhi.
 EB:F3.
 Vittoria, mio cuore.
 EB:F101.
 e. Sacred Vocal
 Dives Malus – Oratorio.
 EB:G11.
 Historia de Jonas – Oratorio.
 EB:G14.
 Hodie Simon Petrus.
 LB:G327.
 Jephte – Oratorio.
 EB:G12, G13.
 Judicium Salomonis – Oratorio.
 EB:G12, G13.

CARLETON, Nicholas (16th. cent.)
 c. Keyboard
 Praeludium.
 LR:D14.

CARLETON, Richard (1558–1638)
 d. Secular Vocal.
 Calm was the air (Triumphs of Oriana)
 LR:Gd34.

CARMINA BURANA (13th. cent. German)
  d/e. Secular Vocal/Sacred Vocal
  3. Ecce torpet (WALTHER VON CHATILLON)
  AA:E9, E12.
  5. Flete flenda.
  AA:E12.
  8. Licet eger cum egrotis (WALTHER VON CHATILLON)
  AA:E9, E10, E12, E14, E17.
  11. Ave nobis venerabilis Maria.
  AA:E12.
  11. In terra summus Rex.
  AA:E12, E16.
  12. Procurans odium.
  AA:A2, E8, E10, E11, E12.
  14. O variom fortune.
  AA:E9.
  15. Ave Maria gratia plena.
  AA:E15.
  15. Celum non animum.
  AA:E9, E10.
  15. Deus in nomine tuo.
  AA:E15.
  16. Michi confer venditor.
  AA:E14, E17.
  16. Planctus Mater Domine: Flete fidelis anime – Planctus ante nascia.
  AA:E15.
  18. Ave domina mundi.
  AA:E15.
  18. Regali ex progenie.
  AA:E15.
  18. Sanctissima et gloriosa.
  AA:E15.
  19. Fas et nefas.
  AA:E8, E10, E12, E16.
  22. Homo qui vigeas.
  AA:E9, E10, E12.
  24. Iste mundus duribundus.
  AA:A2, E11.
  26. Si vocatus ad nupcias.
  AA:E14.
  30. Dum iuventus floruit.
  AA:E8, E9.
  31. Vite perdite (PETER VON BLOIS)
  AA:A2, E8, E9, E11, E16.
  34. Conductus.
  AA:E15.
  34. Deduc Sion, uberrimus.
  AA:E12.
  37. In Gedeonis area.
  AA:E8, E12, E16, E17.
  47. Crucifigat omnes.
  AA:E9, E10, E12.
  52. Nomen a solemnibus.
  AA:E8, E10, E11, E14, E17.
  63. Olim sudor Hercules.
  AA:E10, E13.
  71. Axe Phebus aureo.
  AA:A2, E9, E10, E11, E16.
  73. Clauso Chronos.
  AA:E12, E16.
  79. Estivali sub ferrore.
  AA:E8.
  85. Veris dulcis in tempore.
  AA:E8.
  88a. Jove cum Mercurio.
  AA:E8.
  90. Conspexit.
  AA:E8, E17.
  90. Exit diloculo.
  AA:E8, E10, E12, E17.
  107. Chramer gib diu varwe mir.
  AA:E8, E17.
  108. Vacillantis trutine.

AA:E11, E14.
116. Sic mea fata canendo solo.
AA:A2, E8, E11.
119. Dulce solum natalis patrie.
AA:A2, E8, E11, E16.
131. Dic Christi veritas.
AA:E8, E10, E14.
131a. Bulla fulminante.
AA:E10, E14.
143. Ecce gratum.
AA:E9, E17.
146. Tellus flore.
AA:E9.
147a. Sage, daz ihr dirs.
AA:E8.
151. Virent prata hemiata.
AA:E11, E13, E16.
153. Fulget dies celebris.
AA:E8, E12.
153. Tempus transit gelidum.
AA:E8, E12, E17.
159. Veris dulcis in tempore.
AA:E14.
161. Diu werllt frort sih uber al.
AA:E8.
168a. Nu gruonet aver diu heide (NEIDHARDT VON REUENTHAL)
AA:E9, E17.
179. Tempus est jocundum.
AA:E9, E17.
185. Ich was ein chint so wolgetan.
AA:A2, E11, E16.
196. In taberna quando sumus.
AA:E11, E16.
200. Bacche qui venies.
AA:E11, E12, E16.
211. Alte clamat epicurus.
AA:E11, E17.
211a. Nu lebe ich.
AA:E11.
215–215a. Officium lusorum 'Gambler's Mass.'
AA:E13.
Planctus Maria Virginae (GOTTFRIED VON BRETEUILL)
AA:E8.
Initium Sancti Evangelium secundum marcas argenti.
AA:E17.

CAROSO, Fabricio (c.1526–c.1600)
  b. Instrumental
  Ballo del fiore.
  SI:C18.
  Barriera – Balletto.
  LR:B21.
  Bassa Ducale.
  SI:C16.
  Bassa Savella.
  LR:C11.
  Celeste giglio – Balletto.
  LR:B21.
  Forza d'amore.
  LR:C9.
  Pavaniglia.
  SI:C18.
  Saltarello.
  SI:C18.

CAROUBEL, Francisque (d.c.1618)
  b. Instrumental
  Branles 1–5.
  EB:B40.
  Branle simple 1–2.
  EB:B40.
  Branle de Montirand 1–2.
  EB:B40.
  Branle de Poictou.

EB:B40.
Courante.
LR:B21.
Galliards.
EB:B40.
2 Gavottes.
AA:D20.
LR:B14.
Partita a 5.
EB:B55.
Passamezze.
EB:B40.
Pavana de Spaigne.
LR:B21.
Suite of Dances (Unsp.)
LR:B25.
Volte.
LR:B21.

CARR, Richard (17th. cent.)
  b. Instrumental
Divisions upon an Italian Ground.
LB:B229, B249, B278, B279.

CARREIRA, Antonio (c.1520–1587)
  c. Keyboard
Fantasia de 8o tono.
EB:E58.
Tiento sobre 'Con que lavare.'
LB:D220.
Tiento de 2o tono.
EB:E58.

CARVALHO, Joao de Sousa (1745–1798)
  c. Keyboard
Allegro.
LB:D215.
Toccata in G min.
LB:D215.

CASANOVES, Narcis (1747–1799)
  c. Keyboard
Paso V.
LR:D13.
Paso VI.
EB:E86.
Paso VII.
LR:D13.
Paso X.
LR:D13.
Sonata V.
EB:E82.
  e. Sacred Vocal
Amicus meus – Responsory.
LB:G194.
Caligaverunt oculi mei – Responsory.
LB:G194.
Tenebrae factae sunt – Responsory.
LB:G194.
Lamentations of Jeremiah.
LB:G193.

CASCIA – see GIOVANNI DA CASCIA = GIOVANNI DA FIRENZE

CASCIOLINI, Claudio (18th. cent.)
  e. Sacred Vocal
Panis angelicus.
LR:F81.

CASERTA – see ANTHONELLO DA CASERTA

CASTELLO, Dario (16th./17th. cent.)
  b. Instrumental
Sonata I per soprano solo.
EB:B56, B57, B58.
LB:B273, B280.

Sonata II.
LR:Gd41.
Sonata IV for 2 violins and continuo (Sonate Concertate, 1629)
EB:B43.

CASTILLEJA (16th. cent.)
  d. Secular Vocal
Cucu.
LR:E28.

CASTRO, Juan de (c.1540–1600)
  d. Secular Vocal
Bonjour mon coeur.
LR:E52.
Desde las torres del alma.
SI:A2.
En haut et en bas.
LR:E55.
Enfans a laborder.
LR:E42.
  e. Sacred Vocal
Angelus ad pastores ait.
LR:F89.

CATO, Diomedes (c.1570–c.1615)
  b. Instrumental – Lute
Chorea Polonica.
EB:F104.
Fantasia (Unsp.)
LR:C17, E57.
EB:E85, G141.
Favorito.
LR:C17, C18.
2 Galliards.
LR:C18.
Praeludium.
LR:C18.
Motet and Fugue.
EB:E85.
Villanella.
LR:C17.

CAURROY, Eustache du (1549–1609)
  b. Instrumental
Fantasia.
LR:A1.
Prince la France te veut.
LR:A1.
Une jeune fillette.
LR:D16.
  e. Sacred Vocal
Te Deum.
EB:G16.

CAUSTUN, Thomas (d.1569)
  e. Sacred Vocal
Magnificat and Nunc dimittis.
LR:Ge31.

CAVALIERI, Emilio de (1550–1602)
  d. Secular Vocal
Godi turba mortal.
LR:E41, E56.
O che nuovo miracolo.
LR:E41, E42, E56.
  e. Sacred Vocal
Rappresentatione di Anima e di Corpo – Oratorio.
LR:F2, F3.

CAVALLI, Francesco (1602–1676)
  b. Instrumental
Sonata a 3 for 2 violins and continuo (Musiche Sacre Concernenti, 1656).
EB:E43.
  d. Secular Vocal
L'alma fiacca svani – Lamenti di Cassandra.

EB:F101.
Son ancor pargoletta.
EB:F101.
Sospiri di foco.
EB:F96.
La Calisto - Opera, 1651.
EB:F5.
L'Ormindo - Opera, 1644.
EB:F6.
e. Sacred Vocal
Cantate Domino.
EB:F96.
Laetatus sum.
EB:G142.
Magnificat.
EB:G142.
Missa 'Concertata.'
EB:G15.
Missa pro defunctis, Requiem.
EB:G14.

CAVAZZONI, Girolamo (c.1525-1560)
c. Keyboard - Organ
Ave maris stella.
LR:D15, F90.
Canzon sopra 'Fault d'argent.'
EB:E59.
Christe redemptor omnium.
LR:D15, F90.
Iste confessor.
EB:E59.
Jesu corona virginum.
EB:E59.
Missa Apostolorum: Kyrie - Christe - Kyrie.
EB:E59.
Missa Domenicalis: Kyrie - Christe.
LR:D15.
Ricercare I.
EB:B59.
Ricercare II.
EB:B59.

CAVAZZONI, Marc Antonio (16th. cent.)
c. Keyboard - Organ
Recercada del 2o tono.
EB:E59.

CAVENDISH, Michael (c.1565-1628)
d. Secular Vocal
Come gentle swains.
LR:Gd32, Gd34.
Down in a valley.
LR:Gd33.
Sly thief.
LR:Gd50.
Wand'ring in this place.
LR:A1.

CAZZATI, Maurizio (c.1620-1677)
b. Instrumental
Sonata a 4 for trumpet, strings and continuo, 'La
   Bianchina.'
EB:B60.

CEBALLOS, Rodrigo (c.1530-1581)
e. Sacred Vocal
Hortus conclusus.
LR:F89.

CECERE, Carlo (fl.1750)
a. Orchestral
Concerto No. 1 in A maj for mandolin and strings.
LB:A224.
Concerto No. 2 in A maj for mandolin and strings.
LB:A224.

CEREROLS, Juan (1618-1676)
d. Secular Vocal
Pues Para en la Sepultura - Tono a 4.
EB:G18.
Vivo yo - Villancico a 4.
EB:G18.
e. Secular Vocal
Missa 'de Batalla.'
EB:G17.
Missa 'de Gloria.'
EB:G17.
Missa pro defunctis, Requiem.
EB:G18.

CERNOHORSKY, Bohuslav (1684-1742)
c. Keyboard - Organ
Fuga (Unsp.)
LB:B313.
Fugue in A min.
LB:E149, E236, E237.
Fugue in C maj.
LB:E236.
Fugue in C min.
LB:E149.
Fugue in D maj.
LB:E149.
Fugue in D min.
LB:E149.
Fugue in F sharp min.
LB:E149.
Fugue in F maj.
LB:E236.
Fugue in G sharp min/D maj.
LB:E236.
Toccata in C maj.
EB:E84.
LB:E149, E237.
e. Sacred Vocal
Laudetur Jesus Christus.
LB:E149.
Quare Domine irasceris.
LB:E149.
Quem lapidaverunt.
LB:E149.
Regina caeli.
LB:E149.

CERTON, Pierre (1510-1572)
d. Secular Vocal
Amour a tort.
LR:F4.
Ce n'est a vous.
LR:F4.
C'est grand pitye.
LR:F4.
De tout le mal.
LR:F4.
En esperant.
LR:F4.
Entre vous gentilz hommes.
LR:F4.
Frere Thibaut.
LR:E58.
Hellas ne fringuerons nous.
LR:F4.
Je l'ay ayme.
LR:F4.
Je ne fus jamais si aise.
LR:E38.
Je ne veulx poinct.
LR:F4.
J'espere et crains.
LR:E52.
La, la, la, je ne l'ose dire.
LR:E32.

Martin s'en alla au Lendit.
LR:F4.
Plus ne suys ce que j'ay este.
LR:F4.
Que n'est elle aupres de moy.
LR:F4.
Si ta beaulte.
LR:F4.
Ung jour que madame dormoit.
LR:E58, F4.
Ung jour ung galland.
LR:E58.
e.Sacred Vocal
Beati quorum - Psalm XXXII.
LR:F91.
Missa 'Sus le pont d'Avignon.'
LR:F4.
Nunc dimittis - Canticle Simeonis.
LR:F91.
Super flumina Babylonis - Psalm CXXXVII.
LR:F91.
Verba mea - Psalm V.
LR:F91.

CESARE, Giovanni Martino (1590-1626)
b.Instrumental
Sonata 'La Augustana' (Musicali Melodie, 1621).
EB:B44.
Sonata 'La Fenice.' (Musicali Melodie, 1621).
EB:B44.
Sonata 'La Foccarina.' (Musicali Melodie, 1621).
EB:B61.
Sonata 'La Gioia.' (Musicali Melodie, 1621).
EB:B44.
Sonata 'La Giorgina.' (Musicali Melodie, 1621).
EB:B61.
Sonata 'La Hieronyma.' (Musicali Melodie, 1621).
EB:B44, B53.
Sonata 'La Massimiliana.' (Musicali Melodie, 1621).
EB:B44.

CESARIS, Johannes (15th. cent.)
b.Instrumental
Bonte biaute.
ER:A11.

CESTI, Marc Antonio (1618-1669)
d.Secular Vocal
Amanti io vi disfido.
EB:F7.
Intorno all' idol mio.
EB:F95.
Lachrime mie.
EB:F7.
Mia tiranna.
EB:F7.
Pria ch'adoro.
EB:F7.

CHABRAN, Carlo Francesco (= CHIABRANO) (1723-c.1751)
b.Chamber and Instrumental
Sonata in G maj for violin and continuo, Op. 1, No. 5.
LB:B314.

CHAMBONNIERES, Jacques Champion de (1602-1672)
c.Keyboard - Harpsichord
Canaris - Gigue.
LB:B324.
Chaconne in F maj.
LB:D232.
Double de Moutier.
SI:C8.
Jeunes Zephirs - Sarabande.
LR:D21.
Rondeau.
LB:D232.

Suite No. 1 in A min.
EB:D3.
Suite No. 2 in C maj.
EB:D3.
Suite No. 3 in D min.
EB:D3.
Suite No. 4 in F maj.
EB:D3.
Suite No. 5 in G min.
EB:D3.

CHAMPAGNE - *see* **THIBAUT DE CHAMPAGNE = THIBAUT DE NAVARRE**

CHANCELLOR OF PARIS - *see* **PHILIPPE LE CHANCELLER**

CHANTILLY CODEX (1380-1390, Ars Nova Motets, etc.)
d.Secular Vocal
Degentis vita - Cum vix artidici.
AA:B1.
Inter densas deserti meditans - Imbrius irriguis.
AA:B1.
Ma tredol rossignol.
ER:A4.

CHARDAVOINE, Jehan (1537-1580)
d.Secular Vocal
Mignonne, allons voir si la rose.
LR:E52, E59.

CHARPENTIER, Marc Antoine (c.1636-1704)
a.Orchestral
La Malade Imaginaire: Overture.
LB:A603.
Medee: Suite.
LB:A225, A603.
Nuit (from Nativitatem Domini).
EB:G21.
b.Instrumental
Sonata a 6.
EB:G25.
e.Sacred Vocal
Beatus vir.
EB:G27.
GLoria in excelsis Deo.
LR:Ge34.
Lamentations of Jeremiah.
EB:G19, G20.
Magnificat.
EB:G22, G23.
Mass in G min.
EB:G24.
Messe de minuit.
EB:G25, G136.
Messe pour les trespasses.
EB:G26.
Miserere des Jesuits.
EB:G26.
3 Noëls.
EB:G23.
O amor, o bonitas, o charitas.
EB:G24.
Pange lingua.
LR:Ge34.
Responsories for Tenebrae.
EB:G19, G20.
Salve regina.
LR:Ge34.
EB:G21.
Seniores populi (Responsories for Tenebrae).
EB:G21.
Stabat mater.
LR:Ge34.
Te Deum.
EB:G21, G22, G23.
LB:G39.

Te Deum: Prelude.
LB:B206, B212.
Te Deum: Triumphal March.
LB:A658.
Tenebrae factae sunt (Responsories for Tenebrae).
EB:G21.
Veni creator spiritus.
LR:Ge34.
Extremum Dei Judicum – Oratorio.
EB:G27.
Le Fils Prodigue – Oratorio.
EB:G28.
Sainte Cecile, Vierge et Martyre – Oratorio.
EB:G28.

CHASTELAIN, Charles (c.1490–1578)
  d. Secular Vocal
  Je ne desir que la mort.
  LR:E44.

CHATELAIN DE COUCY (1160–1203)
  d. Secular Vocal
  A vous amants.
  AA:D16.
  Li novais tens.
  AA:D22.

CHATILLON – see WALTHER VON CHATILLON

CHAUMONT, Lambert (1635–1712)
  c. Keyboard – Organ
  Suite No. 3 in G min.
  EB:E78.

CHEDEVILLE, Esprit Philippe 'L'Aine' (1696–1762)
  b. Instrumental
  Duo Galante for recorder and continuo: Rondeau.
    Gavotte. Menuet I. Cotillon.
  LB:B282.
  Laissez paitre vos betes.
  LB:A593.
  Musette.
  LB:A593.

CHEDEVILLE, Nicolas 'Le Cadet' (1705–1782)
  b. Instrumental
  Le Printemps, ou les Saisons Amusants for hurdy gurdy.
  LB:A226.
  Suite No. 5 in G maj for 4 recorders.
  LB:B281.

CHILCOTT, Thomas (d.1776)
  c. Keyboard – Harpsichord
  Suite No. 1 in G min.
  LB:D217, D223.

CHRETIEN DE TROYES (1135–1183)
  d. Secular Vocal
  D'amours qui m'a tolu a moi.
  AA:D16.

CHRZANOWA, Mikolaj z (d.1555)
  e. Sacred Vocal
  Protexisti me Deus.
  LR:E57, F92.

CIAJA – see DELLA CIAJA, Bernadino Azzolino

CICONIA, Johannes (1335–1411)
  d. Secular Vocal
  Aler m'en veus.
  AN:B7.
  Chi nel servir.
  AN:B7.
  Lizadra donna.
  AN:B7.
  ER:A6.
  O felix templum.

ER:A6.
O Padua sidus praeclarum.
ER:A14.
O rosa bella.
AN:B7.
Per quelle strada.
AN:B7.
Le Ray au soleil.
AN:B7.
Sus un' fontayne.
AN:B7.
Una Panthera.
AN:B7.
Venetia mundi splendor.
ER:A14.
  e. Sacred Vocal
  Albane misse celitus.
  AN:B7.
  Credo.
  AN:B7.
  Doctorem principium – Melodia suavissima.
  ER:B6.
  Gloria.
  AN:B7.
  ER:B6.
  O virum – O lux – O beata Nicholae.
  ER:B6.
  Ut per te omnes – Ingens alumnus Padue.
  ER:A6, B6.

CIMA, Gian Paolo (b.1570)
  b. Instrumental
  La Capriccio a 4.
  EB:B6.
  La Novella.
  LR:D18.
  Sonata in D min for recorder and continuo.
  EB:B56, B57.
  LB:B260, B283.
  Sonata in D min for oboe (violin) and continuo.
  EB:E84.
  Sonata in G min for recorder and continuo.
  LB:B260, B283.
  Sonata a 3 for 2 violins, viola da gamba and continuo.
  EB:B43, B45, B62.
  Sonata a 4 in C maj.
  EB:B6.
  Sonata per cornetto e tromba.
  EB:B61.
  Sonata per il violina e violone for violin, viola da gamba
    and continuo.
  EB:B43.

CLARKE, Jeremiah (1670–1707)
  b. Instrumental
  English Suite in D maj for trumpet and strings.
  LB:B214.
  King William's March.
  LB:B219.
  The Prince of Denmark's March – Trumpet Voluntary.
  LR:Gc6.
  LB:A598, A649, A657, A659, B206, B212, B219.
  Suite in D maj for trumpet and strings.
  LB:A661.
  c. Keyboard
  Almand in D maj.
  LB:D217.
  Jigg in A maj.
  LB:D217.
  Round O in A maj.
  LB:D217.
  Suite in D maj: 1st. Movement.
  LB:E194.
  d. Secular Vocal
  Alas, here lies poor Alonso.

EB:F94.
The Glory of Arcadian.
LR:Gd26.
In her brave offspring.
LR:Gd26.

CLAUDIN – *see* DE SERMISY, Claudin.

CLEMENS NON PAPA, Jacobus (1510–1556)
  d. Secular Vocal
  Au joly bois.
  LR:E42.
  La Belle Marguerite.
  LR:E60.
  Iuvons beau iue.
  LR:E50.
  Je prens en gre.
  LR:E42, E54.
  e. Sacred Vocal
  Ego flos campi.
  LR:F82.
  O crux benedicta.
  LR:F80.
  O quam moesta dies.
  LR:E32.
  Pastores loquebantur.
  LR:F82.

CLERAMBAULT, Louis-Nicholas (1676–1749)
  c. Keyboard – Organ
  Suite du 1re ton.
  LB:E150, E151.
  Basse et dessus de trompette (Suite du 1re ton).
  LB:E201, E211.
  Suite du 2em ton.
  LB:E150, E151.

CLUNY – *see* BERNARD DE CLUNY

COBBOLD, William (1560–1639)
  d. Secular Vocal
  With wreaths of rose and laurel (Triumphs of Oriana).
  LR:Gd34.
  You traitors all.
  LR:Gd43.

COCCIOLA, Giovanni Battista (c.1557–1633)
  e. Sacred Vocal
  Super flumina Babylonis.
  EB:G141.
  Tibi laus, tibi gloria.
  EB:G141.
  Veni dilecti mi.
  EB:G141.
  Veni sponsa Christi.
  EB:G141.

CODAX, Martim (13th. cent.)
  d. Secular Vocal – Cantigas de Amigo
  Ay Deus, se sab'ora.
  AA:D4, D7.
  Ay ondas que en vin veer.
  AA:D4, D7.
  Eno sagrado en vigo.
  AA:D7.
  Man did'ei comigo.
  AA:D4, D7.
  Mia yrmana fremosa.
  AA:D4, D7.
  Ondas do mar de Vigo.
  AA:D4, D7.
  Quantas sabedes amar.
  AA:D4, D7.

COELHO, Manuel (1555–1635)
  c. Keyboard
  Tiento I de 1o tono.

LB:D215.

COINCY – *see* GAUTIER DE COINCY

COLOMBE – *see* STE. COLOMBE, Le Sieur de

COLOMBINA – *see* CANCIONERO DE LA COLOMBINA

COLONNA, Giovanni Paolo (1637–1695)
  b. Instrumental
  Sonata
  EB:E59.
  e. Sacred Vocal
  Beatus vir.
  EB:G29.
  Dixit Dominus.
  EB:G29.
  O lucidissima dies.
  EB:B60.
  Missa a 5vv.
  EB:G29.

COMPERE, Loyset (c.1450–1518)
  d. Secular Vocal
  Et dunt revenis vous.
  LR:Gf1.
  Scaramella.
  ER:A6.
  Vat'ens, regret.
  ER:A8.
  e. Sacred Vocal
  Crux triumphans.
  ER:B7.
  O bone Jesu.
  ER:A3.
  Quis numerare – Da pacem.
  LR:A2, E32.
  Virgo celesti.
  LR:A1, E24.

COMPTESSA DE DIA – *see* BEATRICE DE DIA

CONCEICAO, Francisco Diego de (16th./17th. cent.)
  c. Keyboard – Organ
  Falsas medio registro de 2o tono.
  EB:E58.
  Medio registro de 2o tono accidental.
  EB:E57.

CONON DE BETHUNE (c.1160–1219)
  d. Secular Vocal
  Ahi! Amours.
  AA:D22.
  Chanson legere a entendre.
  AA:D16.

CONRADI, Johann Gottfried (d.c.1700)
  b. Instrumental – Lute/Guitar
  Suite in A min.
  EB:C6.
  Suite in C maj.
  LB:C21.

CONSTANZI (18th. cent.)
  d. Secular Vocal
  Lusina la speme – Aria.
  LB:F80.

COOKE, John (15th. cent.)
  e. Sacred Vocal
  Alma proles.
  LR:A4.
  Stella caeli extirpavit.
  ER:B3.

COOPER, John – *see* COPERARIO, Giovanni.

LB:B260, B261, B286.

CORKINE, William (17th. cent.)
b. Instrumental
Corantos I and II.
LR:Ga19.
3 Corantos.
LR:Ga1.
Galliard.
LR:Ga1.
If my complaints.
LR:Ga1.
Monsieur's Almain.
LR:Ga1.
New descants upon old grounds.
LR:Ga19.
Pavane.
LR:Ga1.
The Punke's Delight.
LR:Ga1, Ga19.
Walsingham.
LR:Ga19.
Whoope doe me no harme goodman.
LR:Ga1.
d. Secular Vocal
Away, away.
LR:Gd24.
Come live with me and be my love.
LR:Ga1, Gd51.
EB:B37.
He that hath no mistress.
LR:Gd24.

CORNAGO, Juan (15th. cent.)
d. Secular Vocal
Gentil dama.
LR:A8.
Pues que Dios.
LR:A8.
Senore, qual soy venido.
LR:A8.

CORNET, Pierre (c.1580–1635)
c. Keyboard – Organ
Ad te clamamus.
EB:E28.
Corranta.
EB:E28.
Courante.
EB:E28.
Courant with variations.
EB:E88.
Eia ergo.
EB:E28.
Fantasia du 1re ton.
EB:E28.
Fantasia du 2me ton.
EB:E28.
Fantasia du 3me ton.
EB:E28.
Fantasia du 5me ton.
EB:E28.
Fantasia du 8me ton.
EB:E28, E88.
Salve regina.
EB:E28.
O Clemens.
EB:E28.
Pro fine.
EB:E28.
Tantum ergo.
EB:E28.
Toccata du 3me ton.
EB:E28, E77.
LB:E210.

CORNYSHE, William (c.1468–c.1523)
b. Instrumental
Fa la sol.
LR:Ga17, Gf5.
Fancy.
LR:Gf2.
b. Secular Vocal
Adieu mes amours.
LR:Gf2.
Ah! Robin.
AA:D17.
LR:Gd38, Gd52, Gf2, Gf4, Gf6.
Ay beshrew you.
LR:Gf3, Gf5.
Blow thy horn hunter.
LR:Gf2, Gf4, Gf6.
Hoyda, jolly Rutterkin.
LR:Gd52, Gf3, Gf4.
My love she mourneth.
LR:Gf7.
Woefully arrayed.
LR:Gf3, Gf5.
e. Sacred Vocal
Ave Maria.
ER:B2.
LR:Gf5.

CORREA DE ARAUXO, Francisco (1576–1663)
c. Keyboard – Organ
Canto lleno.
EB:E89.
3 Glosadas sobre el Canto lleno de la Immaculada Conception.
EB:E27, E30, E90.
Lauda Sion ~ Hymn.
EB:E86.
Tiento in A maj.
EB:E27.
Tiento in D maj.
EB:E27.
Tiento lleno de 4o tono.
EB:E90.
Tiento pequene y facil de 7o tono.
EB:E90.
Tiento V de 5o tono.
EB:E30.
Tiento X de medio registro de baxon de 10o tono.
LR:D13.
EB:E29, E66, E86.
Tiento XV de 4o tono.
EB:E29, E30, E57.
Tiento XVI de 4o tono.
EB:E29, E30.
Tiento XXIII de 6o tono.
LR:D13.
EB:E30.
Tiento XXVI de medio registro de tiple.
EB:E30.
Tiento XXVIII de medio registro de tiple de 7o tono.
EB:E29.
Tiento XXXIV de medio registro de baxones de 1o tono.
EB:E29.
Tiento XXXIV de medio registro de baxones de 1o tono.
EB:E29.
Tiento XXXVII de medio registro de baxon de 9o tono.
LR:D13.
EB:E29, E57.
Tiento XLIII de medio registro.
EB:E30.
Tiento XLVII de medio registro de tiple de 8o tono.
EB:E29.
Tiento LII de medio registro entero de 1o tono.
EB:E29.
Tiento LIV de medio registro de dos tiples de 7o tono.

LR:D13.
EB:E29, E79.
d. Secular Vocal
Todo el Mundo en general.
SI:A2.

CORRETTE, Gaspard (c.1660–c.1720)
 c. Keyboard – Organ
Gloria in excelsis Deo.
LB:E212.
Messe du 8me ton.
LB:E150, E197.

CORRETTE, Michel (1709–1795)
 a. Orchestral
Concerto in C maj for hurdy gurdy and orchestra, 'Les recreations du berger fortune.'
LB:A614.
Concerto in D min for harpsichord (or organ), flute and strings, Op. 6, No. 6.
LB:A228, A229.
Concerto in E min for flute and strings, Op. 4, No. 6.
LB:A228.
Concerto in G maj for flute and strings.
LB:A227.
 b. Chamber and Instrumental
Menuets I and II.
LB:B323.
'Le Phenix' for 4 bassoons and continuo.
LB:A635.
Les Sauvages et la Furstemburg.
LB:A228.
Sonata in A maj for viola d'amore and continuo.
LB:A310.
Sonata in D maj for cello and harpsichord, 'Les Delices de la Solitude.'
LB:A228.
Sonata in D maj for violin and harpsichord, 'Les Jeux Olympiques.'
LB:A228, B250.
La servante au bon tabac.
LB:A593, B259.
 c. Keyboard – Organ
Carillon in F maj.
LB:E232.
Magnificat du 8em ton.
LB:E230.
Michaut qui causoit ce grand bruit (Noël).
LB:E232.
Nouveau Livre de Noëls, 1753.
LB:E152.
Noël Provencal.
LB:E231, E232.
Ou s'en vont ces gays bergers (Noël).
LB:E232.
Vous qui desirez sans fin (Noël).
EB:E82.

CORTECCIA, Francesco (1504–1571)
 d. Secular Vocal
Ingredere felicissimis.
LR:A2, E32.

CORTONA, LAUDARIO DI (13th. cent. Italian, Lauds Hymns).
 e. Sacred Vocal.
1. Venite e laudare.
PS:A24.
AA:C5.
2. Laude novella sia cantata.
PS:A24.
AA:C5.
3. Ave donna santissima.
AA:C5.
4. Madonna Santa Maria.

AA:C5.
6. Ave regina gloriosa.
AA:C5.
7. Dal ciel venne messonovello.
AA:C5.
8. Altissima luce col grande splendore.
AA:C5.
9. Fami cantar l'amor di la beata.
AA:C5.
10. O Maria d'omelia se' fontana.
AA:C5.
11. Regina sovrana di gran pietade.
AA:C5.
12. Ave Dei genitrix.
AA:C5.
13. O Maria Dei cella.
AA:C5.
14. Ave vergene gaudente.
AA:C5.
15. O Divina Virgo flore.
AA:C5.
16. Salve, salve virgo pia.
AA:C5.
17. Peccatrice nominata.
AA:C5.
18. Vergene donzella da Dio amata.
AA:C5.
19. Cristo e nato et humanato.
AA:C5.
20. Gloria in cielo e pace 'n terra.
AA:C5.
21. Stella nuova 'n fra la gente.
AA:C5.
22. Plangiamo quel crudel basciare.
AA:C5.
23. Ben crudel e spietoso.
AA:C5.
24. De la crudel morte de Cristo.
PS:A24.
AA:C5.
25. Dami conforto Dio ed alegranza.
AA:C5.
26. Onne home ad alta voce.
PS:A24.
AA:C5.
27. Jesu Christo gloriosi.
AA:C5.
28. Laudamo la resurrectione.
AA:C5.
29. Spiritu Sancto dolze amore.
AA:C5.
30. Spiritu Santo glorioso.
AA:C5.
31. Spiritu Sancta da servire.
AA:C5.
32. Alta Trinita beata.
PS:A24.
AA:C5.
33. Troppo perde il tempo.
PS:A24.
AA:C5.
34. Sto. e alegro et lazioso.
AA:C5.
35. Oime lasso e fredde lo mio coro.
AA:C5.
36. Chi vol lo mondo desprezzare.
AA:C5.
37. Laudar voglio per amore.
PS:A24.
AA:C5.
38. Sia laudato S. Francesco.
AA:C5.
39. Ciascun che fede sente.
AA:C5.

40. Magdalena degna da laudare.
AA:C5.
41. L'Altro prense Arcangelo lucente.
AA:C5.
42. Facciomo laude a tutti sancti.
AA:C5.
43. San Iovanni al mond'e nato.
AA:C5.
44. Ogn'om canti novel canto.
AA:C5.
45. Amore dolze senza pare.
AA:C5.
46. Benedicti et laudati.
AA:C5.
47. Salutiam divotamente.
AA:C5.
Christo risusciti in tutti i cuori.
PS:A24.
Concordi laetitia.
PS:A24.
Martir glorioso, aulente flore.
PS:A24.
O spes mea.
PS:A24.
O virgo pulcherrima.
PS:A24.

COSTA (16th./17th. cent.)
  b.Instrumental
Ricercare XXIV (Music de Joye).
LR:B26.

COSTELEY, Guillaume (1531–1606)
  c.Keyboard – Organ
Fantasie.
LR:D16.
  d.Secular Vocal
Helas, helas, que de mal.
LR:A1.
Je veux aimer ardentement.
LR:E52.
Mignonne, allons voir si la rose.
LR:E52.
La Terre les eaux va buvant.
LR:E52.

COSYN, Benjamin (16th./17th. cent)
  b.Instrumental
The Goldfinch, for viol and harpsichord.
SI:C21.

COUCY – see CHATELAIN DE COUCY

COURVILLE – see THIBAUT DE COURVILLE

COUPERIN, Armand Louis (1725–1789)
  b.Chamber and Instrumental
Fantasias in D min, A min and D min for viola d'amore and
continuo.
LB:B225.
Sonata No. 3 in F maj for harpsichord with violin.
LB:D109.
  c.Keyboard – Harpsichord
L'Arlequin, ou La Adam (Suite in G maj).
LB:D109.
L'Intrepide (Suite in G maj).
LB:D109.
La De Boisgelou (Suite in G maj).
LB:D109.

COUPERIN, Francois (1668–1733)
  b.Chamber and Instrumental
L'Apotheose de Corelli ' Sonate en trio.
LB:B122.
L'Apotheose de Lully – Sonate en trio.
LB:A225.

Duo in G maj for 2 bassoons.
LB:A635.
Concerts Royaux, Nos. 1–4.
  1 in G maj; 2 in D maj; 3 in A maj; 4 in E min.
LB:B116.
Concert Royal No. 3 in A maj.
LB:B118, B119.
Concert Royal No. 4 in E min.
SI:A1.
Nouveaux Concerts, Nos. 1–10 (5–14).
  1 in F maj; 2 in B flat maj; 3 in G min; 4 in G maj; 5 in E
  maj; 6 in A min; 7 in C min; 8 in A maj; 9 in G maj; 10
  in D min.
LB:B116.
Nouveaux Concert No. 3 in G min (7).
LB:B117.
Nouveaux Concert No. 4 in G maj (8), 'Dans la Gout
  Theatral.'
LB:A169.
Nouveaux Concert No. 5 in E maj (9).
LB:B117, B221, B252.
Nouveaux Concert No. 9 in G maj (13).
LB:B117.
Nouveaux Concert No. 10 in D min (14).
LB:B117.
Les Nations.
  1. La Francoise. 2. L'Espagnole. 3. L'Imperiale. 4. La
  Piemontaise.
LB:B120, B121.
Les Nations: L'Espagnole.
LB:B267.
Les Nations: La Piemontaise: Allemande. Air tendre.
  Gigue.
SI:C5.
Piece de Violes No. 1 in E min.
LB:B115.
Piece de Violes No. 2 in A maj.
LB:B115.
Sonate en trio, 'L'Astree.'
LB:B118, B119, B122, B251.
Sonate en quatuor, 'Les Fastes.'
LB:B118, B119.
Sonate en trio, 'La Steinkerque.'
LB:B118, B119, B221.
Sonate en quatuor, 'La Sultane.'
LB:A603, B317, B326.
Sonate en quatuor, 'La Visionnaire.'
LB:B118, B119.
Pieces de Clavecin en concert, Arr. cello, harpsichord
  and strings.
LB:A230.
Pieces de Clavecin en concert, Arr. Bazelaire.
LB:A169.
  c.Keyboard – Harpsichord
Book 1, Ordre 1 (1–18).
  1. Allemande, L'Auguste. 2. Courante I. 3. Courante II.
  4. Sarabande, La Majestueuse. 5. Gavotte. 6. Gigue.
  La Milordine. 7. Menuet. 8. Les Silvans. 9. Les
  Abeilles. 10. La Nanette. 11. Sarabande, Les
  Sentimens. 12. La Pastourelle. 13. Les Nonettes. 14.
  Gavotte, La Bourbonnoise. 15. La Manon. 16.
  L'Enchanteresse. 17. La Fleurie, ou la Tendre
  Nanette. 18. Les Plaisirs de St. Germain en Laye.
LB:D116, D117, D118, D120.
Book 1, Ordre 2 (19–40).
  19. Allemande, La Laborieuse. 20. Courante I. 21.
  Courante II. 22. Sarabande, La Prude. 23.
  L'Antonine. 24. Gavotte. 25. Menuet. 26. Canaries.
  27. Passapied. 28. Rigaudon. 29. La Charolaise. 30.
  La Diane. 31. La Terpsichore. 32. La Florentine. 33.
  La Garnier. 34. La Babet. 35. Les Idees Heureuses.
  36. La Mimi. 37. La Diligente. 38. La Flateuse. 39. La
  Voluptueuse. 40. Les Papillons.
LB:D118, D119, D120.

Branle de Basque.
EB:E31.
Chaconne in C maj.
LB:E217.
Chaconne in D min.
EB:E31, E32, E82.
Chaconne in G min.
PS:B2.
Chaconne (Unsp.)
EB:D35.
Duo.
EB:E32.
Fantasia.
EB:E31.
Fantasia in C maj.
EB:E32.
Fantasia in G min.
LB:E197, E216.
Fantasia XXII.
EB:E32.
Fantasia XXIII.
EB:E32.
Fantasia XXVII.
EB:E32.
Passacaille.
EB:E31, E32.
LB:D232.
Pastourelle in D min.
LB:E197, E216.
La Piemontaise.
LB:D232.
Sarabande en canon.
EB:E31.
Suite in A min.
EB:D4, D34, D36.
Suite in B flat maj.
SI:C8.
Suite in D maj.
EB:D4.
Suite in F maj.
EB:D4, D5.
LB:D233.
Suite in F min.
LB:D141.
Suite in G min.
EB:D4.

COURTOIS, Jean (16th. cent.)
   d.Secular Vocal
Venite populi.
LR:E32.

CRACOVIENSIS, Nicolaus (16th. cent.)
   b.Instrumental.
Hungarian Dance (Lublin Tablature).
LR:B27.

CRAUS, Stephan (15th./16th. cent.)
   b.Instrumental – Lute
Chorea und Auff und nider.
LR:C17.
Fuchs beiss mich nicht – Pavane.
LR:C9.
Tantz und Hupff auf.
LR:C17.
Die Trunken pinter.
LR:C17.

CRECQUILLON, Thomas (d.1557)
   d.Secular Vocal
Avons en est.
LR:E44.
Chanson.
LR:D21.
Content desir.

LR:E42.
Toutes les nuictz.
LR:E36.
Ung gay bergier.
LR:E42.

CREMA, Joan Maria da (16th. cent.)
   b.Instrumental – Lute
La Bertoncina.
LR:C25.
La Bolognese.
LR:C25.
La Louetta.
LR:C25.
Ricercar VIII.
LR:C25.
Ricercar IX.
LR:C25.

CROCE, Giovanni (1557–1609)
   e.Sacred Vocal
Ave virgo.
LR:F84.
Dialogue de chori angeli.
LR:F87.
In Monte Oliveti.
LR:E40.
O vos omnes, qui transitis per viam.
LR:E47.
Tristis est anima mea.
LR:E40.

CROES – *see* DE CROES, Henri Jacques.

CROFT, William (1678–1727)
   b.Instrumental
Sonata in G maj for recorder and continuo.
LB:B288.
Voluntary for organ and trumpets.
LB:B219.
   c.Keyboard – Harpsichord
Allemande and Gavotte in E min.
LB:D217.
Sonata in C min.
LB:D216, D227.
Ground.
LR:Gc8.
Sarabanda.
LR:Gc6.
Suite in A maj.
EB:D1.
Suite in C min.
EB:D1.
Trumpet tune from Bonduca.
LB:B219.
   d.Secular Vocal
Ah, how sweet.
EB:F94.
My time.
LR:Gd26.
Who would value pleasure.
EB:F94.
   e.Sacred Vocal
The Burial Service.
LB:G319.

CRONER, Daniel (1656–1740)
   c.Keyboard
Tablature for harpsichord (clavichord), 1682.
EB:E33.
Tablature for organ, 1681.
EB:E33.

CRUCE – *see* PETRUS DE CRUCE.

CRUGER, Johann (1598–1663)
  e. Sacred Vocal
  Lobet den Herren.
  EB:G132.
  Nun danket all und bringet Ehr.
  LR:F101.

CRUZ, Agostinho da (c.1590–1633)
  c. Keyboard – Harpsichord
  Verso de 8o tono por do sol re.
  LB:D215.

CSUKEI, Istvan (16th. cent.)
  d. Secular Vocal
  After the death of many kings (Hofgreff Songbook,
    1552-3).
  LR:A5.

CUTTING, Francis (1583–1623)
  b. Instrumental – Lute
  Almaine.
  LR:Gb4, Gb5, Gb6.
  Galliard.
  LR:Gd19.
  SI:C17.
  Greensleeves.
  LR:Gb4, Gb5, Gb8, Gb9, Gd39, Gd51.
  Packington's Pound.
  LR:Gb4, Gb8.
  Raleigh's Galliard.
  LR:Gd29.
  Squirrel's Toy.
  LR:Gb6.
  Walsingham.
  LR:Gb4, Gb5, Gb6, Gd18, Gd45.

D'ACOURT (15th. cent.)
  d. Secular Vocal
  Je demande ma bienvenue.
  LR:A4.

DAGGERE, William (15th./16th. cent.)
  d. Secular Vocal
  Downberry down.
  LR:E60, Gf2.

D'AGINCOURT, Francois (1684–1758).
  c. Keyboard – Harpsichord
  Autre Menuet (Suite in D min).
  LB:D144.
  La Bleville (Suite in D min).
  LB:D144.
  La Caressante (Suite in D min).
  LB:D144.
  La Couperin.
  LB: D231.
  Courant (Suite in D min).
  LB:D144.
  La Couronne (Suite in D min).
  LB:D144.
  Les Dances Provencales (Suite in D min).
  LB:D144.
  La Magnifique (Suite in D min).
  LB:D144.
  Menuet et Double (Suite in D min).
  LB:D144.
  Le Pattelin (Suite in D min).
  LB:D144.
  La Sautillante (Suite in D min).
  LB:D144.
  La Sensible (Suite in D min).
  LB:D144.
  La Syncopee (Suite in D min).
  LB:D144.

DALL'ABACO, Evaristo Felice (1675–1742)
  b. Instrumental
  Sonata in G min for mandolin and harpsichord; Op. 1, No.
    5.
  LB:C28.

DALLA CASA, Girolamo (fl.1584)
  b. Instrumental
  Alla dolc' ombra (after De Rore).
  LR:B2.
  Ancore che col partire (after De Rore).
  LR:E36.
  Beato me direi (after De Rore).
  LR:B2.

DALUA (16th. cent.)
  e. Sacred Vocal
  Ut queant laxis.
  LR:E26.

DALZA, Joanambrosio (d.1508)
  b. Instrumental – Lute
  Calata ala Spagnola.
  LR:B16, B25, C26.
  Pavana Ferrerese.
  LR:B10, E24.
  Piva.
  LR:C24, C26.
  Recercare.
  LR:A1, C24.
  Saltarello.
  LR:C24, C26.
  Suite Ferrarese.
  LR:A1.
  Tastar de corde.
  LR:A1, C24.

DAMETT, Thomas (15th. cent.)
  e. Sacred Vocal
  Beata Dei genitrix.
  ER:B3.

DANDRIEU, Jean Francois (1682–1738)
  c. Keyboard – Harpsichord
  L'Aflige (Ordre 2).
  LB:D145.
  La Bouillonante (Ordre 3).
  LB:D145.
  Les Characteres de la Guerre (Ordre 1).
  LB:D145.
  Les Cascades (Ordre 3).
  LB:D145.
  La Contrariante (Ordre 2).
  LB:D145.
  La Coquete (Ordre 1).
  LB:D145.
  L'Empresse (Ordre 4).
  LB:D145.
  La Fastueuse (Ordre 5).
  LB:D145.
  La Fete de Village (Ordre 5).
  LB:D145.
  Les Fifres (Ordre 4).
  LB:D145.
  Les Folies Amusantes (Ordre 1).
  LB:D145.
  La Fugitive (Ordre 3).
  LB:D145.
  La Gemissante (Ordre 2).
  LB:D145.
  L'Harmonieuse (Ordre 1).
  LB:D145, D221.
  La Lyre d'Orphee.
  LB:D231.
  La Melodieuse (Ordre 1).
  LB:D145.

La Musete (Ordre 1).
LB:D145, D221.
La Plaintive (Ordre 1).
LB:D145.
Le Rappel des Oiseaux (Ordre 2).
LB:B324, D145.
La Sensible (Ordre 4).
LB:D145.
Les Tendres Reproches.
LB:D231.
Les Tourbillons (Ordre 2).
LB:D145, D221, D231.
c. Keyboard – Organ
A minuit (Noël).
LB:E213.
Basse de cromorne.
LB:E160.
Basse et dessus de trompette.
LB:E160.
Chantons de voix hautaine (Noël).
LB:E231, E232.
Chretien qui suivez l'eglise (Noël).
LB:E213.
Cromorne en taille.
EB:E90.
Duo en cor de chasse.
LB:E160.
Flutes.
LB:E160.
Fugues I and II.
EB:E90.
Fugue sur l'Ave maris stella.
LB:E160.
Joseph est bien marie (Noël).
LB:E213, E231.
Magnificat.
EB:E90.
LB:E197, E218.
Musette.
LB:E160.
Offertoire.
EB:E90.
LB:E160.
Offertoire pour le Jour de Pacques.
LB:E212.
Plein jeu de 1re ton.
EB:E90.
LB:E160.
Recit de nazard.
LB:E160.
Si c'est pour etre la vie.
LB:E231.
Trio.
EB:E90.
Trio avec pedal.
LB:E160.

D'ANGLEBERT, Jean-Henri (1628–1691)
c. Keyboard – Harpsichord
Prelude in D min.
EB:B9.
Suite in D maj.
SI:C4.
Suite in D min.
EB:D6.
Suite in G maj.
EB:D6.
Suite in G min.
EB:D6.
Le Tombeau de M. de Chambonnieres.
LB:D232, D234.
c. Keyboard – Organ
Fugues. Nos. 1–5.
EB:E34.

Quartet on the Kyrie.
EB:E34.

DANICAN-PHILIDOR, Anne (1681–1728)
b. Instrumental
Sonata in D min for recorder and continuo.
LB:B274, B289.
Suite No. 1 in G min for trumpet and organ (Arr. from Suite for oboe and continuo).
LB:B222.

DANIEL, Arnaut (12th./13th. cent.)
d. Secular Vocal
Il mot son plan e prim.
AA:D6.

DANYEL, John (1564–1625)
b. Instrumental
A Fancy.
LR:Gb9.
EB:C8.
Mistresse Anne Green, her leaves be green.
LR:Gb7.
Passymeasures Galliard.
LR:Gb9.
EB:C8.
Rosamunde Pavan.
LR:Gb9.
d. Secular Vocal – Songs for Lute, Viol and Voice, 1606
Can doleful notes?
LR:Gd5.
Coy Daphne fled.
LR:Gd5.
Dost thou withdraw thy grace.
LR:Gd5, Gd24.
EB:F103.
Drop not mine eyes.
LR:Gd5.
Eyes look no more.
LR:Gd5, Gd48.
Grief keep within.
LR:Gd5.
Have all our passions.
LR:Gd5.
He whose desires are still abroad.
LR:Gd5, Gd24.
I die whenas I do not see.
LR:Gd5.
If I could shut the gate.
LR:Gd5, Gd24.
Let not Cloris think.
LR:Gd5.
Like as the lute delights.
LR:Gd5, Gd27, Gd48.
No, let chromatic tunes.
LR:Gd5.
Now the Earth, the Sky, the Air.
LR:Gd5.
Stay, cruel, stay.
LR:Gd5.
Thou pretty bird.
LR:Gd5.
Time, cruel time.
LR:Gd5, Gd19.
Uncertain certain turns.
LR:Gd5.
What delight can they enjoy.
LR:Gd5, Gd48.
Why canst thou not.
LR:Gd5.

DAQUIN, Louis-Claude (1694–1772)
c. Keyboard – Harpsichord
Allemande (Book 1).
LB:D146.

L'Amusante (Book 1).
LB:D146.
Les Bergeres (Book 1).
LB:D146.
Le Coucou (Book 1).
EB:D35.
LB:D146, D221, D234.
Courante (Book 1).
LB:D146.
Le Depit genereux (Book 1).
LB:D146.
Les Enchainements (Book 1).
LB:D146.
La Guitare (Book 1).
LB:D146.
L'Hirondelle (Book 1).
LB:D146.
La Joyeuse (Book 1).
LB:D146.
La Melodieuse (Book 1).
LB:D231.
Les Plaisirs de la Chasse (Book 1).
LB:D146.
Ronde Bachique (Book 1).
LB:D146, D221.
La Tendre Silvie (Book 1).
LB:D146.
Les Tourbillons.
LB:D224.
Les Vents en courroux (Book 1).
LB:D146.
c. Keyboard – Organ
Noel in D min sur les jeux d'anches, sans tremblant (1).
LB:E161, E162, E231.
Noel in D min en dialogue, duo, trio (2).
LB:E161, E162.
Noel in G maj en musette, en dialogue, en trio (3).
LB:E161, E162, E202.
Noel in G maj en duo sur les d'anches sans tremblant (4).
LB:E161, E162, E202.
Noel in D min en duo (5).
LB:E161, E162.
Noel in D min sur les jeux d'anches sans tremblant et en duo (6).
LB:E161, E162, E163.
Noel in D min en trio et en dialogue (7).
LB:E92, E161, E162.
Noel etranger in G maj sur les jeux d'anches sans tremblant et en duo (8).
LB:B209, E92, E161, E162, E163, E197, E216.
Noel in D maj sur les flutes (9).
LB:E161, E162, E163, E202, E231.
Noel in G maj grand jeu et duo (10).
LB:E92, E161, E162, E163, E184, E232.
Noel in D min en recit et en taille (11).
LB:E161, E162, E163, E231, E232.
Noel in A min grand jeu et duo – Suisse (12).
LB:E161, E162, E163, E188, E214, E219, E220, E232.

D'AUVERGNE, Antoine (1713–1797)
  b. Chamber and Instrumental
  Concert de Simphonie a 4 No. 1 in B flat maj.
  LB:B123.
  Concert de Simphonie a 4 No. 2 in F maj.
  LB:B123.
  Concert de Simphonie a 4 No. 3 in B min.
  LB:B123.

DAVY, Richard (d.1519)
  d. Secular Vocal
  Joan is sick and ill at ease.
  LR:Gf7.
  e. Sacred Vocal
  Psalm XLVII.
  LR:Ge33.

St. Matthew Passion.
ER:B4.

DAZA, Esteban (16th. cent.)
  b. Instrumental – Vihuela
  Fantasia de passos largos.
  LR:E61.
  Fantasia por el 1o tono a 4.
  LR:E61.

DE BOUSSET, Jean-Baptiste (1662–1725)
  d. Secular Vocal
  Air a boire.
  LB:F81.

DE CROES, Henri Jacques (1705–1786)
  b. Chamber and Instrumental
  Sonatas en Trio, Op. 3, Nos. 1–6.
    1. in A min; 2. in F maj; 3. in G min; 4. in D min; 5. in G maj; 6. in F maj.
  LB:B124.

DE FESCH, Willem (1687–1757)
  b. Chamber and Instrumental
  Sonatas for oboe and continuo, 1725, Nos. 1–6.
  LB:B125.
  d. Secular Vocal
  Tu fai la superbetta.
  LB:F81.

DE GEMBLOUX, Johannes Franchois (= GEMBLACO) (15th. cent.)
  b. Instrumental
  Trumpet Intrada.
  LR:Ga11.

DE GRIGNY, Nicolas (1672–1703)
  c. Keyboard – Organ
  Ave maris stella – Hymn.
  LB:E168, E169, E170.
  O solis ortus cardine – Hymn.
  LB:E168, E169, E170.
  Pange lingua – Hymn.
  LB:E167, E168, E169, E170.
  Veni creator spiritus – Hymn.
  LB:E167, E168, E169, E170.
  Verbum supernum – Hymn.
  LB:E168, E169, E170.
  La Messe I (Livre d'Orgue, 1699).
  LB:E164, E165, E170.
  La Messe I: Excpts.
  LB:E167.
  La Messe II (Livre d'Orgue, 1699).
  LB:E166.
  Basse de trompette ou de cromorne (Gloria).
  EB:E66.
  Cromorne en taille.
  LB:E187.
  Dialogue a 2 tailles de cromorne et 2 dessus de cornet pour la Communion.
  EB:E66.
  Dialogue de flutes pour l'Elevation.
  EB:E66.
  Dialogue sur les Grands Jeux (Amen du Gloria).
  EB:E66.
  Recit de tierce pour le Benedictus.
  EB:E66.

DE LA BARRE, Joseph (1633–1678)
  b. Chamber and Instrumental
  Suite in G maj for flute and continuo, Book 1, No. 2.
  LB:B126.
  Suite in D min for flute and continuo, Book 1, No. 5.
  LB:B126.
  Suite in G maj for flute and continuo, Book 2, No. 9.
  LB:B126.

c.Keyboard – Organ
Sarabande.
EB:E76.

DE LA CROIX – *see* **PETRUS DE CRUCE**

DE LA GROTTE, Nicolas (c.1530–c.1600)
d.Secular Vocal
J'ay bien mal choisi.
LR:E43.
Je suis amour.
LR:E44.
Quand ce beau printemps je voy.
LR:E52.
Quand le gril chante.
LR:E44.

DE LA RUE, Pierre (1460–1518)
d.Secular Vocal
Mijn hert.
ER:A4, A8.
LR:A2.
EB:B35.
Pour ung jamais.
LR:A1.
e.Sacred Vocal
Gaude virgo.
ER:B9.
Laudate Dominum.
ER:B9.
Missa 'Ave Sanctissima Maria': Sanctus.
ER:A2.
Missa pro defunctis, Requiem.
ER:B8.
Pater de caelis.
ER:B9.
Salve regina.
ER:B9.
Vexilla regis – Passio Domini.
ER:A8.

DE LA TORRE, Francisco (c.1470–1520)
b.Instrumental
Danza alta.
ER:A8.
LR:B10, B16, B24, D17.
EB:D33.
La Spagna.
LR:A1, E24.
d.Secular Vocal
Dime, triste corazon.
LR:E62.
Pampano verde.
LR:E31.
e.Sacred Vocal
Adoramus te, Senor.
LR:A1, E24.
Pascua d'Espiritu Santo.
LR:E25.

DE LAVIGNE, Philibert (c.1700–1750)
b.Chamber and Instrumental
Sonata in C maj for recorder (or oboe) and continuo, 'La Barsan.'
LB:B241, B274.

DE LEEUW, Cornelis (1613–1685)
e.Sacred Vocal
Een kindeken is ons gheborn.
LR:F117.

DELLA CIAJA, Bernadino Azzolino (1671–1744)
c.Keyboard – Organ
Ricercar in C maj.
LB:E238.
Ricercar in D min.

LB:E238.
Ricercar in F maj.
LB:E238.

DE MACHY, 'Monsieur' (17th. cent.)
b.Chamber and Instrumental
Suite No. 1 in D min for solo viol (1635).
EB:B10.
Suite No. 4 in D maj for solo viol (1635).
EB:B10.

DE MONTE – *see* **LAMBERT DE MONTE**

DE MONTE, Philippus (1521–1603)
d.Secular Vocal
Comme la tourterelle.
LR:E52.
Porta il buon villanel.
AN:B1.
La Premier jour de mois de may.
LR:E52.
Quella fera son'io.
AN:B1.
Stella del nostro mar a l'apparir de sol.
LR:F93.
e.Sacred Vocal
Laudate Dominum.
LR:F82.
Missa a 4vv.
LR:F5.
Missa 'Mon coeur se recommend a vous.'
LR:F5.
O bone Jesu.
LR:F83.
O suavitas et dulcedo.
LR:F82, F93.

DE REIS, Gaspar (16th./17th. cent.)
c.Keyboard – Organ
1o Concertado sobre o canto chao as avessas.
EB:E58.
3o Concertado sobre o canto chao as avessas.
EB:E58.
Concertado a 3 com dous las.
EB:E58.
Concertado sobre a 6o tono.
EB:E57.
Tencao pues mi sol se aussenta morire de pensa.
EB:E58.
Tencao sobre a 5o kyrio de Missa Sancta Maria.
EB:E58.
3 Tencaos.
EB:E58. *

DE RIPPE, Albert (c.1480–1551)
b.Instrumental – Lute
Douce memoire.
LR:C4.
Fantasia I.
LR:C4.
Fantasia II.
LR:C4.
Fantasia XIII.
LR:C4.
Fantasia XVI.
LR:C4.
Fantasia XVIII.
LR:C4.
Fantasia XXII.
LR:C4.
Fantasia XXV.
LR:C4.
Galliarde.
LR:C4.
Galliard L'Amirale.

LR:C4.
O passi sparsi.
LR:C4.
On en dira ce qu'en voudra.
LR:C4.
Verbum iniquum.
LR:C4.

DE RORE, Cipriano (1516–1565)
  d.Secular Vocal (Including Instrumental Arrangements)
  A la dolc' ombra (see DALLA CASA).
  LR:B28.
  Anchor che col partire (see DALLA CASA).
  LR:E39.
  EB:B41.
  Beato me direi (see DALLA CASA).
  Come la notte.
  LR:E39.
  Datemi pace.
  LR:E39.
  De la belle contrade.
  LR:A1.
  Hor che l'aria.
  LR:E39.
  Non e lasso martire.
  LR:E39.
  Non gemme, non fin' oro.
  ER:A6.
  O altitudo divitarum.
  LR:F82.
  O sonno.
  LR:F94.
  Pero piu ferm.
  LR:B28.

DE SAYVE, Lambertus (1549–1614)
  d.Secular Vocal
  Da poiche tu crudel.
  AN:B1.
  e.Sacred Vocal
  Kyrie.
  LR:F93.

DE SERMISY, Claudin (c.1490–1562)
  d.Secular Vocal (Including Instrumental Arrangements)
  Allez souspirs.
  LB:B227.
  Amour me poingt.
  AA:A1.
  Amour me voyant.
  LB:B227.
  C'est a grand tort.
  LR:E42.
  Content desir.
  LR:A1.
  D'etre amoureux.
  LR:E44.
  D'ou vient cela, belle.
  LR:E44.
  Du bien qu'oeil absent ne peut choisir.
  ER:A7.
  Il me suffit.
  LR:E44.
  Jouissance vous donneray.
  SI:C7.
  Languir me fait.
  LR:A2, E22, E50.
  Las, je m'y plains.
  LR:A1, E24.
  O douce amour.
  LR:E36.
  Puisqu'en amour.
  ER:A7.
  Quosque non reverteris.
  LR:A2, E32.

Tant que vivray.
LR:E38, E44, E59, E67, Gd52.
Tu disais que j'en mourrais.
LR:E58.

DE VISEE, Robert (1650–1725)
  b.Chamber and Instrumental
  Suite in A min for flute, lute and bass viol (1716).
  EB:B11.
  Suite in G maj for violin, harpsichord and bass viol
    (1716).
  EB:B11.
  Suite in G min for flute, harpsichord, theorbo and bass
    viol (1716).
  EB:B11.
  b.Instrumental – Lute
  Air des Matelots de M. de Lully.
  LB:C30.
  Chaconne in F maj for theorbo (1716).
  EB:B11.
  Chaconne des Harlequins de M. de Lully.
  EB:C1.
  Courante.
  EB:C9.
  Les Demons d'Alceste de M. de Lully.
  EB:C1.
  Entree d'Apollon de M. de Lully.
  EB:C1.
  Entree des Espagnoles de M. de Lully.
  EB:C2.
  Les Folies d'Espagne – Variations.
  LR:C10.
  Gigue grave.
  EB:C9.
  La Grotte de Versailles de M. de Lully.
  EB:C1.
  LB:C30.
  La Montsermeil.
  EB:C9.
  La Muzette.
  EB:C2, C9.
  Prelude.
  EB:C1, C9.
  Les Silvains de M. de Couperin.
  EB:C1, C2.
  Les Sourdines D'Armide de M. de Lully.
  EB:C1.
  LB:C30.
  Suite in A maj.
  EB:C7.
  Suite in A min.
  EB:C1.
  Suite in C min.
  EB:C2.
  Suite in D maj.
  EB:C2.
  Suite in D min.
  EB:C2, C5.
  LB:B290, C24, C26, C29.
  Suite in F sharp min.
  EB:C1.
  Suite in G maj.
  EB:C1.
  LB:C23.
  Tombeau de Du But.
  EB:C9.
  Tombeau de M. Mouton.
  EB:C1, C9.
  Tombeau de Tonty.
  EB:C9.
  Tombeau de Vieux Gallot.
  EB:C9.
  La Venitienne de M. de Forqueray.
  EB:C9.

DE VITRY, Phillippe (1291–1361)
  d./e. Ars Nova Motets
  Colla iugo – Bona conduit – Libera me.
  AN:A12.
  Cum statua – Hugo, Hugo, princeps.
  AA:B1.
  Firmissime – Adesto – Alleluia.
  AN:A12.
  Impudentor circumivi – Virtutibus laudibus.
  AA:B1.
  Tribum – Quoniam – Merito hoc patimur.
  AN:A12.
  Tuba sacre fidei – In arboris – Virgo sum.
  AN:A12.
  Vos qui admiramini – Gratissima – Gaude gloriosa.
  AN:A12.

DE VOIS, Pieter (16th./17th. cent.)
  b. Instrumental
  Pavane de Spanje (Der Goden Fluit-hemel, 1644).
  EB:B40.

DE WERT, Giaches (1535–1569)
  d. Secular Vocal
  Un jour je m'en allai.
  LR:E22.
  Valle, che de lamenti miei.
  LR:E46, Gd25.
  Vezzosi augelli.
  LR:Gd25.

DEFRONCIACO (14th./15th. cent.)
  e. Sacred Vocal
  Kyrie. Jesu dolcissime (APT MS.)
  AN:B5.

DELALANDE, Michel Richard (1657–1726)
  a. Orchestral
  Concert de trompettes pour les festes sur le canal de
    Versailles (see Symphonies pour les Soupers du Roy,
    Suite No. 1.)
  EB:A14.
  Symphonies pour les Soupers du Roy.
    Suite No. 1: 1. Concert des trompettes pour les festes
      sur la canal de Versailles. 2. Caprice No. 3. 3.
      Fantasie ou caprice No. 2. 4. Caprice No. 1 ou
      caprice de Villers.
    Suite No. 2: 1. Chaconne en echo. 2. Musette de
      Cardenia. 3. Aria. 4. Musette pour les hautbois. 5.
      Fanfare. Symphonies de Te Deum.
  EB:A14.
  e. Sacred Vocal
  Deus in adjutorium.
  EB:G31.
  Deus meus rex.
  EB:G32.
  Exaltabo te.
  EB:G32.
  Lecons de Tenebres.
  EB:G30.
  Sacris solemnis.
  EB:G16.
  Usquequo Domine.
  EB:G31, G32.

DELONEY, Thomas (16th./17th. cent.)
  d. Secular Vocal
  The Great Galleazo.
  LR:Gd43.
  The Queen at Tilsburie.
  LR:Gd43.

DEMANTIUS, Johannes Christoph (1567–1643)
  b. Instrumental
  Andantino.
  LR:F106.

Galliard.
  LR:B10, B17, B18.
  EB:F105.
  Intrada.
  LR:B22.
  Polnischer Tanz.
  LR:B10, B17, B18.
  d. Secular Vocal
  Diese Nacht hatt ich eine Traum.
  EB:F105.
  Tympanum militaire (Excpt).
  LR:A6.
  Zart schönes Bild.
  EB:F105.
  e. Sacred Vocal
  St. John Passion.
  EB:G33, G138.

DENSS, Adrian (late 16th. cent.)
  b. Instrumental – Lute
  Passamezzo.
  LR:C19.

DEPANSIS (14th./15th. cent.)
  e. Sacred Vocal
  Et in terra pax (APT MS)
  AN:B5.

DERRING, Richard (c.1580–1630)
  b. Instrumental
  Pavan.
  LR:Ga14.
  d. Secular Vocal
  Country Cries.
  LR:Gd53.
  e. Sacred Vocal
  Factus est silentium.
  LR:Ge35.
  Gaudent in caelis.
  LB:G327.
  Jesus dulcis memoria.
  LR:F88, Ge32.
  O bone Jesu.
  LB:G327.
  O vos omnes.
  LR:Ge36.
  Quem vidistis.
  LR:F117.

DESMARETS, Henri (1661–1741)
  b. Instrumental
  Menuet.
  LB:B323.
  Passapied.
  LB:B323.

DES PRES – see **JOSQUIN DES PRES**

DIA – see **BEATRICE DE DIA**

DIEUPART, Charles Francis (1670–1740)
  b. Chamber and Instrumental
  Suite in A maj for recorder and continuo.
  LB:B229, B230.
  Suite in A min for recorder and continuo.
  LB:B289.
  Suite in E min for recorder and continuo.
  LB:B284.
  Suite in F min for flute, viola da gamba and lute.
  LB:B269.
  Suite in G maj for recorder and continuo.
  LB:B291, B292, B229.

DIJON – See **GUIOT DE DIJON**

D'INDIA, Sigismondo (c.1580–1629)
  d. Secular Vocal

Ahi chi fia che consoli.
EB:F9.
Alla guerra.
EB:F9.
Amico, hai vinto.
EB:F8.
Ancidetemi pur, dogliosi affanni.
EB:F8, F93.
Apertamente dice la gente.
EB:F9.
Bacciator dubbioso.
EB:F99.
Chi nudrisca tua speme.
EB:F8, F9.
Com' e soave cosa.
EB:F93.
Crude Amarilli.
EB:F98, F99.
Dove potro mai gir tanto lontano.
EB:F9.
Fresche erbette novelle.
EB:F9.
Giunto a la tomba.
EB:F8, F9.
Intenerite voi, lagrime mie.
EB:F98.
La mia fili crudel.
EB:F9.
La tra 'l sangue e la morti.
EB:F9.
Langue al vostro languir.
EB:F8.
O leggiadr' occhi.
EB:F8, F9.
O primavera, gioventu dell' anno.
EB:F100.
Occhi della mia vita.
EB:F8.
Osculare o beata peccatrix.
EB:F9.
Partita dell' amata.
EB:F99.
Piangeno al pianger mio.
EB:F9.
Pianto.
EB:F99.
Porto celato.
EB:F9.
Quella vermiglia rosa.
EB:F8.
Son gli accenti che ascolto.
EB:F8.
Se bel rio, se bell' auretta.
EB:F93.
Su, su prendi la cetra.
EB:F9.
Torna il serena Zefiro.
EB:F8.
Voi ch' ascoltate.
EB:F9.
Vostro fui, vostro son e saro vostro.
EB:F100.
e. Sacred Vocal
Dilectus meus loquitur mihi.
EB:F9.
Domine Deus meus.
EB:F9.
Ecce sponsus venit.
EB:F9.
Isti sunt duae olivae.
EB:G139.
Tui recordatio.
EB:F9.

DIRUTA, Girolamo (c.1560–1630)
  c. Keyboard – Organ
  Ricercar per organo.
  LR:A6.
  Toccata in the Ionian Mode.
  LB:E239.

DLUGORAJ, Adalbert Wojciech (1550–1619)
  b. Instrumental – Lute
  Ballet.
  LR:C19.
  Carola Polonesa.
  LR:C18.
  Chorea Polonica.
  LR:C17, C18, C19.
  Fantasia.
  LR:C16, C17, C18.
  Finale.
  LR:C17.
  2 Finales.
  LR:C15, C18.
  Hajdu dance.
  LR:C19.
  Kowaly.
  LR:C18.
  Villanella I.
  LR:C16.
  Villanella II.
  LR:C16.
  Villanella Polonica.
  LR:C17, C18.
  EB:D2, F104.

DOLLE, Charles (18th. cent.)
  b. Chamber and Instrumental
  Sonata in A min for viol and continuo.
  SI:C18.
  Sonata in G maj for viol and continuo.
  SI:C17.
  Suite in C min for viol and continuo, Book 1, No. 2.
  LB:B127.

DONATI, Baldassare (c.1530–1603)
  d. Secular Vocal
  Villanella alla Napolotana.
  LR:E29.
  e. Sacred Vocal
  Domine ne in furore – Psalm VI.
  EB:G137.
  In te, Domine, speravi.
  EB:G139.

DONATO DA FLORENTIA (= FIRENZE) (14th. cent.)
  d. Secular Vocal
  Come da lupo.
  ER:A4.
  Senti tu d'amor.
  AN:B6.

DORNEL, Louis Antoine (1685–1765)
  b. Chamber and Instrumental
  Sonata en quatuor in D min for recorder, flute, oboe and
    continuo.
  LB:B275.
  Sonata a 3 dessus in B flat maj.
  EB:B64.
  Suite No. 1 in C min for recorder and continuo, 'Livre de
    Symphonies.'
  LB:B293.
  Trio Sonata in D maj, Op. 3, No. 2.
  LB:B325.

DOWLAND, John (1563–1626)
  b. Instrumental – Consort and Lute Pieces
  Almaine – Unnamed Piece.
  LR:Gb3.

LB:B306.
Round Battell Galliard.
LR:Ga5, Gb4, Gb5, Gd9.
Semper Dowland, semper dolens.
LR:Gb3, Gb6, Gb9, Gd10, Gd11, Gd12, Gd21.
EB:F105.
The Shoemaker's Wife.
LR:Gb3, Gc8, Gd9.
Sir George Whitehead's Almain.
LR:C12, Gd11, Gd42.
Sir Henry Gifford's Almain.
LR:Gb3.
Sir Henry Gifford's Galliard.
LR:Gb1.
Sir John Smith's Almain.
LR:Gb3, Gd9, Gd21.
Sir John Souch's Galliard.
LR:Gb2, Gb4, Gd29.
Sir Robert Sidney's Galliard.
LR:Gd31.
Solus cum sola Pavan.
LR:Ga6.
Sorrow come.
LR:E63.
Susanna Fair Galliard.
LR:Ga5.
Tarleton's Gigge.
LR:Ga5.
Tarleton's Resurrection.
LR:C10, Gd9, Gd11, Gd21.
Volta a 4.
LR:Ga5.
EB:B39.
Walsingham.
LR:Gb4, Gb8.
Were every thought an eye.
LR:Ga5.
d. Secular Vocal
First Book of Songs, 1597 (B1).
Second Book of Songs, 1600 (B2).
Third Book of Songs, 1603 (B3).
A Pilgrim's Solace, 1612 (PS).
A Musical Banquet, 1614 (MB).
A Shepherd in a shade (B2).
LR:E50, Gd7.
All ye whom love or fortune (B1).
LR:Gd6.
Awake, sweet love (B1).
LR:E55, Gd6, Gd10, Gd24.
Away with these self-loving lads (B1).
LR:Gd6, Gd42.
Behold a wonder here (B3).
LR:Gd8.
Burst forth my crystal tears (B1).
LR:Gd6.
By a fountain where I lay (B3).
LR:Gd8.
Can she excuse my wrongs (B1).
LR:Gd6, Gd9, Gd10, Gd11, Gd12, Gd19, Gd28, Gd38,
  Gd55.
EB:F91, F105.
Clear or cloudy (B2).
LR:Gd7.
Come again sweet love (B1).
LR:E55, Ga6, Gd6, Gd9, Gd10, Gd12, Gd22, Gd24.
Come away, come sweet love (B1).
LR:Gd6, Gd9, Gd28.
Come heavy sleep (B1).
LR:Gd6, Gd9, Gd18, Gd26, Gd28.
Come when I call (B3).
LR:Gd8.
Come ye heavy states of night (B2).
LR:Gd7, Gd11.
Daphne was not so chaste (B3).

LR:Gd8.
Dear if you change (B1).
LR:Gd6, Gd55.
Die not before thy day (B2).
LR:Gd7.
Faction that ever dwells (B2).
LR:Gd7.
Far from triumphing court (MB).
LR:Gd12, Gd30, Gd31.
Farewell too fair (B3).
LR:Gd8.
Farewell unkind (B3).
LR:Gd8.
Fie on this feigning (B3).
LR:Gd8.
Fine knacks for ladies (B2).
LR:E35, Gd7, Gd10, Gd56.
EB:F106.
Flow my tears (B2).
LR:E42, Gd7, Gd9, Gd12, Gd24.
EB:F106.
Flow not so fast ye fountains (B3).
LR:Gd8, Gd9, Gd10, Gd12.
From silent night (PS).
LR:Gd9.
Go crystal tears (B1).
LR:Gd10, Gd24.
Go nightly cares (PS).
LR:Gd9.
His golden locks (B1).
LR:Gd6.
Humour, say what mak'st thou here (B2).
LR:Gd7.
I must complain (B3).
LR:Gd8.
I saw my lady weep (B2).
LR:Gd7, Gd9, Gd18, Gd26, Gd27, Gd39.
If floods of tears (B2).
LR:Gd7.
If my complaints (B1).
LR:Ga6, Gd6, Gd9.
If that a sinner's sighs (PS).
LR:Gd9, Gd11, Gd18, Gd54.
In darkness let me dwell (MB).
LR:Gd9, Gd12, Gd21, Gd28, Gd30, Gd31, Gd42.
EB:F103.
In this trembling shadow (PS).
LR:Gd27, Gd54.
It was a time when silly bees (B3).
LR:Gd8, Gd29.
Lady if you so spite me (MB).
LR:Gd10, Gd12, Gd24, Gd30, Gd31.
EB:F103.
Lasso mia vita (PS).
LR:Gd9, Gd42.
Lend your ears to my sorrow (B3).
LR:Gd8.
Love stood amazed (B3).
LR:Gd8.
The Lowest trees have tops (B3).
LR:Gd8, Gd21.
Me, me and none but me (B3).
LR:Gd8, Gd9, Gd10.
Mourn, day is with darkness fled (B2).
LR:Gd7.
My thoughts are winged with hopes (B1).
LR:Gd6.
Now cease my wand'ring eyes (B2).
LR:Gd7.
Now, o now I needs must part (B1).
LR:Gd6, Gd11, Gd18, Gd42, Gd54, Ge36.
O sweet woods (B2).
LR:Gd7.
O what hath overwrought? (B3).

LR:Gd8.
Praise blindness eyes (B2).
LR:Gd7.
Rest awhile you cruel cares (B1).
LR:Gd6.
Say, love, if ever thou didst find (B3).
LR:Gd8, Gd9, Gd21, Gd28.
EB:F105.
Shall I strive with words to move (PS).
LR:Gd10.
Shall I sue (B2).
LR:Gd7, Gd9, Gd10, Gd11, Gd12, Gd18, Gd24, Gd26.
Sleep, wayward thoughts (B1).
LR:Gd6.
Song to the lute (?)
LR:Gd21.
Sorrow stay (B2).
LR:Ga6, Ga7, Gd7, Gd9, Gd10, Gd21, Gd38.
Stay, time (PS).
LR:Gd55.
Sweet stay a while (PS).
LR:Gd28, Gd55.
Tell me true love (PS).
LR:Gd10.
Then sit thee down (B2).
LR:Gd7.
Think'st thou then (B1).
LR:Gd6.
SI:B1.
Time stands still (B3).
LR:Gd7, Gd29.
Time's eldest son (B2).
LR:Gd7, Gd21.
Toss not my soul (B2).
LR:Gd7.
Unquiet thoughts (B1).
LR:Gd6.
Weep you no more sad fountains (B3).
LR:Gd8, Gd9, Gd12, Gd24, Gd55.
What if I never speed (B3).
LR:Gd8, Gd9, Gd10, Gd36.
What poor astronomers are they (B3).
LR:Gd8.
When others sing Venite (B2).
LR:Gd7.
When Phoebus first did Daphne love (B3).
LR:Gd8, Gd10.
White as lilies was her face (B2).
LR:Gd7.
Whoever thinks or hopes (B1).
LR:Gd6.
Wilt thou unkind (B1).
LR:Gd6, Gd9, Gd18, Gd21, Gd26.
Woeful eyes (B2).
LR:Gd7.
Would my conceit (B1).
LR:Gd6.
e.Sacred Vocal – Sacred Songs and Lamentations
An heart that's broken.
LR:Ge12.
I shame at mine unworthiness.
LR:Ge12.
A Prayer for the Queen's most excellent Majesty.
LR:Ge12.
Sorrow, come.
LR:Ge12.
Thou mighty God.
LR:Gd12.
Mr. Henry Noell's Lamentations.
    Lord Consider my distress. Lord hear my prayer. Lord
    in thy wrath. Lord, turn not away. O Lord, on whom I
    do depend. Where righteousness doth say.
LR:Ge12.
Psalm XXXVIII: Put me not to rebuke, O Lord.

LR:Ge12.
Psalm C: All people that on earth do dwell.
LR:Ge12.
Psalm CIV: My soul doth praise the Lord.
LR:Ge12.
Psalm CXXX: Lord, to thee I make my moan.
LR:Ge12.
Psalm CXXXIV: Behold and have regard.
LR:Ge12.

DRAGHI, Giovanni Battista (b.c.1640)
    b.Instrumental
    Sonata a 3.
    EB:B65.
    c.Keyboard
    Ground 'Scocca pur.'
    LB:D217.
    Ground in C min.
    EB:D30.

DRAGONI, Giovanni (1540–1598)
    e.Sacred Vocal
    Missa 'Cantantibus Organis Caecilia': Kyrie. Qui tollis
        peccata mundi.
    LR:F95.

DUBEN, Andreas (c.1597–1662).
    c.Keyboard – Organ
    Preambulum.
    EB:E91.
    Preambulum in F maj.
    LB:E198.

DU FAULT, Francois (d.1670)
    b.Instrumental – Lute
    Pavane in E min.
    EB:C3.
    Sarabande and Gigue.
    LR:E44.
    Suite in A min.
    EB:C3.
    Suite in C maj.
    EB:C3.
    Suite in C min.
    EB:C3.
    Suite in G min.
    EB:C3, C6.

DUFAY, Guillaume (1400–1474)
    **d.Secular Vocal – Chansons and Instrumental
    Arrangements**
    Adieu ces bons vins de Lannoys.
    ER:A17.
    LR:A4.
    Adieu m'amour.
    AA:A2.
    AN:A3.
    ER:A15.
    L'Alta bellezza tua.
    ER:A11.
    La Belle se siet.
    ER:A12, A17.
    LR:A4.
    Belle, veullies moy retenir.
    ER:A16.
    Bien veignes vous.
    ER:A11.
    Bon jour, bon mois.
    ER:A11, A15, A17.
    LR:A4.
    Ce moys de May soyons lies et joyaux.
    AN:B4.
    ER:A12, A15.
    Ce jour de l'an.
    ER:A15.

C'est bien raison.
ER:A11.
Craindre vous vueil.
ER:A15.
La Dolce vista.
ER:A11.
Les Douleurs, dont me sens tel somme.
ER:A16.
Dona gentil, bella come l'oro.
ER:A16.
Dona i ardenti ray.
ER:A11.
Donnes l'assault.
ER:A12, A16.
LR:A4.
Franc cuer gentil.
AA:A2.
AN:A3.
ER:B19, B23.
LR:A4, B11.
Helas, et quant vous verray.
AN:B4.
Helas! mon dueill.
ER:A11, A12, A15.
J'attendray tant qu'il vous playra.
ER:A15.
J'ay mis mon cuer et ma pensee.
ER:A11, A16.
Je languis en piteus martire.
ER:A16.
Je me complains piteusement.
ER:A16, B15.
Je veuil chanter de cuer joyaux.
AN:B4.
Je vous pris.
ER:A11.
Mon chier amy.
ER:A11, A16.
Mon cuer me fait tous dispenser.
ER:A17.
LR:A4.
Navre je suis.
ER:A12, B15.
Par droit je puis.
ER:A12, A17.
LR:A4.
La Plus Mignonne de mon cuer.
ER:A16.
Pour l'amour de ma douce amye.
ER:A15, A17.
LR:A4.
Puisque vous estez campieur.
ER:A16.
Quel fronte signorille.
ER:A6, A15.
Resveillies vous et faites chiere lye.
ER:A16.
Se la face ay pale.
AA:A2.
AN:A3.
ER:A15, A17.
LR:A4.
Trop lonc temps ai reste en desplaisir.
ER:A16.
Vergine bella.
ER:A12, A15, A17.
LR:A3, A4, E63, F91.

e. Sacred Vocal – Latin Motets
Alma redemptoris mater.
ER:B22.
Anima mea liquefacta est.
ER:B15.
Audie benigne.
ER:B21.

Ave maris stella.
ER:B21.
Ave regina caelorum.
ER:B15, B23.
Ave virgo.
ER:A11, B22.
Benedicamus Domino.
ER:B40.
Christe redemptor omnium.
ER:A15.
Ecclesia militantis.
ER:A11, B15.
Gloria resurrexit Dominus.
ER:B15.
Lamentatio Sanctae Matris Ecclesiae Constantinopoli-
    tanae.
ER:A11, A12, A16.
Magnanimae.
ER:A15.
Magnas me gentes.
LR:A4.
Magnificat sexti toni.
ER:B21.
Mirandas parit haec urbs.
ER:A15.
Moribus et genere Christo coniuncte Johannes.
ER:A11.
Nuper rosarum flores.
ER:A14.
O gemma, lux et speculum.
ER:A15.
Qui latuit.
ER:A11.
Salve regina.
ER:B21.
Supremum est mortalibus.
ER:A14, B22.
Vasilissa, ergo gaude.
ER:B22.
Veni creator spiritus.
ER:A11.

**e. Sacred Vocal – Masses and Isolated Mass
Movements**
Missa 'Ave regina caelorum.'
ER:B10, B11.
Missa 'Caput.'
ER:B12, B13.
Missa 'Ecce ancilla Domini.'
ER:B11, B14, B15.
Missa 'L'Homme arme.'
ER:B16.
Missa 'L'Homme arme': Kyrie.
ER:A5.
Missa 'Sancti Jacobi.'
ER:B17.
Missa 'Se la face ay pale.'
ER:B18.
Missa 'Sine nomine.'
ER:B19, B20.
Credo.
ER:A11.
Gloria.
ER:A11.
Gloria ad modum tubae.
AA:A1.
ER:B21.
Kyrie.
ER:A11, B21.
Kyrie paschale 'lux et origo.'
ER:B21.
Sanctus.
ER:A11.
Sanctus papale.
ER:B21.

DUMAGE, Pierre (c.1676–1751)
  c.Keyboard – Organ
  Basse de trompette.
  LB:E160.
  Duo (Suite du 1re ton).
  LB:E151, E160.
  Fugue (Suite du 1re ton).
  LB:E151, E160.
  Grand jeu (Suite du 1re ton).
  LB:E151, E160, E197, E211.
  Plain jeu (Suite du 1re ton).
  LB:E151, E160, E197.
  Recit (Suite du 1re ton).
  LB:E151, E160.
  Recit de tierce en taille (Suite du 1re ton).
  LB:E160.
  Tierce en taille (Suite du 1re ton).
  LB:E197.
  Trio (Suite du 1re ton).
  LB:E151, E160.

DUMONT, Henri (1610–1684)
  b.Instrumental
  Sinfonia (Motets a deux voix...1668).
  EB:G35.
  Sinfonia V (Motets a deux, trois et quatre voix...1681).
  EB:G35.
  Sinfonia XXIII (Motets...1681).
  EB:G35.
  Sinfonia XXVIII (Motets...1681).
  EB:G35.
  c.Keyboard
  Allemande.
  EB:D37, G35.
  SI:C7.
  Allemande grave.
  EB:D37.
  Pavane in D min.
  EB:E76.
  LB:D232.
  SI:C2, C13.
  Prelude I (Meslanges, 1657).
  EB:G35.
  Prelude V (Meslanges, 1657).
  EB:G35.
  Prelude XII (Meslanges, 1657).
  EB:G35.
  e.Sacred Vocal
  Benedictus.
  EB:G34.
  Domine non secundum (Motets a deux voix, 1668).
  EB:G35.
  In lectulo meo (Motets a deux voix, 1668).
  EB:G35.
  Magnificat.
  EB:G34.
  Missa 'Royale': Credo. Sanctus. Ite, missa est.
  PS:A71.
  Nisi Dominus.
  EB:G34.
  O aeterne misericors Deus (Motets a deux voix, 1668).
  EB:G35.
  O fideles (Motets a deux voix, 1668).
  EB:G35.
  Panis angelicus (Motets a deux voix, 1668).
  EB:G35.
  Regina divina (Motets a deux, trois et quatre voix...1681).
  EB:G35.

DUNSTABLE, John (c.1380–1453)
  b.Instrumental
  Fantasia a 3 for viols.
  SI:C2, C13.
  Puzzle Canon III.
  LR:Gf6.

  d.Secular Vocal
  O rosa bella.
  ER:B23, B24.
  LR:A1, E64.
  e.Sacred Vocal
  Alma redemptoris mater.
  ER:B24.
  Ave maris stella.
  ER:B23, B24.
  Ave regina caelorum.
  LR:Gd36.
  Beata mater.
  ER:A11, B22.
  Credo a 4vv–Gloria a 4vv.
  ER:B3.
  Preco proheminencie.
  ER:B22.
  Quam pulchra es.
  ER:B6, B23.
  Salve scema sanctitatis – Salve salus servulorum – Cantant caeli agmina.
  ER:B3.
  Salve regina misericordie.
  ER:B22.
  Sancta Maria succurre miseris.
  ER:B24.
  Veni creator spiritus.
  ER:B24.
  Veni sancte spiritus.
  ER:B22, B23, B24.

DUPHLY, Jacques (1715–1789)
  c.Keyboard – Harpsichord
  Allemande (Book 1).
  LB:D111, D144.
  La Boucon (Book 1).
  LB:D111, D144.
  Chaconne (Book 3).
  LB:D111, D147.
  La De Drummond (Book 2).
  LB:D110.
  La De Vatre (Book 2).
  LB:D110.
  La Felix (Book 2).
  LB:D110, D147.
  La Forqueray (Book 3).
  LB:D110, D147, D231.
  La Lanza (Book 2).
  LB:D111.
  La Larare (Book 1).
  LB:D144.
  Legerement (Book 1).
  LB:D144.
  Medee (Book 3).
  LB:D110.
  Menuets (Book 1).
  LB:D144.
  Menuets in E min (Book 2).
  LR:D19.
  La Millettina (Book 1).
  LB:D110, D144.
  La Pothuin (Book 4).
  LB:D111.
  Rondeau (Book 1).
  LB:D110, D144.
  Suite in F maj (Book 3).
  LB:D148.
  La Victoire (Book 2).
  LB:D110.

DURANTE, Francesco (1684–1755)
  a.Orchestral
  Concerto Grosso No. 5 in A maj for strings and continuo.
  LB:A588.
  b.Instrumental

Gagliarda in A min.
LB:C31.
d. Secular Vocal
Alme, voi che provaste.
LB:F23.
Amor, Metilde e morta.
LB:F23.
Danza fanciulla gentile.
EB:F95.
Dormono l'aure estive.
LB:F23.
Fiero acerbo destin.
LB:F23.
Metilde alma mia.
LB:F23.
Metilde, mio tesoro.
LR:F23.
Qualor tento scoprire.
LB:F23.
Son io, Barbara donna.
LB:F23.

DURON, Sebastian (1660–1716)
c. Keyboard – Organ
Gaitilla de mano izquierda.
LR:D13.
EB:E79.
d. Secular Vocal
Salir el Amor del Mundo – Zarzuela: Sodieguen,
  Descausen.
EB:F97.

DUTERTRE, Etienne (16th. cent.)
b. Instrumental
Branle d'Ecosse.
LR:E43.
Pavane and Galliard.
LR:B12.

EAST, Michael (c.1580–c.1648)
d. Secular Vocal
Farewell sweet woods and mountains.
LR:Gd33.
Hence stars (Triumphs of Oriana).
LR:Gd34, Gd35.
No haste but good.
LR:Gd32.
Quick, quick, away!
LR:Gd32.
Sweet muses, nymphs and shepherds sporting.
LR:Gd33.
Thyrsis, sleepest thou?
LR:Gd33.

EBELING, Johann Georg (1637–1679)
e. Sacred Vocal
Die Güldne Sonne.
LR:F101.
EB:G132.
Du meine Seele.
LR:F101.
Warum sollt ich mich denn grämen.
LR:F101.

EBERLIN, Johann Ernst (1702–1762)
c. Keyboard – Organ
Toccata and fugue in A min.
LB:E239.
Toccata III (9 Toccate e Fughe, 1747).
EB:E56.
Toccata VI (9 Toccate e Fughe, 1747).
EB:E56.

EBREO DA PESARO, Guglielmo (d.c.1475)
b. Instrumental
Bassa danza a 2.

LR:B16.
Falla con misuras – Bassa castiglia.
AA:A2.
LR:A3, B29.
La Spagna – Basse danse.
LR:B29.

ECCARD, Johann (1553–1611)
e. Sacred Vocal
Ich lag in tiefer Todesnacht.
LR:F122.
Ich steh an deiner Krippen hier.
LR:F112, F113, F124.
O Freude über Freude.
LR:F107.
Ubers Gebirg.
LR:F107, F112, F118, F123.
Vom Himmel hoch.
LR:F104, F121.

ECCLES, Henry (1670–1742)
b. Instrumental
Sonata in F maj for recorder and continuo.
LB:B288.

ECCLES, John (1668–1735)
d. Secular Vocal
Hither turn thee gentle swain (The Judgement of Paris,
  1701).
SI:C2.
The Jolly breeze.
EB:F94.
Nature fram'd thee sure.
EB:F94.
O, the mighty power of love.
LR:Gd26.
Wise Nature.
EB:F94.

EDWARDS, Richard (1522–1566)
d. Secular Vocal
Where gryping griefs.
LR:A1, E24, Gd27, Gd45, Gd46, Gd51.

EGIDIUS VON RHENIS (15th. cent.)
d. Secular Vocal
Wie lieblich ist der Mai.
ER:A23.

ELEONORA LANYI MS (17th. cent. Hungarian)
b. Instrumental
Dances.
LR:A7.

ENCINA, Juan del (1468–1529)
d. Secular Vocal
A tal perdida tan triste.
LR:E31.
Ay triste que vengo.
LR:A3, A8.
Congoxa mas.
LR:E25, E66.
Cucu.
LR:E28.
Fata la parte.
ER:A4.
LR:A2, E28, E65.
Hoy comamos.
LR:B14.
Levanta Pascual.
LR:A8.
Mas vale trocar.
LR:E29, E66.
Mi libertad en sosiego.
LR:E27.
Pues que jamas.

LR:E66.
Qu'es de ti, desconsolado.
ER:A26.
LR:A8.
Romerico.
LR:E62.
Si abra en este baldres.
LR:A8, E25, E28.
Tan buen ganadico.
LR:E28.
Todos los bienes.
LR:E64.
Triste Espana.
ER:A14.
LR:A2, E26.

ENGELBURG MS (14th. cent. German)
  e. Sacred Vocal
  Ad regnum – Noster cetus.
  AA:C3.
  Congaudent turba (Benedicamus).
  AA:C3.
  Cum natus esset Jesus.
  AA:C3.
  Hodie progreditur.
  AA:C3.
  Unicornis captivator.
  AA:C3.

EPINAL – see GAUTIER D'EPINAL

EPISCOPIUS, L. (16th. cent.)
  d. Secular Vocal
  Laet varen alle fantasie.
  EB:B35.

ERBACH, Christian (1570–1635)
  c. Keyboard – Organ
  Canzon a 4 del 4o tono.
  EB:E81.
  Canzona noni toni.
  LR:D21.
  LB:E197.

ERFURT MS (14th. cent. German)
  e. Sacred Vocal
  Gloria in excelsis Deo.
  AA:C3.
  Hely, hely.
  AA:C3.

ERLEBACH, Philipp Heinrich (1657–1714)
  e. Sacred Vocal
  Siehe, ich verkündige euch grosse Freude.
  EB:G131.

ESCHENBACH – see WOLFRAM VON ESCHENBACH

ESCOBAR, Pedro de (d.1514)
  d. Secular Vocal
  Ora, sus, pues que ansi es!
  LR:E65.
  e. Sacred Vocal
  In Epiphaniae Domini.
  LR:F96.
  In Nativitate Domini.
  LR:F96.
  Las mis penas, madre.
  LR:E27, E31.
  Sumens illud.
  LR:E26.
  Virgen bendita sin par.
  LR:E26.

ESCURIEL, Jehan de L' (= LESCURIEL) (d.1304)
  d. Secular Vocal

Amours, cent mille merciz.
AA:D19.

ESQUIRI – see JEHAN D'ESQUIRI.

ESQUIVEL DE BARAHONA, Juan (c.1565–c.1613)
  e. Sacred Vocal
  Veni Domine, et noli tardare.
  LR:F89.

ESTERHAZY, Pal (1635–1713)
  e. Sacred Vocal
  Harmonia Caelestis, 1711.
    1. Sol recedit igneus. 2. Laetare cor meum. 3. Puer
    natus in Bethlehem. 4. Nil canitur iucundius. 5.
    Dulcis Jesu, quid hoc rei. 6. Jesu care, matris nate. 7.
    Jesu dulcede cordium. 8. Jesu, parve, recens nate.
    9. Quando cor nostrum visites. 10. Nolite timere
    incolae. 11. O quam dulcis es mi Jesu. 12. Jesu
    praesentia. 13. Infinitae, infinitae. 14. Jesu rector
    admirabilis. 15. O Jesu delectabilis. 16. Dormis Jesu
    dulcissime. 17. O suavissime. 18. Jesum ardentibus.
    19. Cur fles Jesu. 20. O Jesu admirabilis. 21. Jesu
    cur sic pateris. 22. Jesus hortum ingreditur. 23. Jesu
    te sequar fletibus. 24. Surrexit Christus hodie. 25.
    Ascendit Deus in jubilo. 26. Veni Sancte spiritus. 27.
    Veni, veni O sancte spiritus. 28. Pange lingua
    gloriosi. 29. Veni creator spiritus. 30. O nitida stella
    Maria. 31. O quam pulchra es Maria. 32. Ave maris
    stella. 33. Salve O Maria, tu gratia plena. 34. Maria
    fons aquae vivae. 35. Ave rosa sine spina. 36. O
    Maria, mater pia. 37. Dic beatae virgini. 38. Ave, ave
    dulcis. 39. Tota dulcis es Maria. 40. Amoris
    flammula. 41. Triumphate, triumphate. 42. Lingua
    dic trophaea. 43. O Maria gratiosa. 44. O quem
    gustum sentio. 45. Maria, quid sentio. 46. Ubi, ubi
    commeraris. 47. Saule, Saule. 48. Sancte Dei
    triumphate. 49. O mors.
  EB:G36.
  Ave Maris stella (Harmonia Caelestis).
  LR:A5.
  Jesu dulcedo (Harmonia Caelestis).
  LR:A5.
  Sol recedit (Harmonia Caelestis).
  LR:A5.

ETIENNE DE MEAUX (13th. cent.)
  d. Secular Vocal
  Le jolies temps d'estey.
  AA:D21.
  Trop est mes maris jalos.
  AA:D21.

EWALDT (17th. cent.)
  c. Keyboard – Organ
  Allein zu dir, Jesu Christ (Pelpin Tablature).
  EB:E35.

EYCK – see VAN EYCK, Jakob.

FABER, Johann Christoph (fl.1730)
  b. Chamber and Instrumental
  Parties sur les flutes dous a 3 for alto, tenor and bass
    recorders.
  LB:B284.

FABRICIUS, Petrus (1587–1651)
  b. Instrumental – Lute
  Chorea Polonica.
  EB:B66.
  Der Elmoyer Tanz.
  LR:C9.
  Es ist ein Bauer in Brunnen gefallen.
  LR:C9.
  Gut Gesell und du musst wandern.
  LR:C9.
  Polnischer Tanz.

LR:C9.
Studentenlob.
LR:C9.
Studententanz.
LR:C9.

FACOLI, Marco (16th. cent.)
  b. Instrumental
  Aria della Comedia Nuovo.
  LR:D14.
  Hor ch'io son gionto quivi.
  LR:D14.
  Padoana terza dita la Finetta.
  LR:D14.
  S'io m'accorgo ben mio.
  LR:D14.

FAIDIT, Gaucelem (1170–1230)
  d. Secular Vocal
  Fortz chausa es.
  AA:D5, D9, D12, D22.
  Vos quem semblaitz.
  AA:D1.

FAIGNIENT, Nicolaus (16th. cent.)
  d. Secular Vocal
  De segheninghe.
  EB:B35.

FALCKENHAGEN, Adam (1697–1761)
  b. Instrumental – Lute
  Duetto.
  EB:C8.
  Suite No. 1 in C min.
  LB:C15.
  Suite No. 5 in F maj.
  LB:C15.

FALCONIERI, Andrea (1586–1656)
  d. Secular Vocal
  Vezzosette e care pupillette.
  SI:C3.

FALLAMERO, Gabriele (16th. cent.)
  d. Secular Vocal
  Vorria madonna.
  LR:F94.

FANTINI, Girolamo (1602–1645)
  b. Instrumental
  Brando in B flat maj for trumpets and thoroughbass.
  EB:B67.
  Capriccio IX in B flat maj.
  EB:B67.
  Capriccio X in F maj.
  EB:B67.
  Sonata in B flat maj for 2 trumpets.
  EB:B67.
  Sonata a due tromba detta 'La Guicciardini.'
  EB:B47.
  Sonata I detta del 'Colloreto' for trumpet and continuo.
  EB:B59.
  LB:B214.
  Sonata II detta del 'Gonzaga' for trumpet and continuo.
  EB:B59.
  LB:B214.
  Sonata III detta del 'Niccolini' for trumpet and continuo.
  EB:B59.
  Sonata V detta del 'Aldimari' for trumpet and continuo.
  EB:B59.
  Sonata VI detta del 'Morone' for trumpet and continuo.
  EB:B59.
  Sonata VII in C maj for trumpet and continuo.
  LB:B214.
  Sonata VIII detta del 'Nero' for trumpet and continuo.
  EB:B59.

  c. Keyboard – Organ
  L'Imperiale.
  LR:F90.

FARINA, Carlo (c.1600–1640)
  b. Instrumental
  Capriccio Stravagante a 4. 'Kurtzweilig Quodlibet.'
  EB:B50.
  LB:B317.
  Pavane.
  EB:A31, B41.
  Sonata detta La Polacca for 2 violins and continuo (Libro
    primo delle Pavane...1626).
  EB:B52.
  Sonata III detta la Moretta for 2 violins and continuo
    (Libro primo delle Pavane...1626).
  EB:B43.

FARKAS, Andras (16th. cent.)
  d. Secular Vocal
  As the Lord God (Verse Chronicle, 1538).
  LR:E49.
  Come, let us remember (Hofgreff Songbook, 1552–3).
  LR:A5.

FARMER, John (1565–1605)
  d. Secular Vocal
  A little pretty bonny lass.
  LR:E60, Gd50.
  Fair Nymphs, I heard one telling (Triumphs of Oriana).
  LR:Gd20, Gd34, Gd35.
  Fair Phyllis I saw sitting all alone.
  LR:E46, Gd25, Gd32.
  O stay, sweet love.
  LR:Gd33.

FARNABY, Giles (1565–1640)
  c. Keyboard
  Fantasia (Unsp.)
  LR:D20, Gc12.
  EB:D34.
  Fantasia X.
  LR:Gc4.
  EB:D39.
  Fantasia XXVII.
  LR:Gc4.
  EB:D39.
  Farmer's Pavan.
  LR:Gc4.
  EB:D39.
  The Flatt Pavan.
  LR:Gc4.
  EB:D39.
  Galiarda.
  LR:Gc6.
  His Conceit.
  LR:Gc6.
  His Dream.
  LR:Ga11, Gc6.
  His Humour.
  LR:Gc6.
  His Rest.
  LR:Ga11, Gc6.
  His Toye.
  LR:Ga6, Gd39.
  Lachrymae Pavan.
  LR:Gc4, Gc16.
  EB:D39.
  Lord Souch's Masque.
  LR:Gc6.
  Loth to depart.
  LR:Gc6, Gc9.
  EB:D24, D36.
  Mal Simms.
  LR:Gc4.

EB:D39.
A Masque.
LR:Ga9, Gc11.
Meridian Alman.
LR:Gc4, Gc6.
EB:D39.
Muscadin.
LR:Gc4, Gc6, Gc9.
EB:D39.
The New Sa-hoo.
LR:Ga11, Gc6, Gc13.
Nobody's Gigge.
LR:Gc8.
The Old Spagnoletta.
LR:Ga11, Gc4 Gc6.
EB:B40, D39.
LB:D220.
SI:A2, B2.
Pawle's Wharfe.
LR:D20, Gc12.
EB:B37.
Praeludium.
LR:Gc4.
EB:D39.
Quodling's Delight.
LR:D20, Gc12.
Rosasolis.
LR:Gc4, Gc6, Gc7.
EB:D37, D39.
Spagnioletta.
LR:Gc6.
Tell me, Daphne.
LR:Ga11, Gc4, Gc6.
EB:D39, E66.
Tower Hill.
LR:D20, Gc4, Gc6, Gc12, Gd39.
EB:B37, D39.
A Toye.
LR:Ga11, Gc4, Gc13.
EB:D24.
Up tails all.
LR:D20, Gc4, Gc12.
EB:D39.
Why aske you?
LR:Gc4, Gc10.
EB:D39.
Woody-cock.
LB:D233.
d. Secular Vocal
Pearce did dance with Petronel.
LR:Gd33.
Pearce did love fair Petronel.
LR:Gd33.
Construe my meaning.
LR:Gd20, Gd32.

FARRANT, Richard (d.1581)
  b. Instrumental
Four-note Pavan.
LR:Ga10.
  e. Sacred Vocal
Hide not thy face.
LR:Ge31.
Lord, for thy tender mercy's sake.
LR:Ge35.

FARTHING, Thomas (c.1475–1520)
  d. Secular Vocal
Hey, now, now.
LR:Gf1.

FASCH, Johann Friedrich (1688–1758)
  a. Orchestral
Concerto in C maj for bassoon, strings and continuo.
LB:B270.

Concerto in D maj for trumpet, 2 oboes and strings.
LB:A232, A594, A647, A660, A663, A664, A665.
Concerto in D min for guitar and strings.
LB:A231.
Sinfonia in A maj for strings and continuo.
LB:A232.
  b. Chamber and Instrumental
Sonata in B flat maj for recorder, oboe, violin and continuo.
LB:B295.
Sonata in G maj for 2 recorders and continuo.
LB:B296.

FAULT – *see* DU FAULT, Francois.

FAWKYNER (15th./16th. cent.)
  e. Sacred Vocal
Gaude rosa.
ER:B2.

FAYRFAX, Robert (1465–1521)
  d. Secular Vocal
Benedicite, what dreamed I?
LR:Gf3, Gf5.
I love, unloved.
LR:A1, E24, Gf3.
Most clear of colour.
LR:Gf3.
Somewhat musing.
LR:Gf1, Gf3.
That was my woe.
LR:A1, Gf3.
  e. Sacred Vocal
Magnificat 'O bone Jesu.'
LR:Gf5.

FEGEUX – *see* LE FEGEUX, Francois.

FELSZTYNA, Sebastian z. (c.1480–1544)
  e. Sacred Vocal
Alleluia ave Maria.
LR:F92.
Alleluia, felix es sacra virgo Maria.
LR:E37, F92.

FERNANDEZ DE HUETE, Diego (17th./18th. cent.)
  b. Instrumental
La Tarantella.
EB:B63.

FERRABOSCO, Alfonso I (1543–1588)
  b. Instrumental – Lute
Spanish Pavan.
LR:C24.

FERRABOSCO, Alfonso II (c.1575–1628)
  b. Instrumental
Almain (Misc.)
LR:Ga1, Ga19, Gd37.
EB:B39.
Coranto (Misc.)
LR:Ga1, Ga19.
Dovehouse Pavan.
LR:Gd37, Gd40.
EB:B39.
Fantasy in F maj.
LR:Gd37, Gd44.
Fantasias I and II.
LR:Ga13.
Four-Note Pavan.
LR:Ga10, Ga17, Ga21.
EB:A31.
LB:A606.
Galliard.
LR:Ga1, Ga19.
Pavan (Unsp.)

LR:C11, C16, Gd19.
LB:B294.
SI:C15.
d. Secular Vocal
Come my Celia.
LR:Gd28.
If all these cupids.
LR:Gd28.
It was no policy.
LR:Gd28.
So beauty on the waters.
LR:Gd28.
Yes were the loves.
LR:Gd28.

FERRABOSCO, Matthia (1550–1616)
    d. Secular Vocal
Che giovarebbe.
LR:F94.
Se si spezzasse.
LR:F94.

FERRAGUTI, Beltrame (15th. cent.)
    d. Secular Vocal
Excelsa civitas vincentia.
ER:A14.

FESCH – see DE FESCH, Willem

FESTA, Sebastiano (1490–1545)
    d. Secular Vocal
Quando ritrova.
LR:E25, E56.
L'Ultimo di mi Maggio.
LR:Gd25.

FEVIN, Antoine de (c.1474–1512)
    d. Secular Vocal
Faulte d'argent.
ER:A4.

FEVRE – see LE FEVRE, Jacques

FIGUIERA, Ghilhelm (13th. cent.)
    d. Secular Vocal
D'un sirventes far.
AA:D11.

FINCK, Heinrich (1445–1527)
    b. Instrumental
Tanz.
LR:E68.
    d. Secular Vocal
Ach herzigs Herz.
LR:E68.
Greiner zanner.
LR:E67.
Ich stuend an einem morgen.
LR:E67.
Ich werd erlöst.
LR:E67.
Der Ludel und der Hensel.
LR:E67.
O schönes Weib.
LR:A6, E67.
Sauff aus und machs nit lang.
LR:E35, E68, E69.
    e. Sacred Vocal
Missa 'Dominicalis.'
ER:B45.
Veni sancte spiritus – Veni creator spiritus.
LR:E37.

FINGER, Godfrey (1656–1723)
    b. Instrumental
Divisions on a ground for recorder and continuo.
LB:B297.

Sonata in G min for recorder and continuo. Op. 3. No. 4.
SI:C19.
Sonata No. 3 in A maj for viol and harpsichord.
SI:C12.
Sonata No. 4 in D min for viol and harpsichord.
SI:C10.
Sonata No. 5 in A maj for viol and harpsichord.
SI:C21.
Suite in A maj for violetta, viol and harpsichord.
SI:C14, C16.
    c. Keyboard – Harpsichord
Sonata No. 2 in F maj for harpsichord.
SI:C16.
    d. Secular Vocal
Calms appear when storms are past (Venus's Song in
    'The Pilgrim.')
SI:C17.

FIOCCO, Joseph Hector (1703–1741)
    c. Keyboard – Harpsichord
Suite No. 1.
LB:D149(Excpt.), D150.
Suite No. 2.
LB:D149(Excpt.), D151.
Adagio (Suite No. 1.).
LB:D149.
Allegro (Suite No. 1).
LB:D149.
Allemande (Suite No. 2).
LB:D149.
Andante (Suite No. 1).
LB:D149.
L'Angloise. (Suite No. 1).
LB:D115.
La Franchoise (Suite No. 1).
LB:D149.
La Fringante (Suite No. 2).
LB:D149.
Gavotte I and II (Suite No. 2).
LB:D149.
Gigue (Suite No. 2).
LB:D149.
L'Inconstante (Suite No. 1).
LB:D115, D149.
L'Inquiet (Suite No. 2).
LB:D149.
L'Italiene (Suite No. 1).
LB:D115, D149.
La Legere (Suite No. 2).
LB:D149.
Minuet I and II (Suite No. 2).
LB:D149.
La Musette (Suite No. 2).
LB:D149.
La Plaintive (Suite No. 2).
LB:D115, D149.
Les Promenades (Suite No. 2).
LB:D115.
Sarabande (Suite No. 2).
LB:D149.
La Villageoise (Suite No. 2).
LB:D115, D149.
Vivace (Suite No. 1).
LB:D149.
    c. Keyboard – Organ
Andante.
EB:E88.
LB:B212.
Gavotte.
EB:E78, E88.
    e. Sacred Vocal
Jubilate Deo – Cantatá.
LB:G188, G197.
Missa Solemnis in D maj.
LB:G197.

FIORENZA, Nicola (1659–1722)
a. Orchestral
Concerto in D maj for flute, strings and harpsichord.
LB:A637.
Siciliana in C min for strings and harpsichord.
LB:A637.

FIORINO, Gasparo (16th. cent.)
d. Secular Vocal
Se tua belta infinitia.
LR:E53.

FIRENZE – see GIOVANNI DA FIRENZE

FIRENZE – see LORENZO DA FIRENZE

FISCHER, Johann (1646–1716)
b. Instrumental
Bourree.
LB:B323.
Gigue.
LB:B323.

FISCHER, Johann Caspar Ferdinand (1650–1746)
a. Orchestral
Suite No. 6 in F maj for strings (Journal de Printemps).
LB:A615.
c. Keyboard – Harpsichord and Organ
Chaconne in F maj.
EB:D36.
Euterpe (Musikalischer Parnassus).
LB:D152.
Final (Musikalischer Blumenstrauss).
LB:E197.
Fuga III (Musikalischer Blumenstrauss).
LB:E197.
Fuga VI (Musikalischer Blumenstrauss).
LB:E197.
Praeludium (Musikalischer Blumenstrauss).
LB:E197.
Praeludium VI (Musikalischer Blumenstrauss).
LB:D152.
Praeludium and fugue in B min.
EB:E56.
Praeludium and fugue in C maj.
EB:E92.
Praeludium and fugue in C min.
EB:E56.
Praeludium and fugue in D maj.
EB:E56.
Praeludium and fugue in E flat maj.
EB:E56.
4 Ricercares for Advent, Quadragesima, Easter and
Pentecost.
EB:E75.
Suite VI in D maj (Musikalischer Blumenbüschlein).
EB:D32.
LB:D222.
Suite VIII (Musikalischer Blumenbüschlein).
LB:D152.
Suite IX in D min (Musikalischer Blumenbüschlein):
Passacaglia.
LB:D225.
Uranie (Musikalischer Parnassus).
LB:D152.

FLECHA, Matteu 'The Elder' (1481–1553)
d. Secular Vocal
La Bomba.
LR:E65.
Le Gerizona – Baille Cantado.
LR:E30.
La Guerra – Ensalada: Instrumental Excpt.
AN:B15.
LR:B24.
La Justa – Ensalada.

LR:E3.
La Justa – Ensalada: Instrumental Excpt.
LR:B24.
La Negrina – Ensalada.
LR:E3.
N'eulalia vol gonella.
AN:B15.
Riu, riu, chiu.
LR:E23.
Teresica hermana.
LR:E23.
Vella, de vos aom amoros.
LR:E3.
Verbum caro.
LR:E23.

FLOR, Christian (1626–1697)
c. Keyboard – Organ
Preludes I and II.
EB:E91.

**FLORENCE MS (12th./13th. cent. French – Notre Dame
School).**
e. Sacred Vocal
Ave virgo virginem.
AA:B2.
Benedicamus Domino.
AA:A2, A3, B2.
ER:B19.
LR:B11.
Cum animadverterem.
AA:B8.
Flos in monte cernitur.
AA:B8.
Judea et Jerusalem.
AA:B2, B5.
Novus miles sequitur.
AA:B8.
ER:B1.
Veris ad imperia.
AA:B8, D3, D5, D19.
Vetus abit littera.
AA:B2.

FLORENTIA – see GHERARDELLO DE FLORENTIA

FO, Jacopo (15th./16th. cent.)
d. Secular Vocal
Tua volsi esser sempre mai.
LR:A3, E25.

FOGLIANO, Giacomo (c.1473–1548)
d. Secular Vocal
L'Amor donna.
ER:A4.
LR:A2.
c. Keyboard
Ricercare II and III.
LR:D18.

FOLQUET DE MARSELHA (1150–1230)
d. Secular Vocal
Sitot me soi.
AA:D2.
Vida.
AA:D2.

FONTAINE, Pierre (1380–1450)
b. Instrumental
La Fille Guillemin.
LR:B11, B13.
J'ayme bien celui.
LR:A4.
Sans faire – Basse danse.
LR:B11, B13.
La Spagna – Basse danse.
LR:B11, B13.

FONTANA, Giovanni Battista (d.c.1631)
 b.Instrumental
 Sonata I for recorder and continuo.
 EB:B42, B68.
 Sonata II for recorder and continuo.
 EB:B56.
 Sonata XV for recorder and continuo.
 EB:B45.
 Sonata a 3 violins and continuo (Sonate a 1, 2, 3...1641)
 EB:B52.
 Sonata for violin and continuo (Unsp.)
 LR:A1.

FONTANA, Vincenzo (fl.1550)
 d.Secular Vocal
 Madonna mia pieta.
 LR:E36.

FORBES, John (17th. cent.)
 d.Secular Vocal
 When cannons are roaring ('Cantus, Songs and Fancies',
  1666).
 LR:Gd47.

FORD, Thomas (1580–1648)
 b.Instrumental
 Forget-me-not, for 2 lyra viols.
 AA:A1.
 The Pill to purge melancholy.
 SI:B2, C20.
 d.Secular Vocal
 Fair, sweet, cruel.
 LR:Gd55.
 e.Sacred Vocal
 Almighty God.
 LR:Gd18, Gd54.

FOREST, John (d.c.1446)
 e.Sacred Vocal
 Qualis est dilectus.
 ER:B6.

FORQUERAY, Antoine (1671–1745)
 b.Chamber and Instrumental
 Suite No. 1 in D min for viol and continuo.
 LB:B128.
 Suite No. 2 in G maj for viol and continuo.
 LB:B128.
 Suite No. 3 in D maj for viol and continuo.
 LB:B127.
 Suite No. 5 in C min for viol and continuo.
 EB:B9
 c.Keyboard – Harpsichord
 La Bellemont.
 LB:D147.
 La Couperin.
 LB:D147.
 La Laborde.
 LB:D147.

FORSTER, Christoph (1693–1745)
 b.Chamber and Instrumental
 Concerto in E flat maj for horn and organ.
 LB:B220.

FORSTER, Georg (1510–1568)
 d.Secular Vocal
 Herzliebster Wein.
 LR:B30.
 Vitrum nostrum gloriosum.
 LR:A1, E24.
 e.Sacred Vocal
 Vom Himmel hoch.
 LR:F103, F118.

FORSTER, John (?) (17th./18th. cent.)
 b.Instrumental

March and Gigue.
 LB:B277.

FORSTER (?) (18th. cent.)
 b.Chamber and Instrumental
 Sonata in C min for oboe and continuo.
 LB:B228.

FRANCESCHINI, Petronio (c.1650–1680)
 a.Orchestral
 Sonata a 7 in D maj for 2 trumpets and strings.
 LB:A666.

FRANCISCUS – *see* **ANDRIEU, Francescus.**

FRANCISQUE, Antoine (1570–1605)
 c.Keyboard
 Branles de Montirande.
 LR:D16.

FRANCK, Melchior (1573–1639)
 b.Instrumental
 Galliarda a 5.
 EB:B46.
 Intrada.
 EB:B38, G132.
 Intrada in G maj.
 LR:F108.
 Partita a 6 in A min.
 EB:B67.
 Partita a 5 in A min.
 EB:B55, B67.
 Pavana a 5.
 EB:B46.
 Pavane and Galliard.
 LR:B10, B17, B18.
 e.Sacred Vocal
 Jesu, du zartes Kindelein.
 LR:F118.

FRAUENLOB – *see* **HEINRICH VON MEISSEN**

FREDERICK THE GREAT (1712–1786)
 a.Orchestral
 Concerto No. 4 in D maj for flute and strings.
 LB:A233.
 Sinfonia in D maj for 2 flutes, 2 oboes, 2 horns, strings
  and continuo.
 LB:A628, A629.
 b.Chamber and Instrumental
 Sonata in B min for flute and continuo.
 SI:A1.
 Sonata in D min for flute and continuo.
 LB:A44.
 Sonata No. 7 in E min for flute and continuo.
 LB:A233, B239.
 Sonata No. 11 in D min for flute and continuo.
 LB:B238.

FREILLON-PONCEIN, Jean-Pierre (18th. cent.)
 b.Instrumental
 Les Embarass de Paris.
 LB:B272.
 Prelude for solo flute.
 LB:B272.

FREITHOFF, Johann Henrik (1713–1767)
 b.Chamber and Instrumental
 Sonata in A maj for 2 flutes and continuo.
 LB:B311.
 Sonata in E maj for violin and continuo.
 LB:B311.

FRESCOBALDI, Girolamo (1583–1643)
 b.Instrumental – Libro delle Canzoni per canto solo, 1620
 3 Canzonas.
 LB:B202.

b. Instrumental – Libro delle Canzoni I, 1628.
Canzon per due bassi.
EB:B57.
Canzon per canto e due bassi.
EB:B57.
2 Canzoni per canto solo.
EB:B57.
Canzona per canto solo.
EB:B58, G56.
Canzon per due canti.
EB:B57.
Canzona per spinettina sola 'La Vittoria.'
EB:B58.
Canzona I a 4 detta la Bonuisia (sopra Ruggieri).
EB:B6, B44, B61.
Canzona II detta La Bernardinia (sopra La Romanesca).
EB:B6, B45, B58, B61.
LB:B260, B283, C31.
Canzona III detta La Lucchesina.
EB:B6, B61.
Canzona IV a 4.
LR:D15.
EB:B6, B45, E36.
Canzona V a 4.
EB:B6.
Canzona VI a 4.
EB:B6, D7.
Canzona VIII detta L'Ambitiosa.
EB:B53.
Canzona XIX detta La Capriola.
EB:B58, B61.
Canzona XX detta La Liparella.
EB:B61.
Canzona XXI detta La Tegrimuccia.
EB:B61.
Canzona XXII detta La Nicolina.
EB:B61.
Canzona XXXV detta L'Allessandra.
EB:B6.
Canzona XXXVI detta La Capponcina.
EB:B6.
Canzona XXXVII detta La Sardina.
EB:B6.'
Canzona detta L'Altera.
EB:B58.
Canzona detta La Arnulfina.
EB:B44.
Canzona detta La Nobile.
EB:B44.
b. Instrumental – Libro delle Canzoni II, 1628
Toccata per spinetto e violino.
EB:B57, B58.
b. Instrumental – Canzone da Sonare, 1634
5 Canzoni da Sonare a due canti con basso continuo.
EB:B12.
Canzone per due canti.
AA:A1.
Canzona IV per basso solo.
AA:A1.
b. Instrumental – Diletto Musicale
Canzona III for recorder and continuo.
LB:B297.
Canzona V for recorder and continuo.
LB:B297.
c. Keyboard – Recercari e Canzoni, 1615
Ricercar I.
SI:C8.
Ricercar X sopra La fa sol la re.
SI:C8, C13.
c. Keyboard – Primo Libro di Capricci, 1624
Capriccio sopra Ut re mi fa sol la.
EB:D7, E37.
Capriccio sopra La sol fa mi re ut.
EB:D7.

Capriccio sopra La sol fa re mi.
EB:D7.
Capriccio sopra La Bassa Fiamenga.
EB:D7, D9.
Capriccio sopra l'aria 'Or che noi rimena.'
EB:D7, D8.
Capriccio di durezze.
EB:D7, D8.
Capriccio sopra un soggetto.
EB:B47, D7.
Capriccio sopra l'aria di Ruggiero.
EB:D7.
Capriccio sopra il Cuchu.
EB:D7, E66.
Capriccio sopra la Spagnoletta.
EB:D7.
Capriccio cromatico con ligature al contrario.
EB:D7, D8.
Capriccio obligo di cantare la quinta parte.
EB:D7.
c. Keyboard – Fiori Musicali, 1635. (*See also* e. Sacred Vocal)
Bergamasca.
EB:E37, E63, E93, G38.
LB:E212.
Capriccio sopra La Girometta.
EB:E37, G38.
Toccata avanti il Ricercare.
EB:E90.
Toccata avanti il Ricercare e Ricercare cromatico doppo il Credo.
EB:E36.
Toccata cromatica per l'Elevazione.
EB:E36, E93.
Canzona doppo l'Epistola (Messa della Domenica).
EB:B53.
Ricercare doppo il Credo (Messa della Domenica).
EB:E36.
Toccata avanti la Messa della Domenica.
EB:E63.
Toccata avanti la Messa della Domenica e tre Kyrie.
EB:E36.
Toccata per l'Elevazione (Messa della Madonna).
EB:E36, E37.
c. Keyboard – Libro di Toccate, Canzoni...II, 1637
Canzona II.
EB:D8.
c. Keyboard – Toccate d'intavolatura...I, 1637
Canto Partite sopra Passacagli.
EB:D9.
Partita XIV sopra l'aria della Romanesca.
EB:D8, D9.
Toccata I.
EB:D8.
Toccata VIII.
LR:Gd41.
Toccata IX.
EB:D8, D9, D34.
Toccata X.
LR:D15.
EB:D9.
Toccata XII.
EB:D8.
c. Keyboard – Toccate d'intavolatura...II, 1637
Canzona III.
EB:D9.
Canzona IV.
EB:E37.
Canzona VI.
EB:E37.
Toccata I.
EB:D8, D38, E36.
Toccata II.
EB:E36, F100.

Toccata III da sonarsi alla levatione.
EB:D7, E37, F100.
Toccata IV da sonarsi alla levatione.
LR:D15.
EB:B44, E37, E70.
LB:D81.
Toccata V.
EB:E36, E37.
Toccata VI.
EB:E37.
Toccata VII.
EB:E36.
Toccata VIII di durezza e ligature.
EB:E36, B44.
Toccata IX.
EB:D9, D38.
Toccata X.
LB:D213.
c. Keyboard – Miscellany
Ancidetemi pur d'Archadelt passagiato.
EB:D8.
Aria detta la Frescobalda.
EB:F100.
Ave maris stella – Hymn.
EB:E82.
Balletto III.
EB:D8, D37.
Balletto e Corrente.
LR:B10.
Canzona.
EB:E70, E91.
Capriccio Pastorale.
EB:E36.
LB:E182.
SI:C16.
Corrente I.
LR:B10.
Corrente II.
LR:B10.
Corrente III.
LR:B10.
Corrente IV.
LR:B10.
Gagliarda III.
EB:E36.
Iste confessor – Hymn.
LR:D15.
Partita sopra l'aria di Folia.
LB:D81.
Partita sopra l'aria di Ruggiero.
EB:D29.
LB:D213.
Preambulum.
EB:E91.
Recercare.
EB:E89.
Ricercare con l'obligo di cantare la quinta pars.
EB:E90.
Toccata (Unsp.)
LR:A1.
EB:D35, E91.
Toccata V (Turin MS).
LR:D15.
d. Secular Vocal
Cosi mi disprezzate – Aria di Passacaglia.
LR:Gd41.
EB:F99.
Dunque dovro – Aria di Romanesca.
EB:F99.
Intro nave dorata.
LR:Gd41.
Se l'aura spina.
LR:Gd42.
EB:F96, F99.

Ti lascio, anima mea – Aria di Ruggiero.
EB:F99.
e. Sacred Vocal – Sonnetti Spirituali, 1630
Dove sparir o ratto idi serani?
EB:G137.
Maddalena alla croce.
EB:G137.
Ohime, che fur, che sono?
EB:G137.
e. Sacred Vocal – Fiori Musicali, 1635
Messa della Apostoli.
EB:G38.
Messa della Domenica.
EB:G37.
Messa della Madonna.
EB:G37.
Messa a 8 sopra l'aria della Monicha.
EB:G39.

FREUNDT, Cornelius (c.1535–1591)
e. Sacred Vocal
Wie schön singt uns.
LR:F107, F121.

FRIDERICI, Daniel (1584–1638)
e. Sacred Vocal
Ein Kind ist uns geborn.
LR:F106.

FROBERGER, Johann Jacob (1616–1667)
c. Keyboard – Harpsichord and Organ
Canzona in F maj.
EB:E92.
Canzona IV.
EB:D12.
Capriccio in G maj.
EB:E92.
Capriccio VI.
EB:E95.
Capriccio VIII.
EB:D12, E56, E95.
Capriccio XIII.
EB:D12.
Capriccio XVI.
EB:E95.
Fantasia.
EB:E95.
Fantasia in G maj.
LB:E197.
Fantasia I.
EB:D12.
Fantasia II in E min.
EB:D11, D12.
Fantasia V.
EB:D12.
Lamentation on the Death of Ferdinand III.
EB:D10, D11.
Ricercare.
EB:E81.
Ricercare in E min.
EB:E63.
LB:E197.
Ricercare in G min.
EB:E92.
Ricercare I.
EB:E56.
Ricercare II.
LR:D19.
Ricercare VI.
EB:D12, E95.
Ricercare XI.
EB:D12.
Sarabande.
EB:D35.
Suite in D maj.

LB:D227.
Suite in F maj.
EB:D36.
Suite I in A min.
EB:D10, D11.
Suite II in A maj.
EB:D10.
Suite III in G min.
EB:D10.
Suite IV in A min.
EB:D10.
Suite V in D maj.
EB:D10.
Suite VI in C maj.
EB:D10.
Suite XII in C maj.
EB:D13.
Suite XV in A min.
EB:D11.
SI:C14.
Suite XVIII in G min.
EB:D13.
Suite XIX in C maj.
EB:D34.
Suite XX in D maj.
EB:D11.
Toccata.
EB:E70, E80.
Toccata capriccio.
EB:E94.
Toccata II.
EB:D12.
Toccata III in G maj.
EB:D11.
Toccata VII.
EB:D12.
Toccata VIII.
EB:D12.
Toccata IX.
EB:D12.
Toccata X in F maj.
EB:D11.
Toccata XII in A min.
EB:D11.
Toccata XXIII.
EB:D13.
Tombeau sur la Mort de M. de Blancheroche.
EB:D13, D37.

FRYE, Walter (d.1475)
   b. Instrumental
   Tout a par moy.
   LR:C24.
   e. Sacred Vocal
   Ave regina caelorum.
   ER:B23.
   LR:A6.

FUENLLANA, Miguel de (1500–1579)
   b. Instrumental – Lute and Vihuela
   Contrapunto sobre el tiple deste villancico de Fuenllana.
   LR:C15.
   Duo.
   LR:C5.
   Duo Contrapunto.
   LR:C5.
   Duo sobre un tema de Morales.
   LR:C5.
   2 Fantasias.
   LR:E61.
   Fantasia de 8o tono.
   LR:C5.
   Fantasia de redobles galanos.
   LR:C5.
   Fantasia para vihuela de 5 ordenes.

LR:C5.
Pleni de la 'Missa de Hercules' (after Josquin).
LR:C15.
Si amores me han de matar (after Flecha).
LR:C15.
Tiento de 8o tono.
LR:C5.
Tiento de 2o tono.
LR:C5.
Tiento de 6o tono.
LR:C5.
4 Tientos.
LR:E27.
   d. Secular Vocal
   De los alamos vengo.
   LR:E51.
   Perdida de Antequera.
   LR:E62.
   Vos me matastes. (after Vasquez).
   LR:E61, E62.

FUHRMANN, Georg Leopold (16th. cent.)
   b. Instrumental
   Intrada Hassleri.
   LR:E54.

FUX, Johann Josef (1660–1741)
   a. Orchestral
   Constanza e Fortessa – Opera, 1723: Orchestral Suite.
   EB:A32.
   b. Chamber and Instrumental
   Rondeau a 7 for violincello piccolo, bassoon, violin, 3
     violas and basso continuo. (Concentus Musico-
     Instrumentalis, 1701).
   LB:A234.
   Serenade a 8 for 3 clarinos, 2 oboes, bassoon, 2 violins,
     viola and basso continuo. (Concentus Musico-
     Instrumentalis, 1701).
   LB:A234.
   Sinfonia in F maj for recorder, oboe and basso continuo.
   LB:B275, B298.
   Sinfonia II for 4 violins, 3 oboes, 2 viols, double-bass,
     bassoon and harpsichord (Concentus Musico-
     Instrumentalis, 1701).
   EB:B51.
   Sinfonia VII for recorder, oboe, viol and harpsichord
     (Concentus Musico-Instrumentalis, 1701).
   EB:B51.
   Sonata a 4 for violin, cornet, posaune, dulcian and organ
     (Concentus Musico-Instrumentalis, 1701).
   LB:A234.
   c. Keyboard
   Ciaconna in D maj.
   LB:D87.
   Harpeggio and fugue in G maj.
   LB:D87.
   Parthie in G min.
   EB:D39.
   LB:D235.
   Sonata V.
   EB:E56.
   Sonata VI.
   EB:E94.
   Suite in A min.
   LB:G87.
   e. Sacred Vocal
   Ad te Domine levavi.
   LR:F80.

GABRIEL, Mena (late 15th. cent.)
   d. Secular Vocal
   A la caza, sus, a caza.
   LR:E31.
   De la dulce.
   LR:E25.

GABRIELI, Andrea (1510–1586)
  c.Keyboard – Harpsichord and Organ (Including Instrumental Arrangements)
Canzona.
EB:E70.
Canzon Ariosa.
LR:D10, D15.
Canzon Francese.
LR:A1.
EB:G137.
Canzon sopra 'Qui la dira.'
LR:B3.
Capriccio sopra il Pass'e mezzo antico.
LR:D10.
Intonazione del 8o tono.
LR:D15.
Pour ung plaisir – Fantasia.
LR:E42.
Preambulum quarti e terti toni.
LR:D10.
Ricercare.
LR:E37.
EB:G57.
Ricercare arioso.
EB:E66.
Ricercare arioso I and III.
LR:D10.
Ricercare arioso II and IV.
LR:F86.
Ricercare del 2o tono.
LR:B28, F90.
Ricercare del 12o tono.
LR:D10.
LB:B299.
Toccata del 10o tono.
LR:D10.
  d.Secular Vocal
O passi sparsi – Madrigal.
LR:F87.
  e.Sacred Vocal
Angelus ad pastores ait.
EB:G98.
Ave regina.
LR:F85.
Egremini et videte.
LR:F84.
Heu mihi.
LR:F85.
Jubilate Deo.
LR:F84.
Laudate Dominum.
LR:F85.
Maria stabat.
LR:F84.
O rex gloriae.
LR:F84.
O sacrum convivium.
LR:F94.
Sancta et immaculata.
LR:F85.
Te Deum patrem ingenitum.
LR:F84.

GABRIELI, Giovanni (1557–1612)
  b.Instrumental – Canzoni and Sonatas, 1597, 1608, 1615
Canzon I primi toni a 8 (1597) (K.C52).
LR:B5, B6, F7.
LB:A616, A657.
Canzon II septimi toni a 8 (1597) (K.C53).
LR:A6, B4, B5, F10.
Canzon III septimi toni a 8 (1597) (K.C54).
LR:B4, B5, B6.
Canzon IV noni toni a 8 (1597) (K.C55).

LB:A616.
Canzon V duodecimi toni a 8 (1597) (K.C56).
LB:B6.
Sonata VI 'pian e forte' a 8 (1597) (K.C57).
LR:B4, B5, F9, F86, F90.
Canzon VII primi toni a 10 (1597) (K.C58).
LR:B3, B5.
Canzon IX duodecimi toni a 10 (1597) (K.C60).
LR:B3, B5.
Canzon X duodecimi toni a 10 (1597) (K.C61).
LR:B3, B5.
Canzon XI in echo duodecimi toni a 10 (1597) (K.C62).
LR:B5, B6.
Canzon XIII septimi toni et octavi toni a 12 (1597) (K.C64).
LR:B4, B5, Ga14.
Canzon XIV noni toni a 12 (1597) (K.C65).
LR:B5, F7.
Sonata XV octavi toni a 12 (1597) (K.C66).
LR:B4, B5.
Canzon XVI quarti toni a 15 (1597) (K.C67).
LR:B5.
Canzon a 10 (Unsp.) (1597).
LR:F90.
Canzon XXII 'Sol sol la sol fa mi' a 8 (1608) (K.C69).
LR:F86.
Canzon prima a 4 'La Spiritata' (1608) (K.C43).
LR:B3, B6, D15.
EB:A34, B39.
LB:A616, B299.
Canzon secunda a 4 (1608) (K.C44).
LR:B3, B6.
Canzon quarta a 4 (1608) (K.C46).
LR:B6.
Canzon XXIV a 8 (1608).
LR:B3.
Canzon XXVII a 8 (1608).
LR:B3.
Canzon I a 5 (1615) (K.C70).
LR:B3, B4.
EB:B39.
LB:A616.
Canzon III a 6 (1615) (K.C72).
LR:B3.
Canzon IV a 6 (1615) (K.C73).
LR:B4.
EB:B39.
Canzon V a 7 (1615) (K.C74).
LB:A591.
Canzon VII a 7 (1615) (K.C76).
LR:B3, B4.
Canzon VIII a 8 (1615) (K.C77).
LR:B4.
LB:A591.
Sonata XIII a 8 (1615) (K.C81).
LR:B4.
Canzon XVI a 12 (1615) (K.C84).
LR:F87.
Sonata XIX a 15 (1615) (K.C87).
LR:B4.
Sonata XX a 22 (5 Choirs) (1615) (K.C88).
LR:B6.
Sonata XXI con tre violini (1615) (K.C89).
LR:B4.
EB:B52.
Canzon a 4 (1615) (Unsp.)
LR:B28.
Canzon a 5 (1615) (Unsp.)
LR:B20, B28.
Canzon a 6 (1615) (Unsp.)
LR:B20, B28.
Canzon a 7 (1615) (Unsp.)
LR:B20.
Canzon in F min a 8 (2 Choirs) (Unsp.)

EB:B55.
Canzon a 8 (Unsp.)
LR:F87.
LB:A616.
Lieto godea sedendo – Madrigal.
EB:B57.
LB:C31.
Ricercare sopra Re fa mi do a 4.
LR:B3.
c. Keyboard
Canzon II (for organ).
LR:D10.
Fantasia del quarti e quinti toni.
LR:D10.
Fantasia del sexti toni.
EB:E66.
Fuga del noni toni.
LR:D10, D15.
Intonazione d'organo.
LR:F90.
Ricercare del primi toni.
LR:E54.
Ricercare del sexti toni.
EB:B39.
Ricercare del decimi toni.
LR:D10.
Ricercare V.
LR:D10.
e. Sacred Vocal – Sacrae Symphoniae, 1597–1615
Angelus ad pastores ait.
LR:F10, F86.
Angelus Domine descendit.
LR:F8.
Audi Domine hymnum.
EB:G57.
Audite principes.
LR:F86.
Beata es virgo.
LR:F84.
EB:G143.
Buccinate in neomenia.
LR:F6, F10.
Cantate Domino.
LR:F7, F84.
Deus, Deus meus.
LR:F84.
Deus in nomine tuo.
EB:G57.
Diligam te Domine.
LR:F7, F85.
Domine exaudi orationem meam.
LR:F7.
Ego rogab ad patrem.
LR:F7.
Ego sum qui sum.
LR:F8, F85.
Exultat jam angelica.
LR:F84.
Hoc tegitur.
LR:F8.
Hodie Christus natus est.
LR:F8, F10, F85, F105, F122.
Hodie completi sunt.
LR:F10.
In ecclesiis.
LR:F6.
Jam non dicam vos servos.
LR:F8.
Jubilate Deo.
LR:F8, F77.
Jubilate Deum.
LR:F7.
Jubilemus.
LR:F85.

Magnificat a 14.
LR:F6, F7, F90.
Magnificat a 17.
LR:F6, F8.
Maria Virgo.
LR:F9.
Miserere mei, Deus.
LR:F7.
Misericordia.
LR:F6.
Misericordias Domini.
LR:F8.
Nunc dimittis.
LR:F8.
O Domine Jesu Christe.
LR:F8, F10.
EB:G143.
O Jesu mi dulcissime.
LR:F8.
EB:G143.
O magnum mysterium.
LR:F10, F86, F114.
Omnes gentes, plaudite manibus.
LR:F10.
Plaudite omnis terra.
LR:F7, F85.
Quem vidistis pastores.
LR:F6, F86.
Quis est iste.
LR:F9, F90.
Regina caeli.
LR:F8.
Sacro tempo d'honor.
LR:F94.
Salvator noster.
LR:F86.
Sancta et immaculata virginitas.
LR:F8.
Sancta Maria, sucurre miseris.
LR:F9.
Sanctus Dominus Deus.
LR:A1.
Surrexit Christus.
LR:F6.
Suscipe.
LR:F6.
Virtute magna.
LR:F7, F85.

GABRIELLI, Domenico (1659–1690)
b. Instrumental
Canon for 2 cellos.
LB:B309.
Ricercare VII in D min for cello.
EB:B45.
Sonata in D maj for trumpet and organ.
LB:B205.
Sonata a 4 for trumpet and continuo.
EB:B60.

GABUZIO, Giulio Cesare (1555–1611)
c. Keyboard – Organ
Surge amica mea – Bicinium.
LR:D18.

GAGLIANO, Marco da (c.1582–1642)
d. Secular Vocal
La Daphne – Opera, 1608.
EB:F11.
Alma mia dove t'en vai.
EB:F10.
Bonta del ciel eterna.
EB:F10.
Cantai un tempo.
EB:F10.

Chi nudrisce tua speme.
EB:F10.
Fanciuletta ritrosetta.
EB:F10.
In un limpido rio.
EB:F10.
Io vido in terra angelici costumi.
EB:F10, F93, F99.
Mie speranze lusinghiere.
EB:F10, F93.
Mira fillede mia.
EB:F10.
O vita nostra al fin polvere et ombra.
EB:F10.
Valli profonde.
EB:F10, F96, F98.
e. Sacred Vocal
Crocem tuam adoramus, Domine.
EB:F10.
Jesu nostra redemptio.
EB:F10.
Magnificat.
EB:F10.
Monstra te esse matrem.
EB:F10.
O beata trinitas.
EB:F10.
Pastor levate su (per la Nativita del Nostro Signore).
EB:F10, G137.
Princeps gloriosisimme.
EB:F10.

GALILEI, Michelangelo (16th. cent.)
 b. Instrumental
Corrento.
LR:C9.

GALILEI, Vincenzo (1520–1591)
 b. Instrumental – Lute
Anchor che col partire.
LR:E39.
Capriccio a due voci.
LR:B20.
Contrapunto.
LR:B20, C22, E2.
Contrapunto I.
LR:C24.
Contrapunto II.
LR:C24.
Duo tutti di fantasia.
LR:C26.
Fantasia.
LR:C24, Gd42.
LB:C31.
Fuga a l'unisono.
LR:C12.
Il vostr gran valore.
LR:C9.
Io mi son giovinetta.
LR:C9.
Ricercare.
LR:C9, C20.
Saltarello.
ER:A7.

GALKA, Jedrzej (c. 1450)
 d. Secular Vocal
Lied auf Wiklew.
ER:B46.

GALLOT, Jacques (c. 1600–1656)
 b. Instrumental – Lute
Le Bout de l'an de M. Gaultier.
EB:C9.
La Dauphine.

EB:C9.
La Divine.
EB:C9.
Le Doge de Venice.
EB:C9.
Prelude.
EB:C9.
Suite in D min.
EB:C6.
Le Tombeau de Madame.
EB:C9.
Le Tombeau de Muses.
EB:C9.

GALLUS – *see* HANDL-GALLUS, Jacobus.

GALUPPI, Baldassare (1706–1785)
 a. Orchestral
Concerto in D maj for flute and strings.
LB:A638.
Concerto No. 1 in F maj for harpsichord and strings.
LB:A235.
Concerto No. 3 in C maj for harpsichord and strings.
LB:A235.
Concerto No. 5 in G maj for harpsichord and strings.
LB:A235.
Concerto No. 7 in C min for harpsichord and strings.
LB:A235.
 b. Chamber and Instrumental
Sonata in G maj for flute, oboe and continuo.
LB:B244, B300.
 c. Keyboard – Harpsichord
Passatempo al cembalo, Nos. 1–6 (1781).
  1 in F maj; 2 in A maj; 3 in C min; 4 in D maj; 5 in B flat
  maj; 6 in E maj.
LB:D154.
Sonata (Unsp.)
EB:E93.
Sonata No. 9 in F min.
LB:D153.
Sonata No. 10 in G min.
LB:D153.
Sonata No. 34 in C min.
LB:D153.
Sonata No. 38 in C min.
LB:D153.
Sonata No. 43 in A min.
LB:D153.
Sonata No. 55 in C maj.
LB:D153.
Sonata No. 59 in F sharp min.
LB:D153.
 e. Sacred Vocal
Magnificat in G maj.
LB:G198.

GANASSI, Silvestro (15th. cent.)
 b. Instrumental
Ricercare.
ER:A4.

GARCIMUNOS (15th./16th. cent.)
 d. Secular Vocal
Pues bien para esta.
ER:A26.

GARDANE, Antonio (1509–1569)
 b. Instrumental
Fornarina galiarda.
LR:E28.
L'Herba fresca gagliarda.
LR:E28.
La Notte gagliarda.
LR:E28.
 c. Secular Vocal

Anchor che col partire.
LR:E39.
Le Cuer de vous.
AA:A1.

GARDANO – *see* GARDANE, Antonio.

GARSI DA PARMA, Santino (1540–1604)
   b.Instrumental – Lute
   Aria del Gran Duca.
   LR:C9, C23.
   Ballo del Serenissimo Duca di Parma.
   LR:C9, C23.
   La Cesarina.
   LR:C23.
   Corenta.
   LR:C9, C23.
   Gagliarda Manfredina.
   LR:C23.
   La Lisfeltina.
   EB:B41.
   La Mutia.
   LR:C23.
   LB:B321.
   La ne mente per la gola.
   LR:C23.

GASCONGNE, Mathieu (16th. cent.)
   e.Sacred Vocal
   Bone Jesu dulcissime.
   LR:E32.

GASTOLDI, Giovanni Giacomo (1550–1622)
   b.Instrumental
   Bicinia.
   ER:A7.
   LB:B272.
   Capriccio a due voci.
   LR:B20.
   Mascherata.
   LR:Gd25.
   d.Secular Vocal
   Amor vittoriose.
   LR:E22.

GAULTIER, Denis 'Le Jeune.' (c.1603–1672)
   b.Instrumental – Lute
   Allemande in D maj.
   EB:C10.
   Le Chevre.
   EB:C9.
   Cleopatre amante.
   EB:C9.
   Courante.
   LB:B297.
   Courante in D maj.
   EB:C10.
   Narcisse.
   EB:C8.
   Prelude.
   LB:B297.
   Prelude in D maj.
   EB:C10.
   Sarabande in D maj.
   EB:C10.
   Sarabande.
   EB:C8.
   Suite I in D maj (Rhetorique des Dieux).
   EB:C4.
   Suite II in A maj (Rhetorique des Dieux).
   EB:C4.
   Suite XII in A min (Rhetorique des Dieux).
   EB:C4.
   Suite in G maj (Rhetorique des Dieux).
   EB:C10.

Tombeau de Mademoiselle Gaultier.
EB:C9.

GAULTIER, Ennemonde 'Le Vieux' (c.1575–1651)
   b.Instrumental – Lute
   Canaries.
   EB:C8, C9.
   LB:B297.
   Courante.
   EB:C9.
   Courante in D maj.
   EB:C10.
   Gigue in D maj.
   EB:C10.
   Prelude.
   EB:C9.
   Sarabande in D maj.
   EB:C10.
   Testament de Mezangeau.
   EB:C9.
   Tombeau de Mezangeau.
   EB:C9.
   LB:B297.

GAUTIER DE COINCY (1177–1236)
   d.Secular Vocal (Including Instrumental Arrangements)
   Amours qui bien set enchanter (M de ND).
   AA:D23.
   Chanson a la vierge.
   LR:B14.
   LB:B259.
   D'une amour quoie et serie (M de ND).
   AA:D23.
   Efforcier m'estuet ma voiz (M de ND).
   AA:D23.
   Entendez tuit ensemble (M de ND).
   AA:D23.
   Hui matin a l'ajournee (M de ND).
   AA:D23.
   Ja pour hyver, pour noif ne pour gelee (M de ND).
   AA:D23.
   Las, las, las, par grand delit.
   AA:D20.
   Ma viele (M de ND).
   AA:D16, D23.
   LR:E59.
   Mere Dieu, virge senee (M de ND).
   AA:D23.
   Les Miracles de Notre Dame (M de ND).
   AA:D23.
   Quant ces flourettes florir voi (M de ND).
   AA:D23.
   Qui que face retrouenge nouvele (M de ND).
   AA:D23.
   Reyne celestre (M de ND).
   AA:D23.
   S'amour dont sui espris (M de ND).
   AA:D23.
   Talenz m'est pris ovendroit (M de ND).
   AA:D23.

GAUTIER D'EPINAL (12th. cent.)
   d.Secular Vocal
   Commencemens de dolce saison bel.
   AA:D6.

GAUTIER DE MARSEILLES, Pierre (c.1643–1697)
   b.Instrumental
   Suite in E min for recorder and continuo.
   LB:B293.
   Suite in E min for recorder and continuo: Passacaille.
   Sommeil.
   EB:B69.

GAWARA, Walentyn (17th./18th. cent.)
  e. Sacred Vocal
  Per merita Sancti Adalberti.
  LR:F92.

GAY, John (1685-1732)
  d. Secular Vocal
  The Beggar's Opera. 1728.
  LB:F24.

GEMBLACO = GEMBLOUX – see DE GEMBLOUX,
Johannes Franchois.

GEMINIANI, Francesco (1680-1762)
  a. Orchestral
  Concerto Grosso in D maj for 2 flutes and continuo. Op.
    2, No. 4.
  LB:B275.
  Concerti Grossi, Op. 3, Nos. 1-6.
    1 in D maj; 2 in G min; 3 in E min; 4 in D min; 5 in B flat
      maj; 6 in E min.
  LB:A236.
  Concerto Grosso in G min, Op. 3, No. 2.
  LB:A607.
  Concerto Grosso in E min, Op. 3, No. 3.
  LB:A587, A596, A608.
  Concerto Grosso in D min, 'La Follia' (Arr. of Corelli's Op.
    5, No. 12).
  LB:A595.
  b. Chamber and Instrumental
  Sonata No. 1 in E min for oboe and continuo.
  LB:B228, B254.
  Sonata in E min for recorder and continuo.
  LB:B266.
  Sonatas for cello and continuo, Op. 1, Nos. 1-6.
    1 in A maj; 2 in D min; 3 in C maj; 4 in B flat maj; 5 in F
      maj; 6 in A maj.
  LB:B129.
  Sonata in D min for cello and continuo, Op. 5, No. 2.
  LB:B309.
  Sonata No. 1 in C maj for cello, guitar and continuo.
  LB:B130.
  Sonata No. 2 in C min for cello, guitar and continuo.
  LB:B130.
  Sonata No. 3 in D maj for cello, guitar and continuo.
  LB:B130.
  Sonata No. 4 in D min for cello, guitar and continuo.
  LB:B130.
  Sonata No. 6 in E min for cello, guitar and continuo.
  LB:B130.
  Sonata No. 10 in G min for cello, guitar and continuo.
  LB:B130.

GENTIAN (16th. cent.)
  d. Secular Vocal
  Celle qui a facheux mari.
  LR:E58.
  Je suis Robert.
  LR:Gd52.

GEOFFROY, Jean-Nicolas (1633-1694)
  c. Keyboard – Harpsichord
  Suite in C min.
  EB:D5.
  Suite in F min.
  EB:D5.
  c. Keyboard – Organ
  Kyrie.
  EB:E31.
  Lucis creator.
  EB:E31.
  Marche.
  EB:E31.
  2 Minuets.
  EB:E31.
  Offertoire grave.

  EB:E31.
  Ouverture d'Isis.
  EB:E31.

GERHARDT, Paul (17th. cent.)
  e. Sacred Vocal
  Lutheran Songs.
  LR:F101, F102.

GERRARDE, Gervaise (17th. cent.)
  b. Instrumental
  Gigue (Manchester MS).
  SI:C20.
  Pavan (Manchester MS).
  SI:C20.

GERVAISE, Claude (1505-1555)
  b. Instrumental
  Allemande.
  LR:B10, B27, Gd58.
  LB:B259.
  Branle.
  LR:B10, B17, B18.
  LB:B259.
  Branle de Bourgogne.
  AA:D20.
  LR:B14, B16, B25, B26, D16, E63.
  LB:B259.
  Branle de Champaigne.
  LR:B12, B14, B16, B25, B27, D16, E63.
  Branle simple.
  LR:B12, E43.
  LB:B259.
  'Danceries' (Unsp.)
  ER:A7.
  Et d'ou venez.
  LR:E54.
  Galliard.
  AA:D20.
  Pavan and Galliard de la Guerre.
  LR:Gd43.
  LB:B272.
  Pavane d'Angleterre.
  LR:B14.
  Pavane and Galliard d'Angleterre.
  LR:B10.
  LB:B259.
  Suite of Dances (Misc.)
  LB:B205, B207, B213.
  La Volunte – Basse danse.
  LR:B10.

GESIUS, Bartholomäus (1560-1613)
  e. Sacred Vocal
  Christum wir sollen loben.
  LR:F123.
  Ein Kind geborn.
  LR:F111, F123.
  Freut euch, ihr lieben Christen.
  LR:F109, F112.
  Ich steh an deiner Krippen.
  LR:F121.
  O Christe, Morgensterne.
  EB:G132.

GESUALDO, Carlo 'Principe de Venosa' (1560-1613)
  b. Instrumental
  Canzona francese.
  LR:A1.
  Gagliarda del Principe de Venosa.
  LR:B10, B21.
  d. Secular Vocal
    Madrigals for 5vv. 1594, Book 1.
    Madrigals for 5vv. 1594, Book 2.
    Madrigals for 5vv. 1595, Book 3.
    Madrigals for 5vv. 1596, Book 4.

Madrigals for 5vv, 1611, Book 5.
Madrigals for 5vv, 1611, Book 6.

Book 1
Amor, pace non chere.
LR:E4, E5.
Baci soavi e cari.
LR:E4, E5.
Bell' angioletta.
LR:E4, E5.
Com' esser puo.
LR:E4, E5.
Felice primavera.
LR:E4, E5.
Gelo ha madonna il seno.
LR:E4, E5.
Madonna, io ben vorrei.
LR:E4, E5.
Mentre madonna.
LR:E4, E5.
Mentre, mia stella.
LR:E4, E5.
Non mirar, non mirar.
LR:E4, E5.
O dolce mio martire.
LR:E4, E5.
Questi leggiadri.
LR:E4, E5.
Se da si nobil mano.
LR:E4, E5.
Si gioioso mi fanno.
LR:E4, E5.
Son si belle le rose.
LR:E4, E5.
Tirsi morir volea.
LR:E4, E5.

Book 2
All' apparir di quelle.
LR:E4, E5.
Candida man.
LR:E4, E5.
Caro amoroso meo.
LR:E4, E5.
De le odorate spoglie.
LR:E4, E5.
Hai rotte e sciolto.
LR:E4, E5.
In piu leggiardro velo.
LR:E4, E5.
Non e questa la mano.
LR:E4, E5.
Non mai non cangere.
LR:E4, E5.
Non mi toglia il ben mio.
LR:E4, E5.
O come e gran martire.
LR:E4, E5.
Se cosi dolce e il duolo.
LR:E4, E5.
Se per lieve fevita.
LR:E4, E5.
Se taccio il duol s'avanza.
LR:E4, E5.
Sento che nel partire.
LR:E4, E5.

Book 3
Ahi, disperata via.
LR:E4, E5.
Ahi, dispietata e cruda.
LR:E4, E5.
Ancidetemi pur.
LR:E4, E5.
Crudelissima doglia.
LR:E4, E5.
Deh, sa gia fu crudel.

LR:E4, E5.
Del bel de' bei vostri occhi.
LR:E4, E5.
Dolce spirto d'Amore.
LR:E4, E5.
Dolcissime sospiro.
LR:E4, E5.
Donna, se m'offendete.
LR:E4, E5.
Languisco e moro.
LR:E4, E5.
Meraviglia d'amore.
LR:E4, E5.
Non t'amo o voce ingrata.
LR:E4, E5.
Se piange oime.
LR:E4, E5.
Se vi miro pietosa.
LR:E4, E5.
Sospirava il mio core.
LR:E4, E5.
Veggio, si dal mio sole.
LR:E4, E5.
Voi, volete ch'io mora.
LR:E4, E5.

Book 4
A voi, mentre il mio core.
LR:E4.
Ahi, gia mi discoloro.
LR:E4, F11.
Arde il mio cor.
LR:E4.
Che fai meco, mio cor.
LR:E4.
Cor mio, deh, non piangete.
LR:E4.
Dunque non m'offendete.
LR:E4.
Ecco, morire dunque.
LR:E4, F11, F22.
Invan dunque, o crudele.
LR:E4, F11.
Io tacero.
LR:E4, F11.
Luci serene e chiare.
LR:E4.
Mentre gira costei.
LR:E4.
Moro, e mentre sospire.
LR:E4.
O sempre crudo amore.
LR:E4.
Or, che in gioia.
LR:E4.
Quando di lui.
LR:E4.
Questa crudele e pia.
LR:E4.
Se chiudete nel core.
LR:E4.
Il sol, qualor piu splende.
LR:E4.
Sparge la morte.
LR:E4.
Tal' or sano desio.
LR:E4.
Volgi, mia luce.
LR:E4.

Book 5
Asciugate i begli occhi.
LR:E4.
Correte, amanti, a prova.
LR:E4.
Deh, coprite il bel sono.

LR:E4.
Dolcissima mia vita.
LR:E4, F11, F22.
Felicissimo sonno.
LR:E4.
Gioite voi col canto.
LR:E4.
Itene, o miei sospiri.
LR:E4, F11.
Languisca al fin.
LR:E4.
Ma tu, cagion.
LR:E4.
Merce, grido piangendo.
LR:E4.
O dolorosa gioia.
LR:E4.
O tenebroso giorno.
LR:E4.
O voi, troppo felici.
LR:E4.
Occhi del mio cor vita.
LR:E4.
Poiche l'avida seta.
LR:E4.
Qual fora, donna.
LR:E4.
Se tu fuggi.
LR:E4.
Se vi duol il mio duolo.
LR:E4.
S'io non miro non moro.
LR:E4.
T'amo, mia vita.
LR:E4.
Tu m'uccidi, o crudel.
LR:E4.

Book 6
Al mio gioir il ciel si fa serene.
LR:E4.
Alme d'amor rubelle.
LR:E4.
Ancide sol la morte.
LR:E4.
Ancor che per amart.
LR:E4.
Ardita Zanzaretta.
LR:E4.
Ardo per te, mio bene.
LR:E4.
Belta, poi che t'assenti.
LR:E4.
Candido e verde fiore.
LR:E4.
Chiare risplendor suolo.
LR:E4.
Deh come invan sospiro.
LR:E4.
Gia piansi nel dolore.
LR:E4.
Io parto e non piu dissi.
LR:E4.
Io pur respiro.
LR:E4.
Mille volte il dio moro.
LR:A1, E4, E5.
Moro, lasso, al mio duolo.
LR:E4, F11, F22.
O dolce mio tessoro.
LR:E4.
Quando ridente e bella.
LR:E4.
Quel no crudel.
LR:E4.

Resta di darma noia.
LR:E4.
Se la mia morte brani.
LR:E4.
Tu piangi, o filia mia.
LR:E4.
Tu segui, o bella Cleri.
LR:E4.
Volan quasi farfallo.
LR:E4.

e. Sacred Vocal
Responsories for Tenebrae.
LR:F12, F13, F14, F15, F16, F17, F18, F19, F20, F21.
Aestimatus sum (Sabbato Sancto).
LR:F12, F20, F21.
Amicus meus (Feria Quinta).
LR:F12, F13, F15.
Animam meam dilectam (Feria Sexta).
LR:F12, F16, F17.
Astiterunt reges terrae (Sabbata Sancta).
LR:F12, F20, F21.
Caligaverunt oculi mei (Feria Sexta).
LR:F12, F18, F19.
EB:G143.
Ecce quomodo moritur justus (Sabbato Sancto).
LR:F12, F20, F21.
Ecce vidimus (Feria Quinta).
LR:F12, F13, F15.
Eram quasi agnus innocens (Feria Quinta).
LR:F12, F14, F15.
In Monte Oliveti.
LR:F12, F13, F15.
Jerusalem surge (Sabbato Sancto).
LR:F12, F18, F21.
Jesum tradidit impius summis (Feria Sexta).
LR:F12, F18, F19.
Judas mercator pessimus (Feria Quinta).
LR:F12, F13, F15.
O vos omnes (Sabbato Sancto).
LR:F11, F12, F20, F21, F22, F88.
Omnes amici mei (Feria Sexta).
LR:F12, F14, F17.
Plange quasi virgo (Sabbato Sancto).
LR:F12, F18, F21.
Recessit pastor noster (Sabbato Sancto).
LR:F12, F20, F21.
Seniores populi consilium fecerunt (Feria Quinta).
LR:F12, F14, F15.
Sepulto Domino (Sabbato Sancto).
LR:F12, F20, F21.
Sicut ovis (Sabbato Sancto).
LR:F12, F18, F21.
Tamquam ad latronem existis (Feria Sexta).
LR:F12, F16, F17.
Tenebrae factae sunt (Feria Sexta).
LR:F12, F16, F17.
EB:G143.
Tradiderunt me in manus impiorum (Feria Sexta).
LR:F12, F18, F19.
Tristis est anima mea (Feria Quinta).
LR:F12, F13, F15.
Una hora non potuistis vigilare mecum (Feria Quinta).
LR:F12, F14, F15.
Unus ex discipulis meis (Feria Quinta).
LR:F12, F14, F15.
Velum templi scissum est. (Feria Sexta).
LR:F12, F16, F17.
Vinea mea electa (Feria Sexta).
LR:F12, F16, F17.
e. Sacred Vocal – Other Motets
Ave dulcissima Maria.
LR:F11, F22, F88.
Ave regina.
LR:F11, F88.

Benedictus.
LR:F12, F19.
Hei mihi Domine.
LR:F11, F22, F88.
Miserere.
LR:F12, F19.
O crux.
LR:F11, F88.

GHERARDELLO, DE FLORENTIA (14th. cent.)
    d.Secular Vocal
    I'vo bene a chi vol bene a me.
    AN:B8.
    Tosto che l'alba.
    AN:B3.
    LR:A4.
    e.Sacred Vocal
    Agnus Dei.
    AN:B5.
    Et in terra pax.
    AN:B5.

GHEYN – see VAN DEN GHEYN, Matthias

GHISELIN, Johannes (= VERBONNET) (1455–1511)
    b.Instrumental
    L'Alfonsina.
    LR:E53.
    d.Secular Vocal
    Ghy syt wertste boven al.
    ER:A1.
    Helas hic motet mi liden.
    ER:A6.

GHIZEGHEM – see HAYNE VAN GHIZEGHEM

GIACOBBI, Girolamo (c.1567–1629)
    e.Sacred Vocal
    Exultate Deo.
    LR:E60.

GIAMBERTI, Giuseppe (b.c.1600)
    e.Sacred Vocal
    O bel lagrimette.
    EB:G137.

GIBBONS, Christopher (1615–1676)
    c.Keyboard – Organ
    Verse for double organ.
    EB:F107.

GIBBONS, Ellis (1573–1603)
    d.Secular Vocal
    Long live fair Oriana (Triumphs of Oriana).
    LR:Gd34.
    Round about her charret (Triumphs of Oriana).
    LR:Gd34.

GIBBONS, Orlando (1583–1625)
    b.Instrumental – Consort
    Fantasia.
    LR:Ga18.
    Fantasia a 4 with 'Ye Greate Dooble Bass.'
    SI:B1.
    Fantasia a 6.
    LR:Ge14.
    SI:C19.
    Fantasias (Royal) Nos. 1–X, XII, XIV, XV.
    LR:Ga7.
    In Nomine in D min.
    LR:Gd44.
    In Nomine a 4.
    LR:Ga7, Ga11, Ga16, Ga21.
    In Nomine a 5.
    LR:Ge14.
    Royal Pavane.
    LR:Ga11.

c.Keyboard (Musica Britannica, MB XX)
Alman in C maj (Cosyn Virginal Book).
LR:Gc6.
Alman (33).
LR:Gc5.
Alman (37).
LR:Gc5.
Coranto (40).
LR:Gc5.
Fancy in A maj.
EB:E82.
A Fancy (3).
LR:Gc5, Gc11.
Fantasia (8).
LR:Gc5.
Fantasia (10).
LR:Gc5.
Fantasia in 4 parts (12).
LR:Gc5, Gc6.
Fantasia in A min (Cosyn Virginal Book).
LR:Gc6, Gc15.
Fantasia in D min (5).
LR:Gc11.
LB:E240.
Fantasia in D min (6).
LR:Gc11.
Fantasia for organ.
LR:Ga19.
French Almain.
LR:Gc6.
French Ayre (32).
LR:Gc6.
Galliard.
LR:B21, Gc10.
Galliard in C maj (Parthenia).
LR:Gc6.
Galliard in D maj (Cosyn Virginal Book).
LR:Gc6.
Galliard (19).
LR:Gc5.
Galliard (21).
LR:Gc5.
Galliard (22).
LR:Gc5.
A Ground (26).
LR:Gc5, Gc15, Gc17.
Italian Ground (27).
LR:Gc5, Gc6.
The King's Jewel – Alman (36).
LR:Gc5.
EB:E82.
Lady Hatton's Galliard (20).
LR:Gc6.
Lincoln's Inn Masque (44).
LR:Gc5.
My Lord Salisbury's Pavan and Galliard (Parthenia).
LR:Gc6, Gc9, Gd40.
My Lady Salisbury's Pavan (18).
LR:Gc5.
Pavan.
LR:Ge14.
EB:D24.
Pavan (16).
LR:Gc5, Gc11.
Pavan (17).
LR:Gc5, Gc10.
Pavan.
LR:Gd18.
Praeludium in G maj.
EB:E64.
LB:D214.
Prelude (1).
LR:Gc5, Gc6.
The Queen's Command (28).

LR:Gc5.
SI:C3.
Verse (4).
LR:Gc5.
A Voluntary.
LR:Gc17.
Welcome Home – Masque.
LR:Gc6.
The Woods so Wild (29).
LR:Gc6, Gc9.
d. Secular Vocal (Madrigals and Motets of 5 Parts, 1614)
Ah dear heart (MM).
LR:Gd13, Gd32, Ge14.
The Cries of London.
LR:Gd52.
Dainty fine bird (MM).
LR:Gd13, Ge14.
Do not repine fair sun.
LR:Gd53.
Fair is the rose (MM).
LR:Gd13.
Fair ladies that to love. (MM).
LR:Gd13.
Fairest nymph.
LR:Gc9.
Farewell all joys (MM).
LR:Gd13.
How art thou thralled (MM).
LR:Gd13.
I feign not friendship (MM).
LR:Gd13, Gd36.
I see ambition never pleased (MM).
LR:Gd13.
I tremble not at noise of war (MM).
LR:Gd13.
I weigh not Fortune's frown (MM).
LR:Gd13.
Lais now old (MM).
LR:Gd13.
'Mongst thousands good (MM).
LR:Gd13.
Nay, let me weep (MM).
LR:Gd13.
Ne'er let the sun (MM).
LR:Gd13.
Now each flowery bank (MM).
LR:A1, Gd13.
O that the learned poets (MM).
LR:Gd13, Gd32.
The Silver Swan (MM).
LR:Gd13, Gd20, Gd32, Gd56, Ge14.
Trust not too much fair youth (MM).
LR:Gd13.
What is our life? (MM).
LR:Gd13, Gd29, Gd32, Ge14.
EB:F108.
Yet if that age (MM).
LR:Gd13.
e. Sacred Vocal
A Song of Joy unto the Lord we sing (Hymn of the Church, 47).
LR:Ge15.
Almighty and everlasting God.
LR:Ge16.
Behold thou hast made my days.
LR:Gd18, Ge14.
Blessed are all they.
LR:Ge16.
Come kiss me with those lips of thine (Hymn of the Church, 9).
LR:Ge15.
Drop, drop, slow tears.
LR:Ge30, Ge39.

Glorious and powerful God.
LR:Ge13, Ge16.
Great King of Gods.
LR:Gd18, Ge14.
Great Lord of Hosts.
LR:Gd40.
Hosanna to the Son of David.
LR:F119, Ge15, Ge35.
How sad and solitary now (Hymn of the Church, 24).
LR:Ge15.
I am the Resurrection.
LR:Ge15.
Jubilate and Te Deum (2nd. Service).
LR:Ge13.
Lord, grant grace.
LR:Ge16.
Lord, I will sing to Thee (Hymn of the Church, 20).
LR:Ge15.
Lord, Thy answer I did hear (Hymn of the Church, 31).
LR:Ge15.
Lord, we beseech Thee.
LR:Ge15.
Now in the Lord my heart doth pleasure take (Hymn of the Church, 4).
LR:Ge15.
Now shall the praises of the Lord be sung (Hymn of the Church, 1).
LR:Ge15.
O clap your hands.
LR:Ge15.
O God, the King of Glory.
LR:Gd40.
O Lord, I lift my heart.
LR:Ge16.
O Lord, how do my woes increase.
LR:Ge16.
O Lord in Thy wrath.
LR:Gd18, Ge14, Ge15, Ge35.
O Lord of Hosts and God of Israel (Hymn of the Church, 22).
LR:Ge15.
Oh my love, how comely now (Hymn of the Church, 13).
LR:Ge15.
Praise the Lord.
LR:Ge15.
Prayer to Hezekiah.
LR:Gd18, Ge14.
Preces and Psalm CXLV.
LR:Ge13, Ge16.
The Secret Sins.
LR:Gd18, Ge14.
See, the Word is incarnate.
LR:F117, Ge13, Ge15.
Sing praises Isr'el to the Lord (Hymn of the Church, 3).
LR:Ge15.
Sing unto the Lord.
LR:Ge16.
The Song of Moses.
LR:Gd18, Ge13, Ge14.
This is the Record of John.
LR:Ge13, Ge16.
LB:G319, G320.
Thou God of wisdom.
LR:Ge34.
Thy beauty, Israel, is gone (Hymn of the Church, 5).
LR:Ge15.
We praise Thee.
LR:Ge16.
When one among the twelve there was (Hymn of the Church, 67).
LR:Ge15.
Who's this, that leaning on her friend (Hymn of the Church, 18).
LR:Ge15.

GIBBS, Thomas (17th. cent.)
  c. Keyboard
    The Lord Monck's March (Playford's 'English Dancing
      Master.')
    EB:D30.

GIELNIOWA, Ladyslaw z (d.1505)
  e. Sacred Vocal
    Jesus Psalter.
    ER:B46.

GIGAULT, Nicolas (1627–1707)
  c. Keyboard – Organ
    Fugue du 1re ton.
    EB:E34.
    Fugue a 3 du 1re ton.
    EB:E34.
    Fugue du 3me ton.
    EB:E34.
    Fugue on the Kyrie.
    EB:E34.
    Kyrie des doubles.
    EB:E34.
    Prelude du 1re ton.
    EB:E34.
    Tu solus altissimus.
    EB:E34.

GILES, Nathaniel (c.1558–1633)
  d. Secular Vocal
    Cease now vain thoughts.
    LR:Gd44.

GILLEBERT DE BERNEVILLE (c.1255–1280)
  d. Secular Vocal
    De mois doleros vos chant.
    AA:A1, D15, D21.

GILLES, Henri (14th. cent.)
  d. Secular Vocal
    Ida capillorum – Portio nature – Ante thronum trinitas.
    AA:B1.
    Rathel plorat – Ha! fratres.
    AA:B1.

GILLES, Jean (1669–1705)
  e. Sacred Vocal
    Laudate nomen Domini – Psalm CXXXV.
    EB:G40.
    Laetatus sum – Psalm CXXII.
    EB:G40.
    Paratum cor meum – Psalm CVIII.
    EB:G40.

GINTZLER, Simon (c.1490–c.1550)
  b. Instrumental – Lute
    Ricercare IV.
    LR:C9.

GIOVANELLI, Ruggiero (1560–1625)
  e. Sacred Vocal
    Et in spiritum (Missa 'Cantantibus Organis Caecilia.')
    LR:F95.

GIOVANNI DA CASCIA = GIOVANNI DA FIRENZE

GIOVANNI DA FIRENZE (14th. cent.)
  d. Secular Vocal
    Appress' un fiume chiaro.
    AN:B8.
    Con bracchi assai.
    AN:B9.
    Da, da, da a chi avaeggia.
    AN:B9.
    De' come dolcemente.
    AN:B6.
    Nel boscho senza folglie.

    LR:E35.
    Per ridd' andano.
    AN:B8.
    Tosto che l'alba.
    AN:B8.

GIROUST, Francois (1738–1799)
  e. Sacred Vocal
    Magnificat.
    LR:E29.

GISTOU, Nicolo (d.1609)
  b. Instrumental
    Galliard.
    LR:B23.
    Paduana.
    LR:B23.
  d. Secular Vocal
    Ma ben arde nel core.
    LR:E19.
    Quel Augellin che canta.
    LR:E19.

GIULIANO, Giuseppe (18th. cent.)
  a. Orchestral
    Concerto in B flat maj for mandolin and strings.
    LB:A224.

**GLOGAUER LIEDERBUCH (late 15th./early 16th. cent.
German.)**
  d. Secular Vocal (Including Instrumental Arrangements)
    Al vol.
    ER:A22, A23.
    LR:E35.
    Der Bauern schwanz – Rubinus.
    ER:A23.
    Bonum vinum.
    ER:A23.
    Bruder Konrad.
    ER:A23.
    Czanner greyner.
    ER:A22.
    Else el se mundo.
    ER:A22.
    Elzeleyn, lipstis elzeleyn.
    ER:A22.
    LR:E35.
    Es gingen drei Bauern.
    ER:A23.
    Es suftzt eyne fraw so zere.
    ER:A22.
    Dy ezels krone.
    ER:A22.
    Hostu mich obbirwünden.
    ER:A22.
    Ich byns irfrewth.
    ER:A22.
    Ich sachz eyns mols.
    ER:A22.
    LR:E64.
    In fewirsch hitcz.
    ER:A22.
    LR:E64.
    Dy Katczen pfothe.
    ER:A22, A23, A24.
    Die Liebe ist schöne.
    ER:A23.
    Der Neue Bauernschwanz.
    LR:E25.
    Mole graviti criminum.
    ER:A22.
    Dy Nacht dy wil verbergen sich.
    ER:A22.
    O wie gern und doch entbern.
    ER:A23.

Der Pfawin swancz.
ER:A22.
Seh hin meyn hertz.
ER:A22.
Der Sonnen glanz.
ER:A24.
Vitrum nostrum.
ER:A23.
LR:E35.
Der Wechter an der czynnen.
ER:A22.
Das Yeger horn.
ER:A22, A23.

GODRIC – *see* **ST. GODRIC.**

GOETZ, Johann (15th. cent.)
  b. Instrumental
  Boumgartner – Basse danse.
  LR:B11, B13.
  Vil lieber zit – Basse danse.
  LR:B11, B13.

GOMBERT, Nicolas (1490–1556)
  c. Keyboard
  Fabordon glosada.
  LR:D13.
  Fabordon llana.
  LR:D13.
  d. Secular Vocal
  Je suis trop ionette.
  LR:E42.
  Musae Jovis – Circumdederunt me (Deploration sur la
    Mort de Josquin.)
  ER:B30.
  e. Sacred Vocal
  Ave regina.
  LR:F82.
  Caeciliam cantate.
  LR:A1.

GOMOLKA, Mikolaj (c.1535–1591)
  e. Sacred Vocal
  Melodies from the Polish Psalter: Psalms I–CL.
  LR:F24.
  Melodies from the Polish Psalter (Misc.)
  LR:F23.
  Boze czemus mnie opuscil – Psalm XXII.
  LR:F97.
  Boze, ktory slug nigdy przepomnisz swoich.
  LR:F97.
  Naklon o Panie uszu swoich – Psalm LXXXVI.
  LR:F97.
  Niescie chwale mocarze – Psalm XXIX.
  LR:E66.
  Nieszczescie dusze trapi – Psalm LXXXVIII.
  LR:F97.
  Sluchaj co zywa – Psalm XLIX.
  LR:E66.
  Szczesliwy ktory – Psalm I.
  LR:E66.
  Uslysz prosby moje – Psalm.
  ER:B45.
  Wsiadaj z dobrym sercem – Psalm XX.
  LR:E66.

GORCZYCKI, Grzegorz Gerwazy (1664–1734)
  e. Sacred Vocal
  Completorium.
  LB:G199.
  Ecce nunc benedicite.
  LB:A617.
  Illuxit sol.
  LB:G328.
  In virtute tua.
  LB:G328.

Iudica me Deus.
LB:G328.
Laetatus sum.
EB:G144.
LB:G328.
Missa 'Paschalis.'
LB:G199.

GORNER, Johann Gottlieb (1697–1778)
  d. Secular Vocal
  Der Kuss.
  LB:F81.
  Der ordentliche Hausstand.
  LB:F81.

GORZANIS, Giacomo de (1525–1575)
  b. Instrumental – Lute
  La dura partita.
  LR:C25.
  Passamezzo e Paduana.
  LR:C9.

GOSSWIN, Anton (1540–1594)
  d. Secular Vocal
  Am abend spat, lieb' Brüderlein.
  LR:E70.

GOSTENA, Giovanni Battista dalla (c.1530–1589)
  d. Secular Vocal
  Tu che dal mio dolor.
  LR:E40.

GOTTFRIED VON BRETEUILL (13th. cent.)
  e. Sacred Vocal
  Planctus Maria Virginae (CARMINA BURANA).
  AA:E8.

GOUDIMEL, Claude (c.1510–1572)
  d. Secular Vocal
  Il me semble que la journee.
  LR:E52.
  Quand j'apercoy ton beau chef jaunissant.
  LR:E52.
  e. Sacred Vocal
  Psalm CII: Grant me my Lord my prayer.
  LR:A6, A7.

GRANCINI, Michelangelo (1605–1669)
  e. Sacred Vocal
  Dulcis Christe.
  EB:G135.

GRANDI, Alessandro (1577–1630)
  e. Sacred Vocal
  Cantabo Domine.
  EB:G56, G137.
  O beata benedicite.
  EB:G139.
  O quam tu pulchra es.
  EB:F96, G56.
  O sacrum convivium.
  EB:G135.
  O vos omnes.
  EB:F96, G139.

GRANDRUE, Eustache (17th. cent.)
  d. Secular Vocal
  Lors que tes beaus yeux mignonne.
  LR:E48.

GRATIANI, Bonifacio (1605–1664)
  e. Sacred Vocal
  Salve regina.
  EB:F92.

GRAUN, Carl Heinrich (1704–1759)
  d. Secular Vocal
  Das Töchterlein.

LB:F81.
Montezuma – Opera: Erra quel nel nobil core.
LB:A628.

GRAUN, Johann Gottlieb (1703–1771)
　　a. Orchestral
　　Concerto in B flat maj for bassoon and strings.
　　LB:A63.
　　Concerto in C min for oboe and strings.
　　LB:A237.
　　Concerto in F maj for flute, strings and continuo.
　　LB:A629.
　　Concerto in G min for oboe and strings.
　　LB:A237.

GREAVES, Thomas (17th. cent.)
　　d. Secular Vocal
　　Come away, sweet love (Songs of Sundrie Kindes,
　　　1604).
　　LR:Gd20, Gd32.

GREENE, Maurice (1696–1755)
　　b. Instrumental
　　Introduction and trumpet tune for trumpet and organ.
　　LB:B212.
　　Suite of Voluntaries (With BOYCE).
　　LB:B223.
　　c. Keyboard – Harpsichord and Organ
　　Lesson in D maj.
　　LB:D214.
　　Overture in D maj.
　　EB:D30.
　　Voluntary in C min.
　　EB:E65.
　　Voluntary No. 8 in D min.
　　LB:E184.
　　e. Sacred Vocal
　　Blessed are those.
　　LB:G327.
　　Lord, let me know mine end.
　　LR:Ge37.
　　LB:G322.

GREETING, Thomas (17th. cent.)
　　b. Instrumental
　　The Nightingale (The Pleasant Companion for the
　　　Flageolet, 1680).
　　EB:B56.

GREFF, Valentin – see BAKFARK, Balint.

GREFINGER, Wolfgang (c.1480–1515)
　　d. Secular Vocal
　　Ach Gott wem soll ichs klagen.
　　LR:E67.
　　Ich stell leicht ab.
　　ER:A23.
　　LR:E67.
　　Wol kumbt de May.
　　LR:E67.

GREITER, Mathias (c.1500–c.1550)
　　d. Secular Vocal
　　Es wollt ein Jäger Jagen.
　　LR:E35.

GRENON, Nicolas (1385–1450)
　　d. Secular Vocal
　　La plus jolie et la plus belle.
　　ER:A11.
　　e. Sacred Vocal
　　Nova vobis gaudia.
　　ER:B6.

GRIGNY – see DE GRIGNY, Nicolas.

GRIMACE, 'Magister' (14th. cent.)
　　d. Secular Vocal

A l'arme, a l'arme.
AN:A2.

GROSSI, Carlo (17th. cent.)
　　e. Sacred Vocal
　　Cantata Ebraica in dialogo (1681).
　　EB:G145.

GROTTE – see DE LA GROTTE, Nicolas.

GUAMI, Gioseffo (c.1540–1611)
　　b. Instrumental
　　Canzon 'La Accorto' a 4.
　　LR:B3.
　　Canzon 'La Battaglia'.
　　LR:B3.
　　Canzon 'La Brillantina.'
　　LR:A1, E24.
　　Canzon 'La Chromatica.'
　　LR:B3.
　　Canzon 'La Guamini' a 4.
　　LR:B3.
　　Canzon 'La Luchesina.'
　　LR:D18.
　　LB:E233.
　　Canzon XXV a 8.
　　LR:B3.
　　EB:G139.
　　Canzon (Unsp.) for organ.
　　LR:F90.

GUEDRON, Pierre (1565–1621)
　　d. Secular Vocal
　　Cesses mortels de soupirer.
　　LR:E48.
　　Donc ceste merveille.
　　LR:E44.
　　Quel espoir de guarir.
　　LR:E48.
　　Si jamais mon ame blessee.
　　LR:E48.
　　Si le parler et le silence (Dowland's 'Musical Banquet.')
　　LR:Gd30, Gd31.
　　Vous que le Bonjour rappelle (Dowland's 'Musical
　　　Banquet.')
　　LR:Gd30, Gd31.

GUENIN, Marie-Alexandre (1744–1835)
　　b. Instrumental
　　Sonata in D maj for harpsichord with violin, Op. 5, No. 1.
　　LB:D148.

GUERRERO, Francisco (1528–1599)
　　b. Instrumental
　　Hermosa Catalina.
　　SI:A2.
　　d. Secular Vocal
　　Dexo la venda.
　　LR:E30.
　　En tanto que de rosa.
　　SI:A2.
　　e. Sacred Vocal
　　A un nino llorando (Canciones y Villanescas Espirituales)
　　LR:F96.
　　Ave virgo sanctissima.
　　LR:F89.
　　Canite tuba in Sion.
　　LR:F96.
　　Magnificat.
　　LR:F89.
　　O Domine Jesu Christe.
　　LR:F89.
　　Ojd, ojd, una cosa divina (Canciones y Villanescas
　　　Espirituales)
　　LR:F96, F104.
　　Pastores loquebantur.

LR:F96.
Salve regina.
LR:F89.
Virgen sancta (Canciones y Villanescas Espirituales)
LR:F96.

GUERRERO, Pedro (16th. cent.)
b. Instrumental
La Perra mora.
LR:E30.

GUIGNON (18th. cent.)
b. Chamber and Instrumental
Sonata in A maj for flute and continuo, Op. 1, No. 8.
LB:B268.

GUIDO D'ARREZZO (992–1050)
e. Sacred Vocal
Ut queant laxis resonate.
AA:B8.

GUILAIN, Jean Adam (18th. cent.)
c. Keyboard – Organ
Suite du 1er ton.
LB:E171, E172.
Suite du 2em ton.
LB:E171, E172.
Suite du 3em ton.
LB:E171, E172, E219.
Suite du 4em ton.
LB:E171, E172.

GUILHEM DE CABESTANH (12th. cent.)
d. Secular Vocal
Vida.
AA:D2.

GUILLAUME D'AMIENS (13th. cent.)
b. Instrumental
Rondeau (Unsp.)
LB:B273.
d. Secular Vocal
C'est la fins.
AA:D15.
LR:E66.
E dame jolie.
LR:E66.
Pour mon cuer.
LR:E66.
Prendes i garde.
AA:D15.
Vos n'aler mie.
AA:A3.

GUILLAUME LE HEURTEUR (early 16th. cent.)
b. Instrumental
Hellas! amour (Attaingnant's 'Chansons Musicales,'
  1533).
AA:A1.
Mon petit cuer (Rhaw's 'Bicinia gallica et latina', 1545).
AA:A1.
Troys jeunes bourgeoises.
LB:B227.

GUILLAUME LE VINIER (13th. cent.)
d. Secular Vocal
Espris d'ire et d'amor.
AA:A3.

GUILLET, Charles (1600–1654)
c. Keyboard – Organ
Fantasie III.
LR:D16.

GUIOT DE DIJON (1200–1230)
d. Secular Vocal
Chanterai pour mon coirage.

AA:D21, D22.

GUIRAUT DE BORNELH (c.1150–c.1230)
d. Secular Vocal
Leu chansonet'e vil.
AA:D3.
Reis glorios.
AA:A3, D4, D5, D6.
Si us quer conselh.
AA:D1.

GUIRAUT D'ESPANHA DE TOLOZA (13th. cent.)
d. Secular Vocal
Ben volgra, s'esser poges.
AA:A1, D8.

GULIELMUS – *see* EBREO DA PESARO, Guglielmo.

GUMPELZHAIMER, Adam (1559–1625)
e. Sacred Vocal
Gelobet seist du.
LR:F109, F112, F122.
Nun freut euch.
LR:F108, F112.
Vom Himmel hoch.
LR:F108, F111, F123.

GUSSAGO, Cesario (c.1550–1625)
b. Instrumental
Sonata 'La Leonora.'
LR:E45, F87.

GUYARD (15th. cent.)
d. Secular Vocal
M'y levay par ung matin.
ER:A4.

HACQUART, Carolus (c.1649–1730)
b. Instrumental
Sonata for 2 viols and continuo, Op. 3, No. 7.
EB:B35.
Sonata in F maj, Op. 3, No. 2.
EB:B325.

HAGEN, Joachim Bernhard (18th. cent.)
b. Instrumental – Lute
Duetto.
EB:C8.
Sonata in B flat maj.
LB:C30.
Sonata in C min.
LB:C15.

HALES, Robert (d.1616)
d. Secular Vocal
O Eyes, leave off your weeping (Dowland's 'Musical
  Banquet.')
LR:Gd30, Gd31.

HALLE – *see* ADAM DE LA HALLE.

HAMAL, Jean-Noel (1709–1778)
e. Sacred Vocal
In exitu Israel – Psalm CXIII.
LB:G200.
Judith Triumphans – Oratorio, 1756.
LB:G201.

HAMMERSCHMIDT, Andreas (c.1612–1675)
d. Secular Vocal
Die Kunst des Küssens.
LB:F81.
e. Sacred Vocal
Alleluja! Freut euch, Christen alle.
LR:F114, F118.
Ihr lieben Hirten.
LR:F108.

O Freundlicher.
LR:A6.

HANDEL, Georg Friedrich (1685–1759)
a.Orchestral – Fireworks and Water Music
Music for the Royal Fireworks, 1749.
LB:A65, A239, A240, A241, A242, A243, A244, A245,
A246, A247, A248, A249, A250, A251, A252, A253,
A254, A255, A256, A257, A258, A639.
Music for the Royal Fireworks: Bourree.
LB:B322.
Music for the Royal Fireworks: La Rejoissance.
LB:E201.
Music for the Royal Fireworks, Arr. Hamilton Harty.
LB:A255, A256, A257.
The Water Music, 1717.
LB:A239, A249, A259, A260, A261, A262, A263,
A264, A265, A266, A267, A268, A269, A270, A271,
A272, A273, A274, A275.
The Water Music: Trumpet Suite No. 2 in D maj.
LB:A596, A651, A663.
The Water Music: Trumpet Suite No. 2 in D maj: Alla
hornpipe.
LB:B322.
The Water Music: Suite (Misc.)
LB:A249, A250, A251, A252, A253, A254, A255,
A256, A257, A258, A276, A277.
The Water Music: Prelude and Hornpipe.
LB:A657.
The Water Music, Arr. Hamilton Harty.
LB:A255, A256, A257.
a.Orchestral – Concerti Grossi, Opp. 3 and 6
Concerti Grossi, Op. 3, Nos. 1–6.
1 in B flat maj; 2 in B flat maj; 3 in G maj; 4 in F maj; 5 in
D min; 6 in D maj.
LB:A279, A280, A281, A282, A283, A284, A285,
A286.
Concerto Grosso in B flat maj, Op. 3, No. 1.
LB:A594.
Concerto Grosso in G maj, Op. 3, No. 3.
LB:A332.
Concerto Grosso in F maj, Op. 3, No. 4.
LB:A245.
Concerto Grosso in D maj, Op. 3, No. 6.
LB:A245.
Concerti Grossi, Op. 6, Nos. 1–12.
1 in G maj; 2 in F maj; 3 in E min; 4 in A min; 5 in D maj;
6 in G min; 7 in E flat maj; 8 in C min; 9 in F maj; 10 in
D min; 11 in A maj; 12 in B min.
LB:A285, A286, A287, A288, A289.
Concerto Grosso in G maj, Op. 6, No. 1.
LB:A290.
Concerto in F maj for organ and orchestra, Arr. Op. 6, No.
1.
LB:A326.
Concerto Grosso in F maj, Op. 6, No. 2.
LB:A290.
Concerto Grosso in E min, Op. 6, No. 3.
LB:A291.
Concerto Grosso in E min, Op. 6, No. 3: Polonaise.
LB:B322.
Concerto Grosso in A min, Op. 6, No. 4.
LB:A291.
Concerto Grosso in D maj, Op. 6, No. 5.
LB:A170, A293, A606.
Concerto Grosso in G min, Op. 6, No. 6.
LB:A253, A292, A317.
Concerto Grosso in G min, Op. 6, No. 6: Larghetto.
LB:B322.
Concerto Grosso in B flat maj, Op. 6, No. 7.
LB:A292.
Concerto Grosso in C min, Op. 6, No. 8.
LB:A293.
Concerto Grosso in F maj, Op. 6, No. 9.
LB:A293.

Concerto in B flat maj for trumpet and strings, Arr. Op. 6,
No. 9.
LB:A336.
Concerto Grosso in D min, Op. 6, No. 10.
LB:A170, A290.
Concerto in D min for organ and strings, Arr. Op. 6, No.
10.
LB:A326.
Concerto Grosso in A maj, Op. 6, No. 11.
LB:A291.
Concerto Grosso in B min, Op. 6, No. 12.
LB:A290, A582.
Concerto Grosso in B min, Op. 6, No. 12: Largo-Allegro.
LB:A617.
a.Orchestral – Concertos for organ, Opp. 4 and 7
Concertos for organ and orchestra, Op. 4, Nos. 1–6.
1 in G min; 2 in B flat maj; 3 in G min; 4 in F maj; 5 in F
maj; 6 in B flat maj.
LB:A294, A295, A296, A297, A298, A299, A300,
A301, A302, A303, A304.
Concerto in G min for organ and orchestra, Op. 4, No. 1.
(1).
LB:A305, A306, A307, A308, A309, A310.
Concerto in B flat maj for organ and orchestra, Op. 4, No.
2 (2).
LB:A239, A306, A307, A308, A311, A312, A313.
Concerto in G min for organ and orchestra, Op. 4, No. 3
(3).
LB:A239, A306, A307, A308, A311.
Concerto in G min for organ and orchestra, Op. 4, No. 3:
Gavotte.
LB:B322.
Concerto in F maj for organ and orchestra, Op. 4, No. 4
(4).
LB:A307, A308, A309, A312, A313, A314, A315,
A316, A317, A590.
Concerto in F maj for organ and orchestra, Op. 4, No. 4:
Adagio-Allegro.
LB:A617.
Concerto in F maj for organ and orchestra, Op. 4, No. 5
(5).
LB:A309, A310, A314, A318, A319.
Concerto in F maj for harp and orchestra, Arr. Op. 4, No.
5.
LB:A201, A275, A614.
Concerto in B flat maj for organ and orchestra, Op. 4, No.
6 (6).
LB:A314, A315, A318, E235.
Concerto in B flat maj for harp and orchestra, Arr. Op. 4,
No. 6.
LB:A239, A275.
Concerto in B flat maj for 2 lutes and strings, Arr. Op. 4,
No. 6.
LB:A327.
Concerto in B flat maj for recorder and strings, Arr. Op. 4,
No. 6.
LB:A328.
Concertos for organ and orchestra, Op. 7, Nos. 1–6.
1 in B flat maj; 2 in A maj; 3 in B flat maj; 4 in D min; 5 in
G min; 6 in B flat maj.
LB:A294, A295, A296, A297, A298, A299, A300,
A301, A302, A303, A304.
Concerto in B flat maj for organ and orchestra, Op. 7, No.
1 (7).
LB:A239, A316, A318, A320.
Concerto in A maj for organ and orchestra, Op. 7, No. 2
(8).
LB:A315, A317, A318, A321.
Concerto in B flat maj for organ and orchestra, Op. 7, No.
3 (9).
LB:A309, A311, A316, A319, A321, A322.
Concerto in B flat maj for organ and orchestra, Op. 7, No.
3: Siciliana.
LB:E194.

Concerto in D min for organ and orchestra, Op. 7, No. 4 (10).
LB:A312, A315, A316, A321, A322, A323, A594.
Concerto in D min for harp and strings, Arr. Op. 7, No. 4.
LB:A201, A239.
Concerto in G min for organ and orchestra, Op. 7, No. 5 (11).
LB:A320, A322, A323.
Concerto in B flat maj for organ and orchestra, Op. 7, No. 6 (12).
LB:A320, A322, A323.
Concerto in F maj for organ and orchestra, 'The Cuckoo and the Nightingale.' (13).
LB:A229, A294, A296, A297, A298, A299, A300, A301, A310, A312, A313, A319, A323, A324, A325, A597, E191.
Concerto in A maj for organ and orchestra (14).
LB:A294, A296, A297, A298, A299, A300, A301, A310, A324, A325, A326.
Concerto in D min for organ and orchestra (15).
LB:A294, A295, A296, A297, A298, A299, A300, A301, A324, A325.
Concerto in F maj for organ and orchestra (16).
LB:A294, A295, A296, A297, A298, A299, A300, A301, A325.

a. Orchestral – Other Orchestral Works
Concerto Grosso in C maj, 'Alexander's Feast.'
LB:A241, A275, A284, A292.
Concerto No. 1 in B flat maj for oboe and strings.
LB:A202, A331, A332, A334.
Concerto No. 1 in B flat maj for oboe and strings: Siciliano.
EB:B47.
LB:B322.
Concerto No. 1 in B flat maj for trumpet and strings (Arr.)
LB:A239, A333, A339.
Concerto No. 1 in B flat maj for trombone and strings (Arr.)
LB:B217.
Concerto No. 2 in B flat maj for oboe and strings.
LB:A202, A331, A332, A334, A338.
Concerto No. 2 in B flat maj for trumpet and strings (Arr.)
LB:A239, A33, A339, A669.
Concerto No. 3 in G min for oboe and strings.
LB:A197, A202, A331, A332, A334, A335, A337, A338, A594, A630, A634.
Concerto No. 3 in G min for trumpet and strings (Arr.)
LB:A239, A333, A339, A652, A668.
Concerto in E flat maj for oboe and strings (Attrib. WOODCOCK).
LB:A624.
Concerto a due cori No. 1 in B flat maj.
LB:A246, A329, A330.
Concerto a due cori No. 2 in F maj.
LB:A239, A240, A241, A245, A247, A251, A329, A330.
Concerto a due cori No. 3 in F maj.
LB:A239, A240, A244, A251, A329, A330.
Concerto Grosso in F maj for horn and organ (Arr. Concerto a due cori No. 3 in F maj.)
LB:B220.
Concerto in B min for viola and orchestra (CASSADESUS).
LB:A64.
Concerto in D maj for 2 horns, strings and continuo.
LB:A331.
Concerto in D maj for 2 trumpets, 4 horns, 2 oboes, bassoon, tympani, organ and strings.
LB:A243.
Concerto in D maj for 2 violins, cello and strings.
LB:A335.
Concerto in D min for flute, violin, cello and strings.
LB:A335.
Concerto in D min for trumpet and strings, Arr. Op. 1, No. 9.

LB:A650.
Concerto in F maj for 2 horns, 2 oboes, bassoon and strings.
LB:A243, A334.
Concerto in F maj for 4 horns, 2 oboes, bassoon and strings.
LB:A243.
Overture in D maj.
LB:A331.
Sonata for organ and strings, 'The Triumph of Time.'
LB:A298, A313.
Concerto a 4 in D min for oboe, violin and continuo.
LB:B244.
Sonata a 5 for violin, strings and continuo.
LB:A332.
Suite in D maj for trumpet, strings and continuo.
LB:A648, A658.
Love in Bath (Arr. Beecham).
LB:A278.

b. Chamber and Instrumental – Sonatas Op. 1
Sonata in E min for recorder and continuo, Op. 1, No. 1a.
LB:B132, B133, B136.
Sonata in E min for recorder and continuo, Op. 1, No. 1b.
LB:B131, B132, B134, B135.
Sonata in E min for violin and continuo, Op. 1, No. 1b.
LB:B142.
Sonata in G min for recorder and continuo, Op. 1, No. 2.
LB:B131, B135, B136, B137, B138, B139, B140, B302.
Sonata in F maj for trumpet and organ, Arr. Op. 1, No. 2.
LB:B218.
Sonata in A maj for violin and continuo, Op. 1, No. 3.
LB:B142, B143, B145, B146, B315.
Sonata in A maj for trumpet and organ, Arr. Op. 1, No. 3.
LB:B208.
Sonata in A min for recorder and continuo, Op. 1, No. 4.
LB:A600, B131, B135, B136, B137, B138, B139, B140, B235, B249, B253, B294, B301.
Sonata in G maj for recorder and continuo, Op. 1, No. 5.
LB:B131, B132, B133, B134, B135, B136.
Allegro in F maj for oboe and continuo, Op. 1, No. 5.
LB:B131, B228.
Sonata in G min for oboe and continuo, Op. 1, No. 6.
LB:B141, B256.
Sonata in G min for trumpet and organ, Arr. Op. 1, No. 6.
LB:B210.
Sonata in G min for violin and continuo, Op. 1, No. 6.
LB:B142, B146.
Sonata in G min for trombone and organ, Arr. Op. 1, No. 6.
LB:B217.
Sonata in C maj for recorder and continuo, Op. 1, No. 7.
LB:E131, B135, B136, B137, B138, B139, B140, B287.
SI:C9.
Sonata in C min for oboe and continuo, Op. 1, No. 8.
LB:A618, B131, B137, B141, B264.
Sonata in B min for recorder and continuo, Op. 1, No. 9.
LB:B132, B133, B134, B135, B136.
SI:C3.
Tempo di minuet in D min for recorder and continuo, Op. 1, No. 9.
LB:B131.
Sonata in G min for violin and continuo, Op. 1, No. 10.
LB:B142, B143, B145, B146.
Sonata in G min for violin and continuo, Op. 1, No. 10: Adagio.
LB:B322.
Sonata in F maj for recorder and continuo, Op. 1, No. 11.
LB:B131, B135, B136, B137, B138, B139, B140, B146, B272, B277, B291.
Sonata in F maj for violin and continuo, Op. 1, No. 12.
LB:B142, B143, B145, B146.
Sonata in F maj for trumpet and organ, Arr. Op. 1, No. 12.
LB:B208.
Sonata in D maj for violin and continuo, Op. 1, No. 13.

LB:D159.
Gavotte in G maj (Aylesford I).
LB:D159.
Minuet in A min (Aylesford I).
LB:D159.
Minuet in D maj (Aylesford I).
LB:D159.
Passapied in A maj (Aylesford I).
LB:D159.
Aylesford Pieces II (Excpts).
LB:D161.
Partita in A maj (Youthful Pieces).
LB:D160.
Minuet in G min (Unsp. Aylesford).
LB:D65.
Pieces for Clay's Musical Clock.
LB:E216.
10 Pieces for Mechanical Clock.
LB:A305.
d.Secular Vocal – German Arias, Italian Cantatas
Das Zitterude Glanzer der spielende Wellen.
LB:F29.
Die Ihr aus duklen Gruften den eitlen Mammon grabt.
LB:F29.
Flammende Rose Zierde der Erden.
LB:F29.
In de angenehmen Buschen.
LB:F29.
Kunft'ger Zeiten elttier Kummer.
LB:F29.
Meine Seele hort im Sehen.
LB:F29, F78.
Single, Seele, Gott zum preise.
LB:F29.
Susse Stille, sanfte Quelle ruhiger Gelassenhelt.
EB:F92.
LB:F29, F78.
Susser Blumen Ambra Flocken.
LB:F29.
Ah che troppo inegale.
LB:F26.
Armida abbandonata.
LB:F25, G66.
Beato in ver.
LB:F28.
Cuopre tal volta in cielo.
LB:F21.
Dalla guerra amorosa.
LB:F21.
Delirio amoroso.
LB:F27.
Dolce pur d'amore l'affano.
LB:F83, G182.
Donna che in ciel.
LB:G219.
Figlio d'alte speranza.
LB:F25.
Langue geme.
LB:F28.
Nel dolce del' oblio.
LB:F25, F26, F27.
Parti, l'idolo mio.
LB:F28.
Sento la che ristretto.
LB:F28.
Silete venti.
LB:F26.
Spande ancor a mio dispetto: Theme and Variations in G min.
LB:B320.
Tanti strali.
LB:F28.
Una alma innamorata.
LB:F25.
d.Secular Vocal – Odes

Look down Harmonious Saint – Praise of Harmony.
LB:F26, F78.
Ode for the Birthday of Queen Anne, 1713.
LB:F32.
Ode for St. Cecilia's Day, 1739.
LB:F30, F31, G208.
Ode for St. Cecilia's Day, 1739: Trumpet Voluntary.
LB:B219.
d.Secular Vocal – Secular Oratorios, Operas
Acis and Galatea – Secular Oratorio, 1720.
LB:F33, F34, F35, F36.
Acis and Galatea: O ruddier than the cherry.
LB:B227.
Admeto – Opera, 1727.
LB:F37.
Admeto: Overture.
LB:A342, A343.
Admeto: Cangio d'aspetto.
LB:F49.
Agrippina: Overture.
LB:A330, A340.
Alcina: Overture.
LB:A242, A255, A276, A340, A343, A346.
Alcina: Ballet Music.
LB:A346.
Alcina: Ah! mio cor! schernito sei.
LB:F48.
Alcina: Tirana gelosia.
LB:F48.
Alcina: Tornami a vagheggiar.
LB:F48.
Alcina: Verdi prati.
LB:F49.
Alexander Balus: Convey me to some peaceful gloom.
LB:F49.
Alexander's Feast – Secular Oratorio, 1736.
LB:F38, F39.
Alexander's Feast: Overture.
LB:A342.
Il Allegro ed il Penseroso – Secular Oratorio, 1740.
LB:F40.
Almira: Ballet Music.
LB:F82.
Amadigi: Sinfonia.
EB:F109.
Amadigi: D'un sventurato amante...Pena tiranna io sento al core.
EB:F109.
Amadigi: Ah! spietato!
EB:F109.
Amadigi: Mi deride l'amante...Destero dall' empia Dite.
EB:F109.
Amadigi: Addio, crudo Amadigi!...Io gia sento l'alma in sen.
EB:F109.
Ariana: Overture.
LB:A330.
Ariodante: Overture.
LB:A276, A344, A346.
Ariodante: Sinfonia Pastorale.
LB:A346.
Ariodante: Ballet Music.
LB:A346.
Ariodante: Orchestral Suite.
LB:A171.
Arminio: Overture.
LB:A345.
Atalanta: March.
LB:A246.
Atalanta: Care selve.
LB:F49.
Berenice: Overture.
LB:A244, A255, A276, A334, A344, A590.
Berenice: Minuet.
LB:A581.

The Choice of Hercules – Secular Oratorio, 1745.
LB:F41.
The Choice of Hercules: Overture.
LB:A342.
Deidamia: Overture.
LB:A340, A345.
Ester: Overture.
LB:A343, A344.
Faramondo: Overture.
LB:A276, A345.
Giulio Cesare: Overture.
LB:A345.
Giulio Cesare: Minuet.
LB:A345.
Giulio Cesare: Aure, deh, per pieta.
LB:F42.
Giulio Cesare: Da tempeste il legno infranto.
LB:F42, F48.
Giulio Cesare: Piangero, la sorte mia.
LB:F42, F48.
Giulio Cesare: Priva son d'ogni conforte.
LB:F42.
Giulio Cesare: Se pieta di me non senti.
LB:F42.
Giulio Cesare: Si, spietata, il tuo rogore sveglia.
LB:F42.
Giulio Cesare: Sperai ne m'ingannai.
LB:F42.
Giulio Cesare: Tu la mia stella sei.
LB:F42.
Giulio Cesare: Va tacito e nascosto.
LB:F42.
Giulio Cesare: V'adoro, pupille.
LB:F42, F48.
Giulio Cesare: Venere bella.
LB:F42.
Lotario: Overture.
LB:A342, A343.
Orlando: Overture.
LB:A343.
Ottone: Overture.
LB:A342, A343.
Ottone: Da speranza e giunto in porto.
LB:F49.
Ottone: Vieni, o figlio.
LB:F49.
Partenope – Opera, 1730.
LB:F43.
Partenope: Overture.
LB:A343.
Partenope: Voglio dire.
LB:F49.
Il Pastor Fido: Pour les Chasseurs I and II.
LB:A346.
Poro: Overture.
LB:A343.
Radamisto: Overture.
LB:A340, A345.
Rinaldo – Opera, 1711.
LB:F44.
Rinaldo: Overture.
LB:A340, A344.
Rinaldo: March and Battle.
LB:A344.
Rinaldo: Lascio ch'io piango.
LB:F49.
Rodelinda: Overture.
LB:A242, A340.
Rodelinda: Dove sei.
LB:F49.
Rodrigo: Orchestral Suite.
LB:A171.
Scipione: Overture.
LB:A276, A345.
Semele – Opera, 1744.

LB:F45.
Semele: Overture.
LB:A345.
Serse (Xerxes) – Opera, 1738.
LB:F46.
Serse: Ombra ma fui.
LB:A658, B206.
Sosarme – Opera, 1732.
LB:F47.
Sosarme: Overture.
LB:A344.
Sosarme: Alle sfere della gloria.
LR:Gd3.
Sosarme: In mille dolci modi.
LR:Gd3.
Sosarme: M'opporro da generoso.
LR:Gd3.
Sosarme: Per le porte del tormento.
LR:Gd3.
Sosarme: Tu caro, caro sei.
LR:Gd3.
Susanna: Overture.
LB:A340.
Tesseo: Overture.
LB:A342, A344.

e. Sacred Vocal – Chandos Anthems
CA1. O be joyful in the Lord.
LB:G202.
CA2. In the Lord I put my trust.
LB:G203, G204.
CA3. Have mercy upon me, O God.
LB:G203.
CA4. O sing unto the Lord a new song.
LB:G205.
CA5. I will magnify Thee, O Lord.
LB:G202, G204.
CA6. As pants the Hart for cooling streams.
LB:G205, G206, G208.
CA9. O praise the Lord with one consent.
LB:G207, G208.
CA10. The Lord is my light.
LB:G206, G208, G319.
CA11. Let God arise.
LB:G207, G208.

e. Sacred Vocal – Coronation Anthems
The King shall rejoice.
LB:G208, G209, G210, G211, G252, G319.
Let thy hand be strengthened.
LB:G208, G209, G210, G211.
My heart is inditing.
LB:G208, G209, G210, G211.
Zadok the priest.
LB:G208, G209, G210, G211, G215, G218, G252, G253, G320.

e. Sacred Vocal – Other Anthems, Psalms, etc.
Alleluia (fragment).
LB:F83.
Amen (fragment).
LB:F83.
Blessed are they that consider the poor – Foundling Hospital Anthem, 1749.
LB:F32.
Dettingen Te Deum.
LB:G213, G214.
Dixit Dominus – Psalm CIX.
LB:G216, G217, G218.
Gloria in excelsis Deo.
LB:B206.
Salve regina.
LB:G219.
Sing unto God – Wedding Anthem.
LB:G78.
Utrecht Te Deum and Jubilate.
LB:G215.

The Ways of Zion do mourn - Funeral Anthem for Queen
  Caroline.
LB:G212.

e. Sacred Vocal - Oratorios
Belshazzar's Feast - Oratorio, 1745.
LB:G239, G240.
Belshazzar's Feast: Overture.
LB:A242, A340.
Belshazzar's Feast: Sinfonia.
LB:A345.
Deborah - Oratorio, 1733.
LB:G241.
Israel in Egypt - Oratorio, 1739.
LB:G242, G243, G244, G245.
Israel in Egypt: He gave them hailstones.
LB:G253.
Israel in Egypt: He spake the word.
LB:G253.
Israel in Egypt: Moses and the children of Israel.
LB:G252.
Jephta - Oratorio, 1752.
LB:G246, G247.
Jephta: Overture.
LB:A242, A340.
Jephta: Sinfonia.
LB:A344.
Jephta: When his loud voice.
LB:G253.
Joseph: Overture.
LB:A342, F26.
Joshua: March.
LB:A246.
Judas Maccabaeus - Oratorio, 1747.
LB:G248.
Judas Maccabaeus: Overture.
LB:A345.
Judas Maccabaeus: Father of Heaven.
LB:G185.
Judas Maccabaeus: For Zion lamentation make.
LB:G252.
Judas Maccabaeus: Mourn ye afflicted children.
LB:G252.
Judas Maccabaeus: O Father whose almighty voice.
LB:G252.
Judas Maccabaeus: See the conquering hero comes.
LB:G252, G253.
Judas Maccabaeus: Daughter of Zion (Tochter Zion).
LR:F121.
The Messiah - Oratorio, 1742.
LB:G220, G221, G222, G223, G224, G225, G226,
  G227, G228, G229, G230, G231, G232, G233, G234,
  G235(E), G236(E), G237(E).
The Messiah - Oratorio, Arr. W.A.Mozart.
LB:G238.
The Messiah: Overture.
LB:A239, A276.
The Messiah: Comfort ye.
LB:A239.
The Messiah: Every valley.
LB:A239.
The Messiah: O thou that tellest.
LB:A239, G185.
The Messiah: For unto us a Child is born.
LR:F105.
LB:A239, G253.
The Messiah: Pastoral Symphony.
LR:F121.
LB:A239, A242, A276, A581, A609.
The Messiah: There were shepherds.
LB:A239.
The Messiah: Glory to God.
LB:A239.
The Messiah: Rejoice greatly.
LB:F48.

The Messiah: And he shall feed.
LB:A239.
The Messiah: He was despised.
LB:G185.
The Messiah: The Lord gave the word.
LB:A239.
The Messiah: How beautiful are the feet.
LB:F48.
The Messiah: Why do the nations.
LB:A239.
The Messiah: Alleluia.
LB:A239, E209, G253.
The Messiah: I know that my redeember liveth.
LB:A239, F48.
The Messiah: Worthy is the lamb.
LB:A239, G253.
The Messiah: Amen.
LB:A239.
La Resurrezione - Oratorio, 1708.
LB:G249.
Samson: Awake the trumpet's lofty sound.
LB:B219.
Samson: Hear Jacob's voice.
LB:G252.
Samson: Let the bright seraphim.
LB:F48, G252.
Samson: Let their celestial concerts.
LB:G252.
Samson: Return, O God of hosts.
LB:G185.
Samson: To song and dance.
LB:G252.
Samson: With plaintive note.
LB:F48.
Saul - Oratorio, 1739.
LB:G250.
Saul: Overture.
LB:A276.
Saul: Instrumental Suite.
LB:A341.
Saul: Gird on thy sword.
LB:G253.
Solomon - Oratorio, 1749 (Arr. Beecham).
LB:G251.
Solomon: Overture.
LB:A276, A344.
Solomon: Sinfonia 'Arrival of the Queen of Sheba.'
LB:A344, A590, A598, A601.
Solomon: May no rash intruder.
LB:G253.

HANDL-GALLUS, Jacobus (1550-1591)
  d. Secular Vocal
Harmonia Morales - Motets, 1590.
LR:E6.
Moralia - Motets, 1586.
LR:E6.
  e. Sacred Vocal
Adoramus te, Jesu Christe.
LR:F79.
Ave Maria.
LR:F82.
Canite tuba in Sion.
LR:F82.
Ecce concipes.
LR:F115.
Ecce quomodo moritur justus.
LR:E47, F81.
Jesu dulcis memoria.
LR:E60.
Missa 'Ad imitationem Pater Noster.'
LR:F98.
Missa 'super Elizabethae Impletum est tempus.'
LR:F95.
Omnes de Saba.

LR:F113.
Pueri concinite.
LR:F98, F125.
Resonet in laudibus.
AN:B2.
Si tibi gratia.
LR:F98.

HANFF, Johann Nikolaus (1630–1706)
c. Keyboard – Organ
Ein feste Burg ist unser Gott.
EB:E77.
Helf mir Gottes gute preisen.
EB:E77.

HARANT, Krystof (1564–1621)
e. Sacred Vocal
Crucifixus a 3vv.
LR:F25.
Maria Kron.
LR:F25.
Missa a 5vv.
LR:F25.
Qui confidunt in Domine.
LR:F25.

HASPROIS, Johannes Simon (= HASPRE) (1360–1428)
d. Secular Vocal
Puisque je sui fumeux.
ER:A11.
Ma doulce amour.
AA:A2.
AN:A2, A3.

HASSE, Johann Adolf (1699–1783)
a. Orchestral
Concerto in G maj for flute, strings and continuo.
LB:A640.
Concerto in G maj for mandolin and orchestra.
LB:A614.
b. Instrumental
Sonata in G maj for mandolin and harpsichord.
LB:C28.
d. Secular Vocal
Canzoni da batelo (Venetian Gondolier Songs).
LB:F50.
Arminio – Opera, 1745/53: Overture.
LB:A640.
Arminio: Son par sola una volta...Se col pianto.
LB:A640.
La Clemenza di Tito – Opera, c.1731: Allegro ma non
troppo, Act III.
LB:F79.
La Clemenza di Tito: Tardi savvede d'un tradimento.
LB:F79.

HASSE, Nicolaus (c.1650)
c. Keyboard – Organ
Allein Gott in der Höh' sei Ehr'.
EB:E38.
Jesus Christus unser Heiland.
EB:E38.
Komm Heiliger Geist, Herre Gott.
EB:E38.

HASSLER, Hans Leo (1564–1612)
b. Instrumental
Canzon.
LR:C12.
3 Intradas.
LR:B10, B17, B18.
Intrada V.
EB:B38.
d. Secular Vocal
Ach weh des Leiden.
LR:E65.

Hertzlieb zu dir allein.
LR:E65.
Ihr Musici, frisch auf!
LR:E22.
Im Kuhlen Maien.
LR:E22.
Jungfrau, dein schon Gestalt.
LR:E22, E65.
Mein lieb will mit mir kriegen.
LR:E22.
Tanzen und springen.
LR:E65.
e. Sacred Vocal
Angelus ad pastores ait.
LR:F114, F122.
Cantate Domino canticum novum.
LR:F26.
Christe, du bist der helle Tag.
EB:G132.
Christum wir sollen loben schon – A solis ortus cardine.
LR:F103.
Domine Dominus noster.
LR:F26.
Missa octavi toni a 8vv.
LR:F26.
Missa secunda a 4vv.
LR:F27.
Nun komm der Heiland Heiland – Veni redemptor
gentium.
LR:F103.
O sacrum convivium.
LR:F26.
Resonet in laudibus.
LR:F103.
Verbum caro factum est.
LR:F105, F122, F126.
Vom Himmel hoch.
LR:F103.

HAUSSMAN, Valentin (c.1588–c.1614)
b. Instrumental
Catkanei.
LR:B21.
Danse Allemande I–III.
LR:B10.
Deutscher Tanz mit Nachtanz.
EB:B46.
Galliard.
LR:B21.
Neue artige und liebliche Tantze.
LR:B30.
Paduan.
LR:B21.
Partita a 5 in G maj.
EB:B67.
Partita.
LR:B25.
Pavan and Galliard.
EB:B46.
Pavan.
EB:G132.
Tantz.
LR:B21.

HAYNE VAN GHIZEGHEM (15th. cent.)
d. Secular Vocal (Including Instrumental Arrangements)
A la audience.
ER:A2.
Amors, amors trop me fiers.
ER:A13.
De quatre nuits.
ER:A5.
De tous biens plaine.
ER:A1, A13.
LR:Gf6.

Gentil gallans.
ER:A7.
Mon souvenir de vous.
ER:A5.
Pour ce que j'ay jouy.
ER:A13.

HEBERLE, Anton (18th. cent.)
  b. Instrumental
  Sonata brillante for recorder solo.
  LB:B307.

HECKEL, Wolff (b.1515)
  b. Instrumental
  Mille regretz (after Josquin).
  LR:A1.
  Nach willen dein.
  LR:A1.
  Proportz auff den Ungarischen Tantz.
  LR:C17.
  Ungarescha.
  LR:A5, B27, C17.

HEER SONGBOOK (Compiled by Johannes Heer, c.1510)
  d/e. Secular and Sacred Vocal (Including Instrumental
  Pieces)
  Adieu soulas.
  LR:E72.
  Es gieng guot tröscher.
  LR:E35, E72.
  Es sass ein meitlein unde spann.
  LR:E72.
  Exputandi tempus est.
  LR:E72.
  La Gran pena.
  LR:E72.
  Guillaume se va chaufer.
  LR:E72.
  Hans, der het ein wib genommen.
  LR:E72.
  Min herz lidt schmerz und grosse not.
  LR:E72.
  La Mora – Carminum.
  LR:E72.
  O praeclara virginum.
  LR:E72.
  Sancta Trinitas.
  LR:E72.
  Sy j'ayme mon amy.
  LR:E72.
  Unser meister het ein magd.
  LR:E72.
  Verlangen hart.
  LR:E72.
  Die Vollen brueden.
  LR:E72.

HEINICHEN, Johann David (1683–1729)
  a. Orchestral
  Pastorale in A maj per la notte della Nativitate Christi.
  LB:A640.
  Concerto a 8 for 4 recorders and strings.
  LB:A636.
  Concerto in C maj for 4 flutes and strings: Allegro.
  LB:B259.

HEINRICH VON MEISSEN (= FRAUENLOB) (d.1318)
  d. Secular Vocal
  Ez waent ein narrenwise.
  AA:D25.
  Ob ich di Wahrheit lerne.
  AN:B1.

HEINTZ, Wolff (c.1520)
  d. Secular Vocal
  Da trunken sie.

LR:E64.

HELLENDAAL, Pieter (1721–1799)
  a. Orchestral
  Concerto in E flat maj for strings and continuo. Op. 2, No.
  3.
  LB:A595.

HELLINCK, Lupus (1495–1541)
  d. Secular Vocal
  Comp alle voort by twee by dry.
  EB:B35.
  e. Sacred Vocal
  Capitan Herrgt.
  LR:F78.

HELMONT, Charles Joseph van (1715–1790)
  c. Keyboard – Organ
  Fugue in E min.
  EB:E78.
  LB:E210.
  Fugue in G maj.
  EB:E78.
  e. Sacred Vocal
  Accensa furore – Motet.
  LB:G188.

HENRY VIII (1491–1547)
  b. Instrumental
  Consort II.
  LR:Gf6.
  Consort IV.
  LR:Ga17.
  Consort VIII.
  LR:Gf6.
  Consort XII.
  LR:Ga17.
  Consort XIII.
  LR:Gf6.
  Consort XVI.
  LR:Gf6.
  Fantasia a 3.
  SI:C13.
  2 Fantasias a 3.
  SI:C11.
  d. Secular Vocal
  Adieu madame et ma maistresse.
  LR:Gf7.
  En vray amour.
  LR:Ga17, Gf6.
  Gentil prince de renom.
  LR:Gf6.
  Green grow'th th'holy.
  AA:C1.
  Helas madame.
  LR:Gf6, Gf7.
  If love now reigned.
  LR:Ga17, Gf6.
  SI:C11.
  Pastime with good company.
  LR:E60, Gf2, Gf4, Gf6.
  SI:C11.
  Taunder knaken.
  LR:Gf2, Gf6.
  SI:B2.
  Without discord and both accord.
  SI:C11.

HEREDIA, Sebastian Aguilera de (c.1565–1627)
  c. Keyboard – Organ
  Ensalada.
  LR:D13.
  Pange lingua.
  LR:D13.
  EB:E79.
  Salve de lleno.

LR:D13.
EB:E79.
Tiento de falsas de 4o tono.
LR:D13.
EB:E79.
Tiento lleno de 1o tono.
LR:D13.
EB:E79.

HERMAN, Johan (16th. cent.)
e. Sacred Vocal
Lobt Gott, ihr Christen.
LR:F112.

HERMANN VON SALZBURG (14th. cent.)
b. Instrumental
Das Nachthorn.
AA:A1.
Der Trumpet.
AA:A1.
Untarn slaf tut den sumer vol.
AA:A1.
d. Secular Vocal
Dem allerliebsten schonen Weib.
AN:B1.
Hor, hor, liebste Frau.
AN:B1.
Spielmannlied.
LR:B29.

HERMANNUS CONTRACTUS (1013–1054)
e. Sacred Vocal
Alma redemptoris mater (Marian Antiphon).
ER:B23.

HERTEL, Johann Wilhelm (1727–1789)
a. Orchestral
Concerto a 6 for trumpet, oboe and strings.
LB:A19.
Concerto in B flat maj for trumpet and strings.
LB:A650.
Concerto a 5 in D maj for trumpet, 2 oboes, 2 bassoons
and continuo.
LB:A647, A660.
Concerto in D maj for trumpet, oboe, bassoon, and
strings.
LB:A336.
Concerto in E flat maj for trumpet and orchestra.
LB:A336.
Sonata a 4 in E flat maj for trumpet and strings.
LB:A658.

HESSEN – *see* MORITZ VON HESSEN.

HEUDELINE, Louis (fl.1701)
b. Chamber and Instrumental
Suite No. 1 in D min for viol and continuo.
SI:C21.

HEUGEL, Hans (early 16th. cent.)
d. Secular Vocal
Entlaubet ist der Walde.
ER:A24.

HEURTEUR – *see* GUILLAUME LE HEURTEUR

HEWITT, James (18th. cent.)
c. Keyboard
The Battle of Trenton.
LB:E191.

HIDALGO, Juan (1612–1685)
d. Secular Vocal
Atiende y da.
EB:F97.
Ay corazon amante.
EB:F97.

Ay que me vio.
EB:F97.
Con tanto respecto adoran.
EB:F97.
Credito es de mi decoro.
LB:F84.
Cuydado pastor.
LB:F84.
De las luces que en el mar.
LB:F84.
Peynandose estave un olmo.
EB:F97.
Tonante Dios.
LB:F84.
Trompicavanlas amor.
LB:F84.

HILTON, John (I) (d.1608)
d. Secular Vocal
Fair Oriana (Triumphs of Oriana).
LR:Gd34.

HILTON, John (II) (1599–1657)
b. Instrumental
Fantasia I.
EB:B65.
Fantasia II.
EB:B65.
Fantasia III.
EB:B65, B69.

HINGSTON, John (d.1683)
c. Keyboard – Organ
Voluntary for double organ.
EB:F91.

HOFHAIMER, Paul (1459–1537)
b. Instrumental
Carmen.
LR:F78.
Carmen in re.
LR:E67.
Carmen in sol.
LR:E63.
Carmen Magistri Pauli.
LR:D21, E67.
c. Keyboard
Recordare.
LB:E239.
Salve regina.
LR:D17.
Salve virgo.
ER:A23.
d. Secular Vocal (Including instrumental arrangements)
Ach lieb mit Lied.
LR:E68.
Cupido hat.
LR:E67.
Ein frohlich wesen.
ER:A1.
Freundlicher Trost.
ER:A23.
Greiner zanner.
ER:A23.
LR:E67.
Der Hunt.
LR:E67.
Man hat bisher.
LR:E67.
Mein herz hat sich mit lieb verpflicht.
ER:A23.
Mein herzigs A.
ER:A23.
Meins Traurens ist.
LR:B30.

Nach willen dein.
LR:A1, E67.
Die Prünlein di da vliessen.
ER:A23.
Zucht, Ehr und Lob.
LR:E68.

HOLBORNE, Anthony (1550–1602)
  b.Instrumental – Consort
As it fell upon a holy eve.
LR:C24, Ga17.
EB:B13.
The Choice.
LR:Ga17.
EB:B13.
The Countess of Pembroke's Paradise.
LR:Ga8, Gd29.
The Cradle – Pavan.
LR:F117, Ga8, Gd43.
Dances and Ayres a 5 – Suite (Unsp.)
LB:B227, B281, B286.
The Fairy Round.
AA:A1.
LR:Ga13, Ga15, Ga17, Gb4, Gb8.
EB:B13.
Farewell Galliard.
LR:Gd29.
The Funerals – Pavan.
LR:B21, Ga10, Ge36.
Galliard (Unsp.)
LR:B10, Ga8, Ga10, Ga13, Ga16, Ga17, Ga21, Gb4, Gb5, Gb6.
SI:A2, B1.
Galliard for cittern and bass.
AA:A1.
Heart's Ease.
LR:Gb4, Gb8, Ge36.
Heigh ho, holiday – Coranto.
LR:B21, Ga8, Ga10, Ga14, Ga16, Gb4, Gb8, Gd37, Gd39.
EB:B13.
LB:B259.
Heres Paternus.
LR:Ga8.
SI:A2.
Holborne's Almain.
LR:Ga8.
The Honiesuckle – Almain.
LR:B10, Ga10, Ga15, Ga16.
EB:B13.
The Image of Melancholy.
SI:B2.
Last will and testament.
EB:B13.
SI:A2.
Lullabie – Galliard.
LR:Ga17.
The Mariegold.
EB:B13.
Muy Linda.
LR:Ga8.
SI:A2.
The New Year's Gift.
LR:F117, Gd43.
EB:B13.
The Night Watch.
LR:Ga15, Ga16, Gd48, Ge36.
EB:B13.
LB:B259.
SI:A2.
Noel's Galliard.
LR:B21, Ga8.
EB:B13.
LB:B259.
Pavan.

LR:Ga16, Gb4, Gb5.
Pavan and Galliard (J61, J131).
LR:Ga8.
Pavan and Galliard (J64, J125).
LR:Ga8.
Pavan and Galliard.
LR:B10, Gd48.
SI:B1.
Pavana ploravit.
LR:Ga13.
Prelude.
LR:Gd37.
Quadro Pavan and Galliard.
LR:Ga8.
Sedet sola.
LR:Ga13.
The Sighes.
LR:Ga16.
Suite for 2 flutes, viola da bracchio, viola da gamba and trombone.
LR:E63.
The Teares of the Muses.
LR:Gd37.
Tinternell.
SI:A2.
The Wanton.
LR:B10, Ga8.
EB:B13.
The Widowe's Mite.
LR:Gd19.
EB:B39.
The Woods so Wild – Galliard.
LR:Ga8.
  d.Secular Vocal
My heavy sprite, oppressed with sorrow's might (Dowland's 'Musical Banquet.')
LR:Gd30, Gd31.
When daffodils begin to peere.
LR:Gd23.

HOLCOMBE (17th./18th. cent.)
  c.Keyboard – Harpsichord
3 Airs.
LB:D223.

HOLLIS (17th. cent.)
  b.Instrumental
John Blunderville's Last Farewell.
LR:Gb7.

HOLMES, John (d.1602)
  d.Secular Vocal
Thus bonny-boots (Triumphs of Oriana).
LR:Gd34, Gd35.

HOMILIUS, Gottfried August (1714–1785)
  e.Sacred Vocal
So gehst du nun, mein Jesus hin.
LB:G321.

HOOPER, Edmund (c.1553–1621)
  c.Keyboard
Alman (Fitzwilliam Virginal Book).
LR:Gc6.

HORTENSA – see CANCIONERO HORTENSA.

HORVATH, Andras Szkharosi (16th. cent.)
  d.Secular Vocal
Do not grieve (Hofgreff Songbook, 1552–3).
LR:A5.

HOTTETERRE, Jacques 'Le Romain.' (1680–1761)
  b.Instrumental
Ecos for solo flute, Op. 2.
LB:A600.
Prelude for solo flute.

LB:B272.
Prelude in A min for recorder and continuo.
LB:B269.
Prelude in F maj for recorder and continuo.
LB:B269.
Sonata in D maj for oboe and continuo, Op. 5, No. 3.
LB:B241.
Suite for 3 recorders.
LB:B281.
Suite in E min for recorder and continuo.
LB:B189.
Suite No. 1 in F maj for 2 flutes and continuo.
LB:B267, B274.
Suite in B flat maj for recorder and continuo, Op. 2.
LB:A600.
Trio Sonata in C maj for 2 oboes and continuo, Op. 3.
LB:A600.
Trio Sonata in C maj for 2 recorders and continuo, Op. 3.
No. 5.
LB:B284.
Bouree d'Achille (Methode pour la Musette, Op. 10).
LB:A600.

HOTTETERRE, Jean (d.c.1691)
  b.Instrumental
  Contredanse.
  LB:A593, B259.
  Marche.
  LB:A593, B259.
  La Noce Champetre: Excpts.
  LB:A593, B282, B324.

HOTTETERRE, Louis (18th. cent.)
  b.Instrumental
  Bourree.
  LB:B323.

HOWETT, Gregory (1550–1614)
  b.Instrumental – Lute
  Fantasia.
  LR:C11, C13, C16.

HOYOUL, Balduin (1548–1594)
  d.Secular Vocal
  Anchor che col partire.
  LR:E39.

HUGARD, 'Monsieur.' (fl.1754)
  b.Chamber and Instrumental
  Suite No. 4 for viol and continuo.
  SI:C20.

HUME, Tobias (d.1645)
  b.Instrumental
  I am melancholy.
  SI:C20.
  Musical Humours.
  LR:Ga19.
  Musicke and Mirthe.
  LR:A1.
  Touch me lightly and tickle me quickley.
  LR:Gd19.
  d.Secular Vocal
  Tobacco, tobacco.
  LR:Gd49.

HUMPREY, Pelham (1647–1674)
  e.Sacred Vocal
  A Hymn to God the Father.
  EB:F103.

HUNT, Thomas (16th./17th. cent.)
  d.Secular Vocal
  Hark! Did ye ever hear? (Triumphs of Oriana).
  LR:Gd34, Gd35.

ILEBORGH, Adam (15th. cent.)
  c.Keyboard – Organ
  Mensura trium notarum.
  LR:D17.
  Sequitur mensura notarum einsdem tenoris.
  LR:D17.

INDIA – *see* D'INDIA, Sigismondo.

INGEGNERI, Marco Antonio (c.1547–1592)
  e.Sacred Vocal
  O bone Jesu, miserere nobis.
  LR:F81.

INGLOT, William (16th./17th. cent.)
  b.Instrumental
  The Leaves be Green.
  LR:A1.

INSULIS, Franco de (14th. cent.)
  b.Instrumental
  Je ne vis pas.
  AA:A2.
  AN:A3.

IPPOLITO, (16th. cent.)
  b.Instrumental
  Canzon sopra 'Susanna.'
  LR:E54.

ISAAC, Heinrich (=Arigo) (1450–1517)
  b.Instrumental
  A la battaglia.
  ER:A2.
  Bruder Konrad.
  LR:A1.
  Carmen saecularis.
  ER:A7.
  Carmen in fa.
  LR:F78.
  Carmen in sol.
  LR:F78.
  La mi la sol.
  LR:B30, E63, Gf2.
  La Mora.
  LR:E69.
  Palle, palle.
  LR:A1.
  d.Secular Vocal (Including instrumental arrangements)
  Donna di dentro di tua casa.
  ER:A1, A6.
  LR:A2.
  E qui la dira.
  LR:E25.
  Es het ein Baur ein Tochterlein.
  LR:A2, E63, E68.
  Freundtlich und mild.
  LR:B30.
  Ich stuend an einem Morgen.
  LR:E68.
  Imperii proceres.
  ER:A14.
  LR:A2, E32.
  Innsbruck, ich muss dich lassen.
  LR:A2, A3, E22, E54, E68, E69.
  LB:A641.
  Helogierons nous.
  LR:E69.
  La la hö hö.
  LR:A1, E24.
  Maudit soyt.
  LR:E69.
  Ne piu bella di queste.
  LR:A1.
  O Venus bant.
  LR:B30.

Quis dabit capiti meo aquam.
ER:A14, B7.
Suesser vatter.
LR:F78.
Tmeiskin vas iunch.
LR:B22.
Un di lieto giama.
ER:A6.
Wann ich des morgens fru auffstehe.
LR:B30.
Zwishen Berg und Tiefem Tal.
EB:E88.
e. Sacred Vocal
Introitus in Nativitate Domine.
LR:F103.
Missa 'La bernadina': Agnus Dei.
ER:A2.
O Maria, mater Christi.
ER:B7.
Quis dabit pacem.
LR:A1.
Regina caeli laetare.
ER:B7.
Sancti spiritus assit nobis.
LR:E32.
Tota pulchra es.
ER:B7.

ISAAC, Heinrich – *see also* **KLEBER** and **KOTTER.**

ISTVANFFY CODEX (16th./17th. cent. Hungarian.)
b. Instrumental – Lute
El Burata.
LR:C20.
Paduana.
LR:C20.
Wo sol ich mich hinkehren.
LR:C20.

IVES, Simon (1600–1662)
b. Instrumental
Ayre.
SI:A1.
Coranto.
SI:A1.
The Fancy.
SI:A1.
Pavan.
SI:A1.
The Virgin.
LR:Gd46.
SI:A1.

IVREA CODEX (1360–1370, Ars Nova Motets)
d. Secular Vocal
Clap, clap, par un matin – Sus Robin.
AA:B1.
Febus mundo oriens – Lanista – Cornibus.
AA:B1.
O Philippe, Franci qui generis – O bone dux.
AA:B1.
Les ormel a la turelle – Mayn se leva – Je n'y saindai.
AA:B1.

JACHET DE MANTUA (16th. cent.)
e. Sacred Vocal
O angele Dei.
LR:E32.

JACINTO (17th. cent.)
c. Keyboard
Toccata in D min.
LB:D215.

JACOPO DA BOLOGNA (1300–1365)
d. Secular Vocal

A quil'altera – Creatura gentil – Veel de dio.
AN:B3.
Di nuovo e giunto.
AA:A1.
AN:B3, B10.
Fenice fu.
AN:B9.
In verde prato.
AN:B8.
I'sent'za.
AN:B6.
Lucida petra.
AN:B3, B8.
Nell' acqua chiara.
AN:B8.
Non al so amante.
AN:B8.
O dolce appress' un bel perlaro.
AN:B8.
Oselletto selvaggio.
AN:B4.
Tanto soavemente.
AA:A1.
Vola el bel sparver.
AN:B6.

JACOTIN, Jacques (d.1529)
d. Secular Vocal
Je suis desheritee.
LR:E38.
A Paris a trois fillettes.
LR:E33.
Voyant souffrir.
LB:B227.

JACQUES DE CAMBRAI (1260–1290)
d. Secular Vocal
Retrowange novelle.
AA:D21.

JANITSCH, Johann Gottlieb (1708–1763)
b. Chamber and Instrumental
Quartet in F maj for flute, violin, oboe, cello and continuo.
LB:B244.
Quartet in G min for violin, oboe, viola and continuo,
'Passions Quartet.'
LB:B225.

JANNEQUIN, Clement (c.1475–1560)
d. Secular Vocal
Aller me fault.
LR:D16.
L'Allouette.
LR:Gf1.
L'Amour la mort et la vie.
LR:E7.
Au joli jeu.
LR:E71.
Baisez moy test.
LR:E7.
Bel aube pin verdissant.
LR:E52.
Le Caquet des femmes.
LR:E58.
Le Chant des oyseaux.
LR:E45, E50, E71.
Les Cris de Paris.
LR:A1.
De son amour.
LR:E42.
L'Espoir confus.
LR:E7.
Fiez-vous-y.
LR:E38.
Frere Frappart Trousse.

LR:E58.
La Guerre – La Battaille de Marignan.
LR:E33, E37, E47.
LB:A591.
Guillet un jour.
LR:E7.
Il estoit une fillette.
LR:B26, E7.
Il me suffit de temps passe.
LR:E58.
J'ai trop soudainement.
LR:E42.
Je n'en feray rien.
LR:E58.
Jehanneton fut l'altre jour.
LR:E7.
Las qu'en congneust.
LR:E7.
M'amye a eu de Dieu.
LR:E7.
Non fer ay.
LR:E58.
Or, vien, ca vie, m'amye.
LR:E58.
O fortune n'estoirs tu pas contente.
LR:E7.
Ou mettra l'on.
LR:E7.
Petite nymphe folastre.
LR:E52, E71.
Plus ne suys.
LR:E7.
Pour quoy tournes-vous vos yeux.
LR:E52.
Reveillez-vous coeurs endormis.
LR:D13, E47.
Robin couche a mesme terre.
LR:E58.
Secooez moy.
LR:E7, E58.
Sy celle la qui oncques.
LR:E7.
Si come il chiaro sole.
LR:E7.
Tetin refraict plus blanc.
LR:E58.
Tresves d'amours.
LR:E54.
Une belle jeune espousee.
LR:E7.
Ung gay bergier.
LR:E7.
Ung jour Colin.
LR:E58.
Un jour Robin.
LR:E7, E58.
Va rossignol.
LR:E7.
Voici le bois.
LR:E52.

JAPPART, Jean (16th. cent.)
d. Secular Vocal
Il est de bonne heure ne.
LR:Gf1.
Ve mozza mia.
LR:E55.

JARZEBSKI, Adam (c.1590–c.1649)
b. Chamber and Instrumental
Complete Chamber Works – Canzonas and Concertos.
EB:B14.
Canzona I a 4 for strings and continuo.
EB:B15.
Canzona II a 4 for strings and continuo.

EB:B15.
Canzona III a 4 for strings and continuo.
EB:B15.
Canzona IV a 4 for strings and continuo.
EB:B15, B144.
Canzona V a 4 for strings and continuo.
EB:B15.
Concerto I a 3 for strings and continuo.
EB:B16.
Concerto 'La Bentrovata' a 3 for strings and continuo.
EB:B15.
Concerto 'Berlinesa' a 3 for strings and continuo.
EB:B16.
Concerto 'Chromatica' a 3 for strings and continuo.
EB:B15.
Concerto 'La Sentinella' a 3 for strings and continuo.
EB:B15.
Concerto 'Spandesa' a 3 for strings and continuo.
EB:B16.
d. Secular Vocal
Susanna videns.
EB:F104.

JEFFREYS, George (d.1685)
b. Instrumental
Fantasia a 3, No. 5.
LR:Ga16.

JEHAN D'ESQUIRI (13th. cent.)
d. Secular Vocal
Jolivete et bone amore.
AA:A1.

JEHANNOT DE LESCUREL (d.1304)
d. Secular Vocal
Gracieusette.
AA:A1.
A vous, douce debonnaire.
AN:A1.

JELICH, Vincent (17th. cent.)
b. Instrumental
Ricercare in F min for trumpet and trombone.
EB:B67.

JENKINS, John (1592–1678)
b. Instrumental
All in a garden green – Fantasia.
SI:B1.
Almain.
LR:Ga18.
Almain a 4.
SI:C16.
Ayre a 4.
SI:C8, C13, C14.
Courante a 4.
SI:C14, C16.
Fancy Ayre Sett No. 6 in G min.
EB:B17.
Fantasia a 4.
LR:Ga18.
Fantasia VIII in A min for 3 viols.
SI:C19.
Fantasia in C maj.
LR:Gd37.
Fantasia XV in D maj for 5 viols.
SI:C21.
Fantasia in D min.
LR:Gd44.
EB:B17.
Lady Catherine Audley's Bells.
EB:B17.
A New Year's Gift to TC.
EB:B17.
Pavan.
LR:Ga18.

Pavan a 4.
SI:C16.
Pavan in G maj.
LR:F117.
Pavan in G min.
EB:B17.
Sarabande a 4.
LR:Ga18.
SI:C14.
The Seige of Newark.
SI:B2.
Sett of Ayres in C min.
EB:B17.
Suite of Ayres in C maj.
EB:B17.
Suite in D min. 'Divisions.'
EB:B17.

JEZIERSKI, Kazimierz (17th./18th. cent.)
　　e. Sacred Vocal
Vigiles pastores.
LB:G329.

JIMENEZ – *See* **XIMENEZ, Jose.**

JOHN IV KING OF PORTUGAL (1604–1656)
　　e. Sacred Vocal
Crux fidelis.
LR:F79, Ge39.

JOHNSON, Edward (16th./17th. cent.)
　　c. Keyboard
Johnson's Medley.
EB:D36.
　　d. Secular Vocal
Come blessed bird (Triumphs of Oriana).
LR:Gd34.
Eliza is the fairest queen (Triumphs of Oriana).
LR:Gd42, Gd54.

JOHNSON, Heinrich Philip (1717–1779)
　　b. Chamber and Instrumental
Trio Sonata in E min.
LB:B1.

JOHNSON, John (c.1540–c.1595)
　　b. Instrumental
The Delight Pavan and Galliard.
LR:Gb9.
A Dumpe.
LR:C24, Gb9.
Fantasia.
LR:Gb4, Gb5.
The Flatt Pavan.
LR:Gd21, C22.
The Flatt Pavan and Galliard.
LR:C24.
EB:C8.
SI:A2.
Galliard to the Flatt Pavan.
SI:C2.
Greensleeves.
LR:Gb9, Gd39.
SI:A2.
Rogero.
LR:Gb9, C22.
Tinternell.
LR:C24.
La Vecchia Pavan and Galliard.
LR:C22.
EB:C8.

JOHNSON, Robert (c.1583–1633)
　　b. Instrumental
Alman.
LR:Ga15, Gb6, Gc6, Gd33.

SI:C1.
2 Almains.
LR:Gb4, Gb5.
Carman's Whistle.
LR:Gb4, Gb5.
Chi passa per sta strada.
LR:E20.
The Fairy Masque.
LR:Ga13.
The Satyres Masque.
LR:Gd19, Gd41.
The Temporiser.
LR:Ga10.
Treble to a ground.
LR:C12.
The Witty Wanton.
LR:Ga10.
　　d. Secular Vocal
Away delights.
LR:Gd37.
Care-charming sleep.
LR:Gd52.
Dear, do not your fair beauty wrong.
LR:Gd41.
Full fathom five.
LR:Gd42, Gd45, Gd46.
Hark, hark, the lark.
LR:Gd51.
Have you seen the white lily grow.
LR:Gd41.
How wretched is the state.
LR:Gd41.
O let us howle.
LR:Gd49.
Where the bee sucks.
LR:Gd18, Gd38, Gd42, Gd45, Gd46.

JOMMELLI, Niccolo (1714–1774)
　　b. Chamber and Instrumental
Trio Sonata in D maj for flute, oboe and continuo.
LB:B300.

JONES, Robert (1577–1617)
　　d. Secular Vocal
Fair Oriana seeming to wink (Triumphs of Oriana).
LR:Gd34.
Farewell, dear love.
LR:Gd23, Gd51.
Love is a Babel.
LR:Gd28.
Love is a pretty frenzy.
LR:Gd28.
Now what is love?
LR:Gd28.
Sweet Philomel.
LR:Gd24.
To sigh and to be sad.
LR:Gd19.
What if I seek for love of thee?
LR:Gd37.
Whither runneth my sweet heart.
LR:Gd19.

JOSQUIN DES PRES (1442–1527)
　　b. Instrumental
La Bernadina.
ER:A2, B24.
LR:E53.
Carmen gallicum Ludovici XI regis Francorum.
LR:A2, E32.
Fanfare.
ER:B24.
Fantasia.
LR:B22.
Kyrie (for organ).

LR:D13.
La Spagna.
ER:A2.
Vive le roy.
ER:A2, B24.
LR:E63.
d. Secular Vocal
Adieu mes amours.
ER:A1, A18.
LR:D19, E38.
Allegez moy, doulce plaisant brunette.
ER:A1, B44.
LR:E38.
Au joly jeu.
LR:E60.
Basies moy.
ER:B24.
Bergerette savoysienne.
ER:A18.
Cuers desolez par toute nation.
ER:A18, B24, B29, B44.
LR:A2, E32.
De tous biens plaine.
ER:A1.
Deploration sur la mort de Johannes Ockeghem.
ER:A18, B24, B43, B44.
El Grillo e buon cantare.
ER:A1, A18, B24.
LR:E45.
Epitaphe de l'amant vert.
SI:C15.
Fault d'argent.
ER:A18.
LR:E21.
Fortuna desperata.
ER:A1.
Guillaume sa va.
ER:A1.
L'Homme arme (Attrib.)
LR:E53.
Je ne suis tenir d'aimer.
ER:B44.
Ma bouche rit.
LR:A6.
Mille regretz.
ER:A18, B29, B44.
LR:A1, E21, E38, E63.
Per Giunio.
LR:F81.
Petite camusette.
ER:B24, B44.
Plaine de dueil.
ER:A18.
Recordans de mia segnora.
ER:A18.
Regretz sans fin.
ER:A18, B44.
Scaramella va allá guerra.
ER:A1, A6, A18.
Se congie prens.
ER:B44.
Tenez moy en voz bras.
ER:A18.
Une Mouse de Biscaye.
LR:E38.
e. Sacred Vocal – Motets
Absalom fili mi.
ER:B25.
Absolve, quaesumus, Domine.
LR:A2, E32.
Alma redemptoris mater.
ER:B32.
Ave Christe immolata.
ER:B26.

Ave Maria.
ER:B29, B31.
Ave nobilissima creatura.
ER:B32.
Ave vera virginitas.
LR:F81.
Benedicta es caelorum regina.
ER:A3, B31, B32.
De profundis.
ER:A3, B33.
Domine, ne in furore.
ER:B33.
Dominus regnavit.
ER:B26, B31, B33.
Ecce tu pulchra es.
LR:F83.
Huc me sydero-Plangent eum.
ER:B30.
Illibata Dei virgo nutrix.
ER:B32.
In te, Domine, speravi.
ER:A18.
LR:E54.
Inviolata, integra et casta es, Maria.
ER:A3, B31.
Miserere mei, Deus.
ER:B31.
Missus est Gabriel angelus.
ER:B32.
Mittit ad virginem.
ER:B25.
O Jesu, fili David.
ER:B33.
O virgo virginum.
ER:B32.
Praeter rerum seriem.
ER:B29.
Salve regina.
ER:B25.
Tu pauperum refugium.
LR:E37.
Tu solus, qui facis mirabilia.
ER:B25, B31.
LR:F80.
Tulerunt Dominum.
ER:B26, B29.
e. Sacred Vical – Masses and Mass Movements
Missa 'Ave maris stella.'
ER:B25.
Missa 'De beata virgine.'
ER:B26, B27.
Missa 'Gaudeamus.'
ER:B28.
Missa 'L'Homme arme, super voces musicales.'
ER:B29, B30.
Missa 'Pange lingua.'
ER:B8.
Credo super 'De tous biens.'
ER:A2.

JUDENKUNIG, Hans (c.1450–1526)
    b. Instrumental – Lute
Ach Elslein, liebstes Elselein.
LR:C9.
Christ der ist erstanden.
LR:A1.
Ellend bringt payn.
LR:C13.
Hoff dantz.
LR:C13.
Ein Niederländischer Rundtanz.
LR:C9, C19.
Von edler Art.
LR:E68.

Welscher Tanz 'Rossina'.
LR:C9, C19.
Wo soll ich mich hinkehren.
LR:C9.

JULLIEN, Gilles (1650-1703)
c. Keyboard - Organ
Suite du 1re ton: Cromorne en taille. Dialogue. Fugue
renversee a 5. Prelude du 1re ton. Prelude a 5.
EB:E34.

JUSTINUS, Pater (18th. cent.)
c. Keyboard - Organ
Soldier's March.
LB:E191.

KAJONI, Janos (17th. cent.)
e. Sacred Vocal
Dies irae (Organo Missale).
LR:A5.

KAJONI CODEX (17th. cent. Hungarian)
b. Instrumental
Miscellaneous Collections.
LR:A5, B27, E49.
EB:B70.
Apor Lazar Tancza.
LR:A5.
2 Choreas.
LR:A5.
Lapoczkas Tancz.
LR:A5.
Otodik Tancz.
LR:A5.
LB:B273.
d. Secular Vocal
Hungary, Transylvannia.
LR:A5.
The song of the Wife of Lupul, the Voivode.
LR:E49.

KAPSBERGER, Giovanni Girolamo (c.1575-1661)
b. Instrumental - Lute
Canzona II.
LB:C30.
Gagliarda III.
EB:B56.
Toccata VI.
EB:B56.
Toccata VII.
LB:C30.
d. Secular Vocal
Io ama, io ardo, io moro.
EB:F100.
Io mi parto cor mio.
EB:F100.
O cor sempre dolente.
EB:F100.
e. Sacred Vocal
Nigra sum.
EB:G137.

KARGEL, Sixtus (c.1540)
b. Instrumental - Lute
Fantasia.
LR:C9.

KARLSPERKA, Daniel Karolides z (16th. cent.)
e. Sacred Vocal
Psalm XCVI.
LR:F99.

KEISER, Reinhard (1674-1739)
b. Chamber and Instrumental
Sonata I a 3 for flute, oboe and continuo.
EB:E84.

d. Secular Vocal
Der Hochmuthige Croesus - Music Drama, 1705:
Excerpts.
Overture.
Croesus Herrsche.
Prangt die allerschonste Blume.
Kleine Vog; ein, die ihr springet.
Seht, wie Herr Elcius ist ein Politicus.
Mein Katchen ist ein Madchen.
Ballet von Bauren und Baurenkindern.
Ich sa', auf wilde Wellen.
Ihr stummen Fische.
Gotter, ubt Barmherzigkeit.
LB:F82.
e. Sacred Vocal
St. Mark Passion, 1704.
LB:G254.

KELLER, Gottfried (d.1704)
b. Instrumental
Prelude for solo flute.
LB:B272.

KELLNER, David (c.1670-1748)
b. Instrumental - Lute
Fantasia in A min.
LB:C21.
Fantasia in C maj.
LB:C21.

KELLNER, Johann Peter (1705-1772)
c. Keyboard - Organ
Was Gott tut, das ist wohlgetan.
LB:E229.

KEMPIS - *see* A KEMPIS, Thomas

KERCKHOVEN, Abraham van den (1627-1702)
c. Keyboard - Organ
Fantasy in C maj.
EB:E39.
Fantasy in C min (352).
LB:E189.
Fantasy in C min (354).
LB:E189.
Fantasy in E min (355).
LB:E189.
Fugue in A min.
EB:E39.
LB:E210.
Fugue in C maj.
EB:E39.
Prelude and fugue.
EB:E77.
Prelude and fugue in D min.
EB:E39.
4 Versets.
EB:E88.
5 Versets du 5me ton.
EB:E39.
5 Versets on Salve Regina.
EB:E39.

KERLE, Jakobus de (c.1531-1591)
e. Sacred Vocal
Missa 'Regina caeli': Sanctus. Hosanna. Benedictus.
LR:F98.
Responsorium pro concilio I.
LB:G318.

KERLL, Johann Kaspar (1627-1693)
b. Instrumental
Sonata in F maj for 2 violins and continuo.
EB:B36.
c. Keyboard - Organ and Harpsichord
Canzona.

EB:E77, E94.
Canzona in C maj.
LB:E197.
Canzona I in D min.
EB:D39.
LB:D235.
Canzona II.
EB:E56, E92.
Canzona III.
EB:E92.
LB:E223.
Capriccio Cucu.
EB:E65, E95.
Ciaconna in C maj.
EB:D31, D39.
LB:D235.
Passacaglia.
EB:E95.
Toccata con durezza e ligatura.
EB:E56.
Toccata tutta de salti.
EB:E94.
Toccata I.
EB:D39.
LB:D235.
Toccata III.
EB:D39.
LB:D235.

KEUTZENHOFF (16th. cent.)
  d. Secular Vocal
  Frisch und frohlich wolln wir leben.
  LR:E69.

KINDERMANN, Johann Erasmus (1616–1655)
  b. Instrumental
  Intrada in C maj.
  EB:F110.
  Ritornello in D maj.
  EB:F110.
  Sinfonia in E maj.
  EB:F110.
  c. Keyboard – Organ
  Magnificat in 8o tono.
  LB:E197.
  d. Secular Vocal
  Nurenburg Quodlibet.
  EB:F110.
  e. Sacred Vocal
  Ach Herr wie lang.
  EB:F110.
  Nun so singen wir.
  EB:F110.
  Wachet auf.
  EB:F110.

KING, Robert (17th./18th. cent.)
  d. Secular Vocal
  Celinda.
  EB:F94.

KIRBYE, George (c.1565–1634)
  d. Secular Vocal
  See what a maze of error.
  LR:Gd32.
  Sorrow consumes me.
  LR:Gd20.
  With angel's face (Triumphs of Oriana.)
  LR:Gd34.

KIRNBERGER, Johann Philip (1721–1783)
  b. Chamber and Instrumental
  Sonata in G maj for flute and continuo.
  LB:B238, B298.
  e. Sacred Vocal

An den Flüssen Babylons.
LB:G321.

KLABON, Krzysztof (1550–1616)
  d. Secular Vocal
  Songs from the Kaliopy Slowienskiej.
  LR:E57, E66.
  As the Trojans (Kaliopy Slowienskiej).
  ER:B45.
  Hear me, all ye nations (Kaliopy Slowienskiej).
  ER:B45.
  Triumph, faithful followers (Kaliopy Slowienskiej).
  ER:B45.

KLEBER, Leonhard (1490–1556)
  c. Keyboard – Organ and Harpsichord
  Die Brünle (after Isaac).
  ER:A19.
  Die Brünnlein, die da fliessen.
  LR:D14.
  Decem precepta trium in sol (after Isaac).
  ER:A19.
  Fantasia in fa.
  LR:D21.
  Fortuna in mi (after Isaac).
  ER:A19.
  Frater Conradus (after Isaac).
  ER:A19.
  In meinem Sinn (after Isaac).
  ER:A19.
  Praeludium.
  ER:A23.
  Preambulum in G maj.
  EB:E66.
  Zucht, Ehr und Lob.
  LR:D14.
  Zwischen Berg und tiefem Tal (after Isaac).
  ER:A19.

KNUPFER, Sebastian (1633–1676)
  d. Secular Vocal
  O heller Glantz du güldnes Licht.
  EB:F111.

KOBIERKOWICZ, Jozef (18th. cent.)
  e. Sacred Vocal
  Dormi mei redemptio.
  LB:G329.
  Musae piae.
  LB:G329.

KOHAUT, Karl (1726–1782)
  a. Orchestral
  Concerto in F maj for guitar and strings.
  LB:A327.

KOTTER, Johannes (c.1485–1541)
  c. Keyboard
  Adieu mes amours (after Isaac).
  ER:A19.
  Aus tiefer not.
  LR:F78.
  Benedictus (after Isaac).
  ER:A19.
  Fantasia in ut.
  LR:D19.
  Fortuna in min (after Isaac).
  ER:A19.
  Ein Frölich wesen (after Isaac).
  ER:A19.
  Graciensi plaisat (after Isaac).
  ER:A19.
  In meinem Sinn (after Isaac).
  ER:A19.
  La Martinella (after Isaac).
  ER:A19.

La Mora (after Isaac).
ER:A19.
Nach willen dein.
ER:A23.
Nil n'est plaisier (after Isaac).
ER:A19.
Proemium in re.
LR:D19.
Si dedero (after Isaac).
ER:A19.
Si dormiero (after Isaac).
ER:A19.
Spaniol Kochersperger.
LR:E68, E69.
LB:D220.
Tristitia vestra (after Isaac).
ER:A19.

KRAKOWA, Mikolaj z (16th. cent.)
  b.Instrumental
Choreas I and II.
LR:E66.
  c.Keyboard
Hayducky Dance.
EB:E85.
Preambulum.
EB:E85.
  e.Sacred Vocal
Ad novem saltus.
LR:E66.
Alec nade mna wenus.
LR:E37.
Ave Jerarchia.
EB:E85.
Rex.
LR:E66.
Salve regina.
LR:F92.
Wesel sie Polska korona.
ER:B45.
LR:F92.
Zaklulam sie tarnem.
LR:E66.

KREBS, Johann Ludwig (1713-1780)
  a.Orchestral
Concerto in B min for harpsichord, oboe and strings.
LB:A237.
Concerto in G maj for guitar and strings.
LB:A231.
  b.Chamber and Instrumental
Fantasia in C maj for flute and organ.
LB:B215, E174.
Fantasia No. 1 in F maj for oboe and organ.
LB:E174.
Fantasia No. 2 in F maj for oboe and organ.
LB:E174.
Fantasia in F min for oboe and organ.
LB:B210, B215, E174.
Suite in G min for flute.
LB:B226.
  c.Keyboard – Organ: Free Organ Works
Fantasia and fugue in G min.
LB:E173.
Fugue on B.A.C.H.
LB:E173.
Impromptu.
LB:E173.
Largo.
LB:E218.
Prelude and fugue in C maj.
EB:E68.
Toccata and fugue in A min.
LB:E173.
Trio in C min.

LB:E224, E225.
Trio in F maj.
LB:E173.
  c.Keyboard – Organ: Choral-based Organ Works
Ach Gott! erhör mein Seufzen.
LB:E225.
Allein Gott in der Höh' sei Ehr'. (Klavierübung 1).
LB:E188.
Christ lag in Todesbanden (Klavierübung 4).
LB:E173.
Es ist gewisslich an der Zeit (Horn and organ).
LB:B224, E174.
Freu dich sehr o meine Seele.
LB:E173.
Gott der Vater wohn uns bei (Trumpet and organ).
LB:B224, E174.
Herr Jesu Christ, meins lebens licht (Oboe and organ).
LB:E174.
Herzlich lieb (Trumpet and organ).
LB:B224, E173, E174.
Ich hab in Gottes Herz und Sinn (Oboe and organ).
LB:E174.
In allen meinen Taten (Clarino and organ).
LB:B222, E174.
Jesu meine Freude (Oboe and organ).
EB:B53, E56.
LB:B222, E174, E188.
Jesus meine Zuversicht (Klavierübung 13).
EB:E56.
Komm' Heiliger Geist (Oboe and organ).
LB:B214, E174.
Kommt her zu mir, spricht Gottes Sohn (Oboe and organ).
LB:E174.
Liebster Jesu, wir sind hier. (Trumpet and organ).
LB:B213, B224.
Meine Seel ermuntre dich (Oboe and organ).
LB:E174.
O Gott, du frommer Gott (Oboe and organ).
LB:E174.
Von Gott will ich nicht lassen (Klavierübung 11).
EB:E56.
LB:E188, E225.
Wachet auf, ruft uns die Stimme (Trumpet and organ).
LB:B213, B214, B223, B224, E174.
Was mein Gott will (Trumpet and organ).
LB:B224.
Wenn mein stündlein ver handen ist.
LB:E173.
Wir glauben all' an einen Gott.
LB:E173.
Zeuch ein zu deinen.
LB:E173.
  e.Sacred Vocal
Erforsche mich Gott.
LB:G321.

KRIEGER, Adam (1634-1666)
  d.Secular Vocal
Amanda, darf man dich wohl küssen.
EB:F111.
Hör, meine Schöne.
EB:F111.
Ich habe mir die welt.
EB:F111.
Ich will es nicht achten.
EB:F111.
Komm Galathea.
EB:F111.
Wievel Stunden.
EB:F111.

KRIEGER, Johann (1652-1735)
  c.Keyboard – Organ
Praeludium and Ricercare in A min.

EB:E92.
Toccata in D maj.
EB:E92.

KRIEGER, Johann Philipp (1649–1725)
  b. Chamber and Instrumental
  Partita for oboes.
  LB:A639.
  c. Keyboard – Organ
  Toccata and fugue in A min.
  EB:E92.
  d. Secular Vocal
  Coridon in Nöten.
  LB:F81.
  Flora – Opera, 1687: Die Losung ist Geld. Freien ist kein
    Pferdekauf.
  EB:F110.
  Im Dunkeln ist gut munkeln.
  LB:F81.
  Ein Küssgen in Ehren.
  LB:F81.
  Procris – Opera, 1689: Wers Jagen recht begreifen will.
  EB:F110.
  Die Schlimmen Männer.
  LB:F81.

KRUMLOVSKY, Jan (18th. cent.)
  b. Chamber and Instrumental
  Partita for viola d'amore and double-bass.
  LB:B312.

KUHLAU, Friedrich (1786–1832)
  b. Chamber and Instrumental
  Duo in G min for 2 flutes.
  LB:B226.

KUHNAU, Johann (1660–1722)
  c. Keyboard – Harpsichord
  Biblical Sonatas, Nos. 1–6.
    1. Der Streit zwischen David und Goliath.
    2. Der von David vermitelst der Music curierte Saul.
    3. Jacobs Heyrath.
    4. Der todtkranke und wieder gesunde Hiskias.
    5. Der Heyland Isaelis.
    6. Jacobs Tod und Begräbnis.
  LB:D162, D163.
  Partita No. 3 in E maj.
  EB:F111.
  e. Sacred Vocal
  Der Gerecht kommt un – Cantata.
  LB:G126.
  Tristis est anima mea.
  LB:G325.

KUHNEL, August (1645–c.1700)
  b. Chamber and Instrumental
  Sonata in E min for 2 viols and continuo (Sonate e Partite,
    1698).
  EB:B48.

KUNGSBERGER (15th. cent.)
  e. Sacred Vocal
  Urbs beata.
  LR:F78.

KUSSER, Johan Sigismund (1660–1727)
  a. Orchestral
  Ouverture (Suite).
  LR:A6.

LAIRD OF COLL (= John Garve Maclean) (17th. cent.)
  b. Instrumental
  The Royal Lament.
  EB:F107.

LALANDE – see DELALANDE, Michel-Richard.

LALLOUETTE, Jean Francois (1651–1728)
  e. Sacred Vocal
  O mysterium ineffabile.
  LR:F27.

LAMBE, Walter (1452–1500)
  e. Sacred Vocal
  Nesciens mater.
  ER:B2.
  Salve regina.
  SI:D4.

LAMBERT DE MONTE (17th. cent.)
  c. Keyboard – Organ
  Motet magnum triumphum.
  PS:A47.

LAMBRANZI, Grigorio (17th. cent.)
  b. Instrumental
  The Dancing School – Dances, c.1640.
  EB:B13.
  Bolognesa.
  EB:B13.
  Dimo Jesu.
  EB:B13.
  La Disamecita.
  EB:B13.
  Entree.
  EB:B13.
  Genio.
  EB:B13.
  Hurlo Bacho.
  EB:B13.
  Logi.
  EB:B13.
  Narcisin.
  EB:B13.
  Ruberto.
  EB:B13.

LANDINI, Francesco (c.1325–1397)
  d. Secular Vocal
  Adieu, adieu, dous dame.
  AN:B11.
  L'Alma mie piange.
  AN:B12.
  Amar si gli alti.
  AN:B12.
  Amor c'à, tuo sugetto.
  AN:B12.
  Angelica belta.
  ER:A7.
  Anna, donna.
  AN:B4.
  Cara mie donna.
  AN:B9, B12.
  Caro signor, palesa.
  AN:B6.
  Che pena e quest' al cor.
  AN:B11.
  Chi pregio vuol.
  AN:B4.
  Chosi pensoso.
  AN:B11, B12.
  LR:A4.
  De dinmi tu.
  AN:B9, B11, B12.
  De! non fugir.
  AN:B12.
  Donna, i' prego.
  AN:B6.
  Donna, s'i t'i fallito.
  AN:B11.
  Donna'l tuo partimento.
  AN:B9.

Ecco la primavera.
AN:B9.
ER:A4, A24.
Giunta vaga bilita.
AN:B9.
Gram pian' agli.
AN:A3, B10, B11, B12.
ER:A4.
LR:A4, B11.
Guard' una volta.
AN:B12.
I prieg amor.
AN:A3, B11.
LR:B11.
I'veggio ch' a natura.
AN:B12.
In somm' alteca.
AN:B6.
Ma' non s'andra.
AN:B11.
Musicha son.
LR:A4.
Non avra ma' pieta.
AN:B11.
Non do la colp' a te.
AN:B12.
O fanciulla giulia.
AN:B11.
Ochi dolente mie.
AN:B6.
Per allegrezza.
AA:A2.
AN:A3.
LR:B11.
Per seguir la speranza.
AN:B12.
Perche di novo solgno – Vendetta far dovrei – Perche tuo
   servo.
AN:B12.
Poi che da te mi convien.
AA:A1.
Questa fanciulla amor.
AN:B9, B10, B11.
LR:A4.
Se la minica mie.
LR:A4.
Si dolce non sono.
AN:B12.
S'i' ti son stato.
AN:B4.
Una colomba candida.
AN:B11.
Va pure amore.
AA:A2.
AN:A3.
LR:B11.

LANES, Mathieu (1660–1725)
   c. Keyboard – Organ
   Rondeau.
   EB:E66.

LANGA – *see* SOTO DE LANGA, Pedro Francisco

LANIERE, Nicholas (1588–1666)
   d. Secular Vocal
   Mark how the blushful morn.
   SI:A1, B1.
   Though I am young.
   EB:F112.

LANTINS, Arnoldus de (15th. cent.)
   d. Secular Vocal
   In tua memoria.
   ER:A6, B23.
   Puisque je voy.

ER:A11.
   e. Sacred Vocal
   Gioria.
   ER:A11.
   Tota pulchra es.
   ER:B6.

LAPICIDA, Erasmus (c.1450–1547)
   b. Instrumental
   Tander naken.
   LR:B30.
   d. Secular Vocal
   Ach edles N, mein einger Trost.
   LR:B30.

LAPPI, Pietro (d.c.1630)
   b. Instrumental
   Canzona 'La Negrona.'
   EB:G139.
   Canzona 'La Seraphina.'
   LR:Ga14.

LARGATO (16th. cent.)
   d. Secular Vocal
   D'Aquel fraire flaco.
   LR:E28.

LAS HUELGAS CODEX (12th./14th. cent.)
   e. Sacred Vocal
   Ave Maria.
   AA:C6.
   Belial vocatur.
   AA:B2.
   Casta catholica.
   AA:C6.
   Catholicorum concio.
   AA:C3, C6.
   LR:A8.
   Christi miseratio (Agnus trope).
   AA:C6.
   Cleri caetus (Sanctus trope).
   AA:C6.
   De castitati thalamo.
   AA:C6.
   Ex illustri nata prosapia.
   AA:C6.
   LR:A8.
   Exultemus et laetemur.
   AA:C6.
   Flavit auster.
   AA:C6.
   Ihesu clementissime.
   AA:C6.
   Novis cedunt vetera.
   AA:C6.
   O monialis concio.
   AA:C6, D12.
   Omnium in te.
   AA:C6.
   Planctus cigne – Clangam filii.
   AA:D12.
   Plange, Castella misera.
   AA:C6, D12, E6.
   Quis dabit capiti.
   AA:C6, D12, E6.
   Resurgentis.
   AA:C6.
   Rex obit.
   AA:C6, D12.
   Sanctus.
   AA:B2.
   Sane per omnis (Benedicamus).
   AA:C6.
   Tristor et cuncti tristantur.
   AA:D12.
   Victimae paschali laudes.

AA:B2.
Virgini matri (Benedicamus).
AA:C6.
Virgo parit puerum.
AA:C6.

LASSUS, Orlando (1530–1594)
b.Instrumental
Bicinium.
LR:E70.
Chanson a 5.
LR:E54.
Madrigal dell'Eterna.
LR:Ga11.
2 Ricercares a 2.
LR:B28.
d.Secular Vocal – French Chansons
A ce matin.
LR:E8.
Ardant amour.
LR:E8.
Avecques vous mon amour finira.
LR:E8.
Bonjour mon coeur.
LR:E22, E36, E52.
De vous servir.
LR:E9.
Du cors absent.
LR:E9.
En esquoir vis.
LR:E9.
En un chasteau.
LR:E8.
En un lieu ou l'on ne void gontte.
LR:E9.
Fleur de quinze ans.
LR:E8.
Fuyons tous.
LR:E9.
Gallans qui par terre.
LR:E11.
Hatez vous.
LR:E9.
Helas, quel jour.
LR:E9.
L'Heureux amour.
LR:E8.
Il estoit une religieuse.
LR:E9.
J'ay cherche la science.
LR:E9.
Je l'ayme bien.
LR:E8, E71.
Je suis quasi prest.
LR:E9.
Las, voulez vous.
LR:E8.
Monsieur l'abbe.
LR:E8.
Le Mort est jeu.
LR:E9.
La Nuict froide et sombre.
LR:E8, E11, E36, E45, E70.
O faible esprit.
LR:E11.
O tems divers.
LR:E9.
O vin en vigne.
LR:E8.
Orsus filles.
LR:E9.
Petite folle.
LR:E9.
Quand mon mary.
LR:E8, E11, E22, E71.

Qui bien se mire.
LR:E9.
Qui dort ici?
LR:E8.
Sauter, danser, faire les tours.
LR:E8.
Scais du dir l'Ave.
LR:E9.
Si du malheur.
LR:E9.
Si je suis brun.
LR:E8.
Si le long temps.
LR:E8, F94.
Si par souhait.
LR:E8.
Si vous n'estes un bon point.
LR:E9.
Sovons joyeux.
LR:E8.
Le Tems passe.
LR:E9.
Le Temps peut-bien.
LR:E9.
Trop endured.
LR:E9.
Un advocat dit a sa femme.
LR:E8, F94.
Un doux nenny.
LR:E9.
Un jour vis un foulon.
LR:E8, E71.
Le Vray amy.
LR:E9.
Vray Dieu.
LR:E9.
d.Secular Vocal – German Lied.
Am Abend spat beim kühlen Wein.
LR:E70.
Audite nova – Der Bauer von Eselkirchen.
LR:E29.
Ein guten rat.
LR:E65.
Die fasstnacht ist ein' schöne Zeit.
LR:E70.
Im Mayen hört man die hanen krayen.
LR:E70.
d.Secular Vocal – Italian Madrigals, etc.
A voi Guglielmo.
LR:E70.
Al gran Guilielmo.
LR:F94.
Amor che ved'ogni pensier.
LR:E11.
Ardo si.
LR:E11.
Come la notte.
LR:E11.
Hor che la nuova e vaga primavera.
LR:F87.
Hor vi riconfortate.
LR:E11.
Il grave de l'eta.
LR:E11.
Io ti vorria.
LR:E22.
2 Madrigals (Unsp.)
LR:B22.
Matona mia cara.
LR:A1, E11, E20, E22, E40, E70, Gd25.
O fugace dolcezza.
LR:E70.
S'io ti vedess' una sol.
LR:E22.
Trionfo del Tempo (10vv in 2 choirs).

LR:F87.
Vedi l'aurora.
LR:E70.
d. Secular Vocal – Miscellaneous works
Cathalina, apra finestra (Moresken).
LR:A1.
Heroum soboles (for Karl V).
LR:E32.
Moresken.
LR:E10.
Prophetiae Sibyllarum.
LR:E10.
Sybilla Europea.
LR:E70.
e. Sacred Vocal – German texts
Ich ruf zu dir.
ER:B33.
Der Tag der ist so freudenreich.
LR:E70.
Wie lang, O Gott.
LR:F94.
e. Sacred Vocal – Latin texts: Motets, etc.
Adoramus te (Unsp.)
LR:F77.
Adoramus te I a 3.
ER:B13.
Adoramus te II a 3.
ER:B13.
Adoramus te III a 5.
ER:B13.
Agimus tibi gratias a 3.
ER:B13.
Agimus tibi gratias a 4.
ER:B13.
Alleluia, laus et gloria.
ER:B13.
Alma redemptoris mater.
LR:F9, F34.
Angelus ad pastores ait.
LR:F111, F113.
Angelus Domini.
LR:F35.
Ave Maria.
LR:F9.
Ave regina caelorum.
LR:F33.
Beatus homo.
ER:B13.
Beatus vir.
ER:B13.
Cor justus.
ER:B13.
Deus, Domine, ne in furore tuo (Penitential Psalm).
LR:F33.
Domine convertere.
LR:F29.
Domine, exaudi orationem meam (Penitential Psalm).
LR:F30, F34.
Emendemus in melius.
LR:F35.
Expectatio justorum.
ER:B13.
Hodie apparuit in Israel.
LR:F125.
In convertendo.
LR:F29.
In hora ultima.
ER:B33.
LR:F94.
In me transierunt.
ER:B33.
In monte Oliveti.
LR:F29.
In pace in idipsum dormiam.

ER:B13.
Indica mihi, cur me ita judices (Lamentations of Job).
LR:F88.
Jubilate Deo.
LR:F81.
Lagrime di San Pietro (1594).
LR:F36.
Lamentations of Job.
LR:F37.
Lauda Sion salvatorem.
LR:F29, F31.
Magnificat 'Praeter rerum seriem.'
LR:F9.
Miserere Domine.
LR:F29.
Miserere mei (Penitential Psalm).
LR:F33.
Multarum hic resonat.
LR:F35.
Musica Dei donum.
LR:F31.
Numquid sicut dies hominis dies tui (Lamentations of Job).
LR:F88.
O mors, quam amara est.
LR:F33.
Oculus non vidit.
ER:B13.
Omnes de Saba venient.
LR:F34.
Parce mihi Domine (Lamentations of Job).
LR:F88.
Pater Abraham.
LR:F35.
Pater noster a 6vv.
LR:F35.
Peccavi quid faciam tibi (Lamentations of Job).
LR:F88.
Princeps Marte potens.
LR:F94.
Pronuba Iuno.
ER:B13.
Qui sequitur me.
ER:B13.
Quid prodest homini.
LR:F35.
Resonet in laudibus.
LR:F104, F113.
Salve regina.
LR:F33, F34.
Si bona suscepimus.
LR:F35.
Stabant justi.
LR:F35.
Taedet animam meam vitae meae (Lamentations of Job).
LR:F88.
Tristis est anima mea.
LR:F29, Ge39.
LR:G326.
Tui sunt caeli.
LR:F34, F80.
Veni dilecte mi.
LR:F35.
Verba mea auribus.
LR:F35.
Verbum caro a 3.
ER:B13.
Verbum caro a 4.
ER:B13.
e. Sacred Vocal – Masses
Missa super 'Bell' Amfitrit' altera.'
LR:F29, F30.
Missa 'Dixit Joseph': Gloria.
LR:C26.

Missa pro defunctis, Requiem.
LR:F32.
Missa 'Puisque j'ay perdu.'
LR:F31.
Missa super 'Thibaut.'
LR:F28.

LAURENCINI (17th. cent.)
  b.Instrumental
  Fantasia.
  LR:Gb7.

LAURENTIUS THE ELDER (15th. cent.)
  d.Secular Vocal
  Mij heeft een piperken.
  ER:A4.
  LR:A2.

LAURENTIUS DE FLORENTIA = LORENZO DA FIRENZE

LAVIGNE – *see* DE LAVIGNE, Philibert

LAWES, Henry (1596–1662)
  d.Secular Vocal
  Angler's Song.
  LR:Gd46.
  Beauty and love once fell at odds.
  SI:B1.
  Go, lovely rose.
  LR:Gd41.
  Man's life is but vain.
  LR:Gd41.
  The Primerose.
  LR:Gd46.
  Sweet, stay awhile.
  LR:Gd41.
  SI:B2.

LAWES, William (1602–1645)
  b.Instrumental – Consort Setts
  Consort Sett in 3 parts No. 1 in G min for 2 bass viols and
    organ (101–103).
  EB:B19.
  Consort Sett in 3 parts No. 3 in A min for violin, bass viol
    and organ (120–122).
  EB:B19.
  Consort Sett in 3 parts No. 8 in D maj for violin, bass viol
    and organ (135–137).
  EB:B19.
  Consort Sett in 4 parts No. 2 in G maj for 2 violins, bass
    viol and organ (141–143).
  EB:B19.
  Consort Sett in 4 parts No. 3 in A min for 2 violins, bass
    viol and organ (144–146).
  EB:B19.
  Consort Sett in 4 parts No. 8 in D maj for 2 violins, bass
    viol and organ (159–161).
  EB:B19.
  Consort Suite in 5 parts No. 1 in G min for viols and organ
    (Mus. Brit. XXI:1).
  EB:B18.
  Consort Suite in 6 parts No. 1 in C min for viols and organ
    (Mus. Brit. XXI:4).
  EB:B18.
  Consort Suite in 6 parts for 2 violins, 2 violas, viol and
    cello.
  EB:B54.
  In Nomine (from Consort of 6 parts, No. 6.)
  EB:B54.
  Consort Suite No. 8 in G maj for violin, division viol,
    theorbo, harp and organ (Mus. Brit. XXI:9).
  EB:B18.
  Sonata No. 1 in G min for 2 violins, bass viol and organ
    (Mus. Brit. XXI:15).
  EB:B18.
  Sonata No. 7 in D min for 2 violins, viol and organ.

EB:B54.
Sonata No. 8 in D maj for violin, bass viol, harp and organ
  (Mus. Brit. XXI:14).
EB:B18.
  b.Instrumental – Miscellaneous pieces
  Almain.
  SI:C8, C20.
  Almain for lute.
  EB:C8.
  Ayre.
  SI:C20.
  Coranto.
  SI:C8.
  Corants I and II for lute.
  EB:C8.
  Pavan.
  SI:C20.
  Sarabande.
  SI:C8.
  The Triumph of Peace.
  LR:Ga13.
  d.Secular Vocal
  Beauty in eclipsa.
  EB:F12.
  Cuoids, weary of the court.
  EB:F12.
  Gather ye rosebuds.
  LR:Gd46.
  EB:F12, F91, F112.
  My Clarissa.
  EB:F12.
  See how in gathering.
  EB:F112.
  e.Sacred Vocal
  Justitiae sacrum.
  EB:F12.
  When man for sin.
  EB:F12.

LAYOLLE, Francois (early 16th. cent.)
  e.Sacred Vocal
  Missa 'Ces fascheux sotz.'
  LR:F38.

LEBEGUE, Nicolas (1630–1702)
  c.Keyboard – Harpsichord
  Gavotte and Double.
  SI:C19.
  c.Keyboard – Organ
  Les Cloches.
  LB:E191, E211.
  Elevation in G maj.
  EB:E41.
  LB:E165.
  Magnificat du 4me ton.
  EB:E41.
  Offertoire in F min.
  EB:E41.
  Sinfonia in F min.
  EB:E41.
  LB:E165.
  Suite du 1re ton (Excpts.)
  EB:E40.
  Suite du 2me ton.
  EB:E40.
  LB:E165.
  Suite du 6me ton.
  EB:E41.
  Suite du 6me ton (Excpts.)
  EB:E40.
  Variations sur un Noël.
  EB:E64.

LECHNER, Leonhardt (c.1553–1606)
  d.Secular Vocal

Nach meiner Lieb' viel' hundert Knaben trachten.
LR:E70.
e. Sacred Vocal
Allein zu dir, Herr Jesu Christ.
EB:G138.
Deutsch Sprüch von Leben und Tod, Nos. 1-15.
LR:F40.
Historia der Passion (1593).
LR:F39.
Das Hohelied Salomonis - 6 Motets.
LR:F40.
Johannes Passion.
LR:F40.
Missa tertia a 5vv.
LR:F39.
Nun schein, du Glanz der Herrlichkeit.
LR:F112.

LECLAIR, Jean Marie (1697-1764)
  a. Orchestral
Concertos for violin (or flute) and strings, Op. 7, Nos.
  1-6.
    1 in D min; 2 in D maj; 3 in C maj; 4 in F maj; 5 in A min;
    6 in A maj.
LB:A347.
Concerto in C maj for violin and strings, Op. 7, No. 3.
LR:A348, A349, A351, A643.
Concerto in C maj for oboe and strings, Op. 7, No. 3.
LB:A642.
Concerto in F maj for violin and strings, Op. 7, No. 4.
LB:A348.
Concerto in A min for violin and strings, Op. 7, No. 5.
LB:A349.
Concerto in A maj for violin and strings, Op. 7, No. 6.
LB:A348.
Concertos for violin (or flute) and strings, Op. 10, Nos.
  1-6.
    1 in B flat maj; 2 in A maj; 3 in D maj; 4 in D min; 5 in E
    min; 6 in G min.
LB:A347.
Concerto in B flat maj for violin and strings, Op. 10, No. 1.
LB:A350.
Concerto in A maj for violin and strings, Op. 10, No. 2.
LB:A350.
Concerto in G min for violin and strings, Op. 10, No. 6.
LB:A349, A350.
  b. Chamber and Instrumental
Sonata in C maj for flute and continuo, Bk. 1 (Op. 1), No.
  2.
LB:B151, B152.
Sonata in E min for flute and continuo, Bk. 1 (Op. 1), No.
  6.
LB:B151.
Sonata in E min for flute and continuo, Bk. 2 (Op. 2), No.
  1.
LB:B151, B152.
Sonata in C maj for flute and continuo, Bk. 2 (Op. 2), No.
  3.
LB:B151.
Sonata in G maj for flute and continuo, Bk. 2 (Op. 2), No.
  5.
LB:B151.
Sonata in D maj for flute and continuo, Bk. 2 (Op. 2), No.
  8.
LB:B151, B276.
Sonata in B min for flute and continuo, Bk. 2 (Op. 2), No.
  11.
LB:B151.
Sonata in G min for flute and continuo, Bk. 2 (Op. 2), No.
  12.
LB:B152.
Sonata in G min for violin and harpsichord, Bk. 2 (Op. 2),
  No. 12: Adagio.
LB:D221.
Sonatas for 2 violins without continuo, Op. 3, Nos. 1-6.

LB:B154.
Sonata in E min for flute and continuo, Bk. 4 (Op. 9), No.
  2.
LB:B151.
Sonata in D maj for flute (or violin) and continuo, Bk. 4
  (Op. 9), No. 3.
LB:B152, B315, B318.
Sonata in G maj for flute and continuo, Bk. 4 (Op. 9), No.
  7.
LB:B151, B268.
Sonata in G min for 2 violins and continuo, Op. 12, No. 5.
LB:B153.
Sonata in B flat maj for 2 violins and continuo, Op. 12,
  No. 6.
LB:B153.
Overture in D maj for 2 violins and continuo, Op. 13, No.
  2.
LB:B153.
Overture in A maj for 2 violins and continuo, Op. 14.
LB:B153.

LEETHERLAND, Thomas (16th./17th. cent.)
  b. Instrumental
Pavane in G min.
LR:Gd44.

LEEUW - *see* DE LEEUW, Cornelis

LE FEGEUX, Francois (16th. cent.)
  d. Secular Vocal
Petit sein ou l'amour.
LR:E43, E48.

LE FEVRE, Jacques (17th. cent.)
  d. Secular Vocal
N'emprisonne pas.
LR:E43, E44.

LEFFLOTH, Johann Matthäus (1705-1731)
  a. Orchestral
Concerto in D maj for trumpet and organ (Arr. of
  Concerto for harpsichord and violin).
LB:B222.

LEGRANT, Johannes (15th. cent.)
  d. Secular Vocal
Entre vous nouveaux maries.
ER:A7.
LR:A3.

LEGRENZI, Giovanni (1625-1690)
  b. Instrumental
Sonata for 2 trumpets, 'La Buscha', Op. 8.
LB:A662.
Sonata in D maj for 2 viols and continuo, Op. 10, No. 5.
EB:B62.
Sonata V for 4 viols and continuo (La Cetra, 1682).
EB:B51.
Sonata VI in E min for strings.
LB:A588.

LEIGHTON, William (d.c.1616)
  e. Sacred Vocal
Almighty God.
LR:Gd54.

LEJEUNE, Claude (1527-1600)
  b. Instrumental
Fantasia.
LR:D16, E45.
  d. Secular Vocal
L'Autre jour.
LR:E58.
La Belle aronde.
LR:E45.
Fie re cruelle.
LR:A1, E24.

O Rose, reyne des fleurs.
LR:E45.
O villanella.
ER:A6.
Les Octonaires de la Vanitie et Inconstance du Monde.
LR:E13.
Le Printemps.
LR:E12.
Un gentil amoureux.
LR:E33.
Une pouce.
LR:E33.
e. Sacred Vocal
Missa 'Ad placitum.'
LR:F41.

LEMLIN, Lorenz (c.1495–c.1539)
d. Secular Vocal
Der Gutzgauch auf dem Zaune sass.
LR:B30.

LEO, Leonardo (1694–1744)
a. Orchestral
Concerto in A maj for cello and strings.
LB:A352.
d. Secular Vocal
Pensi l'iniquio figlio (Aria from Act 1 of Brivio's 'Demofoonte.')
LB:F79.

LEONIN (= LEONINUS) (12th. cent.)
e. Sacred Vocal
Alleluia: Pascha nostrum immolatus est Christus.
AA:B1, B2.
Gaude Maria virgo.
AA:B1.
Haec dies.
AA:B9.
Locus iste.
AA:B1.
Viderunt omnes.
AA:B1.

LEOPOLD I (1640–1705)
e. Sacred Vocal
Regina caeli a 5 (Mense Maio, 1655).
EB:B51.

LEOPOLITA, Marcin (d.1589)
b. Instrumental
Ricercare.
EB:E85.
e. Sacred Vocal
Cibavir eos.
LR:E57.
Mihi autem.
LR:F92.
Missa 'Paschalis'.
LR:F42.
Resurgente Christe Domino.
EB:E85.

LE ROUX, Gaspard (1660–1707)
c. Keyboard – Harpsichord
Suite No. 2 in D maj for 2 harpsichords.
EB:D14.
Suite No. 3 in A min for 2 harpsichords.
EB:D14.
Suite No. 5 in F maj for 2 harpsichords.
EB:D14.
LB:D227.
Suite No. 6 in F sharp min for 2 harpsichords.
EB:D14.

LE ROY, Adrien (c.1520–1599)
b. Instrumental
Allemande and Double.

LR:C15.
Branle de Bourgogne.
LR:B16, E38.
Branle de Poictou.
LR:C11.
Branle Gai.
LR:C15.
Fantasia II.
LR:C15.
Lorayne.
LR:E54.
Passamezze.
LR:C11, C14, C15.
Quand le gril chant.
LR:E43.
Si je m'en vais.
LR:C11.
LB:B259.

LE SAGE DE RICHEE, Phillip Franz (b.c.1695)
b. Instrumental – Lute
Ouverture.
EB:C5.

LESCUREL – *see* **JEHANNOT DE LESCUREL**

LEUTSCHAU CODEX (17th. cent. Hungarian)
b. Instrumental
Various pieces.
EB:B70.

LHERITIER (16th. cent.)
e. Sacred Vocal
Ave Maria.
LR:F115.

LIBAN, Jarzy (1464–1546)
e. Sacred Vocal
Ortus de Polonia.
LR:F92.

LIBRE VERMELL (14th. cent. Spanish)
e. Sacred Vocal
Ad mortem festinamus.
AN:B17, B18.
Cuncti sumus.
AA:A2.
AN:B15, B17, B18.
Goigs de Nostra Donna.
AA:A2.
AN:B15, B18.
Imperaritz de la Cuita joiosa.
AA:A2.
AN:B15, B17, B18.
Laudeamus virginem.
AN:B17, B18.
Mariam matrem.
AN:B15, B18.
O virgo splendens.
AN:B17, B18.
Splendens ceptigera.
AN:B17, B18.
Stella splendens.
AN:B17, B18.

LICHFIELD, Henry (17th. cent.)
d. Secular Vocal
I always loved to call my lady Rose.
LR:E29.

LILIUS, Franciszek (1600–1657)
e. Sacred Vocal
Jubilate Deo omnis terra.
LB:G328.
Missa 'brevissima.'
EB:G146.

LIMBURGIA, Johannes de (15th. cent.)
  e. Sacred Vocal
    Surge propera amica mea.
    ER:B6.

LINDEMAN, Ole Andreas (1769–1857)
  b. Instrumental
    Canon a 4.
    LB:B311.

LINLEY, Thomas (1756–1778)
  c. Keyboard
    Allegretto.
    LB:D223.

LINUS MS (16th./17th. cent. Hungarian.)
  b. Instrumental
    Dances.
    LR:A7.

LISLEY, John (fl.1600)
  d. Secular Vocal
    Fair Cythera presents her doves (Triumphs of Oriana).
    LR:Gd34.

LOBO, Alonso (1555–1617)
  e. Sacred Vocal
    O quam suavis est.
    LR:F89.

LOCATELLI, Pietro Antonio (1695–1764)
  a. Orchestral
    Concerto Grosso in F min, 'Christmas', Op. 1, No. 8.
    LB:A610, A611.
    Concerto in D maj for violin and strings, Op. 3, No. 1.
    LB:A354.
    Concerto Grosso in F maj, Op. 7, No. 12.
    LB:A20.
  b. Chamber and Instrumental
    Sonatas for flute and continuo, Op. 2, Nos. 1–12.
      1 in C maj; 2 in D maj; 3 in B flat maj; 4 in G maj; 5 in D
      maj; 6 in G min; 7 in A maj; 8 in F maj; 9 in E maj; 10 in
      G maj; 11 in D maj; 12 in G maj (2 flutes).
    LB:B155.
    Trio Sonata in E maj for 2 flutes and continuo.
    LB:B299.
    Trio Sonata in D min, Op. 5, No. 5.
    LB:A609, B285.

LOCHAMER LIEDERBUCH (1455–1460, German)
  d. Secular Vocal
    Der Summer.
    ER:A24.
    Der Walt hat sich entlaubet.
    ER:A24.
    Ich spring au disem ringe.
    ER:A4.

LOCKE, Matthew (1622–1677)
  b. Instrumental
    The Flatt Consort for my Cousin Kemble – Fantasia a 3.
    SI:C6, C13.
    Music for His Majesty's Sackbutts and Cornetts.
    LR:Ga14.
    EB:A15, A34.
    Suite No. 1 for recorder(s) and continuo.
    EB:B65.
    Suite No. 2 for recorder(s) and continuo.
    EB:B65, B69.
  c. Keyboard
    Suite in C maj.
    LR:Gc7.
    Suite No. 4 in D maj.
    EB:D30.
    3 Voluntaries in A min.
    LR:Gc6.
    Voluntary in D min.

    LR:Gc6.
    Voluntary in F maj.
    LR:Gc6.
    Voluntary in G maj.
    LR:Gc6.
  d. Secular Vocal
    The Tempest – Incidental Music, 1674.
    EB:A15.
    The Tempest: Lilk. Curtain Tune.
    LB:A601.

LOCSE VIRGINAL BOOK (16th./17th. cent. Hungarian)
  c. Keyboard
    Miscellaneous Dances.
    LR:A5, B27.

LOEILLET, Jacques (1685–1748)
  a. Orchestral
    Concerto in E flat maj for trumpet and strings (Arr. of
      Concerto in E flat maj for oboe and strings).
    LB:A667.

LOEILLET, Jean-Baptiste 'of Ghent' (1688–1717)
  b. Chamber and Instrumental
    Sonata in A min for recorder and continuo, Op. 1, No. 1.
    LB:B156.
    Sonata in D min for recorder and continuo, Op. 1, No. 2.
    LB:B156, B157.
    Sonata in G maj for recorder and continuo, Op. 1, No. 3.
    LB:B156.
    Sonata in B flat maj for recorder and continuo, Op. 3, No.
      9.
    LB:B156.
    Sonata in A maj for recorder and continuo, Op. 3, No. 11.
    LB:B157.
    Sonata in F min for recorder and continuo, Op. 4, No. 11.
    LB:B156.
    Sonata in C maj for trumpet and organ (Arr. of Sonata in
      C maj for recorder and continuo).
    LB:B205.

LOEILLET, Jean-Baptiste 'of London' (1680–1730)
  b. Chamber and Instrumental
    Quintet in B min for 2 flutes, 2 recorders and continuo.
    LB:B296.
    Sonata in A min for flute and continuo, Op. 1, No. 1.
    LB:B290.
    Sonata in G maj for trumpet and organ, Arr. Op. 1, No. 2.
    LB:B211.
    Sonata in C min for recorder and continuo, Op. 1, No. 5.
    LB:B229, B286, B292.
    Sonata in C maj for oboe and continuo, Op. 2.
    LB:B248.
    Sonata in G maj for recorder and continuo, Op. 2.
    LB:B229, B278.
    Sonata in F maj for recorder, oboe and continuo, Op. 2,
      No. 2.
    LB:B157, B295.
    Sonata in G min for trombone and organ (Arr. Sonata for
      recorder, oboe and continuo, Op. 2, No. 3.)
    LB:B215.
    Sonata in C min for recorder, oboe and continuo, Op. 2,
      No. 6.
    LB:B157.
    Sonata in C maj for trumpet and organ (Arr. of
      movements from 12 Solos for Flute, Op. 3.)
    LB:B224.
    Sonata in G min for recorder and continuo, Op. 3, No. 3.
    LB:B277.
    Sonata in E min for oboe and continuo, Op. 5, No. 1.
    LB:B241.
  c. Keyboard – Harpsichord and Organ
    Allemande in D maj.
    LB:B157.
    Aria and Gigue.
    EB:E84.

Cebel in G min.
LB:B157.
Corente-Sarabande-Gigue.
LB:B323.
Gavotte.
LB:E210.
Gigue.
EB:E88.
Hornpipe in G min.
LB:B157.
Slow Air in E min.
LB:B157.

LOGY, Johann Anton (1650–1721)
   b.Instrumental – Guitar
Gigue-Chaconne-Gigue.
EB:C7.
Partita in A min.
LB:C16.
6 Pieces for guitar.
LB:C27, C29.

LOFFELHOLTZ, Christoph (1572–1619)
   c.Keyboard – Organ
Es het ein Baur sein freylein verlohren.
LR:D14.
Die kleine Schlacht.
LR:D14.

LOHET, Simon (c.1550–1611)
   c.Keyboard – Organ
Canzona in E min.
PS:A47.
Fugue in C min.
PS:A47.
Fugue in G min.
PS:A47.

LONGUEVAL, Antoine de (early 16th. cent.)
   e.Sacred Vocal
Passio Domini nostri Jesu Christi secundum Matthaeum.
EB:G33.

LOPEZ, Miguel (1669–1723)
   c.Keyboard – Organ
5 Versos de medio registro.
EB:E90.
Versos de 4o tono.
LR:D13.
Versos de 7o tono.
LR:D13.
EB:E86.
Versos para l'entrada de la 'Salve.'
LR:D13.

LOQUEVILLE, Richard de (d.1418)
   d.Secular Vocal
Quant compaignons s'en vont jouer.
AN:B2.
   e.Sacred Vocal
Sanctus.
ER:A11.

LORENZO DA FIRENZE (= LAURENTIUS DE FLORENTIA) (14th. cent.)
   d.Secular Vocal
Come in sul fonte.
AN:B6.
Dolgomi a voi.
AN:B3.
O tu chara scientia.
LR:A4.
Per larghi prati.
LR:A4.
Sento d'amor la flamma.
LR:B29.

e.Sacred Vocal
Benedictus.
AN:B5.
Sanctus.
AN:B5.

LOSY – *see* **LOGY, Johann Anton**

LOTTI, Antonio (1667–1740)
   b.Chamber and Instrumental
Trio Sonata in A maj for flute, oboe d'amore and
   continuo.
LB:B251, B300.
Trio Sonata in F maj for recorder, viola da gamba and
   continuo.
LB:B303.
   c.Keyboard – Organ
Variazione su un tema natalizio.
LB:E182.
   d.Secular Vocal
Pur dicesti, o bocca bella.
EB:F95.
LB:F80.
   e.Sacred Vocal
Crucifixus.
LR:Ge39.
LB:G187.
Missa III in A maj for 4vv.
LB:G255.
Regina caeli.
LR:F81.

LUBECK, Vincent (1654–1740)
   c.Keyboard – Organ
In dulci jubilo.
EB:E60.
Prelude and fugue in C maj.
EB:E96.
Prelude and fugue in D min.
EB:E72.
Prelude and fugue in E maj.
EB:E60, E61, E68, E71, E72, E73.
LB:E226.
Prelude and fugue in G min.
EB:E72.
   e.Sacred Vocal
Willkommen süsser Brautigam.
LR:F109.

LUBLIN, Johannes von (early 16th. cent.)
   b./c.Instrumental and Keyboard (Tablatura, 1537/48)
Ad novem saltus.
LR:D21, E57.
Chorea.
LR:E54.
Conradus.
LR:D21, E57.
Hajdu Dance.
LR:D21.
Rex.
LR:E57.
Rocha el fusa.
LR:E57.
Tablatura (Excpts.)
LR:E67.
Taniec.
LR:E57.

LUCCHINETTI, Giovanni Bernardo (18th. cent.)
   c.Keyboard – Organ
Concerto for 2 organs.
LB:E233.

LULLY, Jean-Baptiste (1632–1687)
   a.Orchestral
Air pour le Carousel de Monseigneur.

LB:A639.
Suite in C maj for strings (Arr.)
LB:A615.
a./d. Stage Works
Alcidiane et Polexandre – Ballet, 1658: Excpts.
EB:A16.
SI:C19.
Amadis de Gaule – Opera: Orchestral Suite.
EB:A17.
Les Amants Magnifiques – Comedie, 1670: Orchestral
Suite.
EB:F109.
L'Amour Malade – Ballet, 1657: Derniere Entree: Une
Noce de Village.
LB:B323.
Le Bourgeois Gentilhomme – Comedie Ballet, 1670.
EB:F13.
Le Bourgeois Gentilhomme: Orchestral Suite.
LB:A585.
Les Musiciens du Roy: Orchestral Suite.
EB:A32.
e. Sacred Vocal
Miserere.
EB:G41.
Te Deum.
EB:G41.

LUPI, Didier (16th. cent.)
b. Instrumental
Cantus firmus.
LR:E54.
d. Secular Vocal
Tu as tout seul, Jean.
LR:E58.

LUPO, Thomas (c.1598–1642)
b. Instrumental
Fancy a 5.
LR:Ga17.
Fancy a 6.
SI:C18.
Shews and nightly revels.
LR:Gd19.

LUPRANO, Filippo de (16th. cent.)
d. Secular Vocal
Quercus iunta columna es.
LR:E32.
Se me grate.
ER:A4.

LUYTON, Carl (1557–1620)
d. Secular Vocal
Perch' io t'habbia guardate.
AN:B1.

LUZZASCHI, Luzzasco (1545–1607)
c. Keyboard
Toccata del 4o tono.
LR:E53.
d. Secular Vocal
Aura soave.
LR:E14.
Ch'io non t'ami.
LR:E14.
Cor mio deh non languire.
LR:E14.
Deh vieni ormai.
LR:E14.
Io mi son giovinetta.
LR:E14.
Non sa che sia dolore.
LR:E14.
O dolcezze amarissime d'amore.
ER:A4.
LR:E14.

O primavera.
LR:E14.
Occhi del pianto mio.
LR:E14.
Stral pungente d'amore.
LR:E14.
T'amo mia vita.
LR:E14.
Troppo ben puo.
LR:E14.

MACE, Thomas (1613–c.1709)
b. Instrumental – Lute
A Fancy, Prelude or Voluntary.
AA:A1.
Suite in D min.
LR:C9.

MACHADO, Manuel (16th. cent.)
d. Secular Vocal
Que bien siente Galatea!
SI:A2.

MACHAUT, Guillaume de (c.1300–1377)
b. Instrumental
Ballade.
LR:F91.
Hoquetus.
AN:B1.
Hoquetus David.
AA:B1.
AN:A4, A6.
LB:B272.
Double Hoquet.
AN:A7.
d. Secular Vocal (Including instrumental arrangements.)
Amours me fait desirer.
AN:A1, A3, A8.
Ce qui soutient moy.
AN:A4.
Chanson Roiale.
AN:A4.
LB:B259.
Comment au'a moy.
AA:A1.
AN:A5.
Comment peut on mieuss ses maus dir.
AN:A6.
Dame a vous sans retollir.
AN:A4, A5.
Dame comment.
AN:A9.
Dame de qui toute ma joye vient.
AN:A4.
Dame je suis silz.
AN:A6.
Dame se vous m'estes.
AA:A1.
AN:A1.
Dame vostre doulez viaire.
AN:A9.
De bon espoir – Puis que la douce.
AN:A1.
De petit po.
AN:A3, A9.
LR:B11.
De toutes flours.
AN:A1, A6, A9, B4.
Donnez Signeurs.
AN:A9.
Douce dame jolie.
AA:D20.
AN:A1, A4, A8, B2.
Douce dame tant com' vivray.
AN:A4.

Doulz viaire gracieus.
AN:A6, A9.
Fons, tocius.
AN:A6.
Foys porter.
AN:A8.
Gais et Jolis.
AN:B4.
Hareu! hareu! – Helas! ou sera pris confors.
AN:A1.
Honte, paour, douptance meffair.
AN:A6.
J'aim le flour.
AN:B10.
Je suis aussi.
AN:A3.
LR:B11.
Joie plaisance.
AN:A5.
Lasse! – Se j'aim mon loyal aim – Pour quoy.
AA:B1.
La Lay de la Fontaine.
AN:A5.
Loyaute.
AN:A5.
Ma chiere dame.
AA:A2.
ER:B19.
LR:B11.
Ma fin est mon commencement.
AN:A1, A4.
Mes esperis se combat.
AN:A1, A4, A9.
Moult sui de bonne heure nee.
AN:A6.
Muls me doit avoir merveille.
AN:A8.
Nesque on pourroit.
AN:A3.
LR:B11.
Phyton, le mervelleus serpent.
AN:A1.
Plange, regni respublica.
AN:A7.
LR:A4.
Plourez dame.
AN:A4.
Plus dur que dyamant.
AN:A4.
LR:F91.
Quant en moy.
AN:A6.
Quant j'ay l'espart.
AN:A1.
Quant je ne vois ma dame.
AN:A9.
Quant je sui mis.
AA:A1.
AN:A1, A5.
Quant ma dame.
AN:A8.
Quant Theseus – Ne quier veoir.
AN:A1, A6, B4.
Qui promesses – Ha! Fortune.
AA:B1.
Rose liz.
AN:A4, A9.
Sans coeur dolens.
AN:A4.
Se je souspir.
AN:A1, B1, B10.
Tant doucement.
AN:A8.
Tels rit au main qui au soir pleure.
AN:A4, A5.

Tres bonne et belle.
AN:A3.
LR:B11.
Tres douce dame.
AN:A8.
Trop plus est belle – Biaute paree – Se je souspir.
AN:A1.
Tuit mi penser.
AN:A4.
e. Sacred Vocal
Bone pastor, qui pastores.
AN:A7.
Christe, qui lux es – Veni creator spiritus.
AA:B1.
Messe de Notre Dame.
AN:A7, A8, A9, A10, A11.
O livoris feritas.
AN:A7.
Veni creator spiritus.
AN:A7.

MACHY – *see* **DE MACHY, 'Monsieur'**

MACQUE, Jean de (c.1550–c.1614)
c. Keyboard
Canzon alla francese.
EB:E77.
Gagliards I and II.
EB:D31.

MAGE – **DUMAGE, Pierre**

MAHU, Stefan (c.1490–1540)
d. Secular Vocal
Es gieng ein wolgezogner Knecht.
ER:A25.

MAINERIO, Giorgio (c.1545–1582)
b. Instrumental
L'Arboscello Ballo Furlano.
EB:G139.
Ballo Anglese.
ER:A6.
EB:G139.
Ballo Francese.
ER:A6.
LR:E63.
EB:G139.
Ballo Milanese.
LR:E63.
La Billiarda – Saltarello.
LR:B28.
Galgliarda.
LR:E63.
La Lavandra – Galliard.
LR:B20.
EB:G139.
La Parma – Saltarello.
LR:B28.
Pass'e mezzo della paganina.
LR:B20, E63.
EB:G139.
Pass'e mezzo Moderna.
EB:G139.
Putta nera ballo furlano.
LR:B20, B28, E28.
Schiarazula Marazula.
LR:B21, B25, B28.
EB:G139.
Tedescha – Saltarello.
ER:A6.
LR:B21.
EB:G139.
Tedescha I and II.
LR:B20.

Ungarescha - Saltarello.
ER:A6.
LR:B20, B21, B25, B28, E63.
La Zanetta.
EB:G139.

MALVEZZI, Cristofano (1547-1597)
  b.Instrumental
Sinfonia a 6.
LR:E41.
  d.Secular Vocal
A voi reali amanti.
LR:E41.
Coppia gentil.
LR:E41.
Dal vago e bel sereno.
LR:E41, E56.
Dolcissime sirene.
LR:E41.
E noi con questa bella diva.
LR:E41.
Io che l'onde raffreno.
LR:E41.
Lieto solcando il mare.
LR:E41.
Noi che cantando.
LR:E41.
O fortunato giorno.
LR:E41, E56.
O qual risplende nube.
LR:E41, E56.
Or che le due grand' alme.
LR:E41.

MANCHESTER MS (17th. cent. English)
  b.Instrumental
Woodicock with variations.
SI:C21.

MANCHESTER MS - see GERRARDE and SHERLIE

MANCHICOURT, Pierre de (c.1510-1564)
  b.Instrumental
Amour organ - Bicinium (Rhaw's 'Bicinia gallica et latina')
AA:A1.

MANCINI, Francesco (1672-1732)
  b.Instrumental
Concerto (Sonata) in D min for recorder and continuo.
LB:A632, B266.
Concerto (Sonata) in E min for recorder and continuo.
LB:A632.
  e.Sacred Vocal
Agnus Dei (Missa 'Cantantibus Organis Caecilia')
LR:F95.

MANCINUS, Thomas (1550-c.1611)
  d.Secular Vocal
Anchor che col partire.
LR:E39.

MANFREDINI, Francesco (1688-1748)
  a.Orchestral
Concerto Grosso in D maj, Op. 3, No. 9.
LB:A588.
Concerto Grosso in C maj for 2 violins, cello, strings and continuo. 'Con una Pastorale per il Santissimo Natale', Op. 3, No. 12.
EB:A33.
LB:A353, A609, A610, A611.
Concerto Grosso in F min, Op. 8, No. 1.
LB:A353.
Concerto in D maj for 2 trumpets and strings.
LB:A587, A625, A654.

Concerto in D maj for 2 trumpets, harpsichord, organ and strings.
LB:A662.

MANGON, Johannes (d.c.1578)
  e.Sacred Vocal
Salve regina.
LR:F80.

MARAIS, Marin (1656-1728)
  a.Orchestral
Alcyone - Orchestral Suite.
LB:A337.
  b.Instrumental
Chaconne in D maj for 2 viols and continuo (Book I, 1686).
EB:B26.
Le Basque.
EB:B68.
Les Folies d'Espagne for viol and continuo (Book II, 1701).
EB:B24.
LB:B235, B252, B258, B269.
Le Matelotte.
EB:B68.
Sonata a la Maresienne.
LB:B326.
Le Sonnerie de Ste. Genevieve du Mont a Paris for viol and continuo (1723).
EB:B9, B20.
LB:A599, B326.
Le Tombeau de M. de Ste. Colombe for viol and continuo (Book II, 1701).
EB:B9.
Suite in B min for flute, harpsichord and viol (Book IV, 1717).
EB:B27.
Suite in B flat maj for recorder and continuo.
EB:B21.
Suite in C maj for flute, viol and continuo.
EB:B20.
Suite in C maj for recorder and continuo.
EB:B23.
Suite in C min for recorder and continuo.
EB:B22.
Suite in D maj for recorder and continuo.
EB:B22.
Suite in E min for recorder, lute and viol (Book IV, 1717).
EB:B27.
Suite in E min for viol and continuo.
LB:B277.
Suite in F maj for recorder, harpsichord, theorbo and viol (Book III, 1711).
EB:B27.
Suite in F maj for viol and continuo: 2 Minuets (Book III, 1711).
SI:C3.
Suite in G min for recorder and continuo. (1).
EB:B21.
Suite in G min for recorder and continuo. (2).
EB:B23.
Suite in D maj for viol and continuo.
EB:B20.
Suite in D min for 2 viols and continuo (Book I, 1686).
EB:B26.
Suite in D min for viol and continuo: Prelude and Minuet (Book I, 1686).
SI:C1.
Suite in G maj for 2 viols and continuo (Book I, 1686).
EB:B1, B26.
Suite in B min for viol and continuo (Book II, 1701).
EB:B24.
Suite d'un Gout Etranger for viol and continuo (Book IV, 1717).
EB:B25.

Le Table de l'Operation de la Taille (1717).
EB:B50.
Les Voix Humaines for viol and continuo (Book II, 1701).
EB:B24.

MARC, Thomas (fl. 1724)
Instrumental
Sonata No. 1 in D min for viol and harpsichord.
SI:C4.
Sonata No. 3 for viol and harpsichord.
SI:C7.
Suite for viol and harpsichord.
SI:C1.

MARCABRU, Jehan (1100–1150)
d. Secular Vocal
L'Autrier, just una sebissa.
AA:D5, D8, D9, D13.
Pax in nomine Domine.
AA:A3, D4, D22.
Vida.
AA:D13.

MARCADE, Nicolas (16th. cent.)
d. Secular Vocal
Pour avoir fille en marriage.
LR:E29.

MARCELLO, Alessandro (1684–1750)
a. Orchestral
Concerto in C min or D min for oboe and strings.
LB:A338, A355, A357, A589, A621, A626, A630,
A642, A644, A645.
Concerto in C min for trumpet and strings (Arr. Oboe
Concerto).
LB:A653.
Concerto in D min for 2 guitars and strings (Arr. Oboe
Concerto).
LB:A671.

MARCELLO, Benedetto (1686–1739)
a. Orchestral
Concerti a 5 for strings and continuo, Op. 1, Nos. 1–12.
1 in D maj; 2 in E min; 3 in E maj; 4 in F maj; 5 in B min;
6 in B flat maj; 7 in A min; 8 in F maj; 9 in A maj; 10 in
C maj; 11 in E flat maj; 12 in G maj.
LB:A356.
Concerto a 5 in D maj for strings and continuo, Op. 1, No.
1.
LB:A355.
Concerto a 5 in F maj for strings and continuo, Op. 1, No.
4.
LB:A355, A607.
Concerto a 5 in B flat maj for strings and continuo, Op. 1,
No. 6.
LB:A355.
Introduction-Aria-Presto (Arr.)
LB:A582, A586.
b. Chamber and Instrumental
Sonata in A min for trombone and organ.
LB:B202.
Sonata in B min for flute and continuo.
LB:B226.
Sonata in B min for trombone and organ (Arr. Sonata in A
min for cello and continuo).
LB:B217.
Sonata in G maj for flute and organ.
LB:B215.
Sonata in G maj for trumpet and organ.
LB:B222.
Sonata in G min for recorder and continuo.
LB:B266.
Sonatas for flute and continuo, Op. 2, Nos. 1–12.
1 in F maj; 2 in D min; 3 in G min; 4 in E min; 5 in G maj;
6 in C maj; 7 in B flat maj; 8 in D min; 9 in C maj; 10 in
A min; 11 in G min; 12 in F maj.

LB:B158, B159.
Sonata in F maj for recorder and continuo, Op. 2, No. 1.
LB:B262.
Sonata in D min for recorder and continuo, Op. 2, No. 2.
LB:B263.
Sonata in D min for recorder and continuo, Op. 2, No. 8.
LB:B260, B283.
c. Keyboard – Harpsichord
Sonata in C min.
LB:D164.
Sonata in D maj.
LB:D164.
Sonata in D min.
LB:D164.
Sonata in F maj.
LB:D164.
d. Secular Vocal
Quella fiamma che m'accende.
LB:F80.
e. Sacred Vocal
Psalm II: Donde cotanto fremito.
LB:G256.
Psalm III: Oh Dio perche.
LB:G256.
Psalm VIII: Oh! di che lode.
LB:G256.
Psalm X: Mentre io tutta ripongo.
LB:G256.
Psalm XLI.
LB:G327.

MARCHAND, Louis (1669–1732)
c. Keyboard – Harpsichord
Pieces de Clavecin (Cpte.)
LB:D165.
Suite in E min.
LB:D147.
c. Keyboard – Organ
Pieces d'Orgue (Book 1) (Excpts).
LB:E175, E177, E178.
Basse et dessus de trompette et de cornet (Book 1).
LB:E176.
Dialogue sur les grand jeu (Book 1).
LB:E176, E197, E210.
Recit de tierce en taille (Book 1).
LB:E176.
Recit de voix humaine (Book 1).
LB:E176, E178.
Fond d'orgue in E min (Book 2).
LB:E175, E177, E178.
Grand jeu in A min (Book 2).
LB:E175, E177.
Grand jeu in C maj (Book 2).
LB:E177.
Grand jeu in D min (Book 2).
LB:E177.
Recit in A min (Book 2).
LB:E175, E177, E178.
Recit in D min (Book 2).
LB:E175, E177.
Cromorne en taille (Book 3).
LB:E175, E178.
Grand dialogue in C maj (Book 3).
LB:E175, E176, E177.
Basse de trompette (Book 4).
LB:E175, E176, E217.
Duo (Book 4).
LB:E176.
Fugue (Book 4).
LB:E176.
Recit (Book 4).
LB:E176.
Recit de tierce en taille (Book 4).
LB:E176.
Trio (Book 4).

LB:E176.
Basse de cromorne ou de trompette (Book 5).
LB:E175, E176.
Duo (Book 5).
LB:E176.
Fugue (Book 5).
LB:E175, E176, E177.
Plein jeu (Book 5).
LB:E175, E176, E177.
Recit (Book 5).
LB:E176.
Tierce en taille (Book 5).
LB:E175, E176.

MARELLA, Giovanni Battista (fl. 1730)
  b. Instrumental
  Suite in A maj for 2 guitars.
  LB:C31.

MARENZIO, Luca (1553–1599)
  b. Instrumental
  Sinfonia a 5.
  LR:E41, E56.
  d. Secular Vocal
  Ahi, dispietata morte.
  EB:G142.
  Amatemi ben mio.
  LR:E71.
  Bascia mi.
  LR:E63.
  Belle ne fe natura.
  LR:E41, E56.
  Chi dal delfino.
  LR:E41, E56.
  Due rose.
  LR:E45.
  Estote fortes.
  LR:E40.
  I must depart all hapless.
  SI:A2.
  Ma per me lasso.
  EB:G142.
  Madonna sua merce.
  LR:E71.
  EB:G141.
  O figlie di Piero.
  LR:E41, E56.
  O mille volto.
  LR:E41.
  O valoroso Dio.
  LR:E41.
  O voi che sospirate.
  LR:A1.
  Occhi lucente.
  LR:A1.
  Qui di carne si sfama.
  LR:E41.
  Scaldava il sol.
  LR:E71.
  EB:G142.
  Se nelle voci nostre.
  LR:E41, E56.
  Tirsi, morir volea.
  EB:G141.
  Zefiro torna, e'l bel tempo rimena.
  LR:E47.
  e. Sacred Vocal
  Innocentes pro Christo infantes.
  LR:F100.

MARESCHAL, Samuel (1554–1640)
  c. Keyboard
  Ballet joly.
  LR:D19.

MARGARET OF AUSTRIA'S DANCE BOOK (1480–1530)
  b. Instrumental
  La Danse de Cleves.
  ER:B19.
  LR:B11.
  L'Esperance de Bourbon.
  ER:A8, B19.
  LR:B11.
  Filles a marier.
  ER:B19.
  LR:B11.
  La Franchoise nouvelle.
  ER:A8.
  Il me fait mal.
  ER:A8.
  Roti boully ioeulx.
  ER:A8.
  Sans faire – Basse danse.
  ER:A8, B19.
  LR:B11.

MARIN, Jose (1619–1699)
  d. Secular Vocal
  Aquella Sierra Nevada.
  EB:F97.

MARINI, Biagio (1597–1665)
  b. Instrumental
  Balletto I (Sonate, Symphonie, Canzoni... 1629).
  EB:B28.
  Balletto II for 2 violins, viola and continuo (1655).
  EB:B49.
  Canzone 'La Foscarina' (Affetti Musicale... 1617).
  EB:B44.
  Capriccio for 2 violins and continuo, Op. 8 (1629).
  EB:B52.
  Corrente IX (1629).
  EB:B28.
  Eco a 3 violins and continuo, Op. 8 (1629).
  EB:B52.
  Gagliarda I (1629).
  EB:B28.
  Passacaglio a 4 for 2 violins, viola, cello and continuo,
    Op. 22 (1655).
  EB: B52.
  Sinfonia II for 2 violins and continuo (1629).
  EB:B28.
  Sinfonia V for 2 violins and continuo (1629).
  EB:B28.
  Sonata I for 2 violins and continuo, Op. 8, No. 1 (1629).
  EB:B28.
  Sonata II for 2 violins and continuo, Op. 8, No. 2 (1629).
  EB:B28.
  Sonata III for violin and continuo, Op. 8, No. 58 (1629).
  EB:B28.
  Sonata IV for violin and continuo, Op. 8, No. 59 (1629).
  EB:B28.
  Sonata sopra 'La Monicha' for 2 violins, cello and
    continuo, Op. 8. (1629).
  EB:B52.
  d. Secular Vocal
  La Lagrime d'Erminia, Op. 6.
  EB:B28.

MARJEVOLS – *see* SICART MARJEVOLS, Bernart.

MARSON, George (*c.* 1553–1632)
  d. Secular Vocal
  The Nymphs and Shepherds danced (Triumphs of
    Oriana).
  LR:Gd34, Gd35.

MARTI, Joseph (1719–1793)
  e. Sacred Vocal
  Magnificat.
  LB:G194.

MARTIN, Richard (1570–1618)
  d. Secular Vocal
  Change thy mind since she doth change (Dowland's
    'Musical Banquet')
  LR:Gd30, Gd31.

MARTIN, Antonio (17th. cent.)
  b. Instrumental
  Canarios.
  EB:F97.
  La Chacona.
  EB:F97.
  Diferencias sobre las 'Folias.'
  EB:F97.

MARTIN Y COLL, Antonio (17th. cent.)
  b. Instrumental
  El Villano.
  LR:E30.
  Danza del hacha.
  LR:E30.
  c. Keyboard
  Battalla de 5o tono.
  LB:E191.

MARTINI, Giovanni Battista (1706–1784)
  a. Orchestral
  Concerto in G maj for flute and strings.
  LB:A638.
  b. Instrumental
  Elevazione in E maj.
  LB:B204.
  Toccata, largo and Sonata 'Al Post Communio' (From the
    Intermezzo 'Impressario dell Canarie.')
  LB:B204.
  c. Keyboard – Organ
  Elevazione II.
  EB:E59.
  Fuga.
  EB:E59.
  Gavotta.
  LB:E182.
  Largo.
  LB:E238.
  Sonata sui flauti I.
  EB:E59.
  LB:E241.
  Sonata sui flauti III.
  EB:E59.
  e. Sacred Vocal
  Caeli chori resonate.
  LB:A592.

MARTONFI MS (17th. cent. Hungarian)
  b. Instrumental
  Dances.
  LR:A7.

MASCHERA, Florentio (c. 1540–c. 1580)
  b. Instrumental
  Canzona 'La Maggio.'
  LR:E54.

MASINI, Lorenzo (14th. cent.)
  d. Secular Vocal
  Non perch' i' speri, donna.
  AN:B8.

MASSAINO, Tiburtio (1550–1609)
  b. Instrumental
  Canzona XXXIV a 8.
  LR:F87, Ga14.

MATTEIS, Nicola (17th. cent.)
  b. Instrumental
  Ayre with Divisions for recorder and continuo.
  LB:B263.

Ground after the Scottish Humour.
  LB:B291.

MATTEO DA PERUGIA (d.c. 1418)
  d. Secular Vocal (Including instrumental arrangements)
  Belle sans per.
  AN:B13.
  Dame d'honour.
  AN:B13.
  Dame que j'ayme.
  AN:B13.
  Dame souvrayne.
  AN:B13.
  Gia da rete d'amor.
  AN:B13.
  Helas merci.
  AN:B13.
  Ne me chaut.
  AN:B13.
  Pour bel accueil.
  AN:B13.
  Pres du soloil.
  AN:B13.
  Se je me plaing.
  AN:B13.
  Sera quel zorno mai.
  AN:B13.
  Trover ne puis.
  AN:B13.

MATTHESON, Johann (1681–1764)
  b. Chamber and Instrumental
  Sonata No. 4 in G min for recorder and continuo.
  EB:B64.
  c. Keyboard – Harpsichord
  Suite No. 1.
  LB:D166.
  Suite No. 6.
  LB:D166.
  Suite No. 9.
  LB:D166.
  Suite No. 11.
  LB:D166.
  d. Secular Vocal – Stage Works
  Boris Goudenow – Music Drama, 1710.
    Hochbeglüchte Zeiten.
    Empor! Empor! soll mein steter Wahlspruch bleiben.
    Vorrei scordarmi del Idol mio.
    Schau Boris uns in Gnaden an.
  LB:F82.

MAUDIT, Jacques (1557–1627)
  d. Secular Vocal
  Eau vive, source d'amour.
  LR:E48.

MAXYLEWICZ, Wincenty (1685–1746)
  e. Sacred Vocal
  Gloria tibi trinitas.
  LB:G328.

MAYNARD, John (b.1577)
  d. Secular Vocal
  The XII Wonders of the World (1611).
    1. The Courtier. 3. The Soldier. 4. The Divine. 6. The
    Merchant. 7. The Country Gentleman. 8. The Batche-
    lor. 9. The Married Man. 10. The Wife, 11. The
    Widow. 12. The Maid.
  LR:Gd49.

MAZZOCCHI, Domenico (1592–1665)
  e. Sacred Vocal
  Giunto alla cuna (Ottave Per la Natività di N.S.)
  EB:F100.

McGIBBON, William (1690–1756)
  b. Instrumental

Gilliecrankie.
EB:B37.
Sonata No. 5 in G maj.
LB:B327.

MEAUX – see ETIENNE DE MEAUX.

MEDINACELLI – see CANCIONERO MEDINACELLI.

MEGLI, Domenico Maria (16th./17th. cent.)
d. Secular Vocal
Se di farmi morire (Dowland's 'Musical Banquet.')
LR:Gd30, Gd31.

MEISSEN – see HEINRICH VON MEISSEN.

MEISTER ALEXANDER (13th./14th. cent.)
d. Secular Vocal
Owe daz nach liebe gat.
AA:A1.

MELII, Pietro Paolo (da Reggio) (c.1500–c.1600)
b. Instrumental – Lute
Capriccio chromatico.
LR:C9, C10.
Capriccio detta 'Il Gran Matias.'
LR:C10.

MENALT, Gabriel (d.c.1687)
c. Keyboard – Organ
Tiento de falsas de 6o tono.
LR:D13.
EB:E79.

MERKER, Mathaeus (16th./17th. cent.)
b. Instrumental
Galliard.
LR:B23.
2 Paduanas.
LR:B23.

MERSENNE, Martin (1588–1648)
b. Instrumental
Branle pour la musette.
LR:B12.
Passacaille.
LR:B12.
Vaudeville.
LR:B12.

MERTEL, Elias (c.1561–1626)
b. Instrumental – Lute
Ballet.
LR:C9.
Praeludium.
LR:C9.
Sowünsch ich ihr ein gute Nachte.
LR:C9.

MERUCO, Johannes de (14th. cent.)
d. Secular Vocal
De home vray.
AN:A2.

MERULA, Tarquinio (d.c.1625)
b. Instrumental
Canzona 'La Cattarina.'
EB:B45, B69.
Canzona 'La Chirardella.' (Warsaw).
EB:B29.
Canzona 'La Chremesca.' (Warsaw).
EB:B29.
Canzona 'La Ciria.' (Warsaw).
EB:B29, G141.
Canzona 'La Livia.' (Warsaw).
EB:B29.
Canzona 'La Loda.' (Warsaw).
EB:B29.

Canzona 'La Lusignuola.' (Warsaw).
EB:B29.
Canzona 'La Marcha.' (Warsaw).
EB:B29.
Canzona 'La Merula.' (Warsaw).
EB:B29.
Canzona 'la Monteverde.' (Warsaw).
EB:B29.
Canzona 'L'Orbina.' (Warsaw).
EB:B29.
Canzona 'La Pelegrina.' (Warsaw).
EB:B29.
Canzona 'La Piva.' (Warsaw).
EB:B29.
Canzona 'La Strada.'
EB:B45, B69.
c. Keyboard
Cromatico ovvero capriccio.
EB:E56.
Toccata del 2o tono.
EB:D31.

MERULO, Claudio (1533–1604)
b. Instrumental
Canzona francese.
LR:A1.
Canzona 'La Leonora.'
EB:B58, E93.
c. Keyboard
Canzona 'La Zambeccara.'
EB:D29.
LB:D213.

MESANGEAU, Rene (c.1600–c.1639)
b. Instrumental – Lute
Suite.
EB:C10.

MESSAUS, Guillielmus (1585–1640)
e. Sacred Vocal
Laet ons met herten.
LR:F117.
Saligh, heyligh Bethlehem.
LR:F117.

MESTRES (17th. cent.)
c. Keyboard – Organ
4 Pieces.
EB:E86.

MICA, Frantisek Vaclav (1694–1744)
d. Secular Vocal
Abgesungen betrachtungen – Sepolchro, 1727.
Duse hrisna pospichej (Aria of the Compassion).
Slys, Adame, slys, hrisniku (Recitative of Christ).
Budiz tobe veca chvala (Choral Finale).
LB:F79.
Bellezza e decoro – Cantata, 1729: Cosi suol iride belle.
LB:F79.
Der Glorreiche Nahmen Adami – Cantata.
Nevim kde zustal Mars (Recitative of Mars).
Veliky bozsky Mars (Aria of Mars).
At'se tak deje (Recitative and Aria of the Air).
LB:F79.
Nel giorno Natalizio – Cantata, 1732: Sinfonia.
LB:F79.
Operosi terni colossi moles – Cantata, 1735.
Triumfantem jubilantem Marcomanna aquillam audio
– Iuncta si est gemma auro (Recitative and Aria.)
LB:F79.
L'Origine di Jaromerice in Moravia – Opera, 1730.
Jako ptacek jarniho casu (Aria).
Tenkrat zlatym pismen (Recitative and Aria).
LB:F79.

MICHNA, Adam (c.1600–1676)
  e. Sacred Vocal
  Christmas Music.
  LB:G189.
  Dies kleine Kindelein (Capella Regia Musicalis, 1694).
  LR:F116.
  Easter Music.
  LB:G257.
  Magnificat.
  EB:G43.
  Missa 'Sancti Venceslai.'
  EB:G43.
  Schlaf ein, so sang dem lieben Sohn die Mutter (Capella
    Regia Musicalis, 1694.)
  LR:F116.

MICO, Richard (c.1590–1661)
  b. Instrumental
  Pavane a 5.
  SI:C21.

MIELCZEWSKI, Marcin (d.1651)
  b. Chamber and Instrumental
  Canzona I for strings and continuo.
  EB:B16.
  Canzona II for strings and continuo.
  EB:F104.
  Canzona III a 3 for strings and continuo.
  EB:B15, B16.
  Canzona IV a 3 for strings and continuo.
  EB:B16.
  Canzona for 2 violins, cello and harpsichord.
  EB:G45.
  e. Sacred Vocal
  Benedictio et claritas.
  EB:G146.
  Deus in nomine tuo.
  EB:F104, G147.
  Magnificat (Vesperae Dominicalis).
  EB:G45.
  Triumphalis dies.
  EB:G146.
  Veni Domine.
  EB:G147.
  Vesperae Dominicalis.
  EB:G44.

MILA, Lluis (16th. cent.)
  b. Instrumental
  Pavana III.
  AN:B15.

MILAN, Luis (c.1500–c.1561)
  b. Instrumental – Lute/Vihuela
  Fantasia (Unsp.)
  ER:A26.
  LR:C10, C15, C21, C24.
  Fantasia I.
  LR:C8, C20; E61.
  LB:C27, C29.
  Fantasia II.
  LR:C8, C20.
  LB:C27, C29.
  Fantasia III.
  LR:C8, C20, C29.
  Fantasia IV.
  LR:C8.
  Fantasia V.
  SI:C10.
  Fantasia VIII.
  LR:C7, C8.
  Fantasia IX.
  LR:C7.
  Fantasia X.
  LR:C6, C8.

Fantasia XI.
AA:A1.
LR:C6, E26.
Fantasia XII.
LR:C6, C8.
Fantasia XIII.
LR:C8.
Fantasia XV.
LR:C27.
Fantasia XVI.
LR:C6, C7.
Fantasia XXII.
LR:C7.
Pavana (Unsp.)
ER:A26.
SI:B2.
Pavane I.
LR:B16, C6, C7, E61.
Pavane II.
LR:B16, B25, C6, C27.
Pavane III.
LR:C6, C27.
Pavane IV.
LR:C6, C7, E61.
Pavane V.
LR:C6, C7.
Pavane VI.
LR:C6, C7, E61.
Tiento I.
LR:C7.
Tiento IV.
LR:C10.
d. Secular Vocal
Aquel caballero, madre.
LR:E26, E62.
Con pavor recordo el moro.
LR:E61.
O gelosia d'amanti.
LR:E61.
Quien amores ten.
LR:E31.
Sospirastes Baldovinos.
LR:A8.
Toda mi vida os ame.
LR:E31, E62.
SI:B2.
Ved, comadres, que dolencia.
LR:E27.

MILANDRE, L. Th. (18th. cent.)
  b. Chamber and Instrumental
  Andante and Minuet in D maj for viola d'amore and
    continuo.
  LB:B310.

MILANES (17th. cent.)
  d. Secular Vocal
  Dexa la aljava.
  EB:F97.

MILANO, Francesco Canova da (1497–1543)
  b. Instrumental – Lute
  Canon.
  LR:C26.
  La Cara cosa – Pavana.
  LR:C25.
  La Dispietata – Pavana chiamata.
  LR:C25.
  Fantasia I.
  LR:C25, Gb4, Gb8.
  Fantasia II.
  LR:C25, Gb4, Gb8.
  Fantasia III.
  LR:C25, C26, Gb4, Gb8.
  Fantasia IV 'La Campanella.'

LR:Gb4, Gb8.
Fantasia V.
LR:Gb4, Gb8.
Fantasia VI.
LR:C26, Gb4, Gb8.
Fantasia VII.
LR:Gb4, Gb8.
Fantasia VIII.
LR:Gb4, Gb8.
Fantasia in C maj.
LB:C22.
Fantasia in G min.
LB:C22.
Fantasia (Unsp.)
LR:C23, E21.
LB:C20.
2 Fantasias (Unsp.)
LR:C22, E36.
Fantasia for 2 lutes (after Matelart).
LR:B20.
Gagliarda.
LR:C25.
Ricercare (Unsp.)
LR:C9, E36.
LB:B294.
Ricercare I.
LR:C10.
Ricercare II.
LR:C10.
Ricercare 'La Compagna.'
LR:C10, C11.
LB:C20.
Saltarello.
LR:C25.
La Spagna.
LR:C22.

MILLOT, Nicolas (16th. cent.)
  d. Secular Vocal
  Susanne un jour.
  LR:E54.

MILTON, John (c.1563–1647)
  d. Secular Vocal
  Fair Oriana in the morn (Triumphs of Oriana).
  LR:Gd34.

MILWID, Antoni (18th. cent.)
  a. Orchestral
  Sinfonia Pastorella 'Tuba mirum.'
  LB:G258.
  e. Sacred Vocal
  Sub tuum praesidium I and II.
  LB:G258.

MISSA 'CANTANTIBUS ORGANIS CAECILIA'
  See DRAGONI, GIOVANELLI, MANCINI, PALESTRINA,
    SANTINI, STABILE, SURIANO.
  LR:F95.

MODENA, Julius de (b.1498)
  b. Instrumental
  2 Fantasias.
  LR:B28.
  Ricercare a 4.
  LR:A1.
  Ricercare V (Music de Joye).
  LR:B26.
  Ricercare VIII (Music de Joye).
  LR:B26.
  Ricercare X (Music de Joye).
  LR:B26.
  Ricercare XIII (Music de Joye).
  LR:B26.
  Ricercare XVI (Music de Joye).
  LR:B26.

Ricercare XVII (Music de Joye).
LR:B26.
Ricercare XXII (Music de Joye).
LR:B26.
c. Keyboard
Tiento de 4o tono.
LR:D13.

MODERNE, Jacques (d.1551)
  b. Instrumental
  Branle de Bourgogne.
  LR:B14.
  3 Branles de Bourgogne.
  LR:B10, B17, B18.
  Branle Gay nouveau.
  LR:B10, B17, B18.
  Pavan 'La Battaille.'
  LR:A2, E32.

MOLINARO, Simone (c.1565–c.1613)
  b. Instrumental – Lute
  Ballo detto il Conte Orlando.
  LR:B21, C12, C16, C23.
  Fantasia (Unsp.)
  LR:C16.
  Fantasia I.
  LR:C23.
  Fantasia IX.
  LR:C23.
  Fantasia X.
  LR:C23.
  Saltarello.
  LR:B21, C12.
  2 Saltarellos.
  LR:C16, C23.

MOLINS – see PIERRE DES MOLINS.

MOLTER, Johann Melchior (c.1695–1765)
  a. Orchestral
  Concerto in A maj for clarinet and strings.
  LB:A358, A360.
  Concerto in B flat maj for flute and strings.
  LB:A359.
  Concerto in B flat maj for flute d'amore, strings and
    continuo.
  LB:A623.
  Concerto in D maj for clarinet and strings (1).
  LB:A358.
  Concerto in D maj for clarinet and strings (2).
  LB:A358.
  Concerto in D maj for trumpet and strings (1).
  LB:A359.
  Concerto in D maj for trumpet and strings (2).
  LB:A359.
  Concerto in D maj for 2 trumpets and strings.
  LB:A359.
  Concerto in G maj for clarinet and strings.
  LB:A358.
  Concerto in G maj for flute and strings.
  LB:A359.
  Concerto No. 1 for trumpet, 2 oboes, strings and
    continuo with bassoon.
  LB:A664.

MONDONVILLE, Jean-Joseph Cassanea de (1711–1772)
  b. Chamber and Instrumental
  Pieces de Clavecin avec Voix ou Violon, Op. 5.
    Regna terrae. Cantate Deo. In decachordo psalterio.
    Benefac. Domine. Laudate Dominum. Paratum cor
    meum. In Domino laudabitur. Quare tristis es, anima
    mea. Spera in Deo. Protector meus.
  LB:B160.
  Pourquoi mon ame...Esperez en Dieu (Recitative and Aria
    from Pieces de Clavecin avec Voix ou Violon, Op. 5.)
  LB:D148.

e. Sacred Vocal
Cantate Domino.
LB:G259.

MONACHUS, Guilelmus (15th. cent.)
b. Instrumental
Gymel.
ER:A7.

MONARI (17th. cent.)
c. Keyboard – Organ
Sonata IX.
EB:E59.
Sonata X.
EB:E59.
Sonata XI.
EB:E59.

MONIOT D'ARRAS (1190–1239)
d. Secular Vocal
A une ajornee.
LR:B14.
Ce fu en mai.
AA:D15, D20.
LR:E59.

MONK OF MONTAUDON (1152–1200)
d. Secular Vocal
Mout m'enoja s'o auzes dire (Fort m'enoia).
AA:D4, D9.

MONN, Georg (1717–1750)
a. Orchestral
Concerto in D maj for harpsichord and orchestra.
LB:A604.

MONRO, George (d.1731)
d. Secular Vocal
My lovely Celia.
LR:Gd22.

MONTAUDON – *see* MONK OF MONTAUDON

MONTCASSIN CHANSONNIER (15th. cent. Spanish)
d. Secular Vocal
Si em llevi bon mati.
AN:B15.

MONTE – *see* DE MONTE, Philippus.

MONTECLAIR, Michel Pignolet de (1666–1737)
b. Chamber and Instrumental
Concert No. 2 for flute and continuo.
LB:B268.
Concert No. 4 for oboe, harpsichord and viol.
LB:F54.
Concert No. 4 for oboe, harpsichord and viol: Les Ondes.
Chaconne.
LB:B254.
d. Secular Vocal
La Badine – Cantata (1709).
LB:F54.
Pan et Syrinx – Cantata (1709).
LB:F54.

MONTEVERDI, Claudio (1567–1643)
d. Secular Vocal – Madrigals Book I, 1587
A che tormi il ben mio.
EB:F14.
All' hora i pastori.
EB:F14
Almo divino raggio.
EB:F14
Amor per tua merce.
EB:F14.
Amor s'il tuo ferire.
EB:F14.

Ardi o gela.
EB:F14.
Ardo si ma non t'amo.
EB:F14.
Arsi e alsi.
EB:F14.
Baci soavi e cari.
LR:Gd52.
EB:F14.
Ch'ami la vita mia.
EB:F14
Donna s'io miro vol.
EB:F14
Filli cara e amata.
EB:F14.
Fumia la pastorella.
EB:F14.
La vaga pastorella.
EB:F14.
Poi che del mio dolore.
EB:F14.
Questa ordi il laccio.
EB:F14.
Se nel partir da voi.
EB:F14.
Se per havervi oime.
EB:F14.
Se pur non ti consenti.
EB:F14.
Tra mille fiamme.
EB:F14.
Usciam Ninfe.
EB:F14.
d. Secular Vocal – Madrigals Book II, 1590
Ecco mormorar l'onde.
LR:E45, E47, E71.
EB:F33, F37.
S'andasse amor a caccia.
EB:F37.
d. Secular Vocal – Madrigals Book III, 1592
Ch'io non t'ami, cor mio.
EB:F15.
Io pur verro.
EB:F15.
La Giovinetta pianta.
EB:F15.
La tra'l sangue.
EB:F15.
Lumi miei, cari lumi.
EB:F15.
Ma dove o lasso me.
EB:F15.
O come e gran martire.
EB:F15.
O dolce anima.
EB:F15.
O primavera, gioventu dell'anno.
LR:E11.
EB:F15.
O Rossignuol.
EB:F15, F30.
Occhi un tempo mia vita.
EB:F15.
Ond'ei di morte.
EB:F15.
Perfidissimo volto.
EB:F15.
Rimanti in pace.
EB:F15.
Se per estremo ardore.
EB:F15.
Sovra tenere herbette.
EB:F15.
Stracciami pur il core.

Perche fuggi.
EB:F18, F33.
Si i languidi miei sguardi (Lettera amorosa).
EB:F18, F25, F46, F93.
Se'l vostro cor.
EB:F18.
Se pur destina (Partenza amorosa).
EB:F18.
Soave libertate.
EB:F18.
Tirsi e Clori.
EB:F18, F30, F32.
Tornate o baci cari.
EB:F18.
Tu dormi, ah crudo cor!
EB:F18, F23.
Vaga su spina.
EB:F18, F28.
Vorrei baciarti.
EB:F18, F32.

d. Secular Vocal – Madrigals Book VIII, 1638
Altri canti d'amor.
EB:F19, F29.
Altri canti di Marte.
EB:F19, F36.
Amor dove e la fe.
EB:F19.
Ardo avvampo.
EB:F19, F36.
Il Ballo dell' Ingrate.
EB:F21, F22.
Introduzione al ballo dell'Ingrate.
EB:F20, F25, F28.
Combattimento di Tancredi e Clorinda.
EB:F22, F23, F24, F25, F26.
Dolcissimo Uscignolo.
EB:F19, F37.
Ei l'armi cinse.
EB:F25.
Gira il nemico.
EB:F19.
Hor ch'el ciel.
EB:F19, F29, F30, F33, F36.
Mentre vaga angioletta.
EB:F28.
Movete al mio bel suon.
EB:F25, F36.
Ninfa che scalza i piedi.
EB:F28.
Non havea Febo ancora – Lamento della Ninfa.
LR:E50, Gd52.
EB:F19, F23, F33, F35.
Non partir ritrosetta.
EB:F19.
Vago angeletto.
EB:F19.
Volgendo il ciel.
EB:F25.

d. Secular Vocal – Madrigals Book IX, 1651
Ardo, ardo e scoprir ahi.
EB:F32.
Bel Pastor.
EB:F20, F31, F33.
Di far sempre gioire.
EB:F32.
Non voglio amare.
EB:F28.
O mio bene.
EB:F28.
Se vittorie si belle.
EB:F28.

d. Secular Vocal – Canzonette a tre voci, 1584
Il mio martir.
EB:F20.

Io mi vivea.
EB:F20.
Qual si puo dir.
EB:F27.
Raggi dov'el mio bene.
EB:F27.
Son quest'i crespi crini.
EB:F27.

d. Secular Vocal – Scherzi Musicali a tre voci, 1607
Amorosa pupilletta.
EB:F34.
Clori amorosa.
EB:F27, F34.
Damigella tutta bella.
EB:F34, F35.
De la Belleza.
EB:F34.
Dolce miei sospiri.
LR:E22.
EB:F34, F35.
Fugga il verno dei dolori.
LR:E22.
EB:F20, F34.
I bei legami.
EB:F20, F34.
La pastorella mia.
EB:F34.
La violetta.
EB:F34.
Lidia spina del mio core.
EB:F34.
Non cosi tosto io miro.
EB:F34.
O rosetta, che rosetta.
EB:F34.
Quando l'alba in Oriente.
EB:F34.

d. Secular Vocal – Scherzi Musicali a 1 e 2 voci, 1632
Ecco di dolce raggi.
EB:F31, F34.
Eri gia tutta mia.
EB:F31, F96.
Et e pur dunque vero.
EB:F27, F31.
Io ch'armato sin' hor.
EB:F20, F34.
Maladetto sia l'aspetto.
EB:F31, F32, F34, F96.
Quel sguardo sdegnosetto.
EB:F31.
Zefiro torna e di soavi accenti.
LR:F22.
EB:F28.

d. Secular Vocal – Quarto Scherzo delle ariose vaghezze, 1624
La mia Turca.
EB:F31, F33, F34.
Ohime ch'io cado.
EB:F31, F33.
Si dolce e il tormento.
EB:F31, F32.

d. Secular Vocal – Stage Works
Incoronazione di Poppea – Opera, 1642.
EB:F39.
Incoronazione di Poppea: Concert Suite.
EB:F45.
Incoronazione di Poppea: A dio, Roma.
EB:F46, F47.
Incoronazione di Poppea: Disprezzata regina.
EB:F46, F47.
Incoronazione di Poppea: Tu che dagli avi miei.
EB:F46.
Orfeo, favolo in musica – Opera, 1607.
EB:F40, F41, F42.

Orfeo: Misc. Excpts.
LB:B321.
Orfeo: Concert Suite.
EB:F45.
Orfeo: Mira, deh mira.
EB:F46.
Orfeo: Toccata.
AA:A1.
LR:E56.
Il Ritorno d'Ulisse in patria – Opera, 1641.
EB:F43, F44.
e. Sacred Vocal – Various Collections, 1615–1651
Adoramus te, 6vv (1620).
LR:F22.
Cantate Domino, 2vv (1615).
EB:G47.
Cantate Domino, 6vv (1620).
LR:F22.
Christe redemptor.
LR:F114.
Currite populi, solo voice and b.c. (1625).
EB:F96.
Domine ne in furore tuo, 6vv (1620).
LR:F22.
Ecce sacrum paratum, solo voice and b.c. (1625).
EB:G47.
Ego flos campi, solo voice and continuo (1624).
EB:G47.
Exulta filia Sion, solo voice and b.c. (1629).
EB:F96, G46, G47, G48.
Exultent caeli (1629).
LR:F86.
Fugge, fugge anima mea, 2vv, violin and b.c. (1620).
EB:G47.
O beatae viae, 2vv and b.c. (1620).
EB:G47.
O bone Jesu, 2vv and b.c. (1627).
EB:E47.
O quam pulchra es, tenor and b.c. (1625).
EB:G47.
Sacrae Cantiunculae, 1–26.
EB:G50.
Salve O regina, soprano and b.c. (1624).
EB:G47.
Salve regina, tenor and b.c. (1627).
EB:G47.
Venite, venite, 2vv and b.c. (1624).
EB:G48.
e. Sacred Vocal – Selva Morale e Spirituale, 1640
Beatus vir, 5vv.
EB:G46.
Confitebor tibi Domine, 3vv.
EB:G47.
Crucifixus, 4vv.
EB:G48.
Gloria, 7vv.
LR:E47.
EB:G46, G48, G54.
Jubilet tota civitas, solo voice (dialogue).
EB:G47.
Laudate Dominum in sanctis ejus, solo voice.
EB:G47.
Laudate Dominum omnes gentes, 8vv.
LR:F84.
EB:G46, G54.
Laudate pueri, 5vv.
LR:Ge33.
EB:G54, G55.
O ciechi ciechi, 5vv and 2vln.
EB:F36.
Pianto della Madonna, solo voice (on 'Lamento d'Ariana')
EB:G47.
Salve regina, 4vv and b.c.
EB:G46.

Salve regina, 3vv.
EB:G48.
Ut queant laxis, solo voice and 2vln.
EB:G55.
e. Sacred Vocal – Masses (see also 'Vespers.')
Missa a 4vv (SMS) (1640).
EB:G53, G54, G55, G56.
Missa a 4vv e Salmida Cappella (1650).
EB:F17, G55.
e. Sacred Vocal – Vespro della Beata Vergine (1610)
Vespro della Beata Vergine (Cpte.)
EB:G58, G59, G60, G61, G62, G63, G64, G65.
Missa 'In illo Tempore'.
EB:G57, G58.
Audi, caelum, verba mea.
EB:G46, G58, G59, G60, G61, G62, G63, G64, G65.
Ave Maris stella.
EB:G58, G59, G60, G61, G62, G63, G64, G65.
Dixit Dominus Domino meo.
EB:G58, G59, G60, G61, G62, G63, G64, G65.
Domine ad adjuvandum.
EB:B63, G58, G59, G60, G61, G64, G65.
Duo Seraphim.
EB:G47, G58, G59, G60, G61, G62, G63, G64, G65.
Laetatus sum.
EB:G58, G59, G60, G61, G62, G63, G64, G65.
Lauda Jerusalem.
EB:G58, G59, G60, G61, G62, G63, G64, G65.
Laudate pueri.
EB:G58, G59, G60, G61, G62, G63, G64, G65.
Magnificat a 6vv.
EB:G49, G51, G52, G53, G58, G59, G61, G62, G63, G64, G65.
Magnificat a 7vv.
EB:G49, G58, G60, G64.
Nigra sum.
LR:F90.
EB:G47, G58, G59, G60, G61, G62, G63, G64, G65.
Nisi Dominus.
EB:G58, G59, G60, G61, G62, G63, G64, G65.
Pulchra es.
EB:G47, G58, G59, G60, G61, G62, G63, G64, G65.
Sancta Maria, ora pro nobis.
EB:G58, G59, G60, G61, G62, G63, G64, G65.

MONTPELLIER CODEX (13th. cent. French, Ars Antiqua Motets)
d. Secular Vocal
Chose Tassin.
AA:D14.
El mois de mai – De sedebant bigami.
AA:B1.
ER:A24.
En Mai – L'autre jour – He! resvelle toi.
AA:B1.
S'on me regard – Prennes i garde.
AA:B1, D15.
e. Sacred Vocal
Alle psallite cum luya.
AA:A3, B1, B2.
Ave regina – Alma redemptoris – Alma Sabbati.
AN:A12.
De sedebant bigami – Kyrie.
AA:B2.
Deus in adiutorum.
AA:B2, B3.
Epiphanium Domino canamus.
AA:C2.
In Marie miserie – Gemma pudicie.
AA:B1.
O virgo pia.
ER:A5.
Salve virgo virginum – Omnes.
AA:B2.

MONZINO, Bernado (16th./17th. cent.)
  b.Instrumental – Lute
  Contrapunto I and II.
  LR:C26.

MORALES, Cristobal de (c.1500–1553)
  e.Sacred Vocal
  Andreas Christus famulus.
  LR:F45.
  De antequera sale el moro.
  LR:E31.
  Emendemus in melius.
  LR:F45.
  Exulta es Sancta Dei genetrix.
  LR:F44.
  Jubilate Deo omnis terra.
  LR:F45.
  Lamentabatur Jacob.
  LR:F45.
  Magnificat de 2o tono.
  LR:F45.
  Magnificat de 3o tono.
  LR:F96.
  Missa 'L'Homme arme.'
  LR:F43.
  Missa 'Quaeramus cum pastoribus.'
  LR:F44.
  O crux, ave, spes unica.
  LR:F89.
  O vos omnes.
  LR:Ge39.
  Pastores, dicite, quidnam vidistis.
  LR:F45, F104.
  Puer natus est.
  LR:F96.

MORATA, Gines de (16th. cent.)
  d.Secular Vocal
  Aqui me declaro.
  SI:A2.

MORITZ VON HESSEN (1572–1632)
  b.Instrumental
  Fuga a 4.
  EB:F105.
  Galliard.
  ER:A23.
  Galliarda Brunsvicese.
  EB:F105.
  Galliarda del Sopradetto.
  EB:F105.
  Intrada a 4.
  EB:B55.
  Pavane a 5.
  EB:B55.
  Pavane.
  LR:C13, C16.
  Pavana del F.Segario.
  EB:F105.
  Pavana del povero soldato.
  EB:F105.
  Pavana del Tomaso di Canora.
  EB:F105.
  d.Secular Vocal
  Aventuroso piu d'altro torreno.
  EB:F105.

MORLEY, Thomas (1557–1603)
  b.Instrumental
  Balowe – Pavan.
  LR:Ga13, Gd15.
  La Caccia a 2.
  LR:Ga16.
  EB:B47.
  SI:C3, C13.

La Coranto.
LR:Ga12, Ga20, Ge36.
Il Doloroso – Fantasia a 2.
SI:C8.
A Fancy.
LR:Ga12.
LB:B306.
Fantasia a 2.
LR:Ga17.
Fantasia a 3 in G maj.
LR:Gd46.
The Frogg Galliard.
LR:Gd15, Gd21, Ge36.
Galliard.
LR:Ga12.
La Girandola a 2.
LR:Ga16.
Joyne Hands.
LR:Ga12, Gd18, Gd21, Gd54.
EB:B39.
Il Lamento a 2.
LR:Ga16.
LB:B306.
SI:C6, C13.
Lesson a 4.
LR:Gd46.
Lord Souche's March.
LR:Ga12, Gd54.
Pavan.
LR:Gb4, Gb5, Gb6.
La Rondinella.
LR:Gd21.
The Sacred End Pavan and Galliard.
LR:Gd15.
La Sampogna.
EB:B47.
La Sirena.
SI:C6, C13.
Sola soletta.
LR:Ga13, Gd18, Gd54.
La Tortorella – Fantasia.
LR:Ga17, Ga18.
La Volta.
LR:Ga12, Ga20.
  c.Keyboard
  Alman.
  LR:Gc8, Gd19.
  EB:D37.
  Lachrymae.
  LR:Gc15.
  Nancie.
  LR:Ga12.
  Pavan and Galliard.
  LR:Ga15, Gc16.
  d.Secular Vocal
  A painted tale.
  LR:Gd14.
  About the Maypole.
  LR:Gd15.
  Absence, hear though my protestation.
  LR:Ga12, Gd14, Gd55.
  April is my Mistress' face.
  LR:Gd32, Gd56.
  Arise, awake (Triumphs of Oriana).
  LR:Gd15, Gd34, Gd35.
  Can I forget.
  LR:Gd14.
  Come, sorrow, come.
  LR:Gd14.
  Daemon and Phyllis.
  LR:Gd56.
  Faire in a morn.
  LR:Gd14.
  Fire! Fire!

LR:Gd32, Gd56.
Hard by a crystal fountain (Triumphs of Oriana).
LR:Gd15, Gd34, Gd35, Gd40.
Ho, who comes here?
LR:Gd15.
I saw my lady weeping.
LR:Gd14, Gd27.
It fell on a summer's day.
LR:E55.
Leave, alas, this tormenting.
LR:Gd56.
Love took his bow.
LR:Gd15.
I love, alas.
LR:Gd56.
It was a lover and his lass.
LR:Gd14, Gd18, Gd38, Gd39, Gd45, Gd46, Gd55.
Love winged my hopes.
LR:Gd14.
My bonny lass she smileth.
LR:Gd32, Gd36, Gd50, Gd56.
Now is the gentle season.
ER:A24.
Now is the month of Maying.
LR:Ga12, Gd15, Gd20, Gd25, Gd32, Gd56.
O grief, even on the bud.
LR:Gd56.
EB:F108.
O Mistress mine.
LR:Ga12, Gd14, Gd15, Gd18, Gd21, Gd23, Gd42, Gd45,
    Gd46, Gd51, Gd54.
See, mine own sweet jewel.
LR:Gd19.
Shoot, false love, I care not.
LR:E60.
She straight her light.
LR:Gd14.
Sing we and chant it.
LR:Gd32.
Sleep, slumbring eyes.
LR:Ga12, Gd14.
Thirsis and Milla.
LR:Gd14.
Those dainty daffadillies.
LR:Gd56.
Though Philomena lost her love.
LR:Gd25, Gd56.
What if my mistress.
LR:Gd14.
Whither away so fast?
LR:Gd20.
Who is it that this dark night?
LR:Gd14.
Will ye buy a fine dog.
LR:Gd14.
With my love my life was nestled.
LR:Gd14.
EB:F92.
You that wont to my pipes sound.
LR:Gd15.

e. Sacred Vocal
Agnus Dei.
LR:Gd15.
I call with my whole heart – Psalm CXIX.
LR:Gd15.
Laboravi gemitu meo.
LR:F88, Ge32.
Let my complaint.
LR:Gd15.
Nolo mortem peccatoris.
LR:Gd15, Ge34, Ge37, Ge39.
O amica mea.
LR:Gd15.
Out of the deep.

LR:Gd15, Ge30.

MORNABLE, Anthoine de (b.c.1515)
　　d. Secular Vocal
Je ne scay.
LR:E33.

MORTON, Robert (1440–1475)
　　b. Instrumental
La Perontina.
　　d. Secular Vocal (Including instrumental arrangements)
Cousine trop vous m'abuses.
ER:A13.
Le Souvenir de vous.
ER:A13, A17.
LR:A4, C24.

MOSTO, Giovanni Battista (c.1540–1597)
　　d. Secular Vocal – Madrigals Book I, 1595
Pastorale (Misc.)
LR:A6.
Al dolce mormorare.
LR:E15.
Al mio languir.
LR:E15.
Ameni praticelli.
LR:E15.
Apri il mio cor.
LR:E15.
Dal suo dorato – Clorinda.
LR:E15.
De la voce.
LR:E15.
Disse Amarilli.
LR:E15.
Dolce cantava.
LR:E15.
Fuor di due labra.
LR:E15.
Lieta e contenda Irene.
LR:E15.
Mentre l'aura – Hor perche.
LR:E15.
Nacque d'un bel diamante.
LR:E15.
O sonno – Ov'e il silentio.
LR:E15.
Quando l'amate.
LR:E15.
Quella candida mano.
LR:E15.
Sfidi tu forse.
LR:E15.
Sta il crudo cor – Cosi Natura.
LR:E15.

MOULINIE, Etienne (1600–1670)
　　d. Secular Vocal
Enfin la beaute que j'adore.
LR:E48.
Je suis ravi de mon Uranie.
LR:E48.
Paisible et tenebreuse nuit.
LR:E48.
Quelque merveilleuse chose.
LR:E44, E48.

MOULU, (16th. cent.)
　　d. Secular Vocal
Amy souffrez.
LR:E38.

MOURET, Jean-Joseph (1682–1738)
　　a. Orchestral
Airs a Danser: Entre. Air de Paysan. Menuet. 2
    Passapieds.

SI:C12.
Suite No. 1 – Fanfares for 2 trumpets, violins, oboes, tympani and continuo.
LB:B221.
Suite No. 1: Rondeau.
LB:A580.
Suite No. 2 – Sinfonies de chasse for 2 violins, oboe and horn.
LB:A634.

MOUTON, Charles (1626–c.1710)
b.Instrumental – Lute
L'Amant content.
EB:C5.
La Belle Iris.
EB:C10.
La Bizare.
EB:C10.
Les Cabrioles.
EB:C9.
Canarie.
EB:C9.
La Cheangeante.
EB:C10.
Le Dialogue des Graces sur Iris.
EB:C5, C10.
Gavotte.
EB:C9.
La Mallassis.
EB:C5, C10.
Le Mouton.
EB:C10.
La Princesse.
EB:C9.
Prelude.
EB:C9.
La Promenade.
EB:C10.
Tombeau de Gogo.
EB:C9.
Tombeau de Madame.
EB:C9.

MOUTON, Jean (c.1495–1522)
d.Secular Vocal
La, la, la l'oysillon du bois.
LR:A1.
e.Sacred Vocal
Exultet coniubilando – Glorio Christo canamus.
LR:E32.
Missa 'Alleluia.'
LR:F46, Gf1.
Nesciens mater virgo virum.
ER:A3.
Noe, noe, noe, psallite.
LR:F127, Gf1.
Non nobis, Domine, non nobis.
ER:A14.
LR:A2.
Quaeramus cum pastoribus.
ER:B7.
Qui dabit oculis nostris.
LR:E32.

MOYREAU, Christophe (18th. cent.)
c.Keyboard – Organ
Les Cloches d'Orleans.
LB:E230.

MUDARRA, Alonso (c.1520–1580)
b.Instrumental
Diferencias sobre 'Condo claros.'
LR:C5, C6, C10, E30, E61.
Fantasia (Unsp.)
LR:C15, C16.

LB:C32.
Fantasia y Gallarda.
LR:E30.
Fantasia I de pasos largos.
LR:C5.
Fantasia II para desenvoler las manos.
LR:C5.
Fantasia V.
LR:C5.
Fantasia X que contrehaze la harpa en la manera de Ludovico.
LR:C5, C6, C10, C15, C21, C27, E61, Gd43.
LB:C20.
Fantasia XXV de 8o tono.
LR:C5.
Fantasia XXVI de 8o tono.
LR:C5.
Fantasia XXVII sobre fa mi fa re ut.
LR:C5.
Gallarda.
LR:C5, C6, D21.
LB:C32.
Guarda me las vacas – Romanescas.
LR:B16, C6.
Pavana.
LR:C10.
Pavane de Alexandre.
LR:C5, C6, C10.
Pavana para guitarra al temple nuevo.
LR:C5.
Tiento.
LR:A8, E26.
EB:D28.
d.Secular Vocal
Claros y frescos rios.
LR:A8, E26, E51, E62.
SI:A2.
Dulces exuviae.
LR:A1.
Gentil Cavallero.
LR:E51.
Si me llaman.
LR:A8, E62.
Triste estava el rey David.
LR:A8, E62.
Ysabel, Ysabel, perdiste la tu faxa.
LR:E61, E62.

MUDGE, Richard (1718–1783)
a.Orchestral
Concerto in D maj for trumpet and strings.
LB:A661.

MUFFAT, Georg (1653–1704)
a.Orchestral
Concerto 'Victoria maesta.'
LB:A604.
Concerto in D min for strings 'Bona Nova.'
EB:B4.
Sonata in G maj for strings (Armonico Tributo, No. 5.)
EB:A18.
Sonata in G min for strings (Armonico Tributo, No. 2.)
EB:A18, B49.
Suite in D min for strings 'Nobilis juventus' (Florilegium II–1).
EB:A18.
Suite in E maj for strings 'Indissolubilis Amicitia'.
EB:B4.
Suite in G maj for strings 'Laeta poesis' (Florilegium II–2).
EB:A18.
c.Keyboard – Organ
Aria in C maj (Nova Cyclopeias Harmonica).
EB:E92.
Passacaglia in G min (Apparatus Musico-organisticus).
EB:E94.

Toccata No. 1 in D min (App. Mus.)
LB:A617, E189.
Toccata No. 2 in G min (App. Mus.)
EB:E42, E56.
Toccata No. 3 in A min (App. Mus.)
EB:E42.
Toccata No. 6 in F maj (App. Mus.)
EB:E84.
LB:E239.
Toccata No. 7 in C maj (App. Mus.)
EB:E42.
LB:E211, E223.
Toccata No. 9 in E min (App. Mus.)
EB:E42.
Toccata No. 10 in D maj (App. Mus.)
EB:E42.
Toccata No. 11 in A maj (App. Mus.)
EB:E63.
LB:E197.
Toccata No. 12 in B flat maj (App. Mus.)
EB:E42, E73, E95.
6 Versetti.
LB:E239.

MUFFAT, Gottlieb (1690–1770)
  b.Instrumental
  Arlequin.
  LB:F79.
  Paysan.
  LB:F79.
  c.Keyboard – Harpsichord
  Suite IV in B flat maj.
  EB:D14.

MULLER, Marianus (1724–1780)
  c.Keyboard – Organ
  Prelude and fugue in E flat maj.
  LB:E239.
  Sonata in A maj for 4 organs 'Pastorale per il Santo
    Natale.'
  LB:B203.
  Sonata in B flat maj for 4 organs 'Per la Pentecoste.'
  LB:B203.
  Sonata in C maj for 4 organs 'Per la festa di Pasqua.'
  LB:B203.

MUNDAY, John (1563–1630)
  c.Keyboard – Harpsichord
  Bonny sweet Robin (Fitzwilliam Virginal Book).
  LR:D20, Gc8, Gc12.
  SI:B2.
  Fantasia.
  LR:Gc14.
  d.Secular Vocal
  Lightly she whipped (Triumphs of Oriana).
  LR:Gd34, Gd35.
  Were I a king.
  LR:Gd56.

MUNDAY, William (c.1529–c.1591)
  e.Sacred Vocal
  O Lord, the maker of all things.
  LR:Ge35.

MUNNINCKX, Guillielmus (15th./16th. cent.)
  e.Sacred Vocal
  O soeten nacht, seer land verwacht.
  LR:F117.

MURCIA, Santiago de (17th./18th. cent.)
  b.Instrumental
  Tarentelas.
  EB:B63.

MURRIN, Jacobus (14th. cent.)
  e.Sacred Vocal

Patrem omnipotem (APT MS)
AN:B5.

MURSCHHAUSER, Franz Xavier Anton (1663–1738)
  c.Keyboard – Organ
  Aria pastoralis variata.
  LR:F108.
  LB:E197, E216.
  Gegrüsset seist du.
  LB:E216.
  Lasst uns das Kindlein wiegen.
  LB:E216.
  Octi-tonicum III.
  EB:E92.
  Preambulum and fugue.
  EB:E77.

MUSET, Colin (1200–1265)
  d.Secular Vocal
  Chanson du Mai.
  LR:B19.
  En Mai quant li rossignolet.
  AA:D15.
  LB:B273.
  Quant je voy yver retourner.
  AA:A1, D19, D20.
  LR:A3, E64.
  Sire cuenz, j'ai viele.
  AA:D16.

MUSICA ENCHIRIADIS (9th. cent.)
  e.Sacred Vocal
  Benedicamus Domino.
  AA:A3.
  Nos qui vivimus.
  AA:A3, B4, B9.
  Rex caeli Domini.
  AA:A3, B3, B4, B9.
  Sit Gloria Domine.
  AA:A3, B3.
  Te humiles famuli.
  AA:B3.
  Tu patris sempiternus.
  AA:B3.

MUSICAL BANQUET – *see* LR:Gd30, Gd31.

NAICH, Ubert (16th. cent.)
  b.Instrumental – Lute
  Canti di voi le ladi.
  LR:C26.

NANINO, Giovanni Maria (1544–1607)
  d.Secular Vocal
  Erano i capei d'oro e l'aura sparsi.
  LR:E47.

NANTERMI, Oratio (b.c.1550)
  c.Keyboard – Organ
  Partita alla quarta bassa.
  LR:D18.

NARDINI, Pietro (1722–1793)
  a.Orchestral
  Concerto in A maj for violin and strings.
  LB:A605.
  Concerto in E flat maj for violin and strings.
  LB:A361.
  Concerto in E min for violin and strings.
  LB:A351.
  b.Chamber and Instrumental
  Sonata in B flat maj for violin and continuo.
  LB:B314.
  Sonata in D maj for violin and continuo.
  LB:B161.
  Trio Sonata in C maj for flute, oboe and continuo.

LB:B300.

NARES, John (1715-1783)
  c.Keyboard – Harpsichord
  Lesson No. 2 in D maj.
  EB:D30.
  Lesson No. 3 in B flat maj.
  LB:D217.
  e.Sacred Vocal
  The souls of the righteous.
  LB:G327.

NARVAEZ, Luis de (1500–c.1555)
  b.Instrumental – Vihuela/Lute. (Seis Libros del Delphin de Musica)
  Arde coracon arde (Book V).
  LR:C7.
  Baxo de contrapunto de 8o tono.
  LR:E51.
  Baxo de contrapunto (Book VI).
  LR:C7, C10.
  Diferencias sobre 'Conde claros' (Book VI).
  LR:C7, C10, E61.
  Diferencias por otra parte (Book VI).
  LR:C7.
  Diferencias sobre 'Guardame las vacas' (Book VI).
  LR:B24, C6, C7, C10, C21, C27, E51.
  LB:C32.
  Diferencias sobre 'O gloriosa Domine' (Book IV).
  LR:C7, E51.
  Fantasia (Unsp.)
  LR:A1, C6.
  Fantasia V (Book I).
  LR:C7.
  Fantasia V (Book II).
  LR:C7.
  Fantasia VI (Book II).
  LR:C7.
  Mille regrets – Cancion del Emperador (after Josquin) (Book III).
  LR:A1, B24, C6, C7, C10, E51, E61.
  Otras tres diferencias hechas por otra parte.
  LR:E51.
  Ya se asiente el Rey Ramiro (Book V).
  LR:C7, E61.
  d.Secular Vocal
  Con que la lavare.
  LR:E62.
  Romance del Rey moro que perdio Alhama.
  LR:E30.

NASCUS, Giovanni (d.1561)
  e.Sacred Vocal
  Incipit lamentatio.
  LR:F98.

NASSARE, Pablo (d.1730)
  c.Keyboard – Organ
  Tiento a cuatro, partido de mano derecha.
  LR:D13.

NAUDOT, Jacques-Christophe (= Jean-Jacques) (1710–1762)
  a.Orchestral
  Concerto in G maj for recorder, 2 violins and strings. Op. 17, No. 5.
  LB:A631, A646, B295.
  b.Chamber and Instrumental
  Sonata in G maj for recorder and continuo.
  LB:B289.

NAVARRE – *see* THIBAUT DE NAVARRE.

NAVARRO, Juan (c.1525–1580)
  e.Sacred Vocal
  In passione positus.

LR:F89.

NAVAS, Juan de (17th. cent.)
  d.Secular Vocal
  La Rosa que reyna.
  LB:F84.

NEGRI, Cesare (= Cesare NEGRI MILANESI) (1536–c.1604)
  b.Instrumental – Lute
  Baletto.
  LR:B25.
  Alemana d'amore.
  LR:C25.
  Bianca fiore.
  LR:C9, C23, C25.
  Catena d'amore.
  LR:C9, C25.
  La Fedelta d'amore.
  LR:C25.
  La Gratie d'amore.
  LR:C25.
  La Nizzarda.
  EB:B41.
  Spagnoletta.
  LR:C9, C23.

NEITHARDT VON REUENTHAL (1180–1240)
  d.Secular Vocal
  Blozen wir den anger ligen sahen.
  AA:D25.
  Furste Friderich.
  AA:D25.
  Der May hat menig hercze.
  AA:A3.
  AN:B2.
  ER:A24.
  Meie, din lichter schin.
  AA:D25.
  ER:A24.
  Meinzit.
  AA:D25.
  ER:A24.
  LB:B273.
  Nu gruonet aver diu heide (CARMINA BURANA)
  AA:E9, E17.
  Winder, diniu meil.
  ER:A24.
  Winder wie ist nu dein kraft.
  AA:A3, D15.
  AN:B2.
  LR:B29.

NERI, Massimilliano (17th. cent.)
  b.Instrumental
  Sonata a 4.
  EB:B57.

NESBETT, John (15th./16th. cent.)
  e.Sacred Vocal
  Magnificat.
  ER:B2.

NEWARK, William (c.1450–1509)
  d.Secular Vocal
  The farther I go, the more behind.
  LR:Gf4.

NEWMAN (16th. cent.)
  c.Keyboard
  Pavan (Mulliner Book).
  LR:Gc6.
  EB:E56.
  SI:C11, C13.

NEWSIDLER, Hans (c.1508–1563)
  b.Instrumental – Lute

Ach lieb mit Leid (Ein newes Lautenbüchlein, 1544).
LR:E68.
Ach Gott (1544).
LR:E54.
Bettlertanz (Ein newgeordnet künstlich Lautenbüch,
1536).
LR:C9, E68.
Branle (1544).
ER:A23.
Elslein, liebes Elselein (1536).
LR:C21.
LB:B306.
Entlaubet ist der Walde (1544).
LR:E68.
Der Fuggerin Tanz (1536).
LR:C9.
Ein Guter Gassenhauer (1544).
LR:E68.
Ein Guter Venezianer Tantz (1544).
LR:C17.
Ein guter Welscher Tanz – Wascha Mesa (1536).
ER:A23.
LR:B16, B25, C9, C11, C13, C16, C17, C21.
Hupfauff (1536).
LR:B25.
Ich klag' den Tag (1544).
LR:C16, E68.
Ich sag adieu (1536).
LR:C9.
Judentantz (1544).
ER:A23.
LR:B11, B13, B16, C13, C16, C17, D17.
Mein Herz hat sich mit Lieb' verpflicht (1544).
LR:C11, C16.
Nach willen dein (1536).
LR:C21.
Ein Niderlandisch Tenzlein (1536).
LR:C21.
Der Polnisch Tantz.
LR:C17.
Preambel (1536).
LR:C9, C11, C13, C21.
Der Zeuner Tanz (1536).
LR:B11, B13, D17.

NICHOLSON, Richard (d.1639)
b.Instrumental
The Jew's Dance.
LR:E20, Ga20.
d.Secular Vocal
The Cuckoo Song.
SI:C19.
In a merry May morn.
LR:E63.
Sing, shepherds all (Triumphs of Oriana).
LR:Gd34.
e.Sacred Vocal
No more good herdsman of thy song.
SI:B2.

NICOLAI, Johann Michael (1629–1685)
b.Instrumental
Sonata in B flat maj for violin, 2 viols and continuo.
EB:B36.

NICOLO DA PERUGIA (14th. cent.)
d.Secular Vocal
Dappoi ch'el sole.
AN:B3.
O sommo specchio.
AN:B3.

NIELSEN, Hans (16th./17th. cent.)
d.Secular Vocal
Cor mio, deh non piagnete.

LR:E19.
Occhi miei.
LR:E19.
T'amo mia vita.
LR:E19.

NINOT LE PETIT (16th. cent.)
d.Secular Vocal
Mon ami m'amait promis.
LR:E58.

NIVERS, Guillaume-Gabriel (1632–1714)
c.Keyboard – Organ
Suite du 2me ton.
EB:E41.
Suite du 4me ton.
EB:E2.
Ad coenam.
LB:E197.
Christe redemptor omnium.
LB:E197, E216.
Jesu nostra redemptio.
LB:E197.
O lux beata trinitas.
LB:E197.
Veni sancte spiritus.
LB:E197.

**NOELS DE NOTRE DAME DES DOMS, AVIGNON (16th.
cent.)**
d./e.Secular/Sacred Vocal (Including instrumental
arrangements)
Aquesto niue en me levant.
AA:D20.
Courres bregado.
LR:B14.
L'Enfant de Dieu.
LR:B14.
Lou paure Satan.
LR:B14.
Ma bono bregado.
LR:B14.
Nostro Damo aquesto niue.
AA:D20.
Quant li bergie.
AA:D20.
Ure placas votre troupeu.
LR:B14.
Vautre que sias assembla.
LR:B14.
Voues ausi la verita.
LR:B14.

NOLA, Giovanni Domenico da (1510–1592)
d.Secular Vocal
Chi chi li chi.
ER:A4.
LR:Gd25.
Chi la gagliarda.
LR:E36, Gd25.
Madonna nui sapimo.
LR:E25.
Tri ciechi siamo.
LR:E56.

NORCOMBE, Daniel (1576–1620)
d.Secular Vocal
With Angel's face (Triumphs of Oriana).
LR:Gd34.

NORMINGER, Augustus (c.1560–1613)
b.Instrumental
Allemande.
LR:B12.
Danse des bergers.
LR:B14.

Tantz Adelich unnd from.
LR:D14.
Ungaresca (Tablaturebuch, 1598).
LR:A5.
e. Sacred Vocal
Viel Freuden mit sich bringet.
LR:D14.
Von Gott will ich nicht lassen.
LR:D14.

NORRIS, Ralph (after 1576)
d. Secular Vocal
The Sturdy Oak.
LR:Gd43.

NOTKER LE BEGUE (= BALBULUS) (c.840–912)
e. Sacred Vocal
Alleluia: Dominus in Sion.
AA:A3.
Christus hunc diem (Sequence).
AA:A3.

NOTRE DAME, SCHOOL OF (c.1160–1250) (See also BAMBURG, MONTPELLIER)
e. Sacred Vocal
Alleluia: Christus resurgens.
AA:B10.
Alleluia: Non vos relinquam.
AA:B3.
Ave gloriosa mater salvatoris.
AA:B2.
Dic Christi veritas.
AA:B10.
AN:A11.
Dominator Domine.
AA:A3, B4.
Domino fidelium.
AA:A3, B4, B5.
Egressus Jesus.
AA:B2.
Flos filius.
AA:A2, A3.
Flos ut rosa floruit.
AA:B2.
Homo luge – Homo miserabilis – Brumas e mors.
AA:B2.
Homo qui vigeas – Homo qui vigeas – Et gaudebit.
AA:B3.
In illo tempore: Egressus Jesus.
AA:B2.
Jube domne benedicere – Primo tempore.
AA:B2.
Kyrie magne Deus potencie.
AA:B2.
Lux vera lucis radium.
AA:B2.
Pater noster commiserans.
AA:B10.
AN:A11.
Salve virgo virginum.
AA:B2.

NOVELLA, Guilhem Augier (1185–1240)
d. Secular Vocal
Belle dona cara.
AA:D9.
Ben volgra.
AA:D11.

OBRECHT, Jacob (1450–1505)
b. Instrumental
Recercare.
ER:A7.
La Strangetta.
LR:E25.

Tsaat een meskin.
ER:A2.
LR:E25, E37.
d. Secular Vocal
Ein frohlich wesen.
ER:A1.
Helas mon bien.
EB:E88.
LB:B273.
Ic draghe de mutze clutze.
ER:A4.
LR:A1, A2, E24.
Mijn morken gaff.
LR:A1.
e. Sacred Vocal
Beata es Maria.
ER:B9.
Haec Deum caeli.
ER:A3.
Laudemus nunc Dominum.
ER:A3.
Missa 'Caput.'
ER:B34.
Missa 'Fortuna desperata.'
ER:B35.
Missa super 'Maria zart.'
ER:B36.
Missa 'Sub tuum praesidium.'
ER:B37.
Pater noster.
LR:A1.
Salve crux.
ER:B9, B34.
Salve regina.
ER:B9.

OCHSENKUHN, Sebastian (1521–1574)
b. Instrumental – Lute
Innsbruck, ich muss dich lassen.
LR:C9, C13.

OCKEGHEM, Johannes (c.1425–c.1495)
d. Secular Vocal
Au travail suis.
ER:B38.
Deploration sur la mort de Binchois.
ER:A5, A13.
Fors seulement.
ER:B41.
Ma bouche rit.
ER:A1.
Ma maitresse.
ER:A13, B38.
LR:E37.
Morton et Hayne (Attrib.)
ER:A13.
Petite camusette.
ER:A8.
Prenez sur moi.
ER:A1.
e. Sacred Vocal
Alma redemptoris mater.
ER:B38.
LR:F104.
Ave Maria.
ER:B38.
Intemerata Dei mater.
ER:A3, B39.
Missa 'Au travail suis.'
ER:B38.
Missa ''Cuiusvis toni.'
ER:A5.
Missa 'Ecce ancilla Domini.'
ER:B39, B40.
Missa 'Fors seulement.'

ER:B41.
Missa 'Ma maitresse.'
ER:B38.
Missa 'Mi-mi.'
ER:B37, B41.
Missa pro defunctis, Requiem.
ER:B42, B43.
Ut heremitas solus.
LR:B22.

O'KEOVER, John (d.1663)
  b. Instrumental
Fantasia.
LR:Ga21.

OLAGUE, Bartolomeo de (17th. cent.)
  c. Keyboard
Xacara.
EB:D33.

OROLOGIO, Alessandro (c.1550–1633)
  b. Instrumental
2 Intradas a 5.
LR:B20.
  d. Secular Vocal
Occhi miei.
AN:B1.
LR:F93.

ORTEGA (16th. cent.)
  d. Secular Vocal
Pues que me tienes, Miguel.
LR:E30.

ORTIZ, Diego (c.1510–1558)
  b. Instrumental
Doulce memoire (after Sandrin).
LR:A1, B24.
O felichi occhi miei (after Arcadelt).
LR:B24, C24, E39.
LB:B294.
Recercadas sobre 'Doulce memoire', Nos. 1–4.
LR:B7, B8.
Recercadas sobre 'O felichi occhi miei', Nos. 1–4.
LR:B7, B8.
Recercadas for solo viol, Nos. 1–4.
LR:B7, B8.
Recercadas sobre 'La Spagna', Nos. 1–6.
LR:B7, B8.
Recercada II sobre canto llano 'La Spagna.'
LR:B24.
Recercada IV sobre canto llano 'La Spagna.'
LR:B24.
Recercadas sobre tenores Italien, Nos. 1–8.
LR:B7, B8.
Recercada I – Passamezzo antiguo.
LR:A3.
LB:B306.
Recercada II – Passamezzo moderno.
LR:A3, B24, C22, C24, E2.
LB:B294, B306.
SI:A2.
Recercada III – Passamezzo moderno.
LR:B29.
Recercada IV – La Folia.
ER:A26.
LR:E26.
LB:B294, B231.
Recercada V – Passamezzo antiguo.
ER:A26.
LR:B24.
Recercada VI – La Romanesca.
ER:A26.
LR:B24.
SI:A2.
Recercada VII – La Romanesca.

LR:E26.
Recercada VIII – La Folia.
LR:E30.
Recercada 'Quinta pars.'
LR:B7, B8.
LB:B306.
Recercada (Unsp.)
LR:A1, A8, C24, E20, E27.

OSIANDER, Lucas (1534–1604)
  e. Sacred Vocal
Christus, wir sollen loben schon.
LR:F104, F122.

OSWALD VON WOLKENSTEIN (c.1377–1445)
  d. Secular Vocal
Ach senliches leiden.
ER:A20, A21.
Ain graserin.
ER:A20.
Du ausserweltes.
ER:A21.
Durch barburei, Arabia.
ER:A20.
Es fuegt sich.
ER:A21.
Es nahent.
ER:A21.
Fröleich geschrai.
ER:A21.
Froleichen so well wir.
ER:A20.
Frölich zärtlich.
ER:A21.
Gar wunniklaich.
ER:A4.
Gelück und hail.
LB:B321.
Her wiert uns durstet.
ER:A20.
LR:E35.
In Suria.
ER:A4, A20.
Ir alten weib.
ER:A20.
Kum, liebster man.
ER:A21.
Der Mai mit lieber zal.
ER:A20, A21, A24.
Nu huss.
ER:A21.
Der Oben swebt.
ER:A21.
Sag an, herzlieb.
ER:A20.
Stand auff, Maredal.
ER:A20, A21.
Wach auf, mein hort.
ER:A21.
Wer die augen.
ER:A21.
Wol auf und wacht.
ER:A20.
  e. Sacred Vocal
Ave Maria o Mater.
LR:A6.

OTHMAYR, Caspar (1515–1553)
  d. Secular Vocal
Ein Beurisch Tanz.
LR:E68.
Mir ist ein fein's braun's Maidelein.
LR:E22, E29, E68.
  e. Sacred Vocal
Vom Himmel hoch.

LR:F103.

PACELLI, Asprillo (1570–1623)
  d. Secular Vocal
   Chaire lucide stille.
   LR:E71.
   Il di ch'apersi.
   LR:E71.
   Indarn' hai madre.
   LR:E71.
   Non giacinto o narcisi.
   LR:E71.
  e. Sacred Vocal
   Alma redemptoris mater.
   EB:G141.

PACHELBEL, Johann (1653–1706)
  a. Orchestral
   Canon and Gigue in D maj for strings and continuo.
   LB:A442, A583, A590.
   Canon in D maj for strings and continuo.
   EB:A19.
   LB:A232, A580, A581, A585, A589, A599, A601,
    A619, A641.
   Gigue in D maj for strings and continuo.
   LB:B322.
   Suite (Partita) in B flat maj for strings and continuo.
   EB:A19.
   LB:A232.
   Suite in G maj for strings.
   EB:A19, LB:A232.
  b. Instrumental
   Suite in F sharp min for lute.
   LB:C13.
  c. Keyboard – Harpsichord and Organ: Free Works
   Arietta in F maj.
   EB:E46.
   Ciacona in C maj.
   EB:B39.
   LB:D235.
   Ciacona in D maj.
   EB:E84.
   Ciacona in D min.
   EB:E46, E64.
   Ciacona in F maj.
   EB:E68.
   LB:E204.
   Ciacona in F min.
   EB:E43, E44, E45, E46, E72, E80.
   LB: A641, B324, E200, E222, E234.
   Fantasia (Unsp.)
   EB:E94.
   Fantasia in G min.
   EB:E45, E46.
   Fugue in C maj.
   EB:E92.
   Fugue in D maj.
   EB:E46.
   Fugue in D min.
   EB:E46.
   Hexachordum Apollinis: Partitas 1–6. (Arias).
   EB:E43.
   Aria V.
   EB:E65.
   LB:B305.
   Aria (Partita) VI – Aria Sebaldina.
   EB:E44, E46, E95.
   LB:D225, E202.
   Magnificat in 9th. tone.
   EB:E46.
   Magnificat Fugues (Unsp.)
   EB:E91.
   Magnificat Fugue II.
   EB:E46.
   Magnificat Fugue IV.

EB:E56.
Magnificat Fugue V.
EB:E56.
Magnificat Fugue X.
EB:E46, E56.
Magnificat Fugue XIII.
EB:E56.
Prelude, Fugue and Chaconne in D maj.
EB:E69, E81.
LB:E202.
Ricercare in C min.
EB:E44, E45, E46, E75.
LB:E197.
Ricercare in D min.
EB:E89.
Ricercare in F sharp min.
EB:E46.
Toccata in C maj.
EB:F110.
LB:E197.
Toccata in E min.
EB:E44, E46, E92.
Toccata (Unsp.)
EB:E81.
LB:E219.
Toccata and fugue in B flat maj.
EB:E56.

  c. Keyboard – Organ: Chorale-based Works
   Ach Gott, vom Himmel sieh darein.
   EB:E46.
   Alle Menschen müssen sterben.
   EB:E56.
   Allein Gott in der Höh' sei Ehr'.
   EB:E46, E81, F110.
   Christ lag in Todesbanden.
   EB:E46.
   Christus, der ist mein Leben.
   EB:E44, E46, E63.
   Da Jesus an dem Kreuze stand.
   EB:E44, E46.
   Der Tag, der ist so Freudenreich.
   LR:F115.
   Durch Adams Fall ist ganz verdedt.
   LB:E219.
   Ein feste Burg ist unser Gott.
   EB:E92.   •
   Es woll uns Gott.
   EB:E46.
   Gelobet seist du, Jesu Christ.
   LR:F115.
   Herzlich tut mich verlangen.
   EB:E81.
   Komm, Gott, Schöpfer.
   EB:E46, E92.
   Meine Seele erhebet den Herren.
   LR:F115.
   Nun komm, der Heiden Heiland.
   EB:E46, E92.
   Nun lob meine Seele.
   EB:E46.
   O Lamm Gottes unschuldig.
   EB:E44, E72.
   Vater unser Himmelreich.
   EB:E44.
   Von Himmel hoch da komm' ich her.
   LR:F115.
   EB:E44, E46, E67.
   LB:E205, E216.
   Was Gott tut, das ist so wohlgetan.
   EB:E45.
   Was mein Gott will.
   EB:E46.
   Wen wir in höchsten Nöten sein.
   EB:E46.

Werde munter, mein gemute.
EB:E45.
LB:E197.
Wie schön leuchtet der Morgenstern.
EB:E44, E67, E96.
LB:E197, E216.
Wir glauben all an einem Gott.
EB:E44, E46.

PACHELBEL, Wilhelm Hieronymous (1686-1764)
  c.Keyboard – Organ
Toccata in G maj.
LB:E197, E216.
Meine Seele, lass es gehen.
EB:E91.

PACOLINI, Giovanni (16th. cent.)
  b.Instrumental – Lute
La Bella Franceschina.
LR:A1, E24.
La Gamba.
LR:E20.
Padoana commun.
LR:A1.
Padoana de tute parti.
LR:E20.
Padoana Gentil Madonna.
LR:E20.
Padoana Milanese.
LR:E20.
Passamezzo commun.
LR:A1.
Passamezzo della battaglia.
LR:C12.
Passamezzo Milanese.
LR:E20.
Passamezzo – Saltarello.
LR:C26.
Saltarello della traditora.
LR:C12.
Saltarello Milanese.
LR:C12.

PADUA – *see* **BARTOLINO DA PADUA**

PAIX, Jakob (1556-1623)
  b.Instrumental
Der Keyserin Tantz.
LR:D14.
Saltarello.
LR:B16.
Schiarazula Marazula.
LR:B16.
Ungarescha.
LR:A5, B16, B27, D21.

PALACIO – *see* **CANCIONERO DE PALACIO**

PALAZI/TOMIER (13th. cent.)
  d.Secular Vocal
Si col flacs molins torneja.
AA:D11.

PALERO, Francisco- Fernandez (1523-1597)
  c.Keyboard – Harpsichord
Paseabase el rey moro.
EB:D28.
  d.Secular Vocal
Mire Nero de Tarpeya – Romance II.
LR:E30.
EB:D28.

PALESTRINA, Giovanni Pierluigi da (1526-1594)
  b.Instrumental (Including Keyboard)
Ricercare del 1o tono.
EB:E82.
LB:B299.

2 Ricercari a 4.
LR:B28.
8 Ricercari sopra li tuoni a 4.
EB:B12.
  d.Secular Vocal
Chiare fresche e dolci acque.
LR:E47.
I raghi fiori.
LR:E71.
O che splendor.
LR:E71.
Ogni belta, madonna.
LR:E29.
Vestiva i colli.
LR:E42.
  e.Sacred Vocal – Motets, etc.
Adoramus te Christe.
LR:F59, F63, F64.
Alleluia tulerunt Dominum.
LR:F55.
Alma redemptoris mater.
LR:F56, F59.
Ascendit Deus.
LR:F57.
Ave Maria.
LR:F54, F59, F60.
Ave regina caelorum.
LR:F59, F64, F69.
Ave verum corpus.
EB:G56.
Canite tuba.
LR:F54.
Cantabo Domino.
LR:F100.
Confitemini Domino.
LR:F59.
Crux fidelis.
LR:F63.
Dominus Jesus in qua nocte.
LR:F56.
Dum aurora finem daret.
LR:F52.
Ecce quomodo moritur.
LR:F63.
Ego sum panis vivus.
LR:F57.
Et in terra pax (Missa 'Cantantibus Organis Caecilia.')
LR:F95.
Exultate Deo.
LR:F48, F62.
Gloriosi principes terrae.
LR:F59.
Haec dies.
LR:F59, F79.
EB:G136.
Hodea beata virgo Maria.
LR:F65.
Hodie Christus natus est.
LR:F48, F54, F98.
Hymnus in adventu Dei.
LR:F62.
Illumina oculos meos.
LR:F57.
Improperia.
  Ecce lignum crucis (Chant). Popule meus. Quid ultra
     debui. Crucem tuam (Chant). O crux ave.
LR:F53, F64.
Improperium expectavit.
LR:F100.
In monte Oliveti.
LR:F63.
Jesu rex admirabilis.
LR:F62, F64.
Jubilate Deo.

LR:F54, F57.
Laetus Hyperboream.
LR:A6.
Lamentatio (Sabbato Sancto).
LR:F63.
Lauda Sion salvatorem.
LR:F51.
Laudate Dominum.
LR:F57.
Litaniae de Beata Virgine Maria.
LR:F65.
Loquebantur variis linguis.
LR:Ge37.
Magnificat.
LR:F48, F62, F65, F69.
EB:G50.
O bone Jesu.
LR:F47.
O magnum mysterium.
LR:F51, F54.
O vos omnes.
LR:F63.
Omnes amici mei.
LR:F63.
Oratio Jeremia Prophetae.
LR:F47, F55, F57.
Paucitas dierum.
LR:F55, F100.
Peccantem ne quotidie.
LR:F56.
Peccavimus.
LR:F48.
Popule meus.
LR:E40, F63.
Pueri Hebraeorum.
LR:F57, F59, F64.
Quam pulchra es (Song of Songs).
LR:F60.
Recordare mei.
LR:F77.
Rex admirabilis.
LR:F81.
Salve regina.
LR:F59.
Senex puerum portabat.
LR:F65.
Sicut cervus desiderat.
LR:F40, F47, F48, F52, F79, F83.
Song of Songs, Nos. 1–29.
    1. Osculetur me. 2. Trahe me post te. 3. Nigra sum, sed formosa. 4. Vineam meam non custodi. 5. Si ignoras te. 6. Pulchrae sunt genae tuae. 7. Fasciculus myrrhae. 8. Ecce tu pulchra es. 9. Tota pulchra es. 10. Vulnerasti cor meum. 11. Sicut lilium inter spinas. 12. Introduxit me rex. 13. Laeva eius. 14. Vox dilecti mei. 15. Surge, propera amica mea. 16. Surge, amica mea, speciosa mea. 17. Dilectus me5s mihi. 18. Surgam et circuibo civitatem. 19. Adjuro vos. 20. Caput eius aurum optimum. 21. Dilectus meus descendit in hortum suum. 22. Pulchra es, amica mea. 23. Quae est ista, quae progreditur. 24. Descendi in hortum meum. 25. Quam pulchra sunt gressus tui. 26. Duo ubera tua. 27. Quam pulchra es, et quam decora. 28. Gutter tuum sicut vinum optimum. 29. Veni, dilecte mi, agrediamur in agrum.
LR:F66, F67.
Stabat mater.
LR:F53, F56, F58, F65.
LB:G319.
Sub tuum praesidium.
LR:F59.
Super flumina Babylonis.
LR:F47.
Surge illuminare.

LR:F69.
Surrexit pastor bonus.
LR:F59.
Tenebrae factae sunt.
LR:F63.
Terra tremuit.
LR:F57, F80.
Tribulationes.
LR:F48.
Tu es Petrus.
LR:F48, F51, F60.
Tui sunt caeli.
LR:F54.
Unus ex discipulis meis.
LR:F63.
Veni sponsor Christi.
LR:F62.
Vexilla regis.
LR:F63.
Vos dilecti mei.
LR:F100.
Vulnerasti vor meum.
LR:F100.
  e. Sacred Vocal – Masses
Missa 'Ad fugam': Kyrie. Gloria.
PS:A71.
Missa 'Aeterna Christi munera.'
LR:F47, F48.
Missa 'Assumpta est Maria.'
LR:F49.
Missa 'Brevis.'
LR:F49, F50.
EB:G136.
Missa 'De Beata Virgine.'
LR:F51, F52.
Missa 'Gia fu chi m'ebbe cara.'
LR:F46.
Missa 'Hodie Christus natus est.'
LR:F53, F54.
Missa 'Papae Marcelli.'
LR:F50, F55, F56, F57, F58.
Missa 'Papae Marcelli': Kyrie.
LB:G326.
Missa 'Sine Nomine' (Missa 'Mantovana.')
LR:F59.
Missa 'Tu es Petrus.'
LR:F60, F61, F68.
Missa 'Veni sponsa Christi.'
LR:F62.

PALIGON, Marcin (16th. cent.)
  e. Sacred Vocal
Rorate caeli.
LR:F92.

PALOU – *see* BERENGUER DE PALOU

PAMINGER, Leonhard (1495–1567)
  e. Sacred Vocal
Resonet in laudibus – In dulci jubilo – Omnis modus jocundetur.
LR:F103, F104.

PARABOSCO, Girolamo (1520–1567)
  b. Instrumental
Ricercare XIV 'Da pacem Domine.' (Music de Joye).
LR:B26.
  c. Keyboard – Organ
Benedictus.
LR:D18.

PARADIES, Domenico (1707–1791)
  c. Keyboard
Sonata No. 6 in A maj.
EB:D30.

PARCHAM, Andrew (17th. cent.)
   b. Chamber and Instrumental
   Solo (Suite) in G maj for recorder and continuo.
   EB:B56.
   LB:B229, B267, B279, B288, B291, B292.

PARKER, Martin (17th. cent.)
   d. Secular Vocal
   When the King enjoys his own again.
   EB:F107.

PARMA – *see* GARSI DA PARMA, Santino.

PARSONS, Robert (d.1570)
   b. Instrumental
   Trumpets.
   LR:Ga9.
   d. Secular Vocal
   Joan quoth John.
   LR:Gd49.
   No grief is like to mine.
   LR:Gd51.
   Pandolpho – Pour down, you pow'rs divine.
   LR:Gd51.
   e. Sacred Vocal
   Ave Maria.
   LR:F88, Ge32, Ge35, Ge38.

PASCHA, Edmund (1714–1772)
   e. Sacred Vocal
   Harmonia Pastorales – Christmas Mass in F maj.
   LB:G260.
   Prosae Pastorales – Christmas Carols.
   LB:G260.

PASQUINI, Bernardo (1637–1710)
   c. Keyboard
   3 Arie.
   LB:E238.
   Bergamasca.
   EB:E47.
   Canzone francese.
   EB:E47, E56.
   Capriccio.
   EB:E47.
   Partite diverse di Follia.
   LR:D20.
   EB:E47, E66, E87.
   LB:D220, E235.
   Passacaglia.
   EB:E47.
   Pastorale.
   LB:E182.
   Ricercare.
   EB:E56.
   Toccata VII.
   EB:E94.
   Toccata in C maj.
   EB:E47.
   Toccata in D min.
   EB:E47.
   Toccata in E min.
   EB:E47.
   Toccata in E min con 'lo scherzo del cucco.'
   EB:E47.
   Toccata in G maj.
   EB:E47.
   LB:E238.
   Variazione in G min.
   EB:E47.

PASSEREAU (1490–1547)
   d. Secular Vocal
   A ung Guillaume.
   LR:E58.
   Il est bel et bon.

LR:E33, E50, Ga11.
   Je n'en puis plus durer.
   LR:E58.
   Marie monstroit.
   LR:E58.
   Pourquoy donc.
   LR:E58.
   Saincte Barbe mon compere.
   LR:E58.

PAUMANN, Conrad (1409–1473)
   b. Instrumental
   Ascensus simplex.
   AA:A1.
   Ellend du hast.
   AA:A1.
   LR:E64.
   Mit gantzem willen.
   LR:D17.
   EB:D36.
   Quant ieu congneu a ma pensee.
   LR:D17.

PAUMGARTNER (15th. cent.)
   c. Keyboard
   Andante.
   EB:D36.

PEDERSON, Mogens (c.1585–1623)
   d. Secular Vocal
   Care lagrime mie.
   LR:E19.
   Ecco la primavera.
   LR:E19.
   Lasso io prima morire.
   LR:E19.
   Moriro, cor mio se nel partir.
   LR:E19.
   Non fuggir.
   LR:E19.
   O che soave baccio.
   LR:E19.
   Udite, amanti.
   LR:E19.
   e. Sacred Vocal – Danish Works
   Aleneste Gudi Himmerig.
   EB:G66.
   Fader vor Gudi Himmerig.
   EB:G66.
   Forlen os freden nadelig.
   EB:G66.
   Kyrie om Paske.
   EB:G66.
   Med konnig David klage.
   EB:G66.
   Nu bede vi den Helligand.
   EB:G66.
   e. Sacred Vocal – Latin Works
   Ad te levavi.
   EB:G66.
   Deus misereatur nostri.
   EB:G66.
   Laudate Dominum.
   EB:G66.
   Missa a 5vv.
   EB:G66.
   Victimae paschali laudes.
   EB:G66.

PEERSON, Martin (c.1580–c.1650)
   c. Keyboard
   Alman.
   LR:B10.
   SI:C7.
   The Fall of the leaf.

ER:A24.
LR:D14, Gc13, Gc14.
EB:B37.
LB:D214.
Piper's Pavan.
LR:B10, Gc16.
The Primerose.
LR:D14, Gc13, Gc14.
SI:C7.
d. Secular Vocal
Sing, love is blind.
LR:Gd53.
Look up, fair lids.
LR:Gd37.

PEIROL D'ALVERGNA (c.1167–1235)
d. Secular Vocal
Quant amors trobet partit.
AA:D10.

PEKIEL, Bartolomiej (d.1670)
e. Sacred Vocal
Audite mortales (Dialogues for Advent).
EB:G45.
Dulcis amor.
EB:F104.
Magnum nomen Domini.
EB:G142, G144.
Missa 'Brevis.'
EB:G67.
Missa 'Pulcherrima.'
LR:F42.
Resonet in laudibus.
EB:G142, G144.

PELAIA, Giovanni Francesco (16th. cent.)
d. Secular Vocal
Dialogo di amante e amore.
LR:E53.

PENALOSA, Francisco de (c.1470–1528)
d. Secular Vocal
Por las Sierras de Madrid.
LR:E28.

PEPUSCH, Johann Christoph (1676–1752)
b. Chamber and Instrumental
2 Preludes for recorder.
LB:B291.
Sonata in A min for violin and viola da gamba.
LB:B303.
Sonata in D min for recorder and continuo.
LB:B297, B303.
Sonata in F maj for recorder and continuo.
LB:B229, B267, B278, B279.
Sonata in G maj for recorder and continuo: Allegro.
LB:B259.
Trio Sonata in G min for 2 flutes and continuo.
LB:B226.

PERAZA, Francisco (1564–1598)
c. Keyboard – Organ
Medio registro alto de 1o tono.
LR:D13.
LB:E219.

PERGOLESI, Giovanni Battista (1710–1736)
a. Orchestral – *see* **RICCIOTTI**
b. Chamber and Instrumental (Attrib.)
Trio Sonata No. 12 in F maj.
LB:B285.
d. Secular Vocal
Aria di Martia.
EB:F101.
Se tu m'ami.
EB:F101.

LB:F80.
La Serva Padrona – Intermezzo, 1733.
LB:F51, F52, F53.
e. Sacred Vocal
Confitebor tibi, Domine.
LB:G261.
In coelestibus regnis.
LB:G261.
Magnificat.
LB:G272.
Mass in F maj.
LB:G264.
Miserere II.
LB:G262.
Missa Romana.
LB:G263.
Salve regina.
LB:G261, G265, G271.
Stabat mater.
LB:G266, G267, G268, G269, G270, G271.

PERI, Jacopo (1561–1633)
d. Secular Vocal
Belissima regina.
EB:F98.
Dunque fra torbid' onde.
LR:E41.
O durezza di Ferro.
EB:F98.
Tra le donne.
EB:F98.
Euridice – Opera, 1600.
EB:F48.

PEROTIN (= PEROTINUS) (c.1180–1236)
e. Sacred Vocal (Including Instrumental Arrangements)
Adjuva me a 4.
SI:C6.
Alleluia Nativitas.
AA:B10.
Alleluia: Pascha nostrum immolatus est.
AA:B2, D19.
Beata viscera.
AA:A3.
Benedicamus Domino.
AA:B2.
Haec dies a 3.
SI:C2.
Mors...
AA:B9.
Organum (Instrumental).
LR:D17.
Sederunt principes.
AA:B1, B10.
AN:A11.
Viderunt omnes.
AA:B1, B10.
Vir perfecte a 2.
SI:C2.
Virgo...
ER:A5.

PERRIN D'AGINCOURT (12th./13th. cent.)
d. Secular Vocal
Quant voi en la fin d'estey.
AA:A3.

PERRINET (14th. cent.)
e. Sacred Vocal
Kyrie (APT MS).
AN:B5.

PERTI, Giocomo (1661–1756)
e. Sacred Vocal
Aestuat mundi mare.

EB:B60.
San Petronio preconizzato da Dio vescovo di Bologna –
Oratorio: Quando si belle.
EB:B60.

PERUGIA – *see* **MATTEO DA PERUGIA**

PERUGIA – *see* **NICOLO DA PERUGIA**

PERUSIO, Matthieu da (14th. cent.)
d. Secular Vocal
Andray soulet.
AN:A2.
Le Greygnour bien.
AN:A2.

PESARO – *see* **EBREO DA PESARO, Guglielmo.**

PESENTI, Martino (c.1600–c.1647)
b. Instrumental – Correnti, Gagliarde e Balletti...1645
Balletto IV.
EB:B57.
Balletto V.
EB:B57.
Balletto XX.
EB:B57.
Gagliarda II.
EB:B57.
Gagliarda X.
EB:B57.

PESENTI, Michele (c.1475–1521)
d. Secular Vocal
Ben mille volte al di'.
LR:E53.
Non mi doglio gia d'amore.
LR:E53.

PETER VON BLOIS (13th. cent.)
d. Secular Vocal
Vite perdite (CARMINA BURANA)
AA:E8, E9, E11, E16.

PETRUS DE CRUCE (d.1299)
d. Secular Vocal
Aucun ont trouve – Lonc tans.
AA:A3, B1.
Je cuidoie bien metre – Si l'aim si bien.
AA:A3.
S'amours eust point de poer.
AA:D19.

PEUERL, Paul (c.1570–c.1625)
b. Instrumental
Partita a 4 in D min for brass.
EB:B67.

PEVERNAGE, Andreas (1543–1591)
e. Sacred Vocal
Gloria in excelsis Deo (Grosses Weihnachtsgloria.)
LR:F108.

PEZ, Johann Christoph (1664–1716)
a. Orchestral
Concerto Pastorale in D maj for violin, strings and
continuo.
LR:F111.
Concerto Pastorale in F maj for 2 flutes, violin, 2 viols and
continuo.
EB:A33.
b. Chamber and Orchestral
Trio Sonata in D min for 2 recorders and continuo.
LB:B304.

PEZEL, Johann Christoph (= PEZELIUS) (1639–1694)
b. Instrumental
Ceremonial Brass Music, 1685.
EB:A34.

Sonata I for wind instruments.
EB:F111.
Sonata XXXIX for wind instruments: Adagio.
EB:F111.
Sonata in C maj for trumpet and organ.
LB:B223.
Sonatina IV in C maj for 2 trumpets and continuo.
LB:B214.
Sonatina V in C maj for 2 trumpets and continuo.
LB:B214.

PHALESE, Pierre (1510–1573)
b. Instrumental (*see also* individual titles in
ANONYMOUS)
Allegez moy.
LR:C22, E2.
Allemande.
LR:B27, E55.
Allemande d'Anvers.
LR:B27.
Allemande de Liege.
LR:B9.
Allemande 'Smedelijn.'
LR:B27.
L'Arboscello ballo furlano.
LR:B10, B17, B18.
Au joly bois – Pavan and Galliard.
LR:E42.
La Battaglia – Galliard.
LR:E42.
La Battaglia – Pavan.
LR:E64.
Branle.
LR:E64.
Branle de Bourgogne.
LR:B9, B27.
Branle de Champagne.
LR:B9, B19.
Branle de la Guerre.
LR:E55.
Branle de la suite du contraint legier.
LR:B27.
Branle de Poictou.
LR:B9, B10.
La Brune – Galliard.
LR:B9.
Chi passa per sta strada.
LR:E20.
Fantasia.
LR:B9.
Fortune helas pourquoy.
LR:E54.
Galliard.
LR:B16.
Galliard Ferrarese.
LR:E54, F94.
Galliard Laroque.
LR:B9.
Galliard Traditore.
LR:B9, B25.
Grace et vertu.
LR:C22, E2.
Hoboken Danse.
LR:B9.
Passamezzo.
LR:B10, B16.
Passamezzo la doulce.
LR:E55.
Passamezzo d'Italie and Galliard.
LR:B9, B16.
Pavan and Galliard Ferrarese.
LR:B9, F94.
La Rocha el fuso – Pavan and Galliard.
LR:E42.

Saltarello.
LR:B16.
Schiarazula marazzula.
LR:B9.

PHILIDOR – *see* DANICAN-PHILIDOR, Anne.

PHILIPPE LE CHANCELLOR (13th. cent.)
  e. Sacred Vocal
  Mundus a mundita.
  AA:B8.

PHILIPS, Peter (c.1560–1628)
  b. Instrumental
  Chromatic Pavan and Galliard.
  LR:C16.
  Galliard.
  LR:Gd54.
  Pavane.
  LR:Gd54.
  Pavane.
  LR:Gd54.
  Pavana Dolorosa.
  LR:Ga15.
  Passamezzo Pavan.
  LR:Ga10.
  Philips's Pavan.
  LR:Gd21.
  Philips's Pavan and Galliard.
  LR:Gb9.
  e. Sacred Vocal
  Ascendit Deus.
  LR:F88, Ge32, Ge35.

PICCHI, Giovanni (c.1575–c.1630)
  c. Keyboard – Harpsichord
  Ballo detta il Picchi.
  EB:D15.
  Ballo alla Polacha.
  EB:D15.
  SI:C18.
  Ballo ditti il Stefanin.
  EB:D15.
  Ballo Ongaro.
  LR:A5, B27, E55.
  EB:D15.
  Padoana ditta la Ongara.
  LR:A6.
  EB:D15.
  Pass'e mezzo antico di sei part.
  EB:D15.
  Saltarello del ditto Pass'e mezzo.
  EB:D15.
  Il Suo saltarello.
  SI:C18.
  Toccata.
  EB:D15, D31.
  Todesca.
  EB:D15.

PICCININI, Alessandro (c.1566–1638/9)
  b. Instrumental – Lute
  Canzona.
  LR:C12.
  Corrente.
  LB:C30.
  Toccata I.
  AA:A1.
  LR:C26.
  Toccata X.
  LB:C30.

PIERCE, Edward (16th. cent.)
  b. Instrumental
  The Queen's Galliard.
  LR:Gd42.

PIERO, 'Magister.' (DA FIRENZE) (14th. cent.)
  d. Secular Vocal
  Con dolce brama.
  AN:B9.
  Sovra un fiume regale.
  AN:B8.

PIERRE DES MOLINS (15th. cent.)
  d. Secular Vocal
  Amis tous dous.
  AN:A1.
  De ce que fol pense.
  SI:C6.

PIETRAGRUA, Carlo (b.c.1665)
  d. Secular Vocal
  Tortorella.
  LR:Gd42.

PIGNOLET DE MONTECLAIR – *see* MONTECLAIR, Michel Pignolet de

PILKINGTON, Francis (1562–1638)
  d. Secular Vocal
  Amyntas with his Phyllis fair.
  LR:Gd54.
  Come all ye.
  LR:Gd27.
  Have I found her.
  LR:Gd54.
  Music's dear solace.
  LR:Gd27.
  Rest, sweet nymphs.
  LR:D21, Gd26, Gd27.
  Sweet Philida.
  LR:Gd50.

PISADOR, Diego (1508–1557)
  b. Instrumental – Vihuela/Lute
  Pavan in E min.
  LB:C20.
  Pavana muy llana.
  LR:C27.
  Villanesca.
  LR:C27.
  d. Secular Vocal
  Aquellas sierras madre.
  LR:E61.
  En la fuente del rosel.
  LR:E31, E61, E62.
  Partense partiendo.
  LR:E61.
  Romance de Abinderraez 'La Manana de San Juan.'
  LR:E30.
  Si la noche haze escura.
  LR:E61.
  Si te vas a Banar Juanica.
  LR:E61.

PISENDEL, Johann Georg (1687–1755)
  b. Chamber and Instrumental
  Sonata for violin without bass: Largo.
  LB:A640.

PISTOLETA (1150–1200)
  d. Secular Vocal
  Sirventois (Instrumental Arrangement).
  LR:B29.

PITONI, Giuseppe (1657–1743)
  e. Sacred Vocal
  Laudate Dominum.
  LR:F81.

PLANSON, Jehan (c.1559–c.1615)
  d. Secular Vocal
  Chambriere, chambriere.

LR:E58.
Nous etions trois jeunes filles.
LR:E38, E58.
La Rousee de joly mois de may.
LR:E55.

PLATTI, Giovanni Benedetto (1690–1763)
a. Orchestral
Concerto in G min for oboe, strings and continuo.
LB:A644.
b. Chamber and Instrumental
Suite in A maj for trumpet and organ (Arr. of Suite for
    violin and harpsichord).
LB:B222.

PLAYFORD, John (1623–1686)
b. Instrumental ('The English Dancing Master', 1651)
Argeers.
EB:F91.
Boatman.
EB:F91.
Cobler's Jigg.
LB:B323.
Cuckold's all in a row.
EB:B37.
Daphne.
EB:F91.
The Dressed ship.
LR:E34.
Fandango.
LR:E34.
Gavotte.
LB:B323.
Goddesses.
AA:D17.
LR:Gd47.
EB:F107.
Green Garters.
LR:E34.
Greensleeves and Pudding Pyes.
LB:B323.
Greenwood/Dargason.
AA:D17.
How can I keep my maidenhead.
LB:B323.
Hyde Park.
EB:B37.
In '88.
LR:Gd47.
Jack Pudding.
EB:F91.
Jog on.
LR:Gd23.
EB:B37.
Kempe's Jigg.
EB:F91.
Light o' Love.
EB:B37.
Maiden Lane.
EB:B37.
Merry milkmaids we.
EB:B37.
Newcastle.
EB:B37, F91.
The North Country Maid's Resolution and Love to her
    Sweetheart (Cavalilly Man) ('The Dancing Master',
    1670).
EB:F107.
Once I loved a maiden fair.
EB:F91.
The Parson's Farewell/Goddesses.
AA:D17.
LR:Gd47.
Prince Rupert's March.
EB:F107.

Rufty tufty.
EB:F91.
Running Footman.
LB:B323.
St. Martin's.
LR:Gd47.
Sally's Fancy/The Maiden's Blush.
AA:D17.
Staines Morris.
EB:F91.
The Sturdy Oak.
LR:Gd43.
Vive le roy.
EB:F107.
Woodicocke.
EB:B37, F91.

PODBIELSKI, Jan (fl.1650)
c. Keyboard – Harpsichord
Praeludium in D min.
EB:D2, D35, E85.

POGLIETTI, Alessandro (1641–1683)
c. Keyboard
Balletto.
LB:B323.
Capriccio 'über das Hennergeschrey.'
LR:D21.
Französische Handküsse.
EB:D35.
Galopp und Flucht.
EB:B35.
Toccatina sopra la Ribellione di Ungheria.
LR:A6.

POHLE, David (1624–1695)
b. Instrumental
Sonata in A maj for 2 violins and continuo. 'Nun danket
    alle Gott.'
EB:B36.

POLAK, Jakub (c.1545–1605)
b. Instrumental – Lute
Branle.
EB:D2.
Courante.
LR:C17.
EB:D2.
Galliard.
EB:D2.
Praeludium.
LR:C18.

PONCE, Juan (15th./16th. cent.)
d. Secular Vocal
Ave color vini clari.
LR:E28, E65.
Todo mi bien e perdido.
LR:E27.

PONS D'ORTAFA (13th. cent.)
d. Secular Vocal
Si ay perdut.
AA:D4.

PORCAIRAGUES – *see* AZALAIS DE PORCAIRAGUES

PORPORA, Nicolo (1686–1768)
a. Orchestral
Concerto in G maj for cello and strings.
LB:A362.

PORTA, Francesco della (c.1610–1666)
e. Sacred Vocal
Corda deodabimus.
EB:G139.

PORTER, Walter (c.1595–1659)
  d. Secular Vocal
  Thus sang Orpheus to his lute.
  LR:A1.

POWER, Leonel (d.1445)
  e. Sacred Vocal
  Anima mea liquefacta est.
  ER:B6.
  Ave regina caelorum.
  ER:B3.
  Beata progenies.
  ER:B3.
  Gloria a 5vv.
  ER:B3.
  Opem nobis.
  ER:B1.

PRAETORIUS, Hieronymous (1560–1629)
  e. Sacred Vocal
  O vos omnes.
  EB:G138.

PRAETORIUS, Jacob (1586–1651)
  c. Keyboard – Organ
  Allein Gott in der Höh' sei Ehr'.
  EB:E74.
  Preambulum in F maj.
  EB:E60.

PRAETORIUS, Michael (1571–1621)
  b. Instrumental – Terpsichore, 1612
  Aufmarsch.
  LR:E34.
  Ballet.
  EB:B13, B30, B66.
  LB:B295.
  Ballet des Angloises.
  EB:B40.
  Ballet des Baccanales.
  EB:G68.
  Ballet des Coqs.
  EB:G68.
  LB:B259, B272.
  Ballet des Matelotz.
  EB:G68.
  Ballet de Monsieur de Nemours.
  EB:B40.
  Ballet des Sorciers.
  EB:B63.
  Bourree.
  EB:B13, B30, G68.
  3 Branles doubles.
  AA:A1.
  Branle de la Royne I and II.
  LR:E66.
  Branle de Village.
  EB:B40.
  Canarie.
  LR:B29, E45.
  EB:B40.
  Courante.
  AA:D20.
  LR:E66.
  EB:B30, B40, B66.
  LB:B259, B295.
  Courante de Monsieur de Terme.
  EB:B66.
  Courante de Monsieur Wustrow.
  EB:G68.
  Dorftanz.
  LR:E34.
  Entree.
  EB:B30.
  Fastnachtstanz.

  EB:B13.
  Feuertanz.
  LR:E34.
  EB:B13.
  Galliard.
  LR:E66.
  EB:B40.
  Galliard de la Guerre.
  LR:B21, B25.
  Galliard de Monsieur Wustrow.
  LR:B21, B25.
  Gavotte.
  LR:E66.
  EB:B30.
  Hohnentanz.
  EB:B13.
  Introduction and Courante.
  EB:B13.
  LB:B259.
  Mascarada.
  EB:B66.
  Passamezze.
  EB:G68.
  La Passapieds de Bretaigne.
  LB:B295.
  Pavane de Spaigne.
  LR:E45.
  EB:B40, G68.
  LB:B295.
  Philou.
  EB:B40.
  Reprinse.
  LR:B21.
  EB:G68.
  La Rosetta.
  LR:E45, E66.
  Sarabande.
  EB:G68.
  LB:B295.
  Schiffertanz.
  LR:E34.
  Schreittanz.
  LR:E34.
  Spagnioletta.
  LR:E54.
  EB:B13, B30, G68.
  Suite of Gavottes.
  EB:B13.
  LB:B259.
  Tanz der Bauern.
  LR:E34.
  Tanz der Bauerinnen.
  LR:E34.
  EB:B13.
  Tanz der Fischer.
  LR:E34.
  EB:B13.
  La Volte.
  LR:B14, E45.
  EB:B30, B40, B66, G68.
  Die Windmühle.
  LR:E34.
  b. Instrumental
  Partita a 4vv.
  EB:B55.
  c. Keyboard – Organ
  Sinfonia in G min.
  EB:E60.
  d. Secular Vocal
  Der Winter ist ein strenger gast.
  ER:A24.
  e. Sacred Vocal
  A solis ortis cardine.
  LR:F123.

EB:E60.
Allein Gott in der Höh' sei Ehr'.
EB:G68.
Als der gütige Gott.
EB:G69.
Alvus tumescit.
EB:E60.
Aus tiefer Not.
EB:G68.
Christ unser Herr.
EB:F105.
Christus der uns selig macht.
EB:G68.
Den die Hirten lobetan.
LR:F108, F109, F112, F122.
Der Engel sprach zu den Hirten.
LR:F118.
Der Tag vertreibt.
EB:G132, B66.
Ein feste Burg ist unser Gott.
LB:G326.
Ein kind geborn zu Bethlehem.
LR:F105, F123.
EB:G69.
En natus est Emmanuel.
LR:F115.
Erhalt uns, Herr, bei deinem Wort.
EB:G68.
Es ist ein Ros entsprungen.
LR:F103, F104, F106, F107, F109, F111, F112, F118,
   F121, F123.
Gott der Vater wohn uns bei.
EB:G68.
In dulci jubilo.
LR:F107, F109, F112, F123, F124, F125.
In natali Domine.
LR:F104, F107, F109, F118.
Lobt Gott ihr Christen alle gleich.
AA:A1.
LR:F118.
Morgenstern ist aufgedrungen.
LR:F112.
Omnis mundis jocundetur.
EB:G69.
Psallite.
LR:F104, F106, F112.
Resonet in laudibus.
EB:G68.
Singt, ihr lieben Christen alle.
LR:F114.
Uns ist geborn ein Kindelein.
LR:F118.
Vater unser in dem Himmel.
LB:E207.
Vom Himmel hoch.
LR:F108, F112.
Vom Himmel hoch, da komm ich her.
EB:G69.
Wie schön leuchtet der Morgernstern.
LR:F118.

PRENTZL (17th. cent.)
  b. Instrumental
  Sonata in C maj for trumpet and organ.
  LB:B223.

PRES - *see* **JOSQUIN DES PRES**

PRIOLI, Giovanni (c.1575–1629)
  b. Instrumental
  Canzona I a 12.
  EB:G139.

PUJOL, Juan (c.1573–1626)
  e. Sacred Vocal
  Laudate Dominum.

LR:F89.

PULITO (17th./18th. cent.)
  b. Instrumental
  Concerto No. 4 for sackbutt and organ.
  LB:B202.
  Concerto No. 5 for sackbutt and organ.
  LB:B202.

PURCELL, Daniel (1660–1717)
  b. Instrumental
  Sonata in F maj for recorder and continuo.
  LB:B288.
  Sonata in G min for recorder and continuo.
  LB:B291.
  d. Secular Vocal
  Dialogue between Thirsis and Daphne.
  EB:F94.
  I spy Celia.
  EB:F94.
  Lovely charmer (The Island Princess).
  EB:F94.
  Mad Bess.
  EB:F94.
  O ravishing delight.
  LR:Gd26.
  Thy genius, lo!
  EB:F94.

PURCELL, Henry (1658–1695)
  b. Instrumental
  Chaconne (Dioclesian).
  EB:F49.
  Chaconne – 2 in one upon a ground.
  EB:B65.
  Chaconne in F maj – 3 parts upon a ground.
  EB:B64.
  LB:B281.
  Chaconne (Chaconny) in G min, Z730.
  EB:A21, F57, F77, G75.
  LB:A583, A606, A619, B327.
  Chaconne (Fantasia) in D maj – 3 parts upon a ground,
     Z731.
  EB:B54.
  LB:A186, B227.
  Fantasia I a 3 in D min, Z732.
  EB:B31.
  Fantasia II a 3 in F maj, Z733.
  EB:B31.
  Fantasia III a 3 in G min, Z734.
  EB:B31.
  SI:C1, C13.
  Fantasia IV a 4 in G min, Z735.
  EB:B31.
  Fantasia V a 4 in B flat maj, Z736.
  EB:B31.
  Fantasia VI a 4 in F maj, Z737.
  EB:B31.
  Fantasia VII a 4 in C min, Z738.
  LR:Ga16.
  EB:B31.
  Fantasia VIII a 4 in D min, Z739.
  EB:B31.
  Fantasia IX a 4 in A min, Z740.
  EB:B31.
  Fantasia X a 4 in E min, Z741.
  EB:B31.
  Fantasia XI a 4 in G maj, Z742.
  LR:Gd44.
  EB:B31.
  Fantasia XII a 4 in D min, Z743.
  LR:Gd44.
  EB:B31.
  Fantasia XIII a 5 upon one note in F maj, Z745.
  EB:B31.

In Nomine a 6 in G min, Z746.
EB:B31.
In Nomine a 7 in G min, Z747.
LR:Gd44.
EB:B31.
March and Canzona, Z860 (Funeral Music for Queen Mary).
EB:A34.
Overture in D min for 2 violins, viola and continuo, Z771.
EB:B54.
Overture and Suite in G maj for 2 violins, viola and continuo, Z770.
EB:B54.
Overture in G min for 2 violins, 2 violas and continuo, Z772.
EB:B54.
Pavane and Trio in A min for 2 violins and continuo (The Fairy Queen).
EB:F50.
Pavan in A maj.
EB:F57.
Pavan in A min for 2 violins and viol, Z749.
EB:B54, F57.
SI:C15.
Pavan in B flat maj for 2 violins and viol, Z750.
EB:B54, F57.
SI:C15.
Pavan in G min for 3 violins and viol, Z752.
EB:B54, F57.
Pavan in G min.
EB:F57.
Prelude in D min for recorder and continuo.
LB:B302.
Sinfonia I.
EB:B65, B69.
Sinfonia II.
EB:B65.
Sonata in C maj for trumpet and organ.
LB:B212.
Sonata No. 1 in D maj for trumpet and strings.
LB:A651, A652, A665, A668.
Sonata No. 2 in D maj for trumpet and strings.
LB:A652, A668.
Sonata in D maj for trumpet and continuo (Unsp.)
EB:F77.
LB:A670, B211.
Sonata in F maj for trumpet and organ.
LB:B221.
Sonata No. 3 in A min for 2 violins and continuo, Z804 (1697).
EB:B54.
Sonata No. 9 in F maj for 2 violins and continuo, 'The Golden', Z810 (1697).
EB:A21.
Sonata in G min for violin, bass viol and organ.
EB:F57.
Suite from the Fairy Queen: Rondeau. Dance of the Fairies. Chaconne.
LB:C23.
Suite of Dances (Unsp.)
LB:A649, B324.

c. Keyboard – Harpsichord, Organ, etc.
Air in C maj, 'The Cebell', Z630.
EB:B47, D1, D18, E48.
Air in D min, ZT675.
EB:D1, D18.
Air in D min, ZT676 ('The Double Dealer.')
EB:D18, D19, D24, E48.
Air in F maj.
EB:E48.
Air in G maj, Z641.
EB:D18.
Air, ZT693/2 ('Abdelazar'.)
EB:D18, D19.

Air (Unsp.)
LR:Gc8.
EB:E49.
Air ('Distressed Innocence.')
SI:B2.
Air ('The Indian Queen.')
EB:D1.
Allemande in C maj.
EB:E48.
Allemande in D maj, Z665/2.
EB:E48.
Bouree in D maj ('Abdelazar.')
EB:D19.
Canary, ZT677 ('The Indian Queen.')
EB:D18, D19.
Canary.
LR:Gc8.
Chaconne, ZT680 ('Timon of Athens.')
EB:D18, D19.
Entree.
EB:E49.
Fanfare.
EB:E49.
Gavotte, ZD219/1.
EB:D18.
Gigue in C maj, Z665/5.
EB:D19.
Gigue, ZT686.
EB:D19.
Gigue in G min (Attrib. Morgan).
EB:D19.
Grand Air.
EB:E49.
Ground in D min, ZD222 ('Celebrate the Festival'.)
EB:B54, D18, D19, D23.
Ground in C min, ZD221.
EB:D18, D19.
Ground in C min, ZT681 ('Ye tuneful muses.')
EB:D18, D19.
Ground in Gamut, Z645.
LR:Gc13.
EB:D16, D18, D19, E49.
SI:C20.
Hornpipe, ZT683 ('Abdelazar.')
EB:D18, D19.
Hornpipe, ZT685 ('The Old Batchelor.')
EB:D18, D19, D23, D24.
Hornpipe (Unsp.)
LR:Gc13.
EB:D35.
Jig, ZD223.
EB:D18.
Jig, ZT686 ('Abdelazar.')
EB:D18.
March, Z647.
EB:D18, D23.
March in C maj, ZT687.
EB:E48, D18.
Martial Air and Cebell.
EB:E49.
Lesson in A maj, Z665.
EB:D24.
Lesson in A min, Z654.
EB:D23.
March in C maj, Z647.
EB:D24.
March, Z648.
EB:D18.
March.
EB:E49.
Minuet in C maj, ZD230.
EB:E48.
Minuet, Z649.
EB:D16, D18, D19, D23, D24, D39.

Minuet, Z650.
EB:D16, D18, D23, D24, D39.
Minuet, Z651.
EB:D16, D18.
Minuet, ZT688 ('Raise the Voice.')
EB:D16, D18, D23, D24.
Minuet ('Distressed Innocence.')
SI:B2.
Minuet (Unsp.)
LR:Gc13.
EB:E49.
A New Ground, ZT682 ('Welcome to all the pleasures.')
EB:B54, D18, D23, D24, E83, F51.
A New Irish Tune, Z646 ('Lilliburlero.')
EB:D18, D23, D24, D30.
New Minuet, ZT689.
EB:D18, D24.
A New Scotch Tune, Z655.
EB:D23, D24.
Overture ('The Indian Queen.')
EB:D1.
Overture ('The Virtuous Wife.')
EB:D19.
Pavane.
LB:B322.
Prelude in A min.
EB:D35.
Prelude, Z633 (Alternative to Suite No. 4).
EB:D18.
Prelude in C maj, Z665/1.
EB:D19.
Prelude in G maj, Z720.
EB:E48.
Prelude in G min (Brit. Mus.)
EB:D18.
Prelude and Air.
EB:E49.
Prelude and Cebell.
EB:E67.
The Queen's Dolour, Z670.
EB:D18, E48, E49.
LB:B205.
Rigadoon, Z653.
EB:D18, D19, D23.
Rondeau ('Distressed Innocence.')
SI:B2.
Round O, ZT684 ('Abdelazar.')
EB:D18, D19.
LB:A601.
Sarabande with Division, Z654.
EB:D18, D19.
Sefauchi's Farewell, Z656.
EB:B54, D16, D18, D23, D24, E49.
Solemn Overture.
EB:E49.
Song Tune, ZT694.
EB:D18, D23, D24.
Song Tune, ZT695.
EB:D18.
Suite of Lessons: Prelude-Almande-Corant-Sarabande-
    Jig, Z665.
EB:D18.
Suites for harpsichord, Nos. 1–8, Z660–663, 666–669.
    1. in G maj; 2 in G min; 3 in G maj; 4 in A min; 5 in C maj;
    6 in D maj. 7 in D min. 8 in F maj.
EB:D16, D17, D18, D19, D20, D21, D22, D23, D39.
Suite No. 1 in G maj, Z660.
LR:Gc13.
Suite No. 2 in G min, Z661.
EB:D24, D30.
Suite No. 5 in C maj, Z666.
LR:Gc13.
Suite No. 5 in C maj, Z666: Prelude in C maj.
EB:E49.

Suite No. 6 in D maj, Z667.
LR:Gc13.
EB:B54.
Suite No. 7 in D min, Z668.
EB:D37.
Suite from the Indian Queen: Overture. Airs I–III. Trumpet
    Tune.
EB:D1.
Toccata in A min.
EB:D24.
Trumpet Tune in D maj ('The Prophetess.')
EB:E48.
Trumpet Tune, ZS124.
EB:D23.
Trumpet Tune, ZT678 ('The Cebell.')
EB:D18.
Trumpet Tune, ZT697 ('Dioclesian.')
EB:D18.
Trumpet Tune, ZT698 ('The Indian Queen.')
EB:D1, D18.
Trumpet Tune.
PS:A71.
LR:Gc13.
LB:A649.
Tune and Air.
EB:A34.
LB:A657, B212, B219, E220.
Trumpet Voluntary.
EB:E49.
LB:E219.
Trumpet Voluntary in D maj.
LR:F106.
LB:E221.
Verse in the Phrygian Mode, ZS126.
EB:E70.
Voluntary in A maj on the 'Old Hundredth', Z721.
LR:Gc17.
EB:E48.
Voluntary in C maj, Z717.
EB:E48, E70.
Voluntary in D min, Z718.
EB:E48.
LB:B223.
Voluntary in D min for double organ, Z719.
EB:E48, G3.
Voluntary in G maj, Z720.
EB:B68.
LB:E240.
d. Secular Vocal – Catches, Solo Songs and Part Songs
A health to the nut brown lass, Z240.
EB:F52.
Ah! cruel nymph, Z352.
EB:F2, F56.
As Roger last night, Z242.
EB:F112.
Come let us drink, Z245.
EB:F52.
The Fatal Hour, Z421.
EB:F2, F56, F103.
Come shepherds, you that know – Elegy on the Death of
    John Playford, Z464.
EB:F57.
Hark how the wild musicians sing, Z542.
EB:F58.
He that drinks is immortal, Z254.
EB:F112.
Here let my life, Z544/5a (If ever I more riches did
    desire).
EB:F49, F54.
How pleasant is this flowery plain and grove, Z543/2a.
EB:F49.
I gave her cakes and I gave her ale, Z256.
EB:F52, F112.
I loved fair Celia, Z381.

EB:F2.
I saw that you were grown so high, Z387.
EB:F55.
If I ever more riches did desire, Z544.
EB:F52, F54.
If music be the food of love, Z379.
EB:F2, F51, F53, F54, F55.
LB:F83.
Incassum Lesbia, incassum rogas – The Queen's Epicedium, Z383.
EB:F49, F55, F56, F103.
Lost is my quiet for ever, Z502.
EB:F58.
Love arms himself, Z392.
EB:F2.
Love thou can'st hear, Z396.
EB:F2.
Lovely Albinas come ashore, Z394.
EB:F54.
Me, o ye Gods, Z544/4 (If ever I more riches did desire).
EB:F54.
The Miller's daughter, Z277.
EB:F52.
More love or more disdain I crave, Z397.
EB:F55.
My Lady's coachman John, Z260.
EB:F112.
Not all my torments, Z400.
EB:F53, F58.
O how happy's he, Z403 (Z627, 'Dioclesian.')
EB:F50.
O Solitude, my sweetest choice, Z406.
EB:G74.
Of all the instruments, Z263.
EB:F52.
Olinda in the shades, Z404.
EB:F50.
Once, twice, thrice, Z265.
EB:F52.
Pious Celinda, Z410.
EB:F2, F56.
Prithee ben't so sad and serious, Z269.
EB:F52.
Saccharissas grown old, Z507.
EB:F54.
Since time to us so kind does prove, Z272.
EB:F52.
Sir Walter enjoying his damsel, Z273.
EB:F52, F112.
Sweet, be no longer sad, Z418.
EB:F55.
Sylvia, now your scorn give over, Z420.
EB:F55.
There ne'er was so wretched a lover as I, Z513.
EB:F49.
'Tis wine was made to rule the day, Z546.
EB:F58.
'Tis woman makes us love, Z281.
EB:F52.
Tom the tailor, ZD106.
EB:F112.
Under this stone, Z286.
EB:F52.
Upon Christ Church bells in Oxford.
EB:F112.
What hope for us remains now he is gone – Elegy on the Death of Matthew Locke, Z472.
EB:F57.
When the cock begins to crow, ZD172.
EB:F112.
Young John the gardener, Z292.
EB:F52.
Young Thirsis' fate ye hills and groves deplore – Elegy on the Death of Thomas Farmer, Z473.

EB:F56, F57.
d. Secular Vocal – Odes and Occasional Pieces
Come ye Sons of Art away – Birthday Ode for Queen Mary, 1694, Z323.
EB:F61, G42, G71.
Overture, Z323/1.
EB:A21.
Sound the trumpet, Z323/3a.
EB:F54, G133.
Strike the viol, Z323/5a.
EB:F49.
Laudate Ceciliam – Hymn on St. Cecilia's Day, 1683, Z329.
EB:F52, F58.
Love's Goddess sure was blind – Birthday Ode for Queen Mary, 1692, Z331.
EB:F59, F60, F61.
Many, many such days, Z331/7a.
EB:F54.
Sweetness of Nature, Z331/4.
EB:F54.
Welcome to all the pleasures – Ode on St. Cecilia's Day, 1683, Z339.
EB:F59.
Beauty, thou scene of love, Z339/8a.
EB:F54.
The Bashful Thomas, Z333/4b ('The Yorkshire Feast Song, 1690.')
LR:Gd46.
Be welcome then, great sir, Z324/11a ('Welcome song to His Majesty, 1683.')
EB:F54.
Hail, gracious Gloriana, Z320/6a ('Arise my muse' – Birthday Ode for Queen Mary, 1690).
EB:F54.
'Tis Nature's voice, Z328/4 ('Hail bright Cecilia' – Ode on St. Cecilia's Day, 1692).
EB:F56.
LB:F83, G182.
In vain the am'rous flute, Z328/10b ('Hail bright Cecilia' – Ode on St. Cecilia's Day, 1692).
EB:F54.
d. Secular Vocal – Incidental Music and Stage Works
Abdelazar, or the Moor's Revenge – Incidental Music, 1695, Z570.
EB:F78.
Abdelazar: Orchestral Suite.
EB:A20, A21.
Amphitryon, or the Two Sosias – Incidental Music, 1690, Z572.
EB:F81.
Bonduca, or the British Heroine – Incidental Music, 1695, Z574.
EB:F79.
Circe – Incidental Music, 1685, Z575.
EB:F79.
Dido and Aeneas – Opera, 1689, Z626.
EB:F62, F63, F64, F65, F66, F67, F68.
Distressed Innocence, or the Prince of Persia – Incidental Music, 1690, Z577.
EB:F78.
SI:B2.
Don Quixote – Incidental Music, 1694/5, Z578.
EB:F80.
The Fairy Queen – Semi Opera, 1692, Z629.
EB:F69, F70, F71.
The Gordian Knot Untied – Incidental Music, 1691, Z597.
EB:F78.
The Gordian Knot Untied: Orchestral Suite.
EB:A32.
The History of Dioclesian, or the Prophetess – Incidental Music, Z627.
EB:A20.

The Indian Queen - Incidental Music, 1695, Z630.
EB:F72, F73.
The Indian Queen: Overture.
EB:A21.
LB:A598.
King Arthur, or the British Worthy - Opera, 1681, Z628.
EB:F74, F75.
King Arthur: Orchestral Suite.
EB:A17.
The Married Beau, or the Curious Impertinent -
Incidental Music, 1694, Z603.
EB:F78.
The Old Batchelor - Incidental Music, 1691, Z607.
EB:F81.
The Old Batchelor: Orchestral Suite.
EB:A20.
Sir Anthony Love, or the Rambling Lady - Incidental
Music, 1690, Z588.
EB:F79.
The Tempest, or the Enchanted Isle - Opera, 1695, Z631.
EB:F76.
The Virtuous Wife, or Good Luck at Last - Incidental
Music: 1694, Z611.
EB:F81.
The Virtuous Wife: Orchestral Suite.
EB:A20.

**d. Secular Vocal - Songs and Excerpts from Incidental
Music and Operas**
Ah! how sweet it is to love ('The Virtuous Wife', Z611/2).
EB:F51, F55, F81.
Aeolus, you must appear ('The Tempest', Z631/13).
EB:F77.
Arise ye subterranean winds ('The Tempest', Z631/3b).
EB:F58, F77.
As Amoret and Thirsis lay ('The Old Batchelor',
Z607/11).
EB:F56, F81.
Britons strike home ('Bonduca', Z574/16b.)
EB:F79.
Celia that I once was blest ('Amphitryon', Z572/9a).
EB:F81.
Charon, the peaceful shade ('Dioclesian', Z627/6b).
LR:Gd46.
Come away, do not stay ('Dioclesian', Z627/27).
EB:F50, F58.
Come every demon ('Circe', Z575/3a).
EB:F79.
Cynthia frowns ('The Double-Dealer', Z592/10a).
EB:F2.
Divine Andate! president of war ('Bonduca', Z574/14).
EB:F79.
The Earth trembled ('The Indian Queen', Z191/1).
EB:F50, F51.
Fair Iris and her swain ('Amphitryon', Z572/11a).
EB:F81.
Fairest Isle ('King Arthur', Z628/38).
EB:F53, F55.
From rosy bow'rs ('Don Quixote', Z578/9a).
EB:F53, F80.
Genius of England ('Don Quixote', Z578/7b).
EB:F80.
Halcyon days ('The Tempest', Z631/15b).
EB:F77.
Hark how the songsters ('Timon of Athens', Z632/10b).
EB:F49.
Hark the ech'ing air ('The Fairy Queen', Z629/48bc).
EB:F54.
Hear us, great Rugwith ('Bonduca', Z574/11b).
EB:F79.
Hear, ye Gods of Britain ('Bonduca', Z574/12).
EB:F79.
Hear ye sullen powers ('Oedipus', Z583/1b).
EB:F50, F58.
I attempt from love's sickness to fly ('The Indian Queen',

Z630/17h).
EB:F51, F53.
I see she flies me everywhere ('Aureng-Zebe', Z573/1b).
EB:F51, F55.
I'll sail upon the dog star ('A Fool's Preferment', Z571/6).
EB:F51, F55.
In vain Clemen ('Sir Anthony Love', Z588/4).
EB:F79.
Jack thou'rt a toper ('Bonduca', Z574/10).
EB:F79.
Lads and lasses ('Don Quixote', Z578/8).
EB:F80.
Let the dreadful engines ('Don Quixote', Z578/3a).
EB:F80.
Let the fifes and the clarions ('The Fairy Queen',
Z629/29).
EB:F54.
Lovers who to their first embraces go ('Circe', Z575/4a).
EB:F79.
Lucinda is bewitching fair ('Abdelazar', Z570/10).
EB:F78.
Man that is for the woman made ('The Mock Marriage',
Z605/3).
EB:F51, F55, F103.
Music for a while ('Oedipus', Z583/2).
EB:F50, F51, F53, F55, F56, F58, F103.
No more, sir, no more ('Sir Anthony Love', Z588/3).
EB:F79.
Nymphs and shepherds come away ('The Libertine',
Z600/1b).
EB:F55.
O lead me to some peaceful gloom ('Bonduca',
Z574/17a).
EB:F51, F53, F79, F106.
One charming night ('The Fairy Queen', Z629/13b).
EB:F49, F54.
The Plaint ('The Fairy Queen', Z629/40ab).
EB:F50, F53.
Pluto, arise! ('Circe', Z575/6).
EB:F79.
Pursuing beauty ('Sir Anthony Love', Z588/2b).
EB:F79.
Retir'd from any mortal's sight ('King Richard II', Z581).
EB:F49, F53, F56.
See, see, the heavens smile ('The Tempest', Z631/16b).
EB:F77.
See where repenting Celia lies ('The Married Beau',
Z603/10).
EB:F78.
Shepherd, shepherd, leave decoying ('King Arthur',
Z628/16b).
EB:F49.
Since from my dear Astrea's sight ('Dioclesian', Z627).
EB:F51, F53, F56, F106.
Since times are so bad ('Don Quixote', Z578/6a).
EB:F80.
Sing all ye muses ('Don Quixote', Z578/1a).
EB:F80.
Sing, sing, ye Druids ('Bonduca', Z574/13b).
EB:F79.
Sweeter than roses ('Pausanias', Z585/1).
EB:F2, F51, F53, F55, F56.
Take not a woman's anger ill ('The Rival Sisters',
Z609/11).
EB:F51.
Their necessary aid you use ('Circe', Z575/2a).
EB:F79.
There's nothing so fatal ('A Fool's Preferment', Z571/2).
EB:F103.
There's not a swain on all the plain ('Rule a wife and have
a wife', Z587).
EB:F55.
Thrice happy lovers ('The Fairy Queen', Z629/39b).
EB:F53.

Thus at the height we love ('Amphitryon', Z572/1↑b).
EB:F81.

Thus to a ripe consenting maid ('The Old Batchelor',
Z607/10).
EB:F49, F81.

Thy genius lo! ('The Massacre of Paris', Z604 – *see* Daniel
Purcell).
EB:F94.

To arms ('Bonduca', Z574/15b).
EB:F79.

Turn then thine eyes, Z425 ('The Fairy Queen',
Z629/50c).
EB:F55.

'Twas within a furlong ('The Mock Marriage', Z605/2).
EB:F103.

Wake, Quivera ('The Fairy Queen', Z630/4b).
EB:F50.

We must assemble by a sacrifice ('Circe', Z575/1b).
EB:F79.

What shall I do? ('Dioclesian', Z627/18b).
EB:F77.

When the world first knew creation ('Don Quixote',
Z578/2).
EB:F80.

Why should men quarrel? ('The Indian Queen',
Z630/4d).
EB:F49.

With this sacred charming wand ('Don Quixote',
Z578/4b).
EB:F80.

Ye twice ten hundred deities ('The Indian Queen',
Z630/13a).
EB:F50.

Your awful voice I hear ('The Tempest', Z631/14a).
EB:F77.

e. Sacred Vocal – Services and Funeral Music

Benedicite, Z230M3 – Service in B flat maj.
EB:G3.

Funeral Music for Queen Mary, 1695, Z17AB, Z27, Z58
(*see* Anthems).
EB:A34, G70, G71, G72, G80.

Jubilate, Z232.
EB:G72, G73.

Te Deum, Z232.
EB:G72, G73, G136.

e. Sacred Vocal – Anthems

Behold I bring you glad tidings, Z2.
LR:F114.
EB:G77, G79.

Blessed are they that fear the Lord, Z5.
EB:G70.

Blow up the trumpet in Sion, Z10.
EB:G74, G75.

Hear my prayer, O Lord, Z15.
LR:Ge31.
EB:G70, G74.
LB:G319.

I was glad, Z19.
EB:G3, G77.

In thee, O Lord, do I put my trust, Z16.
EB:G77.

Lord, how long, Z25.
LR:F83.
EB:G78.

Man that is born of woman, Z27 (Funeral Music).
LR:F83.
EB:A34, G73.

My beloved spake, Z28.
EB:G70, G78.

My heart is inditing, Z30.
EB:G75.

My song shall be alway, Z31.
EB:G74.

O give thanks unto the Lord, Z33.

EB:G74, G77, G80.

O God, the King of Glory, Z34.
EB:G80.

O God, thou art my God, Z35.
EB:G75.

O God, thou hast cast us out, Z36.
EB:G75.

O Lord God of hosts, Z37.
EB:G74, G77.

O Lord, rebuke me not, Z40.
EB:G76.

O sing unto the Lord, Z44.
EB:G78.

Praise the Lord, O Jerusalem, Z46.
EB:G76.

Praise the Lord, O my soul, Z47.
EB:G76.

Rejoice in the Lord, Z49.
EB:G70, G75.

Remember not, O Lord, Z50.
LR:F83.
EB:G70, G75.

Save me God, Z51.
EB:G76.

They that go down to the sea in ships, Z57.
EB:G78.

Thou knowest, Lord, the secrets of our hearts, Z58c
(Funeral Music).
EB:A34.

Who hath believed our report, Z64.
EB:G78.

Why do the heathen, Z65.
EB:G76.

e. Sacred Vocal – Sacred Songs and Hymns

Awake, awake, ye dead, Z182.
EB:F49.

The earth trembled, Z197/1.
LB:F83.

Evening Hymn, Z193.
EB:F49, F52, F53, F103.

How long, great God, Z189/1.
LB:F83.

Hymn for Ascensiontide.
EB:G135.

In guilty night, Z134/1.
EB:G73.

Jehova quam multi sunt, Z135/1.
LR:Ge32, Ge33.
EB:G3, G78.

Let the night perish, Z191/1.
EB:F51.

Lord what is man?, Z192/1.
LR:Gd22.
EB:F51, F54, F55.

Morning Hymn, Z198.
EB:F51.

Now that the sun hath veiled his light, Z193/1.
EB:F55.

Sleep, Adam, sleep, Z195.
LR:Gd22.

Tell me some pitying angel – The Blessed Virgin's
Expostulation, Z196.
EB:F92.

With sick and famished eyes, Z200.
EB:F106.

PYGOTT, Richard (c.1485–1552)
d. Secular Vocal
Quid petis, o fili.
LR:Gf1, Gf5.

PYKINI (14th. cent.)
d. Secular Vocal
Plasanche or tost.
AN:A2.

QUAGLIATI, Paolo (c.1555–1628)
  d. Secular Vocal
  Ecco le notte.
  EB:F99.
  La nave felice.
  EB:F99.

QUANTZ, Johann Joachim (1697–1773)
  a. Orchestral
  Concerto in E min for flute and strings.
  LB:A628.
  Concerto in G maj for flute and strings.
  LB:A363, A629, A633.
  b. Chamber and Instrumental
  Sonata in A min for flute and continuo, Op. 1, No. 1.
  LB:B239.
  Sonata in D maj for flute and continuo.
  LB:B226, B238, B255.
  Trio Sonata for viola d'amore, violin and harpsichord.
  LB:B312.
  Trio Sonata in C maj for recorder, flute and continuo.
  LB:A44, B296, B298.
  Trio Sonata in C min for flute, oboe and continuo.
  LB:B251.

QUARLES, Francis (d.1727)
  c. Keyboard
  A Lesson or Voluntary.
  LB:D214.
  d. Secular Vocal
  Hey then, up we go!
  EB:F107.

QUENTIN, Bertin (d.c.1767)
  b. Chamber and Instrumental
  Sonata in D min for recorder and continuo.
  LB:B289.

QUESTENBURG, Johann Adam (1678–1752)
  b. Instrumental
  Menuet.
  LB:F79.
  Rigaudon.
  LB:F79.

RACQUET (17th. cent.)
  c. Keyboard – Organ
  Fantasia.
  EB:E76.

RADOMIA, Mikolaj z. (15th. cent.)
  b. Instrumental
  Instrumental piece.
  LR:E66.
  Piece without words.
  LR:E57.
  e. Sacred Vocal
  Et in terra pax.
  ER:B46.
  Hystorigraphi Acie.
  LR:E57.
  Magnificat.
  ER:B46.
  Patrem omnipotem.
  ER:B46.

RAICK, Dieudonne (1702–1764)
  c. Keyboard – Organ
  Andante and Gigue.
  LB:E210.
  Gavotte.
  EB:E88.

RAIMBAUT DE VAQUEIRAS (1155–1207)
  d. Secular Vocal
  Kalenda maya.
  AA:A3, D3, D5, D8, D10, D18.

  LR:B14.
  Vida.
  AA:D10.

RAIMON DE MIRAVEL (1191–1229)
  d. Secular Vocal
  Estat ai en greu cossirier.
  AA:D1.
  Selh que no vol auzir cancos.
  AA:A2, D9, D13.

RAISON, Andre (1650–1719)
  c. Keyboard – Organ
  Offertoire.
  EB:E2.

RAMEAU, Jean Philippe (1683–1764)
  b. Chamber and Instrumental
  Pieces de Clavecin en concerts, Nos. 1–5.
    1. La Coulicam, La Livri, Le Vezinet.
    2. La Laborde, La Boucon, L'Agacante, Menuet I-II.
    3. La Poupliniere, La Timide, Tambourin.
    4. La Pantomime, L'Indiscrette, La Rameau.
    5. La Forqueray, La Cupis, La Marais.
  LB:B162, B163.
  Piece de Clavecin en concert, No. 1 in C min.
  LB:B122, B258.
  Piece de Clavecin en concert, No. 5 in D min.
  LB:B122.
  Piece de Clavecin en concert, No. 6 in G min, 'La Poule'
    (Arr. Kehr).
  LB:A582, A598.
  c. Keyboard – Harpsichord
  Suite in A min – Premier Livre, 1706.
    Prelude. Allemandes I-II. Courante. Sarabandes I-II.
    Gigue. Venitienne. Gavotte. Menuet.
  LB:D143, D167, D168, D169, D170.
  Suite in D min – Pieces de Clavecin, 1724.
    Les Tendres Plaintes. Les Niais de Sologne. Les
    Soupirs. La Joyeuse. La Follette. L'Entretien des
    Muses. Le Lardon. Les Tourbillons. La Boiteuse. Les
    Cyclopes.
  LB:D167, D168, D169, D172.
  Suite in E min – Pieces de Clavecin, 1724.
    Allemande. Courante. Gigues en rondeau. Le Rappel
    des Oiseaux. La Villageoise. Rigaudons I-II. Musette
    en rondeau. Tambourin.
  LB:D167, D168, D171, D232.
  Suite in A min – Nouvelles Suites de Pieces de Clavecin,
    1728.
    Allemande. Courante. Sarabande. Les Trois Mains.
    Fanfarinette. La Triomphante. Gavotte – Doubles.
  LB:D167, D168, D169, D171.
  Suite in G maj – Nouvelles Suites de Pieces de Clavecin,
    1728.
    Les Tricotets. L'Indifferente. Menuets I-II. La Poule. Les
    Triolets. Les Sauvages. L'Enharmonique.
    L'Egyptienne.
  LB:D167, D168, D169, D172.
  Cinq Pieces de Clavecin, 1741/7.
    La Livri. L'Agacante. La Timide. L'Indiscrete. (La
    Pantomime). La Dauphine (1747).
  LB:D167, D168, D170.
  **c. Keyboard – Harpsichord: Excerpts from Pieces de
  Clavecin**
  Allemande I-II. (Suite in A min, 1706).
  LB:D173.
  Allemande (Suite in A min, 1728).
  LB:D174.
  La Boiteuse (Suite in D min, 1724).
  LB:D81.
  Courante (Suite in A min, 1706).
  LB:D173.
  Courante (Suite in A min, 1728).
  LB:D174.

Les Cyclopes (Suite in D min, 1724).
LB:D142, D174.
La Dauphin (1747).
LB:D173.
L'Egyptienne (Suite in G maj, 1728).
LB:D173, D174.
L'Enharmonique (Suite in G maj, 1728).
LB:D173, D232.
L'Entretien des Muses (Suite in D min, 1724).
LB:D173, D230.
SI:C14.
Fanfarinette (Suite in A min, 1728).
SI:C21.
Gavotte (Suite in A min, 1706).
LB:D81, D173.
Gavotte and Doubles I–II (Suite in A min, 1728).
LB:D174, D234.
Gigue (Suite in A min, 1706).
LB:D173.
Gigues en rondeau I–II (Suite in E min, 1724).
SI:C18.
La Joyeuse (Suite in D min, 1724).
LB:D81, D173.
SI:C14.
Le Lardon (Suite in D min, 1724).
LB:D81.
La Livri (Pieces, 1741).
LB:D231.
Menuets I–II (Suite in G maj, 1728).
LB:D230.
Musette en rondeau (Suite in D min, 1724).
LB:D81, D173, D234.
Les Niais de Sologne et Doubles I–II (Suite in D min, 1724).
LB:D174.
La Poule (Suite in G maj, 1728).
LB:D142, D173, D174, D234.
Prelude (Suite in A min, 1706).
LB:D173.
Le Rappel des Oiseaux (Suite in E min, 1724).
LB:D142, D174, D224, D234.
Sarabandes I–II (Suites in A min, 1706).
LB:D173, D230.
SI:C21.
Les Sauvages (Suite in G maj, 1728).
LB:D174.
Les Soupirs (Suite in D maj, 1724).
LB:D173.
Les Tambourins (Suite in E min, 1724).
LB:A583, D81, D142, D173, D174, D221, D234.
Les Tendres Plaintes (Suite in D min, 1724).
LB:D81, D173, D174, D221.
Les Tourbillons (Suite in D min, 1724).
LB:D173, D230.
La Triomphante (Suite in A min, 1728).
LB:D230, D231.
Les Trois Mains (Suite in A min, 1728).
LB:D174.
La Venetienne (Suite in A min, 1706).
LB:D173.
La Villageoise (Suite in E min, 1724).
LB:D173, D174, D230.

d.Secular Vocal – Ballets and other Stage Works
Acanthe et Cephise – Pastorale, 1751: Marches. Dances.
LB:A603.
Le Berger Fidele – Cantata, 1728.
LB:F55.
Castor et Pollux – Opera, 1737.
LB:F56.
Castor et Pollux: 1er Suite.
LB:F66.
Dardanus – Tragedie Lyrique, 1739: 1er et 2em Suites.
LB:F66.
Les Fetes d'Hebe – Opera Ballet, 1739: 2em. Entree.

LB:F57.
Les Fetes d'Hebe: 3em Entree.
LB:F57, F58.
Hippolyte et Aricie – Opera, 1733.
LB:F59, F60.
Hippolyte et Aricie: Orchestral Suite.
LB:F61.
Hippolyte et Aricie: Air du Rossignol.
LB:F55.
Les Indes Galantes – Opera Ballet, 1735.
LB:F62.
Les Indes Galantes: 1er et 2em Suites.
LB:F66.
Les Indes Galantes: Harpsichord Transcriptions.
LB:D175.
Orphee – Cantata, 1721.
LB:F55.
Les Paladins – Comedie Lyrique, 1760: 1er Suite.
LB:F66.
Platee – Comedie Ballet, 1745.
LB:F63.
Platee: 1er. Suite.
LB:F66.
La Temple de la Gloire – Fete, 1745: 1er Suite.
LB:A238.
La Temple de la Gloire: 2em Suite.
LB:A223.
Zaïs – Ballet Heroïque, 1748.
LB:F64.
Zephyr, ou les Nymphes de Diane – Act de Ballet.
LB:F65.
Zoroastre – Tragedie Lyrique, 1749: 7 Dances.
LB:A48.

RAMSEY, Robert (16th./17th. cent.)
   d.Secular Vocal
   Sleep, fleshly birth.
   LR:Gd32.
   What tears, dear prince, can serve.
   SI:A1.

RANDALL, William (d.1780)
   c.Keyboard
   Dowland's Pavan and Galliard – Lachrymae and Can she excuse.
   LR:Gc9.

RANISH, John Frederick (1693–1777)
   b.Instrumental
   Solo for the German flute.
   LB:B319.

RASELIUS, Andreas (c.1563–1602)
   e.Sacred Vocal
   Also hat Gott die Welt geliebt.
   LR:F126.

RASI, Francesco (1575–1620)
   d.Secular Vocal
   Indarno Febo.
   EB:F98.

RATHGEBER, Valentin (1682–1750)
   c.Keyboard – Organ
   Aria Pastorella in C maj.
   LB:E239.
   Aria Pastorella in G maj.
   LB:E239.
   Schlag Aria in D min.
   LB:E239.
   Schlag Aria in E flat maj.
   LB:E239.
   Schlag Aria in E flat maj.
   LB:E329.
   Schlag Aria in F maj.
   LB:E239.

Schlag Aria in G maj.
LB:E239.
d. Secular Vocal
Augsburgisches Tafelkonfect.
LB:F67.
Von den Weibsbildern (Augsburgisches Tafelkonfect).
LB:F81.

RAUCH, Andreas (1592–1656)
d. Secular Vocal
All lust und Freud.
LR:A6.

RAVENSCROFT, Thomas (c.1590–1633)
b. Instrumental
3 Country Dances
d. Secular Vocal
By the bank as I lay.
LR:Gd57.
EB:F112.
He that will an alehouse keep.
LR:Gd45, Gd57.
Jinkin the Jester (Arr. Warlock).
LR:Gd57.
The Maid she went a-milking (Arr. Warlock).
LR:Gd57.
Malt's Come Down (Arr. Warlock).
LR:Gd57.
The Marriage of the Mouse and the Frog.
EB:F112.
Martin said to his man.
LR:Gd58.
Now Robin, lend to me thy bow.
AA:D17.
Of all the birds.
EB:F112.
The Owl.
EB:F91.
Remember O thou Man.
EB:F112.
Rustic lovers.
LR:Gd53.
Sing after, fellows.
LR:Gd33.
The Three Ravens.
EB:F112.
Tomorrow the fox will come to town.
LR:Gd33.
SI:A2.
Trudge away quickly.
EB:F112.
We be soldiers three.
LR:Gd47.
EB:F112.
We be three poor marriners.
LR:Gd43.
EB:F112.
What hap had I to marry a schrow (Arr. Warlock).
LR:Gd57.
Yonder comes a courteous night.
LR:Gd49.

REBEL, Jean-Ferry (1666–1747)
b. Chamber and Instrumental
Sonata No. 3 in D maj for recorder and continuo.
LB:B293.
Sonata No. 6 in B min for recorder and continuo.
LB:B293.
Le Tombeau de M. de Lully.
LB:B326.

REDFORD, John (1485–1543)
c. Keyboard – Organ
2 Versets on the Te Deum.
EB:E66.

e. Sacred Vocal
Rejoice in the Lord (Attrib. *See also* ANONYMOUS)
LR:Ge37.

REGNART, Jacob Francois (1530–1600)
d. Secular Vocal
Ardo si, ma non t'amo.
AN:B1.
LR:F93.
Ich hab vermeint.
AN:B1.
Nach meiner Lieb.
LR:F94.
Nun bin ich einmal frei.
AN:B1.
Petite nymph folastre.
LR:E52.
Si je trepasse.
LR:E52.
Venus, du und dein Kind.
AN:B1.
LR:F94.
Villanella.
LR:B27.

REICHE, Johann Gottfried (1667–1734)
b. Instrumental
Ablasen.
LB:A212.

REINA CODEX (14th./15th. cent.)
d. Secular Vocal
En wyflye beildt ghestadt.
AN:B4.
Or sus vous dormez trop.
AN:B4.

REINER, Jacob (1559–1606)
d. Secular Vocal
Behüt euch Gott zu aller Zeit.
LR:E70.

REINKEN, Johann Adam (1623–1722)
c. Keyboard – Organ
An Wasserflüssen Babylon.
LB:E187.
Toccata in G maj.
EB:E61.

REINMAR VON BRENNENBURG (13th. cent.)
d. Secular Vocal
Wol mich des tages.
AA:D25.

REIS – *see* DE REIS, Gaspard

RESINARIUS, Balthazar (1496–1546)
e. Sacred Vocal
Gelobet seist du.
LR:F103.

REUENTHAL – *see* NEITHARDT VON REUENTHAL

REUSNER, Esaias 'The Elder' (1636–1679)
b. Instrumental – Lute
Sonatina (Neue Lautenfrüchte, 1676).
LB:C29.
Suite in A min (Musikalische Taffel-Erlustigung).
EB:C6.
Suite in F maj (Musikalische Taffel-Erlustigung).
LB:C27.
Suite of Dances: Allemande-Courante-Gavotte-Gigue-
Paduan-Sarabande.
LB:B323.
e. Sacred Vocal
Uns ist ein Kindelein heut geborn.
LR:F123, F124.

REUTTER, Karl Georg von (1708-1772)
  a. Orchestral
    Servizio di Tavola.
    LB:A604.

RHAU, Georg (1488-1548)
  d. Secular Vocal
    Ach Elslein, liebes Elselein.
    LR:E68.
    EB:B66.
    Entlaubet ist der Walde.
    LR:E68.
    Mir ist ein feins brauns Maidelein.
    LR:E68.

RHENIS - see EGIDIUS VON RHENIS

RIBERA, Antonio de (16th. cent.)
  d. Secular Vocal
    Por unos puertos arriba.
    LR:E31.

RICCIO, Giovanni Battista (16th./17th. cent.)
  b. Instrumental
    Canzona 'La Rossignola' a 4 pian e forte.
    EB:B64.
    Canzona 'La Grimaneta.'
    EB:B58.
    Canzona per un flautin.
    EB:B58.
    Canzona per flautin e basso.
    EB:B58.
    Canzona per doi flautini.
    EB:B58.
    Sonata a 4.
    EB:B64.

RICCIOTTI, Carlo (1681-1756)
  a. Orchestral - Previously Attributed to Pergolesi.
    Concerti Armonici for strings and continuo. Nos. 1-6.
      1 in G maj; 2 in G maj; 3 in A maj; 4 in F min; 5 in B flat
      maj; 6 in E flat maj.
    LB:A364.
    Concerto Armonico No. 1 in G maj for 4 violins, viola, cello
    and continuo.
    LB:A584, G265.
    Concerto Armonico No. 2 in G maj for 4 violins, viola, cello
    and continuo.
    LB:A612.
    Concerto Armonico No. 4 in F min for 4 violins, viola, cello
    and continuo.
    LB:A598, A605.
    Concerto Armonico No. 5 in B flat maj for 4 violins, viola,
    cello and continuo.
    LB:A607.
    Concerto in B flat maj for mandolin and strings.
    LB:A224.
    Concerto in D maj for flute and strings.
    LB:A364.
    Concerto in G maj for flute and strings.
    LB:A364, A627, A638, A643.

RICHAFORT, Jean (c.1480-c.1547)
  d. Secular Vocal (see also BAKFARK)
    De mon triste desplaisir.
    LR:Gf2.

RICHARD I (1157-1199)
  d. Secular Vocal
    Ja nuns hons pris.
    AA:B3, D17, D22.

RICHARD, Balthazar (17th. cent.)
  b. Instrumental
    Sonata for violin and continuo.
    EB:B35.

RICHARD, Etienne (1621-1669)
  c. Keyboard - Organ
    Prelude in D min.
    EB:E76.

RICHARDSON, Ferdinand (c.1558-1618)
  c. Keyboard
    Pavane (Fitzwilliam Virginal Book).
    LR:Gc8.

RICHEE - see LE SAGE DE RICHEE, Philip Franz.

RICHTER, Johann Christian (17th./18th. cent)
  c. Keyboard - Harpsichord
    Allemande (Clavierbüchlein for W.F. Bach)
    LB:D104.

RIMINI - see VINCENZO DA RIMINI

RIMONTE, Pedro (16th./17th. cent.)
  d. Secular Vocal
    Madre, la mi madre.
    LR:E30.

RIPOLL ABBEY (12th. cent. Spanish)
  e. Sacred Vocal
    Cedit frigus.
    AA:A2.
    AN:B15, B18.
    In Gedeonis area.
    AN:B18.

RIPPE - see DE RIPPE, Albert

RIQUIER, Guiraut (1230-1292)
  d. Secular Vocal
    Canco a la Maire de Deus.
    AA:D4.
    Fis e verays.
    AA:D4.
    Jhesu Christ.
    AA:D5, D9.
    Ples de tristor, marritze doloiros.
    AA:D6, D12.

ROBERDAY, Francois (1624-c.1672)
  c. Keyboard - Organ
    Fugue and Caprices. Nos. 1-12.
      1 in G min; 2 in G maj; 3 in C maj; 4 in C maj; 5 in D min;
      6 in D min; 7 in D min; 8 in A min; 9 in F maj; 10 in G
      min; 11 in G min; 12 in D maj.
    EB:E50, E51.
    Fugue and Caprice No. 1 in G min.
    EB:E32, E52.
    Fugue No. 1 in G min.
    EB:E76.
    Fugue and Caprice No. 2 in G maj.
    EB:E32, E52.
    Fugue and Caprice No. 3 in C maj.
    EB:E32, E52, E89.
    Fugue No. 3 in C maj.
    EB:E76.
    Fugue No. 5 in D min.
    EB:E52.
    Fugue and Caprice No. 8 in A min.
    EB:E66.
    Fugue No. 10 in G min.
    EB:E52, E76.
    Fugue No. 11 in G min.
    EB:E32.
    Fugue No. 12 in D maj.
    EB:E32, E52, E76.
    Fugue and Caprice (Unsp.)
    EB:E86.

ROBERT, Pierre (c.1618-1698)
  e. Sacred Vocal

Nolite me considerare.
EB:G16.

ROBINSON, Thomas (1588-1610)
b. Instrumental – Lute
Bo Peep – A Toye.
LR:Gb9.
A Fancy.
LR:C22.
Fantasia.
LR:Gb9.
A Gigue.
LR:C10.
Merry melancholy.
SI:C20.
A Plaine Song.
LR:Gb9.
The Queen's Good Night.
LR:B306.
Robinson's Riddle.
SI:C20.
Spanish Pavan.
LR:Gb7.
A Toye.
LR:C10, C12, C22.
SI:C20.
Twenty Waies upon the Bells.
LR:C22, C24.

ROBSON, Jean-Jacques (d.1785)
c. Keyboard – Harpsichord and Organ
Prelude.
EB:E39.
Suite.
EB:D37.
Versets du 1re – 8me ton.
EB:E39.

ROGET, Clair Nicolas (fl.1739)
b. Instrumental
Sonata No. 2 in G maj for 2 viols.
SI:C21.

ROGNIONO (16th./17th. cent.)
b. Instrumental
Anchor che col partire (after De Rore).
EB:B41.

ROHACZEWSKI, Andrzej (17th. cent.)
c. Keyboard – Organ
Canzona a 4.
EB:E85.

ROMAN (15th./16th. cent:)
d. Secular Vocal
O voy.
ER:A26.
LR:E28.
Yo con vos senora.
LR:E65.

ROMAN, Johann Helmich (1694-1758)
a. Orchestral
Concerto in B flat maj for oboe and strings.
LB:A366.
Drottningsholms Music.
LB:A367.
Sinfonia No. 20 in E min for strings.
LB:A365.
b. Instrumental
Sonata a 3 in F min.
LB:B1.
c. Keyboard – Organ
Suite No. 2 for organ.
LB:B212.

ROMAN DE FAUVEL (1310-1316, Attrib. Gervaise de Bus)
d./e. Secular Vocal/Sacred Vocal (*see also*
ANONYMOUS)
Ad solitum vomitum.
AN:A15, A16.
Ade costa dormientis.
AN:A15.
Au Dieux.
AN:A15.
L'Autrier de hors Pinguigni.
AN:A15.
Bon vin doit.
AN:A15, A16.
Celi Domina.
AN:A16.
Conditio – O nacio – Mane prima.
AA:D22.
AN:A12.
Douce dame debonnaire.
AA:A3.
AN:A15, A16.
En mon Dieu.
AN:A15.
Fauvel est mal assegne.
AN:A16.
Fauvel nous a fait present.
AN:A15.
Favellandi vivium.
AN:A15, A16.
Garrit Gallus flendo dolorose.
AN:A16.
Flagellaverunt Gallium.
AN:A16.
Gaudet Favellus.
AN:A15.
Grant despit ai je, Fortune.
AN:A16.
In marie miserie.
AN:A15, A16.
In nova fert animus mutatas.
AN:A16.
J'ai fait nouvetement.
AN:A15, A16.
Jhesu, tu dator venie.
AN:A15.
Maria virgo virginum.
AN:A15, A16.
La mesnie fauvelline – J'ai fait nouveletement.
AA:B1.
AN:A16.
Mundus a mundicia.
AN:A15, A16.
O Philippe, prelustris Francorum.
AN:A16.
O variom fortunae lubricum.
AN:A16.
Omnipotens Domine.
AN:A15, A16.
Porchier mieux estre.
AN:A15, A16.
Pour revouvrer elegiance.
AN:A16.
Quant je le voi – Bon vin doit – Cis chans veult boire.
AA:A1, B1.
Quare fremuerunt gentes et populi.
AN:A15, A16.
Quasi non ministerium – Trahunt – Ve, qui gregi.
AA:B1.
AN:A16.
Quomodo cantabimus.
AN:A16.
Quoniam secta latronum.
AN:A15.
Servant regem misericordier.

AN:A16.
Thamus puepere.
AN:A16.
Veritas arpie.
AN:A15.
Virtus moritur.
AN:A15.
Zelus familie – Jhesu tu dator.
AA:B1.

ROMANINI, Antonio (17th. cent.)
c. **Keyboard – Organ**
Exercitium.
LR:Gb7.
Toccata in the Myxolydian Mode.
LB:E239.
Toccata per organo.
LR:A6.

ROMERO, Mateo (d.c.1647)
d. **Secular Vocal**
A la dulce risa del alva – Folia.
LR:E30.
Hermosas y enojadas – Romance a 3.
LB:F84.
Romerico florido – Folia a 2.
LB:F84.

RONCALLI, Ludovico (17th. cent.)
b. **Instrumental – Guitar**
Suite in C maj.
LB:C27.
Suite in G maj.
EB:C7.
Sonata in E min.
LB:C26.

RONTANI (16th. cent.)
d. **Secular Vocal**
Nerinda bella.
LR:A1, E24.

ROQUELAY (16th. cent.)
b. **Instrumental**
Ta bonne grace.
LR:B26, E36.

RORE – see DE RORE, Cipriano

ROSEINGRAVE, Thomas (1690–1766)
c. **Keyboard**
Fugue in G min (Voluntaries and Fugues, 1730).
LR:Gc6.
First Set of Lessons in E flat maj.
LB:D217.

ROSENMULLER, Johann (1619–1684)
b. **Instrumental**
Sinfonia in D maj for 2 violins and continuo.
EB:B36.
Sinfonia XI for 2 violins, 2 violas, 2 viols and continuo.
EB:F111.
Sonata in E min for 2 violins and continuo.
EB:B48.

ROSIER, Carl (1640–1725)
b. **Instrumental**
Sonata in E min for 2 violins and continuo.
EB:B36.

ROSSELLI, Francesco (16th. cent.)
e. **Sacred Vocal**
Adoramus te, Christe.
LR:F81.

ROSSETTER, Philip (1568–1623)
b. **Instrumental**
Almaine.

LR:Gd48.
Galliard.
LR:Gb4, Gb5, Gd48.
d. **Secular Vocal**
No grave for woe.
LR:Gd48.
Shall I come if I swim?
LR:Gd48.
Sweet, come again.
LR:Gd48.
What then is love?
LR:Gd26, Gd28, Gd48, Gd55.
EB:F103, F106.
When Laura smiles.
LR:Gd29, Gd55, Gd57.
Whether men do laugh or weep.
LR:Gd48.

ROSSI, Luigi (1598–1653)
d. **Secular Vocal**
Erminia sventurata.
EB:F82.
Gelosia.
EB:F82.
Lamento della regina di Svezia.
EB:F82.
Lamento di Zaida mora.
EB:F82.
Mentre sorge dal mar.
EB:F82.
Quando spiega la notte.
EB:F82.
Sopra conca d'argento.
EB:F82.
e. **Sacred Vocal**
Giuseppe, figlio di Giacobbe – Oratorio.
EB:G81.

ROSSI, Michelangelo (c.1600–c.1660)
c. **Keyboard**
Toccata in C maj.
LB:E238.
Toccata in F maj.
LB:E238.
Toccata VII in D min.
EB:B58, D38, E66, E93.
LB:D227.
Versetti I and II.
LR:D18.

ROSSI, Salomone (1570–c.1630)
b. **Instrumental**
Norsina – Galliard a 5.
LR:B28.
Sinfonia.
EB:G145.
Sinfonia grave a 5.
LR:B28.
EB:G145.
Sonata a 6.
EB:G145.
Sonata in dialogo detta 'La Viene' for 2 violins and
continuo (Canto primo, 1613).
EB:B43, G145.
Sontata sopra l'aria di Ruggiero for 2 violins and
continuo (Il Terzo libro de sonate, 1623).
EB:B52.
Tanzsätze a 5.
LR:F87.
e. **Sacred Vocal**
The Songs of Solomon.
EB:G145.

ROTENBUCHER, Erasmus (c.1525–1586)
d. **Secular Vocal**
Invitatorium.

LR:E55.

ROTTA, Antonio (c.1495–1549)
  b. Instrumental
  Preambel.
  LR:C20.

ROUSSEAU, Jean Jacques (1712–1778)
  d. Secular Vocal
  Echo.
  LB:F81.
  Le Devin du Village – Chamber Opera, 1752.
  LB:F68.

ROUX – *see* LE ROUX, Gaspard.

ROVENSKY, Vaclav Holan (1644–1718)
  e. Sacred Vocal
  Wilkommen, ershntes, liebliches (Capella Regia
    Musicalis, 1694).
  LR:F116.

ROY – *see* LE ROY, Adrien.

ROYLLART, Phillippe (14th. cent.)
  d. Secular Vocal
  Rex Karole, Johannis genite – Leticie.
  AA:B1.

ROZYCKI, Jacek (d.c.1697)
  e. Sacred Vocal
  Confitebor.
  EB:G147.
  Magnificat.
  EB:F104, G147.
  Magnificemus in cantico.
  EB:G147.

RUDEL, Jauffre (1120–1147)
  d. Secular Vocal
  Lan quan li jorn.
  AA:D8, D9, D13.
  Vida.
  AA:D13.

RUE – *see* DE LA RUE, Pierre

RUFFO, Vincenzo (c.1510–1587)
  b. Instrumental
  La Danza.
  LR:E20.
  Dormendo un giorno – Capriccio.
  LR:B20.
  La Gamba in bassa e soprano – Capriccio.
  LR:B20, E20.
  La Piva.
  LR:E20.
  d. Secular Vocal
  O felici occhi miei.
  LR:E39.

RUGEN – *see* WIZLAW VON RUGEN

RUGGIERI, Giovanni Maria (c.1670–1720)
  b. Instrumental
  Sonata in G min for 2 violins, cello and continuo, Op. 3,
    No. 5.
  EB:B62.

RYCHNOVSKY, Jiri (d.1616)
  e. Sacred Vocal
  Decantabat populus.
  LR:F99.

SABLONARA – *see* CANCIONERO DE SABLONARA

SACHS, Hans (1494–1576)
  d. Secular Vocal
  Der Gülden Ton.

AA:A3.
Nachdem David war redlich.
ER:A4.

SAINTE-COLOMBE, Sieur de (d.1701)
  b. Instrumental
  Concert a 2 violes esgales I 'Le Retrove.'
  EB:B1.
  Concert a 2 violes esgales XVII 'Le Prompt.'
  EB:B1.
  Concert a 2 violes esgales XXVII 'Bourrasque.'
  EB:B32.
  Concert a 2 violes esgales XLI 'Le Retour.'
  EB:B32.
  Concert a 2 violes esgales XLIV 'Tombeau.'
  EB:B1, B32.
  Concert a 2 violes esgales XLVIII 'La Raporte.'
  EB:B32.
  Concert a 2 violes esgales LIV 'La Dubois.'
  EB:B32.

SAINT GODRIC (d.1170)
  e. Sacred Vocal
  Saincte Maria Virgine.
  AA:A3, C1.

SAINT-LUC, Jacques de (b.1616)
  b. Instrumental – Lute/Guitar
  Menuet (From the Suite 'La Naissance du Compte de
    Questenburg.')
  LB:F79.
  Pastourelle.
  LB:F79.

SAINT MARTIAL MS (early 12th. cent. Limoges)
  e. Sacred Vocal. (Organum)
  De monte lapis.
  AA:B3.
  Rex omnia tenens.
  AA:B3.
  Viderunt Hemanuel.
  AA:A3, B4.

SAINT VICTOR MS (13th. cent.)
  e. Sacred Vocal
  Ave Maria.
  AA:B9.

SALADIN, Louis (17th. cent.)
  e. Sacred Vocal
  Canticum Hebraicum (c.1670)
  EB:G145.

SALAVERDE – *see* SELMA Y SALAVERDE, Bartolome de

SALVATORE, Giovanni (fl.c.1600)
  c. Keyboard
  Toccata (Naples MS)
  AA:A1.

SALZBURG – *see* HERMANN VON SALZBURG

SAMMARTINI, Giovanni Battista (1698–1775)
  a. Orchestral
  Concerto in C maj for flute and strings.
  LB:A638.
  Concerto in C maj for viola pomposa and strings.
  LB:A362.
  Sinfonia No. 13 in G maj for strings.
  LB:A612.

SAMMARTINI, Giuseppe (c.1693–1751)
  a. Orchestral
  Concerto in F maj for recorder and strings.
  LB:A328, A605, A645, B260, B287.
  b. Chamber and Instrumental
  Sonata in A min for 2 cellos.
  LB:B309.

Sonata in G maj for recorder and continuo. Op. 13. No. 4.
LB:B266.
Trio Sonata in F maj for recorder and continuo (Unsp.)
LB:B285.
Trio Sonata No. 2 in F maj for recorder and continuo.
LB:B164, B299.
Trio Sonata No. 3 in G maj for recorder and continuo.
LB:B164.
Trio Sonata No. 5 in F maj for recorder and continuo.
LB:B164.
Trio Sonata No. 6 in D min for recorder and continuo.
LB:B164.
Trio Sonata No. 8 in F maj for recorder and continuo.
LB:B164.
Trio Sonata No. 10 in F maj for recorder and continuo.
EB:B69.
LB:B164.

SANDRIN, Pierre (c.1510–c.1565)
   d. Secular Vocal (Including Instrumental Arrangements)
Cancion.
LR:E50.
Ce qui m'est.
LR:E54.
Doulce memoire.
LR:A1, B8.
Quand ieu congneu.
LR:D16.

SANTA CRUZ, Antonio de (17th. cent.)
   b. Instrumental
Jacaras.
LR:E30.

SANTA MARIA, Tomas de (c.1510–1570)
   c. Keyboard – Harpsichord and Organ
Clausulas de 1o tono.
LR:E27.
3 Fantasias.
EB:D28.
4 Fantasias.
LR:E51.
Fantasia de 1o tono.
EB:E82.
Fantasia de 3o tono.
EB:E82.
Fantasia de 8o tono.
EB:E82.
Fantasia I.
LR:E26.
Fantasia XI.
LR:E26.
Fantasia XXV.
LR:E26.

SANTINI, Fortunato (1778–1862)
   e. Sacred Vocal
Sanctus (Missa 'Cantanibus Organis Caecilia.')
LR:F95.

SANZ, Gaspar (1640–1710)
   b. Instrumental – Guitar
6 Airs (Instruccion de musica, 1674).
LB:C26.
Canarios (Suite Espanola).
LR:C10.
EB:C7.
LB:C24.
La Cavalleria de Napoles con dos clarinos.
LR:C10.
Corriente.
EB:C7.
La Esfachata de Napoles.
LR:C10.
Espagnoletta. (Suite Espanola.)
EB:C7.

LB:B323.
Folias (Suite Espanola).
LR:C10.
Fuga al ayre de giga.
LR:C10.
Fuga del 1er tono.
LR:C10.
Gallarda y Villano.
LB:B323.
Gallardas.
LR:C10.
Giga al ayre ingles.
LR:C10.
Maricapolos.
LR:C10.
La Minnona de Cataluna.
LR:C10.
Paradetas.
LR:C10.
Passacalle de la Cavalleria de Napoles.
EB:C7.
LB:B323.
Passacalles por la C, por cruzado y por quinto tono punto
   alto.
LR:C10.
Passacalles por la L, por el dos bemolado y por primer
   tono punto bajo.
LR:C10.
Pavanas (Instruccion de musica, 1674).
LR:C10, C27.
EB:C7.
LB:C24.
Preludio o capricho arpeado por la cruz.
LR:C10, C27.
EB:C7.
Rujero.
LR:C10.
EB:C7.
Sesquialtera.
LR:C10.
Suite Espanola (Canarios-Espagnoletta-Folias-
   Passacalle)
LR:C27.
LB:C32.
Tarantela.
EB:B63.

SARACINI, Claudio (1586–c.1649)
   d. Secular Vocal
De te parto.
EB:F98, F106.
Deh, come invan chiedete.
EB:F98.
Giovinetta vezzosetta.
EB:F98.
Io more.
EB:F98.
Pallidetta qual viola.
EB:F106.
Quest' amore, quest' arsura.
EB:F98.

SAROSPATAK MS (17th./18th. cent. Hungarian)
   d. Secular Vocal
Student Songs.
LR:A7.

SARRI, Domenico (1679–1744)
   a. Orchestral
Concerto in A min for recorder and strings.
LB:A632, A637
   d. Secular Vocal
Sen corre l'agnelletta.
EB:F95.

SARTI, Giuseppe (1729-1802)
  e. Sacred Vocal
  Lob sei dem allerhöchsten Gott.
  LB:G318.

SARTORIO, Antonio (c.1620-1681)
  a. Orchestral
  L'Adelaide - Opera, 1672: Sinfonia for 2 trumpets.
    strings and continuo.
  EB:F109.

SAYVE - see DE SAYVE, Lambertus

SCACCHI, Marco (d.c.1685)
  d. Secular Vocal
  Vivat et floreat rex.
  EB:F104.

SCALA DEI DE TARRAGONA (13th. cent. Spanish)
  e. Sacred Vocal
  Crimina tollis (Agnus trope).
  AA:A2.
  AN:B15.
  Hosanna, sospitati dedit.
  AN:B18.
  Potestati magni.
  AN:B18.

SCARLATTI, Alessandro (1660-1725)
  a. Orchestral
  Concerto (Sonata nono) in A min for recorder, 2 violins
    and continuo.
  LB:A636, A645, B229, B230, B260, B285.
  Concerto in F maj for oboe and strings.
  LB:A626.
  Concerti Grossi (Sonate a quatro) for strings and
    continuo, Nos. 1-6.
      1 in F min; 2 in C min; 3 in F maj; 4 in G min; 5 in D min;
      6 in E maj.
  EB:A22, A23.
  Concerto Grosso No. 1 in F min for strings and continuo.
  EB:A24.
  Concerto Grosso No. 2 in C min for strings and continuo.
  EB:A24.
  Concerto Grosso No. 3 in F maj for strings and continuo.
  EB:A24.
  Concerto Grosso No. 6 in E maj for strings and continuo.
  EB:A24.
  12 Sinfonie di concerti grossi for wind and strings.
      1 in F maj; 2 in D maj; 3 in D min; 4 in E min; 5 in D min;
      6 in A min; 7 in G min; 8 in G maj; 9 in G min; 10 in A
      min; 11 in C maj; 12 in C min.
  EB:A25, A26.
  Sinfonie di concerto grosso No. 1 in F maj for 2 flutes and
    strings.
  EB:A27.
  LB:A637.
  Sinfonie di concerto grosso No. 2 in D maj for trumpet,
    horn (flute) and strings.
  EB:A27.
  LB:A627.
  Sinfonie di concerto grosso No. 3 in D min for flute and
    strings.
  EB:A24.
  Sinfonie di concerto grosso No. 4 in E min for flute, oboe
    and strings.
  EB:A27.
  Sinfonie di concerto grosso No. 5 in D min for 2 flutes
    and strings.
  EB:A27.
  Sinfonie di concerto grosso No. 6 in A min for flute and
    strings.
  EB:A28.
  Sinfonie di concerto grosso No. 7 in G min for flute and
    strings.
  EB:A28.

Sinfonie di concerto grosso No. 8 in G maj for flute and
    strings.
  EB:A27, A28.
  Sinfonie di concerto grosso No. 9 in G min for flute and
    strings.
  EB:A28.
  Sinfonie di concerto grosso No. 10 in A min for flute and
    strings.
  EB:A28.
  Sinfonie di concerto grosso No. 11 in C maj for flute and
    strings.
  EB:A28.
  Sinfonie di concerto grosso No. 12 in C min for flute and
    strings.
  EB:A24, A27.

  c. Keyboard
  Partite sull' aria della Follia.
  LB:D220.
  Toccata del 1o tono.
  EB:E53.
  Toccata in A maj.
  EB:B45.
  LB:E238.

  d. Secular Vocal
  Arsi un tempo (Madrigal)
  EB:F85.
  Caldo sangue. (Sedicia, Re de Gerusalemme - Oratorio,
    1706.)
  LB:G273.
  Cantate Pastorale per la Nativitata.
  EB:F47, G79.
  Canzonetta (Flavio - Opera, 1698).
  EB:F101.
  Cor mio, deh non languire (Madrigal).
  EB:F85.
  E pur vuole il cielo e amore (Cantata).
  EB:F84.
  Endimione e Cintia (Cantata).
  EB:F83.
  Infirmata vulnerata (Cantata).
  EB:F106.
  Intenerite voi (Madrigal).
  EB:F85.
  Mentre su'l carro aurato (Clori e Mirtillo) (Cantata).
  EB:F84.
  Mori mi dici (Madrigal).
  EB:F85.
  No, non ti voglio Cupido. (Cantata).
  EB:F84.
  O morte (Madrigal).
  EB:F85.
  O selce, o tigre, o ninfe (Madrigal).
  EB:F85.
  Or che date (Madrigal).
  EB:F85.
  Questo silenzio ombroso (Cantata).
  EB:F84.
  Sdegno la fiamma (Madrigal).
  EB:F85.
  Se delitto e l'adorati (Pirro e Demetrio - Opera, 1694).
  EB:F101.
  Se florinda e fedele (La Donna Ancore e Fedele - Opera,
    1698).
  EB:F101.
  Sento nel cor (Cantata).
  EB:F95.
  Sia il sole dal gange (Cantata).
  EB:F95.
  Spesso vibra per suo gioco (Cantata).
  EB:F95.
  Splendeano in bel semblante (Cantate).
  LB:F21.
  Su le sponde del tebro (Cantata).
  LB:G273.

Le Violette (Pirro e Demetrio – Opera, 1694).
EB:F101.
e. Sacred Vocal
Domine, refugium factus es nobis.
LB:G274.
O magnum mysterium.
EB:G143.
LB:G274.
St. John Passion (1680/5).
EB:G83.
San Filippo Neri – Oratorio.
EB:G84.
Stabat mater.
EB:G82.

SCARLATTI, Domenico (1685–1757)
a. Orchestral
Sinfonias for flute, oboe and strings, Nos. 1–3.
1 in G maj; 2 in B flat maj; 3 in G maj.
LB:A637.
c. Keyboard – Harpsichord Sonatas
Kk1 in D min, Allegro.
LB:D176, D179, D200.
Kk2 in G maj, Presto.
LB:D176, D185.
Kk3 in A min, Presto.
LB:D176, D199, D230.
Kk4 in G min, Allegro.
LB:D176.
Kk5 in D min, Allegro.
LB:D176.
Kk6 in F maj, Allegro.
LB:D176.
Kk7 in A min, Presto.
LB:D176.
Kk8 in G min, Allegro.
LB:D67, D176, D179, D186.
Kk9 in D min, Allegro.
LB:D176, D179, D189, D184, D201, D202.
Kk10 in D min, Presto.
LB:D176.
Kk11 in C min.
LB:C32, D176, D179.
Kk12 in G min, Presto.
LB:D176, D186.
Kk13 in G maj, Presto.
LB:D176.
Kk14 in G maj, Presto.
LB:D176, D201.
Kk15 in E min, Allegro.
LB:D176, D181.
Kk16 in B flat maj, Presto.
LB:D176.
Kk17 in F maj, Presto.
LB:D176, D200.
Kk18 in D min, Presto.
LB:D176.
Kk19 in F min, Allegro.
LB:D176, D179, D186.
Kk20 in E maj, Presto.
LB:D176, D185, D186, D201.
Kk21 in D maj, Allegro.
LB:D176.
Kk22 in C min, Allegro.
LB:D176.
Kk23 in D maj, Allegro.
LB:D176, D186.
Kk24 in A maj, Presto.
LB:D176, D181, D184, D185, D186.
Kk25 in F sharp min, Allegro.
LB:D176.
Kk26 in A maj, Presto.
LB:D176.
Kk27 in B min, Allegro.
LB:D176, D200.

Kk28 in E maj, Presto.
LB:D176.
Kk29 in D maj, Presto.
LB:D176, D181, D184, D185.
Kk30 in G min, Fuga-Moderato.
EB:D38.
LB:D176.
Kk32 in D min, Aria.
LB:C32.
Kk33 in D maj, Allegro.
LB:D91, D184, D185.
Kk39 in A maj, Allegro.
LB:D177.
Kk41 in D min, Fuga-Andante Moderato.
EB:E53.
Kk42 in B flat maj, Minuetto.
LB:D186, D204.
Kk44 in F maj, Allegro.
LB:C185.
SI:C16.
Kk45 in D maj, Allegro.
LB:D179.
Kk46 in E maj, Presto.
LB:D185.
Kk49 in C maj, Presto.
LB:D179.
Kk50 in F min, Allegro.
LB:D186.
Kk51 in E flat maj, Allegro.
LB:D186.
Kk52 in D min, Andante moderato.
LB:D178, D185, D199, D230.
Kk59 in F maj, Allegro.
LB:D186.
Kk60 in G min.
LB:D186.
Kk62 in A maj, Allegro.
LB:D200.
Kk63 in G maj, Capriccio-Allegro.
LB:D179.
Kk65 in A maj, Allegro.
LB:D198.
Kk70 in B flat maj.
LB:D179.
Kk72 in C maj, Allegro.
LB:D201.
Kk79 in G maj, Allegrissimo.
LB:D198.
Kk83 in A maj, Minuet.
LB:D198.
Kk84 in C min.
LB:D179.
Kk87 in B min.
LB:D177, D179, D184, D228.
Kk96 in D maj, Allegro.
LB:D177, D185, D200, D202.
SI:C3.
Kk107 in F maj, Allegro.
LB:D202.
Kk109 in A min, Adagio.
LB:D197.
Kk110 in A min, Allegro.
LB:D197.
Kk112 in B flat maj, Allegro.
LB:D195.
Kk113 in A maj, Allegro.
LB:D179, D185, D198.
Kk114 in A maj, Con spirito e presto.
LB:D185.
Kk115 in C min, Allegro.
LB:D182, D185, D202.
Kk116 in C min, Allegro.
LB:D185.
Kk119 in D maj, Allegro.
LB:D91, D185.

Kk120 in D min, Allegrissimo.
LB:D185.
SI:C3.
Kk123 in E flat maj, Allegro.
LB:D179.
Kk124 in G maj, Allegro.
LB:D182, D202.
Kk126 in C min.
LB:D201.
Kk127 in A flat maj, Allegro.
LB:D197.
Kk130 in A flat maj, Allegro.
LB:D197.
Kk132 in C maj, Cantabile.
LB:D182, D184, D201.
Kk133 in C maj, Allegro.
LB:D182, D201.
Kk137 in D maj, Allegro.
LB:D195.
Kk138 in D min, Allegro.
LB:D195.
Kk140 in D maj, Allegro non molto.
LB:D181, D185.
Kk141 in D min, Allegro.
LB:D185.
Kk142 in F sharp min, Allegro.
LB:D196.
Kk144 in G maj, Cantabile.
SI:A1.
Kk146 in G maj.
LB:D91, D184.
Kk149 in A min, Allegro.
LB:D181.
SI:A1.
Kk152 in G maj, Allegro.
LB:D195.
Kk153 in G maj, Vivo.
LB:D195, D204.
Kk159 in C maj, Allegro.
LB:D201, D202, D224.
Kk162 in E maj, Andante-Allegro-Allegro.
LB:D177, D196, D228.
Kk163 in E maj, Allegro.
LB:D196.
Kk167 in F maj, Allegro.
LB:D196.
Kk168 in F maj, Vivo.
LB:D196, D204.
Kk169 in G maj, Allegro con spirito.
LB:D184.
Kk170 in C maj, Andante moderato e cantabile-Allegro.
LB:D197.
Kk172 in B flat maj, Allegro.
LB:D193.
Kk173 in B min, Allegro.
LB:D192.
Kk174 in C min, Allegro.
LB:D193.
Kk175 in A min, Allegro.
LB:D91, D185, D202.
Kk176 in D min, Cantabile andante-Allegrissimo.
LB:D191.
Kk178 in D maj, Vivo.
LB:D204.
Kk183 in F min, Allegro.
LB:D196, D199.
Kk184 in F min, Allegro.
LB:D196, D199, D201.
Kk185 in F min, Andante.
LB:D204.
Kk187 in F min, Allegro.
LB:D191.
Kk188 in A min, Allegro.
LB:D192.
Kk189 in B flat maj, Allegro.

LB:D197.
Kk190 in B flat maj.
LB:D197.
Kk191 in D min.
LB:D199.
Kk192 in E flat maj.
LB:D199, D204.
Kk193 in E flat maj.
LB:D199.
SI:A1.
Kk194 in F maj, Andante.
LB:D192.
Kk195 in F maj, Vivo.
LB:D192.
Kk196 in G min, Allegro.
LB:D193.
Kk198 in E min, Allegro.
LB:D191, D201.
Kk199 in C maj, Andante moderato.
LB:D194.
Kk200 in C maj, Allegro.
LB:D194.
Kk201 in G maj, Vivo.
LB:D195.
Kk202 in B flat maj, Allegro-Vivo.
LB:D184, D202.
Kk203 in E min, Vivo non molto.
LB:D192.
Kk206 in E maj, Andante.
LB:D183, D205.
Kk208 in A maj, Andante e cantabile.
LB:D182, D185, D199, D200.
SI:C16.
Kk209 in A maj, Allegro.
LB:D182, D185, D199.
SI:C16.
Kk211 in A maj, Andantino.
LB:D188.
Kk212 in A maj, Allegro molto.
LB:D188, D204, D205.
Kk213 in D min, Andante.
LB:D180.
Kk214 in D maj, Allegro vivo.
LB:D204.
Kk215 in E maj, Andante.
LB:D178, D182, D185, D230.
SI:C3.
Kk216 in E maj, Allegro.
LB:D178, D182, D185, D230.
SI:C3.
Kk217 in A min, Andante.
LB:D187.
Kk218 in A min, Vivo.
LB:D187.
Kk219 in A maj, Andante.
LB:D193.
Kk220 in A maj, Allegro.
LB:D193.
Kk222 in A maj, Vivo.
LB:D205.
Kk225 in C maj, Allegro.
LB:D190.
Kk226 in C min, Allegro.
LB:D190.
Kk227 in B min, Allegro.
LB:D196, D199.
Kk228 in B flat maj, Allegro.
LB:D189.
Kk229 in B flat maj, Allegro.
LB:D189.
Kk232 in E min, Andante.
LB:D190.
Kk233 in E min, Allegro.
LB:D190.
Kk234 in G min, Andante.

LB:D201.
Kk378 in F maj, Allegro.
LB:D193.
Kk379 in F maj, Minuet.
LB:D193.
Kk380 in E maj, Andante commodo.
LB:D67, D180, D184, D204, D224.
Kk381 in E maj, Allegro.
LB:D180.
Kk384 in C maj, Cantabile-Andante.
LB:D192.
Kk385 in C maj, Allegro.
LB:D192.
Kk386 in F min, Presto.
LB:D179, D188.
Kk387 in F min, Veloce e fugato.
LB:D188.
Kk388 in D maj, Presto.
LB:D179.
Kk390 in G maj, Allegro.
LB:D197.
Kk391 in G maj, Allegro.
LB:D197.
Kk394 in E min, Allegro.
LB:D183, D198, D200.
Kk395 in E maj, Allegro.
LB:D183.
Kk396 in D min, Andante.
LB:D190.
Kk397 in D maj, Minuet.
LB:D190.
Kk399 in C maj, Allegro.
LB:D204.
Kk402 in E min, Andante.
LB:D183, D185.
Kk403 in E maj, Allegro.
LB:D183, D185.
Kk404 in A maj, Andante.
LB:D198.
Kk406 in C maj, Allegro.
LB:D179.
Kk407 in C maj, Allegro.
LB:D204.
Kk412 in G maj, Allegro.
LB:D193.
Kk413 in G maj, Allegro.
LB:D193.
Kk418 in F maj, Allegro.
LB:D188.
Kk419 in F maj, piu tosto presto che allegro.
LB:D188.
Kk420 in C maj, Allegro.
LB:D181, D185, D200, D202.
Kk421 in C maj, Allegro.
LB:D185.
Kk422 in C maj, Allegro.
LB:D185, D187.
Kk423 in C maj, Presto.
LB:D185, D187.
Kk424 in G maj, Allegro.
LB:D201.
Kk425 in G maj, Allegro molto.
LB:D198, D201.
Kk426 in G min, Andante.
LB:D179, D185.
Kk427 in G maj, Presto, quanto sia possibile.
LB:D185, D200.
Kk428 in A maj, Allegro.
LB:D185.
Kk429 in A maj, Allegro.
LB:D183, D185.
Kk430 in D maj, Non presto ma a tempo di ballo.
EB:B38.
LB:D183, D201.
Kk431 in G maj, Allegro.

LB:C32.
Kk434 in D min, Andante.
LB:D185, D197.
Kk435 in D maj, Allegro.
LB:D185, D197.
Kk436 in D maj, Allegro.
LB:D185, D197.
Kk441 in B flat maj, Allegro.
LB:D185.
Kk442 in B flat maj, Allegro.
LB:D185.
Kk443 in D maj, Allegro.
EB:B38.
Kk444 in D min, Allegrissimo.
LB:D204.
Kk446 in F maj, Pastorale-Allegrissimo.
LB:D179.
Kk447 in F sharp min, Allegro.
LB:D190.
Kk448 in F sharp min, Allegro.
LB:D190.
Kk450 in G min, Allegrissimo.
LB:D224.
Kk451 in A min, Allegro.
LB:D193.
Kk454 in G maj, Andante spiritoso.
LB:D177, D180.
Kk455 in G maj, Allegro.
LB:D177, D180.
Kk456 in A maj, Allegro.
LB:D189.
Kk457 in A maj, Allegro.
LB:D189.
Kk460 in C maj, Allegro.
LB:D177, D183, D185.
Kk461 in C maj, Allegro.
LB:D179, D183, D185.
Kk464 in C maj, Allegro.
LB:D194.
Kk465 in C maj, Allegro.
LB:D194.
Kk466 in F min, Andante moderato.
LB:D177, D195.
Kk467 in F min, Allegrissimo.
LB:D177, D195.
Kk470 in G maj, Allegro.
LB:D185, D198.
Kk471 in G maj, Minuet.
LB:D185.
Kk474 in E flat maj, Andante e cantabile.
LB:D201.
Kk476 in G min, Allegro.
LB:D198.
Kk478 in D maj, Andante e cantabile.
LB:D180.
Kk479 in D maj, Allegrissimo.
LB:D180, D185.
Kk481 in F min, Andante e cantabile.
LB:D177, D182, D185, D202, D205.
Kk484 in D maj, Allegro.
LB:D196.
Kk490 in D maj, Cantabile.
LB:D178, D182, D185.
Kk491 in D maj, Allegro.
LB:D178, D182, D185, D198, D200.
Kk492 in D maj, Presto.
LB:D178, D182, D185.
Kk495 in E maj, Allegro.
LB:D188, D198.
Kk496 in E maj, Allegro.
LB:D188.
Kk499 in A maj, Andante.
LB:D187.
Kk500 in A maj, Allegro.
LB:D187.

Kk501 in C maj, Allegretto.
LB:D205.
Kk502 in C maj, Allegro.
LB:D205.
Kk505 in F maj, Allegro non presto.
LB:D184.
Kk507 in E flat maj, Andantino cantabile.
LB:D191.
Kk508 in E flat maj, Allegro.
LB:D191.
Kk511 in D maj, Allegro.
LB:D187.
Kk512 in D maj, Allegro.
LB:D187.
Kk513 in C maj, Pastorale.
LB:D182, D185, D205.
Kk518 in F maj, Allegro.
LB:D185, D200.
Kk519 in F min, Allegro assai.
LB:D179, D184, D185, D200.
Kk524 in F maj, Allegro.
LB:D179, D180, D185, D205.
Kk525 in F maj, Allegro.
LB:D180, D185, D205.
Kk527 in C maj, Allegro assai.
LB:D180.
Kk531 in E maj, Allegro.
LB:D177, D204.
Kk532 in A min, Allegro.
LB:D195, D205.
Kk533 in A maj, Allegro assai.
LB:D181, D195.
Kk534 in D maj, Cantabile.
LB:D188.
Kk535 in D maj, Allegro.
LB:D188.
Kk537 in A maj, Prestissimo.
LB:D181.
Kk538 in G maj, Allegretto.
LB:D192.
Kk539 in G maj, Allegro.
LB:D192.
Kk540 in F maj, Allegretto.
LB:D189.
Kk541 in F maj, Allegretto.
LB:D189.
Kk543 in F maj, Allegro.
LB:D201.
Kk544 in B flat maj, Cantabile.
LB:D181, D184, D185.
Kk545 in B flat maj, Prestissimo.
LB:D185.
Kk546 in G min, Cantabile.
LB:D190.
Kk547 in G maj, Allegro.
LB:D190.
Kk552 in D min, Allegretto.
LB:D185.
Kk553 in D min, Allegro.
LB:D181, D185.

c. Keyboard – Miscellaneous Harpsichord Sonatas
Sonata in A min.
LB:D203.
Sonata in B flat maj.
LB:D203.
Sonata in C maj.
LB:D203.
Sonata in D maj.
LB:D203.
Sonata in D min.
LB:D203.
Sonata in E flat maj.
LB:D203.
Sonata in G maj.
LB:D203.

d. Secular Vocal
Tetide auf Skyros – Opera, 1712.
LB:F69.
e. Sacred Vocal
Salve regina.
EB:F47.
Stabat mater.
EB:G143.
LB:G273, G274.

SCHAFFRATH, Christoph (1709–1786)
b. Chamber and Instrumental
Duetto in B flat maj for harpsichord and oboe.
LB:B264.

SCHEIBE, Johann Adolph (1708–1776)
e. Sacred Vocal
Passions Cantata.
LB:G275.

SCHEIDEMANN, Heinrich (c.1596–1663)
c. Keyboard – Organ
Ach Gott, vom Himmel sieh darein.
EB:E75.
Allein zu dir Herr Jesu Christ.
EB:E35.
Ballett.
EB:D31.
Canzona in F maj.
EB:E69.
Durch Adams Fall ist ganz verderbt.
EB:E75.
Ein feste Burg ist unser Gott.
EB:E35.
Es ist das Heil uns kommen her.
EB:E75.
Gott der Vater.
EB:E35.
Herr Christ, der einig Gottes Sohn.
EB:E66.
Jesu, wollt'st uns weisen.
EB:E61.
Jesus Christus unser Heiland.
EB:E35.
Magnificat fantasia.
LB:E207.
Nun bitten wir den Heiligen Geist.
EB:E60.
Preambulum.
EB:E69.
Preambulum in D min.
LB:E187.

SCHEIDT, Samuel (1587–1665)
b. Instrumental – Ludi Musici, 1622, 1625, 1627
Allemande a 4 (LM1–XVI).
EB:B33.
Benedicamus Domino.
LR:Ga21.
Canzona a 10.
EB:B38.
Canzona Aechiopicam.
LR:Ga21.
Canzon Bergamasca a 5 (LM1–XXVI).
LR:D20, Ga14, Ga21, Gc15.
EB:B33, B66, E87.
Canzon cornetto a 4 (LM1–XVIII).
LR:F106.
EB:B33, G86.
Canzon super 'Cautionem Galliacam' a 5 (LM1–XXIX).
LR:Ga21.
EB:B33.
Canzon super 'O Nachbar Roland' a 5 (LM1–XXVIII).
EB:B33.
LB:B271.
Courante a 4 (LM1–XI).

EB:B33.
Courante a 4 (LM1-XIII).
EB:B33.
Courante a 4 (LM1-XVIII).
EB:B33.
Courante Dolorosa.
LR:Ga14.
EB:G86.
Galliard a 5 (LM1-XXIV).
EB:B33.
Galliard a 5 (LM1-XXV).
EB:B33.
Galliard Battaglia a 5 (LM1-XXI).
LR:Ga14, Ga21.
EB:B33, B39.
LB:A657.
Galliard.
LR:E42.
LB:B322.
Intrada a 5 (LM1-XXII).
EB:B33.
Paduan a 4 (LM1-III).
EB:B33.
Paduan a 4 (LM1-V).
EB:B33.
Paduan a 4 (LM1-VI).
EB:B33, B46.
Paduan a 4.
EB:B64.
Pavana Hispanica.
LR:B10.
EB:E60.
LB:D220.
Pavan in A min (1621).
EB:B49.
Prelude.
LB:B272.

b.Instrumental – Miscellaneous Works
Sinfonia in F maj a 3 for 2 trumpet, trombone, organ and
   continuo.
EB:B55.
Sinfonia in G min a 3 for 2 trumpets, trombone, organ
   and continuo.
EB:B55.
Sonata in G maj for recorder and continuo.
EB:B64.
Suite for brass.
EB:A34.
Suite in C maj for 4 recorders.
LB:B281.
Suite in C maj for strings.
LB:A615.

c.Keyboard – Free Works. (Tablatura Nova 1–3.)
Allemande (TN2).
EB:D25.
Cantio Sacra (TN2).
EB:D25, E89.
Courante a 4 (TN1).
EB:D25.
Echo.
EB:E60, E66.
Fantasia a 3 (TN2).
EB:D25.
Modus ludendi.
EB:E60.
Niederlandisch Liedchen (TN1).
EB:D25.
Passamezzo (TN1).
EB:D25, E4.
Toccata in G min.
LB:E198.
Toccata (Unsp.)
LR:D20.
EB:D25, E87, E91.

Variations on a Dutch Song – Niederlandisch Liedchen
   (TN1).
LR:D20.
EB:E87.
Variations on a galliard of Dowland – The King of
Denmark.
LR:D20, E42.
EB:E65, E73, E87.
Von der Fortuna – Cantilena Anglica. (TN2).
EB:D25, E75.

c.Keyboard – Chorale-based Works
Christum wir sollen loben schon.
EB:E60.
Da Jesus an dem Kreuze stund.
LB:E207.
Ein Kindelein ist uns geboren.
EB:E60.
In dulci jubilo.
EB:E60.
Jesus Christus, unser Heiland.
EB:E72.
Vater unser im Himmelreich.
EB:E60.
Veni creator spiritus.
EB:E69.
Warum betrübst du dich, mein Herz.
EB:E72.
Wendet euch um ihr Aderlein.
LR:Ga21.

e.Sacred Vocal
Duo seraphim clamabant.
EB:G85.
Gelobet seist du, Jesu Christ.
LR:F108.
Herr, unser Herrscher.
EB:G85.
In dulci jubilo.
LR:F10, F108.
Jauchzet Gott, alle Land.
EB:G85.
Lobt Gott, ihr Christen.
LR:F108.
Nun komm der Heiden Heiland.
LR:F126.
Nun lob, mein Seel, den Herren.
EB:G86.
O Jesulein zart.
LR:F111, F113.
Puer natus in Bethlehem.
LR:F115.
EB:E74.
Richte mich, Gott.
EB:G85.
Sende dein Licht und deine Wahrheit.
EB:G85.
Surrexit Christus hodie.
LR:F79.

SCHEIN, Johannes Hermann (1586–1630)
   b.Instrumental – Banchetto Musicale, 1617
Allemande a 4.
EB:B46.
Allemande e tripla.
EB:B66.
Galliard a 5.
EB:B46.
Intrada a 4 in C min.
EB:B67.
Paduana a 5.
EB:B46, G132.
Paduana.
AA:A1.
Suite No. 2 a 5 in D maj: Allemande.
LB:B321.

Suite No. 2 a 5 in D maj: Courante.
LB:B322.
Suite No. 3 a 5 in A maj.
LR:B25.
ER:B30.
Suite No. 4 a 5 in D maj.
EB:B30.
Suite No. 5 in G maj.
EB:B30.
Tripla a 4.
EB:B46.
d. Secular Vocal – Musica boscareccia oder Wald-
Liederlein.
Der kühle Maien.
EB:F111.
Die Voglein singen.
LR:E22.
Viel schöner Blümelein.
EB:F111.
Wen Filli ihre Liebestrahl.
LR:E22.
e. Sacred Vocal
Da Jakob vollendet hatte (Israelsbrünnlein).
EB:G87.
Das ist mir Lieb.
LB:G318.
Der Herr hat mich verlassen. (Israelsbrünnlein).
EB:G87.
Die mit Tränen säen (Israelsbrünnlein).
EB:G87.
Ich bin die Wurzel des Geschlechtes David
(Israelsbrünnlein).
EB:G87.
Ich freue mich im Herren (Israelsbrünnlein).
LB:G325.
Ihr Heiligen lobsinget (Israelsbrünnlein).
EB:G87.
Nun danket alle Gott (Israelsbrünnlein).
EB:G87.
LB:G325.
Siehe, nacht Trost war mir sehr bange (Israelsbrünnlein).
EB:G87.
Unser Leben währet siebnzig Jahr (Israelsbrünnlein).
EB:G87.
Vom Himmel hoch.
LR:F112.
Was betrübst du dich (Israelsbrünnlein).
EB:G87.
Zion spricht (Israelsbrünnlein).
EB:G86, G87.

SCHELLE, Johann (1648–1701)
e. Sacred Vocal
Christus ist des Gesetzes Ende.
LB:G325.
Vom Himmel kam der Engel schar.
EB:F111.

SCHENK, Johann (1656–c.1716)
b. Instrumental – Guitar
Ciaconna in G maj (Le Nymphe di Rheno, Op. 8).
EB:B48.
Suite in A min.
LB:B27. C29.

SCHERER, Sebastian Anton (1631–1712)
e. Keyboard – Organ
Intonation I.
LB:E197.

SCHICKHARDT, Johann Christian (c.1680–1762)
b. Chamber and Instrumental
Trio Sonata No. 5 in G maj for 2 recorders and continuo.
LB:B304.

SCHILDT, Melchior (1592–1667)
c. Keyboard
Paduana Lachrymae.
LR:Gc16.
Preambulum in G maj.
EB:E60.
e. Sacred Vocal
Ach mein herzliebes Jesulein.
LR:F122.

SCHLICK, Arnolt (c.1460–c.1525)
b./c. Instrumental and Keyboard
Cupido hat.
ER:A23.
Hoe losteleck.
LR:D17.
Maria zart von edler art.
ER:A23.
LR:D17, F78, F111, F123.
EB:E67, E73.
LB:E218.
Wer gnad durch klaff.
LR:C9.
e. Sacred Vocal
Salve regina.

SCHMELZER, Johann Heinrich (c.1623–1680)
b. Chamber and Instrumental
Balletto a Cavallo: Pieces for 6 trumpets and tympani,
Nos. 1–3.
EB:B46.
Canzone 'Polnische Sackpfeiffen' for 2 violins and
continuo.
EB:B36.
Fechtschuel a 4 ('The School of Fencing.')
LR:B22.
EB:B50.
Lamento on the Death of Ferdinand III for viol. (1657).
EB:B36.
Gavotte tedesca.
EB:B66.
Sonata for violin, bassoon, trombone, double-bass and
harpsichord.
LB:B312.
Sonata I a 8 (Sacro-profanus concentus musicus, 1662).
EB:B34.
Sonata II a 8 (Sacro-profanus concentus musicus,
1662).
EB:B34. •
Sonata III a 6 (Sacro-profanus concentus ˙musicus,
1662).
EB:B51.
Sonata IV a 6 (Sacro-profanus concentus musicus,
1662).
EB:B34.
Sonata VII for 2 violins, 2 violas and continuo (Sacro-
profanus concentus musicus, 1662).
EB:B49.
Sonata IX for 2 violins, 2 violas and continuo (Sacro-
profanus concentus musicus, 1662).
EB:B49.
Sonata X a 4 (Sacro-profanus concentus musicus,
1662).
EB:B51.
Sonata a 3 for 3 violins and continuo (1677).
EB:B34.
Sonata a 3 for violin, clarino, trombone and continuo.
EB:B34.
Sonata a 3 for violin, viola, viol and continuo.
EB:B34.
Sonata a 4 for violin, cornet, trombone, dulcian and
continuo, 'La Caroietta', 1669.
EB:B34.
Sonata a 5 for 2 violins, clarino, bassoon, viol and
continuo.

EB:B34.
Sonata con arie for 3 trumpets, strings and continuo
   (Serenade, 1672).
EB:F109.
Sonata Natalita a 3 chori (1675).
EB:B34.
Sonata a 7.
LB:B227.

SCHMID, Bernhard (c.1520–1594)
   b./c. Instrumental and Keyboard
   Englischer Tanz.
   LR:B16, D14.
   Ein guter neuer Dantz.
   LR:D14, D21.
   Der Imperial – Ein Fürstlicher Hofdantz.
   LR:D14.
   Passamezzo e saltarello.
   LB:E229.
   Tanz du hast mich wollen nemmen.
   LR:B16.
   Wie schön blüht uns der Maie.
   LR:B10, B11, B13, D14.

SCHOLZE, Johann Sigismond (= SPERONTES) (1705–1750)
   d. Secular Vocal
   Blaustrumpflied.
   LB:F81.
   Liebe mich redlich.
   LB:F81.

SCHONDORFF, Philipp (1556–1617)
   e. Sacred Vocal
   Missa super 'usquequo Domine': Gloria.
   LR:F93.

SCHONFELDER, Johannes (15th. cent.)
   b. Instrumental
   Zart schöne Frau.
   ER:A23.

SCHROTER, Leonhard (c.1532–c.1601)
   e. Sacred Vocal
   Freut euch, ihr lieben Christen.
   LR:F112.
   In dulci jubilo.
   LR:F111.
   Joseph, lieber, Joseph mein.
   LR:F125.
   Lobt Gott, ihr Christen.
   LR:F111, F122.
   LB:G326.

SCHULTZ, Johann Christian (1582–1653)
   b. Instrumental
   Paduana and Intrada (Musikalischer Lustgarte, 1617).
   EB:B46.
   d. Secular Vocal
   Nachtwache. (Musikalischer Lustgarte, 1622).
   LR:B30.

SCHUTZ, Heinrich (1585–1672)
   d. Secular Vocal – Italian Madrigals, 1611, SWV 1–19
   O primavera, Gioventu de l'anno, SWV 1.
   EB:F86, F87.
   O dulcezze amarissime d'amore, SWV 2.
   EB:F86, F87.
   Selve beate, SWV 3.
   EB:F86, F87.
   Alma afflitta, SWV 4.
   EB:F86, F87.
   Cosi morir debb'io, SWV 5.
   EB:F86, F87.
   D'orrida selce alpina, SWV 6.
   EB:F86, F87.
   Ride la primavera, SWV 7.

EB:F86, F87.
Fuggio o mio core, SWV 8.
EB:F86, F87.
Feritevi, viperette mordaci, SWV 9.
EB:F86, F87.
Fiamma ch'allaccia, SWV 10.
EB:F86, F87.
Quella damma, SWV 11.
EB:F86, F87.
Mi saluta costei, SWV 12.
EB:F86, F87.
Io more, ecce ch'io moro, SWV 13.
EB:F86, F87.
Sospire che del bel petto, SWV 14.
EB:F86, F87.
Dunque addio, care selve, SWV 15.
EB:F86, F87.
Tornate a cari baci, SWV 16.
EB:F86, F87.
Di marmo, SWV 17.
EB:F86, F87.
Giunto e pur, SWV 18.
EB:F86, F87.
Vasto mar, SWV 19.
EB:F86, F87.

e. Sacred Vocal – Psalms of David, 1619, SWV 22–47
Der Herr sprach zu meinen Herren, SWV 22.
EB:G111.
Warum toben die Heiden, SWV 23.
EB:G51, G111.
Ach Herr, straf mich nicht in deinem Zorn, SWV 24.
EB:G107, G108, G111, G112.
Aus der Tiefe ruf ich, Herr, zu dir, SWV 25.
EB:F105, F108, G111, G113.
Ich freue mich des, das mir geredt ist, SWV 26.
EB:G107, G111.
Herr unser Herrscher, SWV 27.
EB:G107, G111.
Wohl dem, der nicht wandelt im Rat der Gottlossen,
   SWV28.
EB:G111.
Wie lieblich sind deine Wohnunge, Herre Zebaoth, SWV
   29.
EB:G107, G108, G110, G111, G113.
Wohl dem, der den Herren fürchtet, SWV 30.
EB:G111, G112.
Ich hab meine Augen auf zu den Bergen, SWV 31.
EB:G111, G113.
Der Herr ist mein Hirt, SWV 33.
EB:G111, G112.
Ich danke dem Herr von ganzem Herzen, SWV 34.
EB:G111.
Singet dem Herrn ein neues Lied, SWV 35.
LR:F125.
EB:G108, G110, G111.
Jauchzet dem Herren, SWV 36.
EB:G108, G111.
An den Wassern zu Babel, SWV 37.
EB:G111.
Allelujah, lobet den Herren, SWV 38.
LR:F10.
EB:G111, G136.
Lobe den Herren, meine Seele, und vergiss nicht, SWV
   39.
EB:G111.
Ist nicht Ephraim mein teurer Sohn, SWV 40.
EB:G111.
Nun lob meine Seel, den Herren, SWV 41.
EB:G111, G112.
Die mit Tränen säen, SWV 42.
EB:G111.
Nicht uns, Herr, sondern deinem Namen gib Ehre, SWV
   43.
EB:G111.

Danket dem Herre, denn er ist freundlich, SWV 45.
EB:G111, G112.
Zion spricht, der Herr hat mich verlassen, SWV 46.
EB:G111.
Jauchzet dem Herrn, alle Welt, SWV 47.
EB:G111.
e.Sacred Vocal – Cantiones Sacrae, 1625, SWV 53-93
O bone, o dulcis, SWV 53.
EB:G100, G102.
Et ne despicias, SWV 54.
EB:G100, G102.
Deus misereatur, SWV 55.
EB:G102.
Quid commisisti, o dulcissime puer? SWV 56.
EB:F38, G100, G102.
Ego sum pui plaga dolores, SWV 57.
EB:F38, G100, G102.
Ego enin inique egi, SWV 58.
EB:F38, G100, G102.
Quo nate Dei, SWV 59.
EB:F38, G100, G102.
Calicem salutaris accipiam, SWV 60.
EB:F38, G100, G102.
Verba mea auribus percipe, SWV 61.
EB:G101, G102.
Quoniam ad te clamabo, SWV 62.
EB:G101, G102.
Ego dormio, SWV 63.
EB:G101, G102.
Vulnerasti cor meum, SWV 64.
EB:G101, G102.
Heu mihi, Domine, SWV 65.
EB:G101, G102, G109.
In te Domine speravi, SWV 66.
EB:G101, G102.
Dulcissime et benignissime Christe, SWV 67.
EB:G102.
Sicut Moses serpentem in deserto exaltavit, SWV 68.
EB:G80, G101, G102.
Spes mea, Christi Deus, SWV 69.
EB:G101, G102.
Turbator, sed non perturbator, SWV 70.
EB:G102.
Ad Dominum cum tribularer clamavi, SWV 71.
EB:G102.
Quid detur tibi, SWV 72.
EB:G102.
Aspice pater pissimum filium, SWV 73.
EB:G100, G102.
Nonne hic est, SWV 74.
EB:G100, G102.
Reduc, Domine, SWV 75.
EB:G100, G102.
Supereminet omnem scientiam, SWV 76.
EB:G100, G102.
Pro hoc magno mysterio pietatis, SWV 77.
EB:G100, G102.
Domine, non est exaltatum cor meum, SWV 78.
EB:G101, G102.
Si non humiliter sentiebam, SWV 79.
EB:G101, G102.
Speret Israel in Domino, SWV 80.
EB:G101, G102.
Cantate Domino canticum novum, SWV 81.
EB:G101, G102, G107.
Inter brachia salvatoris mei, SWV 82.
EB:G102.
Veni rogo in cor meum, SWV 83.
EB:G101, G102.
Ecce advocatus meus apud te, SWV 84.
EB:G102.
Domine, ne in furore tuo arguas me, SWV 85.
EB:G102.
Quoniam non est in morte, SWV 86.

EB:G102.
Discedite a me omnes, SWV 87.
EB:G102.
Oculi omnium, SWV 88.
EB:G102.
Pater noster, SWV 89.
EB:G102.
Domine Deus, pater caelestis, SWV 90.
EB:G102.
Confitemini Domino, SWV 91.
EB:G102.
Pater noster, SWV 92.
EB:G102.
Gratias agimus, SWV 93.
EB:G102.
e.Sacred Vocal – Beckerscher Psalter, 1626, SWV 97-256
Walts Gott, mein Werk ich lasse, SWV 137.
EB:G132.
Nun will sich scheiden Nacht und Tag, SWV 138.
EB:G132.
e.Sacred Vocal – Symphoniae Sacrae, I, 1629, SWV 257-276
In te, Domine, speravi, SWV 259.
EB:G103.
Venite ad me, SWV 261.
EB:G103.
Jubilate Deo, SWV 262.
EB:G103.
Anima mea liquefacta est, SWV 263.
EB:G103.
Adjuro vos, filiae Jerusalem, SWV 264.
EB:G103.
O quam tu pulchra es, SWV 265.
EB:G103, G109.
Veni di Libano, SWV 266.
EB:G103.
Fili mi, Absalom, SWV 269.
EB:G103, G109.
Buccinate in neomenia tuba, SWV 275.
EB:G103.
Jubilate Deo, SWV 276.
EB:G103.
e.Sacred Vocal – Kleine Geistliche Konzerte, 1636/9, SWV 282-337
Eile, mich. Gott, zu erretten, SWV 282.
EB:G88.
Bringt her dem Herren, SWV 283.
EB:G88.
Ich danke Herrn von ganzem Herzen, SWV 284.
EB:G88, G95.
O Süsser, o freundlicher, SWV 285.
EB:G88, G94.
Der Herr ist Gross, SWV 286.
EB:G88.
O lieber Herre Gott, SWV 287.
EB:G88.
Ihr Heiligen, lobsinget, SWV 288.
EB:G88.
Erhöre mich, wenn ich dich rufe, SWV 289.
EB:G88.
Wohl dem, der nicht wandelt im Rat der Gottlosen, SWV 290.
EB:G88.
Schaffe in mir, Gott, ein reines Herz, SWV 291.
EB:G88.
Der Herr Schauet, vom Himmel, SWV 292.
EB:G88.
Lobet den Herren, SWV 293.
EB:G88, G133.
Eins bitte ich vom Herren, SWV 294.
EB:G88, G94.
Christe Deus adjuva, SWV 295.
EB:G88.

EB:G96, G99.
Das ist je gewisslich wahr, SWV 388.
EB:G96, G98, G105.
Ich bin ein rechter Weinstock, SWV 389.
EB:G96, G99.
Unser wandel ist im Himmel, SWV 390.
EB:G96, G98.
Selig sind die Toten, SWV 391.
EB:G96, G97, G109.
Was mein Gott will, SWV 392.
EB:G96, G98.
Ich weiss, dass mein Erlösser lebt, SWV 393.
EB:G96, G97.
Sehet an den Feigenbaum, SWV 394.
EB:G96, G99.
Der Engel sprach zu den Hirten, SWV 395.
EB:G96, G98, G109.
Auf dem Gebirge hat man ein Geschrei gehöret, SWV 396.
EB:G96, G97, G109.
e.Sacred Vocal – Symphoniae Sacrae III, 1650, SWV 398–418
Mein Sohn, warum hast du uns das angetan, SWV 401.
EB:G120.
Saul, was verfolgst du mich, SWV 415.
EB:G51.
e.Sacred Vocal – Geistliche Gesänge, 1657, SWV 420–431
Die Worte der Einsetzung des heiligen Abendmahls, SWV 423.
EB:G138.
e.Sacred Vocal – Miscellaneous Works and SWV Anh
Ach, Herr, du Schopfer aller Ding.
LR:F114.
Domini est terra.
LR:F88.
EB:G106.
Erbarm dich mein.
LR:F88.
EB:G106.
Exaltavit cor meum.
EB:G109.
Heute ist Christus geboren.
LR:F88.
EB:G106.
Sumite Psalmum, SWV Anh 9.
EB:G80.
Unser Herr Jesus, Ohne SWV.
EB:G107.
Vater Abraham, erbarme dich mein.
EB:G106.
e.Sacred Vocal – Magnificats, Oratorios, other large-scale works
Musikalische Exequien, SWV 279–281.
Nacket bich ich vom Mutterlieb kommen, SWV 279a. Also hat Got die Welt geliebt, SWV 279b. Herr, wenn ich nur dich habe, SWV 280. Herr, nun lässest du deinen Diener, SWV 281.
EB:G114, G115.
Ich beschwöre euch, ihr Töchter zu Jerusalem, SWV 339 (Dialogue).
EB:G86, G120.
Historia der freudenreichen Geburt Jesu Christi, SWV 435.
EB:G116, G117, G118, G119.
Historia... (Christmas Story): Excerpts.
LR:Gd46.
Weib, was weinest du, SWV 443 (Dialogue).
EB:G80, G120.
Es gingen zweene Menschen hinauf, SWV 444 (Dialogue).
EB:G120.
Magnificat anima mea Dominum, SWV 468.
EB:G52, G110, G113.
O bone Jesu, SWV 471.

EB:G106.
Die Seiben Worte Jesu Christi am Kreuz, SWV 478 (7 Last Words).
EB:G120, G121.
St. Matthew Passion, SWV 479.
EB:G122, G123.
St. Luke Passion, SWV 480.
EB:G124, G125.
St. John Passion, SWV 481.
EB:G126.
Meine Seele erhebt den Herren (Deutsches Magnificat).
EB:G51, G107, G108, G110, G142.

SCOTTO, Paolo (16th. cent.)
   d.Secular Vocal
     O fallace speranza.
     LR:A3, E25.

SCOTUS – *see* SCOTTO, Paolo.

SCRONX, Gherardus (17th. cent.)
   c.Keyboard – Organ
     Echo.
     PS:A47.
     EB:E78, E88.
     LB:E191.

SEDANO (16th. cent.)
   d.Secular Vocal
     Viejo malo en la mi cama.
     LR:E28.

SEGER, Joseph Ferdinand Norbert (1716–1782)
   c.Keyboard – Organ
     Fugue in A min.
     LB:E236, E242.
     Fugue in F min.
     LB:E242.
     Partita in F maj.
     LB:D237.
     Prelude and fugue in D maj.
     LB:E237.
     Toccata in E maj.
     LB:E237.

SEIXAS, Carlos (1704–1742)
   c.Keyboard – Harpsichord
     Minuet and Toccata.
     LB:B324.
     Toccata in C maj.
     LB:D215.
     Toccata in C min.
     LB:D215.
     Toccata in D min.
     LB:D215.
     Toccata in F min.
     LB:D215.
     Toccata in G min.
     LB:D215.

SELMA Y SALAVERDE, Bartolome de (1580–1638)
   b.Instrumental
     Canzona XI a 2.
     LB:F84.
     Canzona XIII a 2.
     LB:F84.
     Corrente I.
     LB:F84.
     Corrente II.
     LB:F84.
     Fantasia sobre el canto del caballero.
     LB:F84.

SENAILLE, Jean Baptiste (1687–1730)
   b.Instrumental
     Sonata V for recorder and continuo.
     SI:C7.

Sonata in D min: Allegro spiritoso.
LB:B206.

SENFL, Ludwig (c.1490–1543)
  b.Instrumental
  Bicinia.
  LR:E16.
  2 Carmen.
  LR:E16, F120.
  Carmen in la.
  LR:E16.
  Carmen in re.
  LR:E16.
  Lamentatio – Carmen.
  LR:B30, E16.
  Tandernak.
  LR:E16.
  d.Secular Vocal
  Ach Elslein, liebes Elselein.
  LR:E16, E63, E64, E68, E69.
  EB:B66.
  Die Brünnlein, die da fliessen.
  LR:E16.
  Das G'laut zu Speyer.
  LR:A2, E22, E65, E69, E70, E71.
  Entlaubet ist der Walde.
  ER:A24, E68, E69.
  Es het ein biderman ein weib.
  ER:A25.
  LR:E64.
  Es taget vor dem Walde.
  ER:A25.
  LR:E16, E64, E70.
  Es wollt' ein' Frau zum Weine gahn.
  LR:E70.
  Fortuna – Nasci, pati, mori.
  LR:E70.
  Frau, ich bin euch von Herzen hold.
  LR:E65.
  Herzogs Ulrichs Jagdlied.
  LR:E68.
  Ich armes Käuzlein.
  LR:E65, E70.
  Ich armes meglein klag mich ser.
  ER:A25.
  LR:E16.
  Ich hab' mich redlich g'halten.
  LR:E64.
  Ich klag den Tag.
  LR:E65.
  Ich muss einem Buhlen haben.
  LR:E68.
  Ich schell'mein Horn.
  LR:E16.
  Ich stund an einem morgen.
  ER:A25.
  LR:A2, B30, E16, E69.
  Ich weiss nit was er ihr verhiess.
  ER:A25.
  LR:E16, E69.
  Im bad wol wir recht frolich sein.
  ER:A25.
  Im Maien.
  ER:A25.
  LR:B30, D21, E16, E64.
  Laub, Gras und Blüt.
  ER:A24.
  Lust hab ich g'habt zuer Musica.
  LR:E16.
  Mein Fleiss und Müdh'.
  LR:E16.
  Meniger stellt nach Geld.
  LR:E69.
  Mit Lust tät ich ausreiten.
  LR:E16, E64.

Mit lust tritt ich an.
LR:E68, E69.
Nun wöllt ihr hören neue Mär!
LR:A3.
Patiencia muss ich han.
LR:E70.
Quodlibet II.
ER:A25.
S'io non venni, non importa.
LR:E16.
Unsäglich schermz.
LR:E16.
Von edler Art.
LR:E68.
Wann ich des Morgens früh aufsteh'.
LR:E16.
Was wird es doch des Wunders nich.
LR:B30, E16, E69.
Will niemand singen.
LR:E16.
  e.Sacred Vocal
  Ach Gott, wem soll ich klagen.
  LR:E16.
  Christ ist erstanden.
  LR:F78.
  Da Jesus an dem Kreuze hing.
  LR:F78.
  Gottes Namen fahren wir.
  LR:E69.
  Ich armer Mann.
  LR:E16.
  Non morir sed vivum.
  ER:B33.
  O du armer Judas.
  LR:A2, F78.
  O herre Gotte, begnade mich.
  ER:B33.
  Quis dabit oculis nostris.
  LR:E69.

SENLECHES, Jacob de (15th. cent.)
  d.Secular Vocal
  En ce gracieux tamps joli.
  AA:A2.
  AN:B4, B16.
  Fuions de ci.
  AA:A2.
  AN:B16.

SEPHARDIC ROMANCES (15th. cent. Judeo-Spanish)
  d.Secular Vocal
  El Rey de Franca tres hijas tenia.
  ER:A26.
  El rey que tanto madruga.
  ER:A26.
  Lavava y suspirava.
  ER:A26.
  Morcios los mis moricos.
  ER:A26.
  Nani, nani.
  ER:A26.
  Palestina hermoza.
  ER:A26.
  Paxarico tu te llamas.
  ER:A26.
  Por alli paso un cavallero.
  ER:A26.
  Por que llorax blanca nina.
  ER:A26.
  Pregoneros van y vienen.
  ER:A26.
  La Reina xerifa mora.
  ER:A26.
  Una matica de Ruda.
  ER:A26.

SEPSISZENTGYORGY MS (16th./17th. cent. Hungarian)
   b. Instrumental
     Dances.
     LR:A7.

SERMISY - see DE SERMISY, Claudin.

SHEPPARD, John (c.1520-1563)
   e. Sacred Vocal
     Gaude, gaude, gaude Maria.
     LR:Ge18.
     Haec dies.
     LR:Ge39.
     In manus tuas.
     LR:Ge18.
     In pace.
     LR:Ge18.
     Jesu salvator saeculi.
     LR:Ge18.
     Laudem dicite Deo.
     LR:Ge18.
     Mass 'Cantate Dominum.'
     LR:Ge17.
     Paschal Kyrie.
     LR:Ge18.
     Spiritus Sanctus.
     LR:Ge17.
     Verbum caro.
     LR:Ge18.

SHERLIE, Joseph (17th. cent.)
   b. Instrumental
     Coranto (Manchester MS).
     SI:C20.
     Pavan and Almain (Manchester MS).
     SI:C20.

SHERYNHAM (15th./16th. cent.)
   e. Sacred Vocal
     Ah, gentle Jesu.
     LR:Gf3.

SICART MARJÉVOLS, Bernart (early 13th. cent.)
   d. Secular Vocal
     Ab greu cossire.
     AA:D11.

SICHER, Fridolin (1490-1546)
   c. Keyboard - Organ
     Carmen in G maj.
     EB:E63.
     Christ ist erstanden.
     EB:E63.
     In dulci jubilo.
     EB:E63.
     LB:E218.
     Resonet in laudibus.
     EB:E63.
     LB:E218.
     Uns hertzens grund.
     EB:E63.

SIEFERT, Paul (1586-1666) (See also SIVERT, Paulus)
   c. Keyboard - Harpsichord
     La Mia Barbara Pavan.
     LR:Gc16.

SIMBRACKY, Jan (d.1657)
   e. Sacred Vocal
     O Domine.
     EB:G140.

SIMMES, William (17th. cent.)
   b. Instrumental
     Fantasia.
     LR:Ga21.

SIMONELLI, Matteo (1618-1696)
   e. Sacred Vocal
     Missa 'Buda expugnata.'
     ER:B44.
     Missa 'Buda expugnata': Kyrie.
     LR:A6.

SIMPSON, Christopher (d.1669)
   b. Instrumental
     Divisions in B flat maj.
     LR:Ga19.
     Divisions on a ground in C maj for viol and continuo.
     SI:C8.
     Divisions on a ground in D maj for viol and continuo.
     SI:C4.
     Divisions on a ground in E min for viol and continuo.
     SI:C5.
     Divisions on a ground in G maj for viol and continuo.
     LB:B277.
     Prelude in E min for solo viol.
     SI:C5.
     Prelude and divisions in C min.
     LR:Ga19.

SIMPSON, Thomas (c.1610-c.1677)
   b. Instrumental
     Allemande.
     EB:B39.
     Alman.
     LR:B21, Ga10.
     Bonny sweet Robin - Ricercare.
     LR:Ga10, Ga16.

SIVERT, Paulus (= SIEFERT, Paulus) (1586-1666)
   c. Keyboard - Organ
     Puer natus in Bethlehem.
     EB:E74.

SMERT, Richard (15th. cent.)
   e. Sacred Vocal
     Nowell, nowell - Dieus vous garde.
     LR:F110, F127.

SMITH, John Christopher (1712-1795)
   c. Keyboard
     Lesson No. 7.
     LB:D223.

SMYTHE, Thomas (16th./17th. cent.)
   b. Instrumental
     2 Galliards.
     LR:Gb7.

SOLA, Andres de (16th. cent.)
   c. Keyboard - Organ
     Medio registro de mano derecha.
     LR:D13.
     EB:E79.

SOLAGE (late 14th. cent.)
   d. Secular Vocal
     Fumeux fume.
     AN:A2.
     ER:A11.
     Helas! je voy mon cuer.
     AN:A2.
     S'aincy estoit.
     LR:A4.

SOLER, Antonio de (1729-1783)
   b. Chamber and Instrumental
     Quintet No. 1 in C maj for harpsichord and string quartet.
     LB:B165.
     Quintet No. 2 in F maj for harpsichord and string quartet.
     LB:B165.
   c. Keyboard - Harpsichord (and Organ)
     Concertos for 2 Keyboards, Nos. 1-6.

1 in C maj; 2 in A min; 3 in G maj; 4 in F maj; 5 in A maj;
  6 in D maj.
LB:D211, E179, E180.
Concerto No. 3 in G maj for 2 keyboards.
LB:D229.
Fandango.
EB:D33.
LB:D209.
Sonata in A min, R71.
LB:D207.
Sonata in A min, R118.
LB:D206, D208, D210.
Sonata in B flat maj, M25.
LB:D210.
Sonata in B flat maj, R114.
LB:D210.
Sonata in B flat maj, R119.
LB:D208.
Sonata in B flat maj.
LB:D209.
Sonata in B min, R10.
LB:D207.
Sonata in B min.
EB:D33.
Sonata in C maj, R7.
LB:D208.
Sonata in C maj, 'Del Gallo', R108.
LB:D208.
Sonata in C min, R19.
LB:D206, D210.
Sonata in C min, R47.
LB:D208.
Sonata in C min, R103.
LB:D208.
Sonata in C min.
LB:D209.
Sonata in C sharp min, R21.
LB:D210.
Sonata in C sharp min.
LB:D209.
Sonata in D flat maj, R88.
LB:D207, D208.
Sonata in D maj, R73.
LB:D208.
Sonata in D maj, R74.
LB:D208.
Sonata in D maj, R84.
LB:D206, D207, D210.
Sonata in D maj, R86.
LB:D206, D210.
Sonata in D maj.
LB:D209, D228.
Sonata in D min, R15.
LB:D206, D207.
Sonata in D min, R24.
LB:D206.
Sonata in D min, R39.
LB:D207.
Sonata in D min.
EB:D33.
Sonata in E min, R52.
LB:D210.
Sonata in E min, R113.
LB:D207.
Sonata in F maj, R89.
LB:D206, D210.
Sonata in F maj, R101.
LB:D207.
Sonata in F min, R72.
LB:D207.
Sonata in F sharp maj.
LB:D209.
Sonata in F sharp min, R77.
LB:D207.
Sonata in F sharp min, R85.

LB:D210.
Sonata in G maj, R4.
LB:D207.
Sonata in G maj, R116.
LB:D210.
Sonata in G min, R38.
LB:D206.
Sonata in G min, R81.
LB:D208.
Sonata in G min, R87.
LB:D210.

SOMMER, Johan (16th./17th. cent.)
  b. Instrumental
  Galliard.
  LR:B23.
  Paduana.
  LR:B23.

SOPRON VIRGINAL BOOK (16th./17th. cent. Hungarian)
  c. Keyboard
  Dances.
  LR:B27.

SORGE, Georg Andreas (1703–1778)
  c. Keyboard – Organ
  Toccata per ogni modi.
  EB:E91.

SOTO DE LANGA, Pedro Francisco (1534–1619)
  c. Keyboard – Organ
  Entrada Real.
  AA:A1.
  Tiento.
  EB:D28.
  2 Tientos.
  LR:D13.
  Tiento de 6o tono.
  EB:E70.

SOWA, Jakub (d.c.1600)
  c. Keyboard – Organ
  Salve regina.
  EB:E85.

SPADI, Giovanni Battista (17th. cent.)
  d. Secular Vocal
  Anchor che col partire.
  LR:E39.

SPEER, Daniel (1636–1707)
  b. Instrumental
  Aufzugmusiken I–II for 6 trumpets and tympani.
  EB:B46.
  Hungarian Dances (Musikalisch Türkischer Eulen-
    Spiegel, 1688).
  LR:A5.
  Intrada in B flat maj.
  EB:B67.
  Sonata in E min.
  EB:B67.
  Sonata a 4.
  EB:B39.
  Sonata for 4 trombones and continuo.
  EB:B46.
  Sonata a 5 for 2 trumpets, 3 trombones, organ and bass.
  EB:B55.
  Sonata for cornett and 3 trombones.
  LR:A6.
  Sonata for 2 cornetts and 3 trombones.
  EB:B39.
  Sonata for trumpet and 3 trombones.
  EB:B46.
  Sonatas for wind instruments Nos. I–IV.
  EB:B38.

d. Secular Vocal
Musikalisch-Turkischer Eulen-Spiegel. 1688.
EB:F88.

SPERGER, Johann Matthias (1750–1812)
a. Orchestral
Concerto No. 2 in D maj for trumpet and strings.
LB:A665.

SPERONTES – see SCHOLZE, Johann Sigismond.

SPERVOGEL (13th./14th. cent.)
d. Secular Vocal
Swa eyn vriund.
AA:A3.

SPETH, Johann (c.1664–c.1720)
c. Keyboard – Organ
Toccata V.
EB:E92.

SPINACINO, Francesco (16th. cent.)
b. Instrumental – Lute
La Bernadina.
ER:A2.
J'ay pris amour.
LR:C24.
Je ne fay.
LR:A1, E24.
Ricercare.
LR:C23.
3 Ricercares.
LR:C25.

STABILE, Annibale (b.c.1540)
e. Sacred Vocal
Crucifixus (Missa 'Cantantibus Organis Caecilia.')
LR:F95.
Patrem omnipotentem (Missa 'Cantantibus Organis Caecilia.')
LR:F95.

STACHOWICZ, Damian (d.1729)
e. Sacred Vocal
Litania.
LB:G276.
Missa pro defunctis. Requiem.
LB:G276.
Veni consolator.
EB:G147.
LB:G276.
Veni redemptor.
EB:G144.

STADEN, Johann (1581–1634)
b. Instrumental
Courante.
EB:F110.
Gagliarda.
EB:F110.
Partita a 4 in A flat maj.
EB:B67.
Pavane.
EB:F110.
Processional Piece.
EB:F110, G132.
e. Sacred Vocal
Ach traurigkeit.
EB:F110.
Beata omnes.
EB:F110.
Gaudium mundi vanum.
EB:F110.

STANLEY, John (1713–1786)
a. Orchestral
Concerto in G maj for strings, Op. 2. No. 3.

LB:A595.
Concertos for organ and strings. Op. 10, Nos. 1–6.
1 in E maj; 2 in D maj; 3 in B flat maj; 4 in C min; 5 in A maj; 6 in C maj.
LB:A368.
b. Chamber and Instrumental
Sonata in G maj for flute and continuo.
LB:B245.
Suite of Trumpet Voluntaries.
LB:B223.
Trumpet voluntary in D maj.
EB:B47.
Trumpet Tune in D maj.
LB:A657.
Trumpet Tune (?).
EB:A34.
c. Keyboard – Organ
Voluntary in C maj, Op. 5, No. 1.
LB:E240.
Voluntary in G maj, Op. 5, No. 3.
LB:E227.
Voluntary in D min, Op. 5, No. 6.
LB:E181.
Voluntary in G min, Op. 5, No. 7.
LB:E201.
Voluntary in D min, Op. 5, No. 8.
LB:E181, E184, E211.
Voluntary in G min, Op. 6, No. 2.
LB:E181.
Voluntary in D min, Op. 6, No. 5.
LB:E215.
Voluntary in D maj, Op. 6, No. 6.
LB:E181.
Voluntary in A min, Op. 6, No. 8.
LB:E181.
Voluntary in D maj, Op. 7, No. 5.
LB:E181.
Voluntary in F maj, Op. 7, No. 6.
LB:E181.
Voluntary in A min, Op. 7, No. 7.
LB:E181.
Voluntary in G min, Op. 7, No. 8.
LB:E210.
Voluntary in D maj.
EB:E64.
LB:E203.
Voluntary in D min.
EB:E96.
Voluntary in G maj.
EB:E64, E83.
Voluntary No. 5.
LB:B212.

STRAROMIEYSKI, Janusz (17th./18th. cent.)
e. Sacred Vocal
Laudate pueri.
LB:G328.

STEENWICK, Gisbert (d.1697)
c. Keyboard – Organ
Heligh, saligh Bethlem.
EB:E61.
More palatino.
EB:E61.

STEFANI, Giovanni (16th./17th. cent.)
d. Secular Vocal
Pargoletta che non sai.
EB:B41.

STEFFANI, Agostino (1654–1724)
d. Secular Vocal – Stage Works
La Lotta d'Ercole con Acheleo – Opera: La Lotta for strings and continuo.
EB:F109.

Il Turno – Opera: Il dolce respiro.
EB:F109.

STEFFENS, Johan (16th./17th. cent.)
b. Instrumental
Galliard.
LR:B23.
Paduana.
LR:B23.

STOBAEUS, Johann (1580–1646)
b. Instrumental – Lute
Alia Chorea Polonica.
LR:C17.
Polish Dances from the Lute Tablature.
EB:B66.

STOCKHEM, Johannes (15th. cent.)
b. Instrumental
Brunette.
ER:A9.
Dit le Bourguygnon.
LR:Gf1.
Ha traiste amours.
ER:A9.
LR:Gf1.
Helas ce n'est pas.
ER:A9.
Je suis d'Allemagne.
ER:A9.
LR:A6.
Pourquoi je ne puis dire.
ER:A9.
Rompeltier.
LR:Gf1.

STOLZEL, Gottfried Heinrich (1690–1749)
a. Orchestral
Concerto Grosso in E min.
LB:A369.
Concerto Grosso in G maj.
LB:A369.
Concerto in B flat maj for trumpet and strings.
LB:A370.
Concerto in B min for flute, oboe, strings and harpsichord.
LB:A369.
Concerto in C maj for trumpet and strings.
LB:A370.
Concerto in D maj for flute, oboe, strings and harpsichord.
LB:A369.
Concerto in D maj for trumpet and strings.
LB:A370, A649, A655, A670.
Concerto in D maj for 6 trumpets and strings.
LB:A660.
Concerto in E min for flute, oboe and strings.
LB:A369.
Concerto in E min for trumpet and strings.
LB:A370.
Concerto in F maj for flute, violins, strings and continuo.
LB:A369.
b. Chamber and Instrumental
Sonata in D maj for trumpet and strings.
LB:A370.
c. Keyboard – Harpsichord
Partita in G min (Clavierbüchlein for W.F.Bach).
LB:D104.

STOLTZER, Thomas (1470–1526)
b. Instrumental
Fantasias in 1 and 6 Ton (Octo tonorum melodiae).
LR:F103.
Melodia I (Octo tonorum melodiae).
LR:B30.
Melodia a 5 (Octo tonorum melodiae).

EB:B55.
d. Secular Vocal (Including Instrumental Arrangements)
Entlaubet ist der Walde.
ER:A24, A25.
LR:A2, B30, E67.
Es mut vil leut.
LR:E67.
Ich klag den Tag.
LR:E67, E68.
Ich stund an einem Morgen.
LR:E68.
Ich wünsch all frawen ehr.
LR:E67.
Man sicht nun vol.
LR:E67.
e. Sacred Vocal
Benedicam Dominum in omne tempore – Psalm XXXIII.
LR:A6.
Christum wir sollen loben schone – A solis ortus cardine.
LR:F103.
Erzürne dich nicht – Psalm XXXVII.
LR:A6.
Ex tractu do inocauit.
LR:B29.

STORACE, Bernardo (17th. cent.)
c. Keyboard – Organ and Harpsichord
Aria sopra la Spagnoletta.
EB:D26.
Balletto.
EB:D26.
Balletto della Battaglia.
LR:D21.
EB:D26, E56.
Capriccio sopra Ruggiero.
EB:D26.
Ciaconna.
EB:D26.
Folia.
EB:D26.
Monica.
EB:D26.
Partite sopra il Cinque Passi.
EB:D26.
Romanesca.
EB:D26.
Sonata in D maj.
LB:D223.
Toccata e Canzone.
EB:D26.

STORL, Johann Georg Christian (1675–1719)
b. Instrumental
Sonata for cornett and 3 trombones.
EB:B46.
Sonata and fugue a 4 for 2 trumpets and 2 trombones.
EB:B55.
Sonata and Passacaglia a 4 for 2 trumpets and 2 trombones.
EB:B55.
Sonata for wind (brass) instruments.
EB:B39.

STRADELLA, Alessandro (1642–1682)
b. Chamber and Instrumental
Sinfonia in A min for 2 violins and continuo (No. 15).
EB:A29.
Sinfonia in A min for 2 violins and continuo (No. 16).
EB:A29.
Sinfonia in D maj for strings and continuo.
EB:G127.
Sinfonia in D maj for 2 violins and continuo (No. 17).
EB:A29.
Sinfonia in D maj for 2 violins and continuo (No. 18).
EB:A29.

LR:B9, E54.
Morisque.
LR:B14, Ga11, Ga20, Gd58.
LB:B273.
Ohne fels.
LR:Gd58.
Passe et Medio and Reprinse le Pingue.
LR:Ga20.
Pavan and Galliard.
LR:F94.
Pavan.
ER:A22.
Die Poste.
LR:B29.
LB:B273.
Ronde III.
LR:B9, B25.
Ronde (Unsp.)
AA:D20.
LR:B10, B12, B17, B18, B29, E45, Ga11, Ga20.
Ronde et Saltarello.
LR:B10, B17, B18, F94, Ga20.
Saltarello.
LR:E45.
Sans roche – Bergerette.
LR:B9, E64, Ga20.
LB:B282.
Si pas souffrir – Pavan.
LR:B9, B10, B17, B18.
Wo bistu – Ronde.
LR:E54.

SWEELINCK, Dirck Janszoon (1591–1652)
e. Sacred Vocal
Hoe schoon lichtet de morgensteer.
LR:F117.

SWEELINCK, Jan Pieterszoon (1562–1621)
**c. Keyboard – Organ and Harpsichord: Free Works and
Variations**
Ballo de Granducèa.
LR:E42.
EB:D36, E55, E75.
Echo fantasia.
EB:E64, E65.
Engelsche fortuyn.
EB:D27.
Est-ce Mars?
LR:D20.
EB:D27, D38, E89.
Fantasia (Unsp.)
EB:E25.
Fantasia cromatica.
EB:D27, E72, E75.
Fantasia ut re mi fa sol la.
EB:D27, D38.
Fantasia II.
EB:D27.
Fantasia III.
EB:E55.
Fantasia IV.
EB:E54, E55.
Fantasia V.
EB:E54.
Fantasia VI.
EB:D27.
Fantasia VIII.
EB:E55.
Fantasia IX.
EB:E55.
Fantasia XI.
EB:E55.
Fantasia XII.
EB:E54, E55, E60.
LB:E207.

Fantasia XIII.
EB:E55.
Fantasia XIV.
EB:E55.
Ich fuhr mich uber Rheine.
EB:D27.
Lachrimae Pavan.
LR:E42, D27.
Malle Symen.
EB:D31, E66.
Mein junges leben hat ein ende.
LR:D20.
EB:D27, D28, E66, E81, E87.
LB:D213, E111, E224, E227.
More palatino.
EB:D27.
Onder der Linden Groen.
EB:D27.
LB:E226.
SI:C15.
Pavana hispanica.
EB:B40, D27, E60.
LB:D220.
Pavana Philippi.
EB:D27.
Praeludium in F maj.
EB:E55.
Praeludium and Toccata.
LR:Gc15.
LB:B277.
Prelude for pedal.
EB:E25.
Ricercare.
EB:E25.
Ricercare brevis.
LR:D20.
EB:E55, E87.
Toccata (Unsp.)
LR:D20.
EB:E25, E87, E89.
Toccata in C maj.
EB:E60.
Toccata XV.
EB:D27.
Toccata XVI.
EB:D27.
Toccata XVII.
EB:D38, E54, E55.
LB:E210.
Toccata XVIII.
EB:D27.
Toccata XIX.
EB:D27.
Toccata XX.
EB:E55.
Toccata XXI.
EB:D27, D31.
SI:C1.
Toccata XXII.
EB:E55.
Toccata XXIII.
EB:E55.
Toccata XXIV.
EB:D27.
Toccata XXV.
EB:D27.
Von der Fortuna.
EB:E75, E82.
c. Keyboard – Organ: Chorale-based Works
Allein Gott in der Höh' sei Ehr'.
EB:E55.
Allein zu dir, Herr Jesu Christ.
EB:E25, E55, E60.
Christe qui lux es.

EB:E55.
Da pacem.
EB:E54, E55.
Erbarm dich.
EB:E55.
Ich ruf zu dir.
EB:E55.
Nun freut euch.
EB:E55.
Psalm V.
LR:C13.
Psalm XXIII.
LR:C13.
Psalm XXXVI.
EB:E55.
Psalm CXVI.
EB:E55.
Psalm CXL.
EB:E55.
Puer nobis nascitur.
EB:E54, E55.
Vater unser im Himmelreich.
EB:E55, E60.
Wir glauben alle.
EB:E55.
e. Sacred Vocal
Ab oriente.
EB:G129.
De profundis.
EB:G129.
Gott ist mein Hirt.
LR:F83.
Hodie Christus natus est.
LR:F119, F126.
O Domine Jesu Christe.
EB:G129.
Te Deum.
EB:G129.
Psalm LXXXIV: O Dieu des armes.
EB:G129.
Psalm XC: Tu as ete, Seigneur, notre retrait.
EB:G129.
Psalm CIX: O Dieu, mon honneur et ma gloire.
EB:G129.
Psalm CXXII: Incontinent que j'eus oui.
EB:G129.
Psalm CXXXIV: Ors sus, serviteurs du Seigneur.
EB:G129.
Psalm CXLVI: Sus non ame qu'on benee.
EB:G129.
Psalm CL: Or soit loue l'eternel.
EB:G129.

SZADEK, Tomasz (c.1590–1611)
  e. Sacred Vocal
  Missa 'in melodiam moteti pisneme': Sanctus.
  EB:G144.
  Officium 'Dies et laetitiae.'
  EB:G4.

SZAMOTULY, Waclav z (d.c.1560)
  e. Sacred Vocal (Polish and Latin Works)
  Ach moj niebieski Panie.
  LR:F70.
  Alleluja, chwalcie Pana.
  LR:F70.
  Blogoslawiony czlowiek – Psalm I.
  LR:F70.
  LB:A617.
  Ego sum pastor bonus.
  LR:F70, F92.
  In te, Domine, speravi.
  ER:B45.
  LR:F70, F92.
  LB:A617.

Juz sie zmierzcha.
ER:B45.
LR:F70.
Kryste dniu naszej swialosci.
LR:F70.
EB:G144.
Naklon Panie ku mnie ucho twoje – Psalm LXXXV.
LR:F70, F97.
Nunc scio vere.
LR:E57, F70, F92.
Pochwalmyz wszyscy.
LR:F70.

SZARZYNSKI, Sylwester Stanislaw (17th. cent.)
  b. Chamber and Instrumental
  Sonata in D maj for 2 violins and continuo.
  EB:G144.
  e. Sacred Vocal
  Ave regina.
  EB:G147.
  LB:G277.
  Ad hymnus ad cantus.
  EB:G146.
  LB:G277.
  Gloria in excelsis Deo.
  LB:G277, G329.
  Jesu, spes me.
  EB:G147.
  LB:G277.
  Pariendo non gravaris.
  EB:G144.
  LB:G277.
  Veni Sancte Spiritus.
  LB:G277.

SZEPETHNEKI, Janos (16th. cent.)
  e. Sacred Vocal
  Here I am, my sweet Lord.
  LR:A5.

TALLIS, Thomas (c.1505–1585)
  c. Keyboard – Organ
  Fantasia.
  LR:Gc17.
  Natus est nobis (Mulliner Book).
  LR:Gc6.
  O ye tender babes.
  LR:Gc9.
  e. Sacred Vocal – English Works
  Archbishop Parker's Psalter.
    E'en like the hunted hind the waterbrooks desire.
    Expend, O Lord, my plaint of word.
    God grant we grace, He us embrace.
    Let God arise in majesty.
    Man blest no doubt.
    O come in one to praise the Lord.
    Why brag'st in malice high.
    Why fum'th in sight.
  LR:Ge21.
  Hear the voice and prayer.
  LR:Ge22.
  If ye love me.
  LR:Ge22.
  e. Sacred Vocal – Latin Works
  Audivi vocem.
  LR:Gd36, Ge25.
  Derelinquat.
  LR:Ge24.
  Deus tuorum militum (Hymn).
  LR:Ge23.
  Ecce tempus idoneum.
  LR:Ga18, Ge22, Ge24.
  Ex more docti mistico (Hymn).
  LR:Ga18, Gc27, Ge23.
  Gaude gloriosa.

LR:Ge22.
Honor, virtus et potestas.
LR:Ge21, Ge25.
Iam Christus astra (Hymn).
LR:Ge23.
Iam lucis orto sidere (Hymn).
LR:Gc17, Ge23.
In jeinio et fletu.
LR:Ge24.
In manus tuas.
LR:Ge24.
Iste confessor (Hymn).
LR:Ge23.
Jesu salvator saeculi.
LR:Ge20.
Lamentations of Jeremiah (I-II).
LR:Gd18, Gd39, Ge3, Ge9, Ge22, Ge23, Ge24.
EB:G133.
Loquebantur variis linguis.
LR:Ge22, Ge38.
Magnificat.
LR:Ge21.
Mass 'Puer natus est.'
LR:Ge19.
Mass 'Salve intemerata.'
LR:Ge20.
Miserere nostri.
LR:Ge21.
Nunc dimittis.
LR:Ge20, Ge21.
O nata lux de lumine.
LR:Ge22, Ge24.
LB:G319.
O sacrum convivium.
LR:Ge21, Ge25.
Salvator mundi. (Hymn).
LR:F88, Ge19, Ge23, Ge24, Ge25, Ge32, Ge35.
Salve nos Domine.
LR:Ge20.
Salve regina.
LR:Ge20.
Sancte Deus.
LR:Ge20, Ge24, Ge25.
LB:G320.
Sermone blando angelus (Hymn).
LR:Ge23.
Spem in alium.
LR:Ge22, Ge24.
Suscipe quaeso Domine.
LR:Ge19, Ge21.
Te lucis ante terminum (Hymn).
LR:Ge23, Ge24.
Veni redemptor.
LR:Ge24.
Videte miraculum.
LR:Ge21, Ge24.

TARTINI, Giuseppe (1692–1770)
a. Orchestral
Concerto in A maj for cello and strings.
LB:A352, A373, A377.
Concerto Grosso in A min for strings, D76.
LB:A376.
Concerto in A min for violin and strings, D115.
LB:A372.
Concerto in B flat maj for violin and strings, D117.
LB:A371.
Concerto in D maj for cello and strings.
LB:A372, A613.
Concerto in D maj for flute and strings, D50.
LB:A375.
Concerto in D maj for trumpet and strings (Arr. D53 for
violin in E maj.)
LB:A655.
Concerto in D maj for trumpet and strings.

LB:A378, A648, A652, A668.
Concerto in D maj for violin and strings.
LB:A361.
Concerto in D maj for violin and strings, D82.
LB:A374.
Concerto in D maj for violin and strings, D96.
LB:A371.
Concerto in D maj for violin, strings and organ, D79.
LB:A376.
Concerto in D maj for violin, 2 horns and strings, D21.
LB:A373.
Concerto in D min for violin and strings, D45.
LB:A373.
Concerto in E maj for violin and strings, D48.
LB:A374.
Concerto in E min for violin and strings, D56.
LB:A374.
Concerto in F maj for violin, strings and harpsichord,
D73.
LB:A376.
Concerto in G maj for flute and strings.
LB:A372, A633.
Concerto in G maj for flute and strings (Dub.)
LB:A375.
Concerto in G maj for flute and strings, D78.
LB:A375.
Concerto in G maj for flute and strings, D105.
LB:A375.
Concerto in G maj for violin and strings, D78.
LB:A371.
Concerto in G maj for violin and strings.
LB:A361.
Sinfonia in A maj for strings and continuo.
LB:A627.
Sinfonia Pastorale in D maj for violin and strings.
EB:A33.
Sonata a 4 in A maj for strings and continuo.
LB:A373.
Sonata a 4 in G maj for strings and continuo.
LB:A372.
b. Chamber and Instrumental
Sonatas for violin and cello without continuo, Nos. 1–12.
1 in G maj; 2 in D min; 3 in D maj; 4 in C maj; 5 in F maj;
6 in E min; 7 in A min; 8 in G min; 9 in A maj; 10 in B
flat maj; 11 in E maj; 12 in G maj.
LB:B166.
Sonata in A maj for violin and continuo, Op. 1, No. 1.
LB:B167.
Sonata in G min for violin and continuo, 'Didone
Abandonata', Op. 1, No. 10.
LB:B167, B168, B318.
Sonata in F maj for violin and continuo, Op. 1, No. 12.
LB:B167.
Sonata in C maj for violin and continuo, Op. 2, No. 6.
LB:B167.
Sonata in A min for violin and continuo, Op. 2, No. 7.
LB:B167.
Sonata in G min for violin and continuo, 'The Devil's Trill.'
LB:B161, B167, B314.
Theme and 30 variations from 'L'Arte dell'arco' for violin
and continuo.
LB:B161.
Trio Sonata No. 6 in D maj.
LB:B168.
Trio Sonata No. 10 in C maj.
LB:B168.

TAVERNER, John (1495–1545)
b. Instrumental
In Nomine a 4.
LR:Ga16, Ga17.
e. Sacred Vocal
Christe Jesu pastor bone.
LR:Ge26.
Dum transisset sabbatum.

LR:F79, Ge26, Ge38, Ge39, Gf5.
In pace in idipsum.
LR:Gf5.
Kyrie 'Le Roy.'
LR:Ge26.
Magnificat in the 1st. tone.
SI:D4.
Magnificat in the 6th. tone.
LR:Gf5.
Mass 'The Western Wind.'
LR:Ge25, Ge26.
Master Christi.
LR:Ge25, Ge26.
Quemadmodum.
LR:Gf5.

TAYLOR, 'Master' (16th. cent.)
c. Keyboard
Pavan and Galliard (The Dublin Virginal Book).
EB:E56.

TAYLOR, Silas (16th./17th. cent.)
b. Instrumental
Coranto and Sarabande (Playford's 'Court Ayres', 1655).
EB:F91.

TELEMANN, Georg Philipp (1681–1767)
a. Orchestral
Adagio in G maj for flute, violin and strings.
LB:A599.
Concerto in A maj for flute, violin and strings (Taffel-
musik I).
LB:A379, A380, A386, A387, A388, A389.
Concerto in A maj for flute, harpsichord and continuo.
LB:A390.
Concerto in A maj for oboe d'amore and strings.
LB:A392.
Concerto in A maj for 2 violins, strings and continuo.
LB:A391.
Concerto in A min for 2 flutes and strings.
LB:A389.
Concerto in A min for recorder, viola da gamba, strings
and continuo.
LB:A356, A391.
Concerto in B flat maj for 2 flutes, oboe, violin and
strings.
LB:A392.
Concerto in B flat maj for 2 recorders and strings.
LB:A636.
Concerto in B flat maj for 3 oboes, 3 violins and continuo.
LB:A389, A399, A402, A597.
Concerto in B flat maj for trombone and organ (Arr.
Concerto in D maj for horn, strings and continuo.)
LB:B217.
Concerto in C maj for flute and strings.
LB:A176, A403.
Concerto in C maj for recorder and strings.
LB:A646.
Concerto in C min for trumpet (oboe), strings and
continuo.
LB:A339, A669.
Concerto in D maj for flute and strings.
LB:A176.
Concerto in D maj for horn and organ.
LB:B220.
Concerto in D maj for trumpet and strings.
LB:A394, A412, A652, A656, A659, A663, A666,
A668, A670.
Concerto in D maj for trumpet and organ.
LB:B209.
Concerto in D maj for trumpet, oboe and strings.
LB:A658.
Concerto in D maj for trumpet, 2 oboes and continuo.
LB:A664.
Concerto in D maj for trumpet, 2 oboes and strings.

LB:A394, A594, A647, A650, A664, A665.
Concerto in D maj for trumpet, 2 oboes, bassoon, harpsi-
chord and strings.
LB:A172, A394.
Concerto in D maj for 3 trumpets, 2 oboes and strings.
LB:A392.
Concerto in D maj for 3 trumpets, 2 oboes, timpani and
strings.
LB:A394.
Concerto in D maj for viola da gamba and strings.
LB:A407.
Concerto in D min for flute, oboe and strings.
LB:A392.
Concerto in E flat maj for flute, oboe d'amore, violin and
strings.
LB:A402.
Concerto in E flat maj for 2 horns and strings (Taffel-
musik III).
LB:A383, A384, A386, A387, A388.
Concerto in E min for recorder, flute and strings.
LB:A397.
Concerto in E min for trumpet (oboe), strings and
continuo.
LB:A339.
Concerto in F maj for 4 horns, 2 oboes and strings.
LB:A413.
Concerto in F maj for recorder and strings.
LB:A636.
Concerto in F maj for recorder, bassoon and strings.
LB:A399, A415.
Concerto in F maj for recorder, bassoon, 2 violins, viola
and continuo.
LB:A406.
Concerto in F maj for 3 violins and strings (Taffelmusik II).
LB:A381, A382, A386, A387, A388, A393, A407,
A602.
Concerto Grosso in F maj for wind and strings.
LB:A404.
Concerto in F min for oboe and strings.
LB:A338, A624.
Concerto in F min for trumpet and strings (Arr. of Oboe
Concerto in F min).
LB:A653.
Concerto in G maj for flute and strings.
LB:A403.
Concerto in G maj for oboe and strings.
LB:A642.
Concerto in G maj for trumpet (flute), 2 violins and
continuo.
LB:A339.
Concerto in G maj for viola and orchestra.
LB:A64, A393, A398, A407, A408, A594.
Concerto in G maj for 2 violas and strings.
LB:A365, A407.
Concerto in G min for recorder and strings.
LB:A391.
Concerto in G min for recorder, 2 violins, cello, harpsi-
chord and bass.
LB:A395.
Introduction and Rondeau in D min for flute, violin and
strings.
LB:A599.
Minuet in G min for oboes and strings.
LB:A641.
Overture – Der Getreue Musikmeister.
LB:B219.
Overture in B flat maj for 2 oboes, 2 violins, viola and
strings (Taffelmusik III).
LB:A383, A384, A385.
Overture in C maj, 'Hamburger Ebb und Fluth.'
LB:A390, A396, A409.
Overture in C maj for 3 oboes and strings.
LB:A402, A409.
Overture in D maj for oboe, trumpet, bassoon and strings

(Taffelmusik II).
LB:A381, A382, A385, A410.
Overture in E min for 2 flutes and strings (Taffelmusik I).
LB:A379, A380, A385.
Overture in F sharp min.
LB:A396, A397.
Overture in G maj 'Des Nations Anciens et Modernes.'
LB:A409.
Overture in G min.
LB:A396.
Polish Concerto No. 1 in B flat maj for strings, harpsichord and continuo.
LB:A404, A405.
Polish Concerto No. 2 in G maj for strings, harpsichord and continuo.
LB:A404, A405.
Polish Partita in B flat maj.
LB:A404.
Polish Sonata No. 1 for strings and continuo.
LB:A404, A405.
Polish Sonata No. 2 for strings and continuo.
LB:A404, A405.
Sinfonia in F maj for recorder, viola da gamba and strings.
LB:A402.
Sonata in D maj for trumpet, strings and continuo.
LB:A669.
Suite in A min for recorder and strings.
LB:A328, A393, A397, A400, A401, A403, A406, A411, A414.
Suite in A min for recorder, viola and strings.
LB:A395.
Suite in D maj for viola da gamba, strings and continuo.
LB:A401.
Suite in D maj for 2 oboes, 2 horns and strings.
LB:A408.
Suite in D min for oboe, violin and continuo.
LB:A390.
Suite in E flat maj, 'La Lyra.'
LB:A398.
Suite in E maj for sopranino recorder and strings.
LB:A226.
Suite in F maj for 4 horns, 2 oboes, bassoon and strings.
LB:A639.
Suite in F maj for 2 horns, 2 violins and continuo.
LB:A399.
Suite in F maj for violin and strings.
LB:A615.
Suite in F maj for violin, 2 flutes, 2 oboes, 2 horns and strings.
LB:A398, B267.
Suite in F min for 2 recorders and strings.
LB:A400.
Suite 'Don Quichotte.'
LB:A408.

b.Chamber and Instrumental
Concerto in C maj for 4 solo violins.
LB:A391.
Concerto in D maj for 4 solo violins.
LB:A391.
Concerto in G maj for 4 solo violins.
LB:A399.
Concerto in G min for flute and harpsichord.
LB:B189.
Divertissement in D maj for 2 trumpets.
LB:A649.
Duet in B flat maj for recorder and violino piccolo (GMM).
LB:B190.
Fantasias for solo flute, Nos. 1-12.
   1 in A maj; 2 in A min; 3 in B min; 4 in B maj; 5 in C maj; 6 in D min; 7 in D maj; 8 in E min; 9 in E maj; 10 in F sharp min; 11 in G maj; 12 in G min.
LB:B169, B170, B171.
Fantasia No. 2 in A min for solo recorder.

LB:B229, B292.
Fantasia No. 4 in B flat maj for solo recorder.
LB:B229, B230, B280.
Fantasia No. 3 in B min for solo flute.
LB:B189, B236.
Fantasia No. 5 in C maj for solo recorder.
LB:B229, B265, B292.
Fantasia No. 6 in D min for solo recorder.
LB:B229, B278.
Fantasia in F maj for solo recorder.
LB:B229, B278.
Fantasia No. 12 in G min for solo recorder.
LB:B229, B230, B236, B280.
Fantasias for solo violin, Nos. 1-12.
   1 in B flat maj; 2 in G maj; 3 in F min; 4 in D maj; 5 in A maj; 6 in E min; 7 in E flat maj; 8 in E maj; 9 in B min; 10 in D maj; 11 in F maj; 12 in A min.
LB:B172, B173.
Heldenmusik for brass and organ.
LB:B209, B218, B219.
Introduzzione a 3 in C maj for 2 recorders and continuo (GMM).
LB:B191.
Partita No. 1 in B flat maj for recorder and continuo (KKM).
LB:B182, B184, B287.
Partita No. 2 in G maj for oboe (or flute) and continuo (KKM).
LB:B176, B182, B185.
Partita No. 2 in G maj for flute and continuo (KMM): Tempo di minuetto.
LB:B322.
Partita No. 2 in G maj for flute and continuo (KKM): Siciliana.
LR:F106.
LB:B231.
Partita No. 3 in C min for recorder (or violin) and continuo (KKM).
LB:B182, B185.
Partita No. 4 in G min for oboe and continuo (KKM).
LB:B177, B183, B184.
Partita No. 5 in E min for recorder and continuo (KKM).
LB:B183, B185, B277.
Partita No. 6 in E flat maj for recorder (or violin) and continuo (KKM).
LB:B183, B185.
Quartets for flute, violin, cello and harpsichord, 'Paris', Nos. 1-6.
   1 in D maj; 2 in A min; 3 in G maj; 4 in B min; 5 in A maj; 6 in E min.
LB:B180, B181.
Paris Quartet No. 1 in D maj.
LB:B87.
Quartet in B flat maj for 2 violins, viola, cello and continuo.
LB:B317.
Quartet in D min for recorder, 2 flutes and continuo (Taffelmusik II).
LB:A381, A382, B175, B188, B296.
Quartet in E min for violin, flute, cello and continuo (Taffelmusik III).
LB:A383, A384.
Quartet in G maj for flute, oboe, violin and continuo (Taffelmusik I).
LB:A379, A380, B175, B276.
Scherzo in E maj for 2 flutes and continuo (3 Trietti, 1731).
LB:B191.
Sonatas for 2 flutes without continuo, Nos. 1-6.
   1 in G maj; 2 in E min; 3 in D maj; 4 in B min; 5 in A maj; 6 in E maj.
LB:B174.
Sonata in canon for 2 flutes.
LB:B272.

Sonata No. 2 in E min for 2 flutes.
LB:B226.
Sonata in D min for flute and recorder.
LB:B304.
Sonata (Solo) in A maj for violin and continuo (Taffel-
musik II).
LB:A381, A382.
Sonata in A min for oboe and continuo (GMM).
LB:B241.
Sonata in A min for trombone and organ (Arr. Sonata in A
min for viola da gamba and continuo).
LB:B215.
Sonata in B flat maj for oboe and continuo.
LB:B254, B256.
Sonata in B flat maj for recorder and continuo (GMM).
LB:B139, B178, B186.
Sonata in B maj for oboe and continuo (EM).
LB:B176.
Sonata (Solo) in B min for flute and continuo (Taffel-
musik I).
LB:A379, A380, B237.
Sonata in C maj for flute and continuo.
LB:B189.
Sonata in C maj for oboe and organ.
LB:B210.
Sonata in C maj for recorder and continuo (EM).
LB:B139, B178.
Sonata in C maj for recorder and continuo (GMM).
LB:B139, B178, B184, B186, B187, B294.
Sonata in C maj for viola da gamba and continuo.
LB:B305.
Sonata in C min for flute (or recorder) and continuo (EM).
LB:B188.
SI:C17.
Sonata (Solo) in C min for flute and continuo.
LB:A599.
Sonata in D maj for flute and harpsichord.
LB:B301.
Sonata in D min for recorder and continuo (EM).
LB:B139, B178, B280.
Sonata in D min for recorder and continuo (GMM).
LB:B186.
Sonata in E flat maj for oboe, harpsichord and continuo.
LB:B177, B250.
Sonata (Solo) in E min for oboe and continuo.
LB:B177.
Sonata in E min for recorder and continuo (EM).
EB:B42.
LB:B298.
Sonata in F maj for flute and continuo (EM).
LB:B249.
SI:C20.
Sonata in F maj for recorder and continuo (GM).
LB:A631, B139, B178, B186.
Sonata in F min for bassoon and continuo (GMM).
LB:B188.
Sonata in F min for recorder and continuo (GMM).
LB:B139, B178, B184, B186, B187, B253.
Sonata in G maj for mandolin and harpsichord.
LB:C28.
Sonata in G maj for oboe and continuo.
LB:B254.
Sonata (Solo) in G min for oboe and continuo (Taffel-
musik III).
LB:A383, A384, B176, B177.
Suite in G min for oboe and continuo (GMM).
LB:B176.
Sonata in G min for trumpet and organ (Arr. Sonata in G
min for oboe and continuo.
LB:B224.
Trio Sonata for flute, viola da gamba, cello and harpsi-
chord.
SI:C17.
Trio Sonata in A maj for flute, harpsichord and continuo

(EM).
LB:B191.
Trio Sonata in A min for recorder, oboe and continuo.
LB:B179.
Trio Sonata in A min for recorder, violin and continuo (6
Trios, 1718).
LB:B191.
Trio Sonata in A min for recorder, violin (or viola da
gamba) and continuo (10).
LB:B190.
Trio Sonata in A min for recorder, violin and continuo
(EM).
LB:B190.
Trio Sonata in B flat maj for recorder, harpsichord and
continuo (EM).
LB:B191.
Trio Sonata in C maj for flute, recorder and continuo.
LB:B226, B304.
Trio Sonata in C maj for recorder, violin (or viola da
gamba) and continuo (10).
LB:B190.
Trio Sonata in C min for flute and continuo (EM).
LB:B175.
Trio Sonata in C min for recorder, oboe and continuo
(EM).
LB:B179, B191.
SI:C9.
Trio Sonata in D maj for 2 flutes and continuo (Taffel-
musik III).
LB:A383, A384.
Trio Sonata in D min for flute, oboe and continuo (EM).
LB:B191.
Trio Sonata in D in for recorder, viola da gamba and
continuo. 'Darmstadt.'
LB:B191.
Trio Sonata in D min for recorder, violin and continuo
(10).
EB:B69.
LB:B187, B190.
Trio Sonata in E flat maj for oboe, harpsichord and
continuo (EM).
LB:A390, B188, B232, B264.
Trio Sonata in E flat maj for 2 violins and continuo (Taffel-
musik I).
LB:A379, A380.
Trio Sonata in E maj for flute, violin and continuo (EM).
LB:B191.
Trio in E min for flute, oboe and continuo (Taffelmusik II).
LB:A381, A382, B247, B275.
Trio in E min for recorder, oboe and continuo.
LB:B87, B179, B187.
Trio Sonata in F maj for recorder, oboe and continuo.
LB:B179.
Trio Sonata in F maj for recorder, viola da gamba and
continuo. 'Darmstadt.'
LB:B303.
Trio Sonata in F maj for recorder, viola da gamba and
continuo (EM).
LB:A395, B190, B191.
SI:C18.
Trio Sonata in F min for recorder, violin and continuo
(10).
LB:B190.
Trio Sonata in G min for flute, violin and continuo (EM).
LB:B244.
Trio Sonata in G min for recorder, violin (or viola da
gamba) and continuo (10).
LB:B190.
SI:C3.

c. Keyboard – Harpsichord
Fantasia No. 1 in C maj for solo harpsichord, in the
French Manner.
LB:B189.
Fantasia No. 2 in C min for solo harpsichord, in the

French Manner.
LB:B189.
Fantasia No. 13 in D maj for solo harpsichord, in the
German Manner.
LB:B189.
Fantasia No. 14 in D min for solo harpsichord, in the
German Manner.
LB:B189.
SI:C17.
Fantasia No. 35 in B flat maj for solo harpsichord, in the
Italian Manner.
LB:B189.
Fantasia No. 36 in B flat maj for solo harpsichord, in the
Italian Manner.
LB:B189.
Overture in E flat maj for solo harpsichord (EM).
LB:D212.
Overture in G min for solo harpsichord (EM).
LB:D212.
Partita for solo harpsichord (GMM).
SI:C10.
Solo in C maj for harpsichord (EM).
LB:D212.
Solo in F maj for harpsichord (EM).
LB:D212.
d. Secular Vocal and Stage Works
Das Frauenzimmer.
LB:F81.
Geld.
LB:F81.
Der Landlust – Cantata.
LB:F70.
Die Lieb und auch die Flöh.
LB:F81.
Ein reiches weib.
LB:F81.
Der Schulmeister – Cantata.
LB:F70.
Die ungekämmte Philis.
LB:F81.
Pimpinone – Comic Intermezzo, 1725.
LB:F71, F72.
Pimpinone – Mein Herz erfreut sich in der Brust.
LB:F82.
Pimpinone: Was aber denkt ihr nun zu tun?
LB:F82.
Ven geliebten Augen brennen – Cantata.
LB:F70.
e. Sacred Vocal
Ach Herr, strafe mich nicht – Psalm VI.
EB:G134.
LB:G324.
Deus judicium tuum – Motet.
LB:G279.
Die Ehre des herrlichen Schöpfers zumelden (Der
Harmonische Gottesdienst).
LB:G278.
Du aber Daniel gehe hin – Funeral Cantata.
LB:G76.
Erquikkendes Wunder der ewigen Gnade (Der Har-
monische Gottesdienst).
LB:G278.
Erwachet zum kriegen (Der Harmonische Gottesdienst).
LB:G278.
Ew'ge Quelle, milder strom (Der Harmonische Gottes-
dienst).
LB:F83.
Glaubet, hoffet, leidet, duldet (Der Harmonisches
Gottesdienst).
LB:G278.
Grand Magnificat in C maj.
LB:G280.
Kleine Kantate von Walde an Au (Moralisch Kantaten).
LB:F83.

Lobt Gott, ihr Christen – Cantata.
LR:F105.
EB:G131.
Magnificat in C maj. 'Meine Seele erhebt den Herren.'
LB:G280.
Wie ist dein Name so gross – Motet.
LB:G279.
St. Luke Passion.
LB:G282.
St. Mark Passion.
LB:G283.
Der Tag des Gericht – Oratorio.
LB:G281.

TERANO (14th. cent.)
  b. Instrumental
  Rosetta.
  AN:B9.

TERZI, Giovanni Antonio (16th. cent.)
  b. Instrumental
  Amor e gratioso.
  LR:C26.
  Ballo tedesco e francese.
  LR:C23.
  Canzoni I and II (after Claudio da Corregio).
  LR:C26.
  Canzone francese.
  LR:A1.
  Chi passa.
  LR:C26.
  Contrapunto.
  LR:C26.
  Tre parti di gagliarde.
  LR:C23.

TESSARINI, Carlo (1690–1765)
  a. Orchestral
  Concerto in B flat maj for violin and strings. Op. 1, No. 7.
  LB:F71.

TESSIER, Guillaume (16th. cent.)
  d. Secular Vocal
  In a grove most rich of shade (Dowland's 'Musical
  Banquet.')
  LR:Gd30, Gd31.

THEILE, Johann (1646–1724)
  d. Secular Vocal
  Durchkläre dich, du Silbernacht – Aria.
  EB:F111.
  Was acht ich deine Gunst – Canzonette.
  EB:F111.

THIBAUT DE BLASON (13th. cent.)
  d. Secular Vocal (Instrumental Arrangements)
  Amours que porra.
  AA:A1.

THIBAUT DE COURVILLE, Joachim (1530–1581)
  d. Secular Vocal
  Si je languis d'un martire incogneu.
  LR:E48.

**THIBAUT DE NAVARRE (= THIBAUT DE CHAMPAGNE)
(1201–1253)**
  d. Secular Vocal (Including Instrumental Arrangements)
  Amors me fet commencier une chanson nouvele.
  AA:D24.
  Au tens plain de felonnie.
  AA:D22, D24.
  Ausi comme unicorne sui.
  AA:D24.
  L'autrier nuit en mon dormant.
  AA:D24.
  L'autrier, par la matinee.

AA:D24.
Bons Rois Thiebaut, Sire, conseillez moi.
AA:D24.
Chancon ferai car talent m'en est pris.
AA:D24.
Constume est bien.
AA:D24.
Contre le tens qui devise yver.
AA:D24.
Dame, cist vostre fins amis.
AA:D24.
Dame, ensi est q'il m'encouvient aler.
AA:D24.
De bone amour vient seance et biaute.
AA:D24.
Dex est ensi comme il pellicans.
AA:D24.
Dou tres doux non.
AA:A1.
Emperes ne rois N'ont nul povoir.
AA:D24.
Fueille ne flor ne vaut riens en chantant.
AA:D24.
J'aloie l'autrier errant sanz conpaignon.
AA:D24.
Je mi cuidoie partir.
AA:D24.
Je nos chanter trop tart.
AA:D24.
Li douz pensers et li douz souvenirs.
AA:D24.
Par dieu, Sire de Champagne et de Brie.
AA:D24.
Phelipe, je vous demant.
AA:D24.
Por conforter ma pesance faz un son.
AA:D24.
Por froidure ne por yver felon.
AA:D24.
Pour mau tens ne por geliee.
AA:D24.
Quant fine amour me prie que je chant.
AA:D24.
Robert, veez de perron.
AA:D24
Rois Thiebaut, Sire, en chanter reponnez.
AA:D24.
Seigneurs sachiez qui or ne s'en ira.
AA:D16, D24, E6.
Sire, nel me celez mie.
AA:D24.
Sires, fer faites me jugement.
AA:D24.
Tout autresi con l'entre fet venir.
AA:D24.
Une dolor enosee s'est dedenz mon cuer.
AA:D24.

TIBURTINO, Giuliano (16th. cent.)
b. Instrumental
Recercare a 3 'La sol fa mi fa.'
LR:A1, E24.

TINCTORIS, Johannes (1435–1511)
d. Secular Vocal
Helas le bon temps.
ER:A9.
Vostre regard.
ER:A9.
e. Sacred Vocal
Missa 'tre vocum': Kyrie.
ER:A2.
Virgo Dei.
LR:A6.

TINODI, Sebastian (c.1505–1556)
d. Secular Vocal – Verse Chronicles
About stewards and wine-butlers.
LR:E49.
The Capture of Peter Prini, Istvan Mailat and Balint Torok.
LR:E49.
The Death of Istvan Losonci at Temesvar Fortress.
LR:E49.
On the many drunkards.
LR:A5, E49.
The Seige of Eger.
LR:A5, E49.
Verse Chronicle (Unsp.)
LR:A6.
When Buda was occupied and Balint Torok put in prison.
LR:E49.
You, lieutenants who are in the army.
LR:A5, E49.

TISDALE, William (17th. cent.)
c. Keyboard
Coranto.
LR:Gc15.
Susanne un jour.
LR:Gc15.

TITELOUZE, Jean (1563–1633)
c. Keyboard – Organ
Ad coenam.
LR:D12.
Ave Maris stella.
LR:D11, D12.
EB:E67.
LB:E197, E216.
Exultet caelum.
LR:D11, D12.
Magnificat du 1re ton.
LR:D11.
Pange lingua.
LR:D11.
Urbs Hierusalem.
LR:D12.
Veni creator.
LR:D11, F41.
LB:E197.

TOLAR, Johann Baptiste (= Jan KRTITEL) (17th. cent.)
b. Instrumental
Balletto.
LR:B22.

TOLOZA – *see* GUIRAUT D'ESPANHA DE TOLOZA.

TOMELIN, Joseph (c.1640–1693)
c. Keyboard – Organ
Duo.
EB:E76.

TOMKINS, Thomas (1572–1656)
b. Instrumental – Consort
Almaine.
LR:Ga18, Gd16, Gd53.
Fantasia IX.
LR:Gd16.
Fantasia X.
LR:Gd16.
Fantasia XIV a 3.
SI:C1, C13.
Pavan.
LR:B10, Ga14, Gc10, Gd16.
Pavan I in F maj.
SI:C17.
c. Keyboard – Harpsichord and Organ
Barafostus' Dream.
LR:Gc9.
Clarifica me Pater.

LR:Gc6.
Fancy.
LR:Gc6, Ge27.
EB:E66.
LB:E184.
The Hunting Galliard.
LR:Gc10.
Lady Folliott's Galliard.
LR:Gd40.
Pavan and Galliard 'Earl Strafford.'
LR:Gc6.
Pavan and Galliard in G maj.
LR:Gc6.
Pavan and Galliard in A min.
LR:Gc6.
A Sad Pavan for these distracted times.
EB:B54, F107.
SI:A1.
A Short Verse.
LR:D20, Gc12.
Toy, made at Poole Court.
LR:Gc6.
A Verse in 3 parts.
LR:Ge27.
Voluntary.
LR:Gc6.
EB:E66.
LB:E184.
What if a day.
LR:Gc6.
Worcester Brawles.
LR:Gc6.

d. Secular Vocal
Adieu, ye city-prisoning towers.
LR:Gd33.
The Fauns and Satyrs (Triumphs of Oriana).
LR:Gd34, Gd35.
Music divine.
LR:Gd32.
O let me die.
LR:Gd54.
O let me live.
LR:Gd18, Gd54.
Oft did I marle.
LR:Gd16.
Oyez, has any found a lad.
LR:Gd16, Gd32.
See, see, the shepherd's Queen.
LR:Gd50.
To shady woods.
LR:Gd16.
Too much I once lamented.
LR:Gd16, Gd20, Gd32.
Weep no more thou sorry boy.
LR:E60, Gd50.

e. Sacred Vocal
Above the stars.
LR:Gd16.
Blessed be the Lord of Israel.
LR:Ge27.
Blessed is he.
LR:Ge27.
Deal with me, O Lord.
LR:Ge27.
Glory be to God.
LR:Ge27.
The Heavens declare.
LR:Ge27.
I heard a voice from heaven.
LR:Gd16.
Merciful Lord.
LR:Ge27.
My beloved spake.
LR:Gd16.

O God the proud are risen.
LR:Ge27.
O Lord, graciously accept.
LR:Ge27.
O Lord grant the King.
LR:Ge27.
O sing unto the Lord a new song.
LR:Gd16.
Put me not to rebuke.
LR:Ge27.
Then David mourned.
LR:Ge27.
When David heard that Absalom was slain.
LR:Gd39, Ge35, Ge36.
Withdraw not Thy mercy.
LR:Ge27.

TOPHAM, William (18th. cent.)
  b. Instrumental
  Sonata in C min for recorder and continuo.
  LB:B288.

TORELLI, Giuseppe (1658–1709)
  a. Orchestral
  Concerto a 4 for 2 violins, strings and continuo.
  EB:B60.
  Concerto No. 1 in D maj for trumpet and strings.
  LB:A354, A410, A654, A670.
  Concerto No. 2 in D maj for trumpet and strings.
  LB:A354, A410.
  Concerto No. 7 in G maj for trumpet, strings and
    continuo.
  LB:A662.
  Concerto Grosso in G min, Op. 8, No. 6, 'Christmas.'
  LB:A353, A582, A609, A610, A611.
  Concerto Grosso in E min, Op. 8, No. 9.
  LB:A18.
  Sinfonia in D maj for trumpet and strings.
  LB:A654.
  Sonata a 5 in D maj for trumpet and strings.
  LB:A598, A656, A663, A669.
  Suite No. 7 in D maj for trumpet and strings.
  LB:A666.
  b. Chamber and Instrumental
  Sonata in E min for 2 violins, cello and continuo, Op. 3,
    No. 7.
  EB:B62.

TORRE – see DE LA TORRE, Francisco.

TRABACI, Giovanni Maria (1580–1647)
  c. Keyboard – Organ
  Canzona francesca II.
  EB:E53.
  Canzona francesco VII cromatica.
  EB:E93.
  Consonanze stravaganti.
  EB:E53.
  Ricercare 1o tono con tre Fughe.
  EB:E53.
  Ricercare 6o tono con tre Fughe e suo riversi.
  EB:E53.
  Toccata per l'Elevatione.
  EB:E66.

TRANOSCIUS (= TRANOVSKY, Jiri) (1592–1637)
  e. Sacred Vocal
  Almi parenti omnium.
  EB:G140.
  Jo dies, jo dies.
  EB:G140.

TREBOR, Johannes (14th. cent.)
  d. Secular Vocal
  Quant joyne cuer.
  AA:A2.

AN:B16.
Se Alixandre et Hector.
AA:A2.
AN:B16.

TRIANA (15th. cent.)
d.Secular Vocal
Dinos, madre del donsel.
LR:E62.

THE TRIUMPHS OF ORIANA – Publ. Thomas Morley, 1601.
LR:Gd34, Gd35.

TROMBONCINI, Bartolomeo (c.1470–c.1535)
d.Secular Vocal (Including Instrumental Arrangements)
A la guerra.
EB:F93.
Ben chio amor.
LR:E63.
Che debb'io far?
LR:E47.
Deh per dio non mi far torto.
LR:E53.
Fate ben gents cortesse.
LB:B265.
Hor che'l ciel e la terra.
LR:A1, E24.
Io son l'occello.
LR:E25, E56.
Ostinato vo' seguire.
LR:A1, E24.
Pregori fronde, fiore, aque.
LR:E53.
Se e debile il filio a cui s'altene.
LR:E47.
Vale dira, vale in pace.
LB:B265.
e.Sacred Vocal
Ave Maria, gratia plena.
LR:A1.

TUMA, Frantisek Ignaz Anton (1704–1774)
a.Orchestral
Partita (Suite) in A maj for strings and continuo.
LB:A416.
Partita (Suite) in D min for strings and continuo.
LB:A416, A417, B313.
Sinfonia in A maj for strings and continuo.
LB:A416.
Sinfonia in B flat maj for strings and continuo.
LB:A416.
Sonata in E min for 2 trombones, strings and continuo.
LB:A416.
e.Sacred Vocal
Stabat mater.
LB:G257.

TUNDER, Franz (1614–1667)
c.Keyboard – Organ
Christ lag in Todesbanden.
EB:E38.
Komm, Heiliger Geist, Herre Gott.
EB:E62, E72.
Was kann uns kommen an für Noth.
EB:E35.
e.Sacred Vocal
Hosianna dem Sohne Davids.
LR:F105.
EB:G131.

TURCO, Giovanni de (16th./17th. cent.)
d.Secular Vocal
Occhi belli.
EB:F98.

TURGES, Edmund (15th. cent.)
e.Sacred Vocal
Enforce yourself as Godde's Knight.
LR:Gf4.

TURIN MS (12th.–15th. cent. French Court of Cyprus)
d.Secular Vocal
Je suis trestout.
AN:A14.
Pur haut et liement chanter.
AN:A14.
Pour leaulte maintenir.
AN:A14.
Qui n'a le cuer rainpli.
AN:A14.
e.Sacred Vocal
Credo in unum Deum.
AN:A14.
Gloria in excelsis Deo.
AN:A14.
Hunc diem festis.
AN:A14.

TURINI, Francesco (c.1589–1656)
b.Instrumental
Gagliarda a 3. (Primo libro di Madrigali, 1621).
EB:B45.
Sinfonia a 3 (Primo libro di Madrigali, 1621).
EB:B45.
Sonata in A min for 2 violins and continuo (Primo libro di Madrigali, 1621).
EB:B49.
Sonata (Unsp.)
EB:B45.

TURNHOUT, Jacob (15th. cent.)
d.Secular Vocal
Ghij meijskens.
EB:B35.

TUTILLON (= TUOTILO) (d.915)
e.Sacred Vocal
Omnipotens genitor (Kyrie trope).
AA:A3.

TYE, Christopher (c.1500–1573)
b.Instrumental – Consort
In Nomine.
LR:A1, Ga18.
In Nomine a 5 – 'Cyre.'
LR:Ga16.
In Nomine – 'Trust.'
LR:Ga17.
e.Sacred Vocal
Mass 'Euge bone.'
LR:Ge28.
Mass 'The Western Wind.'
LR:Ge28.

UCCELLINI, Marco (1610–1680)
b.Instrumental
Sonata in B flat maj, Op. 5.
LB:B325.

(DER) UNVERSAGTE (13th. cent.)
d.Secular Vocal
Der Kuninc Rodolph minnet got.
AA:D25.

UPSALA – *see* CANCIONERO DE UPSALA.

URREDA, Juan (WREEDE, Johannes) (15th. cent.)
d.Secular Vocal
De vos i de mi.
LR:A8.
Muy triste sera mi vida.

LR:A8.
Nunca fue pena mayor.
LR:A8.

VADO (17th. cent.)
  d. Secular Vocal
  No te embarques.
  EB:F97.

VAILLANT, Jean (14th./15th. cent.)
  d. Secular Vocal
  Par maintes fois.
  ER:A4.
  LR:A4.
  Tres doulz amis – Ma dame – Cent mille fois.
  AN:A2.

VALDERRABANO, Enriquez de (c.1500–c.1557)
  b. Instrumental
  Diferencias sobre 'Conde claros.'
  LR:C22.
  Diferencias sobre 'Guardame las vacas.'
  LR:E51.
  Diferencias sobre 'La Pavana.'
  LR:C8, E61.
  SI:A2.
  Fantasia XIII.
  LR:C8.
  Fantasia XIV.
  LR:C8.
  Pavana Real (*See also* Diferencias sobre 'La Pavana.')
  SI:A2.
  Soneto VII.
  LR:C8.
  Soneto VIII.
  LR:C8.
  SI:A2.
  Soneto IX.
  LR:C8.
  Soneto XI.
  LR:C8.
  Soneto XIII.
  LR:C8.
  SI:A2.
  Soneto XV.
  LR:C8.
  Viva la Margarita.
  LR:B24.
  d. Secular Vocal
  A monte sale el amor.
  LR:E51.
  De done venis, Amore?
  LR:E51, E62.
  Las tristas lagrimas mias.
  LR:E51.
  Los Bracos traygo cansados.
  LR:E61.
  Qui la dira.
  LR:E61.
  Sepurte guardo.
  LR:E61.
  e. Sacred Vocal
  Hyerusalem, Hyerusalem (after Ortiz).
  LR:E61.

VALENCIANO, Miguel Marti (17th. cent.)
  d. Secular Vocal
  Ay del amor.
  LB:F84.

VALENTE, Antonio (c.1520–c.1580)
  c. Keyboard – Organ
  Lo ballo dell' Intorcia.
  LB:D220.
  La Romanesca.

LR:D20, E27.
EB:E87.
Versi spirituali I–II.
LR:D18.

VALENTINE, Robert (= VALENTINO) (1680–1735)
  a. Orchestral
  Concerto in B flat maj for recorder and strings.
  LB:A632.
  Concerto in C maj for trumpet and strings (Arr. Concerto
    in C maj for oboe).
  LB:A667.
  b. Chamber and Instrumental
  Sonata in B flat maj for recorder and continuo.
  LB:B288.
  Sonata in C maj for trumpet and organ (Arr. Sonata No.
    10 in C maj for oboe and harpsichord).
  LB:B218.
  Sonata in G maj for recorder and continuo.
  LB:B273.

VALET, Nicolas (= VALLET) (c.1583–1642)
  b. Instrumental – Guitar
  Bourree I–II.
  EB:B40.
  Branle de la Royne.
  EB:B40.
  Galliarde.
  LR:C13.
  Les Pantalons.
  LR:E43, E44.
  Prelude.
  LR:C13.
  Slaep, soete slaep.
  LR:C13.

VAN DEN GHEYN, Matthias (1721–1785)
  c. Keyboard – Organ
  Fugue in F maj.
  EB:E78.
  Prelude and fugue in G min.
  EB:E88.
  LB:E225.
  Siciliane.
  EB:E78.

VAN DEN HOVE, Joachim (1567–1620)
  b. Instrumental – Lute
  Galliarde.
  LR:C13.
  Lieto godea.
  LR:C12.

VAN EYCK, Jacob (c.1590–1657)
  b. Instrumental
  Al liebben de Princem haren.
  LB:B253.
  Amarilli mia bella.
  LB:B294.
  Batalli.
  EB:F91.
  LB:B229, B278.
  Blyndshap van mijn vliedt.
  LB:B249.
  Les Bouffons.
  LR:E43.
  LB:B259, B297.
  Bravada.
  LB:B249.
  Come again.
  EB:B42.
  De Lof-zwangh Maris.
  LB:B249, B294.
  De roete roomer tuden.
  LB:B253.
  Doen Daphne d'over schoone Maeght.

EB:F107.
LB:B229, B278, B279, B286.
Echo Fantasia.
EB:B42.
Engels Nachtgaeltje.
LB:B229, B230, B249, B253, B267, B279, B287,
B294, B297.
Lachrymae Pavan.
LB:B229, B249, B253, B279, B280, B292.
Lavigogne.
LB:B302.
Stil, stil een Reys.
EB:B40.
Twede Roosemand.
LB:B253.
Wat zal men op den avond doen?
LB:B280.

VAN WEERBEKE, Gaspar (16th. cent.)
  e. Sacred Vocal
  Panis angelis.
  EB:B35.

VAN WICHEL, Philippus (17th. cent.)
  b. Instrumental
  Sonata I for 2 violins and continuo.
  EB:B35.

VAN WILDER, Philip (15th./16th. cent.)
  d. Secular Vocal
  Je fille quant dieu me donne ce quoy.
  LR:Gf5.

VASQUEZ, Juan (c.1500–c.1560)
  d. Secular Vocal
  De los alamos vengos.
  SI:A2.
  Duelete de mi, Senora.
  LR:E31.
  En la fuente del rosel.
  LR:E62.
  Lagrimas de mi consuelo.
  LR:E65.
  Lindos ojos aveys, senora.
  LR:A1.
  Los bracos traygo cansados – Romance de Don Beltran.
  LR:E30.
  Pues non me quereis – Romance I.
  LR:E30.
  Si me llaman.
  LR:A8.
  Vos me matastes.
  LR:E62.

VAUTOR, Thomas (b.1590)
  d. Secular Vocal
  Mother I will have a husband.
  LR:Gd33, Gd52.
  Shepherds and Nymphs.
  LR:Gd50.
  Sweet Suffolk Owl.
  LR:Gd20, Gd32, Gd56.
  Weep, weep, mine eyes.
  LR:Gd53.

VECCHI, Orazio (c.1540–1605)
  b. Instrumental
  Il Grillo.
  LR:F106.
  Saltarello.
  LR:E63, Ga11.
  Saltavan ninfe.
  LR:Ga9.
  d. Secular Vocal
  L'Amfiparnasso – Madrigal Comedy.
  LR:E17, E18.

Il bianco e dolce cigno.
LR:E39, E71.
Leva la man di qui vezzosa Clori.
LR:E40.
Quando mirai le bella faccia d'oro.
LR:E40.
So ben mi c'ha bon tempo.
LR:Gd42.
EB:B41, F96.
Tiridola non dormire.
LR:E22.

VEJVANOVSKY, Pavel Josef (1640–1693)
  a. Orchestral
  Balletti pro tabula.
  LB:A616.
  Harmonia Romana.
  LB:A616.
  Serenata in C maj for 2 clarinos, strings and continuo
  (1670).
  EB:A30.
  Serenata a 4 in C maj for brass and strings (1680).
  EB:A30.
  Sonata II a 6 in C maj for strings and continuo (1666).
  EB:A30.
  Sonata a 6 in C maj for 3 trombones, strings and
  continuo, 'La Posta' (1667).
  EB:A30.
  LB:A616.
  Sonata a 7 in C maj for 2 clarinos, strings and continuo
  (1666).
  EB:A30.
  Sonata a 7 in C maj for 2 clarinos, strings and continuo
  (1666).
  EB:A30.
  Sonata a 10 in C maj for 2 clarinos, 2 trombones, strings
  and continuo (1666).
  EB:A30.
  Sonata Paschalis in C maj for 2 violins, strings and
  continuo (1666).
  EB:A30.
  Sonata Natalis.
  LB:A616.
  Sonata tribus quandam.
  LB:A616.
  Suite XIV a 6, 'La Campanarum.'
  LB:A615.

VENETO, Francesco (17th. cent.)
  d. Secular Vocal
  Nasce l'aspro mio tormento.
  EB:F93.

VENTADORN – see BERNARD DE VENTADORN.

VENTO, Ivo de (d.c.1575)
  d. Secular Vocal
  Frisch ist mein Sinn.
  LR:E70.
  Ich bin elend.
  LR:F94.
  Ich weiss ein Maidelein.
  LR:E70, F94.
  So wünsch' ich ihr gute Nachte.
  LR:E70.
  Vor etlich wenig Tagen.
  LR:F94.

VENTURINI, Francesco (d.1745)
  a. Orchestral
  Overture in A min for 2 flutes, 2 oboes, bassoon, 2
  violins, strings and continuo, Op. 1.
  EB:F109.

VERACINI, Francesco Maria (1690–1768)
  b. Chamber and Instrumental

Sonata in A min for recorder and continuo.
LB:B260, B283.
Sonata in D min for recorder and continuo, Op. 1, No. 3.
LB:B262.
Sonata in E min for violin and continuo, Op. 1.
LB:B318.
Sonata in F maj for flute and continuo.
LB:B235.
Sonata in G maj for recorder and continuo.
LB:B260, B261.

VERARDI (16th. cent.)
   d. Secular Vocal
     Viva el gran Rey Don Fernando.
     LR:E26.

VERBONNET – *see* **GHISELIN, Johannes.**

VERDELOT, Philippe (d.c.1552)
   d. Secular Vocal
     Amor quanto piu lieto.
     LR:E39.
     Donna, se fera stella.
     LR:E39.
     La bella dona.
     LR:E39.
     Madonna il tuo bel viso.
     ER:A4.
     Madonna, non so dire.
     LR:E39.
     Madonna, per voi ardo.
     LR:E39.
     Madonna, qual certezza.
     LR:A1.
     O dolce notte.
     LR:E39.
     Quelle che sospirand' ogn' hor desio.
     LR:E39.
     Se l'ardor foss' equale.
     LR:E39.
     Trist' Amarilli.
     LR:E39.
   e. Sacred Vocal
     Ave sanctissima Maria.
     ER:A3.

VIADANA, Ludovico Garsi de (1564–1627)
   e. Sacred Vocal
     Exultate justi.
     LR:F81.
     Laetare Jerusalem.
     EB:G135.
     Nocte surgentes vigilemus omnes.
     EB:F93.

VICTORIA, Tomas Luis de (c.1540–1611)
   e. Sacred Vocal
     Ascendus Christus.
     LR:F71.
     Ave Maria.
     LR:F68, F69, F71, F80, F81, F83, F89.
     Beati immaculati.
     LR:F89.
     Domine non sum Dignus.
     LR:F89.
     Due seraphim clamabant.
     LR:F89.
     Estote fortes in bello.
     LR:F71.
     Gaudent in caelis.
     LR:F71.
     Hic vir descipiens mundum.
     LR:F71.
     In annuntiatione benissimae Mariae.
     LR:E27.
     Iste sanctus.

LR:F71.
Jesu dulcis memoria.
LR:F69.
Lauda Sion salvatorem.
LR:F69.
Litanie de Beata Virgine.
LR:F71.
Magnificat primi toni.
LR:F69, F71, F89.
Missa 'O quam gloriosa.'
LR:F71, Ge10.
Missa pro defunctis, Requiem.
LR:F71, F72.
Missa 'pro Victoria.'
LR:F68.
Nigra sum.
LR:E60.
O Ildephonse.
LR:F89.
O magnum mysterium.
LR E27, F96, F119.
O regem caeli.
LR:F98.
O sacrum convivium.
LR:F89.
Officium Hebdomadae Sanctae.
LR:F73, F74.
Pueri Hebraeorum vestimenta.
LR:F79.
Quam pulchri sunt gressus tui.
LR:F89.
Salve regina.
LR:F89.
Sancta Maria.
LR:F89.
Senex puerum portavit.
LR:F89.
Super flumina Babylonis.
LR:F89.
Veni sponsor Christi.
LR:F71.
Vere languores.
LR:F79.
Videte omnes populi.
LR:Ge39.
Vide speciosam.
LR:F80.

VIDAL, Pierre (d.c.1215)
   d. Secular Vocal
     Baron de mon dan covit.
     AA:D3, D5, D10.
     Anc no mori per amor.
     LR:A6.
     Pois tornatz sui en Proensa.
     AA:D9.
     Vida et Razos.
     AA:D10.

VIETORISZ CODEX (17th. cent. Hungarian.)
   b./d. Instrumental/Secular Vocal
     Dances and Songs.
     LR:A5, E55.
     EB:B66, B70.

VILA – *see* **ALBERCH I VILA.**

VINCENT (17th. cent.)
   d. Secular Vocal
     J'aye une fille de village.
     LR:E43.

VINCENT, Thomas (18th. cent.)
   b. Chamber and Instrumental
     Sonata in A min for oboe and continuo, Op. 1, No. 2.
     LB:B228.

VINCENZO DA RIMINI (= VINCENTIUS DE ARIMINO) (14th. cent.)
  d. Secular Vocal
    Ay schonsolato ed amoroso.
    AA:A1.
    In forma quasi.
    AN:B3.

VINCI, Leonardo (1690–1730)
  b. Instrumental
    Sonata in D maj for flute and continuo.
    L:B225, B301.
  d. Secular Vocal – Stage Works
    Didone Abbandonata – Opera, 1735: Sinfonia in F maj.
    LB:F79.

VINDERS, Hieronymous (16th. cent.)
  e. Sacred Vocal
    O mors inevitabilis – Requiem aeternam (Deploration on the Death of Josquin).
    ER:B30.
    LR:A2.

VINIER – *see* GUILLAUME LE VINIER.

VIRGILIANO, Aurelio (16th. cent.)
  b. Instrumental
    Ricercare VI come di sopra (Il Dolcimelo).
    EB:B45.

VISEE – *see* DE VISEE, Robert.

VITALI, Tommaso Antonio (1663–1745)
  b. Chamber and Instrumental
    Chaconne in G min for violin and continuo.
    EB:B68.
    LB:B161, B315.
    Sinfonia for 2 trumpets, 2 oboes, strings and continuo.
    EB:B60.
    Sonata in B min for 2 violins, cello and continuo.
    EB:B62.

VITRY – *see* DE VITRY, Philippe.

VIVALDI, Antonio (1678–1741)
  a. Orchestral – Concertos With Op. Nos: Opp. 3, 4, 6–12
    Concertos for 1, 2 or 4 violins and strings, Op. 3, Nos. 1–12, 'L'Estro Armonico.'
      1 in D maj for 4 vlns; 2 in G min for 2 vlns; 3 in G maj for 1 vln; 4 in E min for 4 vlns; 5 in A maj for 2 vlns; 6 in A min for 1 vln; 7 in F maj for 4 vlns; 8 in A min for 2 vlns; 9 in D maj for 1 vln; 10 in B min for 4 vlns; 11 in D min for 2 vlns; 12 in E maj for 1 vln.
    LB:A418, A419, A420, A421, A422, A426, A427.
    Concerto in D maj for 4 violins and strings, Op. 3, No. 1.
    LB:A423, A508.
    Concerto in G min for 2 violins and strings, Op. 3, No. 2.
    LB:A568.
    Concerto in G maj for violin and strings, Op. 3, No. 3.
    LB:A149, A423, A424, A425.
    Concerto in E min for 4 violins and strings, Op. 3, No. 4.
    LB:A423, A508.
    Concerto in A maj for 2 violins and strings, Op. 3, No. 5.
    LB:A423.
    Concerto in A min for violin and strings, Op. 3, No. 6.
    LB:A351, A423, A424, A425.
    Concerto in F maj for 4 violins and strings, Op. 3, No. 7.
    LB:A508.
    Concerto in A min for 2 violins and strings, Op. 3, No. 8.
    LB:A179, A425, A582, A594.
    Concerto in A min for 2 violins and strings, Op. 3, No. 8: Allegro.
    LB:A617.
    Concerto in D maj for violin and strings, Op. 3, No. 9.
    LB:A423, A424, A425.
    Concerto in D maj for guitar and strings, Arr. Op. 3, No. 9.
    LB:A532.

Concerto in B min for 4 violins and strings, Op. 3, No. 10.
LB:A149, A202, A425, A477, A499, A508, A562, A571, A584, A594.
Concerto in D min for 2 violins and strings, Op. 3, No. 11.
LB:A499, A502, A568, A607.
Concerto in D min for 2 violins and strings, Op. 3, No. 11: Largo e spicato.
LB:A599, A641.
Concerto in E maj for violin and strings, Op. 3, No. 12.
LB:A424.
Concertos for violin and strings, Op. 4, Nos. 1–12, 'La Stravaganza.'
  1 in B flat maj; 2 in E min; 3 in G maj; 4 in A min; 5 in A maj; 6 in G min; 7 in C maj; 8 in D min; 9 in F maj; 10 in C maj; 11 in D maj; 12 in G maj.
LB:A427, A428, A429, A430.
Concerto in B flat maj for violin and strings, Op. 4, No. 1.
LB:A594.
Concerto in G maj for violin and strings, Op. 4, No. 3.
LB:A431, A516.
Concerto in D min for violin and strings, Op. 4, No. 8.
LB:A431, A516.
Concertos for violin and strings, Op. 6, Nos. 1–12.
  1 in G min; 2 in E flat maj; 3 in G min; 4 in D maj; 5 in E min; 6 in D min.
LB:A432, A433.
Concertos for violin or oboe and strings, Op. 7, Nos. 1–12.
  1 in B flat maj for oboe; 2 in C maj for vln; 3 in G min for vln; 4 in A min for vln; 5 in F maj for vln; 6 in B flat maj for vln; 7 in B flat maj for oboe; 8 in G maj for vln; 9 in B flat maj for vln; 10 in F maj for vln; 11 in D maj for vln; 12 in D maj for vln.
LB:A434, A435, A436.
Concerto in B flat maj for oboe and strings, Op. 7, No. 1.
LB:A556.
Concerto in B flat maj for trumpet and strings, 'Il Barocco', Arr. RV40 and Op. 7, No. 1.
LB:A667.
Concerto in C maj for violin and strings, Op. 7, No. 2.
LB:F71.
Concerto in B flat maj for oboe and strings, Op. 7, No. 7.
LB:A555.
Concertos for violin or oboe and strings, Op. 8, Nos. 1–12, 'Il Cimento dell'Armonia e dell'Inventione.'
  1 in E maj, 'La Primavera'; 2 in G min, 'L'Estate'; 3 in F maj, 'L'Autumno'; 4 in F min, 'L'Inverno'; 5 in E flat maj, 'La Tempesta di Mare'; 6 in C maj, 'Il Piacere'; 7 in D min; 8 in G min; 9 in D min for vln or oboe; 10 in B flat maj, 'La Caccia'; 11 in D maj; 12 in C maj for vln or oboe.
LB:A436, A437, A438.
Concertos for violin and strings, Op. 8, Nos. 1–4, 'The Four Seasons.'
LB:A427, A439, A440, A441, A442, A443, A444, A445, A446, A447, A448, A449, A450, A451, A452, A453, A454, A455, A456, A457, A458, A459, A460, A461, A462, A463, A464, A465, A466, A467, A468, A469, A470, A471, A472, A473, A474, A475, A476, A477.
Concerto in E flat maj for violin and strings, 'Il Tempesto di Mare', Op. 8, No. 5.
LB:A478, A479, A480.
Concerto in C maj for violin and strings, 'Il Piacere', Op. 8, No. 6.
LB:A478, A479, A480.
Concerto in D min for violin and strings, Op. 8, No. 7.
LB:A478, A479, A480.
Concerto in G min for violin and strings, Op. 8, No. 8.
LB:A478, A479, A480.
Concerto in D min for violin or oboe and strings, Op. 8, No. 9.
LB:A478, A481, A546.
Concerto in B flat maj for violin and strings, 'La Caccia',

Op. 8, No. 10.
LB:A478, A479, A481.
Concerto in D maj for violin and strings. Op. 8, No. 11.
LB:A478, A481.
Concerto in C maj for violin or oboe and strings, Op. 8, No. 12.
LB:A478, A481, A546, A555, A556, A626.
Concertos for 1 or 2 violins and strings, Op. 9, Nos. 1–12, 'La Cetra.'
  1 in C maj; 2 in A maj; 3 in G min; 4 in E maj; 5 in A min; 6 in A maj; 7 in B flat maj; 8 in D min; 9 in B flat maj for 2 vlns; 10 in G maj; 11 in C min; 12 in B min.
LB:A427, A433, A482, A483, A484.
Concertos for flute and strings, Op. 10, Nos. 1–6.
  1 in F maj; 2 in G min; 3 in D maj; 4 in G maj; 5 in F maj; 6 in G maj.
LB:A485, A486, A487, A488, A489, A490, A491, A492, A493, A494.
Concerto in F maj for flute and strings, 'La Tempesta di Mare', Op. 10, No. 1.
LB:A434, A537, A540, A566, A575.
Concerto in G min for flute and strings, 'La Notte', Op. 10, No. 2.
EB:B50.
LB:A337, A477, A536, A540, A551, A565, A566, A568, A571, A597.
Concerto in D maj for flute and strings, 'Il Gardellino', Op. 10, No. 3.
LB:A566.
Concerto in F maj for flute and strings, Op. 10, No. 5.
LB:A354, A562.
Concertos for violin or oboe and strings, Op. 11, Nos. 1–6.
  1 in D maj; 2 in E min, 'Il Favorito'; 3 in A maj; 4 in G maj; 5 in C min; 6 in G min.
LB:A494.
Concerto in G min for oboe and strings, Op. 11, No. 6.
LB:A540, A541, A620.
Concertos for violin and strings, Op. 12, Nos. 1–6.
  1 in G min; 2 in D min; 3 in D maj; 4 in C maj; 5 in B flat maj; 6 in B flat maj.
LB:A494.
Concerto in G min for violin and strings, Op. 12, No. 1.
LB:A431, A516.

a. Orchestral – Concertos for several instruments and continuo, RV87–108
Concerto in C maj for recorder, oboe, 2 violins and continuo, P81:RV87.
LB:A438, A544, A557, A622.
Concerto in C maj for flute, violin, oboe, bassoon and continuo, P82:RV88.
LB:A534.
Concerto in D maj for recorder, violin, bassoon (or violin) without bass, P198:RV92.
LB:A549, B257.
Concerto in D maj for lute, 2 violins and continuo, P209:RV93.
LB:A231, A327, A527, A529, A531, A565.
Concerto in D maj for guitar and strings, Arr. RV93.
LB:A528, A532.
Concerto in D maj for recorder, violin, oboe, bassoon and continuo, P207:RV94.
LB:A415, A438, A544.
Concerto in F maj for viola d'amore, 2 horns, 2 oboes, bassoon and continuo, P286:RV97.
LB:A518, A523.
Concerto in F maj for flute, violin, bassoon and continuo, P322:RV100.
LB:B168.
Concerto in G min for recorder, oboe and bassoon without bass, P402:RV103.
LB:A534.
Concerto in G min for flute (or violin), 2 violins, bassoon and continuo, 'La Notte', RV104.

LB:A438.
Concerto in G min for recorder, violin, oboe, bassoon and continuo, P403:RV105.
LB:A438, A544.
Concerto in G min for flute, violin, bassoon (or 2 violins), viola and continuo, P404:RV106.
LB:A534, B168.
Concerto in G min for flute, oboe, bassoon and continuo, P360:RV107.
LB:A438, A534, A545.
Concerto in A min for recorder, 2 violins and continuo, P77:RV108.
LB:A438, A537, A540, A543, A544, A547, A549, A554.

a. Orchestral – Concertos, Sinfonias and Sonatas for strings, RV109–169
Sinfonia in C maj for strings and continuo, PS23:RV112.
LB:A497.
Concerto in C maj for strings and continuo, P27:RV114.
LB:A497, A500, A512.
Sinfonia in C maj for strings and continuo, PS2:RV116.
LB:A497.
Concerto in C min for strings and continuo, P422:RV119.
LB:A497, A500, A557, A568, A620.
Concerto in C min for strings and continuo, P427:RV120.
LB:A502, A507, A512.
Concerto in D maj for strings and continuo, P191:RV123.
LB:A507.
Concerto in D maj for strings and continuo, P157:RV124.
LB:A507.
Concerto in D maj for strings and continuo, P197:RV126.
LB:A497, A500.
Concerto in D min for strings and continuo, P280:RV127.
LB:A509.
Concerto in D min for strings and continuo, P294:RV128.
LB:A512.
Concerto in D min for strings and continuo, 'Madrigalesco', P197:RV129.
LB:A495, A497, A507, A566, A567, A568, A572, A574.
Sonata a 4 in E flat maj for strings and continuo, 'Al Santo Sepulchro', P441:RV130.
LB:A438, A497, A509, A566, A570, G304.
Sinfonia in E maj for strings and continuo, PS19:RV131.
LB:A497.
Sinfonia in E maj for strings and continuo, PS13:RV132.
LB:A497, A512.
Concerto in E min for strings and continuo, P113:RV133.
LB:A512.
Sinfonia in E min for strings and continuo, P127:RV134.
LB:A497, A512.
Sinfonia in F maj for strings and continuo, PS17:RV137.
LB:A497.
Concerto in F maj for strings and continuo, P313:RV138.
LB:A497, A500.
Sinfonia in F maj for strings and continuo, PS4:RV140.
LB:A506, A512.
Concerto in F maj for strings and continuo, P291:RV141.
LB:A497, A500.
Sinfonia in G maj for strings and continuo, PS8:RV146.
LB:A512.
Sinfonia in G maj for strings and continuo, PS3:RV149.
LB:A497, A500, A506, A509.
Concerto in G maj for strings and continuo, 'Alla rustica',

P143:RV151.
LB:A495, A502, A512, A574.
Concerto in G min for strings and continuo,
P371:RV152.
LB:A506, A507, A512.
Concerto in G min for strings and continuo,
P394:RV153.
LB:A497.
Concerto in G min for strings and continuo,
P362:RV154.
LB:A497, A500.
Concerto in G min for strings and continuo,
P407:RV155.
LB:A507, A509.
Concerto in G min for strings and continuo,
P392:RV156.
LB:A497.
Concerto in G min for strings and continuo,
P361:RV157.
LB:A438, A497, A500, A512, A545.
Concerto in A maj for strings and continuo,
P235:RV158.
LB:A497, A502, A512.
Concerto in A maj for strings and continuo,
P231:RV159.
LB:A572.
Concerto in B flat maj for strings and continuo, 'Conca',
P410:RV163.
LB:A512.
Concerto in B flat maj for strings and continuo,
P400:RV167.
LB:A512.
Sinfonia in B min for strings and continuo, PS22:RV168.
LB:A497, A512.
Sinfonia in B min for strings and continuo, 'Al Santo
Sepulchro', PS21:RV169.
LB:A438, A495, A509, A570, A572, G304.
Sinfonia in G maj for strings and continuo (Unsp.)
EB:A31.
LB:A613.

a.Orchestral – Concertos for 1 violin and strings,
RV170–391
Concerto in'C maj for violin and strings, P14:RV179.
LB:A504.
Concerto in C maj for violin and strings, P88:RV186.
LB:A505.
Concerto in C min for violin and strings, 'Il Sospetto',
P419:RV199.
LB:A351, A498, A503, A505.
Concerto in D maj for violin and strings, 'Grosso Mogul',
RV208.
LB:A438.
Concerto in D maj for violin and strings, 'Solennita della
S. Lingua di S. Antonio in Padua', P165:RV212.
LB:A511, D221.
Concerto in D maj for violin and strings, P163:RV213.
LB:A86.
Concerto in D maj for violin and strings, P143:RV230.
LB:A503.
Concerto in D maj for violin and strings, 'L'Inquietudine',
P208:RV234.
LB:A495, A498, A567, A570.
Concerto in E flat maj for violin and strings,
P429:RV254.
LB:A20.
Concerto in E maj for violin and strings, 'Il Riposo'/'Per il
Natale', P248:RV270.
LB:A498.
Concerto in E maj for violin and strings, 'L'Amoroso',
P246:RV271.
LB:A495, A497, A498, A501, A503.
Concerto in E min for violin and strings, 'Il Favorito',
P106:RV277.
LB:A498, A503, A506.

Concerto in F maj for violin and strings, 'Per la Solennita
di S. Lorenzo', P290:RV286.
LB:A511.
Concerto in G maj for violin and strings, P107:RV308.
LB:A503.
Concerto in A maj for violin and strings, 'Per il M.
Pisendel', P228:RV340.
LB:A506.
Concerto in A maj for violin and strings, P234:RV350.
LB:A505.
Concerto in A maj for violin and strings, P236:RV352.
LB:A505.

a.Orchestral – Concertos for viola d'amore, RV392–397
(*See also* RV540)
Concerto in D maj for viola d'amore and strings,
P166:RV392.
LB:A518, A519, A520, A523, A525.
Concerto in D min for viola d'amore and strings,
P289:RV393.
LB:A518, A523.
Concerto in D min for viola d'amore and strings,
P288:RV394.
LB:A515, A518, A523.
Concerto in D min for viola d'amore and strings,
P297:RV395a.
LB:A518, A519, A523.
Concerto in A maj for viola d'amore and strings,
P233:RV396.
LB:A362, A518, A519, A523, A592.
Concerto in A min for viola d'amore and strings,
P37:RV397.
LB:A518, A519, A523.

a.Orchestral – Concertos for cello, RV398–424 (*See*
***also* RV484, 498)**
Concerto in C maj for cello and strings, P31:RV398.
LB:A377.
Concerto in C min for cello and strings, P434:RV401.
LB:A497, A501, A608.
Concerto in E flat maj for cello and strings, P424:RV408.
LB:A524.
Concerto in E min for cello and strings, P119:RV409.
LB:A567, A575.
Concerto in G maj for cello and strings, P120:RV413.
LB:A377, A524.
Concerto in G maj for cello and strings, P118:RV414.
LB:A518, A522.
Concerto in G maj for cello and strings, RV415.
LB:A521.
Concerto in G min for cello and strings, RV416.
LB:A521.
Concerto in G min for cello and strings, P369:RV417.
LB:A518, A522.
Concerto in A maj for cello and strings, P35:RV418.
LB:A518, A522.
Concerto in A min for cello and strings, RV420.
LB:A518, A522.
Concerto in A min for cello and strings, P24:RV422.
LB:A230.
Concerto in B min for cello and strings, P180:RV424.
LB:A438, A478, A524, A570.

a.Orchestral – Concerto for mandolin and strings,
RV425
Concerto in C maj for mandolin and strings,
P134:RV425.
LB:A517, A526, A530, A531, A571, A573.
Concerto in C maj for guitar and strings, Arr. RV425.
LB:A528, A532, A671.

a.Orchestral – Concertos for flute, RV426–440
Concerto in D maj for flute and strings, P203:RV427.
LB:A493, A536, A539, A540, A554.
Concerto in D maj for flute and strings, P205:RV429.
LB:A478, A493, A536, A540, A543.
Concerto in F maj for flute, oboe, bassoon and strings,
P261:RV433.

LB:A533, A557.
Concerto in F maj for flute and strings, P262:RV434.
LB:A543.
Concerto in G maj for flute and strings, P104:RV435.
LB:A543.
Concerto in G maj for flute and strings, P140:RV436.
LB:A493, A536, A540, A550.
Concerto in G maj for flute and strings, P118/141:
  RV438.
LB:A493, A537, A540, A550, A567.
Concerto in G min for flute, bassoon and strings,
  P342:RV439.
LB:A557, A596.
Concerto in A min for flute and strings, P80:RV440.
LB:A493, A536, A540, A550, A554.

**a. Orchestral – Concertos for recorder and flautino,
RV441–445**
Concerto in C min for recorder and strings,
  P440:RV441.
LB:A427, A438, A493, A537, A539, A540, A550,
  A551, A560, A633, A646, B260, B286.
Concerto in F maj for recorder and strings, RV442.
LB:A415, A438, A554, A631.
Concerto in C maj for flautino and strings, P79:RV443.
LB:A427, A502, A543, A547, A549, A554, A561,
  A564, A565, A571, A577, A591, A643, B287.
Concerto in C maj for flautino and strings, P78:RV444.
LB:A515, A547, A551.
Concerto in A min for flautino and strings, P83:RV445.
LB:A515, A535, A547, A549, A551, A576, A623,
  B227.

**a. Orchestral – Concertos for oboe, RV446–465 (See
also RV485, 500)**
Concerto in C maj for oboe and strings, P41:RV447.
LB:A540, A541, A555, A559, A644.
Concerto in C maj for oboe and strings, P43:RV448.
LB:A21, A556.
Concerto in C maj for oboe and strings, P50:RV450.
LB:A540, A541, A546.
Concerto in C maj for oboe and strings, P44:RV451.
LB:A540, A542, A556.
Concerto in C maj for oboe and strings, P91:RV452.
LB:A555.
Concerto in D maj for oboe and strings, P187:RV453.
LB:A540, A542, A546, A555.
Concerto in D min for oboe and strings, P259:RV454.
LB:A624, A642.
Concerto in F maj for oboe and strings, P306:RV455.
LB:A540, A542, A556.
Concerto in F maj for oboe and strings, P264:RV456.
LB:A427, A546, A556, A560.
Concerto in F maj for oboe and strings, RV457.
LB:A540, A542.
Concerto in A min for oboe and strings, P42:RV461.
LB:A21, A438, A539, A540, A541, A542, A546, A555,
  A567, A568, A570, A630.
Concerto in A min for oboe and strings, RV463.
LB:A540.

a. Orchestral – Concertos for bassoon, RV466–504
Concerto in C maj for bassoon and strings, P45:RV472.
LB:A552.
Concerto in C maj for bassoon and strings, P90:RV473.
LB:A552.
Concerto in C maj for bassoon and strings, P56:RV475.
LB:A533.
Concerto in C maj for bassoon and strings, P52:RV479.
LB:A558.
Concerto in C min for bassoon and strings,
  P432:RV480.
LB:A553.
Concerto in D min for bassoon and strings,
  P282:RV481.
LB:A562.
Concerto in E min for bassoon and strings, P137:RV484.

LB:A438, A535, A538, A539, A540, A545, A548,
  A553.
Concerto in E min for cello and strings, Arr.
  P137:RV484.
LB:A564.
Concerto in F maj for oboe and strings, Arr.
  P318:RV485.
LB:A644.
Concerto in F maj for bassoon and strings, P299:RV488.
LB:A558.
Concerto in F maj for bassoon and strings, P305:RV489.
LB:A538, A540, A548.
Concerto in F maj for bassoon and strings, P307:RV490.
LB:A552.
Concerto in G maj for bassoon and strings, P128:RV492.
LB:A553.
Concerto in G maj for bassoon and strings, P131:RV493.
LB:A552.
Concerto in G min for bassoon and strings,
  P381:RV496.
LB:A553.
Concerto in A min for bassoon and strings, P72:RV497.
LB:A552, A558.
Concerto in A min for bassoon and strings, P70:RV498.
LB:A427, A538, A540, A548, A559, A560, A586.
Concerto in A min for cello and strings, Arr. P70:RV498.
LB:A352.
Concerto in A min for oboe and strings, Arr. P89:RV500.
LB:A197, A438, A545.
Concerto in B flat maj for bassoon and strings, 'La Notte',
  P401:RV501.
LB:A548, A553, A558, A620.
Concerto in B flat maj for bassoon and strings,
  P382:RV502.
LB:A538, A540.
Concerto in B flat maj for bassoon and strings,
  P387:RV513.
LB:A548, A558.

a. Orchestral – Concertos for 2 violins, RV505–530
Concerto in C min for 2 violins and strings, P436:RV509.
LB:A496.
Concerto in C min for 2 violins and strings, P435:RV510.
LB:A414.
Concerto in D maj for 2 violins and strings, P189:RV512.
LB:A496.
Concerto in D min for 2 violins and strings, P281:RV514.
LB:A414, A496, A528.
Concerto in E flat maj for 2 violins and strings, P423:
  RV515.
LB:A520.
Concerto in G maj for 2 violins and strings, P132:RV516.
LB:A517.
Concerto in G min for 2 violins and strings, P366:RV517.
LB:A496.
Concerto in A min for 2 violins and strings, P2:RV522.
LB:A499.
Concerto in A min for 2 violins and strings, P28:RV523.
LB:A497, A501, A517.
Concerto in B flat maj for 2 violins and continuo, P390:
  RV524.
LB:A562.
Concerto in B flat maj for 2 violins and continuo, P389:
  RV525.
LB:A497.
Concerto in B flat maj for 2 violins and strings,
  P365:RV527.
LB:A497.

**a. Orchestral – Concertos for 2 instruments,
RV531–548**
Concerto in G min for 2 cellos and strings, P411:RV531.
LB:A17, A497, A520, A524, A574.
Concerto in G maj for 2 mandolins and strings, P133:
  RV532.
LB:A327, A526, A530, A531, A571, A577, A589.

Concerto in C maj for 2 flutes and strings, P76:RV533.
LB:A537, A540, A574.
Concerto in C maj for 2 oboes and strings, P85:RV534.
LB:A562, A573.
Concerto in D min for 2 oboes and strings, P302:RV535.
LB:A427, A535, A561.
Concerto in A min for 2 oboes and strings, P53:RV536.
LB:A557.
Concerto in C maj for 2 trumpets and strings,
P75:RV537.
LB:A477, A565, A571, A572, A574, A576, A594,
A616, A654, A655, A656, A662, A669, B209, B224.
Concerto in F maj for 2 horns and strings, P320:RV538.
LB:A413, A533, A572, A575.
Concerto in F maj for 2 horns and strings, P321:RV539.
LB:A354, A427, A533, A561.
Concerto in D min for viola d'amore, lute and strings.
P266:RV540.
LB:A509, A515, A518, A523, A526, A527, A529,
A564, A573.
Concerto in D min for violin, organ and strings, P311:
RV541.
LB:A513, A563, A569.
Concerto in F maj for violin, organ and strings, P274:
RV542.
LB:A497, A513, A563, A576.
Concerto in C maj for oboe, 2 violins, organ and strings,
P36:RV544a.
LB:A513.
Concerto in G maj for oboe, bassoon and strings, P129:
RV545.
LB:A517, A535, A559.
Concerto in A maj for violin, cello and strings, P238:
RV546.
LB:A497.
Concerto in B flat maj for violin, cello and strings, P388:
RV547.
LB:A497, A501, A569, A577.
Concerto in B flat maj for oboe, violin and strings, P406:
RV548.
LB:A557, A576.
Concerto in B flat maj for trumpet and strings, Arr.
P406:RV548.
LB:A378.

a. Orchestral – Concertos for 3 or 4 violins, RV549–553
Concerto in D maj for 4 violins and strings, P146:RV549
– See Op. 3, No. 1.
Concerto in E min for 4 violins and strings, P97:RV550
– See Op. 3, No. 4.
Concerto in F maj for 3 violins and strings, P278:RV551.
LB:A431, A497, A602.
Concerto in A maj 'con violino principale, con altro
violino in lontano, per echo' and strings, P222:RV552.
LB:A179, A497, A564, A565, A566.
Concerto in B flat maj for 4 violins and strings, P367:
RV553.
LB:A497, A499, A508, A516, A577, A592.

**a. Orchestral – Concertos for several instruments,
RV554–580**
Concerto in C maj for violin, organ (or violin), oboe and
strings, P36:RV554.
LB:A563.
Concerto in C maj for 2 oboes, 2 clarinos, 2 recorders, 2
violins, bassoon and strings, 'Per la Solennita di S.
Lorenzo', P84:RV556.
LB:A510, A518.
Concerto in C maj for 2 violins 'in tromba marina', 2
recorders, 2 mandolins, 2 salmoe, violin, 2 theorbos
and strings, P16:RV558.
LB:A518, A526, A530, A573.
Concerto in C maj for 2 oboes, 2 clarinets and strings,
P74:RV559.
LB:A533, A567, A575, A627.
Concerto in C maj for 2 oboes, 2 clarinets and strings.

P73:RV560.
LB:A559, A575.
Concerto in D maj for violin, strings, 2 oboes, 2 horns
and tympani, P444:RV562a.
LB:A598.
Concerto in D maj for 2 violins, 2 cellos and strings,
P188:RV564.
LB:A497, A574.
Concerto in D min for 2 violins, 2 recorders, 2 oboes,
bassoon and strings, P297:RV566.
LB:A575.
Concerto in F maj for violin, strings, 2 oboes, 2 horns and
bassoon, P267:RV568.
LB:A510.
Concerto in F maj for violin, strings, 2 oboes, 2 horns and
bassoon, P273:RV569.
LB:A560.
Concerto in F maj for violin, strings, 2 oboes, 2 tromba da
caccia and bassoon, P319:RV574.
LB:A427, A561.
Concerto in G maj for 2 violins, 2 cellos and strings,
P135:RV575.
LB:A497, A576.
Concerto in G min for violin, 3 oboes, 2 recorders and
bassoon, 'Per S.A.R. di Sassonia', P359:RV576.
LB:A510, A518.
Concerto in G min for violin, strings, 2 oboes and 2
recorders, 'Per l'orchestra di Dresda', P383:RV577.
LB:A510, A518, A533, A575, A640.
Concerto in B flat maj for violin, oboe, salmoe, 3 viols and
strings, 'Concerto Funebre', P385:RV579.
LB:A511, A575.
Concerto in B min for 4 violins and strings, P148:RV580
– See Op. 3, No. 10.

**a. Orchestral – Concertos for several instruments and 2
orchestras, RV581–585**
Concerto in D maj for violin and 2 orchestras, 'Per la
S.Sma Assontione di MV', P164:RV582.
LB:A504, A511.
Concerto in B flat maj for violin in scordatura and 2
orchestras, P368:RV583.
LB:A504, A530.
Concerto in A maj for 4 recorders, 4 violins ans 2
orchestras, P226:RV585.
LB:A504, A563.

**a. Orchestral – Other Concertos, RV761–779, and
RVAnh. (*See also* Chamber and Instrumental)**
Concerto in C min for violin, organ and strings, RV766.
LB:A513.
Concerto in F maj for violin, organ and strings, RV767.
LB:A513.
Concerto in C min for oboe, violin and strings, RVAnh 17.
LB:A438, A570.

**b. Chamber and Instrumental – Sonatas with Op. Nos:
Opp. 1, 2, 5, 13, 14**
Sonatas for 2 violins and continuo, Op. 1, Nos. 1–12.
1 in G min; 2 in E min; 3 in C maj; 4 in E maj; 5 in F maj; 6
in D maj; 7 in E flat maj; 8 in D min; 9 in A maj; 10 in B
flat maj; 11 in B min; 12 in D min, 'La Folia.'
LB:B192, B193.
Sonata in E min for 2 violins and continuo, Op. 1, No. 2.
LB:B285.
Sonata in C maj for 2 violins and continuo, Op. 1, No. 3.
LB:B285.
Sonatas for violin and continuo, Op. 2, Nos. 1–12.
1 in G min; 2 in A maj; 3 in D min; 4 in F maj; 5 in B min;
6 in C maj; 7 in C min; 8 in G maj; 9 in E min; 10 in F
min; 11 in D maj; 12 in A min.
LB:B193, B194.
Concerto in A flat maj for trumpet and strings, Arr. Op. 2,
No. 4.
LB:A378, A412, A649, A655.
Sonatas for 1 or 2 violins and continuo, Op. 5, Nos. 1–6.
1 in F maj; 2 in A maj; 3 in B flat maj; 4 in B min; 5 in B

flat maj; 6 in G min.
LB:B195.
Sonata in F maj for violin and continuo, Op. 5, No. 1.
LB:B194.
Sonata in A maj for violin and continuo, Op. 5, No. 2.
LB:B194.
Sonata in B flat maj for violin and strings, Op. 5, No. 3.
LB:B194.
Sonata in B min for violin and continuo, Op. 5, No. 4.
LB:B194.
Sonata in B flat maj for 2 trumpets and organ, Arr. Op. 5, No. 5.
LB:B221.
Sonatas for musette, vielle (or other instruments) and continuo, 'Il Pastor Fido', Op. 13, Nos. 1-6. (RV54-59). 1 in C maj; 2 in C maj; 3 in G maj; 4 in A maj; 5 in C maj; 6 in G min.
LB:B195, B196.
Sonata in C maj for trombone and organ, Arr. Op. 13, No. 2.
LB:B202.
Sonata in C maj for vielle and continuo, Op. 13, No. 3.
LB:A593.
Sonata in A maj for oboe and continuo, Op. 13, No. 4.
LB:B256.
Sonata in G min for recorder (or flute or oboe) and continuo, Op. 13, No. 6.
EB:B56.
LB:A438, B198, B200, B260, B261, B262, B263.
Sonata in G min for trumpet and organ, Arr. Op. 13, No. 6.
LB:B213.
Concerto in G min for trumpet and strings, Arr. Op. 13, No. 6.
LB:A378.
Sonatas for cello and continuo, Op. 14, Nos. 1-6. 1 in B flat maj (RV47); 2 in F maj (RV41); 3 in A min (RV43); 4 in B flat maj (RV45); 5 in E min (RV40); 6 in B flat maj (RV46).
LB:B195, B197.
Sonata in B flat maj for cello and continuo, RV47, Op. 14, No. 1.
LB:A438, B309.
Sonata in B flat maj for trombone and organ, Arr. Op. 14, No. 1.
LB:B217.
Sonata in A min for cello and continuo, RV43, Op. 14, No. 3.
LB:B89, B198.
Sonata in B flat maj for cello and continuo, RV46, Op. 14, No. 6.
LB:B89, B198.
(*See also* Sonatas for cello and continuo, below.)

b. Instrumental – Sonatas for violin and continuo, RV1–37
Sonata in C maj for violin and continuo, RV2 (Pisendel).
LB:B199.
Sonata in C min for violin and continuo, RV5 (Pisendel).
LB:A432, B199.
Sonata in C min for violin and continuo, RV6 (Pisendel) (Manchester 7).
LB:B199.
Sonata in F maj for violin and continuo, RV19 (Pisendel).
LB:A432, B199.
Sonata in G maj for violin and continuo, RV25 (Pisendel).
LB:A432, B199.
Sonata in A maj for violin and continuo, RV29 (Pisendel).
LB:B199.

b. Instrumental – Sonatas for cello and continuo, RV38–47 (*See also* Sonatas Op. 14, above)
Sonata in E flat maj for cello and continuo, RV39.
LB:B197.
Sonata in G min for cello and continuo, RV42.
LB:A521, B197.
Sonata in A min for cello and continuo, RV44.

LB:B197.
b. Instrumental – Sonatas for flute, recorder and oboe, RV48–53
Sonata in C maj for flute and continuo, RV48.
LB:B200.
Sonata in D min for flute and continuo, RV49.
LB:B200.
Sonata in E min for flute and continuo, RV50.
LB:B200.
Sonata in F maj for recorder and continuo, RV52.
LB:B266, B302.
Sonata in C min for solo oboe, RV53.
LB:B210.
b. Instrumental – Sonatas for 2 instruments, RV60–81
Sonata in C maj for 2 violins and continuo, RV60.
LB:A521.
Sonata in G maj for 2 violins without bass, RV71.
LB:B316.
b. Chamber and Instrumental – Trio Sonatas, RV82–86
Trio Sonata in C maj for violin, lute and continuo, RV82.
LB:A527, A529, A532, A573.
Concerto in A maj for guitar and strings, Arr. RV82.
LB:A528, A569.
Concerto in D maj for flute, cello and continuo, Arr. RV84.
LB:B258.
Trio Sonata in G min for violin, lute and continuo, RV85.
LB:A527, A529, C28.
Trio Sonata in A min for flute, bassoon and continuo, RV86.
LB:B270.
b. Chamber and Instrumental – Miscellaneous Works
Sonata in C min for flute and continuo (Unsp.)
LB:B237.
d. Secular Vocal – Cantatas for solo voice with continuo, RV649–686
Qual per ignoto (alto and b.c.), RV677.
LB:F73.
Amor hai vinto (alto and b.c.), RV683.
LB:F73.
Cessate omai cessate (alto and strings), RV684.
LB:F73, G313.
O mio porpore piu belle (alto and strings), RV685.
LB:F73.
d. Secular Vocal – Serenatas, RV687–694
La Sena Festegiante – Serenata, c.1729, RV693.
LB:F76.
d. Secular Vocal – Operas and Other Stage Works, RV695–740
Armida al campo d'Egitto, RV699: Sinfonia in C maj.
LB:A514.
Arsilda regina di Ponto, RV700: Sinfonia in C maj.
LB:A514.
Bajazet, RV703: Sinfonia in C maj.
LB:A514.
Dorilla in tempe, RV709: Sinfonia in C maj.
LB:A514.
Farnace, RV711: Sinfonia in C maj.
LB:A514.
Giustino, RV717: Sinfonia in C maj.
LB:A514.
Griselda, RV718: Sinfonia in C maj.
LB:A514.
L'Incoronazione di Dario, RV719: Sinfonia in C maj.
LB:A514.
L'Olimpiade – Melodrama, 1734, RV725.
LB:F74.
L'Olimpiade, RV725: Sinfonia in C maj.
LB:A514, A612.
Orlando Furioso – Opera, 1727, RV728.
LB:F75.
Ottone in villa, RV729: Sinfonia in C maj.
LB:A514.
Tito Manlio – Opera, 1719, RV738.

LB:F77.
La Verita in Cimento, RV740: Sinfonia in G maj.
LB:A514.
d. Secular Vocal – Miscellaneous Vocal Items: Arias etc.
Agitata da due venti.
LB:F80.
Chiare onde.
LB:F80.
Da due venti.
LB:F80.
Piango, gemo.
EB:F101.
Sposa son disprezzata.
LB:F80.
Un certo non soche.
EB:F101.
LB:F80.
Vieni, vieni o mio diletto.
LB:F80.
e. Sacred Vocal – Liturgical Works, RV586–622
Messe 'Sacrum' (soloists, chorus, 2 clarini and strings),
  RV586.
LB:G294, G296.
Kyrie (2 choirs and strings), RV587.
LB:G284, G288, G293, G297, G300.
Gloria (soprano, alto, chorus, 2 oboes, trumpet and
  strings), RV588.
LB:G295.
Gloria (soprano, alto, chorus, 2 oboes, trumpet and
  strings), RV589.
LB:A477, G198, G272, G284, G288, G289, G290,
  G291, G292, G293, G294.
Gloria, RV589: Gloria.
LB:G320.
Gloria, RV589: Et in terra pax.
LB:G320.
Gloria, RV589: Gratias agimus tibi.
LB:G320.
Gloria, RV589: Laudamus te.
LB:G320, G327.
Credo (chorus and strings), RV591.
LB:G292, G293, G294, G296.
Domine ad adjuvandum me (2 choirs, 2 oboes and
  strings), RV593.
LB:G284, G300.
Dixit Dominus (2 sopranos, alto tenor, bass, 2 choirs and
  2 orchestras), RV594.
LB:G284, G300, G302, G303, G307.
Dixit Dominus (2 sopranos, alto tenor, bass, chorus,
  trumpet, 2 oboes and strings), RV595.
LB:A432, G301.
Beatus vir (2 sopranos, tenor, 2 choirs, 2 oboes, 2 string
  orchestras), RV597.
LB:G284, G297, G298, G299, G300.
Beatus vir (2 sopranos, alto, chorus and strings), RV598.
LB:G291, G292, G312.
Laudate pueri Dominum (soprano and strings), RV601.
LB:G308.
Laudate pueri Dominum (soprano, chorus and 2 string
  orchestras), RV603.
LB:G313.
In exitu Israel (chorus and strings), RV604.
LB:G294.
Credidi propter quod (choir and organ), RV605.
LB:G294.
Laudate Dominum (choir and strings), RV606.
LB:G294.
Laetatus sum (choir and strings), RV607.
LB:G294.
Nisi Dominus (alto, strings and organ), RV608.
EB:F102.
LB:G295, G305, G311, G314.
Nisi Dominus, RV608: Pastorale.
LB:A599.

Lauda Jerusalem (2 sopranos, 2 choirs and strings),
  RV609.
LB:G284, G292, G298, G300.
Magnificat (2 sopranos, 2 altos, 2 tenors, 2 oboes,
  chorus and strings), RV610.
LB:G284, G289, G319.
Magnificat (soprano, alto, chorus and strings), RV611.
LB:G133, G312, G314.
Salve regina (alto, 2 oboes and 2 string orchestras),
  RV616.
LB:G284.
Stabat mater (alto and strings), RV621.
LB:G303, G304, G305, G306, G307.
**e. Sacred Vocal – Non-Liturgical Works, Introductions,
RV623–642**
Canta in prato (soprano and strings), RV623.
LB:G284, G310.
In furore (soprano and strings), RV626.
B:G284, G308, G309, G310, G312.
Invicti bellate (alto and strings), RV628.
LB:G297, G309, G311, G313.
Longa mala umbrae terrores (alto and strings), RV629.
LB:G306, G311.
Nulla in mundo pax sincera (soprano and strings),
  RV630.
LB:G284, G290, G298, G308, G310.
O qui coeli terraeque (soprano and strings), RV631.
LB:G284, G301, G309, G310.
Canta in prato (soprano and strings) (Intro to Dixit),
  RV636.
LB:A432, G284, G300, G312.
Filiae mestae (alto and strings) (Intro to Miserere),
  RV638.
LB:G304.
Longa mala umbrae terrores (alto and strings) (Intro to
  Gloria), RV640.
LB:G294, G309.
Non in pratis (alto and strings) (Intro to Miserere),
  RV641.
LB:G304.
Te Deum (soprano, alto, chorus and strings), RVAnh38.
LB:G284.
e. Sacred Vocal – Oratorios, RV643–645
Juditha Triumphans devicta Holofernis Barbarie –
  Oratorio, 1716, RV644.
LB:G284, G285, G286, G287.

VIVANCO, Sebastian de (c.1550–1622)
  e. Sacred Vocal
  Stabat mater.
  LR:F89.

VIVARINO, Innocentio (b.1570)
  b. Instrumental
  Sonata I (Primo libro de Moteti, 1620).
  EB:B61.
  Sonata II (Primo libro de Moteti, 1620).
  EB:B61.
  Sonata III (Primo libro de Moteti, 1620).
  EB:B61.

VIVIANI, Giovanni Bonaventura (1638–1693) ·
  b. Instrumental
  Sonata No. 1 in C maj (D maj) for trumpet and organ (or
    strings).
  EB:B59.
  LB:A666, B207, B212, B213, E235.
  Sonata No. 2 in C maj (D maj) for trumpet and organ (or
    strings).
  EB:B59.
  LB:A666, A669, B207, B213.

VODNANSKY, Jan Campanus (1572–1622)
  e. Sacred Vocal
  Favete linguis singuli.

LR:F99.
Psalm XLVI.
LR:F99.

VOELCKEL, Samuel (16th./17th. cent.)
b. Instrumental
2 Courants (Newe Teutsche weltliche Gesanglein).
AA:A1.

VOGELWEIDE – see WALTHER VON DER VOGELWEIDE

VOIS – see DE VOIS, Pieter.

VUILDRE, Philippe de (16th. cent.)
d. Secular Vocal
Je fille quant Dieu.
LR:E33.

VULPIUS, Melchior (1560–1615)
d. Secular Vocal
Die Beste Zeit.
ER:A24.
e. Sacred Vocal
Gleichnisse aus den Evangeliensprüchen, Nos. 1–8.
EB:G130.
Der Tag bricht an.
EB:G132.
Die Helle Sonn.
EB:G132.
Hinunter ist der Sonnen Schein.
EB:G132.
Vom Himmel hoch.
LR:F108.

WAELRANT, Hubert (1517–1595)
d. Secular Vocal
Als ic u vinde.
ER:A4.
O villanella.
LR:E20.
Vorria morire.
ER:A6.

WAGENSEIL, Georg Christoph (1715–1777)
c. Keyboard – Harpsichord
Divertimento in F maj.
EB:D39.

WAGNER, Georg Gottfried (1698–1756)
e. Sacred Vocal
Lob und Ehre und Weisheit und Dank.
LB:G318.

WAISSELIUS, Matthäus (= WAISSEL) (1540–1602)
b. Instrumental – Lute
La Battaglia – Fantasia.
LR:E42.
C'est un grand tort – Fantasia.
LR:E42.
Chi passa – Galliard.
LR:E42.
Deudtscher Tantz.
LR:C13.
Fantasia.
LR:C13.
La Gamba – Galliard.
LR:E42.
Je prens en grey – Fantasia.
LR:E42.
Polish Dances.
LR:C17.
EB:B66.
La Rocha el fuso – Galliard.
LR:E42.
La Traditora – Galliard.
LR:E42.

Ung gay bergier – Fantasia.
LR:E42.

WALTHER, Johann (= WALTER) (1496–1570)
d. Secular Vocal
All morgen ist ganz frisch und neu.
EB:G132.
e. Sacred Vocal
Chorale (Unsp.)
LR:F115.
Christum wir sollen loben schon – A solis ortus cardine.
LR:F103.
Ein Kindelein so lobelich.
LR:F120.
Gelobet seist du.
LR:F103, F123.
In dulci jubilo.
LR:F120.
Josef, lieber, Josef mein.
LR:F103, F109, F112, F118, F120, F127.

WALTHER, Johann Gottfried (1684–1748)
c. Keyboard – Organ: Concertos
Concerto in A min after Torelli.
LB:E234.
Concerto in B min after Sigr. Megck.
EB:E91, E96.
LB:E188, E211, E218.
Concerto in F maj after Albinoni.
LB:E188, E197.
Concerto in G maj.
LB:B204.
c. Keyboard – Organ: Chorales
In dulci jubilo.
LB:E208.
Jesu meine Freude.
EB:E61, E68.
LB:E228.
Lobe den Herren.
LB:E205.
Meinen Jesus lass ich nich.
EB:E74.
Nun komm der Heiden Heiland.
EB:E61.

WALTHER VON CHATILLON (12th./13th. cent.)
d. Secular Vocal
Ecce torpet (CARMINA BURANA).
AA:E9, E12.
Licet eger cum egrotis (CARMINA BURANA).
AA:E9, E10, E12, E14, E17.
e. Sacred Vocal
Ver pacis appertit (Conductus).
AA:B8.

WALTHER VON DER VOGELWEIDE (1160–1230)
d. Secular Vocal
Mir hat her Gerhart Atze ein pfert.
AA:D25.
Nu alrest lebe ich mir werde – Palastinalied.
AA:D22, D25, A3.
ER:A7.
Under der linden an der heide.
AA:D25.
LR:E35.
Wei sol ich den gemyneu.
ER:A7.

WARD, John (d.1641)
b. Instrumental
Fantasia a 5.
LR:Ga17.
Fantasia a 4.
LR:E63.
d. Secular Vocal
Come, sable night.

LR:Gd32.
Out from the vale.
LR:Gd32.
Retire, my troubled soul.
LR:Gd20.

WATHAY, Ferenc (16th. cent.)
  d. Secular Vocal – Verse Chronicle
  Cantio 23: That treats the miserable past and present
    state of the Hungarian Nation.
  LR:E49.

WECK, Hans (c.1495–1536)
  b./c. Instrumental/Keyboard
  Ein Andrer Dancz.
  LR:E68.
  Hopper Tanz.
  ER:A23.
  LR:D19, E68.
  Spanyoler Tancz.
  ER:A8, A23.
  LR:A3.

WECKMANN, Matthias (1619–1647)
  c. Keyboard
  Canzona.
  EB:E94.
  Fantasia.
  EB:E77.
  Komm, Heiliger Geist.
  EB:E60.

WEELKES, Thomas (1575–1623)
  b. Instrumental – Consort
  Fantasia for viols.
  LR:Gd17.
  In Nomine.
  LR:Gd17.
  d. Secular Vocal
  The Andalusian Merchant.
  LR:Gd17.
  As Vesta was from Latmos Hill descending. (Triumphs of
    Oriana).
  LR:Gd34, Gd35, Gd39, Gd40.
  As wanton birds.
  LR:Ga21.
  Cease sorrows now.
  LR:Gd52, Gd56.
  Come sirrah, Jack ho!
  LR:E46, Gd25, Gd56.
  The Cries of London.
  LR:Gd17, Gd53.
  Death hath deprived me.
  LR:Ga21.
  Four arms, two necks.
  LR:Gd25.
  Grace, my lovely one.
  LR:E29.
  Hark all ye lovely Saints.
  LR:E50, Gd25, Gd32, Gd50, Ge36.
  Hark! I hear some dancing.
  EB:B39.
  Hence care, thou art too cruel.
  LR:Gd17, Gd32.
  In pride of May.
  LR:Ga21.
  Lo, country sports that seldom fades.
  LR:Gd33.
  The Nightingale, the organ of delight.
  LR:Gd25.
  O care, thou wilt despatch me.
  LR:Ga21, Gd17, Gd32, Ge36.
  Our country swains in the Morris Dance.
  LR:Gd33.
  Say dear, when will your frowning cease.

LR:Gd20, Gd50.
Since Robin Hood.
LR:Gd25, Gd53, Gd56.
Sing we at pleasure.
LR:Gd32.
Sit down and sing.
LR:Ga21.
Strike it up tabor.
LR:Gd18, Gd45.
Sweet heart, arise.
SI:A2.
To shorten winter's sadness.
LR:Gd17.
Thule, the period of cosmography.
LR:Gd17, Gd53.
Thus sings my dearest jewel.
LR:Gd32.
Welcome, sweet pleasure.
LR:Ge36.
SI:A2.
Whilst youthful sports are lasting.
LR:Gd33.
Why are you ladies staying.
EB:B39.
  e. Sacred Vocal
  All laud and praise.
  LR:Gd17.
  Alleluia, I heard a voice.
  LR:Ge11, Ge33, Ge36.
  Give ear, O Lord.
  LR:F28.
  Gloria in excelsis Deo.
  LR:F119.
  Hosanna to the Son of David.
  LR:F77, F119, Ge11, Ge35.
  O Lord arise.
  LR:Gd17, Ge11.
  O Lord, grant the Queen a long life.
  LR:Ge38.
  When David heard that Absalom was slain.
  LR:Ge35.

WEERBEKE – *see* **VAN WEERBEKE, Gaspar**

WEISS, Sylvius Leopold (1686–1750)
  b. Instrumental – Guitar and Lute
  Bourree.
  LB:C22.
  Chaconne.
  LB:C22, C30.
  Fantasia.
  LR:C10.
  LB:C22, C24.
  Fantasia in C min.
  LB:C18.
  Fantasia in E min.
  LB:A640.
  Passacaille.
  LB:C24.
  Prelude.
  LB:C22, C25, C30.
  Prelude in C min.
  LB:C18.
  Prelude and fugue in C maj.
  LB:C17.
  Rigaudon.
  LB:C30.
  Suite No. 2 for guitar (?).
  LB:C16.
  Suite in A min.
  LB:C20, C21.
  Suite in C min.
  LB:C17.
  Suite in D maj.
  LB:C18.

Suite in D min.
LB:C14, C18, C19, C25.
Suite in G min.
LB:C17.
Tombeau sur la mort de M. Cajetan Baron d'Hartig.
LB:C14, C16.
Tombeau sur la mort de M. Compte de Logy.
LB:C18, C19, C20, C21, C23, C24.

WELDON, John (1676–1736)
d. Secular Vocal
The Wakeful Nightingale.
EB:F94.

WERNER, Gregor (1695–1766)
a. Orchestral
Prelude and fugue in C min for strings.
LB:A604.

WERNICKE, Israel Gottlieb (1755–1836)
b. Chamber and Instrumental
Canon a 5 on B.A.C.H.
LB:B311.
Canon in motu recto, inversu et contrario.
LB:B311.
Canon in ostinato on B.A.C.H.
LB:B311.
Canon on a Norwegian Dance.
LB:B311.

WERT – see DE WERT, Giaches

WHITELOCKE, Bulstrode (1605–1675)
b. Instrumental
Whitelocke's Coranto.
EB:F91.

WHYTE, Robert (d.1574)
c. Keyboard
In Nomine.
LB:D214.
Ut re mi (Chr. Ch. MS).
LR:Gc6.
e. Sacred Vocal
Christe qui lux es.
LR:Ge29.
Domine quis habitavit.
LR:Ge29.
Lamentations of Jeremiah.
LR:Ge29.
Portio mea.
LR:Ge29.
Regina caeli.
LR:Ge29.

WHYTHORNE, Thomas (d.1528)
d. Secular Vocal
As thy shadow.
LR:Gd57.

WICHEL – see VAN WICHEL, Philippus

WIDMANN, Erasmus (1572–1634)
b. Instrumental. (Musikalischer Tugendspiegel, 1613)
Agatha.
LR:B25.
EB:B30.
Anna.
EB:B30.
Clara.
EB:B30.
Magdalena.
LR:B25.
EB:B30.
Regina.
LR:B25.
EB:B30.

Sophie.
EB:B30.
Canzona.
EB:A31.
Galliard.
EB:A31.
Intrada.
EB:A31.

WIGTHORPE, William (16th./17th. cent.)
d. Secular Vocal
I am not, I, of such belief. (MB XXII:55).
LR:Gd37.

WILBYE, John (1574–1638)
c. Keyboard
The Frogg Galliard.
LR:Gc16.
LB:D214.
d. Secular Vocal
Adieu, sweet Amaryllis.
LR:Gd32, Gd56.
Cruel behold my heaving ending.
LR:Gd25.
Draw on sweet night.
LR:Gd32.
EB:F108.
Flora gave me sweetest flowers.
LR:Gd32.
The Lady Oriana (Triumphs of Oriana).
LR:Gd34, Gd35.
Lady when I behold.
LR:Gd52.
O wretched man.
LR:Gd25.
Oft have I vowed.
EB:F108.
Sweet honey-sucking bees.
LR:Gd20, Gd32, Gd39.
Thus saith my Cloris bright.
LR:Gd56.
Weep, weep, mine eyes.
LR:Gd32, Gd39.
EB:F108.
Yet, sweet, take heed.
LR:Gd32.

WILDER – see VAN WILDER, Philip.

WILLAERT, Adrian (1490–1562)
b. Instrumental
E qui la dira.
LR:A1.
Fantasia.
LR:A6, B22.
Passa la nave – Madrigal a 6.
LR:B28.
Ricercare.
LR:E67.
Ricercare a 3.
LB:B28.
Ricercare I (Music de Joye).
LR:B26.
d. Secular Vocal
A quand'.
LR:E67
Allons, allons gay.
LR:E33, E42, E67.
Fault d'argent.
LR:E33.
Madonna, qual certezza.
LR:A1.
O bene mio.
ER:A6.
LR:A2, E22, E67.

O dolce mia vita.
EB:B35.
Villanelle.
LR:E67.
e. Sacred Vocal
Ave regina.
LR:F82.
Benedicta es, caelorum regina.
LR:F75.
In convertendo.
LR:F82.
Magnum hereditatis mysterium.
LR:F75.
O magnum mysterium.
LR:F80, F118.
Pater noster.
LR:F75.
Quem terra, ponthus, ethera.
LR:F75.
Salute te, sancta virgo Maria.
LR:F75.
Victor io salve – Quis curare neget.
LR:A2, E32.

WILLIAMS, William (17th. cent.)
b. Instrumental
Sonata IV in A min.
EB:B65.

WILSON, John (1595–1674)
d. Secular Vocal
Lawn as white as driven snow.
LR:Gd51.
The Merry Month of May.
SI:C14.
Take, o take those lips away.
LR:Gd18, Gd42, Gd45, Gd51.

WINCHESTER MS (10th. cent. English)
e. Sacred Vocal
Alleluia Te martyrum.
AA:B3.

WINSTANLEY, Gerard (17th. cent.)
d. Secular Vocal
The Digger's Song (1649).
EB:F91.

WIPO OF BURGUNDY (d.c.1048)
e. Sacred Vocal
Victimae Paschali laudes (Sequence).
AA:A3.

WIZLAW VON RUGEN (c.1266–1325)
d. Secular Vocal
Ich warne dich, vil junger man gezarte.
AA:D25.
Loibere risen.
AA:D25.
LR:E64.

WOLFENBUTTEL CODEX (early 14th. cent.)
e. Sacred Vocal
A Maria maris stella.
AA:B2.
Ad solitum – Ad solitum – Regnat.
AN:A12.
Ad solitum – Regnat.
AN:A12.
In Rama sonat gemitus (Threnody).
ER:B1.
Kyrie virginitatis amator.
AA:B2.
Verbum bonum et suave (Sequence).
AA:B2.

WOLFRAM VON ESCHENBACH (1170–1220)
d. Secular Vocal
Do man dem Edelen.
AN:B1.

WOLKENSTEIN – see OSWALD VON WOLKENSTEIN

WOODCOCK, Clement (16th. cent.)
b. Instrumental
Browning Fantasy.
ER:A24.
LB:B271.

WOODCOCK, Robert (18th. cent.)
a. Orchestral
Concerto in C maj for flute, strings and continuo.
LR:F106.
Concerto in D maj for flute and strings.
LB:A222.
Concerto in E flat maj for oboe and strings.
LB:A222, A624.

WORCESTER MS (13th. cent. English)
e. Sacred Vocal
Agnus Dei.
AA:C2.
Alleluia psallat.
AA:C2.
Beata viscera.
AA:B2, C2.
Benedictus.
AA:C2.
Fulget caelestis curia.
AA:C2.
Gaude – Inviolata.
AA:C2.
Per te Dei genetrix. (Alleluia).
AA:C2.
Salve sancta parens.
AA:C2.
Sanctus.
AA:C2.
Spiritus procedens (Gloria).
AA:C2.

WOTJA, Jan Ignac Frantisek (18th. cent.)
b. Instrumental
Introduction and Aria for viola da gamba, pardessus de
viol and viola d'amore.
LB:B313.

WREEDE – see URREDA, Juan.

WYATT, Thomas (16th./17th. cent.)
d. Secular Vocal
Blame not my lute.
LR:A1, E24.

WYLKYNSON, Robert (15th. cent.)
e. Sacred Vocal
Salve regina.
ER:B2.
LR:Ge38.
SI:D4.

XIMENEZ, Jose (1601–1672)
c. Keyboard – Organ
Batalla.
EB:E89.
Batalla de 6o tono.
LR:D13.
Batalla de 7o tono.
LR:D13.
Tiento lleno de 1o tono.
LR:D13.

ZACH, Johann (1699–1773)
b. Instrumental
Sonata a 3 stromenti in A maj.
LB:B313.
c. Keyboard – Harpsichord and Organ
Capriccio in C min.
LB:D237.
Fuga d'imitazione in G min.
LB:E236.
Fugue in A min.
LB:E242.
Fugue in D maj.
LB:E236.
Partita in C maj.
LB:D237.
Sonata in A maj.
LB:D237.
e. Sacred Vocal
De Passione Christi.
LB:G257.

ZACHOW, Friedrich Wilhelm (= ZACHAU) (1663–1712)
b. Chamber and Instrumental
Trio in F maj for flute, bassoon and continuo.
LB:B270.
c. Keyboard – Harpsichord and Organ
In dulci jubilo.
EB:E64.
LB:E208.
Prelude and fugue in G maj.
EB:E56, E74.
Suite in B min.
EB:D32.
LB:D222.

ZANETTI, Francesco (17th. cent.)
b. Instrumental
La Mantovana.
EB:B41.
d. Secular Vocal
Fuggi, fuggi, fuggi.
EB:B41.

ZANGUIS, Nicolaus (1570–1620)
e. Sacred Vocal
Congratulamini nunc omnes.
LR:F112.
Magnificat secundi toni.
LR:F93.

ZANOTTI, Camillo (1545–1591)
d. Secular Vocal
Dono licor a bate.
AN:B1.
Tirsi morir volea.
LR:F93.

ZAREVUTIUS, Zacharias (1625–1665)
c. Keyboard – Organ
Postlude on 'Benedicamus Dominicale.'
LB:E239.
Sacred Vocal
Magnificat.
EB:G140.

ZELECHOWSKI, Piotr (17th. cent.)
c. Keyboard – Organ
Fantasia.
EB:E85.

ZELENKA, Jan Dismas (1679–1745)
a. Orchestral
Capriccios Nos. 1–5.
1 in D maj; 2 in G maj; 3 in F maj; 4 in A maj; 5 in G maj.
LB:A578.

Concerto in G maj for oboe, violin, cello, bassoon and
strings.
LB:A578.
Hippocondrie in A maj.
LB:A417, A578, G315.
Overture in F maj.
LB:A578, A579.
Sinfonia Concertante in A min.
LB:A578, A579.
b. Chamber and Instrumental
Sonatas for 2 oboes, bassoon and continuo, Nos. 1–6.
1 in F maj; 2 in G min; 3 in B flat maj; 4 in G min; 5 in F
maj; 6 in C min.
LB:B201.
Trio Sonata in B flat maj for oboe, violin and continuo,
No. 3.
LB:G315.
e. Sacred Vocal
Exurge providentia – Aria.
LB:G315.
In exitu Israel – Motet.
LB:G315.
Kyrie Eleison – Aria.
LB:G315.
Lamentations of Jeremiah.
LB:G316.
Recordare Domine – Aria.
LB:G315.
Testamenti tui – Aria.
LB:G315.

ZELLBELL, Ferdinand (1719–1780)
c. Keyboard – Organ
Prelude in A min.
EB:E74.
Prelude in D min.
EB:E74.
Prelude in E min.
EB:E74.
Prelude in F maj.
EB:E74.
Prelude in G min.
EB:E74.

ZESSO, Johan Baptiste (early 16th. cent.)
d. Secular Vocal
E quando andarete al monte.
LR:A3, E25.

ZIANI, Marc Antonio (c.1653–1715)
e. Sacred Vocal
Alma redemptoris mater.
LB:G324.

ZIELENSKY, Mikolaj (c.1550–1615)
b. Chamber and Instrumental
Fantasia II for strings and continuo.
EB:B16.
Fantasia III for strings and continuo.
EB:B16.
e. Sacred Vocal
Benedicamus Deum caeli (Communiones).
LR:F76.
Deus in simplicitate (Offertoria).
LR:F76.
Domus mea (Communiones).
LR:F76.
Felix namque se (Offertoria).
LR:F76.
Haec dies (Communiones).
LR:F76.
In monte Oliveti (Communiones).
LR:F76.
EB:G144.
Justus ut palma florebit.

EB:G146.
Magnificat.
LR:F76.
O gloriosa Domine (Communiones).
LR:F76.
Offertorium XX (Offertoria).
EB:G142.
Per signum crucis (Communiones).
LR:F76.
Tanto tempore (Offertoria).
LR:F76.
Terra tremuit (Offertoria).
LR:F76.
Viderunt omnes (Communiones).
LR:F76.
Vox in Rama (Communiones).
LR:F76.

ZIPOLI, Domenico (1688-1726)
  c.Keyboard - Harpsichord and Organ
  Canzona.
  EB:E67, E82.
  LB:E241.
  Elevazione in F maj.
  LB:E238.

Partita for solo harpsichord.
SI:C11.
Partita in C maj.
LB:E210.
Pastorale.
EB:E66, E74.
LB:E182, E238.
Suite in G min.
EB:E93.
LB:D228.
Toccata.
EB:E93.
Verso e canzona in C maj.
LB:E238.

ZWIERZCHOWSKI, Mateusz (d.1768)
  e.Sacred Vocal
  Missa pro defunctis, Requiem.
  LB:G317.

ZWINGLI, Huldrych (1484-1531)
  e.Sacred Vocal
  Herr, nun heb den wagen selb.
  LR:A2, E32.

Plainsong Index

PS:A60.
Flores apparuerunt (Gradual).
PS:B16.
Fratres, expurgatum vetus fermentum (Epistle).
PS:A28.
Fudata est domus Domini (Responsory).
PS:A170.
FUNERAL SERVICE.
PS:A45, A46.

Gabriel angelus locutus (Antiphon).
PS:A53.
GALLICAN CHANT (Anthology).
PS:B20, C1, C7.
Gaude et laetar (Transitorium – AMBROSIAN).
PS:B19.
Gaude Maria virgo (Antiphon).
PS:A53.
Gaude Maria virgo (Responsory).
PS:A52, A53.
Gaudeamus omnes in Domino (Introit).
PS:A47.
Gaudent in caelis animae (Antiphon).
PS:B18.
Gaudete in Domino semper (Introit).
PS:A16.
Genealogia Christi (Evangelium).
PS:A15.
Genuit puerpera regem (Antiphon).
PS:A53, B2, B6, B10.
Germinavit radix Jesse (Antiphon).
PS:A52.
Gloria VIII.
PS:B14.
Gloria IX.
PS:A10.
Gloria XI.
PS:A28, A29, A30.
Gloria XV.
PS:B7.
Gloria et honore coronasti (Offertory).
PS:A17.
Gloria, laus et honor (Hymn).
PS:A20, B2, B20.
AA:C3.
Gloria patri genitoque – Szivarvany havasan (Respon
sory with folk variant – HUNGARIAN).
LR:A5.
Gloriosus Dei (Responsory).
PS:A17.
Gustate et videte (Ad Confractionem Panis – MOZARA
BIC).
PS:B21.

Habet in vestimento (Antiphon).
PS:A60.
Haec dies quam fecit (Gradual).
PS:A28, A29, A39, A41, A42, A43, A44, B2.
AA:A3, B4, C3.
Haec dies quam fecit – Alleluia (Antiphon – GALLICAN).
PS:C1.
Haec est domus Domini (Antiphon).
PS:A70.
Hodie Christus natus est (Antiphon).
PS:A15, B16.
LR:F125.
Hodie Maria virgo caelos ascendit (Antiphon).
SI:D3.
Hodie nobis caelorum rex (Responsory).
PS:A5, B6, C7.
Hodie nobis de caelo pax (Responsory).
PS:A5, B2.
Hodie scietas quia veniet (Introit).
PS:B2.

Hodie Simon Petrus acsendit (Antiphon).
PS:B18.
Homo quidam fecit (Responsory).
PS:B6, B17.
Hosanna filio David (Antiphon).
PS:A20, A29.
HYMN TO ST. MICHAEL (?).
PS:B7.
HYMNS (Anthology).
PS:B3, B4.

Ille homo (Confractorium – AMBROSIAN).
PS:B19.
IMPROPERES.
PS:A25, B2.
Improperium expectavit cor meum (Offertory).
PS:A20, A42.
In anniversario Domini Dagoberti Regis (Elegy).
PS:B5.
In Bethlehem Judea (Ante Evangelicum – AMBROSIAN).
PS:B19.
In exitu Israel (Psalm).
PS:A40, B19, C7.
In hoc cognoscent omnes (Antiphon).
PS:A24.
In illo tempore (Gospel).
PS:A28.
In paradisum deducant (Antiphon).
PS:A30, B16.
In principio erat verbum (Responsory).
PS:A5.
In splendoribus sanctorum (Communion).
PS:A10, A43, B2.
Ingrediente Domino in sanctem civitatem (Responsory).
PS:A20, B2.
Intellige clamorem meum (Communion).
PS:A42.
Introibo ad altare (Illatio – MOZARABIC).
PS:B21.
Iste confessor Domini (Hymn).
PS:B16.
SI:D3.
Isten, teged discerunk (Te Deum – HUNGARIAN).
PS:A15.
Ite, missa est (Post Communion).
PS:A10, A28, A30, B14.

Jam Christus astra ascenderat (Hymn).
PS:C1.
Jam toto subitus (Hymn).
PS:A53.
Jerusalem surge et sta (Communion).
PS:B2.
SI:D1.
Jesu corona celsior (Hymn).
PS:C1.
Jesu dulcis memoria (Hymn).
SI:D3.
Jesu nostra redemptio (Hymn).
PS:A36.
SI:D2.
Jesu redemptor omnium (Hymn).
PS:A16.
Jesus tradidit impius (Responsory).
PS:B16.
Jubilamen (Lectio).
PS:A15.
Jubilate Deo universa terra (Offertory).
PS:A16, C1.
Judeae et Jerusalem (Responsory).
PS:A6, B2, B7.
Justorum animae (Offertory).
PS:B7.
Justus ut palma florebit (Gradual).

O quam glorifica (Hymn).
PS:A53.
AA:B4.
O quam gloriosum (Antiphon).
PS:A60.
O quam metuendas est (Antiphon to Magnificat).
PS:A70.
O quam suavis est Domine (Antiphon).
SI:D3.
O quantum in cruce (Antiphon).
PS:A27.
O redemptor sume carmen (Hymn).
PS:B8.
O sacrum convivium (Antiphon).
PS:B17.
O salutaris hostia quae caeli (Hymn).
PS:B14.
SI:D1.
O sapientia quae ex ore (Antiphon).
PS:B16.
O vos omnes (Responsory).
PS:A29, B2, B20.
Occurrent turbae (Antiphon).
PS:A20.
Oculi omnium (Gradual).
PS:B10.
Offerte Domino (Sacrificium – MOZARABIC).
PS:B21.
OFFICE FOR THE DEAD.
PS:A45, A46, B5.
OFFICE FOR THE DEDICATION OF A CHURCH.
PS:A70.
OFFICE FOR THE FEAST OF CORPUS CHRISTI.
PS:A47, A48, A49.
OFFICE FOR THE FEAST OF THE HOLY TRINITY.
PS:A49.
OFFICE FOR THE FEAST OF ST. CECILIA.
PS:A69.
OFFICE FOR THE FEAST OF ST. MICHAEL.
PS:A66.
Omnes amici mei (Responsory).
PS:B2, B20.
Omnes gentes plaudite (Responsory).
PS:C1.
Omnes patriarchae (Antiphon – AMBROSIAN).
PS:B19.
Omnes qui in Christo (Communion).
PS:A17, B2.
Omnes de Saba (Gradual).
PS:A43, B2.
Omnes gentes plaudite manibus (Psalm XLVI – Introit).
PS:A36.
Optatus votis omnium (Hymn).
PS:A36.
Oratio Jeremiah (Lamentations of Jeremiah).
PS:A27, B22.
Oremus dilectissimi nobis (Antiphon).
PS:B18.
Os justi (Gradual).
PS:B10.

Pacem meam (Antiphon – MOZARABIC).
PS:B21.
Pacifice loquebantur (Psalmellus – AMBROSIAN).
PS:B19.
Panem angelorum (Antiphon).
PS:A47.
Pange lingua gloriosi corporis mysterium (Hymn).
PS:A24, B16.
Pange lingua gloriosi lauream certaminis (Hymn – GALLICAN).
PS:C7.
Pange lingua gloriosi praelium (Hymn).
PS:A25.

SI:D2, D3.
Paradisi portae (Antiphon).
PS:A53.
Parce Domine, parce populo tu (Antiphon).
PS:A24, B14.
Parvalus filius (Antiphon).
PS:A4, B2, B6.
Pascha nostrum immolatus est (Communion).
PS:A28, A30, A41, A42, A43, A44.
Passer invenit (Communion).
PS:B16.
Pater noster (Canticle).
PS:A10, A28, B14, B21.
Pater, si non potest (Communion).
PS:A20.
Pax Domini (?).
PS:A10, B14.
Pax in caelo (Psallenda – AMBROSIAN).
PS:B19.
Per quem haec omnia (Doxology).
PS:A10.
Planctus Hugonis abbatia.
PS:B5.
Planctus Karoli.
PS:B5.
Planctus Paulinus d'Aquila.
PS:B5.
Plaude parens Pannonia (BLASIUS POZSONY PSALTER).
LR:A5.
PLAY OF DANIEL (Liturgical Drama).
PS:C2, C3, C4.
PLAY OF HEROD (Liturgical Drama).
PS:C7.
PLAY OF THE THREE MARIES (Liturgical Drama).
PS:C5, C6.
Popule meus quid feci (Antiphon).
PS:B20.
Populus Sion (Introit).
PS:B2.
Post dies octo (Antiphon).
PS:B6.
Postquam surrexit Dominus (Antiphon).
PS:A24.
Posuisti Domine (Offertory).
PS:A47.
PRAGUE EASTER PLAY = PLAY OF THE THREE MARIES (Liturgical Drama).
PS:C5, C6.
Precatus est Moyses (Offertory).
PS:C1.
Procedentum sponsum (Benedicamus trope).
PS:A15.
PROCESSION FOR PALM SUNDAY.
PS:A19, A20.
Propter veritatem (Gradual).
PS:A53.
Psallite Domino (Communion).
PS:A43.
Puer natus est nobis (Introit).
PS:A16, A30, A44, B2, B10.
AA:C3.
Pueri Hebraeorum portantes (Antiphon).
PS:A20, A29, A39.
LR:F79.
Pueri Hebraeorum vestimenta (Antiphon).
PS:A39.
LR:F79.
Pusillanimes confortamini (Communion).
PS:A16.

Quare fremuerunt gentes (Psalm II – Introit).
PS:A30.
Quem terra pontus ethera (Hymn).
SI:D3.

Anonymous Work Index

A biente y siete de marco (16th. cent. Spanish. CANCIO-
NERO DE MEDINACELLI).
SI:A2.

A la fontanella (13th. cent. French).
AA:D17.

A la mode de France et Nonesuch (16th. cent. English).
LR:B10.

A l'entrada del temps clar (13th. cent. French).
AA:D5, D8, D10.

A los banos del amor (15th. cent. Spanish. CANCIO-
NERO DE PALACIO).
ER:A26.

A los maitines era. (16th. cent. Spanish.)
LR:E65.

A madre. (13th. cent. Spanish. CANTIGAS DE SANTA
MARIA).
AA:E7.
LR:A8.

A madre de Jhesucristo (13th. cent. Spanish. CANTIGAS
DE SANTA MARIA).
AA:E4.

A madre do qui liurou (13th. cent. Spanish. CANTIGAS
DE SANTA MARIA).
AA:A3.

A prisai qu'en chantant (13th. cent. French).
AA:A1.

A virgen sempr' accorrer (13th. cent. Spanish. CANTI-
GAS DE SANTA MARIA).
AA:E5.

Absent I am (16th. cent. English).
LR:Gf8.

Accede nuntia (17th. cent. Polish).
EB:E85.

Ach Elslein, liebes Elselein (16th. cent. German).
LR:D14.

Ad honorem regis (12th./13th. cent. Spanish. CALIX-
TINE CODEX).
PS:B22.

Ad mortem festinamus (14th. cent. Spanish. LIBRE
VERMELL).
AN:B17, B18.

Ad regnum – Noster cetus (14th. cent. German. ENGEL-
BURG MS).
AA:C3.

Ad solitum – Ad solitum – Regnat (14th. cent. French
WOLFENBUTTEL CODEX).
AN:A12.

Ad solitum – Regnat (14th. cent. French. WOLFENBUT-
TEL CODEX).
AN:A12.

Ad solitum vomitum (14th. cent. French. ROMAN DE
FAUVEL).
AN:A15, A16.

Ad veniam (13th. cent. Polish. STARY SACZ MS).
AA:B9.

Ade costa dormientis (14th. cent. French. ROMAN DE
FAUVEL).
AN:A15.

Adest Sponsus (12th. cent. French).
AA:B5.

Adieu mes amours (15th. cent. French.)
ER:A1.
LR:E38.

Adieu soulas (16th. cent. French. HEER SONGBOOK).

LR:E72.

Advenit nobis desiderabilis (15th. cent. Franco-Flemish).
ER:A14.

Agincourt Carol – See Deo gracis Anglia.

Agmina militie (13th. cent. Polish. STARY SACZ MS).
AA:B9.

Agniau dous (13th. cent. French).
LR:B19.

Agnus Dei (13th. cent. English. WORCESTER MS).
AA:C2.

Agnus Dei (14th. cent. French. APT MS).
AN:B5.

Agnus Dei (14th. cent. Spanish. MISSA BARCELONA).
AA:A2.
AN:B15.

L'Agricola (16th. cent. Italian).
LR:E20.

Ah, Robin (16th. cent. English).
LR:Gf8.

Ahime sospiri (16th. cent. Italian).
LR:E56.

Airs and Dances of Renaissance Scotland (Trad.
Scottish).
LB:B327.

Al alva venid (15th. cent. Spanish. CANCIONERO DE
PALACIO).
ER:A26.
LR:E25.

Al di dolce ben mio (16th. cent. Italian).
LR:A4, B32.

Al Nino (16th. cent. Spanish).
LR:A8.

Al rebuelo de una garca (16th. cent. Spanish).
LR:E30.

Al vol (15th. cent. German. GLOGAUER LIEDERBUCH).
ER:A22, A23.
LR:E35.

Alas, departing is time for woe (15th. cent. English.)
LR:Gf4.

Alas, what shall I do for love (16th. cent. English. HENRY
VIII MS).
LR:Gf7.

Alca la nina los ojos (16th. cent. Spanish. CANCIONERO
DE UPSALA).
LR:E23.

Alia Fantasia in 6 ton (17th. cent. Polish).
EB:D2.

All hail to the days – To drive the cold winter away (16th.
cent. English. Words: Durfey).
LR:E34.

All in a garden Green (16th. cent. English. BALLET'S
LUTE BOOK).
LR:Gd38, Gd43.
SI:C14.

All the flowers of the broom (16th. cent. English. WIL-
LIAM BLAKE'S LUTE BOOK, 1610).
LR:Gd47.

Alle mijn gepeys (16th. cent. Flemish. EEN SCHOON
LIEDEKENS BOECK. ANTWERP, 1544).
LR:E21.

Alle psallite cum luya (13th. cent. French. MONTPELLIER
CODEX).
AA:A3, B1, B2.
LR:E34.

Allegez moy, doulce plaisant brunette (15th. cent. French).
ER:A1.
Alleluia – Organum a 2 (13th. cent. Hungarian).
LR:A5.
Alleluia: Angelus Domine (11th. cent. French).
AA:A3, B4.
Alleluia: Ave benedicta Maria (14th. cent. Bohemian).
EB:G140.
Alleluia: Christus resurgens – Mors (13th. cent. French. NOTRE DAME).
AA:B10.
Alleluia: Justus ut palma. (12th. cent. French).
AA:B3.
Alleluia: Non vos relinquam (13th. cent. French. NOTRE DAME).
AA:B3.
Alleluia, panna syna porodila (16th. cent. Bohemian. KROLMUS HYMNBOOK).
LR:F99.
Alleluia psallat (13th. cent. English. WORCESTER MS).
AA:C2.
Alleluia: Te martyrum (10th. cent. English. WINCHESTER MS).
AA:B3.
Allemande (16th. cent. French).
EB:E66.
An Allemande Fitt for the Manichorde (16th. cent. English).
LR:Gc6.
Allemande Prince (16th. cent. English).
LR:Gf2.
Almain for 2 lutes (16th. cent. English).
LR:Gd23.
Almand (16th. cent. English).
LR:Gc8, Gd33.
SI:B1.
Almand Real (16th. cent. English).
LR:Gd41.
Almand d'Ungrie (16th. cent. Hungarian).
LR:C17.
Alta estava la pana (16th. cent. Spanish. CANCIONERO DE UPSALA).
LR:E23.
Alta Trinita beata (13th. cent. Italian. CORTONA).
AA:C5.
Alte clamat Epicurus (13th. cent. German. CARMINA BURANA).
AA:E11, E17.
Altissima luce col grande splendore (13th. cent. Italian. CORTONA).
AA:C5.
L'Altro prense Arcangelo lucente (13th. cent. Italian. CORTONA).
AA:C5.
Amen (15th. cent. German. BUXHEIMER ORGAN BOOK).
EB:E66.
L'Amour de moy (15th. cent. French).
LR:E38, E59.
SI:C16.
L'Amor dona, ch'io te porto (16th. cent. Spanish).
LR:E26, E28.
Amor potest – Ad amorem (13th. cent. French. BAMBURG CODEX).
AA:B1, D18.
Amore dolze senza pare (13th. cent. Italian. CORTONA).
AA:C5.
Amours dont je suis espris (13th. cent. French).
AA:D19.
Anchor che col partire (16th. cent. Italian).
LR:E39.
And I were a maiden (15th. cent. English).
LR:Gf4, Gf8.
Andeliku rozhochany (You lovely angel) (12th./14th.

cent. Bohemian).
PS:C6.
Angelus ad virginum (13th. cent. English).
AN:B10.
LR:F120.
Angelus ad virginum (15th. cent. Polish).
ER:B46.
Anglia tibi turbidas (15th. cent. English).
LR:A4.
Anni novi novitas (15th. cent. Bohemian).
AN:B2.
Anno Domini (17th. cent. Polish).
AA:C4.
The Antyk (16th. cent. English).
LR:Gf2.
Apor Lazar Tancza (17th. cent. Hungarian. KAJONI CODEX).
LR:A5.
Aque serven todo' los celestiaes (13th. cent. Spanish. CANTIGAS DE SANTA MARIA).
AA:A3.
Aquel que de voontade (13th. cent. Spanish. CANTIGAS DE SANTA MARIA).
AA:A1.
Aquesto niue en me levant (16th. cent. French. NOELS DE NOTRE DAME).
AA:D20.
Argeers (17th. cent. English. PLAYFORD).
EB:F91.
As I lay (15th. cent. English).
LR:E34.
Asi pod'a Virgen (13th. cent. Spanish. CANTIGAS DE SANTA MARIA).
AA:A2, D9.
Assi como Jesu Christe (13th. cent. Spanish. CANTIGAS DE SANTA MARIA).
AA:E2.
Au boys joli – Galliard (16th. cent. French).
LR:B10, B11, B13, B31.
Au Dieux (14th. cent. French. ROMAN DE FAUVEL).
AN:A15.
Au renouviau (13th. cent. French).
LR:B19.
Au tans d'aost (13th. cent. French).
AA:A1.
L'Auceu en gabiolo (Trad. Provencal).
LR:B19.
Aufzug (16th. cent. German).
LR:F94.
L'Autrier de hors Pinguigni (14th. cent. French. ROMAN DE FAUVEL).
AN:A15.
Ave Dei genitrix (13th. cent. Italian. CORTONA).
AA:C5.
Ave domina mundi (13th. cent. German. CARMINA BURANA).
AA:E15.
Ave donna santissima (13th. cent. Italian. CORTONA).
AA:C5.
Ave gloriosa – Ave virgo regia – Domine (13th. cent. French. BAMBURG CODEX).
AA:B2.
LR:A8.
Ave gloriosa mater salvatoris (13th. cent. French. NOTRE DAME).
AA:B2.
Ave in caelum (16th. cent. Polish).
ER:B46.
Ave Maria (12th. cent. French).
AA:B5.
Ave Maria (Conductus) (13th. cent. French. ST. VICTOR MS).
AA:B9.
Ave Maria (Conductus) (13th. cent. Spanish. LAS

HUELGAS CODEX).
AA:C6.
Ave Maria gratia plena (13th. cent. German. CARMINA
BURANA).
AA:E15.
Ave Maria Keiserin (17th. cent. German).
LR:F80.
Ave maris stella (13th. cent. French).
AA:B8.
Ave maris stella (16th. cent. French).
EB:E76.
Ave nobis venerabilis Maria (13th. cent. German.
CARMINA BURANA).
AA:E12.
Ave regina – Alma redemptoris – Alma Sabbati (14th.
cent. French. MONTPELLIER CODEX).
AN:A12.
Ave regina caelorum (15th. cent. Polish).
AA:C4.
Ave regina gloriosa (13th. cent. Italian. CORTONA).
AA:C5.
Ave vergene gaudente (13th. cent. Italian. CORTONA).
AA:C5.
Ave virgo, gratio plean Dies te salve (16th. cent. Spanish).
LR:E26.
Ave, virgo regia (13th. cent. French).
AA:D19.
Ave virgo virginem (13th. cent. French. FLORENCE
CODEX).
AA:B2.
Axe Phebus aureo (13th. cent. German. CARMINA
BURANA).
AA:A2, E9, E10, E11, E16.
Ay, Linda amiga (16th. cent. Spanish).
LR:E31.
Ay luna que reluzes! (16th. cent. Spanish. CANCIONERO
DE UPSALA).
LR:E23.
Ay, Santa Maria (13th. cent. Spanish. CANTIGAS DE
SANTA MARIA).
AA:E3, E4.
Ay triste que vengo (16th. cent. Spanish).
LR:E31.

Bacche qui venies (13th. cent. German. CARMINA
BURANA).
AA:E11, E12. E16.
Badzwiesiola (Be merry) (15th. cent. Polish).
ER:B46.
The Baffled Knight (16th. cent. English).
SI:A2.
Bagpipe Tune (Trad. Bohemian).
AN:B2.
Baixa dansa Barcelona (15th. cent. Spanish. BRUSSELS
MS).
AN:B15.
Ballad of King Henry and the Miller of Mansfield (Trad.
English).
LR:Gd58.
Ballade de la Reine d'Avril (12th. cent. French).
LR:B12.
Ballata (14th. cent. Italian).
AA:A2, A3.
Ballet (17th. cent. Polish).
EB:B71.
Balletto Polacho (16th. cent. Hungarian).
LR:C18.
Ballo Milanese (16th. cent. Italian).
LR:B11, B18.
Die Bänkelsängerlieder (Sonata) (17th. cent. German).
EB:A19, B38.
The Bannockburn Air (17th. cent. Scottish. SCOTS
MUSICAL MUSEUM, 1796).
EB:F91.

Barafostus' Dream – Divisions (16th. cent. English).
LR:Ga19.
La Bassa Castiglya (15th. cent. Franco-Flemish).
ER:A17.
LR:A4.
Bassa danza a 2 (15th. cent. Italian).
LR:B16.
Bassa danza a 3 (15th. cent. Italian).
LR:B16.
Basse danse (16th. cent. French).
SI:C2.
Basse danse (16th. cent. French. MUSIC DE JOYE-
MODERNE).
LR:B26.
La Battaille – Basse danse (16th. cent. French. MUSIC
DE JOYE-MODERNE).
LR:B26, B31.
Battalla famosa (16th. cent. Spanish).
SI:A2.
Battalla famosa (18th. cent. Spanish).
LR:D13.
Batori Tantz (16th. cent. Hungarian).
LR:C17.
Der Bauern schwanz – Rubinus (15th. cent. German.
GLOGAUER LIEDERBUCH).
ER:A23.
Baxelo un trato (16th. cent. Italian).
LR:A4, B32.
Be peace, ye make me spill my ale (16th. cent. English).
LR:Gf8.
Beata viscera (13th. cent. English. WORCESTER MS).
AA:B2, C2.
Beatus Adalbertus (13th. cent. Polish).
AA:C4.
Beaulte – Basse danse (15th. cent. French. MARIE DE
BOURGOGNE MS, 1405).
LR:B12.
SI:C2.
Begone, sweet night (16th. cent. English).
LR:Gf8.
Belial vocatur (13th. cent. Spanish. LAS HUELGAS
CODEX).
AA:B2.
La Bella Franceschina (16th. cent. Italian).
LR:A1.
Belle Doëtte as fenestre se Siet (13th. cent. French).
SI:C2.
Belle qui tiens ma vie (16th. cent. French).
LR:B31.
Belle, tenes moy (16th. cent. French).
LR:A1, E24.
Belle Ysabellot (13th. cent. French. BAMBURG CODEX).
ER:A5.
Ben ch'io (14th. cent. Italian).
AA:A2.
ER:B19.
LR:B11.
Ben com (13th. cent. Spanish. CANTIGAS DE SANTA
MARIA).
AA:E7.
Ben crudele e spietoso (13th. cent. Italian. CORTONA).
AA:C5.
Ben sab (13th. cent. Spanish. CANTIGAS DE SANTA
MARIA).
AA:E4.
Benedic regem cunctorum (13th. cent. Polish).
AA:C4.
Benedicamus Domino (9th./10th. cent. French.
MUSICA ENCHIRIADIS).
AA:A3.
Benedicamus Domino (11th./12th. cent. Spanish.
CALIXTINE CODEX).
AA:A3, B4.
Benedicamus Domino (13th. cent. French. FLORENCE

CODEX).
AA:A2, A3, B2.
ER:B19.
LR:B11.
Benedicamus Domino (13th. cent. Polish).
AA:C4.
Benedicamus Domino I–II (13th. cent. Polish. STARY
  SACZ MS).
AA:B9.
Benedicti et laudati (13th. cent. Italian. CORTONA).
AA:C5.
Benedictus (13th. cent. English. WORCESTER MS).
AA:C2.
Benedictus (14th. cent. French. APT MS).
AN:B5.
Benvennas Mayo! (13th. cent. Spanish. CANTIGAS DE
  MAYO).
AA:D9.
Biance flor (14th. cent. Italian).
AN:B9.
LR:A4.
The Bird Fancyer's Delight (17th. cent. English. THE
  DIVISION FLUTE).
LB:B265, B282.
El Bisson – Pavan (16th. cent. Spanish).
LR:E25.
Blow thy horn, hunter (16th. cent. English. Attrib.
  CORNYSHE).
LR:Gd58.
Boatman (17th. cent. English. PLAYFORD).
EB:F91.
Bogurodzica – Cantio Polonica (14th. cent. Polish).
AA:C4.
EB:B46.
Ein Böhmischer Tantz (17th. cent. German).
LR:D21.
Bon vin doit (14th. cent. French. ROMAN DE FAUVEL).
AN:A15, A16.
Bonny sweet Robin (16th. cent. English).
AA:D17.
LR:Gd45.
Bonum vinum (15th. cent. German. GLOGAUER LIEDER-
  BUCH).
ER:A23.
La Bounette (16th. cent. English).
LR:Gc6.
Branle (15th. cent. French).
LB:B12.
Branle de Bourges (16th. cent. French).
LR:B12.
Branle de Bourgogne (16th. cent. French).
LR:B25, B26.
LB:B207.
Branle des chevaux (16th. cent. French).
LR:B19.
Branle de Poictou (16th. cent. French).
LR:B10, B11, B13.
SI:C2.
Branle Gai (16th. cent. French).
LR:B13, C20.
Branle simple (16th. cent. French. MUSIC DE JOYE-
  MODERNE).
LR:B26.
2 Branles. (16th. cent. French).
LR:B10, B11.
Breve regnum (15th. cent. Polish).
LR:E66.
EB:G144.
Bruder Konrad (15th. cent. German. GLOGAUER LIE-
  DERBUCH).
ER:A23.
LR:A1.
Bruder Conrad's Tantzmass (16th. cent. German).
LB:B273.

Bryd on brere (14th. cent. English).
AN:B10.
LR:Gd58.
Les Buffons (16th. cent. French. ORCHESOGRAPHIE).
LR:E20, Gd47.
Bulla fulminante (13th. cent. German. CARMINA
  BURANA).
AA:E10, E14.
Buoh vsemohuci (God Almighty) (12th./14th. cent.
  Bohemian).
PS:C6.
Il Burato (16th. cent. Italian).
LR:Gf2, C20.
Bussa la porta (16th. cent. Italian).
LR:E56.
Byla cesta (18th. cent. Moravian).
LR:F116.

Calabaca, no se, buen amor (16th. cent. Spanish).
LR:E28.
Calabaza (15th. cent. French).
LR:B19.
Calata (16th. cent. Italian).
LR:A1.
Caligo terrae – Virgo Maria (14th. cent. English).
AA:B3.
Calleno custure me (16th. cent. English).
LR:Gd45.
Can she excuse? (After Dowland) (16th. cent. English).
LR:Gc16.
Canaries (17th. cent. English. STRALOCH MS. 1627/9).
SI:C1.
5 Canciones para clarinos y trompetas (18th. cent.
  Spanish).
EB:E86.
Candida virginitas (13th. cent. French).
AA:A2, A3.
Canon de l'ete (15th. cent. French).
LR:B14.
Cantio de St. Elizabetha Hungariae Regis Filia (17th.
  cent. Hungarian. LYRA CAELESTIS. 1695).
LR:A5.
Cantio natalita (17th. cent. German).
LR:F111, F124.
Cantico Polonica (*See also* Bogurodzica) (16th. cent.
  Polish).
EB:E85.
Canzona (17th. cent. Polish).
EB:E85.
The Carman's Whistle (16th. cent. English).
LR:Gd23.
La Carocossa (16th. cent. Italian).
LR:A4, B32.
Casta catholica (13th. cent. Spanish. LAS HUELGAS
  CODEX).
AA:C6.
Cathaccio – Galliard (16th. cent. Italian).
EB:E56.
Catholicum concio (12th. cent. German. HAUTRIVE
  GRADUALE).
AA:C3.
Catholicorum concio (13th. cent. Spanish. LAS HUEL-
  GAS CODEX).
AA:C3, C6.
LR:A8.
Un Cavalier di Spagna (16th. cent. Italian).
LR:Gd25.
Ce joli mois de Mai. (15th. cent. French).
SI:C18.
Ce penser qui sans fin tirannise ma vie (16th. cent.
  French. MUSICAL BANQUET).
LR:Gd30, Gd31.
Cedit frigus (Temps Pasqual) (12th. cent. Spanish.
  RIPOLL ABBEY).

AN:A12.
Conditor fut le nonpareil (16th. cent. French).
LR:F127.
Conductus (13th. cent. German. CARMINA BURANA).
AA:E15.
Congaudent catholici (12th./13th. cent. Spanish.
   CALIXTINE CODEX).
PS:B22.
Congaudent hodie (12th. cent. Spanish).
AA:B5.
Congaudent turba (Benedicamus trope) (14th. cent.
   German. ENGELBURG MS).
AA:C3.
Consort IX (16th. cent. English. HENRY VIII MS).
LR:Gf6.
Consort X (16th. cent. English. HENRY VIII MS).
LR:Gf6.
Consort XII (16th. cent. English. HENRY VIII MS).
LR:Gf6.
Consort XIX (16th. cent. English. HENRY VIII MS).
LR:Gf6.
Consort XX (16th. cent. English. HENRY VIII MS).
LR:Gf8.
Consort XXI (16th. cent. English. HENRY VIII MS).
LR:Gf6.
Conspexit. (13th. cent. German. CARMINA BURANA).
AA:E8, E17.
Contre le temps (14th. cent. French).
AN:A2.
Contredanses, Suite of (18th. cent. French).
LB:A593.
Coranto (16th. cent. English).
LR:B10.
SI:B1.
La Cornetta – Pavan (16th. cent. Italian).
LR:A4, B32, E56.
Corten espadas afiladas (16th. cent. Spanish. CAN-
   CIONERO MEDINACELLI).
SI:A2.
Courres bregado (16th. cent. French. NOELS DE NOTRE
   DAME).
LR:B14.
Cracovia civitas (15th. cent. Polish).
ER:B46.
LR:E37.
Credo in unum Deum (13th./15th. cent. French. TURIN
   MS).
AN:A14.
Crimina tollis (Agnus trope) (12th. cent. Spanish. SCALA
   DEI).
AA:A2.
AN:B15.
Cristo e nato et humanato (13th. cent. Italian. CORTONA).
AA:C5.
Cruelle departie (17th. cent. French).
LR:E59.
Crucifigat omnes (13th. cent. German. CARMINA
   BURANA).
AA:E9, E10, E12.
Cuckolds all in row (17th. cent. English. PLAYFORD).
EB:B37.
The Cuckoo (Trad. English).
LR:Gd50.
Le Cuer est bon – Basse danse (16th. cent. French).
LR:B10, B11, B13, B31.
Cum animadverterem (13th. cent. French. FLORENCE
   CODEX).
AA:B8.
Cum natus esset Jesus (14th. cent. German. ENGEL-
   BURG MS).
AA:C3.
Cum sint difficilia (13th. cent. French).
AA:D22.
Cuncti sumus – Ballo rodo (14th. cent. Spanish. LIBRE

VERMELL).
AA:A2.
AN:B17, B15, B18.
Cunctipotens genitor (11th. cent. French).
AA:A3, B4.
Cunctipotens genitor (11th./12th. cent. Spanish.
   CALIXTINE CODEX).
AA:A3, B4, B9.
Curant (17th. cent. Polish).
EB:B71.
Currant (Courant) (16th. cent. English).
LR:C21.
Czanner greyner (15th. cent. German. GLOGAUER LIE-
   DERBUCH).
ER:A22.
Czardas (Trad. Bohemian).
AN:B2.
Czlowiek (17th. cent. Polish).
EB:B71.

Dadme albricias (16th. cent. Spanish. CANCIONERO DE
   UPSALA).
LR:E23, E27, F120.
Dal ciel venne messonovello (13th. cent. Italian.
   CORTONA).
AA:C5.
Dale si le das (15th. cent. Spanish. CANCIONERO DE
   PALACIO).
ER:A4.
LR:A2, E27, E28.
Dallying Alman. (16th. cent. English).
SI:B2.
Dami conforto Dio ed alegranza (13th. cent. Italian.
   CORTONA).
AA:C5.
Dance (16th. cent. English. FITZWILLIAM VIRGINAL
   BOOK).
EB:E66.
Dance Tune for broken consort (13th. cent. English.
   BODLEIAN).
SI:C19.
Danse de cleves (15th. cent. Franco-Flemish. MARGA-
   RET OF AUSTRIA).
ER:B19.
LR:B11.
Danse d'etudiants (16th. cent. French).
LR:B19.
Danse Royal (Ductia) (13th. cent. French).
AN:A3, D19.
AN:A16.
LR:B19.
Danse Royal (Estampie) (13th. cent. French).
AA:A3, D18, D19, D22.
ER:A7.
LB:A593.
3 Danses Royales (13th. cent. French).
AN:B10.
Dantz und der auff und auff (16th. cent. German).
LR:C19.
Danza (16th. cent. Italian).
LR:C9, C17.
Danza alta (16th. cent. Italian).
LR:F120.
Danza – Correnta (16th. cent. Italian).
LR:C9.
Danze e arie (16th. cent. Italian).
LR:C25.
Daphne (16th. cent. English).
LR:Gd35.
EB:F91.
Dargason (Trad. English).
LR:Ge36.
The Dark is my delight (16th. cent. English).
LR:Gd49.

Daunce (16th. cent. English).
Sl:B1.

De castitati thalamo (13th. cent. Spanish. LAS HUELGAS CODEX).
AA:C6.

De grad (13th. cent. Spanish. CANTIGAS DE SANTA MARIA).
AA:E7.

De la crudel morte de Cristo (13th. cent. Italian. CORTONA).
AA:C5.

De la tromba pavan (16th. cent. English).
LR:C12.
EB:C8.

De la vida de este mundo (16th. cent. Spanish).
LR:E31.

De los alamos vengo (16th. cent. Spanish).
LR:E31.

De monte lapis (12th. cent. French. ST. MARTIAL MS).
AA:B3.

De muitas guisas (13th. cent. Spanish. CANTIGAS DE SANTA MARIA).
AA:E4.

De ramis cadunt folia (Autumn Song) (13th. cent. French).
AA:B8.

De sedebant bigami (13th. cent. French. MONTPELLIER CODEX).
AA:B2.

Death is sad for frail man (Funeral Song) (17th. cent. Hungarian).
LR:A7.

Deduc Sion, uberimas (13th. cent. German. CARMINA BURANA).
AA:E12.

Defectus misit nos (16th. cent. Polish).
AA:C4.

Degentis vita – Cum vix artidici (14th. cent. French. CHANTILLY CODEX).
AA:B1.

Deh fosse la qui mecho (16th. cent. Spanish).
LR:E27.

Dela la riviere (15th. cent. French).
LR:B14.

Den besten vogel den ich weiss (15th. cent. German).
ER:A25.
LR:B30.

Den lustelijcken mey (16th. cent. Flemish. EEN SCHOON LIEDEKENS BOECK. ANTWERP, 1544).
LR:E21.

Den meinen sack (15th. cent. German).
ER:A25.

Den Winter comt aen (16th. cent. Flemish. EEN SCHOON LIEDEKENS BOECK. ANTWERP, 1544).
LR:E21.

Deo confitemini (13th. cent. French).
AA:A3.

Deo gracis Anglia (The Agincourt Carol) (15th. cent. English).
AA:C1.
ER:B23.
LR:A4, Gf4.

Depositum – Ad solitum – Regnat (14th. cent. French. BAMBURG CODEX).
AN:A12.

Des hadde een swave een dochterlijn (16th. cent. Flemish. EEN SCHOON LIEDEKENS BOECK, ANTWERP, 1544).
LR:E21.

Des oge (13th. cent. Spanish. CANTIGAS DE SANTA MARIA).
AA:E4.

Deus in adjutorium (12th. cent. French).
AA:B2.

Deus in adjutorium (13th. cent. French. MONTPELLIER CODEX).
AA:B2, B3.

Deus in nomine tuo (13th. cent. German. CARMINA BURANA).
AA:E15.

Deus te salve (13th. cent. Spanish. CANTIGAS DE SANTA MARIA).
AA:E4.

Deus tuorum militum (15th. cent. English).
LR:A4.

Dic Christi veritas (13th. cent. French. NOTRE DAME.)
AA:B10.
AN:A11.

Dic Christi veritas (13th. cent. German. CARMINA BURANA).
AA:E8, E10, E14.

Dietky, v hromadu se sendeme (Children let us get together) (12th./14th. cent. Bohemian).
PS:C6.

Diferencias sobre 'Conde claros' (16th. cent. Spanish).
LR:B24.
EB:D28.

Diferencias sobre 'Las vacas' (16th. cent. Spanish).
LR:B24.
EB:D28.

Dindirindin (16th. cent. Spanish. CANCIONERO DE PALACIO).
LR:E31, E62, E64, E65.

Dio s'e fatto fanciullo (16th. cent. Italian).
LR:F100.

Dit la Bourgignon (16th. cent. French).
LR:E25, E38.

Diu werllt frort sih uber al (13th. cent. German. CARMINA BURANA).
AA:E8.

Division (16th. cent. English).
LR:Gd41.

Dizen a mi (16th. cent. Spanish).
LR:E35.

Dlugoz mnq panno (17th. cent. Polish).
EB:B71.

Dobranoc anusienko (17th. cent. Polish).
EB:F104.

Dolce amoroso focho (16th. cent. Spanish).
LR:E27.

Dominator Domine – Ecce ministerium (13th. cent. French. BAMBURG CODEX).
AA:B1.

Dominator Domine (13th. cent. French. NOTRE DAME).
AA:A3, B4.

Domino fidelium (13th. cent. French. NOTRE DAME).
AA:A3, B4, B5.

Donde se sufra Juana (16th. cent. Spanish).
LR:E26.

Dont vient cela (16th. cent. French).
LR:B31.

Dormi Jesule (17th./18th. cent. Polish).
LB:G329.

Douce dame (14th. cent. French. ROMAN DE FAUVEL).
AA:A3.
AN:A15, A16.

Doulce memoire (16th. cent. French).
LR:E42.

La Doune cella (16th. cent. English).
LR:D20, Gc6.
EB:E87.

Dove son quei fiori occhi (16th. cent. French).
LR:C9.

Dowland's Almayne (16th. cent. English).
LR:Gc16.

The Downfall of Dancing (Trad. English).
LR:Gd58.

The Dressed Ship (16th. cent. English. PLAYFORD).

LR:E34.
Drevo se listem odieva (Foliage is beginning to cover the trees) (12th./14th. cent. Bohemian).
PS:C6.
Dreweries accordes (16th. cent. English).
LR:C12, C24.
Drmes (Trad. Croatian).
AN:B2.
Du meine Seele, singe (16th. cent. German. PAUL GERHARDT).
LR:F102.
Du pist mein hort (15th. cent. German).
AA:A2.
AN:A3.
Ductia (13th. cent. English. READING MS).
AA:D14.
LR:E34.
LB:B272.
Ductia (13th. cent. French).
AN:A16.
ER:A7.
LR:A2, B12, B19, C15, E66.
2 Ductiae (13th. cent. French).
AA:A2, A3.
LR:B11, B13.
The Duke of Milan's Dumpe (16th. cent. English).
LR:Gd51.
The Duke of Somersette's Dompe (16th. cent. English).
LR:Gf6, Gf8.
Dulce solum natalis patrie (13th. cent. German. CARMINA BURANA).
AA:A2, E8, E11, E16.
Dulcissima Maria (16th. cent. Italian).
LR:F91.
Dum iuventus floruit (13th. cent. German. CARMINA BURANA).
AA:E8, E9.
Dum pater familias (12th./13th. cent. Spanish. CALIXTINE CODEX).
PS:B22.
AA:E7.
Duma (15th. cent. Polish).
ER:B45.
Dunaj voda hluboka – Officium (16th. cent. Bohemian).
LR:F99.
Dy nacht dy wil verbergen sich (15th. cent. German. GLOGAUER LIEDERBUCH).
ER:A22.

E dame jolie (13th. cent. French).
AA:A3.
E la don don, verges Maria (16th. cent. Spanish. CANCIONERO DE UPSALA).
ER:A24.
LR:F120.
E su su quel monte (16th. cent. Italian).
LR:E56.
Ecce gratum (13th. cent. German. CARMINA BURANA).
AA:E9, E17.
Ecce quod natura (15th. cent. English).
LR:F110.
Ecce torpet (13th. cent. German. CARMINA BURANA – WALTHER VON CHATILLON).
AA:E9, E12.
Edi beo thu (13th. cent. English).
AA:B3, C1.
LR:E34.
Egressus Jesus (13th. cent. French. NOTRE DAME).
AA:B2.
Eja mea anima (17th. cent. German).
LR:F124.
Ellend du hast (15th. cent. German. BUXHEIMER ORGAN BOOK).
EB:E66.

Else el se mundo (15th. cent. German. GLOGAUER LIEDERBUCH).
ER:A22.
Elslein, liebstes Elselein (15th. cent. German. GLOGAUER LIEDERBUCH).
ER:A22.
LR:A1, D14, E24, E35.
En ma dame ai mis mon cuer (13th. cent. French).
AA:A3.
En ma forest (13th. cent. French).
AA:D15.
En Mai la roussee (13th. cent. French).
LR:B29.
En mai – L'autre jour – He! resvelle toi (13th. cent. French. MONTPELLIER CODEX).
AA:B1.
En non Dieu (14th. cent. French. ROMAN DE FAUVEL).
AN:A15.
En Santa Maria (13th. cent. Spanish. CANTIGAS DE SANTA MARIA).
AA:E4.
En todo tempo faz ben (13th. cent. Spanish. CANTIGAS DE SANTA MARIA).
AA:E5.
En vray amour (16th. cent. French).
LR:Gf8.
En wyflye beildt ghestadt (14th. cent. Flemish. REINA CODEX).
AN:B4.
Endurez le maux (13th. cent. French. BAMBURG CODEX).
AA:D16.
L'Enfant de Dieu (16th. cent. French. NOELS DE NOTRE DAME).
LR:B14.
England be glad (16th. cent. English. HENRY VIII MS).
LR:Gf7, Gf8.
English Dance – Estampie (13th. cent. English. OXFORD–BODLEIAN).
AA:A1, A3, D14, D17.
ER:A4.
LR:C15, E64, Gd58.
LB:B227.
Entlaubet ist der Walde (16th. cent. German).
LR:D14.
Entra mayo y sale abril (16th. cent. Spanish).
LR:E28.
Entree du fol (16th. cent. French).
LR:B10, B11, B13.
Epiphanium Domino canamus (13th. cent. French. MONTPELLIER CODEX).
AA:C2.
Era di maggio (16th. cent. Italian).
LR:E56.
Erhalt uns, Herr, bei deinem Wort (16th. cent. German. PAUL GERHARDT).
LR:F102.
Es fur ein pawr (15th. cent. German).
LR:E35.
Es gieng guot tröscher (16th. cent. German. HEER SONGBOOK).
LR:E35, E72.
Es gingen drei Bauern (15th. cent. German. GLOGAUER LIEDERBUCH).
ER:A23.
Es ist ein Ros entsprungen (16th. cent. German).
LR:F126.
Es ist das Heil uns kommen her (18th. cent. German).
LB:E197.
Es ist ein schnee der walde (15th. cent. German).
ER:A25.
Es sass ein meitlein unde spann (16th. cent. German. HEER SONGBOOK).
LR:E72.

AN:A16.
Flavit auster (13th. cent. Spanish. LAS HUELGAS
   CODEX).
AA:C6.
Flete flenda (13th. cent. German. CARMINA BURANA).
AA:E12.
Flor de lis – Je nepu is – Douce dame (13th. cent. French).
AA:D18.
La Florentine (15th. cent. French. MARIE DE BOUR-
   GOGNE MS, 1405).
SI:C2.
Flos filius (13th. cent. French. BAMBURG CODEX).
AA:D16.
Flos filius (13th. cent. French. NOTRE DAME).
AA:A2, A3.
LR:F91.
Flos florum – Ach, du getruys (15th. cent. Bohemian).
AN:B2.
Flos in monte cernitur (13th. cent. French. FLORENCE
   CODEX).
AA:B8.
Flos is rosa floruit (13th. cent. French. NOTRE DAME).
AA:B2.
Flower of flowers (14th. cent. Bohemian).
AN:B2.
La Folia (16th. cent. Italian).
EB:B37.
Folksong tune (Trad. Bohemian).
AN:B2.
Fortune a bien – Galliard (16th. cent. French).
LR:E38.
Fortune my foe (16th. cent. English).
LR:Gd38.
EB:B37.
La Forze d'Hercole – Pavan (16th. cent. Italian).
LR:A4, B20, B32, D17, E56.
Foweles in the frith (13th. cent. English).
AA:C1.
La Francoise nouvelle (15th. cent. French. MARIE DE
   BOURGOGNE MS, 1405).
SI:C2.
La Franchoise nouvelle (15th. cent. French. MARGARET
   OF AUSTRIA).
ER:A8.
French Tuckato (17th. cent. English. ANNE CROM-
   WELL'S VIRGINAL BOOK, 1638).
EB:F91.
El Fresco ayre (16th. cent. Spanish. CANCIONERO
   MEDINACELLI).
ER:A4.
Frog Galliard (after Dowland) (16th. cent. English).
LR:Gc16.
The Fryar and the Nun (16th. cent. English).
LR:Gd23.
Fugue in A maj (18th. cent. Bohemian. COLLECTION OF
   FRANTISEK HULKA).
LB:E242.
Fugue in A min (18th. cent. Bohemian).
LB:E242.
Fugue in C maj (18th. cent. Bohemian).
LB:E242.
Fugue in C maj (18th. cent. Bohemian. COLLECTION OF
   FRANTISEK HULKA).
LB:E242.
Fugue in C maj (18th. cent. Bohemian. COLLECTION OF
   JAN SLAVIK OF HOROVICE).
LB:E236, E242.
Fugue in C maj de tempore Natalis (18th. cent. Bohe-
   mian. COLLECTION OF JAN SLAVIK OF HOROVICE).
LB:E236.
Fugue in C min for 2 organs (18th. cent. Bohemian).
LB:E242.
Fugue in D maj (18th. cent. Bohemian).
LB:E236, E242.

Fugue in D maj on a theme of F.X. Brixi (18th. cent. Bohe-
   mian).
LB:E242.
Fugue in D min (18th. cent. Bohemian).
LB:E242.
Fugue in D min (18th. cent. Bohemian. COLLECTION OF
   CHLADEK OF RAKOVNIK).
LB:E236.
Fugue in D min ad offertorium (18th. cent. Bohemian.
   COLLECTION OF JAN SLAVIK OF HOROVICE).
LB:E236.
Fugue in E maj on a theme of F.X. Brixi (18th. cent. Bohe-
   mian).
LB:E242.
Fugue in E Phrygian (18th. cent. Bohemian).
LB:E242.
Fugue in E min (Attrib. C.P.E. Bach) (18th. cent. Bohe-
   mian).
LB:E242.
Fugue in E min (18th. cent. Bohemian. COLLECTION OF
   JAN SLAVIK OF HOROVICE).
LB:E236.
Fugue in A maj (18th. cent. Bohemian. COLLECTION OF
   JAN SLAVIK OF HOROVICE).
LB:E236.
Fugue in F min (18th. cent. Bohemian).
LB:E242.
Fugue in F min on a theme of J.S. Bach (18th. cent. Bohe-
   mian. COLLECTION OF CHLADEK OF RAKOVNIK).
LB:E236.
Fugue in G maj (18th. cent. Bohemian. BAKOV COLLEC-
   TION).
LB:E236.
Fugue in G min (18th. cent. Bohemian. COLLECTION OF
   CHLADEK OF RAKOVNIK).
LB:E236.
Fulget caelestis curia (13th. cent. English. WORCESTER
   MS).
AA:C2.
Fulget dies celebris (13th. cent. German. CARMINA
   BURANA).
AA:E8, E12.
Fulget hodie de l'espine (14th. cent. French).
LR:F127.
Fulget nunc natalita (15th. cent. Bohemian).
LR:F116.
Funde de celestibus Hyacinthe (14th. cent. Polish).
AA:C4.

Gabriel from heven-king (13th. cent. English).
AA:C1.
Gaite de la tour (13th. cent. French).
AA:D16.
La Gaiette – Pavan (16th. cent. French. MUSIC DE JOYE).
LR:B26.
Gallarda la Royne d'Escosse (16th. cent. French).
LR:Gd42.
Galliard (16th. cent. French).
LR:B13, C20.
Galliard (16th. cent. French. MUSIC DE JOYE).
LR:B26.
Galliard (16th. cent. English).
LR:Gb9.
LB:C29.
Galliard a la Lyonaise (16th. cent. French).
SI:C14.
A Galyarde (16th. cent. English).
LR:D14.
La Gamba (16th. cent. Italian).
LR:A4, B32, E20.
La Gamba in basso e soprano (16th. cent. Italian).
LR:A4, B32.
Gambler's Mass – Officium Lusorum (13th. cent. German.
   CARMINA BURANA).

AA:E13.
La Garde – Pavane (16th. cent. French).
LR:B10, B11, B13.
Garrit Gallus flendo dolorose (14th. cent. French.
ROMAN DE FAUVEL).
AN:A16.
Die Gassenhauer Dantz (16th. cent. German).
LR:F94.
Gaude – Inviolata (13th. cent. English. WORCESTER
MS).
AA:C2.
Gaudet Favellus (14th. cent. French. ROMAN DE
FAUVEL).
AN:A15.
Gavotte (17th. cent. Belgian).
EB:E88.
Gavotte (17th. cent. English. PLAYFORD).
LB:B323.
Gedeonis area (13th. cent. French).
AA:B5.
Gelassen had eyn sustergen (16th. cent. German).
LR:F78.
Gentil madonna (16th. cent. Italian).
LR:A4, B32.
Gerard's Mistress (17th. cent. English).
EB:D30.
Der Gestraifft Dantz (16th. cent. German/Flemish).
LR:C13, F94.
Gilderoy (16th./17th. cent. Scottish).
EB:B37.
Giorgio – Galliard (16th. cent. Italian).
LR:A4, B32, E56.
Girometta (16th. cent. Italian).
LR:A1.
Gloria (14th. cent. Polish. KRAKOW).
AA:B9.
Gloria in altissimus Deo (17th./18th. cent. Polish).
LB:G329.
Gloria in cielo (Laude) (13th. cent. French).
AA:A3.
Gloria in excelsis Deo (13th./15th. cent. French. TURIN
MS).
AN:A14.
Gloria in excelsis (Responsory) (14th. cent. German.
ERFURT MS).
AA:C3.
Gloria 'n cielo e pace 'n terra (13th. cent. Italian. COR-
TONA).
AA:C5.
Gloria tibi trinitas (16th. cent. English).
EB:E66.
Gloriosus Christus rex humilis (14th. cent. Bohemian).
EB:G140.
Go hert, hert with adversitee (15th. cent. English).
AA:C1.
Go, my flock, go get you hence (16th. cent. English.
MUSICAL BANQUET).
LR:Gd30, Gd31.
Goday, my Lord, Syr Christemass (15th. cent. English).
LR:Gf4.
Goddesses (17th. cent. English. PLAYFORD).
AA:D17.
LR:Gd47.
EB:F107.
Goigs de Nostra Donna (14th. cent. Spanish. LIBRE
VERMELL).
AA:A2.
AN:B15, B17, B18.
Good King Wenceslas – Pavan (16th. cent. Bohemian.
PIAE CANTIONES).
LR:E34.
Gracious mistress of the angels (17th. cent. Hungarian.
CANTUS CATHOLICI, 1651).
LR:A5.

La Gran Pena (16th. cent. Italian. HEER SONGBOOK).
LR:E72.
Grande reif'e que mal venna (13th. cent. Spanish. CAN-
TIGAS DE SANTA MARIA).
AA:D9.
The Grange (17th. cent. English).
EB:D30.
Grant despit ai je, Fortune (14th. cent. French. ROMAN
DE FAUVEL).
AN:A16.
Gray's Inn Masque (16th. cent. English).
LR:Gd42.
The Great Boobee (17th. cent. English).
EB:F91.
Green Garters (16th. cent. English. PLAYFORD).
LR:E34.
Greensleeves (16th. cent. English).
LR:E55, Ga15, Gd45, Gd47.
EB:B37.
LB:B324.
Greensleeves to a ground (16th. cent. English).
LB:B249, B253.
Greensleeves and Pudding Pyes (17th. cent. English.
PLAYFORD).
LB:B323.
Greenwood/Dargason (17th. cent. English. PLAYFORD).
AA:D17.
Grimstock – A Jigg (16th. cent. English).
LR:Gd51.
Ground in B min (17th. cent. English).
LB:D217.
Guarda, dona, el mio tormento (16th. cent. Spanish).
LR:E26.
La Guercia (15th. cent. French).
ER:A2.
Guillaume se va chaufer (16th. cent. French. HEER
SONGBOOK).
LR:E72.
Die Güldne Sonne (16th. cent. German. PAUL GER-
HARDT).
LR:F102.

Hac festo die (13th. cent. Polish).
AA:C4.
Hac in anni janua (13th. cent. French).
AA:A2, A3.
Haec dies (13th. cent. French).
AA:A3.
Hajdu Dances (16th. cent. Hungarian).
LR:A6, B27, E37.
Hans, der het ein wib genommen (16th. cent. German.
HEER SONGBOOK).
LR:E72.
Hark, hark, the lark (16th. cent. English).
LR:Gd46.
Hastu mir (16th. cent. German).
LR:A1.
Haulberroys (16th. cent. French).
LR:C20.
Have you seen but a white lily grow (16th. cent. English).
LR:Gd57.
Hayl Mary, Ful of Grace (15th. cent. English).
LR:F110.
He! Robinet (15th. cent. French).
ER:A4.
Hejnal Krakowska (17th. cent. Polish).
EB:B47.
Helas amy – Basse danse (16th. cent. French. MUSIC DE
JOYE).
LR:B26.
Hely, hely (14th. cent. German. ERFURT MS).
AA:C3.
Henry VIII's Pavan (16th. cent. English).
LR:Gf2.

In einem Kripplein (16th. cent. German).
LR:F126.
In fewirsch hitcz (15th. cent. German. GLOGAUER LIE-
DERBUCH).
ER:A22.
LR:E64.
In Gedeonis area (12th. cent. Spanish. RIPOLL ABBEY).
AN:B18.
In Gedeonis area (13th. cent. German. CARMINA
BURANA).
AA:E8, E12, E16, E17.
In illo tempore (13th. cent. French. NOTRE DAME).
AA:B2.
In marie miserie – Gemma pudicie (13th. cent. French.
MONTPELLIER CODEX).
AA:B1.
In marie miserere (14th. cent. French. ROMAN DE
FAUVEL).
AN:A15, A16.
In nova fert animus mutatas (14th. cent. French. ROMAN
DE FAUVEL).
AN:A16.
In pro (14th. cent. Italian).
AN:B8.
LR:A4.
In questo ballo (16th. cent. Italian).
LR:E56.
In Rama sonat gemitus (12th. cent. French. WOLFEN-
BUTTEL CODEX).
ER:B1.
LR:F120.
In saeculum artifex (13th. cent. French).
ER:A7.
In saeculum vielatoris (13th. cent. French. BAMBURG
CODEX).
AA:A3, B8, D18.
ER:A7.
LB:B272.
In taberna quando sumus (13th. cent. German. CAR-
MINA BURANA).
AA:E11, E16.
In terra summus Rex (13th. cent. German. CARMINA
BURANA).
AA:E12, E16.
In Wilderness (16th. cent. English. RITSON MS).
LR:Gf7.
Initium Sancti Evangelium secundum Marcas Argenti
(13th. cent. German. CARMINA BURANA).
AA:E17.
Inscription from the tombstone of Queen Barbara Radzi-
will (16th. cent. Polish).
LR:E57.
Inter densas deserti meditans – Imbrius irriguis (14th.
cent. French. CHANTILLY CODEX).
AA:B1.
2 Intradas for 2 organs, 2 trumpets, 2 horns and tympani
(18th. cent. German).
LB:B203.
Intrada Pastorale for 2 trumpets, 2 organs, 2 horns and
tympani. (18th. cent. German).
LB:B203.
Io m'accorgo d'un altro amante (16th. cent. Italian).
LR:C11.
Io vorrei fuggir (16th. cent. Italian).
LR:C9.
Istampitta (14th. cent. Italian).
LR:B16.
Istampitta Belicha (14th. cent. Italian).
AN:B14.
Istampitta Ghaetta (14th. cent. Italian).
AN:B9, B10, B14.
LR:A4, B16, B25.
Istampitta Isabella (14th. cent. Italian).
AN:B6, B14.

Istampitta Palamento (14th. cent. Italian).
AN:B14.
Istampitta Principio di Virtu (14th. cent. Italian).
AN:B14.
Istampitta tre fontane (14th. cent. Italian).
AN:A2.
Iste confessor (16th. cent. English).
EB:E66.
Iste mundus duribundus (13th. cent. German. CARMINA
BURANA).
AA:A2, E11.
Italiana – Saltarello (16th. cent. Italian).
LR:B25, C11.

Jack Pudding (17th. cent. English. PLAYFORD).
EB:F91.
J'ai trop aime (15th. cent. French. AMERBACH TABLA-
TURE).
LR:D19.
J'aymeroye mieux dormir seulette (16th. cent. French).
LR:B31.
Ja nao podeis (16th. cent. Portuguese).
LR:A8.
Jacet granum (14th. cent. English).
ER:B1.
J'ai fait nouveletement (14th. cent. French. ROMAN DE
FAUVEL).
AN:A15, A16.
J'ai un cuer – Decebit (13th. cent. French).
AA:D18.
J'ai vu la beaute (14th. cent. French).
LR:E59.
Jamais m'aymeray masson. (16th. cent. French).
LR:B31.
Jancu, Janto (16th. cent. Spanish).
LR:E26.
J'ay prise amours (16th. cent. English).
LR:Gf5.
Je m'en vais a Livarro (17th. cent. French).
LR:B12.
Je ne fay (16th. cent. Franco-Flemish).
LR:A1.
Je ne puis – Amors me tienent – Veritatem (13th. cent.
French).
AA:D22.
Je suis d'Allemagne (15th. cent. French).
ER:A4.
Je suis trestout (13th./15th. cent. French. TURIN MS).
AN:A14.
Je trouvay la fillette (15th. cent. French).
LR:B14.
Je vous... – Cancion (16th. cent. Spanish).
LR:D13.
EB:D28.
Jesu Christe Rex superne (13th. cent. Polish).
AA:C4.
Jesu Kriste, scedry knese (Jesu Christ, bountiful Lord)
(12th./14th. cent. Bohemian).
PS:C6.
Jesu Christo gloriosi (13th. cent. Italian. CORTONA).
AA:C5.
Jesucristo hombre y Dios (16th. cent. Spanish).
LR:D13.
Jesu nostra redemptio (14th. cent. French. APT MS).
ER:B6.
Jesus Christ is risen today (Trad. English).
LR:Ge39.
Jezis, nas spasitel (15th. cent. Bohemian. JISTEBNICKY
KANCIONAL).
AN:B2.
Jezusa umarlego stworzenie plakalo (Lenten Hymn)
(16th. cent. Polish).
LR:F97.
Jezusa meke czcijcie (15th. cent. Polish).

AA:C4.
Jhesu, fili virginis (15th. cent. English).
LR:F110.
Jhesu, tu dator venie (14th. cent. French. ROMAN DE
FAUVEL).
AN:A15.
A Jigge (16th. cent. English).
LR:Gb9.
Jizt mne radost ostava (My joy is waning) (12th./14th.
cent. Bohemian).
PS:C6.
Jog on (16th. cent. English).
LR:Gd23.
EB:B37.
Johannes postquam senuit (Benedicamus trope) (14th.
cent. German. BAMBURG MS).
AA:C3.
John come kiss me now (16th. cent. English).
LR:Gb7.
Le Joli tetin (15th. cent. French).
ER:A4.
Jolietement – Au cuer ai un mal – Je ne m'en repentirai
(13th. cent. French).
AA:D18.
The Jolly Carter (Trad. English).
LR:Gd50.
Josef, liber nefe min (14th. cent. German).
AA:B5.
Joussance (16th. cent. English).
LR:Gd38.
Jove cum Mercurio (13th. cent. German. CARMINA
BURANA).
AA:E8.
Jube Domine (13th. cent. Polish).
AA:C4.
Jube domne benedicere – Primo tempore (13th. cent.
French. NOTRE DAME).
AA:B2.
Judea et Jerusalem (13th. cent. French. FLORENCE
CODEX).
AA:B2, B5.
Julia die experta meas vires (16th. cent. Franco-Flemish).
LR:E32.

Dy Katczen pfothe (15th. cent. German. GLOGAUER
LIEDERBUCH).
ER:A22, A23, A24.
LR:A1.
Kate of Bardie (16th. cent. English).
LR:Ga1.
Kedykolwick terazjestos (17th. cent. Polish).
EB:B71.
Kee yeled yoolad lanoo (Isaiah's Prophecy) (Hebrew
Cantillation).
AA:B5.
Kemp's Jig (16th. cent. English).
LR:B21, C21, E55, Gd21, Gd23, Gd45.
EB:F91.
Kere dame (15th. cent. Franco-Flemish).
ER:A11.
The King's Last Farewell (17th. cent. English. THOMA-
SON TRACTS, 1649).
EB:F107.
The King's Morisck (16th. cent. English).
LR:Ga19.
The King's Pavion (16th. cent. English).
LR:Gf5.
SI:C11.
Klobucky Tanecz (17th. cent. Hungarian. VIETORISZ
CODEX).
LR:A5.
Kommt her, der Königs Aufgebot (16th. cent. German.
PAUL GERHARDT).
LR:F102.

Kristus pan se narodil (18th. cent. Moravian).
LR:F116.
Ktoz, jsu bozi bojovnici (Ye, who are the champions of
God) (12th./14th. cent. Bohemian).
PS:C6.
Kyrie de Angelis (14th. cent. English).
ER:B6.
Kyrie magne Deus potencie (13th. cent. French. NOTRE
DAME).
AA:B2.
Kyrie virginitatis amator (13th. cent. German. WOLFEN-
BUTTEL CODEX).
AA:B2.
Krzyzu swiety i chwalebny (16th. cent. Polish).
LR:F97.

Lady Laudian's Lilt (17th. cent. English. STRALOCH MS,
1627/9).
SI:C17.
Laetare Cantuaria (15th. cent. English).
ER:B1.
Lament of the Virgin (Paraphrase of Planctus by Geoffroi
de St. Victor) (13th. cent. Hungarian).
LR:A5.
Lamento di Tristan and Rotta (14th. cent. Italian).
AA:D17.
AN:B3, B9, B14.
ER:A7.
LR:A4, B14, B16, B25, C15.
The Lancashire Pipes and A Pointe or Prelude to be
played before the Lancashire Pipes (16th. cent.
English).
LR:Ga1.
Lapoczkas Tancz (17th. cent. Hungarian. KAJONI
CODEX).
LR:A5.
Las, je n'eusse (16th. cent. French).
LR:A1.
Lasse, pour quoi refusai (13th. cent. French).
AA:D21.
Laudamo la resurrectione (13th. cent. Italian. CORTONA).
AA:C5.
Laudar voglio per amore (13th. cent. Italian. CORTONA).
AA:C5.
Laude novella sia cantata (13th. cent. Italian. CORTONA).
AA:C5.
Laudeamus virginem (14th. cent. Spanish. LIBRE
VERMELL).
AN:B17, B18.
Lavana y suspirava (15th. cent. Spanish. SEPHARDIC
BALLADS).
ER:A26.
L'e pur morto Feragu (16th. cent. Italian).
LR:A1.
Lei graci dei meissouncie (Trad. Provencal).
LR:B19.
Let us not that young men be (16th. cent. English. HENRY
VIII MS).
LR:Gf7.
Li jalous partout – Tuit cil qui sunt – Veritatem (13th.
cent. French).
AA:D15.
Licet eger cum egrotis (13th. cent. German. CARMINA
BURANA – WALTHER VON CHATILLON).
AA:E9, E10, E12, E14, E17.
Die Liebe ist schöne (15th. cent. German. GLOGAUER
LIEDERBUCH).
ER:A23.
Light o' love (16th./17th. cent. English. PLAYFORD).
EB:B37.
Like to the Damask Rose (17th. cent. English).
EB:F103.
Lilio nadobna (17th. cent. Polish).
EB:B71.

Little Musgrave (Trad. English. WIT RESTORED, 1658).
LR:Gd47.
Llaman a Teresica (16th. cent. Spanish. CANCIONERO
DE UPSALA).
LR:E23.
Lodesana – Galliard (16th. cent. Italian).
EB:E56.
Loemos mui' a Virgen (13th. cent. Spanish. CANTIGAS
DE SANTA MARIA).
AA:E2.
Lonc le rieu de la fontaine (13th. cent. French).
AA:A2.
ER:B19.
LR:B11.
Lord Zouche's March (16th. cent. English).
LR:Ge36.
Lord Willoughby (Trad. English).
LR:Gd58.
Loth to depart (16th. cent. English).
LR:Gd51.
Lou paur satan (16th. cent. French. NOELS DE NOTRE
DAME).
LR:B14.
Ludi Sancti Nicholai: 1. Tres filiae. 2. Iconia Sancti
Nicolai (12th. cent. French. FLEURY).
AA:B6.
Lulay, Lullow, I saw a sweete (15th. cent. English).
LR:F110, F127.
Lully, lullay, thou tiny little child (16th. cent. English).
LR:F120.
Lux hodie – Orientis partibus (Song of the Ass) (13th.
cent. French).
AA:B5.
LR:F127.
Lux vera lucis radium (13th. cent. French. NOTRE DAME).
AA:B2.

Ma bono bregado (16th. cent. French. NOELS DE NOTRE
DAME).
LR:B14.
Ma charmante cadet (13th. cent. French).
AA:D5.
Ma tredol rossignol (14th. cent. French. CHANTILLY
CODEX).
ER:A4.
Macht hoch die Tür. (16th. cent. German).
LR:F126.
Madame d'amours (16th. cent. English. SELDON MS).
LR:Gf1, Gf5, Gf6, Gf8.
Madam defrain (16th. cent. English).
LR:Gf3.
Madonna Santa Maria (13th. cent. Italian. CORTONA).
AA:C5.
La Magdalena – Basse danse (16th. cent. Italian).
LR:B25.
Magdalena degna da laudare (13th. cent. Italian.
CORTONA).
AA:C5.
Maggio valente (16th. cent. Italian).
LR:E56.
Magnie Deus potencie (Kyrie trope) (14th. cent. French).
AA:B8.
Magnificat primi toni (15th. cent. German. BUXHEIMER
ORGAN BOOK).
EB:E66.
The Maid in the moon (17th. cent. Trad. English).
AA:D17.
Maiden Lane (16th./17th. cent. English. PLAYFORD).
EB:B37.
Mais nos faz Sancta Maria (13th. cent. Spanish. CANTI-
GAS DE SANTA MARIA).
AA:A3.
Mall Symms (16th. cent. English).
LR:Gb7.

La Manfredina and Rotta (14th. cent. Italian).
AN:B6, B9, B14.
ER:A7.
LR:E34.
La Manfredina de mau-gouver (14th. cent. French).
AA:D20.
La Manfrolina (16th. cent. Italian).
LR:E20.
Maravillosos et piadosos (13th. cent. Spanish. CANTI-
GAS DE SANTA MARIA).
AA:D9.
El Marchese di Salluzzo (16th. cent. Italian).
LR:E56, A4, B32.
Mari Folksongs (History of Hungarian Music).
LR:A5.
Maria decor florum (16th. cent. Polish).
AA:C4.
Maria en mitissima (14th. cent. Polish. KRAKOW).
AA:B9.
Maria muoter reinu mait (14th. cent. German).
AA:A1.
LR:E64.
Maria virgo virginum (14th. cent. French. ROMAN DE
FAUVEL).
AN:A15, A16.
Mariam matrem (14th. cent. Spanish. LIBRE VERMELL).
AN:B15, B18.
Martyn said to his man (16th. cent. English).
SI:A2.
Mascherada (16th. cent. Italian).
LR:B21, C9, C19.
Die Maruscat Dantz und der auf und auff (16th. cent.
German).
LR:F94.
Mater summi Domine (14th. cent. French).
AA:B8.
Una Matica de Ruda (15th. cent. Spanish. SEPHARDIC
ROMANCES).
ER:A26.
Maudi sie tant de ratun (15th. cent. French).
LR:B14.
A Measure. 16th. cent. English. GILES LODGE LUTE
BOOK, 1570).
SI:C3.
Die Megdlein sinnd von Flandern (16th. cent. German).
LB:B273.
Ein Meidlein tet mir klagen (15th. cent. German. ARNDT
VON AICH LEIDERBUCH).
ER:A22, A25.
Menalca surge (17th./18th. cent. Polish).
LB:G329.
Mentem meam (12th. cent. Spanish).
AN:B18.
Menuet des vielles (18th. cent. French).
LR:B12.
Menuet and Gigue for the lute (18th. cent. French).
SI:C19.
Merry milkmaids we (16th./17th. cent. English. PLAY-
FORD).
EB:B37.
A Merry Moode (16th. cent. English).
LR:Gb9.
La Mesnie Fauveline – J'ai fait noiveletement (14th. cent.
French. ROMAN DE FAUVEL).
AA:B1.
AN:A16.
Meza notte (16th. cent. Italian).
LR:A4, B32.
Mich wundert sehr. (15th. cent. German).
LR:B30.
Michi confer venditor (13th. cent. German. CARMINA
BURANA).
AA:E14, E17.
Michill's Galliard (16th. cent. English. MORLEY'S

CONSORT LESSONS).
LR:Ga20.
Mignonne, allons (16th. cent. French).
LR:A1, E24, E44.
Mij quam eyn hope (15th. cent. Flemish).
ER:A4.
Mijn morken gaf mij een jonck wijff (15th. cent. Flemish).
ER:A1.
The Miller of the Dee (Trad. English).
EB:B37.
Min herz lidt schmerz und grosse not (16th. cent. German. HEER SONGBOOK).
LR:E72.
Minnes (17th. cent. Spanish).
EB:D33.
Miri it is (13th. cent. English).
AA:C1.
Miserere my maker (16th. cent. English).
LR:Gd3, Gd18, Gd26, Gd42.
Missa Barcelona (14th. cent. Spanish).
AN:A13, B16.
Missa Barcelona: Agnus Dei.
AA:A2.
AN:B15.
Missa 'Fuit homo missus' (15th. cent. Flemish).
ER:B20.
Missa 'Sanctissimae trinitas' (15th. cent. Franco-Flemish).
ER:B40.
Missa Tournai (14th. cent. French).
AN:A12, A13.
Mista (Trad. Croatian).
AN:B2.
Mistro Rigo (16th. cent. Spanish).
LR:E20.
Mit Got so woln wirs heben an (16th. cent. German).
LR:A2, F78.
El Mois de mai – De sedebant bigami (13th. cent. French. MONTPELLIER CODEX).
AA:B1.
ER:A24.
Mole graviti criminum (15th. cent. German. GLOGAUER LIEDERBUCH).
ER:A22.
Mon amy – Ronde (16th. cent. French).
LR:B11, B13.
Mon desir – Basse danse (16th. cent. French. SUSATO).
LR:B10, B11, B13, E35.
Monson's Galliard (16th. cent. English).
LR:Gd29.
La Mora – Carminum (16th. cent. German. HEER SONGBOOK).
LR:E72.
Morcios los mis moricos (15th. cent. Spanish. SEPHARDIC ROMANCES).
ER:A26.
La Mourisque – Passamezzo (16th. cent. French).
LR:Gf2.
Mout me fut grief – Robin m'aime – Portare (13th. cent. French).
AA:D15, D18.
Muit' amar deuemos (13th. cent. Spanish. CANTIGAS DE SANTA MARIA).
AA:E3, E5.
Muito devemos varoes (13th. cent. Spanish. CANTIGAS DE SANTA MARIA).
AA:E1.
Muito valuera mais (13th. cent. Spanish. CANTIGAS DE SANTA MARIA).
AA:E1.
Mundus a mundicia (14th. cent. French. ROMAN DE FAUVEL).
AN:A15, A16.
Mundus vergens (13th. cent. French).

AA:B3.
Muscadin (16th. cent. English).
LR:D20, Gc12, Gc14.
Musicorum decus et species (15th. cent. Franco-Flemish).
ER:A11.
Mutato modo geniture (15th. cent. French?).
LR:A4.
My delyght (16th. cent. English. ELIZABETH ROGER'S VIRGINAL BOOK).
LR:D14.
My heartly service – The Plough Song (16th. cent. English).
LR:Gf8.
My Lady Carey's Dompe (16th. cent. English).
LR:D17, D20, Gc9, Gf2.
EB:E87.
My Lady Wynfylde's Rownde (16th. cent. English).
LR:A1.
LB:D216.
My Robin (16th. cent. English).
AA:D17.
SI:B2.
My thousand times beloved (Trad. Welsh).
LB:B324.

Die Nachtegael int Wilde (16th. cent. Flemish. AMSTELREDAMS AMOREUS LIETBOECK, 1589).
LR:E21.
Nancie (16th. cent. English).
LR:Ge36.
Nani, nani (15th. cent. Spanish. SEPHARDIC ROMANCES).
ER:A26.
Nas mentes (13th. cent. Spanish. CANTIGAS DE SANTA MARIA).
AA:E4.
Natus est nobis (16th. cent. English).
EB:E66.
Ne m'oublier mie (13th. cent. French. BAMBURG CODEX).
AA:D16.
Ain Neiderlandisch runden Danz (15th. cent. Franco-Flemish).
ER:A2.
Nembressete Madre de Deus (13th. cent. Spanish. CANTIGAS DE SANTA MARIA).
AA:D9, E4.
LR:A8.
Der Neue Bauernschwanz (15th. cent. German. GLOGAUER LIEDERBUCH).
LR:E25.
New Nothing (16th. cent. English).
LR:Gd23.
Newcastle (16th./17th. cent. English. PLAYFORD).
EB:B35, F91.
Ein Niderlandisch Tenzlein (15th. cent. Franco-Flemish).
ER:A2.
Nie zlodziejem (17th. cent. Polish).
EB:B71, F104.
Niemiec (17th. cent. Polish).
EB:B71.
Night Peece (16th. cent. English).
LR:Gd23.
The Nightingale (16th. cent. English. ELIZABETH ROGER'S VIRGINAL BOOK).
LR:D14.
Nina y vina (15th. cent. Spanish. CANCIONERO DE COLOMBINA).
ER:A26.
No la devemos dormir (16th. cent. Spanish. CANCIONERO DE UPSALA).
LR:E23.
Nobilis humilis (Hymn to St. Magnus) (12th. cent.

English).
AA:A1, A3, B4.
Noci mila (15th. cent. Bohemian).
LB:B273.
Noel (16th. cent. ?).
LR:F104.
Noi si vogliam' partire (16th. cent. Italian).
LR:E56.
Nomen a solemnibus (13th. cent. German. CARMINA BURANA).
AA:E8, E10, E11, E14, E17.
Non avra ma pieta (14th. cent. Italian).
LR:A4.
Non egran causa (13th. cent. Spanish. CANTIGAS DE SANTA MARIA).
AA:E6.
Non orphanum – Et gaudebit (13th. cent. French).
AA:B3.
Non orphanum (13th. cent. Polish. STARY SACZ).
AA:B9.
Non quiero ser monja, non (16th. cent. Spanish).
LR:E28.
Non sofra Santa Maria (13th. cent. Spanish. CANTIGAS DE SANTA MARIA).
AA:E3, E4.
Norabuena vengas menga (16th. cent. Spanish).
LR:E28.
The North Country Maid's Resolution and Love to her Sweetheart (17th. cent. English. PLAYFORD).
EB:F107.
The Norwich Minuet (18th. cent. English).
LB:D214.
Nos qui vivimus (9th./10th. cent. MUSICA ENCHIRIADIS).
AA:A3, B4, B9.
Nostro damo aquesto niue (16th. cent. French. NOELS DE NOTRE DAME).
AA:D20.
Nostra phalans plaudat (13th. cent. Spanish).
AA:E7.
Noun pourrie ana plus mau (Trad. Provencal).
LR:B19.
La Nourrico dou Rei Plang de Nostro Damo (14th. cent. French).
AA:D20.
Nova, nova, Gabriel of hygh degree (15th. cent. English).
LR:F110, F127.
Novel amor (13th. cent. French).
AA:D13.
Novis cedunt vetera (13th. cent. Spanish. LAS HUELGAS).
AA:C6.
Novus miles sequitur (Conductus for St. Thomas of Canterbury) (13th. cent. French. FLORENCE CODEX).
AA:B8.
ER:B1.
Now make we mirth (15th. cent. English).
LR:F127.
Now would I fain (15th. cent. English).
AA:C1.
Nowell – The Borys Hede (15th. cent. English).
LR:F127.
Nowell, nowell – Owt of your sleep (15th. cent. English).
AA:C1.
LR:F110.
Nowell, nowell, tidings true (15th. cent. English).
LR:F120.
Nowell, sing we (16th. cent. English. SELDON MS).
LR:Gf1.
Nowell's Galliard (16th. cent. English).
EB:D24.
Nu gruonet aver diu heide (13th. cent. CAR-MINA BURANA – NEIDHARDT VON REUENTHAL).
AA:E9, E17.
Nu lebe ich (13th. cent. German. CARMINA BURANA).
AA:E11.

Nubas (Medieval Arabo-Spanish).
AA:C7, D4.
Nuevas te traygo (16th. cent. Spanish).
LR:E62.
Nun danket all' und bringet Ehr (16th. cent. German. PAUL GERHARDT).
LR:F102.
Nun danket alle Gott (16th. cent. German. PAUL GER-HARDT).
LR:F102.
Nun freut euch, lieben Christen gmein (18th. cent. German).
LB:E198.
Nun singet und seid froh (16th. cent. German).
LR:F126.
Nun wiegen wir das Kindelein (16th. cent. German).
LR:F111.
The Nutting Girl (Trad. English. Morris Dance).
AA:D17.

O admirable veneris ydolum (14th. cent. English).
LR:Gd58.
O beate Stanislae (13th. cent. Polish).
AA:C4.
O bella piu (16th. cent. Italian. MUSICAL BANQUET).
LR:Gd30, Gd31.
O Bethlehem du kleine Stadt (16th. cent. German).
LR:F126.
O dass ich tausend Zungen hätte (16th. cent. German. PAUL GERHARDT).
LR:F102.
O dear life, when shall it be? (16th. cent. English. MUSICAL BANQUET).
LR:Gd30, Gd31.
O dear little nightingale (17th. cent. Hungarian. VIETO-RISZ CODEX).
LR:A5.
O death, rock me asleep (16th. cent. English).
LR:Gd51.
EB:F92.
O divina virgo flore (13th. cent. Italian. CORTONA).
AA:C5.
O gläubig Herz, gebenebei (16th. cent. German. PAUL GERHARDT).
LR:F102.
O great round blue sky (17th. cent. Hungarian. VIETO-RISZ CODEX).
LR:A5.
O Herr, brich den Himmel auf (16th. cent. Bohemian).
LR:F116.
O homo considera – O homo de pulvere – Filiae Jerusa-lem (14th. cent. English).
AA:B3.
O Jesu Christ (16th. cent. German).
LR:F78.
O Jesu meeke (16th. cent. English).
SI:C2.
O Jesus, fair rose, born to the virgin (17th. cent. Hun-garian. CANTUS CATHOLICI, 1651).
LR:A5.
O lusty May (16th. cent. English).
LR:Gf8.
O Maria Dei cella (13th. cent. Italian. CORTONA).
AA:C5.
O Maria, Deu maire (13th. cent. French – Provencal).
AA:B5.
O Maria d'omelia se' fontana (13th. cent. Italian. CORTONA).
AA:C5.
O Maria maris stella (13th. cent. German. WOLFEN-BUTTEL CODEX).
AA:B2.
O Maria virgo (13th. cent. French).
AA:D19.

O miei giorni fugaci (16th. cent. Italian).
LB:B253.
O mitissa virgo – Quant voi – Virgo virginum (13th. cent.
French. BAMBURG CODEX).
AA:A3, B1.
O monialis concio (Planctus) (13th. cent. Spanish. LAS
HUELGAS CODEX).
AA:C6, D12.
O my heart is sore (16th. cent. English. HENRY VIII'S MS).
LR:Gf7, Gf8.
O najdrozsky kwiatku (My dearest flower) (15th. cent.
Polish).
ER:B46.
LR:E37.
O Phillippe, Franci qui generis – O bone dux (14th. cent.
French. IVREA CODEX).
AA:B1.
O Philippe, prelustris Francorum (14th. cent. French.
ROMAN DE FAUVEL).
AN:A16.
O praeclara virginum (16th. cent. German. HEER
SONGBOOK).
LR:E72.
O przedziwna gladkosci (17th. cent. Polish).
EB:B71, F104.
O quantum solicitor (14th. cent. Bohemian).
PS:C6.
O, que bien que baila Gil! (17th. cent. Spanish).
LB:F84.
O Roma nobilis (11th. cent. Golliard Melody).
AA:A1, B8.
O svalanie Konstantske (O ye Council of Constance)
(12th. cent. Bohemian).
PS:C6.
O tocius Asie (13th. cent. French).
AA:D22.
O 'twas on Monday (Trad. English).
LR:Gd50.
O variom Fortunae lubricum (14th. cent. French. ROMAN
DE FAUVEL).
AN:A16.
O variom fortune (13th. cent. German. CARMINA
BURANA).
AA:E9.
O virgo pia (13th. cent. French. MONTPELLIER CODEX).
ER:A5.
O virgo splendens (14th. cent. Spanish. LIBRE
VERMELL).
AN:B17, B18.
O wie gern und doch entbern (15th. cent. German.
GLOGAUER LIEDERBUCH).
ER:A23.
Obra de 1o tono (17th. cent. Spanish/Portuguese).
EB:E57.
Obras de 1o tono sobre la Salve regina (17th. cent.
Portuguese. PERE ROQUE DE CONCEICAO ORGAN
BOOK).
EB:E58.
Occhi belli (16th. cent. Italian).
LR:Gd41.
Occhi non fu (16th. cent. Italian).
LR:A4, B32.
Officium Lusorum – The Gambler's Mass (13th. cent.
German. CARMINA BURANA).
AA:E13.
Offondo do mar tan chao faz (13th. cent. Spanish.
CANTIGAS DE SANTA MARIA).
AA:D9.
Ogn'om canti novel canto (13th. cent. Italian.
CORTONA).
AA:C5.
Oiet, virgines – Gabriel's Prophecy (12th. cent. French.)
AA:B5.
Oime lasso e fredde lo mio core (13th. cent. Italian.

CORTONA).
AA:C5.
Ojos garcos ha la nina (16th. cent. Spanish. CANCIO-
NERO DE UPSALA).
LR:E23.
Olim in armonia (13th. cent. French. LILLE MS).
AA:B8.
Olim sudor Hercules (13th. cent. German. CARMINA
BURANA).
AA:E10, E13.
Omnia beneficia (13th. cent. Polish. STARY SACZ).
AA:B9.
Omnipotens Domine (14th. cent. French. ROMAN DE
FAUVEL).
AN:A15, A16.
Omnis mundis (15th. cent. Bohemian).
LR:F116.
Omnium in te (13th. cent. Spanish. LAS HUELGAS
CODEX).
AA:C6.
On parole de batre – A Paris – Frese nouvele (13th. cent.
French. BAMBURG CODEX).
AA:A3, B1, D18.
On the Death of His Highness Istvan Bocskai (17th. cent.
Hungarian).
LR:E49.
Once I loved a maiden fair (17th. cent. English.
PLAYFORD).
EB:F91.
Omne homo ad alta voce (13th. cent. Italian. CORTONA).
AA:C5.
Or la truix (13th. cent. French).
AA:D20.
Or sus vous dormez trop (14th. cent. French. REINA
CODEX).
AN:B4.
Oracon com piadade (13th. cent. Spanish. CANTIGAS
DE SANTA MARIA).
AA:E5.
Orientis partibus (Song of the Ass) (13th. cent. French)
(See also Lux hodie – Orientis partibus).
AA:A3, B5.
LR:F120, F127.
Les Ormel a la turelle – Mayn se leva – Je n'y saindai
(14th. cent. French. IVREA CODEX).
AA:B1.
Orsu, orsu car' signori (16th. cent. Italian).
LR:E56.
Otce nas (16th. cent. Bohemian).
LR:F99.
Otödik Tancz (17th. cent. Hungarian. KAJONI CODEX).
LR:A5.
LB:B273.
Ough warder mount (16th. cent. English).
LR:Gf6.
Owr King went forth (15th. cent. English).
AA:C1.

Packington's Pound (16th. cent. English).
LR:Gd38.
EB:B37.
Paduana (16th. cent. Italian).
LR:C20.
Paduana Hispanica (16th. cent. Italian).
LR:C17.
Pagamoszka (17th. cent. Polish).
EB:B71.
Pagar ben (13th. cent. Spanish. CANTIGAS DE SANTA
MARIA).
AA:E2, E4.
Palestina hermoza (15th. cent. Spanish. SEPHARDIC
ROMANCES).
ER:A26.
Pan de miglio (16th. cent. Italian).

LR:E53.
Pange melos lacrimosum (13th. cent. French).
AA:B3.
Parson's Farewell/Goddesses (17th. cent. English. PLAYFORD).
AA:D17.
LR:Gd47.
Parthenia Inviolata – Excerpts (16th. cent. English).
LR:Gc15.
Parti di mal (13th. cent. French).
AA:D22.
Pase el agoa, ma Julieta (16th. cent. Spanish. CAN-CIONERO DE PALACIO).
LR:A3, E31, E64.
Pase et medio (16th. cent. French. SUSATO, 1551).
ER:A24.
Pasli ovce valasi (18th. cent. Morarian).
LR:F116.
Passamezzo (16th. cent. Italian).
LR:C11, C19.
Passa mezzo moderno (16th. cent. Italian).
LR:C9.
Passava amor su arco desarmado (16th. cent. Spanish. MUSICAL BANQUET).
LR:Gd30, Gd31.
Pastheen Fionn (Trad. Irish).
LB:B324.
Pastor caesus in gregis medio (13th. cent. English).
ER:B1.
Pastor gregis (15th. cent. Polish).
ER:B45, B46.
Pastorico, non tu a duermas (16th. cent. Spanish).
LR:E31.
La Pastorella (16th. cent. Italian).
LR:E56.
Pastourelle (13th. cent. French).
AA:D20.
La Pastouro e lou segnour (Trad. Provencal).
LR:B14.
Pastyme with good company (16th. cent. English).
LR:Gf6.
Pater noster commiserans (13th. cent. French. NOTRE DAME).
AA:B10.
AN:A11.
Patrie pacis (15th. cent. English).
LR:A4.
Ein Pauer gab seim son ein weib (15th. cent. German. ARNDT VON AICH LEIDERBUCH).
ER:A22, A25.
Pavan (16th. cent. English).
LR:Gb7, Gc12.
SI:C14.
Pavana de la morto de la Ragione (16th. cent. Italian).
LR:A1.
Pavana el Tedescho (16th. cent. Italian).
LR:A1.
Pavana in passe e mezzo (16th. cent. Italian).
LR:A3.
Pavana Venetiana (16th. cent. Italian).
LR:A1.
Pavane (16th. cent. French).
LR:B11, B13, C20.
Pavane (16th. cent. French. MUSIC DE JOYE).
LR:B26.
Pavane and Galliard (16th. cent. English. DUBLIN VIRGINAL BOOK).
EB:E56.
Pavaniglia (17th. cent. Italian).
EB:B41.
Pavin of Albert (16th. cent. English).
LR:Gf6.
Paxarico tu te llamas (15th. cent. Spanish. SEPHARDIC ROMANCES).

ER:A26.
Peccatrice nominata (13th. cent. Italian. CORTONA).
AA:C5.
Per merita sancti Adalberti (14th. cent. Polish).
AA:C4.
EB:E85.
Per te Dei genitrix (Alleluia trope) (13th. cent. English. WORCESTER MS).
AA:C2.
Perdi la mia rrueca (15th. cent. Spanish. CANCIONERO DE PALACIO).
ER:A26.
Perspice Christicola: Sumer is icumen in (13th. cent. English).
AA:C1.
Peticon (13th. cent. Spanish. CANTIGAS DE SANTA MARIA).
AA:E4.
Le Petit Rouen (16th. cent. English).
LR:Gf5.
Der Petler – Ein guet Dantz (16th. cent. German. MUNICH LAUTENTABALTURE).
LR:D21.
Pezzo Tedesco (16th. cent. Italian).
LR:C9, C19.
Der Pfawin swancz (15th. cent. German. GLOGAUER LIEDERBUCH).
ER:A22.
The Pipes of Rumsey (16th. cent. English).
LR:Ga1.
Pisnicka prikladna (16th. cent. Polish).
LR:D21.
Piva (16th. cent. Italian).
LR:A4, B32.
Planctus cigne – Clangam filii (13th. cent. Spanish. LAS HUELGAS CODEX).
AA:D12.
Planctus Maria virginae (13th. cent. German. CARMINA BURANA – GOTTFRIED VON BRETEUILL).
AA:E8.
Planctus mater Domine: Flete fidelis anime – Planctus ante nascia (13th. cent. German. CARMINA BURANA).
AA:E15.
Plange, Castella misera (13th. cent. Spanish. LAS HUELGAS CODEX).
AA:C6, D12, E6.
Plangiamo quel crudel basciare (13th. cent. Italian. CORTONA).
AA:C5.
Planktus Panny Marie (14th. cent. Bohemian).
PS:C6.
Play of Daniel – *see* PLAINSONG.
Play of Herod – *see* PLAINSONG.
Play of the Three Mary's – *see* PLAINSONG.
Pois aos seus que ama (13th. cent. Spanish. CANTIGAS DE SANTA MARIA).
AA:E1.
Pois que dos reys (13th. cent. Spanish. CANTIGAS DE SANTA MARIA).
AA:E4.
Pokaz mi pieka panno (17th. cent. Polish).
EB:B71.
Polish Dance (16th. cent. Polish).
LR:C17.
Polonaises (17th. cent. Polish).
EB:D2.
Polorum regina – Ballo rodo (14th. cent. Spanish).
AN:B10, B17, B18.
El Pomo de lo pomaro (16th. cent. Italian).
LR:A3.
A Poor soul sat sighing (16th. cent. English).
LR:Gd49.
Por alli passo un cavallero (15th. cent. Spanish. SEPHARDIC ROMANCES).

ER:A26.
Por muy gran fremosura (13th. cent. Spanish. CANTIGAS
DE SANTA MARIA).
AA:E4.
Por que llorax blanca nina (15th. cent. Spanish.
SEPHARDIC ROMANCES).
ER:A26.
Porchier mieux estre (14th. cent. French. ROMAN DE
FAUVEL).
AN:A15, A16.
Porque me nao ves, Joanna (16th. cent. Portuguese).
LR:A8.
Porque trobar (13th. cent. Spanish. CANTIGAS DE
SANTA MARIA).
AA:A2, D6, E1, E4, E5.
Potestati magni (13th. cent. Spanish. SCALA DEI).
AN:B18.
Pour haut et liement chanter (13th./15th. cent. French.
TURIN MS).
AN:A14.
Pour leaulte maintenir (13th./15th. cent. French. TURIN
MS).
AN:A14.
Pour mon cuer (13th. cent. French).
AA:A3.
Pour recouvrer alegiance (14th. cent. French. ROMAN
DE FAUVEL).
AN:A16.
Pour ung plaisir (16th. cent. French).
LR:E42.
Pourquoy donc (16th. cent. French).
LR:B31.
Povstan, povstan, velike mesto Prazske (Rise up ye great
town of Prague) (12th./14th. cent. Bohemian.)
PS:C6.
Pravdo mila, tiezit tebe (Dear truth I'm asking you)
(12th./14th. cent. Bohemian).
PS:C6.
Praeludium VI (16th. cent. English).
LR:Gb7.
Praeludium and Fugue (17th. cent. Polish. WARSAW
TABLATURE).
EB:F104.
Praemir dilatio (13th. cent. French).
AA:B3.
Prague Easter Play – *see* PLAINSONG.
Pray for us, thou Prince of Pes (15th. cent. English).
AA:C1.
Pray for us – In this valley (15th. cent. English).
LR:F127.
Preambulum (17th. cent. Polish).
EB:D2, E85.
Pregoneros van y vienen (15th. cent. Spanish.
SEPHARDIC ROMANCES).
ER:A26.
4 Preludes for solo recorder (17th. cent. English).
LB:B291.
Preludes (17th. cent. Polish).
EB:D2.
Prince Rupert's March (17th. cent. English. PLAYFORD).
EB:F107.
The Prince's Masque (17th. cent. English).
LB:D214.
La Princesse (17th. cent. French).
EB:D31.
Prisoner's Song (13th. cent. French – *see also* RICHARD
I).
AA:D18.
Proch dolor – Pie Jhesu (16th. cent. Franco-Flemish).
LR:E32.
Procurans odium (13th. cent. German. CARMINA
BURANA).
AA:A2, E8, E10, E11, E12.
Proeomium (16th. cent. German).

LR:F78.
Propinan de melyor (15th. cent. Spanish. CANCIONERO
DE COLOMBINA).
ER:A26.
Proportz (16th. cent. German).
EB:E66.
Die Prunle die da fliessen (15th. cent. German).
ER:A25.
LR:A2.
Prussian Grenadier Songs and Marches (18th. cent.
German).
LB:A233.
Psallat chorus – Eximie pater – Aptatur (13th. cent.
French).
AA:B3.
Psalm CXXX (16th. cent. Bohemian).
LR:C17.
Pues no me quereis hablar (16th. cent. Spanish).
EB:D28.
Pulcelete bele et avenant – Je languir – Domino (13th.
cent. French).
AA:A3, D18.
Puzzle Canon (16th. cent. English).
LR:Gf8.

Qual e a santiuigada (13th. cent. Spanish. CANTIGAS DE
SANTA MARIA).
AA:E5.
Quan je voy le duc (14th. cent. Italian).
AN:B9.
Quand li oisilons menu chantent (13th. cent. French).
SI:C6.
Quando retrova – Allemana ripressa (16th. cent. Italian).
LR:E56.
Quant ay lo mon consirat (13th. cent. Spanish).
AA:A2.
AN:B15.
LR:A8.
Quant florist – El mois de Mai – Et gaudebit (13th. cent.
French).
AA:B3.
Quant il rossignols (13th. cent. French).
AA:D20.
Quant je le voi – Bon vin doit – Cis chans veult boire (14th.
cent. French. ROMAN DE FAUVEL).
AA:A1, B1.
Quant li bergie (16th. cent. French. NOELS DE NOTRE
DAME).
AA:D20.
Quant voi l'alloete (13th. cent. French).
AA:D19.
Quant voi revenir (13th. cent. French).
AA:A3.
Quant revient et foille et flor (13th. cent. French).
AA:A2.
Quant revient – L'Autre jour (13th. cent. French).
AA:A3.
Quare fremuerunt gentes et populi (14th. cent. French.
ROMAN DE FAUVEL).
AN:A15, A16.
Quasi non ministerium – Trahunt – Ve, qui gregi (14th.
cent. French. ROMAN DE FAUVEL).
AA:B1.
AN:A16.
Que bien me lo veo (16th. cent. Spanish).
LR:E31.
Que chantez vous (16th. cent. French).
LR:Gd46.
The Queen of Bohemia's Dumpe (16th. cent. English).
SI:A1.
The Queen's Jigge (16th. cent. English).
SI:A1.
The Queen's Masque (17th. cent. English).
LB:D214.

Quem pastores (15th. cent. Bohemian).
LR:F116.
Quen a omagen (13th. cent. Spanish. CANTIGAS DE
SANTA MARIA).
AA:E3, E4.
LR:B19.
Quen a virgen (13th. cent. Spanish. CANTIGAS DE
SANTA MARIA).
AA:E6.
Quen boa dona querra (13th. cent. Spanish. CANTIGAS
DE SANTA MARIA).
AA:E5.
Quen Jesu Christe (13th. cent. Spanish. CANTIGAS DE
SANTA MARIA).
AA:E5.
Quen ouver (13th. cent. Spanish. CANTIGAS DE SANTA
MARIA).
AA:E4.
Quen por servico (13th. cent. Spanish. CANTIGAS DE
SANTA MARIA).
AA:E5.
Quene note (15th. cent. French).
AA:A2.
AN:A3.
Questa fanciull' amore (14th. cent. Italian).
LR:A4.
Qui n'a le cuer rainpli (13th./15th. cent. French. TURIN
MS).
AN:A14.
Qui porroit un guierredon (13th. cent. French).
AA:A1.
Quis dabit capiti (13th. cent. Spanish. LAS HUELGAS
CODEX).
AA:C6, D12, E6.
Quodlibet (16th. cent. Italian).
LR:A4, B32.
Quomodo cantabimus (14th. cent. French. ROMAN DE
FAUVEL).
AN:A16.
Quoniam secta latronum (14th. cent. French. ROMAN
DE FAUVEL).
AN:A15.

Racz Panie Chryste (16th. cent. Polish).
AA:C4.
Radosci wam powiedam (15th. cent. Polish).
AA:C4.
Der Ratten Schwanz (16th. cent. German).
LR:A1.
Recordare Dominum (17th. cent. Polish).
AA:C4.
Recruiting Song (Trad. Bohemian).
AN:B2.
Redit aetus aurea (12th. cent. English).
AA:D17.
Regali ex progenie (13th. cent. German. CARMINA
BURANA).
AA:E15.
Regi regnum glorioso (11th. cent. French).
AA:B4.
Regina sovrana di gran pietade (13th. cent. Italian.
CORTONA).
AA:C5.
La Reina xerifa mora (15th. cent. Spanish. SEPHARDIC
ROMANCES).
ER:A26.
Rejoice in the Lord (16th. cent. English. Attib.
REDFORD).
LR:Ge37.
Remember, O Lord, what is come upon us (16th. cent.
Hungarian. HOFGREFF SONGBOOK).
LR:A5.
Resonet in laudibus (17th. cent. German).
LB:E187.

Resonemus laudibus (14th. cent. French).
LR:F127.
Restoes, restoes (14th. cent. French).
AN:A2.
Resurgentis (Benedicamus) (13th. cent. Spanish. LAS
HUELGAS CODEX).
AA:C6.
Resveillies vous a faites chiere lye (15th. cent. Franco-
Flemish).
ER:A17.
LR:A4.
Retrove (13th. cent. French. *See also* – Estampie).
AA:D14.
LR:D17.
Reveillez-vous (16th. cent. French).
EB:D28.
Rex caeli Domini (9th./10th. cent. MUSICA ENCHI-
RIADIS).
AA:A3, B3, B4, B9.
Rex immense (11th./12th. cent. Spanish. CALIXTINE
CODEX).
AA:B3, B4.
Rex obit (13th. cent. Spanish. LAS HUELGAS CODEX).
AA:C6, D12.
Rex omnia tenens (12th. cent. French. ST. MARTIAL).
AA:B3.
Rex virginum amator (Kyrie trope) (13th. cent. French).
AA:A2, A3.
El Rey de Francia tres hijas tenia (15th. cent. Spanish.
SEPHARDIC ROMANCES).
ER:A26.
El Rey que tanto madruga (15th. cent. Spanish. SEPHAR-
DIC ROMANCES).
ER:A26.
Rigaudon, Deuxieme (18th. cent. French. Publ FEUILLET,
1709).
SI:C11.
Rigaudon des Vaisseaux (18th. cent. French. Publ
FEUILLET, 1709).
SI:C11.
Riu, riu, chiu (16th. cent. Spanish. CANCIONERO DE
UPSALA).
LR:E27, F120, F127.
Robin Hood and the Tanner (Trad. English).
AA:D17.
LR:Gd23.
Robin is to the Greenwood gone (16th. cent. English).
LR:C24.
Robinson's May (16th. cent. English).
LR:C21.
La Roche – Galliard (16th. cent. French).
LR:B10.
La Rocha el fusa – Galliard (16th. cent. Italian).
LR:A3, E25, E42, Gf2.
Rodrigo Martinez (15th. cent. Spanish. CANCIONERO
DE PALACIO).
ER:A4.
LR:A3, E27.
Le Roi a fait (13th. cent. French).
AA:D5.
Le Roi Renaud (15th. cent. French).
LR:E59.
Roma gaudens jubila (13th. cent. French).
AA:A3.
Romanesca (15th. cent. Spanish. CANCIONERO DE
PALACIO).
ER:A26.
La Roquel – Galliard (16th. cent. French).
LR:B11, B13.
Rosa das Rosas (13th. cent. Spanish. CANTIGAS DE
SANTA MARIA).
LR:B19, E34, E62.
LB:B259.
Rosemont (17th. cent. French).

EB:D31.
Le Rossignol (13th. cent. French).
AA:D5.
Le Rossignol (16th. cent. English).
LR:A1, C12, E21, E24, Gd21.
EB:C8.
SI:C2.
La Rote de rode (16th. cent. French).
LR:B31.
Roti boully ioeulx (15th. cent. Franco-Flemish. MAR-
GARET OF AUSTRIA).
ER:A8.
Rotulum et tropus (15th. cent. Bohemian).
LB:B273.
Roundo: A New Round Dance (17th. cent. English.
APOLLO'S BANQUET, 1691).
EB:B56.
Roundo of Mr. Tollet (17th. cent. English. APOLLO'S
BANQUET, 1691).
EB:B56.
La Royne d'Ecosse (16th. cent. English).
SI:A1.
Rozkoszna rozo (17th. cent. Polish).
EB:B71.
Rufty tufty (17th. cent. English. PLAYFORD).
EB:F91.
Running Footman (17th. cent. English. PLAYFORD).
LB:B323.
Rupert's Retreat (17th. cent. English. ELIZABETH
ROGER'S VIRGINAL BOOK, c.1650).
EB:F107.

Sacris solemnis (16th. cent. Spanish).
LR:D13.
Sage, daz ihr dirs (13th. cent. German. CARMINA
BURANA).
AA:E8.
Saint Martin's (17th. cent. English. PLAYFORD).
LR:Gd47.
Saint Thomas honour we (14th. cent. English).
AN:B10.
Sally's Fancy/The Maiden's Blush (17th. cent. English.
PLAYFORD).
AA:D17.
Saltarello (14th. cent. Italian).
AA:A2, D3, D14.
AN:B2, B9, B14.
ER:A4, A7, B19.
LR:A4, B11, B16, C15, E34, E35.
LB:B227, B273.
Saltarello (16th. cent. Italian).
LR:B10, B25.
2 Saltarellos (14th. cent. Italian).
AA:A1.
AN:B3.
3 Saltarellos (14th. cent. Italian).
AN:B8.
Saltarello de la morte de la Ragione (16th. cent. Italian).
LR:A1.
Saltarello de la Pavana (16th. cent. Italian).
LR:A3.
Saltarello del Re (16th. cent. Italian).
LR:D17.
Salutiam divotamente (13th. cent. Italian. CORTONA).
AA:C5.
Salve, salve virgo pia (13th. cent. Italian. CORTONA).
AA:C5.
Salve sancta parens (13th. cent. English. WORCESTER
MS).
AA:C2.
Salve sancta parens (15th. cent. Polish).
ER:B46.
Salve virgo virginum (13th. cent. English).
AN:B10.

Salve virgo virgimun – Omnes (13th. cent. French.
MONTPELLIER CODEX).
AA:B2.
Salve virgo virginum (13th. cent. French. NOTRE DAME).
AA:B2.
Samson dux fortissimae (13th. cent. English).
ER:A4.
San Iovanni al mond'e nato (13th. cent. Italian.
CORTONA).
AA:C5.
Sancta trinitas (16th. cent. German. HEER SONGBOOK).
LR:E72.
Sanctissima et gloriosa (13th. cent. German. CARMINA
BURANA).
AA:E15.
Sanctus (13th. cent. English. WORCESTER MS).
AA:C2.
Sanctus (13th. cent. Spanish. LAS HUELGAS CODEX).
AA:B2.
Sanctus trope (14th. cent. Bohemian).
EB:G140.
Sane per omnia (Benedicamus) (13th. cent. Spanish.
LAS HUELGAS).
AA:C6.
Sans faire – Basse danse (16th. cent. Franco-Flemish.
MARGARET OF AUSTRIA).
ER:A8, B19.
LR:B11.
Sans roche – Bergerette (16th. cent. French).
LR:B11, B13.
Santa Maria amar (13th. cent. Spanish. CANTIGAS DE
SANTA MARIA).
AA:E3, E5.
Santa Maria leva (13th. cent. Spanish. CANTIGAS DE
SANTA MARIA).
AA:D9, E3, E4.
Santa Maria, stela do dia (13th. cent. Spanish.
CANTIGAS DE SANTA MARIA).
AA:E2, E3, E4.
Santa Maria, valed (13th. cent. Spanish. CANTIGAS DE
SANTA MARIA).
AA:E4.
Santo Lorenzo, martyr d'amore (14th. cent. Italian).
AA:A3.
La Scarpa (16th. cent. Italian).
LR:A4, B32.
The Scotch Jigg (16th. cent. English).
SI:C3.
The Scots Marche (17th. cent. English. ELIZABETH
ROGER'S VIRGINAL BOOK, c.1650).
LR:D14.
EB:F91.
Se la face ay pale (15th. cent. Franco-Flemish).
ER:A17.
LR:A4.
Se mai per maraveglia (16th. cent. Italian).
LR:A1.
Se ome fezer (13th. cent. Spanish. CANTIGAS DE SANTA
MARIA).
AA:E3.
Sede, Syon, in pulvere (13th. cent. French).
AA:D22.
Seguidillas en eco: Du visita celoso (16th. cent. Spanish.
CANCIONERO DE SABLONARA).
LR:E30.
Seh hin meyn hertz (15th. cent. German. GLOGAUER
LIEDERBUCH).
ER:A22.
Sei, willkommen, Jesus (16th. cent. German.
LR:F126.
Sellinger's Round (16th. cent. English).
LR:Gd38.
Sen calar (13th. cent. Spanish. CANTIGAS DE SANTA
MARIA).

AA:E4.
Serran, donde dormistes? (16th. cent. Spanish. CAN-
CIONERO DE UPSALA).
LR:E23.
Servant regem misericordier (14th. cent. French.
ROMAN DE FAUVEL).
AN:A16.
The Sheep-shearing (Trad. English).
LR:Gd50.
The Shepherd (17th. cent. English).
LB:D214.
Shepherd's Hey (Trad. English. Morris Dance).
AA:D17.
Shepherd's Tune (Trad. Syrian).
AA:A1.
The Shooting of the guns – Pavan (16th. cent. English).
LR:A1, E24.
La Shy myse (16th. cent. English).
LR:D20, Gc6.
EB:E87.
Si aveis dicho, marido (15th. cent. Spanish. CAN-
CIONERO DE PALACIO).
ER:A26.
Si d'amor pena sentis (15th. cent. Spanish. CANCIO-
NERO DE PALACIO).
ER:A26.
Si em llevi un bon mati (15th. cent. Spanish. MONT-
CASSIN CHANSONNIER).
AN:B15.
Si la noche haze escura (16th. cent. Spanish. CANCIO-
NERO DE UPSALA).
ER:A26.
LR:E23.
Si no's huviera mirado (16th. cent. Spanish. CANCIO-
NERO DE UPSALA).
LR:E23.
Si par souffrir (16th. cent. French).
LR:B31.
Si te vas a banar Juanilla (16th. cent. Spanish. CANCIO-
NERO DE UPSALA).
LR:E23.
Si vocatus ad nupcias (13th. cent. German. CARMINA
BURANA).
AA:E14.
Sia laudato S. Francesco (13th. cent. Italian. CORTONA).
AA:C5.
Siberian Folksongs (History of Hungarian Music).
LR:A5.
Sic mea fata canendo solo (13th. cent. German.
CARMINA BURANA).
AA:A2, E8, E11.
The Sick Tune (16th. cent. English).
LB:C29.
Sine nomine (13th. cent. French. BAMBURG CODEX).
AA:D16.
Sinfonia in D maj for 2 trumpets and continuo (18th.
cent. German).
LB:B214.
Sing we to this merry company (15th. cent. English).
ER:B23.
Sir John Smith's Almaine (16th. cent. English).
LR:Gb6.
Sit gloria Domine (9th./10th. cent. French. MUSICA
ENCHIRIADIS).
AA:A3, B3.
Slicznie pieszczona bogini (17th. cent. Polish).
EB:B71.
Slyste, rytieri bozi (Hear, ye Knights of God) (12th./14th.
cent. Bohemian).
PS:C6.
Small pathes to the greenwood (16th. cent. English).
LR:Gf3.
Soberana Maria (16th. cent. Spanish).
LR:A8, F114.

Soester gloria (16th. cent. German).
LR:F111.
Sol eclysim partitur (Planctus) (13th. cent. Spanish).
AA:D4, E7.
Sol oritur in sydere (13th. cent. French).
AA:B3.
Sola me dexastes (16th. cent. Spanish).
LR:E25, E26.
The Solemn Pavan (16th. cent. English).
LR:Gd19.
Soleta so jo aci (16th. cent. Spanish. CANCIONERO DE
UPSALA).
AN:B15.
ER:A26.
Solo de cornemuse (15th. cent. Bohemian).
AA:A2.
ER:B19.
LR:B11.
Le Soleil luit (Lai) (13th. cent. French).
AA:D16.
Sollt ich meinem Gott nicht singen (16th. cent. German.
PAUL GERHARDT).
LR:F102.
Solus cum sola (after Dowland) (16th. cent. English).
LR:Gc16.
S'on me regard – Prennes i garde (13th. cent. French.
MONTPELLIER CODEX).
AA:B1, D15.
Sonata in G min for recorder and continuo (17th. cent.
English).
LB:B291.
Song of the Ass – *See* Orientis partibus.
Song of the Sybil (Trad. Spanish).
AA:A2, B5.
AN:B15.
Song of the Conquest and Enslavement of Hungarian
Soil (16th. cent. Polish).
LR:E57.
The Song of the Wife of Lupul, the Voivode (17th. cent.
Hungarian. KAJONI CODEX).
LR:E49.
Song on the Death of Sigismund I (16th. cent. Polish).
LR:E57.
Song on the Marriage of Sigismund II (16th. cent.
Polish).
LR:E57.
Der Sonnen glanz (15th. cent. German. GLOGAUER
LIEDERBUCH).
ER:A24.
Sophia nascitur (15th. cent. Bohemian).
LR:F116.
Sopra il fieno colcato (16th. cent. Italian).
LR:F100.
Sorella mia piacente (16th. cent. Italian).
LR:E56.
Souche's March (16th. cent. English) (*See also* – Lord
Zouche's March).
LR:Gd29.
Soun tres filho de la Cientat (15th. cent. French-
Provencal).
LR:B14.
Souvent souspire mon cuer (Estampie) (13th. cent.
French).
LR:A3.
Soy serranica (16th. cent. Spanish. CANCIONERO DE
UPSALA).
ER:A26.
LR:E23.
La Spagna – Basse danse (15th. cent. Franco-Flemish).
AN:A3.
ER:A12, A13, A17, B23.
LR:A4, E25, E38, F120.
Spagnoletta (17th. cent. Italian).
EB:B41.

Spaniol Kochersberg (16th. cent. German).
EB:E66.
Spanish Ladies (16th./17th. cent. English. A GARLAND OF GOOD WILL, 1631).
LR:Gd47.
Spirito Sancta da servire (13th. cent. Italian. CORTONA).
AA:C5.
Spirito Sancto dolze amore (13th. cent. Italian. CORTONA).
AA:C5.
Spirito Santo glorioso (13th. cent. Italian. CORTONA).
AA:C5.
Spiritus procedens (13th. cent. English. WORCESTER MS).
AA:C2.
Splendens ceptigera (14th. cent. Spanish. LIBRE VERMELL).
AN:B17, B18.
Sta notte mi sognava (16th. cent. Italian. MUSICAL BANQUET).
LR:A1, Gd30, Gd31.
Stabat juxta Christi crucem (13th. cent. English).
AA:C1.
Staines Morris Dance (Trad. English).
LR:B10, E34.
EB:F91.
Stala matka bolescina (16th. cent. Polish).
LR:F97.
Stantipes (13th. cent. English. READING MS).
AA:B8.
LB:B321.
Stella nouva 'n fra la gente (13th. cent. Italian. CORTONA).
AA:C5.
Stella splendens (14th. cent. Spanish. LIBRE VERMELL).
AN:B17, B18.
Still O Himmel, still O Erde (17th. cent. German).
LR:F124.
Stingo (17th. cent. English).
AA:D17.
Stomme alegro et lazioso (13th. cent. Italian. CORTONA).
AA:C5.
Strawberry Leaves (16th. cent. English).
LR:Gd35.
Su la rivera (14th. cent. Italian).
AN:B6.
Suite of Dances (16th. cent. French).
LR:B31.
Suite regina (16th. cent. Italian).
LR:A1.
Der Summer (15th. cent. German. LOCHAMER LIEDER-BUCH).
ER:A24.
Sumer is icumen in (14th. cent. English – *See also* Perspice Christicola).
AN:B10.
LR:E64.
Superne regnum (17th. cent. Polish).
AA:C4.
Surrexit Christus Hodie I–II (14th. cent. Polish. KRAKOW MS).
AA:B9.
EB:G144.
Surrexit Christus Hodie (15th. cent. Hungarian).
LR:A6.
Svaty Vaclave (Saint Wenceslas) (12th./14th. cent. Bohemian).
PS:C6.
LB:B273.
Sweet England's pride is gone (16th. cent. English).
LR:Gd29.
Sweet was the song the Virgin sung (16th. cent. English).
LR:F120.
Sy j'ayme mon amy (16th. cent. French. HEER SONG-BOOK).
LR:E72.
Symphia in laudem summi regis (15th. cent. German. LEIPZIG CODEX).
ER:A8.
Synge we to this merry compagne (15th. cent. English).
LR:Gf4.
Syt willekomen, heire Krist (14th. cent. German).
LR:F80.

Tak mowie Ludzie (17th. cent. Polish.)
LR:C20.
Take heed of time, tune and ear (16th. cent. English).
LR:Gd53.
La Tambourina – Galliard (16th. cent. French).
SI:C11.
Tance (17th. cent. Polish).
EB:B71.
T'Anderknaken (15th. cent. Flemish).
ER:A2.
Taniec (16th. cent. Polish. JAN OF LUBLIN TABLATURE).
LR:E37.
Taniec (17th. cent. Polish).
EB:B71.
Taniec Alia Poznanie (17th. cent. Polish).
EB:E85.
Tant que vivray (16th. cent. French).
LR:B31.
La Tantaine (15th. cent. French. MARIE DE BOURGOGNE MS, 1405).
SI:C2.
Tantz XXVI (16th. cent. Polish. DANTZIG TABLATURE).
LR:C20.
2 Tantz und Proportio (16th. cent. Hungarian).
LR:C17.
Tappster, drynker, fill another ale (15th. cent. English).
LR:A4, Gf4.
Tarantella for broken consort (Trad. Italian).
SI:C19.
Tarapata (17th. cent. Polish).
EB:D2.
Te Deum in te Domine (13th. cent. English).
ER:A4.
Te Deum (14th. cent. English).
AA:A1.
Te humiles famuli (10th. cent. MUSICA ENCHIRIADIS).
AA:B3.
Te matrem dei laudamus (16th. cent. Spanish).
LR:D13.
Tellus flore (13th. cent. German. CARMINA BURANA).
AA:E9.
Tempus adest floridum (16th. cent. Bohemian. PIAE CANTIONES).
AN:B2.
Tempus est jocundum (13th. cent. German. CARMINA BURANA).
AA:E9, E17.
Tempus transit gelidum (13th. cent. German. CARMINA BURANA).
AA:E8, E12, E17.
Thamus puerpere (14th. cent. French. ROMAN DE FAUVEL).
AN:A16.
Then they for sudden joy did weep (16th. cent. English).
LR:Gd45.
There is no rose of swych vertu (15th. cent. English).
LR:F110, F120.
This day day daws (15th. cent. English).
AA:C1.
LR:Gf8.
This joyful Eastertide (Trad. English).
LR:Ge39.
This merry pleasant spring. (16th. cent. English).
SI:B1.

Thomas gemma Cantuariae (13th. cent. English).
ER:B1.
Thomason Tracts (English, 1649).
EB:F107.
Those eyes (16th. cent. English).
LR:Gd19.
The Three Ravens (Trad. English).
LR:Gd38.
SI:C6.
Ti dounarai dou noutarry (15th. cent. French-Provencal).
LR:B14, B15.
Tickle my toe (16th. cent. English).
LR:B10.
SI:B2.
Tiento de 1o tono (17th. cent. Spanish/Portuguese).
EB:E57.
Tiento de 6o tono (17th. cent. Portuguese. PERE ROQUE DE CONCEICAO ORGAN BOOK).
EB:E58.
Tijs soezas (13th./15th. cent. Greek. PIERIS ZARMAS).
AN:A14.
Time to pass with goodly sport (16th. cent. English. HENRY VIII MS).
LR:Gf5, Gf7.
Toda noite (16th. cent. Portuguese).
LR:A8.
Toe mpaloe (13th./15th. cent. Greek.PIERIS ZARMAS).
AN:A14.
Tordion (16th. cent. French. MUSIC DE JOYE).
LR:B26.
Le Tour – Galliard (1th. cent. French. SUSATO).
LR:E35.
A Toye (16th. cent. English).
LR:Gd35.
La Traditore – Galliard (16th. cent. Italian).
LR:A4, B32, E20, E25, E42.
Transeamus usque Bethlehem (16th. cent. German).
LR:F111.
Transylvanian Dance (16th. cent. Hungarian).
LR:C19.
Tre fontane (14th. cent. Italian).
LR:A4.
Tres doulce regard (14th. cent. Italian).
ER:A4.
Tres morillas m'enamoran (15th. cent. Spanish. CANCIONERO DE PALACIO).
LR:E30, E31.
Tribum quem (14th. cent. French).
AN:A2.
La Tricotea (16th. cent. French).
LR:A1, E24.
Trinck und gib mir auch (15th. cent. Flemish).
LR:B29.
Triory (16th. cent. French).
LR:B19.
Triste plaisir (14th. cent. French).
LR:B29.
Trompetenmusik zu einem Schauspiel zu Ross (17th. cent. German).
EB:B46.
Tristo et cuncti tristantur (13th. cent. Spanish. LAS HUELGAS CODEX).
AA:D12.
Trop souvent me deuill – Brunette a qui (13th. cent. French).
AA:A3.
Troppo perde il tempor (13th. cent. Italian. CORTONA).
AA:C5.
Trotto (14th. cent. Italian).
AA:A2.
AN:B2, B8, B9.
ER:A7, B19.
LR:B11, B12, B16, E64, Gd58.
Tu patris sempiternus (10th. cent. French. MUSICA ENCHIRIADIS).
AA:B3.
Tuba gallicalis (15th. cent. French).
LR:A4.
A Tune of Mr. Purcell's in Amphitrion (17th. cent. English. APOLLO'S BANQUET, 1691).
EB:B56.
6 Tunes for the instruction of Singing Birds (17th. cent. English).
LB:B291.
The Turtle Dove (Trad. English).
LR:Gd50.

Ungarescha No. 3 (16th. cent. Polish. DANTZIG TABLATURE).
LR:C20.
Ungarescha No. 5 (16th. cent. Polish. DANTZIG TABLATURE).
LR:C20.
Unicornis captivator (14th. cent. German. ENGELBURG MS).
AA:C3.
Unser meister het ein magd (16th. cent. German. HEER SONGBOOK).
LR:E72.
Up I arose in verno tempore (16th. cent. English, RITSON MS).
LR:Gf7, Gf8.
Upon 'La mi re' (16th. cent. English).
LR:Gc6.
EB:E66.
LB:E240.
Urbs beata – In dedicatione (16th. cent. German).
LR:F78.
Ure placas votre troupeu (16th. cent. French. NOELS DE NOTRE DAME).
LR:B14.
Ut tuo propitiatus (11th. cent. French).
AA:A3, B4.

Va pur superba va (17th. cent. Italian).
ER:B41.
Vacillantis trutine (13th. cent. German. CARMINA BURANA).
AA:E11, E14.
Van Thilsken vanden Schilde (16th. cent. Flemish. EEN SCHOON LIEDEKENS BOECK, ANTWERP, 1544).
LR:E21.
Vanden Boonkens (16th. cent. Flemish. EEN SCHOON LIEDEKENS BOECK, ANTWERP, 1544).
LR:E21.
Vautre que sias assembla (16th. cent. French. NOELS DE NOTRE DAME).
LR:B14.
Der Vechlienlin (15th. cent. German).
ER:A25.
Vegnando da Bologna – Pavane (16th. cent. Italian).
LR:Gf2.
Veni sancte spiritus – Da gaudiorum (14th. cent. Bohemian).
EB:G140.
Venid a sospirar (15th. cent. Spanish. CANCIONERO HORTENSA).
ER:A4.
Venite e laudare (13th. cent. Italian. CORTONA).
AA:C5.
Venus tu m'a pris – Basse danse (15th. cent. French).
SI:C2.
Verbum bonum et suave (13th. cent. German. WOLFEN-BUTTEL CODEX).
AA:B2.
Verbum caro – Dies et laetitae (14th. cent. French).
LR:F127.
Verbum caro – In hoc anni circulo (15th. cent. French).

LR:F127.
Verbum caro factum est (Laude) (15th. cent. Italian).
AA:B5.
Verbum caro factum est (17th. cent. German).
LR:F124.
Verbum patris hodie – Verbum patris humanatus (12th. cent. French).
LR:F127.
Verbum patris humanator (12th. cent.)
AA:B4.
Vergene donzella da Dio amata (13th. cent. Italian. CORTONA).
AA:C5.
Veri dulcis (11th. cent. Spanish. BARCELONA).
AN:B18.
Veri floris (13th. cent. Spanish).
AN:B18.
Veris ad imperia (13th. cent. French. FLORENCE CODEX).
AA:B8, D3, D5, D19.
Veris dulcis in tempore (13th. cent. German. CARMINA BURANA).
AA:E8, E14.
Veritas arpie (14th. cent. French. ROMAN DE FAUVEL).
AN:A15.
Verlangen hart (16th. cent. German. HEER SONGBOOK).
LR:E72.
Versos varios (17th. cent. Spanish/Portuguese).
EB:E57.
Vesame y abracame (16th. cent. Spanish).
LR:E35.
Vetus abit littera (13th. cent. French. FLORENCE CODEX).
AA:B2.
Vi los barcos, madre (16th. cent. Spanish. CANCIONERO DE UPSALA).
LR:E23.
Victimae paschali laudes (13th. cent. Spanish. LAS HUELGAS CODEX).
AA:B2.
Viderunt Hemanuel (12th. cent. French. ST. MARTIAL MS).
AA:A3, B4.
Vil hinderlist (15th. cent. German. ARNT VON AICH LIEDERBUCH).
ER:A22.
Vil lieber zit (15th. cent. German. BUXHEIMER ORGAN BOOK).
EB:E66.
La Violetta – Galliard (16th. cent. French).
SI:C14.
Virent prata hemiata (13th. cent. German. CARMINA BURANA).
AA:E11, E13, E16.
Virga da Jesse (13th. cent. Spanish. CANTIGAS DE SANTA MARIA).
AA:E4.
Virgen, madre groriosa (13th. cent. Spanish. CANTIGAS DE SANTA MARIA).
AA:E2, E5.
Virgen Santa Maria, guarda nos (13th. cent. Spanish. CANTIGAS DE SANTA MARIA).
AA:E1.
The Virgin Mary at Midnight (18th. cent. Hungarian).
LR:A5.
Virgini matri (13th. cent. Spanish. LAS HUELGAS CODEX).
AA:C6.
Virgo Maria (14th. cent. English).
AA:B3.
Virgo parit puerum (13th. cent. Spanish. LAS HUELGAS CODEX).
AA:C6.
Virtus moritur (14th. cent. French. ROMAN DE FAUVEL).

AN:A15.
Vite perdite (13th. cent. German. CARMINA BURANA – PETER VON BLOIS).
AA:A2, E8, E9, E11, E16.
Vitrum nostrum (15th. cent. German. GLOGAUER LIEDERBUCH).
ER:A23.
LR:E35.
Vive le Roy (17th. cent. English. PLAYFORD).
EB:F107.
The Voice (16th. cent. English).
LR:Gd51.
Volez-vous que je vous chante (13th. cent. French).
AA:D15, D20.
LR:E59.
LB:B259.
Die Vollen brueden (16th. cent. German. HEER SONGBOOK).
LR:E72.
La Volta (16th. cent. English).
LR:Gd35.
Voues ausi la verita (16th. cent. French. NOELS DE NOTRE DAME).
LR:B14.
Vuestros ojos tienen d'amor (16th. cent. Spanish. MUSICAL BANQUET).
LR:Gd30, Gd31.
Vzhuru, vzhuru cechove (16th. cent. Bohemian).
LR:F99.
Der Walt hat sich entlaubet (15th. cent. German. LOCHAMER LIEDERBUCH).
ER:A24.
Waltham Cross (16th. cent. English).
LR:Ge36.
Wanton season (16th. cent. English).
LR:D14.
Warder mount (16th. cent. English).
LR:Gf6.
Warum sollt ich mich denn grämen (16th. cent. German. PAUL GERHARDT).
LR:F102.
Watkin's Ale (16th. cent. English).
LR:B10, C21, Gd38, Gd47.
The Way the white swan weeps (17th. cent. Hungarian. VIETORISZ CODEX).
LR:A5.
We be soldiers three (16th. cent. English).
LR:Gd18, Gd45.
Der Wechter an der czynnen (15th. cent. German. GLOGAUER LIEDERBUCH).
ER:A22.
Welscher Tanz (16th. cent. German).
LR:E69.
What is't ye lack? (16th. cent. English).
LR:Gd49.
Where be ye my love? (16th. cent. English).
LR:Gf2.
Where to, my sweetheart? (17th. cent. Hungarian. VIETORISZ CODEX).
LR:A5.
Who shall have my fair lady? (16th. cent. English. RITSON MS).
LR:Gf7.
Why ask you? (16th. cent. English).
LR:D20, Gc12.
Why shall not I? (16th. cent. English).
LR:Gf6.
The Willow Song (16th. cent. English).
LR:Gd18, Gd23, Gd42, Gd45, Gd51.
Wilson's Wilde (16th. cent. English).
LR:Gd38, Gd42.
The Wind and the rain (Trad. English).
LR:Gd38, Gd45.
Der Winter will hin weichen (15th. cent. German).

Performer Index

Aachen Cathedral Choir, dir. Günther Pöhl.
LR:F26, F80, F124.
LB:G76, G326.
Abbado, Claudio – See Milan Angelicum Orchestra.
 – See I Solisti del Teatro Alla Scala, Milan.
Abdoun, Georg (baritone).
EB:G16.
LB:G192, G259.
Abel, Bruce (bass).
LB:G139, G160.
Academia Instrumentalis Claudio Monteverdi, dir. Hans
 Ludwig Hirsch.
LB:A11, A572.
Academy of Ancient Music, dir. Christopher Hogwood.
EB:A15, F57, F78, F79, F80, F81.
LB:A22, A35, A54, A236, A268, A488, A574, A596,
 F32, G126, G226, G290, G305.
SI:A1, A2.
Academy of St. Martin-in-the-Fields, dir. Iona Brown.
LB:A482.
Academy of St. Martin-in-the-Fields, dir. George Guest.
EB:G55, G78.
Academy of St. Martin-in-the-Fields, dir. Philip Ledger.
EB:G22.
LB:F41, G2, G133, G171, G319.
Academy of St. Martin-in-the-Fields, dir. Raymond
 Leppard.
LB:F49.
Academy of St. Martin-in-the-Fields, dir. Neville
 Marriner.
EB:A3, A11, F95.
LB:A24, A27, A66, A83, A95, A154, A161, A192, A199,
 A219, A258, A263, A283, A286, A298, A312, A328,
 A330, A334, A346, A408, A409, A422, A427, A430,
 A475, A477, A560, A561, A581, A594, A598, A608,
 A616, A647, A652, A657, A666, A668, B95, B105,
 F36, F78, G50, G85, G109, G174, G224, G246.
Academy of St. Martin-in-the-Fields, dir. David Will-
 cocks.
LB:F31, G83, G204, G206, G207, G208, G211, G230,
 G272, G319, G320.
Academy of St. Martin-in-the-Fields Choir, dir. Neville
 Marriner.
LB:G85, G109, G224.
Academy of Worcester Cathedral, dir. Donald Hunt.
LB:G190.
Accademia Monteverdiana, dir. Dennis Stevens.
AA:C2.
ER:B1.
LR:B10.
EB:F22, G65.
LB:A483.
Accademici di Milano, dir. Piero Santi.
LB:A559.
Accardo, Salvatore (violin).
LB:A371, A494, B16, B193, B195.
Ackermann, Manfred (bass).
LB:G159.
Ackermann, Wilhelm (trumpet).
LB:A660.
Adam, Rosemarie (soprano).
EB:G88.
Adam, Theo (bass-baritone).
LR:F3.

EB:G121, G125.
LB:F10, F12, F16, F82, G47, G64, G69, G87, G91, G92,
 G93, G105, G238.
Addison, Adele (soprano).
LB:G237.
Addison, Sue (sackbutt).
LR:Gd43.
Aets, Karel – See Choeur Concinitie et Schola Cantorum,
 Louvaine.
Aeschbacher, Gerhard (harpsichord).
LB:A132.
Agerich, Martha (soprano).
LB:D61.
Agnel, Henri (lute, cittern, darabouka).
LR:B29.
Agosti, Rashida (contralto).
LR:E4, E5.
Ahlgrimm, Isolde (harpsichord).
LB:D77.
Ahrens, Hans Georg (bass).
LB:G152.
Alain, Marie-Claire (organ).
EB:E40.
LB:A31, A208, A300, A301, A308, A513, B204, B207,
 B208, B216, E10, E11, E12, E13, E14, E135, E138,
 E148, E162, E175, G45.
Alain, Olivier (organ).
LB:E138.
Alan, Hervey (bass-baritone).
EB:F74, F77.
LB:G157.
Alarius Ensemble.
EB:B35, B43, B48.
Alda, Caterina (soprano).
EB:G127.
Aldeburgh Festival Strings, dir. Steuart Bedford.
EB:F64.
Aldwinckle, Robert (harpsichord).
LB:D236.
Ales, Georges (violin).
EB:A27.
All Saint's, Margaret Street, Boy's Choir.
ER:B2, B4.
LR:F127.
Allard, Maurice (bassoon).
LB:A558.
Alldis, John – See John Alldis Choir.
Allegri, Maria Grazia (contralto).
LB:G286.
Allen, Betty (contralto).
LB:G244.
Allen, Roger (organ).
LB:E227.
Allen, Thomas (bass). EB:G71.
LB:F39, F40.
Alpert, Lorenzo (recorder, percussion) (Member of
 HESPERION XX).
SI:A2.
Alsfelder Vocal Ensemble, dir. Wolfgang Helbich.
LR:F27.
LB:G255, G318.
Altena, Marius von (tenor).
EB:F23.
LB:G12, G18, G25, G33.

EB:D9.
LB:A182, A600, B131, B179, B190, B191, D2, D3, D60.
Assisi, Choir of the Papal Chapel of St. Francis of, dir. Alfonso de Ferrara.
PS:A24.
Astle, Jo (recorder).
LR:Gd43.
Astle, Philip – *See* Peasants All.
Atkinson, Lynton (boy treble).
EB:G77.
Atmacayan, Garo (cello, double-bass).
EB:B8.
LB:B196.
Atrium Musicum, Madrid, dir. Gregorio Paniagua.
AA:A2, C6, C7, D4, D24, E4.
AN:B16, B18.
LR:B8, E28.
EB:B63.
Aubrey-Luchini, Andree (soprano).
LB:G256.
Auger, Arleen (soprano).
LR:F3.
LB:F12, F60, G109, G145, G154.
Aulos Ensemble.
LB:B276.
Auriacombe, Louis – *See* Toulouse Chamber Orchestra.
Austrian Radio Chorus and Orchestra, dir. Charles Mackerras.
LB:G238.
Aveling, Valda (harpsichord).
LB:A299, A311, A315, D186.
Avignon Vocal Ensemble, dir. Georges Durand.
LR:F115.
EB:G37, G38, G39, G40.
Ayo, Felix (violin).
LB:A393, A433, A449, A497, B18.

Baccelli, Umberto (horn).
LB:A388.
Bach Choir, dir. Reginald Jacques.
LB:G142.
Bach Choir, dir. David Willcocks.
LR:F10.
LB:G148.
Bachtiar, Alexandra (cello).
LB:B158.
Baciero, Antonio (organ, harpsichord, clavichord).
LR:D1, D2, D3, D4, D5, D6, D7, D8.
Badea, Christian (violin).
LB:B316.
Badev, Gyorgi (violin).
LB:A82, A84.
Badini, Giuliana – *See* Sienna Sinfonia.
Bahr, Gunilla von (flute).
LB:A173, A623, B240, F83.
Bailes, Anthony (lute).
LR:E48, Gd31.
EB:C8, C10, F98.
LB:B297, C15.
Baker, Janet (mezzo-soprano).
LR:Gd22.
EB:F5, F47, F62, F63, F64, F95.
LB:A477, F59, G65, G66, G82, G85, G109, G114, G131, G137, G171, G174, G216, G231, G248, G272, G230.
Baker, Mark (bass).
EB:F68.
Baker-Genovesi, Margaret (mezzo-soprano).
EB:F39, F43.
Bakfark Consort.
LR:A7, E49.
Balcells, Rosa (harp).
LR:E51.

Baldin, Aldo (tenor).
LB:G152, G184.
Balint, B (violin).
LB:A81.
Ball, Christopher (recorder, cornemuse, crumhorn, dulcian, etc).
EB:B13.
Ball, Christopher – *See* Praetorius Consort.
Balmas, Elisabeth (violin).
LB:B194.
Balser, Alfred (horn).
LB:A413.
Baltsa, Agnes (contralto).
LB:G122.
Bamburg Symphony Orchestra, dir. Hanspeter Gmür.
LB:A70.
Banas, Bozena (soprano).
LR:F76.
Banchini, Chiara (violin).
LB:B116, B117.
Banda, Ede (cello).
EB:B7.
LB:B74, B130.
Bannwart, Fr. Roman – *See* Maria Einsiedeln.
Barab, Seymour (viol).
AA:D6.
Barbe, Helmut – *See* Berlin Bach Orchestra.
– *See* St. Nikolai Kantorei.
Barbe, Henriette (harpsichord).
LB:A57, B71, B184, B185, B189, B232.
Barbirolli, John – *See* English Chamber Orchestra.
– *See* Pro Arte Orchestra.
Barcis, Elena (soprano).
EB:F48.
Bardolet, Jordi (boy soprano).
LB:G193.
Barenboim, Daniel – *See* English Chamber Orchestra.
– *See* New Philharmonia Chorus and Orchestra.
Barham, Edmund (tenor).
LB:G295.
Barlay, Zsuzsa (soprano).
LB:G287.
Barlow, Jeremy (recorder, regal, virginal).
EB:B37.
Barmen-Gemarke Kantorei, dir. Helmut Kahlhöfer.
LR:F105, F112.
EB:G9, G51.
LB:F11, G36, G49, G53, G100, G183, G325.
Baron, Samuel (flute).
LB:B188.
Baross, Gabor – *See* Bartok Chorus of the Eotvos Lorand University.
Baroti, Istvan (organ).
LB:E239.
Barrington, Sarah (oboe).
LB:A619.
Barshai, Rudolph – *See* Moscow Chamber Orchestra.
Barsony, Laszlo (viola d'amore).
LB:A529.
Bartel, Reinhold (tenor).
EB:F44.
Bartok Chorus of the Eotvos Lorand University, dir. Gabor Baross.
EB:G142.
Bartoli, Rene (guitar).
LB:B290.
Bartolucchi, Domenico – *See* Sistine Chapel Choir.
Bartonikovi, Hans (oboe).
LB:A665.
Bartonikovi, Josef (oboe).
LB:A665.
Bäss, Hajo (violin) (Member of MUSICA ANTIQUA COLOGNE).
EB:F89.

Bastin, Jules (bass).
LB:G188, G197, G200, G201.
Bate, Jennifer (organ).
LB:E15.
Bath Festival Orchestra, dir. Yehudi Menuhin.
LB:A99, A121, A167, A202, A266, A299, A310, A311,
A315, A320, G65, G66.
Baumann, Christiane (soprano).
LB:G10.
Baumann, Hermann (horn).
LB:A354, A386, B220.
Baumgartner, Rudolf (violin).
LB:A213, A214.
Baumgartner, Rudolf - *See* Lucerne Festival Strings.
Bavarian Radio Symphony Orchestra and Chorus, dir.
Eugen Jochum.
LB:G166.
Bavarian State Orchestra Chamber Ensemble, dir. Hans
Ludwig Hirsch.
EB:G15.
BBC Chorus.
LB:G114.
BBC Singers, dir. John Poole.
EB:G143.
SI:D4.
Beacamp, Rene - *See* Rouen Chamber Orchestra.
Bean, Hugh (violin).
LB:A78, A463.
Beaucoudray, Marc (flute).
LB:B82.
Beaumadier, Jean-Louis (piccolo, flute).
LB:A547.
Beavan, Nigel (bass).
EB:F75.
Bec Hellouin, Choir of the Benedictine Abbey of.
PS:A7, B9.
Beckedorf, Horst (cello).
LB:A521.
Beckensteiner, Jean-Francois (harpsichord, organ).
LB:A620.
Beckett, John - *See* Musica Reservata.
Beckmann, Friedel (contralto).
LB:G140.
Bedford, Steuart - *See* Aldeburgh Festival Strings.
Bedois, Arsene (organ).
EB:E58.
Beecham, Thomas - *See* Royal Philharmonic Orchestra.
Beecham Choral Society.
LB:G251.
Beek, Andrew van der (cornet).
SI:B1.
Beganyi, Ferenc (bass).
LB:G39.
Behrend, Siegfried (guitar).
LR:B25.
LB:A565, A573, C27, C29, C31.
Behrend, Siegfried - *See* Deutsche Zupforchester.
Behrmann, Martin - *See* Spandauer Kantorei.
Beinem, Eduard van - *See* Concertgebouw Orchestra,
Amsterdam.
- *See* London Philharmonic Orchestra.
Belliard, Jean (counter-tenor).
AA:D8, D16, D23.
ER:A13.
LR:E59.
Belsky, Vratislav (chamber organ).
LB:A665.
Benbow, Charles (organ).
LB:E16, E17.
Bence, Margarethe (contralto).
EB:F44.
LB:F7, F8, G62.
Benda, Hans von - *See* Berlin Philharmonic Orchestra.
Bende, Zsolt (baritone).

EB:F88.
LB:G287, G297.
Benelli, Ugo (tenor).
LB:A432, G302.
Bengtson, Stig (flute).
LB:A1.
Benkö, Daniel (lute).
LR:A7, C1, C2, C3, E49.
EB:B66.
LB:A529.
Bennett, William (flute).
LB:A69, A192, A199, A222, A427, A560, A561, A594,
B78, B84.
Beraza, Jacques (organ).
EB:E66.
Berberian, Cathy (soprano).
EB:F39, F40, F46.
Berbie, Jane (mezzo-soprano).
EB:F6.
LB:G309.
Berg, Arne (tenor).
LR:E19.
Berganza, Teresa (mezzo-soprano).
LR:E62.
EB:F101, G82.
LB:G267, G289, G311.
Berger, Franz (violin).
LB:B322.
Berkeley Chamber Singers, dir. Alden Gilchrist.
ER:B16, B41.
Berkes, Kalman (clarinet).
LB:B92.
Berlin Bach Orchestra, dir. Helmut Barbe.
LB:G13.
Blin Bach Orchestra, dir. Helmut Kahlhöfer.
EB:G9.
Berlin Bach Orchestra, dir. Eberhard Wenzel.
LB:G217.
Berlin Brandenburg Orchestra, dir. Rene Klopfenstein.
LB:A23.
Berlin Chamber Orchestra, dir. Helmut Koch.
LB:G93.
Berlin Chamber Orchestra, dir. Vittorio Negri.
LB:A7, A449, F77, G284, G285.
Berlin Chamber Orchestra, dir. Peter Schreier.
LB:F2, F10, F12, F16.
Berlin Ensemble für Alte Musik.
ER:A22.
LR:F103.
Berlin Philharmonic Orchestra (without dir.)
LB:A418.
Berlin Philharmonic Orchestra, dir. Hans von Benda.
LB:A628, A640.
Berlin Philharmonic Orchestra, dir. Wilhelm Brückner-
Rüggeberg.
LB:A640, F82.
Berlin Philharmonic Orchestra, dir. Wilhelm
Furtwängler.
LB:A170.
Berlin Philharmonic Orchestra, dir. Herbert von Karajan.
LB:A88, A90, A93, A166, A287, A412, A441, A495,
A611, G107, G122, G136.
Berlin Philharmonic Orchestra, dir. Raphael Kubelik.
LB:A239, A250, A259.
Berlin Philharmonic Orchestra, dir. Karl Richter.
LB:A242.
Berlin Radio Choir.
LB:F77.
Berlin Radio Soloists, dir. Vittorio Negri.
LB:G284, G285.
Berlin Radio Symphony Orchestra, dir. Lorin Maazel.
LB:G108, G268.
Berlin Symphony Orchestra, dir. Karl Forster.
LB:G153.

Berman, Karel (bass).
LB:G316.
Bernard Thomas Chamber Orchestra, dir. Bernard
  Thomas.
LB:A29, A50, A394, A451, A569, D221.
Bernard, Andre (trumpet).
LB:A19, A333, A378, A664, A670, B213.
Bernard, Claire (violin).
LB:A425, B154, B173.
Bernadin, Anne (soprano).
LB:G295, G303.
Bern Bach Choir, dir. Theo Loosli.
LB:G154.
Bern Chamber Orchestra, dir. Theo Loosli.
LB:G154.
Bernat-Klein, Gundula (soprano).
LR:F108.
EB:G10, G69, G89, G90, G91, G92, G93, G94, G95.
LB:G27, G124.
Bernes, Andre (trumpet).
LB:A571, A589.
Bernstein, Heinz (positive organ, harpsichord).
LR:E68.
Bernstein, Leonard – See New York Philharmonic
  Orchestra.
Berruti, Achille (organ).
EB:B62.
Berry, Walter (bass).
LB:G136, G147, G150, G159.
Bertola, Giulio – See Milan Angelicum Orchestra.
Bessac, Francine (soprano).
EB:G41.
Best, Martin (tenor) (and Martin Best Consort).
AA:D5.
LR:Gd23.
Betoulieres, Jacques (organ).
EB:E32.
Bettens, Ethienne (bass).
LB:G273.
Beuerle, Hans Michael – See Frankfurt Chamber Choir.
Beuron – See St. Martin.
Beusche, Christian (cello).
LB:B245.
Beusker, Gerd (tenor).
LB:G282.
Bevan, Maurice (baritone).
EB:F72, F75, F94, G78.
LB:F34.
Beverley, Mary (soprano).
EB:G23.
SI:A2, B1.
Bevers, Jodie (cello).
LB:B159.
Bex, Robert (cello).
LB:A33.
Beyer, Franz (viola).
LB:A635.
Bianchi, Virginia (bassoon).
LB:A559.
Bickenbach, Christfried (positive organ).
LB:G177.
Bielefeld Children's Choir.
LR:F106.
Biggs, E. Power (organ).
LB:A296, B219.
Bihn, Friedrich – See Hamburg Symphony Orchestra.
Bilgram, Hedwig (harpsichord, organ).
LB:A119, A146, A147, A213, A669, B76, B83, B112,
  B211, B218, B221, B222, B224, G105, G181.
Billeter, Bernhard (organ).
LR:B24.
Bilt, Peter van der (bass).
LB:G239.
Bima, Jeanne Maria (soprano).

LB:G296.
Binkley, Thomas – See Studio der Frühen Musik.
Birchmeier, Oskar (harpsichord).
LB:B301.
Birkeland, Helge (bass).
LB:G240.
Bise, Juliette (soprano).
EB:F42.
LB:G254.
Björkegren, Ulf (tenor).
LB:G74.
Björlin, Ulf – See Drottningholm Theatre Orchestra.
  – See Prague Chamber Orchestra.
  – See Stockholm Baroque Ensemble.
Blachley, Alexander – See Pomerium Musices.
  – See Schola Antiqua.
Blachut, Beno (tenor).
LB:G315.
Black, Neil (oboe).
LB:A175, A192, A222, A427, A560, A561, A567.
Blackley, R. John – See Schola Antiqua.
Blanckenberg, Heinz (baritone).
LB:G146.
Blech, Harry – See London Mozart Players.
Blees, Thomas (cello).
LB:A352, A362, A635.
Bloch, Francoise (viol).
LB:B269.
Blood, Christine (recorder).
SI:C11, C12.
Boatwright, Helen (soprano).
LB:G202, G203, G205.
Bobesco, Lola (violin).
LB:A504, A612, B316, B318.
Boegner, Michele (piano).
LB:A131.
Boeke, Kees (recorder).
LB:B190, B267, B274.
Boekel, Meindert (organ).
LB:E187.
Boepple, Paul – See Dessoff Choirs.
  – See Symphony of the Air.
Boettcher, Wolfgang (cello).
LB:B134, B238.
Bogacchi, Hans (oboe).
LB:A413.
Bogatin, Barbara (cello).
LB:B314.
Boggis, Peter (counter-tenor).
EB:F70.
Böhme, Kurt (bass).
LB:G143.
Bol, Hans (viol).
LB:B157.
Bollen, Ria (contralto).
LB:G198.
Bolliger, Albert (organ).
EB:E46.
Bologna Philharmonic Orchestra, dir. Angelo Ephrikian.
EB:A29.
LB:A507.
Bonaldi, Clara (violin).
LB:B3.
Bonay, Adele (contralto).
EB:F48.
LB:A432, G302.
Bonell, Carlos (guitar).
LB:C23.
Bonifaccio, Maddalena (soprano).
LB:F51.
Bonynge, Richard – See English Chamber Orchestra.
  – See London Symphony Orchestra.
  – See New Symphony Orchestra of London.
Borgonovo, Pietro (oboe).

LB:A6.
Bork, Hanneke van (soprano).
LB:G273.
Bornemann, Eva (contralto).
EB:G88.
LB:G20, G27, G31, G163.
Bosse, Helmut (violin).
LB:B150.
Bössow, Rolf (tenor).
EB:G88, G89, G94, G126.
LB:G235.
Boston Camerata, dir. Joel Cohen.
AA:B5.
ER:A6.
LR:F4.
EB:F34, F68, G25, G145.
Boston Camerata Motet Choir, dir. Joshua Rifkin.
LR:F75.
Boston Pops Orchestra, dir. Arthur Fiedler.
LB:A209.
Both, Andre (horn).
LB:A634.
Bott, Catherine (soprano, psaltery, positive organ).
AA:E17.
Boulay, Laurence (harpsichord, virginals).
EB:D23, G30.
Boulez, Pierre – *See* New York Philharmonic Orchestra.
   – *See* Paris Opera Orchestra.
Boulfroy, Alain – *See* Prague Chamber Orchestra.
Boulin, Sophie (soprano).
LB:A634.
Boult, Adrian – *See* London Philharmonic Orchestra.
   – *See* London Symphony Orchestra.
   – *See* Philomusica of London.
Bouman, Henk (harpsichord, chamber organ) (Member
   of MUSICA ANTIQUA, COLOGNE).
Bourgue, Maurice (oboe).
LB:A15, A589, B201.
Bournemouth Sinfonietta, dir. Kenneth Montgomery.
LB:A25, A56, A276.
Bournemouth Sinfonietta, dir. Ronald Thomas.
LB:A26, A221, A450.
Bournemouth Sinfonietta, dir. Volker Wangenheim.
LB:A587, A624.
Bowen, Kenneth (tenor).
LB:G236.
Bowers-Broadbent, Christopher (harpsichord).
LB:D163.
Bowman, James (counter-tenor).
AN:A7.
LR:Gd10, Gd42, Gd44, Gd48, Gd51, Gf6.
EB:F5, F41, F61, F71, G62, G72, G75.
LB:B227, F32, F37, F41, G144, G230, G245, G250,
   G305.
Boxall, Maria (harpsichord).
SI:C11.
Boyce, Bruce (baritone).
EB:G42, G61.
Boyd Neel Orchestra.
LB:A255, A269.
Boyd Neel Orchestra, dir. Roy Henderson.
LB:G269.
Boyd Neel Orchestra, dir. Anthony Lewis.
EB:F70.
Boyd Neel String Orchestra, dir. Thurston Dart.
LRGa10.
Boyer, Jean (organ).
EB:E1.
Brain, Dennis (horn).
LB:G112.
Brand, Tom (tenor).
LB:F9.
Brandhoff, Ulrich (cornet).
EB:F40.

Brandis, Thomas (violin).
LB:A388, A418, A495, B116, B117.
Brannigan, Owen (bass).
EB:F5, F71.
LB:F24, F35.
Bratislava Chamber Orchestra.
LB:A68.
Bratschke, Detlef (boy soprano).
LB:G59, G68.
Brauer, Herbert (baritone).
LB:F82.
Braun, Matitiahu (violin).
LB:A580.
Braunholz, Bernhard (cello).
LB:A228.
Bream, Julian (lute, guitar).
LR:C7, C16, Gb2, Gb3, Gb4, Gb5, Gb8, Gd39, Gd55.
LB:A327, C9, C24.
Bream Consort.
LR:Gd21.
Brejza, Josef (horn).
LB:A331.
Bremen Bach Orchestra, dir. Hans Heintze.
LB:G27.
Bremen Cathedral Choir.
LB:G27.
Brendel, Alfred (piano).
LB:D62.
Brenner, Roger (sackbut).
SI:A2.
Bressler, Charles (tenor).
LB:G202, G203, G205.
Brett, Charles (counter-tenor).
EB:F61, G22, G63, G71, G72, G78.
LB:G212, G218.
Brewer, Edward (harpsichord).
EB:F54.
LB:B141, B188.
Brewer, Virginia (oboe).
LB:B141, B188.
Bride, Philip (violin).
LB:A602.
Brinkmann, Dorothea (contralto).
EB:G131.
Britten, Benjamin – *See* English Chamber Orchestra.
Brix-Meinert, Ilse (viola d'amore, violin).
LB:B321, B322.
Broadside Band.
LR:Gd23.
EB:B37.
Broadway, Michael (virginals).
SI:C15.
BRockmeier, Willi (tenor).
LB:F67.
Brodard, Michel (bass).
EB:G26.
LB:G118, G301.
Brookes, Oliver (viol, cello).
LR:Gd42.
EB:F61.
LB:B291.
Brosse, Jean-Patrice (harpsichord, organ).
EB:D19, E48.
Brown, Iona (violin).
LB:A27, A427, A482, A581.
Brown, Iona – *See* Academy of St. Martin-in-the-Fields.
Brown, James (oboe).
LB:A567.
Brown, Mark – *See* Pro Cantione Antiqua.
Brown, Wilfred (tenor).
EB:F73, G78.
LB:G147, G215.
Browne, Sandra (mezzo-soprano).
EB:F18.

Brückner-Rüggeberg, Wilhelm – *See* Berlin Philharmonic Orchestra.
Brüggen, Frans (recorder, flute).
LR:E39, Ga16.
EB:B64.
LB:A40, A44, A184, A186, A337, A397, A398, A399, A400, A415, A502, A544, A600, A605, A631, A646, B41, B64, B85, B120, B131, B138, B139, B149, B162, B178, B191, B229, B230, B257, B260, B261, B267, B274, B278, B279, B283, B286, B292, B296, D131.
Brüggen, Frans – *See* Amsterdam Mozart Ensemble.
– *See* Concerto Amsterdam.
Brüggen Consort.
LR:Ga16.
Bruni, Massimo – *See* Prague Chamber Orchestra.
Brunner, Evelyne (soprano).
EB:G27.
Bruscantini, Sesto (baritone).
LB:F52, F75.
Brussels Vocal Quartet.
EB:B35.
Brychcy, Wieslaw (bass).
LB:G199.
Buccarella, Lucio (double-bass).
LB:B201.
Bucher, Joseph (organ).
LB:A324, E18.
Buchhlierl, Hans (boy soprano).
LB:G168.
Büchner, Otto (violin).
LB:A70, A179, A213, A214, B112, B322.
Buckel, Ursula (soprano).
LB:F4, F14, G20, G55, G121.
Buckley, Emer (harpsichord).
LB:D227.
Budai, Livia (contralto).
LR:E42.
LB:G39, G306.
Budapest Madrigal Singers, dir. Ferenc Szekeres.
LR:A5, F81.
LB:F74, G287, G292, G297.
Budapest Philharmonic Orchestra, dir. Miklos Erdelyi.
LR:A6.
LB:A81, A171.
Budapest Philharmonic Orchestra, dir. Istvan Zambo.
LB:G39.
Bufkens, Roland (tenor).
LB:G197.
Buhl, Johannes (cello).
LB:A520, B242, F81.
Bühler, Johannes (cello).
LB:A148.
Bumbry, Grace (contralto).
LB:G225.
Burgess, Grayston (counter-tenor).
AA:C1.
AN:A8.
Burgess, Grayston – *See* Purcell Consort of Voices.
Burgess, Mary (soprano).
LB:G291.
Burgess, Sally (soprano).
LB:F39.
Burmeister, Annelies (contralto).
LB:G105, G284, G285.
Burns, Nancy (soprano).
LB:G16.
Burrowes, Norma (soprano).
EB:F18, F61, F64, F71, G63.
LB:B227, F33, G212, G220.
Burrowes, Stuart (tenor).
LB:A239, G220.
Burton, Miriam (soprano).
LB:G244.

Bust-Nielsen, Lena (recorder).
LR:B23.
Bustamente, Maria-Carmen (soprano).
LR:E51.
LB:F53, G194.
Buttrey, John (tenor).
LB:F34.
Bydgoszcz Philharmonic Choir.
ER:B46.
Bye, Torkil (flute).
LB:B311.
Bylsma, Anner (cello).
LB:A40, A354, A386, A438, A521, A600, B38, B131, B138, B139, B178, B191, B229, B230, B260, B261, B267, B274, B278, B279, B283, B286, B296, B309, G175.

Caballe, Monteserrat (soprano).
LB:F80.
Cable, Jonathan (violone) (Member of MUSICA ANTIQUA, COLOGNE).
Caddy, Ian (bass).
LB:G303.
Caen Chamber Orchestra, dir. Jean-Pierre Dautel.
LB:A603.
Caillard, Phillippe – *See* Phillippe Caillard Choir.
Caillat, Stephane (bass).
ER:A13.
Caillat, Stephane – *See* Paillard Chamber Orchestra.
– *See* Stephane Caillat Vocal Ensemble.
Calabrese, Nane (viola d'amore).
LB:A523.
Caley, Ian (tenor).
LB:F60.
Calvayrac, Albert (trumpet).
LB:A571, A589.
Cambridge Consort, dir. Joel Cohen.
AA:D15.
LR:E38.
Cambridge University Chamber Choir, dir. Richard Marlow.
EB:G33.
Camden, Anthony (oboe, oboe d'amore).
LB:B87, B247, D226.
Camden Wind Ensemble.
LR:F114.
Camerata Academica, Hamburg.
EB:F11.
Camerata Bern, dir. Jörg Ewald Dähler.
LB:A584.
Camerata Bern, dir. Alexander van Wijnkoop.
LB:A8, A237, A578.
Camerata Chamber Choir, dir. Per Enevold.
LR:E50.
Camerata Hungarica, dir. Laszlo Czidra.
ER:A9.
LR:B27, E42, E54, E67.
EB:B66.
Camerata of London.
LR:Gd2, Gd29, Gd38, Gd41.
Cameron, John (bariton).
EB:F74.
LB:F24, G236, G251.
Campanez, Irene (mezzo-soprano).
LB:G286.
Canino, Bruno (harpsichord).
LB:B75, B193, B195, B300.
Canne-Meijer, Cora (contralto).
LB:G281.
Cano, Pablo (harpsichord, clavichord).
EB:D28.
Cantelo, April (soprano).
EB:F73.
LB:F31, G206, G208.

Canticum Novum Chamber Orchestra, dir. Alf Ardal.
LB:A204.
Cantilena, dir. Adrian Shepherd.
EB:A28, A31.
LB:A217, A458, A568, A606.
Cantilena Men's Choir, dir. Edmund Kajdasz.
EB:G4.
Cantores in Ecclesia, dir. Michael Howard.
LR:F66, Ge20.
Cantores Minores Wratislavienses, dir. Edmund Kajdasz.
PS:B17.
LR:E71, F13, F14, F16, F18, F20, F24, F58, F61, F63.
LB:G103, G104.
Cape, Safford – *See* Pro Musica Antiqua.
Capecchi, Renato (baritone).
EB:F93.
LB:F53.
Capella Accademica, Vienna, dir. Eduard Melkus.
LB:A28, A49, A73, A213, A527, G94, G96, G105,
   G288.
Capella Accademica, Vienna, dir. Kurt Redel.
LB:A404.
Capella Accademica, Vienna, dir. August Wenzinger.
LB:A361.
Capella Antiqua, Munich, dir. Konrad Ruhland.
PS:B8.
AA:B2, B8, E10.
AN:A7, A12.
ER:A14, B6, B21.
LR:A2, E32, E39, E70.
EB:F40, G59.
Capella Arcis Varsoviensis, dir. Marek Sewen.
EB:B14.
Capella Bydgostiensis, dir. Stanislaw Galonski.
ER:B46.
LR:E57, F76.
EB:G141.
LB:A180, G199.
Capella Bydgostiensis, dir. Wlodzimierz Szymanski.
LR:E37.
Capella Clementina, dir. Helmut Müller-Brühl.
LB:A551.
Capella Colonensis, dir. August Wenzinger.
LB:A241, A280.
Capella Coloniensis, dir. Gabriele Ferro.
LB:A575.
Capella Coloniensis, dir. Claudio Scimone.
LB:F76.
Capella Cordina, dir. Alejandro Planchart.
ER:B17, B20, B28, B34, B40.
LR:F1, F38, F43.
Capella Cracoviensis, dir. Stanislaw Galonski.
AA:B9.
LB:A617, G258.
Capella Lipsiensis, dir. Dietrich Knothe.
ER:B37.
LR:E68.
Capella Musicale del Duomo di Milano, dir. Luigi
   Benedetti and Luciano Migliavacca.
PS:B19.
Capt, Mauricette (soprano).
LB:G118.
Caracciolo, Franco – *See* Milan Angelicum Orchestra.
   – *See* Rossini Orchestral of Naples.
Caramia, Giacinto (cello).
EB:B62.
Carbow, Ekkehard (harpsichord).
LB:B100.
Cardon, Stephane – *See* Grenoble Instrumental
   Ensemble.
   – *See* Lyon Madrigal Ensemble.
Cardoze, Mireille (violin).
EB:B11.
Carley, Louise (viol).

SI:C2, C3.
Carley, Marie-Therese (viol, tabor).
SI:C2, C12, C14.
Carli, Isabella de (harpsichord).
LB:G256.
Carlos Villa Ensemble.
LB:A358.
Carmel Bach Festival Chorale and Orchestra, dir. Sandor
   Salgo.
LB:G299.
Carmelite Priory Choir, dir. George Malcolm.
EB:G53.
Carmelite Priory Choir, dir. John McCarthy.
PS:B16.
LR:F69.
Carmirelli, Pina (violin).
LB:A433, A497.
Caroldi, Alberto (oboe).
LB:A559.
Carp, David (recorder).
EB:F54.
Casals, Pablo (cello).
LB:B39.
Case, John Carol (baritone).
LB:G147.
Casei, Neda (contralto).
LB:G316.
Casoni, Biancamaria (mezzo-soprano).
EB:G84.
LB:G286.
Cassademunt, Sergei (viol).
LR:B7, Ga7.
Castelli, Christiane (soprano).
LB:F63.
Cattini, Umberto – *See* Milan Angelicum Orchestra.
Caudle, Theresa (cornet).
LR:Gd43.
SI:B1.
Celea, Jean-Paul (double-bass).
LB:A395.
Centurione, Mario (cello).
LB:A497.
Cervera, Marcal (cello).
LB:B165, B252.
Cervera, Montserrat (violin).
LB:B165.
Ceuppens, Maria (soprano).
LB:G201.
Chabay, Leslie (tenor).
LB:G244.
Challan, Annie (harp).
LB:A614.
Chambon, Jacques (oboe).
LB:A10, A12, A232, A664.
Chamonin, Jocelyn (soprano).
EB:G34.
LB:G259, G291.
Channon, David (lute, viol).
SI:C1, C2, C6, C8, C11, C13, C14, C16, C17, C18, C19,
   C20.
Chapelet, Francis (organ).
LR:D13, D20.
EB:E57, E75, E79, E86, E87, E89, E90.
Chapuis, Michel (organ).
LR:F41.
EB:E12, E13, E14, E15, E20, E52, E86, G6.
LB:A84, B118, E9, E19, E20, E21, E80, E87, E103,
   E109, E112, E113, E151, E156, E157, E163, E164,
   E168, E178, G195.
Charbonnier, Jean-Louis (viol).
EB:G30.
Chicago Chamber Orchestra, dir. Dieter Kober.
LB:A274.
Choeur Amici della Polifonia.

LB:F75.
Choeur Concinitie et Schola Cantorum, Louvaine, dir. Karel Aerts.
LR:F64, F125.
Choeur National, dir. Jacques Grimbert.
EB:G106.
Chojnacka, E (harpsichord).
LB:D209.
Chorus Viennensis.
LR:F98.
LB:G3, G14, G21, G22, G25, G29, G33, G34, G37, G63, G111, G156, G169.
Chorzempa, Daniel (organ).
LB:A295, A323, E22.
Christchurch Cathedral Choir, dir. Simon Preston.
LR:F30, F34, Ge5, Ge35.
LB:F32, G126, G226, G245, G290.
Christiansen, Jan (trumpet).
LB:B311.
Christie, William (harpsichord, organ).
EB:D14, F7, F8, F53, F82, G19, G20, G47.
LB:B82, B160, B254, D152, F23, F28, F54.
Christie, William – *See* Arts Florissants Vocal and Instrumental Ensemble.
Christ's Hospital Singers, dir. Malcolm McKelvay.
EB:G133.
Chuchro, Joseph (cello).
LB:B59.
Chung, Kyung-Wha (violin).
LB:B30.
Chwedczuk, Jozef (organ).
EB:E69.
Chwedczuk, Zbigniew – *See* Pomeranian State Philharmonic Orchestra.
Cianella, Yvonne (soprano).
LB:F72.
Cillaro, Carlo Felice – *See* Milan Angelicum Orchestra.
City of London Ensemble.
LB:A80.
Claire, Dom Jean – *See* Solesmes.
Clarion Consort.
EB:B47.
LB:A212.
Clarke, Christina (soprano).
· EB:F69.
Clarke, Patricia (soprano).
EB:F63.
LB:G242.
Clarke, Paul (recorder).
LB:B284.
Clarkson, Julian (counter-tenor).
LB:G243.
Clemencic, Rene (recorder, flute, etc).
LR:E55.
LB:B158, B253, B273, B282, B302.
Clemencic, Rene – *See* Clemencic Consort.
– *See* Musica Antiqua, Vienna.
Clemencic Consort.
AA:A2, D2, D10, D13, E1, E2, E3, E11, E12, E13, E14, E15, E16.
AN:A15.
ER:A8, B10, B12, B14, B19, B35, B42.
LR:B10, B11, B18.
EB:B70, F25, F56.
Clemente, Peter (harpsichord).
LB:B248.
Clerkes of Oxenford, dir. David Wulstan.
PS:C2.
LR:Ge15, Ge16, Ge17, Ge18, Ge19, Ge22, Ge29.
Clervaux, Choir of the Benedictine Abbey of St. Maurice and St. Maur.
PS:A30, B6.
Cleveland Symphonic Winds, dir. Frederick Fennell.
LB:A248.

Clinton, Gordon (bass).
LB:G142.
Cobb, Willard (tenor) (Member of STUDIO DER FRUHEN MUSIK).
Coates, Kevin (mandolin).
LB:C28.
Coates, Reggie (lute, cittern).
SI:A2.
Cochereau, Pierre (organ).
EB:E49.
LB:A671.
Cohen, Joel – *See* Boston Camerata.
– *See* Cambridge Consort.
Coin, Christoph (viol). (Member of HESPERION XX).
LR:Ga7.
EB:B26.
LB:B128.
SI:A2.
Colacicchi, Luigi – *See* Rome Philharmonic Academy Choir.
Cold, Ulrick (bass-baritone).
LR:E19.
EB:F89.
LB:F37, F46, F60, G275.
Cole, Martin (lute).
LR:Gd5.
Collard, Janine (mezzo-soprano).
EB:G32.
LB:G279.
Collegiate Church of St. Mary, Warwick – *See* St. Mary, Warwick.
Collegium Aureum (members of...)
AA:B10.
AN:A11.
ER:B31, B39.
LR:B17, E17, F9, F26, F111, F124.
EB:A12, A17, A33, F30, F58, G1, G60.
LB:G100.
Collegium Aureum, dir. Franzjosef Maier (violin).
LB:A20, A30, A36, A42, A52, A58, A105, A158, A182, A247, A271, A284, A288, A303, A387, A455, A480, A481, B106, F51, F70, G76, G81, G125, G168, G263.
Collegium Aureum, dir. Reinhard Peters.
LB:A53, F3, F26.
Collegium Aureum, dir. Rolf Reinhardt.
LB:A401, A520, A521, F26.
Collegium Aureum, dir. Kurt Thomas.
LB:G1.
Collegium Musicum, dir. Lavard Friisholm.
LB:G275.
Collegium Musicum Italicum, dir. Renato Fassano.
LB:F52.
Collegium Sagittarii.
EB:G120.
Collegium St. Emmeram, dir. Hans-Martin Schneidt.
LB:G152, A165.
Collegium Terpsichore, dir. Fritz Neumeyer.
EB:B30.
Collegium Terpsichore, dir. Joseph Ulsamer.
LR:B25.
Collegium Vocale, Cologne, dir. Hans-Martin Linde.
LR:F2.
Collegium Vocale, Cologne, dir. Colin Tilney.
LR:E1.
Collegium Vocale, Ghent, dir. Philippe Herreweghe.
LR:F35, F83.
EB:G54.
LB:F64, G54, G57, G59, G67, G68, G72.
Collet, Louis (baritone).
EB:G16.
Collins, Anne (contralto).
EB:F15, F18.
LB:G284, G294, G300.

Collot, Serge (viola).
EB:A27.
Cologne Chamber Orchestra, dir. Helmut Müller-Brühl.
LB:A191.
Cologne Children's Choir.
LR:F106.
Cologne Kantorei, dir. Volker Hempfling.
LB:G321, G323.
Cologne Viol Consort.
LR:B2, F118.
EB:B6, B29.
Colombo, Scipio – See Oiseau Lyre Ensemble.
Il Complesso Barocco, dir. Alan Curtis.
LB:F37, F73.
Complesso Barocco di Milano, dir. Francesco Degrada.
EB:F90.
Complesso di Musica Antica, Wroclaw, dir. Eugeniusz
Sasiadek.
EB:G147.
Complesso Veneziana Strumenti Antichi, dir. Pietro
Verardo.
EB:B12.
Con Moto ma Cantabile Chamber Ensemble, dir. Tadeusz
Ochlewski.
EB:B16.
LB:F69.
Concentus Musicus Cantorum, dir. Arthur Maud.
ER:B27, B45.
LR:Gf1.
Concentus Musicus Instrumental Ensemble, dir. Arthur
Maud.
ER:B45.
LR:Gf1.
Concertgebouw Orchestra, Amsterdam, dir. Eduard van
Beinum.
LB:A255, A261.
Concertgebouw Orchestra, Amsterdam, dir. Eugen
Jochum.
LB:G150.
Concerto Amsterdam, dir. Frans Brüggen.
LB:A380, A382, A384, A385, A386, A398, A410,
A415, A631, B267.
Concerto Amsterdam, dir. Anthon van der Horst.
LB:A317, A319, A326.
Concerto Amsterdam, dir. Jaap Schröder.
LB:A295, A323, A349, A354, A438, A570, G44.
Connors, Ursula (soprano).
EB:G65.
LB:F57.
Conrad, Ferdinand (recorder).
LB:B150, B156, B182, B183, B186, B262, B288,
B289, B303, B304, B321, B322.
Conrad, Margrit (contralto).
EB:F42.
LB:G254.
Conrad, Richard (tenor).
LB:F42.
Consorte of Musicke, dir. Anthony Rooley.
LR:A1, E20, E24, Ga2, Ga5, Ga6, Gd4, Gd6, Gd7, Gd8,
Gd13, Gd30, Gd49, Ge12.
EB:B19, B28.
Consortium Classicum.
LB:A357, F29, G71, G80, G99.
Consortium Musicum.
LR:F90, F94.
EB:F105, F109, F110, G119.
LB:G60, G82, G141, G155.
Constantini, Marco (bassoon).
LB:A539.
Cooper, Robert (fiddle, rebec).
AN:B13.
Cooremans, Kamiel – See Audite Nova Choir, Antwerp.
Copenhagen Concentus Musicus.
LB:B187.

Copper Green, John (organ).
EB:E96.
Corazza, Remy (tenor).
LB:G259.
Corboz, Michel – See English Baroque Festival
Orchestra.
 – See Gulbenkian Foundation Chamber Orchestra.
 – See Gulbenkian Foundation Symphinic Choir and
Orchestra.
 – See Lausanne Vocal and Chamber Ensemble.
Coro dei Frati Minori di Busto Arsizio, dir. Fr. Filippo
Cavalleri and Fr. Illuminato Colombo.
PS:A73, A74, A75.
Costa, Othmar – See Walther von der Wogelweide
Chamber Choir.
Cotandrea, Italo (violin).
LB:A393.
Cotogni, Anna Maria (violin).
LB:A497.
Cotrubas, Ileana (soprano).
EB:F5.
LB:F44, G271.
Cotte, Roger (recorder).
ER:A7.
LR:E31.
LB:B272, B324.
Cotte, Roger – dir. of Instrumental Ensemble.
LB:A593, A614, F68.
Cotte, Roger – See Group des Instruments Anciens de
Paris.
Cottret, Bernard (bass).
LB:F68.
Coueffe, Yves (trumpet).
EB:A27.
Coulson, Richard (harpsichord, organ).
EB:B68.
Couraud, Marcel – See Stuttgart Chamber Soloists.
Covey-Crump, Rogers (tenor).
AN:B6.
EB:G14.
Crafoord, Erika (viola).
LB:A148.
Crantz, Gunnar (violin).
LB:A191.
Crass, Franz (bass).
EB:F105.
LB:G60, G71, G80, G92, G114, G141, G155, G164,
G213, G221.
Craven, John (harpsichord).
LB:B284.
Crenne, Christiane (violin).
LB:A602.
Criswell, Michael (boy treble).
LR:Gd46.
Crook, Howard (tenor).
EB:F54.
Cros, Jean (double-bass).
LB:A589.
Crum, Alison (viol, recorder, cornemuse).
LR:Gd5.
Csanky, Emilia (oboe).
LB:A630, B92.
Csapo, Eva (soprano).
LR:F2.
EB:G11.
Cuarteto de Madrigalistas de Madrid.
LR:E23.
Cuberli, Lella (soprano).
LB:F76.
Cuenod, Hughes (tenor).
EB:F5, F6, G49, G64.
Cummings, Douglas (cello).
LB:B43, B87.
Cummings, Henry (bass).

LB:G142.
Cundari, Emilia (soprano).
LB:G261, G314.
Curtis, Alan (harpsichord).
EB:D4, F89.
LB:A40, A42, A44, A118, B51, B181, D12, D56, D109, D131, D148.
Curtis, Alan – See Il Complesso Barocco.
Czech Philharmonic Orchestra, dir. Leopold Stokowski.
LB:A210.
Czech Philharmonic Chorus, dir. Josef Veselka.
PS:C6.
LR:F53, F55, F67, F99, F116.
EB:G43.
LB:E149, G98.
Czech Philharmonic Orchestra, dir. Libor Pesek.
EB:A30.
Czidra, Laszlo (recorder).
LB:A406, A554.
Czidra, Laszlo – See Camerata Hungarica.

Da Camera Vocal Ensemble, dir. Daniel Meier.
ER:A5.
Dael, Lucy van (violin).
EB:F12.
LB:B51, B229, B230, D109, D131, D148.
Dähler, Jörg Ewald (harpsichord).
EB:D13, F55.
LB:A148, A185, A233, A572, A584, B60, B70, B72, B89, B98, B132, B198, B251, B255, B301, D78, D79, D80, D143, D154, D162.
Dähler, Jörg Ewald – See Camerata Bern.
  – See Langnau Church Choir.
  – See South West German Chamber Orchestra.
Dalla Libera, Sandro (organ).
LR:D10.
EB:E36.
Dalton, John (organ).
LB:E91.
Dams, Rita (contralto).
LB:F37.
Danby, Nicholas (organ).
LB:E234.
Danish Royal Opera Choir, dir. Lavard Friisholm.
LB:G275.
Darasse, Xavier (organ).
EB:E41.
LB:A589.
Dart, Thurston (harpsichord, clavichord, virginals, organ).
LR:Gc6, Gd39.
EB:B18.
LB:D21.
Dart, Thurston – See Boyd Neel String Orchestra.
  – See Elizabethan Consort.
  – See Philomusica of London.
Dassow, Klaus-Dieter (violin, viola).
LB:B100.
Dautel, Jean-Pierre – See Caen Chamber Orchestra.
Davia, Frederico (tenor).
EB:F48.
Davan-Wetton, Hilary (organ).
LB:E235.
Davies, Peter (flute, recorder, cornemuse).
AN:B13.
Davies, Ryland (tenor).
EB:F18.
LB:G232, G248, G250.
Davies, Timothy (lute, mandora).
AN:B13.
Davis, Alan (recorder).
LB:B284.
Davis, Andrew (harpsichord).
LB:A134.

Davis, Andrew – See English Chamber Orchestra.
  – See London Symphony Orchestra.
Davison, Arthur – See Virtuosi of England.
Dawson, Anthony (tenor).
EB:G77.
Daxelhofer, Christine (harpsichord).
LB:A148, B98.
Dean, Stafford (bass).
EB:F15, F16, F41, G77.
LB:G250.
Debost, Michel (flute).
LB:A486, A571, B174.
Debray, Lucein (oboe).
LB:A355.
Deckert Knudnsen, Gunhild (violin).
LR:B23.
Decortis, Maria-Louis (soprano).
LB:G201.
Dedoyard, Berthe (harpsichord).
EB:D37.
LB:B316.
Degrada, Francesco – See Complesso Barocco di Milano.
Dejmek, Zdenek – See Janacek Chamber Orchestra.
Delfosse, Michele (harpsichord).
LB:B194, D10, D144.
Deller, Alfred (counter-tenor).
LR:Gd3, Gd9, Gd26.
EB:F53, F69, F75, F106, G42.
LB:F47, G195.
Deller, Alfred – See Deller Consort.
  – See The King's Music.
  – See Stour Festival Chamber Orchestra.
Deller, Mark (counter-tenor).
EB:F69, F75.
Deller Consort.
PS:A31, A40, A52, B5, B20, C1, C5.
AA:B10.
AN:A11.
LR:E17, F11, F15, F17, F19, F21, F41, F88, Gd15, Gd16, Gd17, Gd18, Gd45, Gd50, Gd52, Gd54, Ge2, Ge4, Ge7, Ge14, Ge23, Ge32.
EB:F1, F30, F49, F50, F52, F59, F69, G6, G56, G73, G74, G76.
LB:B118.
Deller Singers.
EB:F72, F75.
Delvallee, Georges (organ).
LB:B202, B315, E233.
Demenga, Catrin (violin).
LB:A148.
Demmeler, Fritz (flute).
LB:A628.
Demus, Jörg (forte-piano).
LB:D219.
Dene, J (bass).
LB:G287.
Denize, Nadine (contralto).
EB:G16.
Depannemaker, Serge (percussion).
AA:D9.
Depoltova, Eva (soprano).
LB:F79.
Depraz, Xavier (bass).
EB:G32.
Deriemaeker, Stanislas (positive organ).
ER:A19.
Dermota, Anton (tenor).
LB:G148.
Deroubaix, Jeanne (mezzo-soprano).
LR:F94.
EB:B51.
Deschenes, Mario (flute).
LB:B226.

Dessoff Choirs, dir. Paul Boepple.
ER:B26.
LB:G244.
Deutsche Zupforchester, dir. Siegfried Behrend.
LB:A573.
Devallier, Lucienne (contralto).
LB:G256.
Devetzi, Vasso (piano).
LB:A123.
Devos, Louis (tenor).
EB:G41, G83.
LB:F62, G188, G197, G200.
Devos, Louis – *See* Musica Polyphonica Ensemble.
Diakov, Anton (bass).
LB:G136.
Diaz, Justino (bass).
LB:G243.
Dickerson, Bernard (tenor).
EB:F16.
Dickey, Bruce (cornet, recorder).
SI:A2.
Dickie, Murray (tenor).
EB:F43.
Dingfelder, Ingrid (flute).
LB:A47, A411.
Dintrich, Michel (guitar).
LB:C20.
Diplock, Cyril (organ).
LB:E220.
Dittmer, Petronella (violin).
EB:B68.
Dobree, G (clarinet).
LB:A358.
Dobrucky, William (violin).
LB:A617.
Dobrzanski, Jerzy – *See* Musicae Antiquae Collegium
    Varsoviense.
    – *See* Warsaw Chamber Orchestra.
Dobsay, Laszlo – *See* Schola Hungarica.
Dobson, Michael – *See* Thames Chamber Orchestra.
Doe, Roger (viol).
LB:B57.
Dohn, Robert (flute).
LB:A227.
Doktor, Paul (viola).
LB:A398.
Döling, Waldemar (harpsichord).
LB:B90, B134, B238, B258.
Doll-Bittlmayer, Suzanne (harpsichord).
LB:A14.
Dolmetsch, Cecile (viol, rebec, soprano).
SI:C1, C2, C3, C4, C5, C6, C7, C8, C10, C11, C12, C13,
    C14, C15, C16, C17, C18, C19, C20, C21.
Dolmetsch, Natalie (viol).
SI:C1, C2, C3, C5, C6, C11, C13.
Dolmetsch Consort.
LR:Gd46.
LB:B277, B281.
SI:C1–C21.
Dombois, Eugen Müller (lute).
LR:C21, E16, Ga3, Gd14.
EB:F40.
LB:A640, C21, F82.
Dombrecht, Paul (oboe).
LB:B176, B191, B228, B244, B275.
Domingues, Oralia (mezzo-soprano).
LB:G286.
Don Smithers Brass Ensemble.
LR:Ga9.
Donath, Helen (soprano).
EB:F39, F105, G7.
LB:A239, F13, F39, G184, G220.
Donnington, Margaret (viol).
SI:C14, C18, C19, C20, C21.

Dooley, Jeffrey (counter-tenor).
EB:F54.
Doormann, Ludwig – *See* Frankfurt Cantata Orchestra.
    – *See* Göttinger Stadtkantorei.
Doppelgatz, Marion (child soprano).
LR:F106.
Dore, Philip (organ).
LB:E194.
Dorigny, Henri (guitar).
LB:A532.
Dorrow, Dorothy (soprano).
EB:G46.
Dover, Ben (curtall, crumhorn, recorder).
SI:A2.
Downes, Ralph (organ).
LB:E23.
Dresden Kreuzchor, dir. Rudolf Mauersberger.
EB:G96, G102, G108, G114, G121, G125.
Dresden Kreuzchor, dir. Günther Ramin.
LB:G117, G325.
Dresden State Orchestra, dir. Vittorio Negri.
LB:A518, A642.
Dreyfus, Huguette (harpsichord, forte-piano).
EB:A27, B2, B8.
LB:A33, B46, B151, B196, D4, D14, D17, D107, D122,
    D185.
Driehuys, Leo (oboe).
LB:A15, A539.
Driesshe, Louis van den (tenor).
LB:G201.
Drottningholm Baroque Ensemble.
LB:A1, A636.
Drottningholm Theatre Orchestra, dir. Ulf Björlin.
LB:A367.
Druce, Duncan (violin).
SI:B2.
Dudley, John (tenor) (Member of LAS HUELGAS
    ENSEMBLE).
AN:A14.
LR:E3, E72.
Dufy, Terence (organ).
LB:E179.
Dufour, Olivier (tenor).
EB:F42, G29.
LB:G115, G118, G127.
Dumond, Arnaud (guitar).
LR:C11.
Dupre, Desmond (lute).
AA:C1.
LR:Gd3, Gd26, Gd45.
EB:F92, F106.
LB:A275.
Durand, Georges – *See* Avignon Vocal Ensemble.
Durand, Guy (recorder, vielle).
ER:A7.
LB:B324.
Dutton, Paul (boy treble).
LB:G327.
Duxberry, John (tenor).
LB:G273.

Earle, Roderick (bass).
EB:F76.
Early Music Consort, London, dir. David Munrow.
AA:A1, B1, D22.
AN:A1, A2, B9.
ER:A1, A2, A3, A12, B18.
LR:A3, E26, E69, Ga20.
EB:F61, G63, G68, G139.
Eastman Brass Quintet.
LR:Ga21.
Eathorne, Wendy (soprano).
EB:F15, F16.
LB:G78, G119, G120.

Ebbinge, Ku (bassoon).
EB:G35.
LB:A600.
Eden, Conrad (organ).
LB:E194.
Eddy, Timothy (cello).
LB:B141, B188.
Edney, John (sackbut).
SI:A2.
Eduard Melkus Ensemble.
LB:A48.
Eetvelde, Jo van (organ).
LB:E210.
Egger, Georg (violin).
LB:A407.
Egmond, Max von (bass-baritone).
AA:D25.
EB:F23, F40, F43, G59, G75.
LB:F17, F37, F60, F64, G3, G5, G6, G12, G14, G18, G21,
    G22, G25, G33, G57, G59, G63, G67, G68, G72,
    G111, G144, G156, G281.
Egmond, Piet van (organ).
LB:E66.
Ehmann, Wilhelm (dir. of vocal ensemble).
EB:G88, G90, G91, G92, G94, G95.
Ehmann, Wilhelm – See Amsterdam Het Kunstmaandor-
    kest.
    – See German Bach Soloists.
    – See German Baroque Soloists.
    – See South West German Chamber Orchestra.
    – See Verstärkter Bläserchor.
    – See Westphallian Kantorei.
Eichberger, Franz Friedrich (harpsichord).
LR:F106.
LB:B287.
Eichberger, Myriam (flute).
LR:F106.
LB:B287.
Eichhorn, Holger (cornet).
EB:B44, B61.
Eichhorn, Kurt (organ).
EB:B44, B61.
Einhorn, Aviva – See Les Musicholiers.
Ekorness, Øyvind (cello).
LB:B311.
Elhorst, Hans (oboe).
LB:A8.
Eliasson, Sven Olof (tenor).
EB:F43.
Elizabethan Consort, dir. Thurston Dart.
EB:B18.
Elizabethan Consort of Viols.
ER:B24.
LR:Gd33, Gd35.
Elkins, Margreta (soprano).
LB:F42.
Ellenbeck, Hans-Dieter (tenor).
EB:G69, G98.
LB:G139, G159.
Elliott, Kenneth (harpsichord).
LR:Gd26.
LB:B4.
Elliott, Paul (tenor).
EB:B41, F72, F75.
LB:F33, G126, G226, G243.
SI:A1, A2, B2.
Elliott, Robert (harpsichord, organ).
EB:F92, F94, F106, G56.
Ellis, Ossian (harp).
AA:C1.
LB:A275.
Elsner, Helma (harpsichord).
LB:B242.
Elvestrand, Magne (harpsichord, organ).

LB:B311.
Elwes, John (tenor).
AN:B13.
EB:F41, F76, G14, G26, G58.
LB:F62, F64, G10, G118.
Ely Cathedral Choir, dir. Arthur Wills.
EB:G3.
LB:G191.
Emil Seiler Chamber Orchestra.
LB:A629.
Emil Seiler Chamber Orchestra, dir. Wolfgang Hofmann.
LB:A564, A565, A643.
Enevold, Margrete (soprano).
LR:E50.
Enevold, Per – See Camerata Chamber Choir.
Engel, Theo – See Frankfurt Bach Orchestra.
Engelhard, Brigitte (harpsichord).
LB:B235.
Engen, Keith (bass).
LB:G79, G93, G105, G121, G134, G135, G151.
English, Gerald (tenor).
AA:C1.
EB:F15, F44, F96, F103.
LB:F3, F59, G250.
English Bach Festival Choir and Orchestra, dir. Jean-
    Claude Malgoire.
LB:G303.
English Bach Festival Chorus.
LB:F60, G295.
English Baroque Festival Orchestra, dir. Michel Corboz.
LB:G295.
English Baroque Soloists, dir. John Eliot Gardiner.
LB:F33.
English Chamber Orchestra, dir. John Barbirolli.
EB:F67.
English Chamber Orchestra, dir. Daniel Barenboim.
LB:A175, A177.
English Chamber Orchestra, dir. Richard Bonynge.
LB:A67, A344, A345, G229.
English Chamber Orchestra, dir. Benjamin Britten.
EB:F71.
LB:A113, G158.
English Chamber Orchestra, dir. Andrew Davis.
LB:A59.
English Chamber Orchestra, dir. Jose-Luis Garcia.
LB:A568.
English Chamber Orchestra, dir. Peter-Lukas Graf.
LB:A185.
English Chamber Orchestra, dir. George Guest.
EB:G72.
English Chamber Orchestra, dir. Philip Ledger.
LB:F39, G319.
English Chamber Orchestra, dir. Laurence Leonard.
LB:A411.
English Chamber Orchestra, dir. Raymond Leppard.
EB:F18, F47, F65.
LB:A43, A96, A127, A134, A154, A223, A225, A238,
    A243, A254, A260, A289, A329, A332, A343, A618,
    F57, G66, G232.
English Chamber Orchestra, dir. Anthony Lewis.
EB:F63.
LB:F59.
English Chamber Orchestra, dir. Charles Mackerras.
EB:F60, F73.
LB:A47, A650, A658, A669, G231, G242, G248, G250.
English Chamber Orchestra, dir. George Malcolm.
LB:A19.
English Chamber Orchestra, dir. Garcio Navarro.
LB:A201.
English Chamber Orchestra, dir. Vittorio Negri.
LB:G284, G294, G300.
English Chamber Orchestra, dir. Simon Preston.
LB:G245.
English Chamber Orchestra, dir. Karl Richter.

LB:A240.
English Chamber Orchestra, dir. Antonio Ros-Marba.
LB:F53, G311.
English Chamber Orchestra, dir. Johannes Somary.
LB:G116, G138, G234.
English Chamber Orchestra, dir. Paul Steinitz.
LB:G7.
English Chamber Orchestra, dir. Henryk Szeryng.
LB:A425, A446.
English Chamber Orchestra, dir. David Willcocks.
LB:G208, G216, G319.
English Chamber Orchestra, dir. Pinchas Zukerman.
LB:A439, A447, A499.
English Concert, dir. Trevor Pinnock.
LB:A38, A163, A189, A457, A478, A595.
English Consort of Viols.
LR:F117, Gd37, Gd44.
SI:B1.
English Symphony Orchestra, dir. John Tobin.
LB:G227.
Engsö, Rune (organ).
LB:E225.
Ensemble Guillaume de Machaut.
AA:D8, D23.
ER:A13.
Ensemble Guillaume Dufay.
AA:B6.
AN:B5.
Ensemble Polyphonique de Mont-Parnasse, dir. Victor
   Martin.
PS:A71.
Ensemble Polyphonique de Paris, dir. Charles Ravier.
LR:E7, E8, E9.
Ephrikian, Angelo – *See* Bologna Philharmonic
   Orchestra.
   – *See* Italian Vocal Quintet.
   – *See* Solistes de Bruxelles.
   – *See* I Solisti di Milano.
   – *See* Vienna State Opera Orchestra and Choir.
Eppel, Henner (flute).
LB:B100.
Equale Brass Ensemble.
EB:G71.
Equiluz, Kurt (tenor).
LR:B30, F3.
EB:F39, F40, F43.
LB:F8, F17, G3, G5, G6, G14, G21, G22, G25, G29, G33,
   G34, G35, G37, G40, G51, G52, G54, G56, G57, G59,
   G63, G67, G68, G72, G76, G111, G132, G144, G155,
   G156, G161, G162, G169, G184, G281.
Erb, Karl (tenor).
LB:G140.
Erdelyi, Miklos – *See* Budapest Philharmonic Orchestra.
Erdman, Jerzy (organ).
EB:E35, E38.
Ericson, Bengt (cello, viol).
EB:B42.
LB:B306, B317.
Erler, Jörg (boy soprano).
LB:G57.
Escolania de Montserrat, dir. Fr. Ireneu Segarra.
LR:F12, F44, F72.
EB:G1, G17, G18, G60.
LB:G193, G263.
Ess, Gunther (baritone).
EB:G124.
Ess, Helen (soprano).
EB:G124.
Esswood, Paul (counter-tenor).
LR:F3.
EB:F39, F43, F46, F60, F62, G58, G77, G127.
LB:F46, G3, G5, G6, G12, G14, G18, G21, G22, G25,
   G29, G33, G34, G37, G40, G51, G52, G54, G56, G57,
   G63, G67, G68, G72, G78, G119, G120, G130, G144,

G169, G187, G227, G231, G239, G242, G246, G247,
   G248, G324.
Estellet-Brun, Michel (organ).
LB:A9.
Estournet, Jean (violin).
LB:A602.
Estrada, Dom Grigorio – *See* Montserrat.
L'Estro Armonico Ensemble.
LB:A577.
Etcheverry, Michaëla (mezzo-soprano).
EB:G30.
Evans, Geraint (baritone).
LB:G147.
Evans, Wynford (tenor).
LR:Gd24, Gd28.
Everett, Timothy (boy soprano).
EB:F64.
Ewerhart, Rudolf (organ).
LR:F90, F111, F124.
LB:A303, B203, G178.
Ewerhart, Rudolf – *See* Santini Chamber Orchestra.
   – *See* Württemburg Chamber Orchestra.
Extempore String Ensemble.
LR:Ga8, Ga15.
Extermann, Marinette (harpsichord).
LB:A297, A307, A318.

Fackert, Alfred (tenor).
LB:G249.
Faerber, Jörg – *See* Württemburg Chamber Orchestra.
Fagius, Hans (organ).
LR:Gc17.
LB:E24, E92, F83.
Fahberg, Antonia (soprano).
EB:F44.
LB:G62.
Falk, Julia (contralto).
LB:G75.
Falvai, Sandor (piano).
LB:A141.
Fantini, Franco (violin).
LB:A432, A474, A504.
Fantipe, Henri-Claude – *See* Solistes de Paris.
Farina, Eduardo (harpsichord).
LB:A235, B167.
Faringer, Solveig (soprano).
LR:F91.
Farncombe, Charles – *See* Handel Opera Society
   Orchestra and Chorus.
Farolfi, Rodolfo (tenor).
LR:E4, E5.
EB:F31, F48.
Fassano, Renato – *See* Collegium Musicum Italicum.
   – *See* I Virtuosi di Roma.
Fassbaender, Brigitte (mezzo-soprano).
LB:G155, G166.
Faulstich, Gerhard (baritone).
LB:G282.
Fehr, Hans Georg (bass).
EB:G124.
Feit, Pierre W. (oboe).
LB:B2.
Felicani, Rodolfo (violin).
LB:B322.
Felix, Gladys (contralto).
EB:G16, G34.
Fennell, Frederick – *See* Cleveland Symphonic Winds.
Fernandez, Huguette (violin).
LB:A206, A576, A620.
Ferracini-Malacarne, Maria-Grazia (soprano).
EB:G49, G64.
LB:G264.
Ferrard, Jean (organ).
LB:E173.

Ferraresi, Cesare (violin).
EB:B62.
Ferrari, Astone (violin).
LB:A12, A445.
Ferrari, Enza (harpsichord).
EB:F93.
Ferraris, Mario (violin).
LB:A432, B192.
Ferras, Christian (violin).
LB:A69, A76.
Ferrier, Kathleen (contralto).
LB:G11, G142, G185, G269.
Ferro, Luigi (violin).
LB:A471.
Feuge, Elizabeth (soprano).
LB:G143.
Feuille, Jacques – *See* Jacques Feuille Ensemble.
Feyerabend, Johannes (tenor).
LB:G31, G70.
Fiedler, Arthur – *See* Boston Pops Orchestra.
Figueras, Montserrat (soprano).
AA:B7, D1.
AN:B17.
ER:A26.
LR:F2.
EB:F97.
LB:F84.
SI:A2.
Figueras, Pilar (soprano).
AA:B7, D1, D2, E1, E2, E3, E15.
Filistad, Adolfo (tenor).
EB:F48.
Finck, Siegfried (percussion).
LR:B25.
Fink, Christian (violin, viola d'amore).
EB:F102.
LB:A369, A599.
Fink, Eric (horn).
LB:B232.
Fink, Johannes (viol).
ER:A4.
LB:B69, B112.
Finke, Eberhard (cello).
LB:F82.
Finnilä, Birgit (contralto).
LB:F77, G30, G45, G124, G138, G161, G238, G284, G285, G294.
Finucane, Tom (lute, recorder).
AA:E17.
Fioroni, Giovanna (contralto).
LB:G261.
Fischer, Eduard – *See* Prague Chamber Soloists.
Fischer, Edwin (piano).
LB:A130, D35.
Fischer, Hans (horn).
LB:A399.
Fischer, Roger (organ).
LB:E206.
Fischer-Dieskau, Dietrich (baritone).
LB:G8, G9, G17, G19, G24, G28, G47, G87, G88, G89, G90, G91, G92, G93, G105, G106, G121, G134, G135, G136, G137, G147, G149, G153, G167, G171, G172.
Fissore, Enrico (bass).
EB:F39, G48, G49, G64.
Fistulatores et Tubicinatores Varsoviensis.
LR:E66.
EB:B71.
Fithian, Bruce (tenor).
EB:F68.
Five Centuries Ensemble.
LR:E14.
EB:F9, F10, F84.
Flagstad, Kirsten (soprano).

EB:F66.
Flebbe, Herta (soprano).
EB:G69, G116, G126.
Fleet, Edgar (tenor).
LB:F59, G215.
Fleet, Edgar – *See* Pro Cantione Antiqua.
– *See* Schola Cantorum, London.
Fleischer, Eva (contralto).
LB:G93.
Fleischmann, Otto (bassoon).
LB:A399, A415, A544.
Florilegium Musicum Ensemble, dir. Hans Ludwig Hirsch.
LB:F71.
La Follia Instrumental Ensemble, dir. Miguel de la Fuente.
EB:A16, A24.
LB:A662.
Fontainbleau Chamber Orchestra, dir. Jean-Jacques Werner.
LB:A348.
Fontenarosa, Renaud (cello).
LB:B37.
Fontgombault, Choir of the Abbey of Notre Dame de.
PS:A70.
Foretti, Cristo (lute).
LB:A523.
Forster, Karl – *See* Berlin Symphony Orchestra.
Forster-Durlich, Dorothea (soprano).
EB:F29.
Fortunato, D'Anna (contralto).
EB:F68.
Foti, Clara (mezzo-soprano).
LR:E4, E5.
EB:G48.
Fournier, Pierre (cello).
LB:A564, B32, B112.
Frager, Malcolm (piano).
LB:D203.
France, Katalin (oboe).
LB:A658.
Francescatti, Zino (violin).
LB:A214.
Francia, Carlo Sforza (organ).
LB:E1.
Francis, Sarah (oboe).
LB:B256.
Frank, Maria (cello).
LB:A529.
Frankfurt Bach Orchestra, dir. Theo Engel.
LB:A195.
Frankfurt Bach Orchestra, dir. Martin Stephani.
LB:A62, A253.
Frankfurt Cantata Orchestra, dir. Ludwig Doormann.
LB:G70.
Frankfurt Chamber Choir, dir. Hans Michael Beuerle.
LR:E18.
Frankfurt Kantorei, dir. Helmuth Rilling.
LB:G184.
Frankfurt Kantorei, dir. Kurt Thomas.
LB:G20, G183.
Frankfurt Madrigal Ensemble.
LB:G282.
Franklin, Brian (viola da gamba).
LR:Gc15.
Franz Liszt Chamber Orchestra and Choir, dir. György Lehel.
LB:G160.
Franz Liszt Chamber Orchestra, dir. Janos Rolla.
LB:A360, A406.
Franz Liszt Chamber Orchestra, dir. Frigyes Sandor.
LR:A6.
EB:G36.
LB:A108, A159, A172, A272, A309, A406, A529, A552, A553, A554, A630, A658, B108, F27, G86,

Gotti, Tito – *See* Lausanne University Choir.
 – *See* Orchestra del Teatro Communale di Bologna.
Göttinger Stadtkantorei, dir. Ludwig Doorman.
LB:G70, G183.
Göttsche, Heinz Markus – *See* Heidelberg Chamber
  Orchestra.
Götze, Werner (tenor).
EB:G121.
Gould, Glen (piano).
LB:D19, D25, D33, D34, D42, D49.
Goverts, Hans (harpsichord).
LB:A29, A50, D221.
Gracis, Ettore – *See* Scarlatti Orchestra of Naples.
Graf, Hedy (soprano).
EB:G69, G131, G235.
Graf, Peter-Lukas (flute).
LB:A185, A191, A363, B70, B71, B91, B98, B132,
  B189, B232, B251, B255, B301, G184.
Graf, Peter-Lukas – *See* English Chamber Orchestra.
Graham-Jones, Ian (viol).
SI:C18, C19, C20, C21.
La Grande Ecurie et la Chambre du Roy, dir. Jean-Claude
  Malgoire.
EB:G23.
LB:A485, A591, A634, F44, F46, F60, G291.
Green, Daryl (soprano).
LB:G243.
Greene, Eric (tenor).
LB:G142.
Greevy, Bernadette (contralto).
LB:F49.
Greifswald Cathedral Choir, dir. Hans Pflugbeil.
EB:G9.
Grenat, Birgit (soprano).
EB:G46, G47.
Genoble Instrumental Ensemble, dir. Stephane Cardon.
EB:G31.
LB:A226, B123.
Griffett, James (tenor).
EB:G23.
Grimbert, Jacques – *See* Choeur National.
Grischkat, Hans – *See* Schwäbian Singkreis.
Grist, Reri (soprano).
EB:B60, F83.
Grobholtz, Werner (violin).
LB:A503.
Groh, Tine (soprano).
EB:G51.
Gröschke, Christa-Sylvia (soprano).
EB:G85.
LB:G139.
Group des Instruments Anciens de Paris, dir. Roger
  Cotte.
LR:E31.
LB:B272.
Gruber, Karl (oboe).
LB:A399, A597.
Grubich, Joachim (organ).
EB:E71, E85.
LB:A306, A314, E28, E114.
Grudin-Brandt, Inger (harpsichord, clavichord).
LB:D81.
Grumiaux, Arthur (violin).
LB:A75, B17, B145, B172.
Grummer, Elisabeth (soprano).
LB:G149, G153.
Grund, P (mandolin).
LB:A531.
Grundy, Owen (bass).
AA:C1.
Guest, George – *See* Academy of St. Martin-in-the-Fields.
 – *See* English Chamber Orchestra.
 – *See* Philomusica of London.
 – *See* St. John's College Choir.

Guglielmo, Giovanni (violin).
LB:B166.
Guildford Cathedral Choir, dir. Bernard Rose.
LR:Ge30.
Guilini, Carlo Maria – *See* Philharmonia Orchestra.
Guillou, Jean (organ).
LB:A23, D22.
Gulbenkian Foundation Chamber Orchestra, dir. Michel -
  Corboz.
LB:A128.
Gulbenkian Foundation Symphonic Choir and
  Orchestra, dir. Michel Corboz.
EB:G21, G26, G27.
LB:G307.
Guignard, Eric (cello).
LB:G278.
Guller, Youra (piano).
LB:D224.
Gulli, Franco (violin).
EB:B62.
LB:A376, A432, B193, B199.
Gümmer, Paul (bass).
EB:G115.
Gundermann, Rony (soprano).
LB:G132.
Gundlich, Etzel (organ).
EB:E43, E84.
Günter, Horst (bass).
LB:G163, G283, G326.
Gunter, Kurt (violin).
LB:B112.
Günther Arndt Choir.
LB:F82.
Gurtner, Heinrich (harpsichord, organ).
LB:A132, B217, E8.
Gütersloh Bach Choir, dir. Hermann Kreutz.
LB:G179.
Gutstein, Ernst (bass).
LR:F3.
Guttmann, Wolfgang (lute).
LR:D21.
Györ Girls' Choir, dir. Miklos Szabo.
ER:B13.
LR:F59.
EB:G36, G50.

Haas, Arthur (harpsichord).
EB:D14.
LB:D56.
Haas, Douglas (organ).
LB:A229.
Haas, Karl – *See* London Baroque Ensemble.
Haasemann, Frauke (contralto).
LR:F108.
EB:G10, G69, G89, G92, G93, G94, G95, G97, G98,
  G99, G112, G115.
LB:G4, G32, G58, G235.
Haebler, Ingrid (forte-piano).
LB:A49, B8, B10.
Haefliger, Ernst (tenor).
AN:A9.
LB:G17, G87, G91, G92, G93, G105, G106, G108,
  G121, G134, G135, G138, G150, G151, G221, G326.
Haertel, Siegfried (bass).
LB:G141, G263.
Haesler, Konrad (cello).
LB:B258.
Haferland, Heinrich (viol).
LR:F108.
LB:B303, B305.
Hagegard, Haken (baritone).
LB:G74.
Hahn, Werner (bass).
LR:D21.

Hoff, Brynjar (oboe).
LB:A204.
Höffgen, Marga (contralto).
LB:G112, G146, G167, G184, G221, G284.
Hoffmann, Grace (contralto).
LB:G223.
Hofmann, Wolfgang - See Emil Seiler Chamber Orchestra.
Hogwood, Christopher (harpsichord, chamber organ, virginals, forte-piano).
LR:Gc1, Gc2, Gc5.
EB:F3, F61, G107.
LB:A328, A427, B7, B9, B129, B155, B233, B291, D1, G196.
SI:A1, A2.
Hogwood, Christopher - See Academy of Ancient Music.
Hokanson, Leonard (piano).
LB:B62.
Holbling, Quido (violin).
LB:A617.
Holl, Robert (bass).
LB:G284, G294, G300.
Hollard, Florian - See Harmonie de Chambre, Paris.
Hölle, Matthias (bass).
EB:G11.
Höller, Günther (recorder).
LB:A645.
Holliger, Heinz (oboe, oboe d'amore).
LB:A8, A15, A19, A43, A213, A237, A332, A540, A541, A542, A578, A618, A642, B116, B117, B177, B201, B246, B252.
Holloway, John (violin).
EB:B58.
Hollweg, Ilse (soprano).
LB:A278.
Hollweg, Werner (tenor).
LB:G159, G247.
Holman, Peter - See Ars Nova.
Holmes, Ralph (violin).
LB:A458.
Holtman, Jacques (violin).
LB:A386.
Holy, Walter (trumpet).
EB:B67.
Homberg, Antoinette van den (violin).
LB:B229, B230, B260.
Honey, Gordon (bass).
SI:C8.
Honge, Paul (bassoon).
LB:A620.
Honegger, Henri (cello).
LB:B35.
Hope-Simpson, R (viol).
LB:D226.
Hopfner, Heiner (tenor).
LB:G152, G165.
Horacek, Jaroslav (bass).
LB:F79.
Horak, Jaroslav (viola d'amore).
LB:B312.
Horak, Jiri (clarino).
EB:A30.
Horne, Marilyn (contralto).
LB:F42, F75.
Horriben, Alison (soprano).
LR:Gd5.
Horst, Anthon van der - See Amsterdam Chamber Orchestra.
 - See Concerto Amsterdam.
Hörtnagel, Georg (double-bass).
EB:G12.
Hortobagyi, György (bassoon).
LB:B92.
Hortus Musicus, dir. Andres Moustonen.

PS:C3.
AA:B4.
AN:B3, B12.
Horvath, Aniko (harpsichord).
EB:D25.
Horvath, Jozsef (tenor).
LB:F74.
Horvath, Laszlo (clarinet).
LB:A360.
Hostettler, Nicole (spinet).
LB:B177.
Howard, Michael - See Cantores in Ecclesia.
Howell, Gwynne (baritone).
LB:G158, G224.
Howells, Anne (mezzo-soprano).
EB:F6.
Howlett, Neil (baritone).
LB:G7.
Huber, Kurt (tenor).
AN:B8.
LR:E16.
EB:G12, G52, G85, G103, G104.
Hübscher, Jürgen (lute).
LR:C12.
Hucke, Helmut (oboe).
LR:A30, A182, A191, A357, A645.
Huddersfield Choral Society.
LB:G210, G233.
Hudemann, Hans-Olaf (bass).
EB:F110, G51, G116.
LB:G70, G73.
Huggett, Monica (violin).
LB:F21.
SI:A1.
Humphrey, Raymond (organ).
LB:E193.
Huneau, Bernard (recorder, flute, crumhorn).
AA:D8, D23.
ER:A13.
LR:B29.
Hungarian Baroque Trio.
LB:B270.
Hungarian Chamber Orchestra, dir. Wilmos Tatrai.
LB:A528, A604, A613.
Hungarian People's Army Male Voice Choir, dir. Istvan Kis.
LR:A6.
Hungarian Radio Orchestra, dir. Lamberto Gardelli.
LB:A467.
Hungarian State Orchestra, dir. Ferenc Szekeres.
LB:F74, G287.
Hunt, Donald (organ).
LB:E194, E214.
Hunt, Donald - See Academy of Worcester Cathedral.
 - See Leeds Parish Church Choir.
 - See Worcester Cathedral Choir.
 - See Yorkshire Sinfonia.
Hunt, Thomas (boy treble).
LB:G327.
Hunt, William (vielle, viol).
AA:E17.
LR:Gd5.
Hünteler, Konrad (flute).
LB:B298.
Hunter, George - See Illinois University Choir.
Hurford, Peter (organ).
LB:E89, E90, E105, E116, E117, E118, E140, E141, E142, E143, E213.
Hürth Gymnasium Choir.
LB:G176.
Hurwitz Chamber Orchestra.
LB:A59.
Hüsch, Gerhard (baritone).
LB:G140.

Huttenlocher, Philippe (bass-baritone).
EB:F42, F55, G21, G26, G27, G29, G41, G49, G64.
LB:F62, G10, G63, G68, G72, G115, G118, G145, G161, G214, G298.
Huys, Johann (harpsichord, virginals, chamber organ, forte-piano).
LR:D19.
EB:F100, G35, G137.
LB:B244, B275, G182.

I Musici.
EB:A4, A9, A23.
LB:A13, A15, A16, A97, A371, A393, A426, A433, A434, A436, A444, A494, A497, A498, A500, A501, A536, A537, A538, A539, A540, A541, A542, A565, A566, A610, A618.
Iadone, Joseph (lute, viol).
AA:E5.
LR:Gd12.
Ihara, Naoko (contralto).
EB:G27.
LB:G10, G307.
Iiyama, Emiko (soprano).
LB:G111.
Illinois University Choir, dir. George Hunter.
ER:B25.
Immerseel, Jos van (harpsichord).
LB:D149, D158.
Instrumental Ensemble of Paris, dir. Louis de Froment.
LB:A625.
Instrumental Ensemble of France, dir. Jean-Pierre Wallez.
LB:A181, A350, A378, A420, A428, A460, A489, A548, A549 A602, A664, A670, F65, G310.
Iranian National Radio and Television Chamber Orchestra, dir. Emil Tchakarov.
LB:A582.
Isaacs, John (viol).
SI:C8, C13.
Isenhardt, Wolfgang (tenor).
LB:G159.
Isoir, Andre (organ).
LR:D11, D12, D16.
EB:E2, E31, E34, E76.
LB:A563, E6, E7, E30, E31, E84, E150, E158, E160, E165, E166, E169, E171, E177, E230, E231.
Italian Radio and Television Chamber Choir, dir. Claudio Scimone.
LB:G296.
Italian Vocal Quintet, dir. Angelo Ephrikian.
LR:E4, E5.
Ito, Ako (guitar).
LB:A532.
Iwanow, Igor (violin).
LB:A592.

Jablonski, Roman (cello).
LB:A230.
Jaccottet, Christianne (harpsichord).
LB:A237, B116, B117, B158, B165, B177, B201, B252
Jackson, Francis (organ).
LB:E213.
Jackson, Nicholas (organ).
LB:E228.
Jacob, Werner (organ).
EB:E60.
LB:E33, E185, E197, E198, E216.
Jacobean Consort of Viols.
LB:G320.
Jacobeit, Irmgard (soprano).
EB:F29, G59.
LB:F9.
Jacobs, Rene (counter-tenor).
EB:F7, F8, F12, F13, F56, F89, F99, F100, G19, G20,

G35, G47, G134, G137.
LB:F22, F23, F28, F37, F43, F64, F73, G25, G33, G34, G182.
Jacobson, Lena (organ).
LR:D14.
EB:E74.
Jacques, Reginald – See Bach Choir.
– See Jacques Choir and Orchestra.
Jacques Choir and Orchestra, dir. Reginald Jacques.
LB:G11, G142.
Jacques Feuille Ensemble.
LR:E12, E13, E58.
Jaffe, Michael – See Waverley Consort.
Jahn, Otto (trumpet).
LB:A660.
Jakowicz, Karel (violin).
LB:A86.
James, David (counter-tenor).
SI:A2.
Janacek Chamber Orchestra, dir. Zdenek Dejmek.
LB:A588.
Jannigro, Vittorio – See Angelicum Orchestra.
Janota, Gabor (bassoon).
LB:A552, A553.
Janowitz, Gundula (soprano).
LB:G92, G107, G124, G136, G164, G221.
Jansen, Jacques (baritone).
LB:F63.
Jappe, Michael (viol).
EB:B57.
LB:B137.
Jaquenod, Jean (organ).
LB:E172.
Jaquet, Marie-Louis (organ).
LR:D17.
EB:B59.
LB:E233.
Jaye Consort of Viols.
LR:B10, Ga18, Gd17, Gd40, Gd53, Ge14.
Jean-Noël Mollard Quartet.
LB:B110.
Jedlicka, Dalibor (bass).
LB:F79.
Jedrzejczak, Janusz (lute).
EB:F104.
Jelden, Georg (tenor).
EB:F110, G115, G119, G124.
LB:F11, G15, G27, G36, G77, G192, G241, G254.
Jelosits, Peter (boy soprano).
LB:G37, G51, G52, G54.
Jenkins, Neil (tenor).
LB:F34, G119, G148, G227.
Jergon, Jan (organ).
EB:E25.
LB:A617.
Jerusalem Music Centre Chamber Orchestra.
LB:A414, A448.
Jespers, Liane (soprano).
LB:G197.
Jetter, Margaret (soprano).
EB:G122.
Jeunesses Musicales Choir.
LR:F52.
LB:G259.
Jeynes, Helen (recorder).
LB:B284.
Jochims, Wilfred (tenor).
EB:G103.
LB:F1, F5, F13, G240.
Jochum, Eugen – See Bavarian Radio Symphony Orchestra and Chorus.
– See Concertgebouw Orchestra, Amsterdam.
Joculatores Upsaliensis.
ER:A24.

LR:E35, E64.
Jodry, Annie (violin).
LB:A348, B154, B315.
John Alldis Choir.
EB:F18.
LB:A239, G220, G222, G284, G285, G294, G300.
Johnson, Patricia (contralto).
EB:F62.
LB:G172.
Jonasova, Jana (soprano).
LB:F79.
Jonen, Alfons (tenor).
EB:F105.
Jones, Geraint – See Geraint Jones Singers and Orchestra.
– See Mermaid Singers and Orchestra.
Jones, Philip (trumpet).
LB:A594.
Jones, Philip – See Philip Jones Brass Ensemble.
Jones, Richard Elfyn (organ).
LB:E181.
Jones, Sterling – See Studio der Frühen Musik.
Jones, Trevor (viol, viola, rebec).
LR:E36.
EB:B19, F3.
SI:A1, A2, B2.
Joppich, Fr. Godehard – See Munsterschwarzach.
Jørkov, Jørn (counter-tenor).
LR:E19.
Jørkov, Jørn (pandora).
LR:B23.
Juhani, Matti (tenor).
LB:G139.
Junghänel, Kee (violin).
EB:G47.
Junghänel, Konrad (lute, theorbo).
EB:F7, F56, F89, G19, G20, G47, G134.
LB:C14, C17, F28.
Junghanns, Rolf (harpsichord, clavichord).
EB:D29.
LB:D6, D8, D83, D213.
Jungmann, Dorothea (soprano).
EB:F13.
Jürgens, Jürgen – See Monteverdi Choir, Hamburg.
Jurinac, Sena (soprano).
LB:G123.

Kagera, Jutta (cello).
LB:B287.
Kägi, Walter (viola).
LB:B98.
Kahlhöfer, Helmut – See Barmen-Gemarke Kantorei.
– See Berlin Bach Orchestra.
– See German Bach Soloists.
Kaine, Carmel (violin).
LB:A192, A199, A598.
Kajdasz, Edmund – See Cantilena Mens' Choir.
– See Cantores Minores Wratislavienses.
– See Wroclaw Radio Chamber Orchestra.
– See Wroclaw Radio Choir.
Kalmar, Magdar (soprano).
LB:F27, G39, G160, G308.
Kameralny Chamber Choir, dir. Antoni Szalinski.
EB:F104.
Kamu, Okku (violin).
LB:A173, A204.
Kantorow, Jean-Jacques (violin).
LB:A451, A569, B152, D221.
Kaplan, György (tenor).
LB:F74.
Kapp, Richard – See New York Philharmonic Virtuosi.
Kaproen Ensemble.
ER:A10.
Karajan, Herbert von – See Berlin Philharmonic

Orchestra.
– See German Opera Chorus.
– See Vienna Singverein Orchestra and Chorus.
Karen-Smith, Linda (contralto).
EB:G79.
Karper, Laszlo Szendrey (guitar).
LB:A528, B130.
Kart, Esther (contralto).
EB:G51.
Kassel Vocal Ensemble, dir. Klaus Martin Ziegler.
LB:G55.
Kastner, Hannes (organ).
LB:E43, G61, G117.
Kastrup, Wilfred (tenor).
LB:G58.
Kaufmann, Eduard (organ).
LB:A442, A583.
Kawalla, Szymon – See Pomeranian State Philharmonic Orchestra.
Kazandjiev, Vassil – See Sofia Chamber Orchestra.
Kecskes, Andras (lute).
LR:A5, A6, C17, C19, C20, E55.
LB:B158, B253, B273.
Kee, Piet (organ).
EB:E61.
LB:E199.
Kehr, Günther (violin).
LB:A228, B242.
Kehr, Günther – See Mainz Chamber Orchestra.
Kejmar, Miroslav (trumpet, clarino).
LB:A572, F79.
Keller, Irma (contralto).
LB:G55.
Keller, Jörg-Neithardt (organ).
LR:F102.
Kelly, Frances (harp).
EB:B13.
Kempff, Wilhelm (piano).
LB:D37, D47, D65, D66.
Kendall, William (tenor).
LB:G243.
Kennard, Julie (soprano).
EB:G143.
Kent, George (organ).
LB:B214, B223.
Kentish, John (tenor).
LB:F47.
Keönch, Boldiszar (tenor).
LB:G39.
Kergonan, Choir of the Benedictine Abbey of.
PS:A41, A53, B7.
Kern, Patricia (mezzo-soprano).
EB:F18.
Kerns, Robert (baritone).
LB:G107.
Kessick, Marlaena (flute).
LB:B300.
Kesteren, John van (tenor).
LB:F7, G121.
Keterlass, Leo (bass).
LB:G150.
Keyte, Christopher (bass).
ER:B4.
EB:F15, F16, F28, F57, F73, F81, G46, G58, G65, G78.
LB:G187, G242, G246, G248, G272, G320.
Kimura, Mihoko (violin).
EB:G47.
Kind, Sylvia (harpsichord).
LR:Gc14.
EB:D35.
LB:D234.
King, Andrew (tenor).
LR:Gd5.
King, Thea (clarinet).

LB:A567.
King's College Choir, dir. Philip Ledger.
LR:F54, F119, Ge39.
EB:G22, G63, G70.
LB:F39, F41, G2, G133, G171, G319.
King's College Choir, dir. Boris Ord.
LR: Ge28.
King's College Choir, dir. David Willcocks.
LR:F10, F50, F65, Gd39, Ge1, Ge13, Ge24, Ge26, Ge31.
EB:G2, G75, G136.
LB:F31, G5, G6, G12, G18, G83, G102, G144, G157,
    G186, G204, G206, G207, G208, G211, G216, G230,
    G272, G319, G320.
The King's Music.
SI:B2.
The King's Music, dir. Alfred Deller.
EB:F72, F75.
The King's Singers.
LR:E33, E46, E60, E65, Gd25, Ge9.
Kipnis, Igor (harpsichord).
LB:A122, D51, D84.
Kirch, Klaus (organ).
LB:G176.
Kirkby, Emma (soprano) (Member of CONSORTE OF
    MUSICKE).
LR:Gd27.
EB:B28, F80.
LB:F32, G126, G196, G226, G246, G290.
Kirkpatrick, Ralph (harpsichord, clavichord).
LB:A129, A213, A214, B321, D48, D85, D86, D106,
    D107, D180.
Kirsch, Dieter (lute).
LR:C12.
Kirschsten, Leonore (soprano).
LB:F8.
Kiskat, Fritz (cello).
LB:B112.
Klamand, Olaj (horn).
LB:A572.
Klebel, Bernhard (oboe).
LB:A399, A597.
Klebel, Bernhard – See Musica Antiqua, Vienna.
    – See Pro Arte Antiqua, Vienna.
Klein, Karl-Heinz (harpsichord).
EB:G15.
Klein, Karl-Heinz (baritone).
ER:A4, A21, A25.
Klein, Markus (boy soprano).
LB:G57, G67.
Klemperer, Otto – See New Philharmonia Orchestra.
    – See Philharmonia Orchestra.
Klenzi, Theresia (mezzo-soprano).
LR:F2.
Klerk, Albert de (organ).
EB:E61, E82.
LB:A317, A319, A326, B210, E187, E207.
Klinda, Ferdinand (organ).
LB:E34.
Klopfenstein, Rene – See Berlin Brandenburg Orchestra.
Klose, Margarethe (contralto).
LB:G143.
Knall, Klaus – See Freiburg Studenten Kantorei.
Knapp, Peter (bass).
EB:G63.
Knibbs, Jean (soprano).
EB:F69, F72, F75, G14.
LB:G243.
Knothe, Dietrich – See Capella Lipsiensis.
Knowles, Geoffrey (organ).
EB:E68.
Kobayashi, Michio (harpsichord).
LB:B246.
Københavns Drengekor, dir. Niels Møller.
EB:G66.

Kober, Dieter – See Chicago Chamber Orchestra.
Kobler, Robert (organ).
LB:E86.
Koch, Helmut – See Berlin Chamber Orchestra.
Koch, Johannes (viol).
LR:F108, F111, F124.
LB:A401, A407, B71, B133, B143, B144, B150, B156,
    B182, B183, B186, B239, B262, B288, B289, B303,
    B304, B305, B321, B322, G178.
Koch, Lothar (oboe).
LB:B248.
Koch, Ulrich (viola d'amore, viola pomposa).
LB:A362, C12.
Kocsis, Zoltan (piano).
LB:A125, A136, A141, A143.
Koehlein-Goebel, Marianne (soprano).
LB:G159.
Koenig, Fernand (bass).
LB:G139.
Kogan, Leonid (violin).
LB:A79, A431, A516, B53.
Kogan, Pavel (violin).
LB:A79, A431, A516.
Köhler, Helga (organ).
EB:G132.
Kohn, Carl Christian (bass).
LB:G153.
Kohnen, Robert (harpsichord). (Member of ALARIUS
    ENSEMBLE).
EB:B35, B43, B48, G134.
LB:B127, B176, B228, B268, D87.
Komosinski, Edward (violin).
LB:A592.
Konecny, Jaroslav (mandolin).
LB:F79.
Koopman, Ton (harpsichord, organ).
LR:E29.
EB:B25, B26, D15, D27, D38, E55, F99.
LB:B63, B114, B115, B128, B325, D150, D151, D229,
    E108, E155, F84.
SI:A2.
Koopman, Ton – See Musica Antiqua.
Kortendiek, Johannes (bass).
EB:G89, G92, G115.
LB:G58.
Kossowski, Edmund (bass).
LB:G317.
Koster, Dijck (cello).
LB:B309.
Kovacs, Denes (violin).
EB:B7.
LB:A81, A467.
Kovacs, Lorant (flute).
LB:B74, B136, B163.
Kovats, Kolos (bass).
LB:F74, G39, G160.
Kozderka, Ladislav (trumpet).
LB:A665.
Kozma, Lajos (tenor).
EB:F40, F46.
Kracow Chamber Orchestra.
LB:A193.
Kraft, Walter (organ).
LB:E119.
Kraemer, Nicholas (organ, harpsichord, virginals).
SI:B2.
Krahmer, Renate (soprano).
LB:G105.
Krapp, Edgar (organ).
EB:B53.
LB:B213.
Kraus, Adalbert (tenor).
LB:G59, G145, G154, G184, G282.
Kraus, Tom (bass-baritone).

LB:G110, G113, G146, G147, G170, G173, G229.
Krebbers, Hermann (violin).
LB:A75.
Krebda, Oldrich (harpsichord).
LB:B312.
Krebs, Helmut (tenor, counter-tenor).
LB:G13, G192, G326.
Kreidler, Dieter (guitar).
LB:C19, C25.
Kremsa, Edgar (double-bass).
LB:A148.
Krenn, Werner (tenor).
LB:F19, G113, G128, G161, G173, G229.
Kretschmar, Helmut (tenor).
EB:F44.
LB:G163.
Kreutz, Hermann – *See* Gütersloh Bach Choir.
   – *See* Heider Kammermusikkreis.
Kronwitter, Seppi (boy soprano).
LB:G40, G51, G52, G81.
Krotzinger, Werner (violin).
LB:A648.
Krüger, Martin (guitar).
LB:C31.
Krukowski, Stanislaw – *See* Wroclaw Radio Choir.
Kruysen, Bernard (baritone).
LB:G49.
Kruzel-Sawa, Marietta (organ).
LB:E219.
Krumbach, Wilhelm (organ).
LR:F111.
LB:E46, E190, E208.
Kubelik, Raphael – *See* Berlin Philharmonic Orchestra.
   – *See* London Philharmonic Orchestra.
Kubiak, Teresa (soprano).
EB:F5.
Küchler, Ingeborg (harpsichord, forte-piano).
LB:A28.
Küchler, Reimer (harpsichord, forte-piano). ·
LB:A28.
Kudlicki, Marck (organ).
LB:A617.
Kuentz, Paul – *See* Paul Kuentz Chamber Orchestra.
Kühl, Detlev (bassoon).
LB:B248.
Kühn Mixed Choir, dir. Pavel Kühn.
LR:F93.
LB:F79, G315.
Kuijken, Barthold (flute) (Member of PARNASSUS
   ENSEMBLE).
LB:A182, B170, B191, B244, B275.
Kuijken, Sigiswald (violin, viol) (Member of ALARIUS
   ENSEMBLE).
EB:A6, A7, A8, B9, B35, B43, B48, F12, G134.
LB:A466, A521, B52, B127, B162, B191, B268.
Kuijken, Sigiswald – *See* La Petite Bande.
Kuijken, Wieland (viol, cello) (Member of ALARIUS
   ENSEMBLE).
LR:E39.
EB:B9, B32, B35, B43, B48, F8, F12, F53, F56, F82,
   G19, G20, G134.
LB:A600, B61, B127, B162, B176, B191, B228, B268,
   F23, F28.
Kulka, Konstanty (violin).
LB:A461, A462, A477, B24.
Kundrtova, Hana (contralto).
LB:F79.
Kunz, Eric (bass-baritone).
EB:G79.
Kunz, Hans (tenor, bass).
LB:G34.
Kunz, Roland (bass).
LB:G13, G27, G84.
Kunz, Hanns-Friedrich (bass).

EB:G122.
Künzel, Johannes (bass).
EB:G9.
Kusche, Benno (bass-baritone).
LB:F81.
Kussmaul, Rainer (violin).
LB:A191.
Kvalbein, Aage (cello).
LB:B311.
Kweksilber, Marijanne (soprano).
EB:F89.
LB:F22, F25, F64, G40.
Kynaston, Nicholas (organ).
LB:A313, E35.

La Fleur, Rolf (lute).
LB:B306.
La Scala Theatre Orchestra, Milan – *See* Solisti del Teatro
   Alla Scala, Milan.
Labric, Pierre (organ).
LB:E221.
Lachner, Herbert (bass).
LR:F3.
Ladysz, Bernard (bass).
LB:G276.
Lagace, Bernard (organ).
EB:E16, E18, E20, E22, E44, E66.
LB:E136.
Lagace, Mireille (organ, harpsichord).
EB:E17, E19, E21, E23.
LB:D26, D52, D58, D112.
Laggar, Peter (bass).
EB:G29.
LB:G326.
Lagorce, Marcel (trumpet).
LB:A655.
Lagoya, Alexandre (guitar).
LB:A671.
Lahrs, Rosemarie (violin).
LB:B322.
Laird, Michael (horn, trumpet, cornet).
LB:A561, A574, A666.
SI:A2.
Laird, Michael – *See* Michael Laird Cornet and Sackbut
   Ensemble.
Laki, Krisztina (soprano).
LB:F43.
Lambden, Judith (harpsichord, spinet).
SI:C17, C18, C19, C20, C21.
Lamy, Jean (cello, viol).
EB:A27.
LB:B151, B195.
Landwehr-Hermann, Gertraud (soprano).
LB:G281.
Landini Consort.
PS:C4.
AN:B6.
LR:F120.
Lane, Elizabeth (soprano).
LR:Gd32.
Lane, Martin (counter-tenor).
LB:G216.
Lang, Hans (cello).
LB:B195.
Lange, Barbara (soprano).
EB:G12, G52.
Lange, Hansjürg (bassoon).
LB:B131, B241.
Lange, Hansjürg – *See* Hamburg Philharmonic
   Orchestra.
Lange, Mathieu – *See* North German Chamber Orchestra.
Langenbeck, August – *See* Stuttgart Cantata Choir.
Langnau Church Choir, dir. Jörg Ewald Dähler.
LB:G254.

Langridge, Philip (tenor).
EB:F39, G62.
LB:F36, F65, G120, G187, G204, G224.
Larde, Christian (flute).
EB:A27.
LB:B151.
Lardrot, Andre (oboe).
LB:B232.
Laroque, Jean-Pierre (bassoon).
LB:A548, A664.
Larrieu, Maxence (flute).
LB:A46, A181, A489, A622, B66.
Larrocha, Alicia de (piano).
LB:D63.
Las Huelgas, Choir of the Cistercian Monastery of Santa
   Maria la Real.
AA:C6.
Las Huelgas Ensemble, dir. Paul van Nevel.
AN:A14.
LR:E3, E72.
Laszlo, Margit (soprano).
LB:G287.
Latchem, Malcolm (violin).
LB:A27, A427.
Laubach Kantorei, dir. Georg Goebel.
LR:F109, F121.
EB:G132.
LB:G325.
Laubenthal, Horst (tenor).
LB:G136, G166.
Laursen, Jørgen (tenor).
LR:E19.
Lausanne Chamber Choir, dir. Kurt Redel.
LB:G280, G283.
Lausanne Chamber Orchestra, dir. Tito Gotti.
EB:G29.
Lausanne University Choir, dir. Tito Gotti.
EB:G29.
Lausanne Vocal and Chamber Ensemble, dir. Michel
   Corboz.
LR:F7, F8.
EB:F32, F33, F42, G49, G64.
LB:G10, G115, G118, G127, G161, G293, G298, G301,
   G312.
Lautenbacher, Susanne (violin).
LB:A196, A407, A473, A635, B25, B26, B27, B143,
   B144, B182, B183, B303.
Lavotha, Elemer (cello).
LB:B240.
Lazzarini, Adriana (contralto).
LB:G256.
Leanderson, Rolf (bass).
LB:F56, F83.
Lear, Evelyn (soprano).
LB:G134, G151, G268.
Leathard, Rosemary (oboe).
SI:C9.
Lecoq, Michel (tenor).
EB:F13.
Ledger, Philip (harpsichord, organ).
LB:A134.
Ledger, Philip – *See* Academy of St. Martin-in-the-Fields.
   – *See* English Chamber Orchestra.
   – *See* King's College Choir.
   – *See* Pro Cantione Antiqua.
Leeds Festival Chorus.
LB:G242, G250.
Leeds Parish Church Choir, dir. Donald Hunt.
LB:G327.
Le Floc, Herve (violin).
LB:A395.
Leguay, Jean-Pierre (organ).
PS:A71.
Leguillon, Bernard (horn).

LB:A331.
Lehane, Maureen (contralto).
EB:F44, G97, G104.
LB:G1, G76, G239, G270.
Lehel, György – *See* Franz Liszt Chamber Orchestra and
   Choir.
Lehotka, Gabor (organ).
LR:A6.
EB:E33, E65.
LB:A309, B108, E36, E37, E202, E239, G297.
Lehrendorfer, Franz (harpsichord, organ).
EB:G15.
LB:A147, B203.
Leib, Gunther (baritone).
EB:G125.
LB:G93.
Leipzig Gewandhaus Orchestra, dir. Rudolph Mauers-
   berger.
LB:G46, G47, G64.
Leipzig Gewandhaus Orchestra, dir. Günther Ramin.
LB:G61, G117, G140.
Leipzig Gewandhaus Orchestra, dir. Kurt Thomas.
LB:G48, G93, G167.
Leipzig Symphony Orchestra, dir. Hans Weissbach.
LB:G143.
Leipzig University Choir.
LB:G143.
Lejeune, Jerome (viol).
EB:G35.
Lemaigre, Philippe (guitar).
LB:C26.
Lemaire, Gery – *See* Solistes de Liege.
Lemgo Marien-Kantorei, dir. Walther Schmidt.
EB:G87.
Lemmen, Günther (viola d'amore).
LB:A515, A520, B310.
Lemnitz, Tiana (soprano).
LB:G140.
Lengert, Claus (boy soprano).
LB:G72.
Leningrad Philharmonic Chamber Orchestra, dir. Lev
   Shinder.
LB:A470.
Lensky, Margaret (contralto).
LB:G273.
Lenthold, Hansjürg (clarinet).
LB:B232.
Leonard, Laurence – *See* English Chamber Orchestra.
Leonhardt, Gustav (harpsichord, organ).
LR:E39, Gc11.
EB:B9, D7, D11, D31, E54, E56, F12, F40, G129.
LB:A30, A42, A44, A118, A133, A138, A142, A144,
   A184, A186, A386, A398, A438, A521, A600, A605,
   B52, B55, B56, B61, B138, B139, B140, B162, B178,
   B191, B229, B230, B260, B261, B267, B274, B278,
   B279, B283, B286, B292, B296, B309, D11, D24,
   D36, D43, D44, D60, D88, D178, D199, D230, E38,
   E187, E189, G175, G178.
Leonhardt, Gustav – *See* La Petite Bande.
   – *See* Vienna Concentus Musicus.
Leonhardt, Marie (violin).
LB:A184, A186, A386, B229, B230, B260.
Leonhardt Consort.
EB:B49, B54, F23, F29, G75.
LB:A44, A118, A133, A138, A142, A144, A184, A186,
   A600, G5, G6, G12, G18, G25, G33, G34, G40, G54,
   G57, G59, G67, G75, G175.
Lepauw, Roger (vielle).
AA:D9.
Leppard, Raymond (harpsichord).
LB:A127, A134.
Leppard, Raymond – *See* Academy of St. Martin-in-the-
   Fields.
   – *See* English Chamber Orchestra.

London Symphony Orchestra, dir. Charles Mackerras.
LB:A245.
London Symphony Orchestra, dir. Leopold Stokowski.
LB:A211, G236.
Long, Nancy (coprano) (Member of LAS HUELGAS ENSEMBLE).
AN:A14.
LR:E3, E72.
Loomis, James (bass).
LB:G273.
Loose, Mia (recorder).
LB:G157.
Looser, Rolf (cello).
LB:B98.
Loosli, Arthur (bass).
LB:G154.
Loosli, Theo - *See* Bern Bach Choir.
  - *See* Bern Chamber Orchestra.
Lopategui, Jose-Luis (guitar).
LR:C27.
Lopes, Jose Oliviera (bass).
EB:G21.
Lopez-Cobos, Jesus - *see* London Philharmonic Orchestra.
Lorengar, Pilar (soprano).
LB:A628.
Lorenz, Dietrich (tenor).
LR:F94.
Lorenz, Siegfried (baritone).
LB:F10, G93.
Los Angeles Philharmonic Orchestra, dir. Pinchas Zukerman.
LB:A91, A351.
Loschi, Mario (oboe).
LB:A51.
Lott, Felicity (soprano).
EB:F64, G22, G71.
LB:G148.
Louis Halsey Singers, dir. Louis Halsey.
EB:G14.
Loup, Francois (bass).
EB:F42, G49, G64.
Loveday, Alan (violin).
LB:A475.
Lubbock, John - *see* St. John's Smith Square Orchestra.
Lübeck Kantorei.
LB:G170.
Luca, Sergio (violin).
LB:B20, B314.
Luccardi, Giancarlo (bass).
EB:F39.
LB:F77.
Luccini, Vera (harpsichord).
LB:A432, B199.
Lucerne Festival Strings, dir. Rudolf Baumgartner.
LB:A32, A89, A129, A214, A423, A442, A477, A564, A565, A583, A643, B322, G47.
Ludwig, Christa (mezzo-soprano).
LB:G92, G107, G136, G147, G153, G164, G268.
Lugano Chamber Music Society Choir and Orchestra, dir. Edwin Loehrer.
LB:G273.
Lugosi, Melinda (soprano).
LB:G292, G297.
Lukomska, Halina (soprano).
LB:F26.
Lumsden, Alan (sackbut).
SI:B1.
Lumsden, David (harpsichord, organ).
EB:F96, F103.
LB:B87, B247, E99.
Lumsden, David - *see* New College Oxford.
Lutz, Volker (harpsichord).
LB:B287.

Lutze, Gert (tenor).
LB:G61, G79.
Luxembourg Madrigal Choir, dir. Daniel Schertzer.
LR:E29.
EB:F17.
Luxembourg Radio Orchestra, dir. Louis de Froment.
LB:A622.
Luxon, Benjamin (baritone).
LR:Gd47.
EB:F18.
LB:F36, G122, G230.
Lynen, Simone (contralto).
LB:G188, G200.
Lyon Madrigal Ensemble, dir. Stephane Cardon.
EB:G31.

Mass, Emil (violin).
LB:A495.
Maazel, Lorin - *See* Berlin Radio Symphony Orchestra.
  - *See* RIAS Chamber Choir.
Mackerras, Charles, dir. of Instrumental and Vocal Ensemble.
LR:F3.
Mackerras, Charles - *See* Austrian Radio Chorus and Orchestra.
  - *See* English Chamber Orchestra.
  - *See* North German Radio Chamber Orchestra.
  - *See* Paul Kuentz Chamber Orchestra.
  - *See* London Symphony Orchestra.
  - *See* Prague Chamber Orchestra.
Mackintosh, Catherine (violin, viol, rebec).
EB:B19.
LB:B7.
SI:A2, B2.
Madin, Suzanne (cello).
LB:B284.
I Madrigalisti di Genova, dir. Leopoldo Gamberini.
LR:E40, E47.
I Madrigalisti di Venezia, dir. Gabriele Bellini.
EB:F20, F21, F26, F27.
Maga, Othmar - *See* South German Philharmonic Orchestra.
Magdalen College Choir, dir. Bernard Rose.
LR:F84, F85, Gd39, Ge27.
LB:G262.
Magyar, Thomas (violin).
LB:A74.
Maier, Franzjosef (violin).
LB:A53, A182, A455, A480, A481, A520, A521, F71.
Maier, Franzjosef - *See* Collegium Aureum.
Mainardi, Enrico (cello).
LB:B322.
Mainz Chamber Orchestra, dir. Günther Kehr.
EB:F24, G79.
LB:A147, A227, A228, A281, A342, A413, A604, A654, A660.
Mainz Christuskirche Choir and Chamber Orchestra, dir. Diethard Hellmann.
LB:G84.
Maisonneuve, Claude (oboe).
EB:A27.
Maitre, Elizabeth (mandolin).
LB:A614.
Maksymiuk, Jerzy - *See* Polish Chamber Orchestra.
Malacarne, Rodolfo (tenor).
EB:F24, G48.
Malaguti, Laerte (bass).
EB:F24, G79.
LB:A604.
Malaniuk, Ira (mezzo-soprano).
LB:G280, G283.
Malcolm, George (harpsichord, organ).
EB:D24, F51.
LB:A24, A66, A69, A117, A121, A124, A137, A140,

Medieval Ensemble of London.
AN:B13.
Medlam, Charles (viol, cello) (Member of MUSICA
   ANTIQUA, COLOGNE).
Meer, Janneke van der (violin).
EB:G134.
LB:B244, F84.
Meer, Richte van der (cello).
LB:B244, B275.
Meer, Ruud van der (bass).
LB:G29, G33, G34, G37, G51, G52, G54, G56, G59,
   G63, G67, G68, G72, G161.
Meier, Daniel – See Da Camera Vocal Ensemble.
Meinecke, Sigfried (viola).
LB:B112.
Meissen, Paul (flute).
LB:B76, B83.
Melis, György (baritone).
LB:G160.
Melkus, Eduard (violin).
EB:B2, B8.
LB:A73, A213, A361, A388, A404, A527, B46, B142,
   B161, B196, F79.
Melkus, Eduard – See Capella Accademica, Vienna.
   – See Eduard Melkus Ensemble.
Melzer, Friedrich (tenor).
AN:A9.
EB:G5, G10, G97.
LB:G16, G241.
Melzer, Hans (cello).
LB:B322.
Mendez, Eke (violin).
LB:A203.
Menuhin, Yehudi (violin).
LB:A69, A76, A202, B23.
Menuhin, Yehudi – See Bath Festival Orchestra.
   – See Menuhin Festival Orchestra.
Menuhin Festival Orchestra, dir. Yehudi Menuhin.
LB:A69, A76, A137, A140, A220, A246, A299, G209.
Merker, Karl-Ernst (tenor).
LB:F82.
Mermaid Singers and Orchestra, dir. Geraint Jones.
EB:F66.
Mermoud, Philippe (cello).
LB:B177.
Mersiovsky, Gertrud (organ).
LR:D9.
EB:E29.
Mertens, C. (harp).
LB:A569.
Mesple, Mady (soprano).
LB:G309.
Messthaler, August (bass).
EB:G117, G146.
Messana, John Angelo (counter-tenor).
LB:G218.
Mestre, Francese (boy alto).
LB:G193.
Meszaros, Janos (bassoon).
LB:B312.
Metzger, Heribert (claviorganum).
LR:D21.
Meurant, Andre (tenor).
EB:G16, G32, G34.
Meyer, Hannes (organ).
LB:B215.
Meyer, Wolfgang (harpsichord).
LB:A628.
Meystre, Marc Philippe (harpsichord).
LB:A148.
Mezo, Laszlo (cello).
LB:A524, B163.
Micanik, Jaroslav (clarino).
EB:A30.

LB:F79.
Michael Laird Cornet and Sackbut Ensemble.
EB:A15.
Michala Petri Trio.
LB:B280.
Michaelis, Bernhard (boy alto).
LR:F111, F123, F124.
EB:F44, G112.
Micheau, Janine (soprano).
LB:F63.
Michel, Catherine (harp).
LB:B254.
Michel, Hannelore (cello).
EB:G12.
Michelow, Sybil (contralto).
LB:G60.
Michelucci, Roberto (violin).
LB:A15, A444.
Mielsch, Hans-Ulrich (tenor).
LR:F111, F123, F124.
EB:G51, G117.
Migdal, Marian (piano).
LB:D153.
Mijajer, Dejan (violin).
LB:A506.
Mijajer, Dejan – See Musici Academici.
Mikulka, Vladimir (guitar).
LB:C1.
Milan Angelicum Orchestra, dir. Claudio Abbado.
LB:A376.
Milan Angelicum Orchestra, dir. Giulio Bertola.
EB:G13, G48.
LB:G261.
Milan Angelicum Orchestra, dir. Franco Caracciolo.
EB:G84.
Milan Angelicum Orchestra, dir. Umberto Cattini.
LB:A51.
Milan Angelicum Orchestra, dir. Carlo Felice Cillario.
EB:G81.
LB:G219, G314.
Milan Angelicum Orchestra, dir. Bruno Martinotti.
LB:A517, G313.
Milan Cathedral Choir – See Capella Musicale del
   Duomo di Milano.
Milan Polyphonic Choir.
EB:F48, G13, G48.
LB:G219, G256, G261, G264.
Milanova, Stoika (violin).
LB:A82, A84, A459.
Miller, Donald (bass).
LB:G202.
Miller, Lajos (baritone).
LB:F74.
Miller, Tess (oboe).
LB:A199.
Milligan, James (bass).
LB:G233.
Miloradovitch, Hazelle (viol).
SI:C20, C21.
Milstein, Nathan (violin).
LB:A505, B14, B15, B29.
Minetto, Maria (soprano).
EB:F46.
LB:G264, G273.
Minnesota Orchestra, dir. Martin Skrowaczewski.
LB:A257.
Minton, Yvonne (contralto).
LB:G113, G234.
Minty, Shirley (contralto).
EB:G65.
LB:F32, G7.
Miranda, Ana-Maria (soprano).
LR:E31.
LB:F50, F68, G198.

Misschaert, Lieven (lute, viol, voice).
LR:E21.
Mitterhofer, Andre (organ).
LB:B205.
Mlejnkova, Vlast (soprano).
LB:G315.
Möhring, Hans Jürgen (flute).
LB:A205.
Molinari-Pradelli, Francesco – *See* Royal Opera House
    Orchestra, Covent Garden.
Molinaro, Ermanno (violin).
LB:B192.
Moll, Kurt (bass).
LB:G8, G90, G93, G155.
Mollard, Jean-Noël – *See* Jean-Noël Mollard Quartet.
Möller, Wouter (cello).
LB:A570, B179, B190.
Molyneux, Shelagh (soprano). (Member of The
    SCHOLARS).
LB:G130.
Monk, Christopher (cornet, recorder).
SI:C17.
Monkewitz, Annelies (soprano).
EB:F24.
Monte Carlo Opera Orchestra, dir. Massimo Freccia.
LB:A46.
Monte Carlo Opera Orchestra, dir. Louis Fremaux.
LB:G192.
Monteverdi Choir, Hamburg, dir. Jürgen Jürgens.
ER:B32.
LR:A2, E22, F104.
EB:F11, F28, F29, F37, F62, F85, F86, G46, G59.
LB:F9, G75, G281.
Monteverdi Choir, London, dir. John Eliot Gardiner.
LR:F22, F86.
EB:F108, G120.
Monteverdi Choir and Orchestra, dir. John Eliot
    Gardiner.
EB:F76, G62, G71.
LB:F58, G212, G218, G243.
Monteverdi Orchestra, dir. John Eliot Gardiner.
LB:A327.
Montgomery, Kenneth – *See* Bournemouth Sinfonietta.
Montini, Lisabeth (contralto).
LB:F67.
Montreal Bach Choir.
LR:E27.
Montreux Festival Choir.
EB:G127.
Montserrat, Choir of the Benedictine Abbey of, dir. Dom
    Grigorio Estrada.
PS:A5.
Montserrat – *See* Escolania de Montserrat.
Morell, Judith (harpsichord).
LB:A580.
Morey, Rita (viol).
SI:C19.
Morgan, Geoffrey (organ).
LR:Ge27.
Morison, Elsie (soprano).
EB:F70, F74, G42, G61.
LB:F24, F40, G233, G251.
Morley Consort, dir. David Munrow.
LR:Ga20, Gd18, Gd54.
Morris, Gareth (flute).
LB:G112.
Morrow, Michael – *See* Musica Reservata.
Moscow Chamber Orchestra, dir. Rudolph Barshai.
LB:A18, A123, A477.
Moscow Philharmonic Orchestra.
EB:A5.
Moscow Radio Symphony Orchestra Ensemble.
LB:A516.
Moser, Edda (soprano).

LR:F3.
LB:F60.
Moses, Susan (cello).
LB:B167.
Moustonen, Andres – *See* Hortus Musicus.
Mozart Boys' Choir.
LB:G247.
Mozzato, Gudo (violin).
LB:A471.
Mueller, Hannelore (viol).
EB:B1.
LB:A233, B200.
Müller, Carl-Heinz (bass).
EB:G89.
LB:G73.
Müller, Eduard (harpsichord, organ).
EB:B57.
LB:A118, A132, A142, A144, A239, A294, A316, B50,
    B112, B113, B142, B322.
Muller, Philippe (cello).
LB:B308.
Müller-Brincken, Jocken (oboe).
LB:A11.
Müller-Bruhl, Helmut – *See* Capella Clementina.
    – *See* Cologne Chamber Orchestra.
Müller-Henser, Franz (bass).
EB:F105, F110.
Müller-Molinari, Helga (contralto).
LB:F43, F76.
Münch-Holland, Gunhild (viol).
LB:B288.
Munchinger, Karl – *See* Stuttgart Chamber Orchestra.
    – *See* Vienna Academy Choir.
Munclinger, Milan (flute).
LB:B6, B81, B122, B147, B237.
Munclinger, Milan – *See* Ars Rediviva.
Munich Bach Choir, dir. Karl Richter.
LB:G79, G121.
Munich Bach Choir and Orchestra, dir. Karl Richter.
LB:G8, G9, G17, G19, G24, G28, G69, G87, G88, G89,
    G90, G91, G92, G93, G105, G106, G134, G135,
    G137, G151, G164, G221.
Munich Bach Orchestra, dir. Karl Richter.
LB:A92, A119, A146, A151, A164, A165, A179, A213,
    A214, A239, A279, A290, A291, A292, A293, A339,
    A669, G41, G43.
Munich Bach Orchestra, dir. Hans Stadlmair.
LB:A533.
Munich Bach Soloists, dir. Hanspeter Gmür.
LB:A70.
Munich Chamber Orchestra, dir. Hans Stadlmair.
LB:A41, A333, A669.
Munich Philharmonic Orchestra, dir. Marc Andrea.
LB:A651.
Munich Soloists.
LB:B103.
Munich State Opera Orchestra, dir. Karl Richter.
LB:G79.
Munich Vocal Soloists, dir. Hans Ludwig Hirsch.
LR:E10.
EB:G15.
Munich Youth Orchestra.
LR:F106.
Munns, Robert (organ).
LB:E192, E211, E224.
Munns, Robert – *See* St. Mary's Parish Church,
    Woodford.
Munrow, David (recorder, flute, wind instruments).
LR:Gd26.
EB:F49.
LB:A328, B227, B291.
Munrow, David – *See* Early Music Consort, London.
    – *See* Morley Consort.
Münster Cathedral Choir.

LR:F111.
Munsterschwarzach, Choir of the Benedictine Abbey of,
    dir. Fr. Godehard Joppich.
PS:A20.
Munteanu, Petre (tenor).
EB:G84.
Murdoch, Mary (oboe).
LB:B148.
Murray, Anne (mezzo-soprano).
LB:G145, G284, G294, G300.
Musica Amorbacensis.
LB:B307.
Musica Antiqua, dir. Ton Koopman.
EB:G54.
LB:F25.
Musica Antiqua, Cologne.
EB:B36, B52.
LB:A391, A632, B93, B153, B326.
Musica Antiqua, Vienna, dir. Rene Clemencic.
AN:B1.
ER:B29.
LR:E6, F99, Gd36.
EB:B46, G57.
LB:A233.
Musica Antiqua, Vienna, dir. Bernhard Klebel.
LR:A6, E45, E63.
EB:F88.
Musica Aurea, Liege.
ER:A23.
LR:B9, Ga12, Gd1, Gd11.
Musica da Camera, Amsterdam.
LB:B325.
Musica da Camera, Prague.
LB:A615.
Musica Dolce Recorder Ensemble.
LB:A636, B271.
Musica Holmiae.
LB:B1, B317.
Musica Polyphonica Ensemble, dir. Louis Devos.
EB:G83.
Musica Reservata, dir. John Beckett.
AA:D18.
ER:A17, B23.
LR:A4, B31, B32, E56, Gd39.
Musica Reservata, dir. Andrew Parrott.
ER:A18.
Musica Reservata, dir. Michael Morrow.
AA:D18.
LR:Gf2.
Musicae Antiquae Collegium Varsovienses, dir. Jerzy
    Dobrzanski.
LB:G277.
Musicae Antiquae Collegium Varsovienses, dir. Stefan
    Sutkowski.
EB:F104, G45, G141, G144.
Les Musicholiers, dir. Aviva Einhorn.
LB:F66.
Musici Academici, dir. Dejan Mijajer.
LB:A506.
Musici di Praga, dir. Frantisek Vajnar.
LB:A417, G315.
Musici Pragenses.
EB:G43.
Musiciens de Paris.
LB:A17, A355.
Musiciens de Provence.
AA:D20.
LR:B12, B14, B15, B19.
LB:B259.
Musikalische Compagney.
EB:B44, B61.
Muti, Riccardo – See New Philharmonia Chorus and
    Orchestra.
Myerscough, Clarence (violin).

EB:F92, F106.

Nabokov, Dmitri (bass).
EB:F23.
Näf, Fritz (tenor).
AN:B8.
LR:E16.
Nait, Giuseppe (tenor).
EB:G48.
National Museum Chamber Orchestra, Sweden, dir.
    Claude Genetay.
LB:A173.
Natorp, Hartwig (cello).
LB:B232.
Navarra, Andre (cello).
LB:B34.
Navarro, Garcia – See English Chamber Orchestra.
NCRV Vocal Ensemble, Hilversum, dir. Marinus
    Voorberg.
EB:G129.
Nedberg, Torleiv (bassoon).
LB:B311.
Nef, Isobel (harpsichord).
EB:D22.
Negri, Vittorio – See Berlin Chamber Orchestra.
    – See Berlin Chamber Soloists.
    – See Dresden State Orchestra.
    – See English Chamber Orchestra.
    – See Orchestra delle Teatro de la Fenice, Venice.
Nelson, Judith (soprano).
EB:F7, F8, F80, F81, F82, F89, G19, G20, G47.
LB:B160, F23, F28, F32, F54, G126, G196, G226,
    G290.
SI:A2.
Nesbitt, Dennis (viol, baryton).
LR:Gd42.
LB:D226.
Netherlands Chamber Orchestra, dir. Kurt Redel.
LB:A518, A522.
Netherlands Chamber Orchestra, dir. Simon Goldberg.
LB:A74.
Netherlands Chamber Orchestra, dir. David Zinman.
LB:A55, A60.
Netherlands Chamber Choir.
LB:G150.
Neudecker, Gustav (horn).
LB:B242.
Neuman, Vaclav – See Prague Chamber Orchestra.
Neumeyer, Fritz (harpsichord, clavichord).
LB:B310, B321, B322, D5, D8, F81.
Neumeyer, Fritz – See Collegium Terpsichore.
Nevel, Paul van – See Las Huelgas Ensemble.
New Chamber Soloists, dir. George Malcolm.
LB:A168.
New College Oxford, Choir of, dir. Edward Higginbottom.
LR:Ge25.
New College Oxford, Choir of, dir. David Lumsden.
LR:F117, Ge8, Ge10.
New England Brass Ensemble.
LB:B219.
New London Consort.
AA:E17.
LR:Gf3, Gf8.
EB:B58.
New Philharmonia Chorus and Orchestra, dir. Daniel
    Barenboim.
LB:G131.
New Philharmonia Chorus and Orchestra, dir. Riccardo
    Muti.
LB:G289.
New Philharmonia Orchestra, dir. Otto Klemperer.
LB:A155, G114.
New Philharmonia Orchestra, dir. Leopold Stokowski.
LB:A463.

EB:F42, G29.
LB:G115, G127.
Persichilli, Angelo (flute).
LB:B159, B236.
Pertis, Zsuzsa (harpsichord).
LR:A6.
EB:D34.
LB:A524, A529, A658.
Perulli, Raphael (viol).
EB:G6.
LB:G195.
Pesek, Libor – See Czech Philharmonic Orchestra.
   – See Prague Chamber Orchestra.
   – See Prague Symphony Orchestra.
Peter, Edwin (tenor).
LB:G254.
Peter, Oscar (flute).
LB:B150, B245.
Peter, Otto (baritone).
LB:G278.
Peters, Karlheinz (bass).
EB:F24.
Peters, Reinhard – See Collegium Aureum.
Petit, Gilbert (trumpet).
LB:A662.
La Petite Bande, dir. Sigiswald Kuijken.
EB:A6, A7, A8, A18.
LB:A466, F43, F61.
La Petite Bande, dir. Gustav Leonhardt.
EB:F13.
LB:F22, F64.
Petrescu, Emilia (soprano).
EB:F41, G8.
Petri, Michala (recorder).
LB:B280.
Petri, Michala – See Michala Petri Trio.
Peysang, Andre (tenor).
EB:F44.
Pfaff, Fr. Maurus – See St. Martin, Beuron.
Pfalz Boys' Choir.
LB:G139.
Pfeiffer, Walter (violin).
LB:A77, B149.
Pflugbeil, Hans – See Griefswald Cathedral Choir.
Philadelphia Orchestra, dir. Eugene Ormandy.
LB:A277, A496.
Philharmonia Orchestra, dir. Carlo Maria Guilini.
LB:A472.
Philharmonia Orchestra, dir. Otto Klemperer.
LB:A100, G147.
Philharmonia Orchestra and Chorus, dir. Otto
   Klemperer.
LB:G223.
Philip Jones Brass Ensemble.
LR:B10, F10, F86, F114, Ga11, Ga14.
EB:B38, G62, G70, G86, G118.
LB:A616, A657.
Philipp Nicolai Kantorei, Unna.
LR:F102.
Phillippe Caillard Choir.
LR:F48.
EB:G32, G34.
LB:G192, G279.
Phillips, Peter – See Tallis Scholars.
Philomusica of London, dir. Adrian Boult.
LB:F35.
Philomusica of London, dir. Thurston Dart.
LR:Ga4.
LB:A102, A275.
Philomusica of London, dir. George Guest.
LB:G187.
Philomusica of London, dir. Anthony Lewis.
EB:F74, F77.
Philomusica of London, dir. Carl Pini.

LB:A550.
Philomusica of London, dir. David Willcocks.
LB:F40, G157, G319.
Picket, Philip (recorder, harp, citole).
AA:E17.
EB:B58.
LB:B263.
Pierlot, Pierre (oboe).
LB:A5, A12, A232, A555, A556, A576, A620, A622,
   A626, A664.
Piguet, Michel (oboe).
LB:A438, A578, B118, B119, B137, B241.
Piguet, Michel – See Ricercare Ensemble, Zurich.
Piguet Oboe Ensemble.
LB:A639.
Pilewski, Witold (bass).
EB:F104, G45.
LB:G329.
Pini, Anthony (violin).
LB:A483.
Pini, Carl (violin).
LB:A483.
Pini, Carl – See Philomusica of London.
Pinnock, Trevor (harpsichord).
LR:Ga19, Gc9.
EB:D30.
LB:A163, A595, B67, D40, D93, D170, D171, D172,
   D211, D216.
Pinnock, Trevor – See English Concert.
Pinto, David (viol).
LR:Gd5.
Pio-Fumagali, Luciana (soprano).
EB:G81.
Pires, Maria-Joas (piano).
LB:A128.
Pischner, Hans (harpsichord).
LB:A180, B47.
Pitch-Axenfeld, Edith (harpsichord).
LB:A195, A618.
Pitter, Zdenek (theorbo).
LB:B312.
Piwkowski, Kazimierz (counter-tenor).
LR:E66.
Piwowarczyk, Marian (trumpet).
LB:E174.
Planchart, Alejandro – See Capella Cordina.
Planyavsky, Alfred (double-bass).
LB:B161.
Planyavsky, Peter (organ).
EB:E95.
Pledge, A. (harpsichord).
LB:D226.
Pleeth, Anthony (cello).
EB:B58.
LB:A478, B7, B129, B155, B233, B263.
SI:A1.
Plümacher, Hetty (contralto).
LB:F20.
Pocaterra, Antonio (cello).
LB:A432, B166, B192, B199.
Pohjola, Paavo (violin).
LB:B240.
Pöhl, Günther (flute).
LB:B90, B258.
Pöhl, Günther – See Aachen Cathedral Choir.
Pohlers, Klaus (flute).
LB:A227, A228, B242.
Pol, Wijnand van de (organ).
EB:E53.
Polish Chamber Orchestra, dir. Jerzy Maksymiuk.
LB:A110.
Polish Philharmonic Choir, dir. Stefan Stuligrosz.
LR:F70.
Pollard, Brian (bassoon).

LB:B191, B296.
Polonska, Elena (harp).
ER:A7.
LB:B324.
Polster, Hermann (bass).
EB:G121.
Pomeranian Philharmonic Madrigal Choir, dir. Stanislaw
    Galonski.
LR:F97.
LB:G199.
Pomeranian Philharmonic Choir.
LR:F76.
Pomeranian State Philharmonic Orchestra, dir. Zbigniew
    Chwedczuk.
LB:G317.
Pomeranian State Philharmonic Orchestra, dir. Szymon
    Kawalla.
LB:G276.
Pomerium Musices, dir. Alexander Blachley.
ER:B15, B38.
Pommerien, Wilhelm (bass).
LR:F108.
EB:G10, G69, G85, G88, G89, G90, G91, G92, G93,
    G94, G95, G97, G98, G99, G103, G104, G112, G131.
LB:G4, G32, G58, G235.
Pommier, Jean-Bernard (piano).
LB:D41, D57.
Ponce, A. (guitar).
LB:A569.
Pongracz, Peter (oboe).
LB:A658.
Pons, Michel (viola d'amore).
LB:A519.
Pontet, Joël (harpsichord).
LB:B77, B79.
Poole, John – See BBC Singers.
Pope, Martin (sackbut).
LR:Gd43.
Pople, Ross (cello).
LB:B148, B168.
Popp, Eberhard – See Martin Luther Kantorei.
Popp, Lucia (soprano).
LB:G131.
Popplewell, Richard (organ).
LB:E196.
Possemeyer, Berthold (tenor).
EB:F11.
Possiedi, Paolo (lute).
LR:C25.
Posta, Frantisek (double-bass).
LB:B312.
Potmesilova, Jaroslava (organ).
EB:E62.
LB:E236.
Potsdam Philharmonic Choir, dir. Stefan Stuligrosz.
PS:A76.
LR:F23.
Potter, John (tenor).
AA:E17.
Poulet, Gerard (violin).
LB:A425.
Poulton, Diana (lute, vihuela).
SI:C2, C3, C7, C10, C11.
Poutet, Joel (harpsichord).
LB:A9.
Praetorius Consort, dir. Christopher Ball.
AA:D19.
EB:B13.
LB:B259.
Pragnell, George (bass).
LB:F45.
Prague Chamber Orchestra.
EB:A32.
LB:A416.

Prague Chamber Orchestra, dir. Ulf Björlin.
LB:A396.
Prague Chamber Orchestra, dir. Alain Boulfroy.
LB:A9, A487.
Prague Chamber Orchestra, dir. Massimo Bruni.
LB:G266.
Prague Chamber Orchestra, dir. Libor Hlavacek.
LB:A64, A443.
Prague Chamber Orchestra, dir. Hans-Martin Linde.
LB:A543.
Prague Chamber Orchestra, dir. Charles Mackerras.
LB:A264.
Prague Chamber Orchestra, dir. Vaclac Neuman.
LB:A120, A126, A135, A139.
Prague Chamber Orchestra, dir. Libor Pesek.
LB:A321.
Prague Chamber Orchestra, dir. Jindrich Rohan.
LB:A525.
Prague Chamber Orchestra, dir. Frantisek Vajnar.
LB:A503.
Prague Chamber Orchestra, dir. Josef Veselka.
LB:E149.
Prague Chamber Soloists, dir. Eduard Fischer.
LB:A285.
Prague Chamber Soloists, dir. Libor Hlavacek.
LB:F79.
Prague Madrigal Singers, dir. Miroslav Venhoda.
PS:C6.
AN:B1.
ER:B11, B29, B36.
LR:E6, E11, F25, F55, F95, F99, F116, Gd36.
EB:F19, G57, G140.
LB:G189, G257, G260.
Prague Radio Symphony Orchestra, dir. Frantisek Vajnar.
LB:A85.
Prague Symphony Orchestra, dir. Libor Pesek.
EB:A30.
Prazak, Josef (viol).
LB:F79.
Presti, Ida (guitar).
LB:A671.
Preston, Simon (harpsichord, organ).
LB:A121, A140, A299, A310, A311, A315, A320.
Preston, Simon – See Christchurch Cathedral Choir.
    – See English Chamber Orchestra.
Preston, Stephen (flute).
LB:A163, A478, A488, A596, B67, B126, B155, B200,
    B233.
SI:A1.
Prey, Herman (baritone).
LR:F3.
LB:F82, G48, G114, G134, G141, G146, G151, G159,
    G166.
Price, margaret (soprano).
LB:G234, G250.
Priday, Elizabeth (soprano).
LB:G243.
Primavera Quintet.
LR:E42.
EB:B66.
Pritchard, John – See Northern Sinfonia.
Pro Arte Antiqua, Prague.
LB:B313, G257.
Pro Arte Antiqua, Vienna, dir. Bernhard Klebel.
AN:B1.
ER:B22.
EB:G43.
LB:G189.
Pro Arte Orchestra, dir. John Barbirolli.
LB:A621.
Pro Arte Orchestra and Chorus, dir. Malcolm Sargent.
LB:F24.
Pro Arte Orchestra, Munich, dir. Kurt Redel.
EB:F102.

Ryan, Mary (flute).
LB:B148, B168.
Ryman, M. (flute).
LB:A180.

Saar Radio Chamber Orchestra, dir. Karl Ristenpart.
LB:A10, A176, A493, A637, G279.
Sacher, Paul – *See* Zurich Collegium Musicum.
Sadlo, Miklos (cello).
LB:B31.
Sage, Sally le (soprano).
LB:G7.
Sai, Franco (tenor).
LB:G296.
Sailer, Friederike (soprano).
EB:F110, F111.
St. Anthony Singers.
EB:F63, F70, F73, F74, G42.
LB:F35, F40, F45, F47, F59.
St. Cecilia Orchestra, dir. Anthony Lewis.
LR:Gd3.
LB:F47.
St.-Clivier, Andre (mandolin).
LB:A571, A589.
St. Ethelreda, Ely Place, London, Choir of.
PS:A61.
St. George's Canzona, dir. John Sothcott.
AA:D17.
AN:B2, B10.
LR:B10, E25, E34.
EB:F91, F107.
St. Hedwig's Cathedral Choir.
LB:G153.
St. Jacobi Choir, Göttingen.
LB:G241.
St. Jacobi Kantorei, Hamburg, dir. Heinz Wunderlich.
LB:G73.
St. John's College Choir, dir. George Guest.
LR:F28, F49, F62, F71, Ge33.
EB:G55, G72, G77, G78.
LB:G187.
St. John's Smith Square Orchestra, dir. John Lubbock.
LB:A601.
St. Jordi Choir and Chamber Orchestra, dir. Oriol
    Martorell.
LB:G194.
St. Lambert Chorale, Verviers.
PS:A47.
St. Margaret's Singers, dir. Richard Hickox.
LR:Ge6.
St. Martin, Beuron, Choir of the Benedictine Abbey of,
    dir. Fr. Maurus Pfaff.
PS:A10, A28.
LB:G326.
St. Mary, Warwick, Choir of the Collegiate Church of, dir.
    Andrew Fletcher.
EB:G23.
St. Mary, Warwick, Choir of the Collegiate Church of, dir.
    Geoffrey Holroyde.
EB:G80.
St. Mary's Parish Church, Woodford, Essex, Choir of, dir.
    Robert Munns.
LR:Ge37.
St. Michaelis Choir, Hamburg.
LB:G163.
St. Nikolai Kantorei, Berlin, dir. Helmut Barbe.
LB:G13, G183.
St. Paul's Cathedral Choir.
LR:Gd39, Ge11.
LB:G148, G322.
St. Peter's Church Choir, Leipzig, dir. Dietrich Knothe.
ER:B37.
St. Peter's School Boys' Choir, Leipzig.
LB:G143.

St. Peter's Singers, dir. David Read.
SI:D2, D3.
St. Thomas Choir, Leipzig, dir. Rudolf Mauersberger.
LB:G46, G47, G64.
St. Thomas Choir, Leipzig, dir. Günther Ramin.
LR:F107, F108.
LB:G61, G117, G140.
St. Thomas Choir, Leipzig, dir. Kurt Thomas.
LB:G48, G93, G95, G167.
Salamonsberger, Reinhard (tenor).
LR:D21.
Salgo, Sandor – *See* Carmel Bach Festival Chorus and
    Orchestra.
Salminen, Marti (bass).
LB:G137.
Salome, Helene (piano).
LB:D108.
Salter, Lionel (harpsichord, forte-piano, organ).
LB:B161.
Salvi, Bruno (harpsichord).
LB:A149.
Salzer, Daniele (harpsichord).
LB:A395.
Sampson, Alastair (organ).
EB:E83.
Sams, Shirley (soprano).
EB:G65.
Samuel, Harold (piano).
LB:D70.
Sanders, John (organ).
LB:E214.
Sandlund, Staffan (bass).
LB:G239.
Sandor, Frigyes – *See* Franz Liszt Chamber Orchestra.
Santa Cruz del Valle de los Caidos, Escolania and Schola,
    dir. Laurentino Säenz de Buruaga.
PS:A29, A72.
AA:E4.
AN:B18.
Santana, Huc (baritone).
LB:F63.
Santi, Piero – *See* Accademici di Milano.
Santini, Nerina (soprano).
EB:F48.
Santini Chamber Orchestra, Münster, dir. Rudolf
    Ewerhart.
EB:F44.
LB:G249.
Santor, Stanislaw (violin).
LB:A592.
Santos, Carlos (harpsichord).
LR:E51.
Santos, Turibos (guitar).
LB:C11.
Sanvoisin, Michel (recorder).
LB:A226, A395, A571.
Sanvoisin, Michel – *See* Ars Antiqua, Paris.
Saorgin, Rene (organ).
EB:E5, E6, E7, E8, E9, E10, E11, E42, E89, G6.
LB:E61, E147, E167, E241.
Saque, Elsa (soprano).
EB:G21.
LB:G307.
Saretzki, Hans-Dieter (tenor).
EB:G99.
Sargent, Malcolm – *See* Pro Musica Orchestra and
    Chorus.
    – *See* Royal Liverpool Philharmonic Orchestra.
Sarti, Gastone (bass).
LR:E4, E5.
EB:F48, F90.
LB:A432, G302.
Sarti, Laura (soprano).
EB:F42.

LR:F108.
EB:G115, G116, G132.
LB:E64.
Schopper, Michael (bass).
LB:G40, G144, G263.
Schortemeier, Dirk (bass).
EB:F13.
Schott, Ulricke (harpsichord).
LB:A119, A146, A213.
Schreiber, Magdalene (soprano).
EB:G122.
Schreier, Peter (tenor).
EB:F83, G121, G125.
LB:F1, F10, F12, F16, G8, G9, G19, G24, G28, G46, G47,
   G64, G69, G71, G80, G87, G88, G89, G90, G91, G92,
   G93, G105, G107, G122, G124, G136, G137, G181,
   G238.
Schreier, Peter – *See* Berlin Chamber Orchestra.
Schrems, Theobald – *See* Regensberg Cathedral Choir.
Schriever, Gerda (contralto).
LB:G47.
Schröder, Jaap (violin).
LB:A236, A349, A354, A386, A398, A438, A570,
   A600, B267.
Schröder, Jaap – *See* Concerto Amsterdam.
Schroyens, Raymond (harpsichord).
LB:B125, B157.
Schüchter, Wilhelm – *See* Hamburg Chamber Orchestra.
Schulz, Walter (cello).
LB:B161.
Schulze, Siegfried (bass).
LB:G140.
Schüphach, Marie-Lise (oboe).
LB:B116, B117.
Schuster, Walther R. (organ).
LB:E223.
Schwäbian Singkreis, dir. Hans Grischkat.
LR:F109, F112, G117.
Schwalbe, Michel (violin).
LB:A441.
Schwarz, Gerald (trumpet).
LB:A580, A656.
Schwarz, Gerald – *See* 'Y' Chamber Orchestra.
Schwarz, Magali (mezzo-soprano).
EB:F42, G29, G49, G64.
LB:G115, G127.
Schwarzer, Horst (baritone).
LB:G241.
Schwarzkopf, Elizabeth (soprano).
EB:F66.
LB:G112, G147, G223.
Schwartzweller, Lisa (soprano).
LB:G73.
Schweizer, Verena (soprano).
LB:G301, G312.
Schwickert, Gernot (boy soprano).
LB:G61.
Scimone, Claudio – *See* Capella Coloniensis.
   – *See* Italian Radio and Television Chamber Choir.
   – *See* I Solisti Veneti.
Scottish Baroque Ensemble.
LB:A585, B327.
Scottish Chamber Orchestra, dir. Paul Tortelier.
LB:A169.
Scotto, Renate (soprano).
LB:F52.
Scovotti, Jeanette (soprano).
LB:F44, F56.
Sebestyen, Janos (harpsichord, organ).
LR:A5, A6.
EB:B7, E47.
LB:A604, B74, B130, B136, B163, D96, D97, D98,
   D99, D100, D161, D210, E62, E182.
Seefried, Irmgard (soprano).

LB:G134, G135.
Seel, Waldemar (horn).
LB:B242.
Segarra, Fr. Ireneu – *See* Escolania de Montserrat.
Segerstam, Leif (violin).
LB:A173.
Segovia, Andres (guitar).
LB:C10.
Seifert, Ingrid (violin). (Member of MUSICA ANTIQUA
   COLOGNE).
EB:F89.
Seiler, Emil (violin).
LB:B321.
Selig, Edith (soprano).
EB:G16, G32.
LB:G279.
Senechal, Michel (tenor).
LB:F63.
Serafim, Fernando (tenor).
EB:G21, G26.
LB:G307.
Serafin, Jozef (organ).
EB:E80.
Sestetto Italiano Luca Marenzio.
EB:F14.
Sewen, Marek – *See* Capella Arcis Varsoviensis.
Seymour, Peter (organ).
LB:E200.
Sgrizzi, Luciano (harpsichord).
LB:B3, D10, D160, D201.
Shacklock, Constance (contralto).
LB:F24.
Shann, Edgar (oboe).
LB:A179, A213, A214.
Shaulis, Zola Mae (piano).
LB:D39.
Shavitz, Carlos (lute).
LR:Gd24, Gd28.
Shaw, Geoffrey (baritone).
EB:F61.
Sheen, Graham (bassoon).
LB:A567.
Shepherd, Adrian – *See* Cantilena.
Sheppard, Honor (soprano).
EB:F69, E72, F75, F92, F94.
LB:B4, F34, G252.
Shindler, Lev – *See* Leningrad Philharmonic Chamber
   Orchestra.
Shirley-Quirk, John (bass-baritone).
EB:F60, F71, G62, G123.
LB:F59, G50, G83, G85, G108, G148, G158, G216,
   G222, G232, G248.
Shulman, Louis (violin).
EB:F54.
Sidey, Anthony (virginals).
SI:C2.
Sidwell, Martindale – *See* London Bach Orchestra.
Siemeling, Marlies (soprano).
LB:A640, F82.
Sienna Sinfonia, dir. Giuliana Badini.
LB:A476.
Silbertin-Blanc, Antoine (organ).
LB:A305.
Sillem, Mauritz (harpsichord).
LB:A669.
Sillito, Kenneth (violin).
LB:A78, A332, A456.
Silos, Santo Domingo de, Choir of the Monastery of, dir.
   Ismael Fernandez de la Cuesta.
PS:B10, B21, B22.
Silva, Joana (soprano).
EB:G21.
LB:G307.
Silver, Millicent (harpsichord).

LB:B256.
Sima, Gabriele (soprano).
LR:D21.
LB:G247.
Simon, Albert – *See* Franz Liszt Chamber Orchestra.
Simpson, Glenda (mezzo-soprano).
LR:Gd2, Gd29, Gd38, Gd41.
Sinclair, Monica (contralto).
LB:F24, F42, G228.
Sinnone, Ileana (soprano).
LB:G313.
Sipple, Peter – *See* Wellesley Chamber Singers.
Sistine Chapel Choir, dir. Domenico Bartolucchi.
LR:F100.
Sjögren, Björn (viola, viola da braccio).
LB:B317.
Skeaping, Joseph (viol).
SI:C11.
Skeaping, Kenneth (viol).
SI:C8, C11, C13.
Skeaping, Lucie (recorder, percussion).
SI:A2.
Skeaping, Roderick (viol, rebec).
EB:F53.
SI:A2, B1, C1.
Skowron, Jullien (vielle, crwth, rebec).
AA:D8, D16, D23.
ER:A13.
LR:B29.
Skram, Knut (bass).
LB:A204.
Skrowaczewski, Martin – *See* Minnesota Orchestra.
Slabak, Jan (trumpet).
LB:A665.
Slama, Frantisek (cello).
LB:B81, B135, B237.
Slechta, Milan (organ, harpsichord).
EB:A30.
LB:A321.
Sloane, Eleanor (violin).
LB:F21.
Slokar, Branimir (trombone).
LB:B215, B217.
Slovak Chamber Orchestra, dir. Bodhan Warchal.
EB:A2.
LB:A353, A617.
Sluis, Mieke van der (soprano).
LB:F64.
Sluys, Josef (organ).
EB:E28, E39.
Smets, Godelieve (harpsichord).
LB:D113, D114.
Smietana, Wojciech Jan (bass).
LR:E66.
Smigelski, Werner (harpsichord).
LB:A628.
Smit-Sibinga, Marijke (harpsichord).
LB:B195.
Smith, Hopkinson (lute, theorbo).
LR:C4, C26.
EB:B24, B25, B26, B56, C2, C3, C4.
LB:B126, B282, B302, C18.
SI:A2.
Smith, Jennifer (soprano).
EB:F76, G26, G41.
LB:F62, G293, G295, G298.
Smith, Kevin (counter-tenor).
LR:E36.
EB:G14, G23, G58.
Smith, Norman (trumpet).
LB:A656.
Smithers, Don (trumpet, cornet).
ER:A4.
EB:F40.

LB:A598.
Smithers, Don – *See* Don Smithers Brass Ensemble.
Snarski, Leon – *See* Gdansk Medieval Academy Choir.
Sneak's Noyse (= Roderick Skeaping, Lucie Skeaping, Reggie Coates, Ben Dover).
SI:A2.
Societe des Concerts du Conservatoire, dir. Hans Rosbaud.
LB:F63.
Söderstrom, Elisabeth (soprano).
EB:F39.
Sofia Chamber Orchestra, dir. Vassil Kazandjiev.
LR:B5.
LB:A82, A84, A459.
Soffel, Doris (contralto).
LB:G154.
Sokol, Ivan (organ).
EB:E91.
LB:E236.
Soldan, Jean (flute).
LB:A583.
Sole, Albert (boy soprano).
LB:G193.
Solesmes, Choir of the Benedictine Abbey of St. Pierre de, dir. Dom Jean Claire.
PS:A2, A3, A37, A49, A69, B2.
Solesmes, Choir of the Benedictine Abbey of St. Pierre de, dir. Dom Joseph Gajard.
PS:A1, A4, A6, A8, A9, A11, A12, A13, A14, A18, A19, A21, A23, A25, A26, A27, A32, A33, A34, A38, A45, A46, A48, A50, A51, A55, A56, A57, A58, A59, A60, A63, B2, B11, B12, B13, B15.
Solistes de Bruxelles.
LB:A612.
Solistes de Bruxelles, dir. Angelo Ephrikian.
LB:A504.
Les Solistes de France, dir. Jean-Claude Hartemann.
LB:A131.
Solistes de Liege, dir. Gery Lemaire.
LB:A667, G188, G197, G200, G201.
Solistes de Paris, dir. Henri-Claude Fantipe.
LB:A532.
Les Solistes Romands, dir. Arpad Gerecz.
LB:A75.
Solisti dell Gruppo Strumentale 'V.L. Campi' di Piacenza, dir. Giuseppe Zanaboni.
LB:B299.
I Solisti del Teatro Alla Scala, Milan, dir. Claudio Abbado.
LB:A98.
I Solisti di Milano, dir. Angelo Ephrikian.
EB:A26, F31, F48.
LB:A356, A419, A432, A474, A504, G264, G304.
I Solisti Veneti, dir. Claudio Scimone.
LB:A2, A4, A6, A12, A224, A235, A372, A373, A374, A375, A421, A429, A435, A440, A469, A479, A484, A491, A508, A509, A510, A511, A512, A513, A514, A523, A530, A555, A556, A557, A558, A609, A638, F55, F75, G271.
Somary, Johannes – *See* English Chamber Orchestra.
Sondberg, Bonna (soprano).
LB:G275.
Sonnleitner, Johannes (chamber organ).
LR:Ga7.
Sorelli, Mariella (harpsichord, organ).
LB:B192, G304.
Sothcott, John – *See* St. George's Canzona.
Sotin, Hans (bass).
LB:G82, G141.
Sous, Alfred (oboe).
LB:A227, A331, A413 B196, B242, F71.
Soustrot, Bernard (trumpet).
LB:A370, B221.
South German Madrigal Choir, dir. Wolfgang Gönnenwein.

LR:E52, F73.
EB:G16.
Stephani, Martin – *See* Frankfurt Bach Orchestra.
  – *See* German Bach Soloists.
Stephens, Derek (harpsichord).
LB:B148, B168.
Stern, Isaac (violin).
LR:A414, A448, A496.
Stevens, Dennis – *See* Accademia Monteverdiana.
Stewart, Charles (bass).
LB:G243.
Stich-Randall, Teresa (soprano).
LB:G108.
Stiftner, Walter (bassoon).
LB:B137, B158, B196.
Stiltz, Manfred (recorder).
LB:A549.
Stilwell, Richard (tenor).
EB:F65.
Stingle, Anton (lute).
LB:A531.
Stockholm Bach Choir.
LB:F30, F38.
Stockholm Bach Choir and Chamber Orchestra, dir.
  Anders Ohrwall.
LB:G74.
Stockholm Baroque Ensemble, dir. Ulf Björlin.
LB:A366.
Stockholm Chamber Choir, dir. Hans-Martin Linde.
LR:F2.
Stockholm Chamber Choir.
LR:E41.
LB:F56, G239.
Stockholm Chamber Ensemble, dir. Jan-Olav Wedin.
LB:A365, A623.
Stöhr, Hörst (double-bass).
LB:B321.
Stoklassa, Gertraut (soprano).
EB:G79.
LB:G241.
Stokowski, Leopold – *See* Czech Philharmonic
  Orchestra.
  – *See* London Symphony Orchestra.
  – *See* New Philharmonia Orchestra.
Stolte, Adele (soprano).
LR:F109.
EB:G89, G90, G91, G92, G93, G94, G95, G112, G115,
  G117.
LB:G47, G93.
Stoltze, Kurt Heinz (harpsichord).
LB:A147.
Stour Festival Chamber Orchestra, dir. Alfred Deller.
EB:F1, F59, F69, G72.
LB:F34.
Stoutz, Edmond de – *See* Zurich Chamber Orchestra.
Strahle, David (viol).
SI:C15.
Strano, Francesco (cello).
LB:A497.
Strehl, Laurenzius (viol).
LB:B116, B117.
Streich, Rita (soprano).
LB:F67.
Stricker, Andre (organ).
LB:E130.
Stringer, Alan (trumpet).
LB:A657, B212.
Strzelecka, Barbara (harpsichord, virginals).
LR:Gc13.
EB:D2.
LB:D141.
Studer, Ulrich (tenor).
LB:G81.
Studio der Frühen Musik, dir. Thomas Binkley.

AA:B6, B7, D3, D7, D11, D12, D14, D21, D25, E6, E7,
  E8, E9.
AN:A5, A6, A16, B7, B11, B14.
ER:A4, A15, A21, A25.
LR:A2, A8, F78.
Studt, Richard (violin).
LB:A199.
Stuligrosz, Stephan – *See* Polish Philharmonic Choir.
  – *See* Potsdam Philharmonic Choir.
Stumpf, Karl (viola d'amore).
LB:A525.
Sturm, Margot (contralto).
LR:D21.
Stuttgart Bach Collegium, dir. Helmuth Rilling.
LR:F101, F102.
EB:G7.
LB:A196, F1, F7, F8, F13, F18, F19, F20, F72, G16, G30,
  G35, G97, G110, G132, G145, G184.
Stuttgart Cantata Choir, dir. August Langenbeck.
EB:G138.
Stuttgart Chamber Orchestra, dir. Karl Munchinger.
LB:A45, A61, A106, A111, A117, A124, A156, A364,
  A461, A468, A477, A590, B101, B107, G113, G128,
  G146, G159, G170, G173.
Stuttgart Chamber Soloists, dir. Marcel Couraud.
LB:A445.
Stuttgart Chamber Soloists.
LB:A352, A407, A629.
Stuttgart Gedächtniskirche Figuralchor, dir. Helmuth
  Rilling.
LR:F101, F105, F108, F122.
LB:F1, F7, F8, F13, F18, F19, F20, G30, G62, G132,
  G180, G183, G184, G240.
Stuttgart Hymnus-Chorknaben.
LR:F108.
LB:F70, G62, G325.
Stuttgart Kirchenmusiktage, dir. Helmuth Rilling.
LB:G240.
Stuurop, Alda (violin).
LB:B229, B230.
Stych, Jan – *See* Martinu Chamber Orchestra.
Suddaby, Elsie (soprano).
LB:G142.
Suk, Josef (violin).
LB:A443, B22, B28, B48, B146.
Sundberg, Stig (horn).
LB:B317.
Sunderland, Raymond (organ).
LB:E194.
Sunnegardh, Thomas (tenor).
LB:G239.
Sutcliffe, Sydney (oboe).
LB:A21, G112.
Sutcliffe, Tom (counter-tenor).
AN:A7.
LB:G144.
Sutherland, Joan (soprano).
LB:F35, F42, F48, G225, G229.
Sutkowska, Maria (soprano).
EB:F104, G45.
LB:G329.
Sutkowski, Stefan (oboe).
LB:A592.
Sutkowski, Stefan – *See* Musicae Antiquae Collegium
  Varsoviense.
  – *See* Warsaw Chamber Orchestra.
Swiatek, Alicja (soprano).
LB:G279.
Sykora, Vaclav Jan (harpsichord).
LB:B312, D215, D237.
Symphoniae Sacrae Sackbutt Ensemble.
EB:G72, G107.
Symphony of the Air, dir. Paul Boepple.
LB:G244.

Syntagma Musicum, dir. Kees Otten.
AN:B4.
ER:A11.
Szabo, Miklos – *See* Györ Girls' Choir.
Szekeres, Ferenc – *See* Budapest Madrigal Singers.
  – *See* Franz Liszt Chamber Orchestra.
  – *See* Hungarian State Orchestra.
Szendrai, Janta – *See* Schola Hungarica.
Szeryng, Henryk (violin).
LB:A83, A425, A446, B12, B13, B49, B111.
Szeryng, Henryk – *See* English Chamber Orchestra.
Sziklai, Erika (soprano).
LR:E42.
Szlek-Consoli, Elizabeth (flute).
LB:E174.
Szökefalvi-Nagy, Katalin (soprano).
LB:G292.
Szostok-Radkowa, Krystyna (mezzo-soprano).
LB:A592, G277, G317, G329.
Szweda, Andrzej (tenor).
LB:G276.
Szybowski, Adam (bass).
LB:G258.
Szymanski, Wlodzimierz – *See* Capella Bydgostiensis.

Tachezi, Herbert (harpsichord, organ).
EB:B20, E92.
LB:A118, A187, A302, A335, A597, B54, B64, B65,
  B85, B149, B220, B257, E2, E132, F71.
Tadeo, Giorgio (bass).
EB:G81, G128.
Tagliavini, Luigi Fernando (harpsichord, organ).
EB:E37.
LB:A51, A149.
Takacs, Klara (mezzo-soprano).
LB:F74, G39, G292, G297.
Tallis Scholars, dir. Peter Phillips.
LR:Ge21, Ge38.
Tappy, Eric (tenor).
EB:F42, G49, G64, G127.
Tarr, Edward (trumpet).
EB:A29, B67.
LB:A654, B214, B223.
Tarr Brass Ensemble.
LB:A639, G273.
Taskin Trio.
LB:B57.
Tassinari, Gastone (flute).
LB:A51.
Tatnell, Roland (counter-tenor).
EB:F60.
Tatrai, Wilmos – *See* Hungarian Chamber Orchestra.
Tatrai Quartet.
LB:B270.
Taverner Choir, dir. Andrew Parrott.
LR:F6.
EB:F79.
Taylor, Christopher (flute).
LB:A550, B73.
Taylor, Joan (soprano).
LB:G269.
Taylor, Paul (tenor).
EB:G143.
Taylor, Paul Arden (recorder, krumhorn).
EB:B13.
Tchakarov, Emil – *See* Iranian National Radio and
  Television Chamber Orchestra.
Tchavdarov, Zahari (viola).
LB:B240.
Tear, Robert (tenor).
AA:C1.
EB:F16, F64, F67, F73, G62, G63, G78.
LB:F36, F39, F41, F59, F78, G2, G85, G109, G116,
  G131, G133, G148, G158, G171, G216, G230, G231,

G239.
Telemann Society Chamber Ensemble.
LR:B1.
Terhoeven, Ursula (mezzo-soprano).
EB:F109.
Terni, Clemente (organ).
EB:E30.
Teutsch, Karol – *See* Warsaw Philharmonic Chamber
  Orchestra.
Thal, Herbert (trumpet).
LB:A654.
Thames Chamber Orchestra, dir. Michael Dobson.
LB:A222.
Thames Chamber Orchestra, dir. David Willcocks.
LB:G148.
Thamm, Hans – *See* South West German Chamber
  Orchestra.
  – *See* Windsbach Boys' Choir.
Theuring, Günther (counter-tenor).
EB:F46.
Thiry, Louis (organ).
LB:E139.
Thoene, Helga (violin).
LB:A640.
Thoene, Walter (harpsichord).
EB:F110, F111.
LB:A357, G177.
Thomas, Bernard (flute, recorder, crumhorn).
LR:E36.
EB:B58.
Thomas, Bernard – *See* Bernard Thomas Chamber
  Orchestra.
Thomas, David (bass).
EB:F11, F76, F80, G23, G58.
LB:F32, F64, G126, G226.
SI:A2.
Thomas, Kurt – *See* Collegium Aureum.
  – *See* Frankfurt Kantorei.
  – *See* German Bach Soloists.
  – *See* Leipzig Gewandhaus Orchestra.
  – *See* St. Thomas Choir, Leipzig.
Thomas, Marjorie (contralto).
LB:G233.
Thomas, Mary (soprano).
LR:Gd32.
EB:F74.
Thomas, Michael (harpsichord).
LB:D226.
Thomas, Ronald (violin).
LB:A199, A450.
Thomas, Ronald – *See* Bournemouth Sinfonietta.
Thomaschke, Thomas (bass).
LB:G247.
Thompson, Adrian (tenor).
LB:G158.
Thorndycraft, Rosemary (violin, viol).
EB:B37.
Thuneman, Klaus (bassoon).
LB:A538, A540, B83, B201.
Thuri, Frantisek (organ).
LB:B237.
Tibor Varga Chamber Orchestra.
LB:A71.
Tichota, Jiri (lute).
LB:F79.
Ticinelli-Fatori, Luciana (soprano).
EB:F90, G49, G64.
Tietze, Ekkehardt (organ).
LB:G61.
Tiffin Choir.
EB:F60.
Tilegant, Friedrich – *See* South West German Chamber
  Orchestra.
Tilney, Colin (harpsichord).

Virtuosi of England, dir. Arthur Davison.
EB:A21.
LB:A21, A78, A101, A267, A313, A456.
Virtuosi di Roma, dir. Renato Fassano.
LB:A471, F52.
Visser, Lieuwe (bass).
LB:G56.
Vodrazka, Jaroslav (organ).
LB:E236, E242.
Vogel, Siegfried (bass).
EB:G125.
Voorberg, Marinus – See NCRV Vocal Ensemble, Hilversum.
Vollenwyder, Erich (harpsichord).
LB:G278.
Vorholz, Dieter (violin).
LB:A520.
Vries, Hans de (oboe).
LB:A546, B179, B210.
Vuichard, Charles (counter-tenor).
EB:G29.
LB:G254.
Vyvyan, Jennifer (soprano).
EB:F70, F71, F77.
LB:F45, G228.

Wachsmuth, Andree (violin).
LB:B165.
Wakefield, John (tenor).
EB:F9.
LB:G222.
Walcha, Helmut (harpsichord, organ).
EB:E72.
LB:B49, D13, D16, D23, D29, D32, D46, D103, D106, E4, E5, E67, E68, E69, E70, E71, E72, E82, E93, E131, E145.
Walevska, Christine (cello).
LB:A518, A522.
Wallace, Ian (bass).
LB:F24, F47.
Wallez, Amaury (bassoon).
LB:A658.
Wallez, Jean-Pierre (violin).
LB:A181, A350, A420, A460, A549, A602.
Wallez, Jean-Pierre – See Instrumental Ensemble of France.
Wallfisch, Ernst (viola, viola d'amore).
LB:A407.
Walter, Wolfgang (claviorganum).
LR:D21.
Walterskirchen, Gerhard (claviorganum).
LR:D21.
Walther von der Vogelweide Chamber Choir, dir. Othmar Costa.
ER:A20.
LR:F39.
Walton, Michael (viol, recorder, spinet).
SI:C1, C2, C3, C4, C5, C6, C7, C8, C9, C11, C13.
Wanami, Takayoshi (violin).
LB:A174.
Wand, Ulrich (boy soprano).
LB:G81.
Wandsworth School Choir.
LB:G158, G248.
Wangenheim, Volker – See Bournemouth Sinfonietta.
Warchal, Bodhan (violin).
LB:A617.
Warchal, Bodhan – See Slovak Chamber Orchestra.
Ward, David (bass).
LB:G157, G225.
Ward, Jocelyn (lute, tabor).
SI:C3, C14.
Ward, Nicolette (viol, recorder).
SI:C15, C16, C17, C19.

Ward, Rosalind (recorder).
SI:C2.
Warfield, William (baritone).
LB:G237.
Warsaw Chamber Orchestra, dir. Jerzy Dobrzanski.
LB:A592, G329.
Warsaw Chamber Orchestra, dir. Stephan Sutkowski.
LB:A562.
Warsaw Philharmonic Chamber Ensemble, dir. A. Markowski.
LB:F15.
Warsaw Philharmonic Chamber Orchestra, dir. Karol Teutsch.
EB:B15.
LB:A86, A230, A306, A314, A324, A405, A462, A586, G265.
Wasser, Ludwig (organ).
LB:G176.
Wassmer, Claude (bassoon).
LB:B264.
Waterfield, Polly (violin).
EB:B19.
SI:A1.
Watkinson, Carolyn (contralto).
LB:F44, F46, G126, G226, G290, G291.
Watson, Lilian (soprano).
EB:F15, F16.
LB:G245.
Watt, Alan (bass).
LB:G245.
Watts, Helen (contralto).
EB:F16.
LB:F40, F41, F45, F47, G2, G111, G113, G116, G128, G129, G133, G147, G157, G170, G173, G184, G215, G222, G232, G295, G303.
Waverley Consort, dir. Michael Jaffe.
LB:Ge36.
Webb, Richard (cello).
LB:B129.
Weddle, Robert (organ).
LB:E201.
Wedin, Jan-Olav – See Stockholm Chamber Ensemble.
Wehrle, Anne-Marie (harpsichord).
LB:B301.
Wehrung, Herrad (soprano).
LR:F108.
EB:G10, G69, G90, G91, G92, G94, G95, G97, G98, G115.
LB:G4, G15, G23, G77.
Weir, Gillian (organ).
EB:E4, E51.
LB:E73, E176.
Weisberg, Arthur (bassoon).
LB:B188.
Weissbach, Hans – See Leipzig Symphony Orchestra.
Weissenberg, Alexis (piano).
LB:D28, D45, D75, D76.
Weissenborn, Günther – See Hannover Rundfunk-orchester of NDR.
Weldon, George – See Royal Philharmonic Orchestra.
Wellesley Chamber Singers, dir. Peter Sipple.
LR:F46, F96.
Wells, Mary (soprano).
EB:F71.
Wendlandt, Hanni (soprano).
LB:G13.
Wenk, Erich (bass).
EB:G9.
LB:F1, F8, F19, F72, G35, G132, G249.
Wenkel, Ortrun (contralto).
EB:F102.
LB:G139.
Wennberg, Gunnar (horn).
LB:B317.

Wenze, Eberhard – *See* Berlin Bach Orchestra.
– *See* Halle Kirchenmusikschule Choir.
Wenzinger, August (viol, cello).
EB:B1.
LB:B112, B140, B142, B321.
Wenzinger, August – *See* Capella Accademica, Vienna.
– *See* Capella Colonensis.
– *See* Schola Cantorum Basiliensis.
Werbowski, Emilian (oboe).
LB:E174.
Wering, Janny van (harpsichord).
LB:A118, A142, A144.
Werner, Jean-Jacques – *See* Fontainbleau Chamber Orchestra.
Westminster Choir.
LB:G237.
Westphallian Kantorei, dir. Wilhelm Ehmann.
LR:F102, F105, F108, F109.
EB:G10, G69, G89, G93, G97, G98, G99, G112, G113, G115, G116, G126, G130, G132.
LB:G4, G31, G32, G38, G58, G101, G183, G235, G325.
Whikehart Chorale.
EB:G110.
White, Ian (viola d'amore).
LB:D226.
White, Willard (bass).
LB:F33.
Whitesides, William (tenor).
EB:F44.
Whitworth, John (counter-tenor).
AA:C1.
EB:F70, F74, G42.
LB:F45.
Wiata, Inia Te (bass).
EB:G78.
Widensky, Peter (chamber organ).
LB:B158, B273.
Widmer, Kurt (bass-baritone).
AN:A9.
EB:G11.
LB:G154.
Wiedle, Wilhelm (boy soprano).
LB:G56, G59, G63, G67, G68, G72, G81.
Wiegand, George (lute).
LR:Gd23.
EB:B37.
Wiemer, Wolfgang (organ).
EB:G132.
Wierzbieki, Wlodzimierz (tenor).
LB:G277.
Wijnkoop, Alexander van (violin).
LB:B232.
Wijnkoop, Alexander van – *See* Camerata Bern.
Wilbraham, John (trumpet).
LB:A169, A594, A598, A616, A647, A657, A666.
Wilbye Consort, dir. Peter Pears.
LR:Gd39.
Wildenblanck, Udo (boy soprano).
LB:F67.
Wilfart, Serge (tenor).
LB:F68.
Wilhelm, Hans (bass).
EB:G122.
Wilhelms, Günther (bass).
EB:G12, G52.
Wilkins, David (chamber organ, harpsichord, virginals).
SI:C1, C5, C6, C7, C8, C11, C13.
Willcocks, David – *See* Academy of St. Martin-in-the-Fields.
– *See* Bach Choir.
– *See* English Chamber Orchestra.
– *See* King's College Choir.
– *See* Philomusica of London.
– *See* Thames Chamber Orchestra.

Williams, John (counter-tenor).
EB:G21, G71.
Williams, John (guitar).
LB:C7.
Williams, John (oboe).
LB:A624.
Williams, Trevor (violin).-
LB:B148, B168.
Williamson, Paul – *See* Peasants All.
Wills, Arthur (organ).
EB:G3.
LB:E217, G191.
Wills, Arthur *See* Ely Cathedral Choir.
Wilson, Alan (harpsichord, organ, ottavina, percussion).
EB:B13, B19.
Wilson, Christopher (lute).
LR:E36, Gd5, Gd43, Gd47.
Wilson, Ian (trumpet, cornet).
LB:A574.
SI:A2.
Windsbach Boys' Choir, dir. Hans Thamm.
LR:F108, F126.
EB:F110, F111, G119.
LB:G15, G71, G80, G325.
Winfield, John (tenor).
LB:G250.
Wingerden, Jeanette van (recorder).
LB:A400, B296.
Winschermann, Helmut (oboe, oboe d'amore).
LB:A194, A195, A205, B183, G49.
Winschermann, Helmut – *See* German Bach Soloists.
Winter, Helmut (organ).
EB:E2, E45, E89.
Winter, Otto (oboe).
LB:A369.
Witsch, Peter (tenor).
LB:G279.
Witsenburg, Edward (harp).
EB:F12.
Wohlfahrt, Erwin (tenor).
EB:F110.
Wolf, Ilse (soprano).
LB:G129, G215.
Wolf-Matthäus, Lotte (contralto).
EB:G51.
LB:G13, G36, G70, G73, G84, G117, G217.
Wolfgang von Karajan Ensemble.
LR:F3.
Wolken, Fritz (bassoon).
LB:A635.
Wollitz, Eduard (bass).
EB:F44.
LB:F11, G53.
Wolteche, Joseph (organ).
EB:G35.
Wood, Christopher (harpsichord).
LB:D157, D221.
SI:C1, C2, C3, C4, C5, C7, C8, C9, C10, C11, C12, C15.
Woodford, Anthony (viol).
SI:C11.
Woodland, Rae (soprano).
LB:G227.
Woodrow, Anthony (double-bass).
LB:B191, B309.
Woods, Jonathan (harpsichord).
EB:D33.
Woolf, Simon (boy soprano).
EB:F60.
Woolley, Robert (harpsichord).
EB:D18.
LB:D140.
Worcester Cathedral Choir, dir. Donald Hunt.
LB:G190.
Woytowicz, Stefania (soprano).

LB:F15, G265.
Wren Consort.
LB:F21.
Wren Orchestra, dir. Bernard Rose.
LB:G262.
Wroclaw Radio Chamber Orchestra, dir. Edmund
Kajdasz.
EB:G44, G146.
LB:G328.
Wroclaw Radio Choir, dir. Edmund Kajdasz.
LR:F42.
EB:G44, G146.
LB:G328.
Wroclaw Radio Choir, dir. Stanislaw Krukowski.
AA:C4.
LR:F92.
LB:A617.
Wroclaw Radio and Television Choir, dir. Stanislaw
Galonski.
LB:G199.
Wührer Chamber Orchestra, dir. Friedrich Wührer.
LB:A338.
Wulstan, David – *See* Clerkes of Oxenford.
Wunderlich, Fritz (tenor).
EB:F111.
LB:G92, G146, G153, G164.
Wunderlich, Heinz (organ).
LB:E74.
Wunderlich, Heinz – *See* Hamburg Chamber Orchestra.
– *See* St. Jacobi Kantorei, Hamburg.
Wuppertal Instrumental Collegium.
LB:G49.
Württemburg Chamber Orchestra, dir. Rudolph
Ewerhardt.
LB:F4, F5, F6.
Württemburg Chamber Orchestra, dir. Jörg Faerber.
LB:A14, A63, A114, A218, A227, A229, A407, A413,
A473, A515, A531, A635, A648, A654, A658, A660,
B287.
Württemburg Chamber Orchestra, dir. Helmuth Rilling.
LB:G62.
Wuyts, Christiane (harpsichord, clavichord, virginals,
clavisimbalum).
EB:D36.
LB:B250, D59, D104.
Wyatt, Walker (bass).
EB:F43.
LB:G18.

'Y' Chamber Orchestra, dir. Gerald Schwarz.
LB:A656.
Yakar, Rachel (soprano).
EB:F13.
LB:F22, F37.
Yano, Shige (soprano).
LB:F82.
Yeatman, Barbara (viol).
SI:C19.
Yepes, Narcisso (guitar, lute).
LR:E62.
LB:A526, A564, B111, C3, C4, C5, C6.
Yorkshire Sinfonia, dir. Donald Hunt.
LB:G252.
Yorkshire Sinfonia, dir. Manoug Parikian.
LB:B99.
York-Skinner, John (counter-tenor).
EB:F61.
LB:F43.
Young, Alexander (tenor).
EB:F60.
LB:F24, G157, G207, G208, G234, G242, G251.

Zabaleta, Nicanor (harp).
LB:A201, A239, B320, D105.

Zaccaria, Nicola (bass).
LB:F75.
Zacharias, Christian (piano).
LB:D177.
Zaepffel, Alain (tenor).
EB:G27.
Zagreb Soloists.
LB:A198, A403, A465, A546.
Zahradnicek, Jiri (tenor).
LB:F79.
Zambo, Istvan – *See* Budapest Philharmonic Orchestra.
– *See* Veszprem Mixed Choir.
Zanaboni, Giuseppe (organ).
LR:D15, D18.
EB:E59.
LB:E75, E76, E238.
Zanaboni, Giuseppe – *See* Solisti dell Gruppo
Strumentale 'V.L. Campi' di Piacenza.
Zanetti, Miguel (piano).
LB:F80.
Zanfini, Renato (oboe).
LB:B300.
Zannerini, Severino (cello).
LB:A372, A373.
Zapf, Gerd (trumpet).
LB:A572.
Zareska, Eugenia (contralto).
LB:G123.
Zartner, Rudolf (organ).
EB:F110.
Zawodna, Irena (soprano).
LB:G277.
Zayas, Rodrigo de (lute, vihuela, guitar, theorbo).
LR:C10, E61.
Zedda, Alberto – *See* Orchestra d'Archi dell Angelicum.
Zelenka, Milan (guitar).
LB:A525.
Zelenka, Rudolf (harpsichord).
LB:F79.
Zempleni, Maria (soprano).
LB:F74, G292.
Zickler, Heinz (trumpet, clarino).
LB:A604, A654, A660.
Ziegler, Klaus Martin (organ).
EB:G8.
Ziegler, Klaus Martin – *See* German Baroque Soloists.
– *See* Kassel Vocal Ensemble.
Zimmer, Roland (lute).
LR:E68.
LB:A518.
Zinman, David – *See* Netherlands Chamber Orchestra.
Zöller, Karlheinz (flute).
LB:A628, A640, B134, B238.
Zosso, Rene (hurdy-gurdy, voice).
AA:D2, D10, D13.
AN:A15, B17.
LB:B196.
Zukerman, Eugenia (flute).
LB:B243.
Zukerman, George (bassoon).
LB:A63, A635.
Zukerman, Pinchas (violin, viola).
LB:A177, A351, A439, A447, A499, B243.
Zukerman, Pinchas – *See* English Chamber Orchestra.
– *See* Los Angeles Philharmonic Orchestra.
Zürcher, Martin (recorder).
LB:B184, B185.
Zürcher Kreis der Engadiner Kantorei St. Maritz, dir.
Hannes Reimann.
EB:G124.
Zurich Bach Choir.
LB:E98.
Zurich Camerata, dir. Räto Tschupp.
LB:A57.

Zurich Chamber Orchestra, dir. Edmond de Stoutz.
LB:A363.
Zurich Collegium Musicum, dir. Paul Sacher.
LB:A377, A565.
Zurich Ricercare Ensemble – *See* Ricercare Ensemble,
  Zurich.

Zylis-Gara, Teresa (soprano).
LR:F3.
EB:F109, G127.
LB:G71, G80, G141, G163, G172, G216.